From the Morgenthau Diaries

Years of War
1941-1945

FROM

The Morgenthau Diaries

Years of War

1941-1945

BY JOHN MORTON BLUM

ILLUSTRATED WITH PHOTOGRAPHS

HOUGHTON MIFFLIN COMPANY BOSTON

1 9 6 7

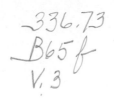
First Printing W

Foreword

THIS VOLUME, the last of three based upon the Diaries of Henry Morgenthau, Jr., carries the account of his public life from Pearl Harbor Day, December 7, 1941, to the occasion of his departure as Secretary of the Treasury on July 18, 1945. In that time Morgenthau, like the others to whom Franklin Roosevelt had conferred responsibilities of government, was preoccupied with the domestic and international problems of the Second World War. This book records the Secretary's activities, examines his policies and his explanations of them, and describes his relationships with his associates.

During the period here surveyed, Morgenthau, as always, was dedicated both to the principles of the New Deal and the interests of the United States as he interpreted them. In the continuing debate about domestic policy, he stood for the extension of social reform, for federal regulation of private economic interests, for federal limitations on the profits of large corporations and the incomes of wealthy individuals, and for voluntary rather than compulsory programs of public finance. Like the President, he subordinated all issues to the dominant purposes of winning the war and constructing a lasting peace. He believed that the volume of American aid to any one of the nation's allies had to accord with the military importance of the recipient and with the efficiency with which that recipient could employ the equipment and supplies it received. On those counts he advocated extensive assistance to the Soviet Union, continued and generous aid to the United Kingdom, but limited

support for China and for the Free French. He believed, too, that
postwar conditions would demand economic as well as political
cooperation among the United Nations, and that the United States
would have to assist its allies in their financial and industrial reconstruction. Unhappy during the war with the appeasement, for whatever purpose, of Nazi sympathizers or collaborators, Morgenthau
considered the eradication of Nazism and the destruction of German
military power the first requisite of peace and of future American
security, and he deemed postwar friendship with Great Britain and
Russia a second essential for reaching those goals.

Morgenthau's intimacy with Roosevelt gave him special opportunities to serve his purposes and the President's, but his influence
during the years of war was relatively less than it had been in the
preceding years of preparation, for the President turned more than
he had before to the military for advice and assistance. Yet Morgenthau remained an important counselor, on whose loyalty Roosevelt
always relied, and the Treasury remained a powerful part of the
federal executive establishment. Disappointed though he was by
some of the President's decisions, Morgenthau played a major role
in shaping others, especially those relating to methods of public
finance, to the planning of wartime and postwar monetary policy,
to the allocation of aid to major allies, to the rescue of Jewish refugees, and to early phases of planning for postwar assistance to Great
Britain and postwar policy in Germany. In the few months in which
he served under President Truman, the Secretary accomplished much
less, for his role in government had depended always primarily upon
his special relationship with Franklin Roosevelt, their mutual affection and mutual trust.

American policy during the war reflected, of course, many influences, many points of view, many differences of opinion among those
in Washington and between them and their counterparts in other
capitals. So, too, Treasury policy responded to the advices of a
number of the Secretary's subordinates as well as to his own predelic-
tions. In the formulation and implementation of every major program of Morgenthau's concern, many views were heard, and the
chorus was often discordant. But Treasury policy, in the making
and in the end, was Morgenthau's responsibility, and national policy
in the making continually felt his weight. An account of his activi-

ties and recommendations, therefore, contributes a necessary ingredi-
ent to the understanding of the workings of American government
during the Second World War. To that end, the Secretary of the
Treasury compiled his Diaries and authorized their use.

*   *   *

This volume, like its predecessors, could not have been written without the authorization of Henry Morgenthau, Jr., who gave me full
access to his records and commented on the entire manuscript, which
was completed not long before his death in February, 1967. His
participation inspirited the project. Occasionally he suggested modi-
fications in my phraseology, always in the interest of clarity, but he
requested a full record, within the limits of available space, of his
activities and his ideas, and of the accompanying support or dissent
of his colleagues. He asked for the deletion of nothing reflecting
upon him, whether favorably or unfavorably, though he did urge
me to respect the privacy of men still alive who spoke openly in his
presence about others, also still alive, whom they disliked. He and
I both depended on the energy and dedication with which his records, the Morgenthau Diaries, had been kept and organized during
his twelve years in office by Henrietta Klotz, his old friend, and Isa-
belle Diamond, her assistant in the task.

The manuscript of this book profited from the efforts of two intelligent and helpful typists, Joan D. Blackmer and Madge B. Ramsey.
Arthur M. Schlesinger, Jr., and Craig Wylie, both of whom read
every chapter, gave me excellent counsel about matters of fact, judgment, and prose, as also, with regard to questions of his particular
concern, did William L. Neumann. Where I have nevertheless erred,
the fault is entirely my own. My research was facilitated by the un-
stinting assistance of the officers of the National Archives, Herman
Kahn particularly, and of the staffs of the Franklin D. Roosevelt
Library, especially Elizabeth B. Drewry and Robert H. Parks, and
the Yale University Library. Twelve years have passed since I began
the research on the first of the volumes of which this is the last. The
encouragement and cheerfulness of my wife made that time seem
much shorter and my disposition less severe.

JOHN MORTON BLUM

Yale University

Contents

Illustrations

From the Morgenthau Diaries

Years of War
1941-1945

I

Strains of War

1941-1945

SICK FROM WORRY, the senior officers of the Treasury Department greeted the Secretary at eleven in the evening on December 7, 1941, when he returned from a Cabinet meeting at the White House. "It is just unexplainable," he said. "And they caught us just as unprepared as the others — just the same. . . . Much worse than anybody realizes. . . . I was with Frank Knox when he got the report from Pearl Harbor, and that telephone conversation was taken down, and I read it, so I know the President read the same one in Cabinet. . . . Knox feels something terrible. . . . Stimson . . . kept mumbling that all the planes were in one place. . . . They have the whole fleet in one place — the whole fleet was in this little Pearl Harbor base. They will never be able to explain it."

Inexplicability contributed to the shock of the Japanese attack that forced the entire nation to face the unlimited emergency of war. For almost four years war dominated the lives of all Americans. The problems of waging war placed an ultimate strain on the federal government, especially on the President and his close advisers. War heightened their sensibilities, stretched their nerves, called forth their last reserves of energy.

1. Emergency Unlimited

Responsibility for protecting the President fell to the Secret Service, a branch of the Treasury, whose Secretary, Henry Morgenthau, Jr.,

1

also counted that President his dearest friend. Morgenthau's first official order after the news from Pearl Harbor doubled the guard at the White House. At all times, he directed, twenty-five uniformed officers were to patrol the grounds and a dozen agents in plain clothes were to be on duty. Following the precedent of the First World War, he planned also to station a detail of soldiers within the gates. The President objected. Men in uniform, he ruled, were to stay outside: "As long as you have one about every hundred feet around the fence, it's all right." Roosevelt rejected, too, Morgenthau's suggestion for placing light tanks at the entrances of the White House, so the Secretary resorted instead, on the advice of General George Marshall, to arming the soldiers in those positions alternately with Garand rifles and submachine guns. He also set up a special air raid shelter in the vault of the Treasury — close to the Secretary's large, stately office — for the President and his immediate family and staff. Checking on his subordinates, Morgenthau that night found only three men patrolling the long block against the back entrance of the White House. He gave Edward Starling, who was supposed to be in charge, "the most terrific dressing down you ever heard of," and the next day, with Roosevelt's consent, had "all responsibilities for supervising the White House Secret Service detail and guards taken away from him."

Morgenthau's second official wartime order closed the borders to all Japanese within the United States and revoked all licenses under which Japanese individuals and firms were doing business. Policing the properties of Japanese nationals involved Foreign Funds Control, an office within the Treasury, in the emotionalism of the West Coast. There deep-rooted hostility to the Japanese generated frenetic rumors about espionage and subversion and frightened demands for repressive treatment not only of local Japanese residents but also of Nisei, American citizens of Japanese descent. On December 10 some of the staff of Foreign Funds Control urged Morgenthau to take over thousands of small businesses owned by Japanese and Nisei in the area between the Pacific Ocean and Utah. "After thinking the matter over during the night," the Secretary decided that proposal "was not only hysterical but impractical." Subversion and espionage were properly the responsibility of the Department of Justice. It was "up to the Treasury simply to carry out its responsibility . . . to the freezing order." He would therefore only send a telegram to all banks in the West asking them "to renew their efforts to get in to us, as quickly as possible, all of these forms, notifying us of any aliens of any country who were doing business in this country, but particularly Germans, Italians and Japanese." Someone with "some horse sense," moreover, had to be sure that the Treasury was not preventing Japanese farmers from providing food for Los Angeles markets. Californians, Morgenthau said, "were so hysterical they wanted the Army to go out and work the truck farms while they put the Japanese into a concentration camp." He would have no part of that: "We have just got to keep our feet on the ground."

"No time," Edward Foley, the Treasury's General Counsel, objected, "to be thinking about civil liberties when the country is in danger."

"Listen," Morgenthau replied, ". . . when it comes to suddenly mopping up 150,000 Japanese and putting them behind barbed wire, irrespective of their status, and consider doing the same with the Germans, I want at some time to have caught my breath. . . . Anybody that wants to hurt this country or injure us, put him where he can't do it, but . . . indiscriminately, no."

Further Treasury orders, issued on December 11, 1941, permitted Japanese nationals in the United States to receive up to a hundred dollars a month for living expenses. Those producing, marketing, or distributing food might engage in all transactions incident to the normal conduct of their business, but they could not withdraw from their accounts during any one week sums greater than their average weekly withdrawals during the previous six months. Further, the business licenses, revoked a week earlier, of Japanese who had resided continuously within the continental limits of the United States since June 17, 1940, were restored on December 15, 1941, except in cases where Treasury agents, after inspection, put suspect enterprises under government control.

The Army's decision early in 1942 to move thousands of Japanese and Nisei to concentration camps appalled Morgenthau. It also presented the Treasury with responsibility for protecting the property of the aliens who had been incarcerated. The department performed that duty through the Federal Reserve Banks, which took care of the businesses and real estate of the Japanese, particularly, as

Morgenthau put it, "to see that they're not victimized, that's the principal thing." His various orders, the Secretary believed, protected the interests of the nation while also protecting, insofar as the temper of the times permitted, the individual rights of the Nisei, as well as those of the Japanese and other enemy aliens.

2. Alien Property

With the coming of war, the Justice Department pressed for exclusive jurisdiction over alien property within the United States. During the months before Pearl Harbor, the Treasury's Foreign Funds Control, operating under a committee on which the Justice and State Departments were also represented, had regulated the use of assets of citizens of the Axis nations and of the nations the Axis had conquered. In order to supervise or eliminate undesirable influences in foreign-owned or dominated businesses, especially the voice of Germans who had acquired large American holdings since 1921, the Treasury had issued some 2500 operating licenses, had closed down a few firms whose activities endangered the national interest, and had taken over the management of more than fifty other firms. But Attorney General Francis Biddle believed that in wartime his department alone should regulate activities which might otherwise damage national security. Any committee, any division of authority, Biddle argued, was bound to be inefficient. Further, the Alien Property Custodian, an officer of the Justice Department, had exercised sole supervision over alien properties during the First World War. That precedent seemed to him appropriate and wise.

Morgenthau disagreed vigorously. Foreign Funds Control, he noted, had an admirable record and an experienced and expert staff. The management of alien properties could not easily be divorced from other functions of the Control, such as the licensing of foreign assets. Most important, Morgenthau distrusted Biddle's appointee as Alien Property Custodian, Leo Crowley. In the early years of the New Deal Crowley, then head of the Federal Deposit Insurance Corporation, had clashed continually with the Treasury and the Federal Reserve System. Crowley, Morgenthau believed, had a deserved reputation for conveniently loose judgment in the distribution of patronage, and the patronage falling to the Alien Property Custodian — the large fees and salaries of government-appointed managers of alien businesses — should especially be assigned to competent executives rather than to political hacks.

In mid-December 1941, Morgenthau took his case to the President. "A great deal of this work depends upon working with the banks," the Secretary said, "and the Treasury organization has done a swell job, and we had the connections. . . . The trouble is . . . some of the bright young men in the Department of Justice . . . aren't satisfied, and they want more power." Morgenthau's suggestion for preserving the interdepartmental committee, Roosevelt said, "sounds fine to me."

Morgenthau went next to Jimmy Byrnes, the adroit South Carolinian whom Roosevelt had appointed to the Supreme Court in June 1941, and now enlisted as his surrogate in the reorganization of the federal government for waging war. To Byrnes, on December 31, Morgenthau complained particularly about Crowley's connections with Victor Emanuel, the versatile entrepreneur whose interests ranged through utilities, chemical, airplane, and other companies. "Jimmy," the Secretary said, "how can a man who is . . . chairman of Standard Gas and Electric, and who is the personal front and representative here for Victor Emanuel, be Alien Property Custodian?"

"You are right," Byrnes replied. ". . . That is the most outrageous thing I ever heard."

"Our boys," Morgenthau continued, "can run this thing and they will run it well and there will be no trouble or scandal of any kind."

Byrnes agreed, but later that day, with Roosevelt's tacit approval, he proposed a compromise which would have left foreign-owned businesses under Treasury direction until the government actually took them over, and would then have placed them within Crowley's office. His "back to the wall," Morgenthau, as he told his staff, "decided to fight it." He did so in a series of reports to the White House about various successful ventures of Foreign Funds Control. The most critical of those reports described the Treasury's investigation of the General Aniline and Film Corporation. For weeks to come, the struggle for control over alien properties focused on the problems of that company.

Immediately after Pearl Harbor the Treasury had sent a group of agents into General Aniline, an American affiliate of the huge German chemicals trust, I. G. Farben Industrie. Inquiries had revealed several dangerous situations, one in the Ozalid Division of General Aniline. The head of that division, one F. W. von Meister, had come to the United States directly from an association with German zeppelin and automobile works. By leasing and servicing blueprinting machines and other equipment for reproducing documents, von Meister had provided access for his subordinates, many of them German aliens, to the drafting rooms of some 3500 industrial plants, including defense installations and experimental laboratories. Ozalid also had contracts for microprinting with the United States Government Archives, some even with the United States Navy. So, too, the Agfa-Ansco Division of General Aniline had obtained access to confidential government military films, some of which were being processed by German aliens. In the opinion of the Treasury, General Aniline had functioned as a cloak for subversive activities. Its annual expenditures of some $60 million, its six thousand and more employees gave the German government, through I. G. Farben, unusual opportunities for concealing German agents for propaganda and other subversive purposes. One man, a confessed Nazi educated in Germany, had received training at General Aniline for the avowed purpose of becoming a confidential assistant to the head of the Camera and Film Division. In other instances young Germans of military age had worked for the company before leaving for Japan or China for purposes the Treasury had not yet ascertained.

On the basis of these and similar disclosures, Morgenthau on January 13, 1942, suspended and barred from company premises various officers who incarnated the influence of I. G. Farben, among them a vice president, a production manager, two divisional general managers, and a divisional secretary. All were naturalized Americans of German descent. The Treasury did not suspend but did place under close supervision another twenty-five officers, all of German origin, twelve of them aliens. Roosevelt, "extremely interested" in Morgenthau's report about General Aniline, told the Secretary that "in case anybody asks you, you can say that the President has read it and his answer is, 'Kill the son of a bitch.' "

Morgenthau needed that vehement support in order to impose

the Treasury's policy on the politician then serving, at Roosevelt's own suggestion, as the acting head of General Aniline. In November 1941, that post with its munificent salary had gone to John E. Mack, a Poughkeepsie, New York, lawyer and Democratic nabob who had thrice placed Roosevelt's name before the party's national conventions. In a memo to the Treasury on January 29, 1942, Mack argued that his first duty was to conserve the company as a going concern essential to the war purposes of the United States until the federal government saw fit to act instead through an Alien Property Custodian. He had brought in William Bullitt, a sometime intimate of Roosevelt and former ambassador to Russia and France, as chairman of the Board of Directors, and both he and Bullitt were eager to purge the company of subversives. But Mack resented the failure of the Treasury to consult him and other company officers before issuing its recent orders. Those orders, he said, unnecessarily shook morale. He particularly criticized the simultaneous suspension of five major officers, and he would not comply with an accompanying directive forbidding any further communication with them.

Before replying to Mack, Morgenthau talked with Bullitt. "I thought that nobody," the Secretary said, "should get more than $50,000 salary and that Mack might be made General Counsel, Bullitt could stay as Chairman of the Board, and then we'd get a first-rate operating man to operate the company. I thought that these enormous fees that they were paying were a disgrace and that the whole thing would reflect on the President. He agreed on that." Mack did not. Eager to hold on to his own job, he also, through his attorneys, urged the establishment of a new plant management committee whose personnel, as he named them, remained almost entirely I. G. Farben men. The Treasury, in contrast, contended that all employees with that background should be eliminated whenever it was possible without impairing the productivity of the corporation.

The Department gained authority to impose a solution on February 16, 1942, when 97 per cent of the shares of General Aniline and Film were put in charge of the Secretary on the ground that "the real interest in these shares is German." Bullitt immediately resigned and returned his pay, observing that he had taken his post only in order to keep an eye on the Germans, but Mack continued in office on full salary, awaiting Morgenthau's next move.

Opposition to Treasury policy now seemed to Morgenthau to threaten from another quarter, for the Secretary suspected that Leo Crowley would follow Mack's preferences if and when General Aniline were transferred to the Alien Property Custodian. Hoping to block Crowley, Morgenthau explained his own position to Harry Hopkins. Roosevelt, the Secretary said on February 26, "wants to be in the position that if I go ahead and clean all of this up, he doesn't know anything about it, and he can say he doesn't know anything about it. . . . I am not going to have any political directors." Nothing in Washington was "ever settled," Morgenthau continued, but if the Treasury succeeded in handling General Aniline, the Department might then retain control over other large alien businesses: "If you do a good job, the President leaves it with you; and if you do a bad job, he takes it away from you. That is the way it should be."

Morgenthau got half the loaf — the half he wanted. The Cabinet the next day discussed the management of the properties of West Coast Japanese who had been imprisoned. "If you were smart," Roosevelt told Morgenthau, "I don't think you would take it." "Mr. President, we don't want it," Morgenthau said. ". . . We thought that these big companies we could handle, but when it comes to these little farms and businesses and so forth, I agree with you, and we don't want it." During their conversation, as the Secretary recalled it, Francis Biddle was leaning over the table, "his face . . . almost purple . . . he was so excited," and intermittently he urged Roosevelt to leave the disposition of the matter with the Director of the Budget, Harold Smith, whom he recognized as his own ally. But the President had a prescription. "The question of actual frozen funds," he said, "that, of course should stay in the Treasury, but the rest of it, I don't see why it should."

After leaving the meeting, Morgenthau concluded that continuing responsibility for foreign funds was as much as the Treasury should rightly undertake. As he put it to his staff: "I will tell you . . . I've put up the fight of my life. . . . I think we are . . . lucky, because . . . we can't look after 50,000, or we can't look after 25,000 people. Now, if they want to throw the big in with the little, I say, let her go. I have done everything that I can, but the President said he is going to leave us frozen funds." He would turn over to the Justice Department the Japanese businesses and with them their larger and more important German counterparts.

To the Secretary's satisfaction, Roosevelt on March 5 also permitted him to "proceed at once with Aniline. . . . Go ahead. . . . Don't wait for anything." At once Morgenthau appointed Robert McConnell president and chief executive officer of General Aniline. McConnell, chairman of the Engineers Defense Board, had had broad experience in business and industry, especially in chemicals. "Our program," Morgenthau wrote him, "envisages the elimination of all things in General Aniline and Film Corporation representing control by German interest. . . . All persons of executive or managerial status who have been connected with I. G. Farben will have to be replaced as soon as possible by men unquestionably devoted to American ideals." Soon thereafter suspect technical personnel should be discharged. But employees were not to be dismissed "simply because they are of German birth or extraction," and "the whole program must be carried out with a view to maintaining, and wherever possible expanding, the operations of the company whose products are so necessary in the war effort."

Crowley's endorsement of those objectives and of McConnell's appointment reconciled Morgenthau to an executive order of March 11, 1942, moving various powers from the Treasury to the Office of the Alien Property Custodian. The order also stipulated that "in the case of any property, or interest therein, subject to the control of the Secretary of the Treasury, when the Alien Property Custodian shall notify the Secretary of the Treasury in writing that he is so directed, the Secretary of the Treasury shall release all control of any such property . . . to the Alien Property Custodian." The Treasury retained responsibility for foreign assets other than business properties, which Biddle would like to have assumed, but in the largest sense, in the controversy between the departments, Biddle and Crowley had won.

Crowley exploited his victory precisely as Morgenthau had feared he might. Sam Rosenman, assisting the President at the White House, blanched at the opportunism of the Alien Property Custodian. "If I had not been acting for the President," Rosenman told

Morgenthau in July 1942, "I don't know what I would have done to Crowley, I was so angry and so mad. . . . Here I was sitting in the capacity of a judge . . . and Crowley comes in . . . and says to me, 'By the way, Judge, I need a couple of good businessmen for Aniline Dye and if there are any friends of yours that you would like to put in there, just let me know and I will be glad to put them into General Aniline and Dye.' . . . It's just like offering me a bribe. . . . I don't know when I have been so angry."

But if Crowley had plums to distribute, McConnell had the authority to set things right at General Aniline, where he quickly cleaned up the Ozalid Division. He removed some forty executives and employees because of doubts about their loyalty, scrubbed out every vestige of German influence, and made the division as safe for government work as was any company in the United States. In every way McConnell fulfilled Morgenthau's expectations. Along with the lawyers within the Treasury itself, McConnell cooperated with Thurman Arnold, head of the Antitrust Division in the Department of Justice, in efforts to dissolve connections between large American corporations and I. G. Farben. Increasingly a supporter of antitrust actions in general, McConnell developed a particular sensitivity about collusion in restraint of trade by American companies which had connections with firms in Europe and South America. Because he opposed Crowley's plans for disposing of stock in several South American firms, McConnell resigned as head of General Aniline in mid-1943. He had by then developed a special interest in the problems that American industry would confront in moving from war to peace, and Morgenthau happily found a place for him within the Treasury to study questions of reconversion. There McConnell quietly worked out plans for easing economic adjustment to peace, for combating international cartels, and particularly for exorcising the influence and breaking up the power of German cartels and their Nazi masters. Indeed through McConnell, the Treasury's experience in General Aniline eventually bore significantly on departmental policy for postwar Germany. More immediately, through McConnell, Morgenthau had made General Aniline a safe and steady contributor to American war production.

3. Producing for War

The sheer volume of American defense production obscured, when war began, the inefficiencies of organization and the conflicts of interest within the economy and the sundry federal agencies concerned with it. Various civilian procurement officers, competing for authority with each other, also constantly clashed with the supply officers of the War and Navy Departments. Some manufacturers were reluctant to abandon commercial enterprises in order to convert their plant to war purposes; others were held back by shortages, particularly of machine tools, gasoline, and rubber. Labor leaders feared that management would make the national emergency an excuse for beating back the union movement, while managers used the national emergency as an excuse for attacking the unions.

Morgenthau had long since relinquished the responsibilities for defense production which he had assumed temporarily in 1940 at Roosevelt's request. Yet Treasury agencies, particularly the Procurement Division, continued to discharge their regular and significant duties in government purchasing, and executives in Washington and in labor and industry were aware of Morgenthau's concern for war production policy.

In mid-December 1941, Philip Murray, the head of the Congress of Industrial Organization, and Walter Reuther, the president of the United Automobile Workers, told Morgenthau that the allocation of military orders had left the Dodge Division of Chrysler Motors with no work. The employees of that division had therefore been laid off. Yet the government, as Morgenthau soon discovered, needed thousands of trucks. The Secretary's further investigations annoyed William Knudsen, the former General Motors executive now chief of the Office of Production Management. Knudsen's admitted dismay over the reduction in passenger car production in turn persuaded Morgenthau that "the Detroit crowd," with its eye on business-as-usual, was crippling OPM. Seeking support elsewhere, the Secretary persuaded Undersecretary of War Robert Patterson on December 28 to order 400,000 Dodge trucks for the Army. "If I didn't accomplish anything else," Morgenthau later noted, "at least I got Patterson to place this additional order which is half the truck capacity for the whole country for one year."

Ensuing discussions in January 1942, revealed Patterson's general discouragement about procurement problems. "As near as I can make out," Morgenthau concluded, "the Army just goes ahead and orders what it wants and pretty well disregards OPM." Patterson wanted to "leave the buying with the Army and Navy," but Murray and Reuther thought the services would then attempt to control wages and other conditions of work. Like Morgenthau, the labor leaders wanted instead to have the President establish a central body, perhaps even a new Cabinet department, for the conversion of industry to war production. Such an agency, they believed, would force selfish corporate interests, particularly the loitering automobile companies, to an all-out effort.

Roosevelt, however, remained cool to proposals for a ministry of supply. Rather, on January 13, 1942, the President established the War Production Board as a successor to the Supply Priorities and Allocations Board. Donald Nelson, the executive director of the defunct board, was to be chairman of the new agency. "His decision as to questions of procurement and production will be final," the President announced. But they were not. The Army and the Navy continued to operate with considerable independence, and within the War Production Board, Nelson lacked the will to control those of his subordinates who were solicitous of the particular industrial interests they had served before coming to Washington.

Morgenthau had special responsibility for silver policy. Wartime prosperity stimulated consumer demand for flatware and other articles made of silver. Furthermore, silver was a vital substitute for nickel, copper, aluminum, and tin, all in short supply and under rationing. Silver served, too, in the manufacture of guns, torpedoes, and electrical, photographic, and pharmaceutical equipment for military use. In order to provide more silver for industry, Morgenthau ceased government purchase of the metal in Canada, and held the Treasury's bids for Mexican silver to thirty-five cents an ounce, an eighth of a cent below market price. Manufacturers then had available substantially the whole Canadian and Mexican supply.

For the crux of the silver problem there was no easy solution. The Silver Purchase Act of 1934 still forced the Treasury to buy the entire American production of the metal at more than twice its market value, and the Silver Committee in the Senate, "twelve men against the nation," had the strength to perpetuate that extraordinary sub-sidy, the strength even to prevent the Treasury from selling its enor-mous hoard of silver for less than 71.11 cents an ounce, the artificial domestic price. Nevertheless, small quantities were sold for engine bearings, military insignia, and solders. The Treasury itself con-sumed 48,900,000 ounces by increasing the percentage of silver in the five-cent piece so as to release nickel and other base metals for crucial industrial purposes. More important, new legislation per-mitted the release of 410 million ounces to foreign governments re-ceiving Lend-Lease assistance.

Even the statute of 1934 did not forbid domestic loans of silver. In response to a request of the War Production Board, Morgenthau in the spring of 1942 had his staff contrive a scheme by which the department could furnish silver for electric conductors in govern-ment-owned aluminum and magnesium plants. That silver would not be consumed but preserved and later returned to the Treasury. This use of the uncoined silver, beyond the small portion needed for backing silver certificates, would "release large quantities of cop-per for other war needs." Moved especially by that consideration, Roosevelt endorsed the plan, which the Attorney General also ap-proved. On May 6, 1942, the Treasury leased to the Defense Plant Corporation 40,000 of the available 47,000 tons of unpledged bul-lion. The Senate Silver Committee did not object, but it soon pre-vented similar loans of the silver bullion earmarked for reserve against circulating certificates.

Six thousand tons of the silver loaned to industry went into silver wire for electromagnets at the top-secret plant at Oak Ridge, Ten-nessee, producing U-235 and plutonium. Morgenthau knew only that the War Department was utilizing the silver in some secret way. Indeed at no time in his years in office did he have any knowledge about developments in atomic energy. On one occasion Secretary of War Henry Stimson told him that in connection with a "very secret matter" he wanted to put $12 million in the Federal Reserve Bank in New York, for which he needed the Treasury's consent. Morgen-thau replied that the War Department had always before told him what was going on, but Stimson said that the matter was "so much more secret than anything else that I've ever had that I don't feel able to do that." Morgenthau was hurt. "If the Secretary of the

Treasury can't be trusted," he said, "he oughtn't to be Secretary of
the Treasury." But Stimson, while sorry to have shocked his associate, insisted that rather than bring the President into the question,
he would deposit the funds in a private bank. "He won't trust me,"
Morgenthau exploded when the conversation ended. "To hell with
him. I am sick and tired of it, anyway." But within a week he was
persuaded of the advantages of having the War Department turn to
the Federal Reserve Bank of New York rather than to a private
bank, and he then assured Stimson that he would arrange the details
with the appropriate officer, who turned out to be General Leslie
Groves. Even after talking with Groves, Morgenthau had only "got
the impression that it's some secret weapon." Twenty years later he
surmised that Roosevelt, knowing of his opposition to poison gas,
was unwilling to tell him about the atomic bomb, the use of which
he would have questioned.

While Morgenthau also disapproved of the continuing diffusion
of federal authority over war production, he had no mandate from
Roosevelt to intercede. Within the reach of Treasury policy, the
Secretary did what he could. As the President knew, he had other
absorbing duties, not the least the responsibility for raising the
money to pay the enormous costs of the battle against the Axis.

4. A Tremendous Program

Financing the costliest war in history imposed severe strains on the
Treasury. One involved an exhausting effort to persuade the balky
Congress to raise taxes high enough to cover one-half the expenses.*
Another related to the "tremendous program," as Morgenthau put
it, to defray the balance of expenses by borrowing. A third grew out
of continual controversy with various federal agencies about Morgenthau's effort to keep the purchase of government bonds on a voluntary basis. Persisting difficulties arose, too, from the attempt to
hold down interest rates on federal securities without thereby increasing wartime inflation.

With the federal government accumulating a huge wartime debt,

---

* Chapter II deals with the Treasury's wartime tax proposals, their failure in
Congress, and their implications for the problem of inflation. That chapter also
covers the debate about voluntarism in the bond program.

a pattern of low interest rates minimized servicing charges and thus the cost of the war to current and future taxpayers. Such a pattern depended upon sustaining the market price of federal securities at par, for if a $10,000 bond carrying a 2½ per cent coupon fell below par, then the actual yield on the bond rose above 2½. In order to keep the securities at par or slightly above it, the Treasury needed and received the cooperation of the Federal Reserve System, which stood ready, as the Board of Governors announced when war began, "to advance funds on United States Government securities at par to all banks."

The department and the system agreed about the need to keep yields low. They agreed, too, on the need to maximize sales to investors other than banks, for in that way the government could absorb corporate and private funds which would otherwise add to inflationary conditions. But the Treasury generally advocated a longer maturity for securities than did some Federal Reserve officers, especially President Allan Sproul of the New York Bank, who believed that the pace of inflation made investors wary of long-range, fixed-income offerings. Yet here again Treasury policy prevailed, for during the early months of the war the market became more and more optimistic, and in May 1942 the Federal Reserve accepted the 2½ per cent bonds scheduled for redemption in 1967–1972 as a bench mark for later issues. Indeed relations between the Treasury and the Federal Reserve were more harmonious during the war than they had ever been during the years of the New Deal.

Even so, Morgenthau was characteristically cautious. When Daniel Bell, the able Under Secretary of the Treasury, urged his chief to ask Roosevelt to state categorically that "we do not intend to pay a higher rate [than 2½ per cent] on any security issued during this war," Morgenthau hesitated. The Federal Reserve, he feared, might get "cold feet." More important, no one could predict what adverse conditions might develop. "I never tied my hands or made a forecast," the Secretary told Bell. ". . . Danny, old boy, I love you, but I won't say that." Instead he and Bell recommended to Roosevelt a more flexible statement: "We can finance our war effort without danger of disruptive inflation and without departing from our low interest rate policy."

Marriner Eccles, the vigorous and voluble head of the Federal Reserve Board, often in the past a hostile critic of the Treasury, gave

his full allegiance to the announced policy, assisted the department
in developing a variety of securities designed to appeal to non-bank
investors, and helped mobilize the Federal Reserve Banks for their
part in the successive war loan drives. Morgenthau would have
liked Eccles to liberalize reserve requirements in New York so as to
facilitate sales of bonds to banks there, and the Secretary would also
have preferred a lower rate for short-term funds than Eccles would
countenance, but those questions were trivial compared to the broad
agreements about general purposes. Eccles even assumed the unfa-
miliar role of the Treasury's defender. In Morgenthau's temporary
absence from Washington in October 1942, Eccles replied to *Time*
magazine which had condemned the Secretary's "customers-be-
damned" insistence on low interest rates. Banks, Eccles said, no
longer had the excess reserves and idle funds of prewar years. They
would therefore no longer heavily oversubscribe Treasury offerings.
"The Secretary of the Treasury," Eccles went on, "was entirely
right . . . in what you stigmatize as his 'little homily on 2 per cent
financing.' " To be sure lots of banks wanted a higher rate, but they
deserved no more because, as the Economic Policy Commission of
the American Bankers Association had admitted, the Federal Reserve System and the Treasury were supplying banks with the reserves with which to buy government securities. Further, it would
be shortsighted for banks to seek abnormal profits from war financing. Rates had to be held down to control the servicing charge on
the debt. In England and Canada, "this basic principle . . . is recognized and adhered to. In effect the governments of those countries are compensating the banks by giving them what amounts to a
living wage, not a large profit-making return, for the services they
are rendering."

Gratefully, Morgenthau told Eccles that "nobody could ask for
more cooperation or better service" than the Federal Reserve had
given the Treasury.

5. Voluntarism — Treasury Style

Except for Morgenthau himself, only Franklin and Eleanor Roosevelt cherished the Treasury's War Bond program. One day early in

1942 the Secretary walked over, as he had so often, from the fine old Treasury building to the White House for luncheon with the President in his office. Almost weekly for nine years the two had sat there together. "Henry," Roosevelt said, "you and I are the only people who understand it. Everybody else is against it, but we are going to do it." What they wanted to do was to persuade the American people voluntarily to buy bonds to finance the war.

A voluntary program, they believed, could raise sufficient funds to meet expenses not covered by tax revenues, and could absorb enough private income to relieve inflationary demands for goods and services in limited supply. A compulsory lending program, they thought, would produce little, if any, more money, while Congress, given the chance, would tend to hold back on income taxes if it enacted a forced lending bill. For 1942, Roosevelt and Morgenthau at first expected the bond drives to produce $8 billion, one billion more than a 10 per cent forced savings tax would have yielded. Equally important, voluntarism would work only if the Treasury mounted a vast sales campaign. Through that campaign, as Morgenthau put it and Roosevelt agreed, the Treasury could "make the country war-minded — there just isn't any other vehicle to do it."

Opponents of the Treasury's policy, men like Marriner Eccles and Budget Director Harold Smith, who considered voluntarism wholly inadequate for combating inflation, continuously underestimated the value placed by Roosevelt and Morgenthau on the psychological aspects of the successive sales drives. Again and again Eccles or Smith or others won the President or the Secretary to temporary or partial support for some kind of compulsory lending,* but always Morgenthau was determined to preserve his machinery for selling the war, which included an Advertising War Council of volunteer copywriters. Fred Smith, an advertising executive whom the Secretary recruited as an assistant, called Morgenthau "the number two advertising man in Washington. His only peer is his boss." Morgenthau, Smith went on, "couldn't lay out an advertisement if his entire apple crop depended upon it. . . . But . . . he has a genius for knowing . . . sweat from bluff. . . . Perhaps the most important advertising decision he ever made was the decision to use *bonds*

---

* See Chapter II which discusses compulsory lending or borrowing schemes as they arose in connection with revenue legislation.

to sell the *war,* rather than vice versa. . . . He simply points out
that people have been trying to sell thrift since the time of Benja-
min Franklin, and not with very great success; while under his plan
of selling the war first and bonds second, people are laying away
more money in a couple of weeks than they had ever before saved."

In April 1942 the Treasury was emphasizing the importance for
its bond sales of voluntary monthly payroll deductions, through
which employees of large corporations contracted to purchase bonds
regularly. Those systematic deductions also, as Morgenthau often
observed, had a healthy, anti-inflationary impact. Roosevelt agreed.
After inspecting the General Motors payroll deduction plan, one of
the most complicated and expensive in the country, the President
said: "I want a sign in everybody's window, not just saying, 'I
bought a war bond,' but that 'I buy a war bond every month.'"

The ongoing sales campaign, directed to that goal, constantly received Morgenthau's personal attention. He ordered his special
bond staff to prepare radio programs not only in English but in
foreign languages for use in cities with large foreign-born populations. He wrote dubious congressmen about the importance to the
Treasury of the advertising sponsored by "public spirited companies
or individuals" who bought hundreds of millions of dollars a year of
bond advertisements. "This is very different from free advertising,"
Morgenthau noted, "in that it provides a substantial amount of revenue to newspapers and magazines. . . . The . . . Bond program
has already given the newspapers many millions of dollars in advertising from banks, department stores, and other institutions. In the
case of radio, our most popular program . . . was sponsored and
paid for by two corporations, and was not in any sense free advertising." Indeed, the generosity of the contributing sponsors had made
it possible for the Treasury to avoid spending "one penny on paid
advertising in newspapers and magazines or on the radio since the
start of our . . . program."

The Department's budget covered other activities, including the
salaries of the professional staff in the bond office and the costs of
promotional films, of which one series featured Walt Disney's Donald Duck. Ordinarily the Treasury also paid for the use of bill-
boards. At least once the layout displeased Morgenthau. "Is it necessary," he complained, "for us to get a Hollywood actress swathed

in mink over a blue-and-white print dress to launch our new bill board campaign? Personally, I think it is awfully cheap. Secondly, I would much rather have a girl from Amalgamated Clothiers Union swathed in a pair of overalls."

In the spring campaign of 1942, Morgenthau for the first time had his staff establish quotas for sales. He wanted quotas for every state and county and an increase in the payroll savings plan to carry it to at least 10 per cent of the gross payroll of every important business firm. As things stood, about 45 per cent of all employees were participating, with an average monthly allotment of about 4.8 per cent of their wages. Morgenthau intended to double that record. To reach groups other than wage earners, he ordered special emphasis on the sale of F and G bonds. Those bonds, written in larger denominations than the smaller E bonds,* carried slightly lower rates of interest but were available for purchase in unlimited quantity by individuals, personal trusts, and corporations.

To launch the spring drive, Morgenthau solicited the assistance of Secretary of Agriculture Claude Wickard, of Philip Murray of the CIO and William Green of the AFL, and of the heads of the National Association of Manufacturers and the United States Chamber of Commerce, all of whom opposed compulsory savings. "We have got to step up the sale of War Bonds," the Secretary said in his own speech for the newsreels on April 20, 1942, "to a billion dollars every month. Every community in this country will have to do its share to reach this quota. All of us who earn regular pay should set aside an average of at least 10 per cent of it every week for buying War Bonds. . . . It's not only smart to be thrifty, but our future depends upon it." To newspapermen, off the record, the Secretary stressed the significance of the campaign for national morale. "There are millions of people," he said, ". . . who say, 'What can we do to help?' . . . Right now, other than going in the Army and Navy or working in a munitions plant, there isn't anything to do. . . . Sixty per cent of the reason that I want to do this thing is . . . to give the people an opportunity to do something. . . . The

* The E bonds, maturing in 15 years, carried an accelerating interest rate to discourage purchasers from redeeming them before maturity. So, for example, a bond costing $18.75 was worth $25 fifteen years later, but much of the increment in its value accrued in the last years of its term. E bonds were available only to individuals and only in limited quantity.

unions have been perfectly swell about this thing. It is the unions who want the volunteer plan as against the forced savings, and they are proud of what they have done. . . . Now, as to inflation, when we tap the thing at the payroll and get the people to put this money in, that is going to take care of this thing . . . the hard way and . . . the democratic way."

That way had its entertaining moments, which the Secretary enjoyed. The April drive had just started when he received a telegram from the faculty director of the campaign at Phillips Academy, Andover, where 99.2 per cent of the students had signed pledges to buy savings stamps* regularly. "I've promised the undergraduate body a congratulatory telegram from you," Frederick S. Allis, Jr., explained. "Will whoever opens this please draft something in the way of a reply with some punch to it and sign Morgenthau's name. I have referred to 'my old friend Henry Morgenthau' in campaign speeches and suggest that your reply begin Dear Fritz stop. This would amuse the little men no end. Please shoot this off right away to make Wednesday's edition of the school newspaper." Morgenthau responded in full spirit. "Dear Fritz," he wired. ". . . Three cheers for Andover. As an old Exeter boy I am deeply impressed. Your record . . . will make other schools sit up and take notice. This is no time however for Andover boys to rest on their oars. The war is costing $120 million every day and the need for savings is much greater than ever before. . . . I suggest therefore that all Andover boys set themselves a quota of at least 10 per cent of their allowances and keep it up until the war is won. Remember the more bonds you buy the more planes will fly." The Secretary's telegram, Allis replied, "did more than anything . . . to personalize . . . our stamp campaign. . . . I was the more pleased to get it because several of my Republican friends . . . assured me that no one ever answered telegrams in Washington these days."

Morgenthau often praised volunteers in the field. During the week in which he wired Allis, he also thanked, among others, Kay Kayser, the bandleader, for participating in bond wagon shows in Chicago; H. W. Anderson, a vice president of General Motors, for sending along a desk set of promotional materials, a "magnificent

---

* Those stamps, in denominations as small as ten cents, could be bought and accumulated until the purchaser had $18.75, the cost of the smallest E bond.

example" for other companies; and Arthur Hays Sulzberger, publisher of the *New York Times,* for an offer to let the Treasury use
the north facade of the *Times* tower for war bond messages. Later
he acknowledged the cooperation of the governors of every state,
and of the British and American military services for assigning war
heroes to appear at various bond rallies.

The whole program, as the Secretary interpreted it, depended
upon good will. "It is . . . against Treasury policy," he warned,
"for anyone connected with the War Savings Staff . . . to use intimidation . . . of any kind to induce people to sign pledges, payroll
authorization cards, or bond applications. . . . We must persuade
people to buy . . . willingly and enthusiastically, by bringing them
to realize that in doing so they serve their country today and themselves tomorrow."

When persuasion faltered, as it did for a time in the promotion of
F and G bonds, the Secretary turned not to threats but to new techniques. "What I am going to do," he told his staff in June 1942, "I
am going to ask the president of the Federal Reserve to call for volunteers among security salesmen all over the United States. . . .
They will be corralled under the president of the Federal Reserve
to go out and do this thing." That reorganization removed some
salesmen from the direct surveillance of the Treasury War Savings
Staff, to the irritation of several of Morgenthau's subordinates, but
the Secretary put efficiency above bureaucratic feelings. Before the
December drive, he had wholly excluded the F and G committees
from the department's supervision, thus leaving his staff free to concentrate on the E bonds, on payroll savings, and on related matters.

Morgenthau had to get results. If he slipped, voluntarism would
fall with him. "Henry has promised to raise $1 billion a month and
he's got his neck out," Roosevelt told the Cabinet on July 10, 1942,
"and let him hang himself if he wants to or else . . . his head goes
caput!"

"This is either the second or third time he has said this at Cabinet," Morgenthau reported to his staff. "And if sometimes I seem a
little unreasonable in my pressure on you, it's remarks like this that
are difficult to take. . . . I know each and every person is doing his
damndest . . . but at times if I get a little overexcited, it's remarks
like that which I think were most unfortunate before the Cabinet.

. . . I had it on the tip of my tongue to say, and almost bit my tongue off, 'However badly we do, Mr. President, it's better than your campaign for rubber.'* But I did not say it and I am glad. There are a lot of things which are going badly for him and I suppose he thought he would take a crack. . . . And sometimes it's awfully hard to take it." Alone with Roosevelt on July 16, Morgenthau "told the President that he had been pretty rough on me at the last Cabinet on War Bonds. . . . 'Well,' he said, 'There isn't a day passes that either Wallace or Miss Perkins doesn't go after me on compulsory savings. . . . What did I say?' I said, 'Forget it, but I thought you were pretty rough.' "

On the whole Morgenthau was optimistic, proud of what the Treasury had accomplished, confident that it could do more as time went by. He was especially grateful to Harold Graves, his assistant for many years, who had built up the bond organization; to Theodore R. Gamble, who had left his chain of theaters to relieve Graves of executive responsibility for the program; and to Peter Odegard, an Amherst political scientist, who had been the director of "Mass Psychology." Those men and their associates, Morgenthau told the press in December, just before the start of a new campaign, "have broken the ground right straight along on radio, moving pictures, newspapers, and magazines in their effort to bring to this country what this whole fight is about. I think they have done a grand job."

The Victory Loan Drive of December, the Secretary reported at its conclusion, far exceeded his expectations. Aiming for $9 billion, the Treasury had raised $12.906 billion, "the biggest amount of money ever raised by any government in such a short time." The campaign had reached a larger proportion of non-bank investors, including purchasers of small E bonds and stamps, than ever before, and broken all records for sales of F and G securities.

This "grand response by the people," as Morgenthau called it, sustained his spirits, impressed the President, and, for the while, protected voluntarism, Treasury style, from the mounting criticisms of its opponents. Yet the Secretary was caught on a treadmill that constantly accelerated, for the costs of war were rising, as was the pace of inflation, and the preservation of voluntarism therefore demanded continuing efforts on an increasing scale.

---

* The production of synthetic rubber had not yet come close to meeting national needs.

6. Two Hundred Billion Dollars

The national debt increased during the Second World War some two hundred billion dollars, most of it borrowed in the six war loan campaigns of 1943, 1944, and the first half of 1945. That increase was more than four times the total of the whole debt outstanding before the war in Europe had begun. The annual servicing charge on the increase, though limited by the low interest rates the Treasury established, nevertheless roughly equaled the relief appropriations of 1935 which had then seemed astronomical to most New Dealers, as well as to their conservative opponents. The courageous revenue legislation that the Treasury recommended and the Congress rejected would have prevented perhaps a third of the increment in the debt, but even if Congress had raised taxes substantially, the Treasury would have had to borrow more money, more quickly than Morgenthau would have cared to contemplate until the actual task fell to him. He and his staff learned while they worked, adjusting their tactics as they applied the experience of each war loan drive to the plans for its successor, as they responded to the changing economic situation in the country and, sometimes negatively, to the suggestions of their critics.

In preparing for the Second War Loan, scheduled for April 1943, Morgenthau increased the authority of the Victory Loan Committees, the creatures of the Reserve banks, at the expense of the authority of his own War Savings staff. The Victory Loan groups were to concentrate, as they had earlier, on F and G bonds, and on those customers who ordinarily made purchases through banks and brokers. "I have got to raise the money," the Secretary told the press. "I have got to use the financial machinery of the country. I have to have their cooperation. . . . That doesn't mean I have sold out to them. It would be very stupid on my part . . . that I should suddenly, at the end of my career, practically sell out to the bankers . . . particularly when all my sympathy is the other way. . . . I don't belong to their club and I have no intention of joining — and they don't want me."

They did want more authority. After the successful completion of the drive, the Federal Reserve System urged an immediate enlargement of its role within the war bond organization. But the New York Federal Reserve Bank, Morgenthau feared, would turn to hardened anti-New Dealers if it could choose the state managers for its area. The Treasury, the Secretary decided, would continue to direct the state organizations, but would consult the presidents of the reserve banks about appointments in their regions. The consolidated Victory Fund Committees and War Savings Staffs would function under state chairmen who were to report directly to the Secretary of the Treasury.

Privately, Morgenthau fretted over lapses of the War Savings organization. In defiance of his explicit orders, officials in that office had launched a campaign specifically to promote savings stamps. The figures compiled by the office, moreover, sometimes contained errors, and its sales record in the months between major bond drives lagged behind the Secretary's expectations. In a long scolding of July 19, 1943, he demanded more vigor and discipline in preparations for the Third War Loan Drive, coming in September and aimed at $15 billion, to be raised entirely from "individual investors, corportations, insurance companies and other non-banking sources."

Morgenthau opened that campaign to "Back the Attack" on September 3 by selling a $100 bond to Winston Churchill, then in the United States. "I will give it to the first American soldier who sets foot in Berlin," the Prime Minister said, though he never did. Marshal Stalin, at Morgenthau's request, sent a special message of his own. But the success of the drive, which exceeded its goal, owed most to the men the Secretary had criticized a few months earlier. The War Finance Division of the Treasury Department had placed promotional material on the radio, in newspapers, general magazines, farm and business and trade publications, and outdoor advertisements. Its campaign had drawn on the assistance of private and business groups who posted reminders in buses and streetcars, in moving picture theaters, on caps of milk bottles, and on matchboxes. For the Third War Loan total advertising in all media ran just short of $24 million, much of it contributed without cost to the Treasury.

Advertising and promotion had measurable results. Among Americans who did not live on farms, 71 per cent had known about the Second War Loan drive; in contrast, 86 per cent were aware of the Third War Loan. The improvement was even more marked among the farm population. The third drive sold bonds to many more people than had the second. Among the non-farm population, only 20 per cent of those gainfully employed had increased their bond purchases in April 1943, whereas 35 per cent did so in September. The fall campaign reached approximately twice as many people as had the campaign of April, while sustaining the percentage of purchases among those solicited. And the proportion of Americans increasing their bond purchases without solicitation grew from 16 to 20 per cent, obviously under the impact of the September effort.

Treasury studies revealed that the motivation of individuals buying bonds remained essentially constant. They bought in order to help a member of the family in the armed service, to invest their money safely, to preserve "the American way of life," to combat inflation, to save for security against the chance of a postwar depression, or to save for some specific postwar use. Few Americans believed the war would soon end, though sales fell off briefly in the short period between the announcement of the surrender of the Italian government and the renewal of German resistance at Salerno and elsewhere in Italy. Japan appeared in many ways a stronger emotional symbol of the enemy than did Germany. Americans felt that the war with Japan would last longer, and they tended to view the Japanese as "ungodly, subhuman, beastly, sneaky, and treacherous." Future drives, the Treasury concluded, would do well to stress the war against Japan and, in the face of rising living costs, to emphasize the need for personal sacrifice.

In October 1943, Morgenthau spent twenty days on battlefields in North Africa and Italy. He had gone, he later said, to get a firsthand view of the war and some idea of what soldiers were thinking. "My only interest in life is to win the war," he told one reporter, "so I spend a lot of time trying to learn about the war. I just want to beat those bastards." He therefore worried about some of the things he saw or heard. For one, as he told the President after he returned, General Mark Clark desperately needed more amphibious craft in Italy. For another, British officers often spoke disparagingly of the Russians. Not the least, Morgenthau found Dakar "the dirtiest outfit I have seen. . . . Possibly as a result, the malaria rate is exceedingly high. Hospitals are inadequate. Prefabricated barracks . . . afford no protection from mosquitoes or from the weather."

But continually the Secretary's thoughts returned to bonds. On

October 23, 1943, broadcasting with General Eisenhower from Allied Headquarters in Algiers, the Secretary assured the American people that their dollars were being well spent. A willingness to pay higher taxes and to buy more bonds would demonstrate the deep involvement of civilians in the fight. Eisenhower agreed that successful bond drives boosted the morale of his troops. Better to inform those troops, Morgenthau arranged for the Armed Forces Radio to carry the best promotional shows of future bond campaigns. He also took steps to sell more bonds to the soldiers themselves, not so much in order to instill in them habits of thrift or to extract from them a fraction of the costs of the war, as to cooperate with military authorities who had found that the average GI had too much cash in his pocket. When the Yanks had less to spend, it reduced friction between American soldiers and the troops of allied nations who had lower pay, and it checked inflation in occupied areas.

Americans at home still had too much to spend. Congress's final and stubborn rejection of the Administration's tax program left corporations and individuals, as 1944 began, with surplus incomes which would push the prices of scarce goods and services to new peaks unless the Treasury succeeded, in its part of the price control program, in absorbing much of that surplus by larger sales of bonds. Morgenthau, while still opposed to compulsory lending, confessed to his staff that he had often been "terribly disappointed" by the results of the voluntary program. A March 1944 report of the Securities and Exchange Commission indicated that some $14 billion of savings had gone into bank balances, which were easily convertible into cash. The bond drives, Morgenthau felt, should have attracted that money. Instead they were failing especially to reach working men earning between $100 and $200 a week. "I am going to raise hell until I get the answer," the Secretary warned his assistants. ". . . I think we have been smart enough now to stay ahead, but all the percentage trends show we are getting less and less of the savings of the country."

Yet for 1944 Morgenthau more than ever before had to look to the banks for help. Previously he had planned a financing in each quarter of the year, but now, as he told his staff, "I want only three, and the last one I want after elections." A large financing during the presidential canvass of the autumn, he believed, would fail to win enthusiasm from Republican Wall Street. But the decision for only three financings, as Dan Bell pointed out, would force the Treasury to borrow proportionately more from the banks than from individuals. "That is all right," the Secretary said. "I would rather borrow it than have them cut my throat." As it worked out, he got the money but he exposed his throat.

During 1944 private and corporate speculators exploited the rhythm of financings that the Treasury and Federal Reserve had established. They did so, as Marriner Eccles explained, by "playing the pattern of rates." Banks sold to the Federal Reserve most of their short-term, low-yield securities as those securities, toward the end of their terms, reached premium prices. With the cash they obtained, the banks then bought longer-term, higher-yield securities. They made those purchases from individuals, corporations, and insurance companies who were taking advantage of what Eccles called "free riding." Those non-bank investors bought heavily in each Treasury bond drive with the assurance that the Reserve System would sustain the value of their purchases. Then, as the bonds they had bought advanced toward maturity, the speculators sold them to commercial banks. Indeed, commercial banks loaned billions of dollars to their customers for precisely that kind of speculation. As a result, securities purchased in one bond drive were frequently sold just before or during the next drive, and within months after the end of a drive, a substantial portion of sales to non-bank investors found its way back to the banks where it contributed to excess reserves. "Countless corporations as well as individuals made a great show of their patriotism in subscribing heavily to . . . war loan drives," Eccles later observed, whereas in fact they were making a guaranteed profit at no risk.

The problem reached a worrying dimension during the Fifth War Loan in mid-1944. As Eccles wrote Morgenthau that August, the Board of Governors in the Federal Reserve System hoped the Treasury would make a stronger appeal for the cooperation of commercial banks, would require subscribers other than banks and dealers to make a down payment of 25 per cent from existing funds, and most important, would concentrate on the lowest denominations of marketable bonds, particularly those with maturity values between $100 and $500, in order to increase sales to permanent investors. Such bonds were not eligible for repurchase by banks at any time.

Morgenthau and Dan Bell, preparing for the Sixth War Loan, believed that it was not yet necessary to alter significantly the pattern of offerings of previous drives. Further, they doubted they could raise enough money if they concentrated on sales of securities ineligible for resale to banks. Though they urged banks voluntarily to discipline speculation, their pleas had little effect. The Sixth War Loan raised some $21 billion, as compared to its goal of $14 billion, but it failed to draw that money from non-inflationary sources. Bank credit supported the purchase of more than $10 billion of government bonds while the Sixth War Loan was in progress or immediately thereafter. Accordingly the increase of holdings by non-bank investors came to only about $11 billion, a little more than half of the total achievement of the drive.

Treasury studies indicated that insurance companies and corporations, rather than private individuals, were responsible for most of the speculation. In an effort to improve the situation, Morgenthau and several of his staff met on March 1, 1945, with representatives of various American life insurance companies. He would prefer to see the industry police itself, the Secretary said, rather than to impose a formula that would prevent insurance companies from subscribing beyond their investment needs during war loans. His visitors agreed, and agreed also to put their own companies and others on their honor in future drives. "What I am trying to do is this," Morgenthau later explained to his assistants. "I would like to leave the financial community in an atmosphere of feeling that what the Treasury has done is fair, extra fair."

Eccles felt the Treasury had not done enough. He believed the Department should have organized the Seventh War Loan to offer the banks $3 billion directly, while also defining all other securities as permanently ineligible for bank purchase. He thought, too, that the Treasury was trying to raise more than it could from corporations. Still, for the "Mighty Seventh," as Morgenthau announced in July 1945, the American people subscribed "a total of $26,313 million. . . . We asked for seven billion dollars in individual subscriptions. We have received a total of $8,681 millions. Finally, and most important of all, we set for the wage earners of the country the difficult goal of $4 billion in E Bonds. The final figures show that E Bond sales have amounted to $3,976 millions."

Unfortunately corporations had continued their speculative practices. While non-bank investors bought some $147 billion of government securities during the wartime bond campaigns, as Eccles later wrote, the actual increment in their holdings was only $93 billion. Commercial banks, on the other hand, while permitted to subscribe for only $10 billion during the drives, increased their holdings by some $57 billion, and the holdings of Federal Reserve banks grew $18 billion. Corporations, the leading culprits, subscribed to about $60 billion, but their actual holdings rose only $19 billion. Insurance companies, in contrast, retained about two-thirds of their subscriptions. As Eccles saw it, bankers, government bond dealers, and brokers made substantial profits by servicing the corporate speculators whose gains were the largest.

Yet even Eccles admitted that some wartime securities had to be sold to banks. Further, the interest rates which he advocated retrospectively for those securities seemed exorbitant to the Treasury. From Morgenthau's point of view, direct sales to banks in the dimension Eccles preferred at the interest rates he proposed would have yielded profits for the banks at least as large as those which instead accrued to the speculators, while higher rates on Treasury bills would have resulted primarily in larger profits for the Federal Reserve System, which acquired them. A substantial part of bond sales, moreover, drew on genuine savings, individual and corporate.

While recognizing the problems Eccles stressed, Morgenthau pointed to gains which, in his view, compensated for the shortcomings of the Treasury's program. The Second World War, he noted, the costliest war in history, had absorbed approximately half of the national product of the United States for three years, twice the percentage absorbed during the First World War. Defense and war spending between July 1940 and July 1945, increased the interest-bearing public debt $211 billion. In raising that sum, the Treasury had followed three basic principles — to borrow money in a manner designed to resist inflation; to offer securities best suited to the needs of the investors; to keep the cost of financing at a reasonable level. In most respects, Morgenthau believed, the Department had succeeded. Of the $211 billion increase, non-bank investors loaned some $122 billion. The $89 billion accumulated in commercial and Federal Reserve banks was larger, Morgenthau wrote, "than I would have wished, just as the proportion of our total funds raised by taxes is smaller than I would have wished." Yet the growth in the holdings of the Federal Reserve banks was balanced by a corresponding growth in currency and commercial bank deposits. During the period of that growth the national product had doubled, and the accompanying volume of business required a larger volume of cash. In June 1940, individuals and business firms in the United States had about 41 cents in currency and demand deposits for every dollar of the annual product of the country. In July 1945, they had 46 cents, an increment so small that Morgenthau did not "believe that it harbors an inflationary hazard."

The Treasury, the Secretary maintained, had offered the small investor "a security entirely free from risk." After the First World War, many of the Liberty Bonds and other issues had sold below par. In contrast, the E, F, and G Bonds of the Second World War were guaranteed to retain their par value, though of course inflation could decrease their real value, as it ultimately did, but primarily in the postwar period.

Unlike any previous major war in American history, the Second World War had been financed at a low level of interest rates — one of Morgenthau's greatest accomplishments in all his years at the Treasury. In the period between the outbreak of the First World War and its end, the average rate of interest on the national debt had risen from 2.36 to 4.22 per cent. In contrast, on July 30, 1939, just before the start of the Second World War, the average rate of interest on the national debt, then some $45 billion, amounted to 2.53 per cent; six years later, with the debt at $257 billion, the average rate had fallen to 1.94 per cent. Those figures understated "the saving in interest cost between this war and the last one," because interest on the securities of the Second World War was not tax free. With the coming of peace, Morgenthau predicted, low interest rates would help to stimulate investment and thus employment. Low interest rates, moreover, as Morgenthau saw it, had the incomparable advantage of minimizing the servicing charge on the war debt, the charge on future generations.

Indeed, Morgenthau concluded, the wartime experience made a

case for enlarging the authority of the Treasury, and diminishing that of the Federal Reserve System, over questions of national finance. The Secretary of the Treasury, he urged, should have responsibility and control over all aspects of fiscal and monetary policy, including those which fell, in existing circumstances, respectively to the Bureau of the Budget or the Board of Governors of the Federal Reserve System. Accordingly he recommended the reinstatement of the Secretary of the Treasury as a full member of the Board of Governors and of the Federal Open Market Committee. With the Secretary participating on those boards, they should take over the functions and powers of the Securities and Exchange Commission. Those and related changes, Morgenthau argued, would eliminate the friction which had on occasion characterized the making of wartime fiscal and monetary decisions.

His recommendations, which the makers of postwar policy rejected, stood in direct opposition to the demands of the business community for reducing Treasury influence in Washington. That view informed an article of 1945 in *Fortune* which blamed the Department for inflation. Taxes, *Fortune* complained, had not been high enough. Prices had soared, especially quotations on equities on the New York stock market. Too much of the public debt was in short-term securities. But, as the Treasury replied, the Department had consistently urged higher taxes which the Congress had refused.* The size of the short-term debt, the Treasury went on, had no effect on consumer spending and therefore was no impetus to inflation. As for prices, they had advanced less during the Second World War than in any other major war in American history, and risen less in the United States than in any other nation on the allied side. Further, while the prices of stocks in New York had moved up almost 90 per cent during the months of war, in 1945 they remained below their 1937 highs, and 45 per cent below their 1930 highs, even though corporate profits were close to their all-time zenith. *Fortune,* the Treasury suggested, "just can't stand prosperity."

Looking back two decades later, Morgenthau reversed none of his wartime judgments. As he had before, so again, he lamented corporate speculation during Treasury bond drives, just as he frowned on other corporate practices that the New Deal had tried to prevent.

* See Chapter II.

But he retained his particular pride in holding down the interest rate on the wartime debt, and his attachment to the easy money policy of his earlier years in office. Most of all he expressed satisfaction with the Treasury's reliance on voluntarism, and with the bond campaigns as instruments for awakening the American people to the implications of the war. He regretted only his signal failure, the failure of the whole executive branch, to bring the Congress to a responsible tax policy, for which he had fought continually while he was also raising the billions of dollars needed to back the attack.

II

Taxation for War

1942-1944

IN THE MONTHS before Pearl Harbor, Morgenthau had been devoting most of his time to the problems of taxation and the control of inflation, which were to continue to harass the Treasury for another two years. With conversion to war production, fewer goods and services became available for civilian consumption, while the accompanying spurt in employment raised personal incomes. Increased taxes, like increased savings, could effectively reduce the spending power of the American people, and thereby help to ease the rise in prices, while the resulting revenue from such taxes might meet — if the Treasury's purpose prevailed — about half the booming costs of war. Morgenthau wanted revenue legislation also to preserve the social goals of the New Deal, to distribute the burden of taxation on the principle of ability to pay, and to prevent any individual or corporation from exploiting the war for personal gain. Those objectives, along with his commitment to voluntarism in the bond program, governed the Secretary's thinking throughout the war, but he subjected his views deliberately to the criticisms of his expert advisers.

On matters of taxation, those advisers included Under Secretary of the Treasury Daniel Bell, whose responsibilities for debt management naturally involved him also in questions relating to revenue. As conservative as Morgenthau in his views about fiscal policy, Bell, like his chief, was prepared to embrace innovations that promised to reduce the need for federal borrowing. Accordingly both men, while hostile to Keynesian economics, accepted suggestions from Keynes's American disciples. One such disciple was Assistant Secretary of the Treasury Harry Dexter White. Though White's responsibilities lay in the area of monetary research and policy, he occasionally spoke out about taxation, and he continually supported the fiscal proposals of Alvin Hansen, the Harvard economist, of Ben Cohen, the President's counselor, and of other proponents of the new economics. Assistant Secretary of the Treasury Herbert E. Gaston, who had been with Morgenthau in various capacities since 1929, gave the Secretary unequaled devotion and understanding. A veteran of agrarian reform movements and a dedicated New Dealer, Gaston, with the Secretary, stressed the importance of taxation as a vehicle for social progress. So, too, did the most influential new member of the Treasury staff, Randolph Paul, who came to the Department just before Pearl Harbor to take charge of the Tax Division and soon thereafter, in July 1942, became General Counsel. An experienced tax lawyer and economist, Paul operated, as one of Morgenthau's friends observed, in the tradition of one of his predecessors, Herman Oliphant — with "brains, imagination, integrity and the willingness to spend himself on a cause." Paul persuaded the Secretary to incorporate Keynesian devices in his recommendations to the President and to the Congress, while he also valued and sustained the general objectives of Morgenthau's wartime revenue programs.

1. The Social Point of View

The President, preparing his budget message of January 1942, endorsed the Treasury's tentative recommendation for $7 billion of new taxes, approximately half the estimated deficit for the coming year. It was "going to require a considerable amount of ingenuity to find that seven billion," as Randolph Paul warned Morgenthau. "This lousy tax system that we have got," the Secretary replied on January 7, 1942, called for all the ingenuity he and the rest of the tax staff could muster. They were to be "bold and brave and intelligent enough" to prepare for Congress an ideal program, "to give the country something fresh."

The Secretary spoke out personally for immediate action to close loopholes through which wealthy men and corporations could avoid federal taxes. "Now that we are at war," he said in an address of January 24 to the City Club of Cleveland, "now that the revenue needs of the government have soared beyond all previous conceptions, it is high time to tax the income of state and municipal securities," and past time to reduce the depletion allowance of 27.5 per cent each year from which oil companies and other mining interests benefited. Those defects in the revenue laws injured national morale, Morgenthau believed, while morale would suffer further if new taxes bore most heavily on small wage earners, as would a sales tax, the device preferred by the Republicans in Congress. "I look at this thing from the social viewpoint," the Secretary told his staff on February 20. ". . . Feeling the way I do at this particular state of the war effort, and until I am convinced that Congress means to close up these billion dollar loopholes . . . I can't sit here and be the fellow to go after the . . . people in the lower one-third."

Yet, as the Secretary had to admit, "there is only one person can save us from a sales tax, and that is if Mr. Roosevelt makes up his mind to a real fight on it." The advocates of a sales tax, or of a gross income tax written to bear heavily on the lowest brackets, emphasized the utility of their proposals for raising revenue and for combating inflation. They realized, too, as did Morgenthau, that tax reform had few champions in Congress or elsewhere. The elimination of the exemptions for state and municipal bonds, whether for outstanding or for future issues, was a "dead duck" according to Arthur Vandenberg of Michigan, then probably the most influential Republican in the Senate. Speaker of the House Sam Rayburn of Texas, whose favored constituents included the oil companies first and any others later, warned Morgenthau that Vandenberg was right and that Congress would also resist any reduction in the percentage of depletion allowance. And the Senate in 1940 and 1941 had already revealed its unwillingness to enact an effective excess profits tax on corporations, another of the Secretary's objectives. As Morgenthau put it ruefully, "I can get all my New Dealers in the bathtub now."

Nevertheless Morgenthau, working from materials prepared by Randolph Paul, made no concessions to politics in his testimony before the House Ways and Means Committee on March 3, 1942. He

asked for the tax reforms he had been advocating and for higher
surtaxes on individual income. To maximize the impact of taxation
on the threat of inflation, Morgenthau recommended, as Paul had
advised, increased social security taxes and a system providing for
collection of income taxes at the source by regular payroll and other
deductions. He stressed the need for raising corporation taxes some
40 per cent, to be achieved largely by remedying defects in the excess
profits schedules. "We are fighting for the maintenance of the very
system of free enterprise which makes corporate profits possible,"
Morgenthau said. "At a time like this, I am confident that incorporated business will willingly pay additional taxes. . . . In the critical months ahead our patriotism . . . must rise above the profit
motive." Yet very high taxes could impair incentive. He therefore
suggested that corporate taxes paid at a rate above 80 per cent be
returned by the government after the war for business use in purchasing additional capital equipment or employing additional
labor. That arrangement would assure revenue and anti-inflationary pressure during the war, and assure funds for reconversion and
economic stimulation after the armistice.

Morgenthau also proposed increases in estate and gift taxes and in
excises selected because the commodities to which they applied were
either luxuries or in scarce supply. In contrast, he said, a general
sales tax "falls on scarce and plentiful commodities alike. It strikes
at necessaries and luxuries alike. . . . It bears disproportionately
on the low income groups. . . . It increases prices and . . . stimu-
lates demands for higher wages."

The Treasury's program drew immediate complaints from the
House Ways and Means Committee which was disinclined to raise
taxes as much or as progressively as the Department deemed necessary. Yet hearings had barely begun before the accelerating pace of
inflation forced Morgenthau and his advisers to demand new and
stiffer policies that separated them still further from their critics on
the Hill.

2. Weeks of Particular Hell

In mid-March 1942, various of Roosevelt's advisers — among others
Vice President Wallace, Secretary of Agriculture Wickard, Budget

Director Harold Smith, Marriner Eccles, and Leon Henderson, the head of the Office of Price Administration — persuaded the President "to order basic staff and command work on the problem of inflation." Morgenthau, a member of the committee appointed to explore that question, disagreed with his colleagues and would not sign the report they sent the White House early in April. The report recommended a sales tax, a lowering of income tax exemptions, and the freezing of wages. The Secretary, no less worried than were the others about inflation, endorsed a six-point program devised by Randolph Paul. It proposed the freezing of prices at current levels; the rapid enactment of the Treasury tax bill; further necessary fiscal measures; wage adjustments to compensate for the rising cost of living; and direct controls over credit, inventory, and residential building. Further, Morgenthau commended the Treasury's voluntary savings program for which Eccles and Smith wanted to substitute compulsory lending. The Secretary summarized his views in a memorandum to Roosevelt of April 3, 1942:

"We should not leave a stone unturned to keep the cost of living as nearly as possible at the present level. You will notice . . . we have not limited ourselves to fiscal measures for we do not believe that fiscal measures alone are adequate to meet the situation. If we adopt a program of strict rationing . . . the amount of money available for federal borrowing will be greatly increased and it will come from sources which will not be inflationary. . . . There are radical points of difference between our conclusions and those of Harold Smith's group. . . . We feel strongly that it would be a mistake to yield to the clamor for a sales tax. . . . A sales tax . . . would get no more revenue but simply have shifted the source of revenue to the lower income groups.

"We object on the same grounds to lowering the personal exemptions. . . . We also . . . are in strong disagreement on the proposal to freeze wages, which we think unnecessary, impractical, and exceedingly dangerous."

Determined "to force a decision," the Secretary was especially angry with the Keynesian economists in Washington. "First they want inflation," he complained, "and they don't want any rationing or anything sensible about finances. They think that the Government can do the thing one day by pumping money in, and the next day they think the Government can do the thing by putting the

brakes on the lower income groups, but I have yet to see a single one
of them make a success of anything that they have undertaken. . . .
I am sick and tired of the whole thing."

Smith, Eccles, and Leon Henderson were equally adamant. Following a futile meeting with Treasury experts on April 7, 1942, they
went straight to the White House to press for their own plan.
"Well," Morgenthau said when he heard about their foray, "I always say when you are doing a tax bill you have got to sleep on the
floor so a fellow can't put a knife in your back." The Smith plan,
the Secretary felt, would kill voluntary savings and wreck any
chance for the recommendations the Treasury had made to the
Ways and Means Committee. Taking his own case to the President
on April 9, Morgenthau found Roosevelt "in sympathy with everything that we wanted," an impression which Eccles — to his distress
— also gleaned. At the Cabinet meeting the next day Henry Wallace "got a little ugly" when the President supported the Treasury.
The Department had, too, Morgenthau learned, the backing of organized labor, but Smith was attempting to woo it away. "These
stupid asses around Harold Smith," Morgenthau told his staff, "in
order to satisfy Labor . . . want to go after the rich people." Smith
was therefore urging a 100 per cent tax on war profits, and Eccles a
95 per cent tax, though the Treasury was certain that anything
above 80 per cent would hurt war production, a conclusion in which
the War and Navy Departments agreed.

Alone with Roosevelt on April 15, Morgenthau said that Smith
was "like a termite undermining the foundation of the Treasury.
. . . I have heard him before a committee publicly say that he
wanted to have the taxing authority of the budget as well as the
expenditure. . . . He is constantly undermining us . . . and I
wish that you would tell him to stop it." Roosevelt made no promises, though he did comment that Harold Smith was a very stick-to-it
person. Still, Morgenthau was satisfied. "The President was very
nice to me about it," he reflected after their meeting. "The last time
I brought up the subject he resented it."

The President was also receptive to most of the Treasury's suggestions for his national address about inflation on April 27, 1942. "I
really am terribly pleased on the President's message," Morgenthau
announced to his morning meeting the next day, "because there is

really everything in there that I fought for; . . . no ceiling on
wages, we fought for rationing, and he has come out for rationing;
we insisted on a ceiling on prices, and he has got that; he was very
fine on the War Bonds; there is nothing about the tax thing that I
couldn't endorse, so I would say that the Treasury got about 95 per
cent compliance from the President, which I think is pretty good."
So it was, especially after what Morgenthau had called "three weeks
of particular hell . . . fighting the boys who wanted compulsory
savings." The Secretary felt "a little weak," but "at least . . . in
the clear."

Further, on April 28 the Office of Price Administration followed
up the President's message with a major change in policy. Before
that date OPA had experimented with selective price controls. Now
it issued a General Maximum Price Regulation — "General Max" in
the phrase of wartime Washington. Effective as far as it went, that
order set the stage for the Price Control Act passed at Roosevelt's
request in October. The new law broadened the field of price controls and provided for the first time for the control of wages. "General Max" and the directives supplementary to it proved themselves
beyond the expectations of their sponsors. The price control program for the duration of the war held the line against inflation more
successfully than did any other facet of government policy. But its
success depended in considerable degree from the first on reducing
inflationary pressures, a major objective of the Treasury's tax recommendations. In April 1942, those recommendations were faring
badly on the Hill.

3. A Most Hostile Committee

The House Ways and Means Committee, antagonistic toward almost every Treasury proposal, was proceeding to write a tax bill of
its own. Indeed the committee never seriously considered closing
tax loopholes or adopting the Department's suggestions for steep
increases on surtaxes on individual income and on estate and gift
schedules. So, too, the committee shrugged off the President's unexpected proposal, one part of his message of April 27, for limiting
individual income after taxes to $25,000 a year for the duration of

the war. As the Treasury saw it, the larger problem was the limitation of excess corporate profits, but on that issue, too, the committee went its own way. By the end of April, Paul conceded that the issue was lost.

The congressmen who were fighting against taxes on individual and corporate wealth had contrived an effective tactic. By beating back the Treasury's recommendations and thereby reducing the revenue the new bill could raise, they could maintain that only a sales tax would provide the funds necessary for the prosecution of the war, only the sales tax would remove from consumer pockets money which would otherwise contribute to inflation. By the end of April, furthermore, as the President's message indicated, the need to control inflation had come to surpass even the need to raise revenue. At that juncture Morgenthau adjusted his own position. As he explained to the White House, the Treasury in March had asked Congress for $7 billion of additional revenue. Now the movement of prices and the cost of war indicated the need for more than $8 billion. Without surrendering any of his previous objectives, Morgenthau therefore recommended one change he had previously opposed. He suggested, as preferable to a sales tax, the lowering of personal exemptions so that the income tax would penetrate further down the scale of earnings and reach the lowest income groups.

On May 7, 1942, Walter George, the Chairman of the Senate Finance Committee, and Robert Doughton, the Chairman of the House Ways and Means Committee, warned the Secretary that his new recommendation would probably fail to forestall the movement for a sales tax. Doughton, moreover, believed it preferable to increase rates on those already paying taxes rather than to lower exemptions so as to extend the base of the income tax itself.

Cool to the Treasury's revised view on exemptions, the Ways and Means Committee also resisted the Department's long-standing proposal for collecting income taxes at the source by regular withholding from payrolls. That scheme, some congressmen believed, would prove "a box of monkeys," impossible of administration. Randolph Paul argued in reply that there would be no difficulty in enforcing withholding at the source if Congress made available the necessary personnel and equipment. Further, as Paul put it to Morgenthau in mid-May 1942, "we believe that the future of the income tax as a substitute for the sales tax in reaching large groups of people depends upon successful collection at the source. Such collection . . . is important also for its anti-inflationary effect and its convenience to the taxpayer. We believe also that it would diminish delinquency in filing returns and paying the tax. For these reasons we think it imperative that collection at the source be introduced and be made to work, whatever new blood may be necessary and whatever revision of machinery may be necessary."

Morgenthau agreed, but he had begun to worry about the adverse effect of withholding at the source on the war bond campaign. Paul originally had hoped that the withholding plan would go into effect on July 1, 1942. As the spring wore on and the Ways and Means Committee continued to sit on the revenue bill, the Secretary came to prefer January 1, 1943 as a starting date. The lassitude of the committee also led him to brood over the political effects of any revenue act. When he made his initial recommendations to Congress in March, he had expected legislation by midsummer. Constant debate and delay indicated by the end of May that no bill could clear the House and the Senate before autumn. In that event, the initiation of withholding at the source, as well as increases in tax rates and reductions in exemptions, might antagonize taxpayers, perhaps lead them to vote against congressmen who shaped the law. In the privacy of his office, Morgenthau on May 25, 1942 confessed his fears. It was too late, he said, to discuss the pros and cons of withholding taxes. He had already made his speech and taken his position in favor of the plan. But now, he said, "I am more interested that we get a Democratic Congress than I am in inflation or anything else, as far as domestic, internal, economic, political situations go. I mean, to me, that, domestically, it is more important than anything else, and it just makes common sense to me that if you should have this thing hit these people before election . . . it may be very harmful to our Democratic congressmen. . . . I will put it on straight political grounds, or, if you want to be noble about it, so that Mr. Roosevelt can carry on for the rest of his term, I strongly recommend that this doesn't go into effect until January 1."

As Randolph Paul reported later that day, Bob Doughton agreed to the January date. "It was put on the ground of convenience to the Commissioner and convenience to the taxpayer," Paul said.

"There was none of this motivation that we discussed in this room." But on all other matters Paul looked gloomy. The Treasury was "being defeated with proper regularity," he said. ". . . It is obvious that this committee . . . is . . . most hostile . . . to any change."

As the Ways and Means Committee finally drafted the Revenue Bill, it contained none of the Treasury's controversial recommendations and it promised to yield, according to departmental estimates, only $6.25 billion additional revenue, far less than the $8.7 billion which Morgenthau considered necessary. "Those fellows," he said, "just don't know there's a war on." Only a sales tax could easily close the financial gap, but Morgenthau and Paul opposed seeking new money in the "wrong form." Further, Sam Rayburn told the Secretary on June 15, 1942, that Roosevelt wanted Congress out of Washington well before the first of November. Therefore no one in the Administration could afford to send up any more suggestions. Instead Rayburn recommended that the Treasury take the six billion it was getting, and hurry the bill out of the House and over to the Senate, where the department would have another chance. "Don't fight too much about this extra revenue," the Speaker said. "If there is going to be a sales tax, let the Senate put it on." That, Morgenthau judged, "was pretty good advice." Conveyed to the President the next day, it "met with his 100 per cent approval." "Keep on sittin' and no sweatin' and no talkin'," Roosevelt said. ". . . Just stay put."

4. A Couple of Whipping Boys

When the bill passed on to the Senate, Morgenthau told the Finance Committee of that body, in his testimony of July 23, 1942, "the people of this country want a courageous tax bill, and want it with the least possible delay." That kind of bill would have to yield $8.7 billion in new revenue, he said, and should include the reforms and the progressive schedules that the Treasury had earlier commended unsuccessfully to the House. Yet those provisions, as Walter George had told the Secretary, evoked little enthusiasm in the Senate. And, while Congress dallied, the continuing advance in prices was provoking demands for higher wages, was disturbing the economy, and impeding the industrial prosecution of the war. New, rapid, and forceful policies were past due "to prevent a calamitous rise in the cost of living."

That phrase, one of Herbert Gaston's, expressed the mood of the Treasury. Accordingly the Department attempted, while the tax bill lay before the Senate, to devise radical schemes to stem inflation. In the process Morgenthau modified, sometimes abandoned, his own established preferences. He came to support tighter government controls than he had ever previously advocated; he agreed, as in the past he had not, to heavy taxation on low income groups; he accepted, in spite of his cautious reluctance, the need for employing technically difficult methods for collecting revenue; he even consented for a season to compulsory rather than voluntary lending. Had the Congress been as resilient as the Secretary, it would have written, as it did not, a dramatic chapter in the history of American public finance.

The Treasury's offensive against inflation began with an analysis of July 20, 1942, in which Harry White urged the need for compulsory savings. At a meeting two days later, White supported Randolph Paul's plea for the collection of taxes at the source. White had no interest in soliciting opinions of industrial workers about that prospect. For 1943, he said, those workers, like other Americans, should pay double taxes, the taxes due on their 1942 income, and their current taxes for 1943, collected by payroll deductions. Obviously they would object; there was therefore no point in polling them, as Morgenthau wanted to. "Harry," the Secretary said, "you really shock me. . . . Are you afraid of what they will think. . . . The little fellow at the bench doesn't get his chance to be heard."

The President, Morgenthau continued, shared his own worry about just how much the government could tap at the source. Deductions from payrolls already included social security, voluntary purchases of savings bonds, union dues, and special items like the community fund. Collections for income taxes would further reduce the take-home pay of the workers, the Secretary said, and "by the time we get all of these things, aren't we asking this man to do too much?"

Voluntary purchases of war bonds would fall off, White replied.

Consequently the government should initiate compulsory lending when tax collections from payrolls began. Unpersuaded, the Secretary insisted on two weeks of further study.

Inflation would not wait. On July 27, 1942, Judge Samuel Rosenman told Morgenthau that the President wanted an executive order freezing both prices and wages, and rolling agricultural prices back from 110 to 100 per cent of parity. Morgenthau feared that Roosevelt and Rosenman were developing a patchwork quilt of controls, with little regard for the needs of union labor. Their "Alice in Wonderland" scheme, the Secretary predicted, would fail. He preferred a more comprehensive and novel approach.

On July 29 the Secretary and his aides took their own proposal to Rosenman. It called for "expenditure rationing" to limit aggregate spending. Each individual or family would be able to spend for consumer goods only that amount of money for which the government had issued coupons. By establishing quotas for coupons, the government could limit total demand, while leaving to consumers the choice of what they bought. Further, as the supply of consumer goods diminished, the government could reduce the volume of coupons issued. The system could also make allowances for variations in family size and income. Though the plan involved serious administrative problems, they seemed no more severe than those already confronting the Office of Price Administration. "There is one thing about the Treasury," Rosenman remarked, "it certainly is resourceful." But as he soon reported to Morgenthau, the President was not "prepared to go that far" without the explicit consent of Congress.

Roosevelt held back partly because he preferred direct controls over prices and wages, partly in the hope that the Senate would make the tax bill an effective anti-inflationary instrument. As July became August and August September, Morgenthau begged the President to "take the bit in your teeth." Now the President held that the steps he contemplated necessitated a reorganization of the executive branch, which he could announce but not put into effect until Congress had had sixty days, under its statutory power, to disapprove his stated plans. "You are daring Congress to tell you that you cannot do it," Morgenthau complained. "I am just laying it before them," Roosevelt said, "and if they do not do something about it the plan goes into effect."

The plan, which Rosenman drafted with some help from Treasury experts, established an Economic Stabilization Administrator, charged with ultimate control over policy connected with profits, prices, wages, rationing, the cost of living, the movements of labor, private credit, subsidies, and related matters. The order establishing the new office provided too that, until the administrator ruled otherwise, all wages were frozen at current levels saving for adjustments necessary to meet the costs of living, to eliminate substandard conditions of living, to correct serious inequalities, or to reward increased productivity. Raises in salaries above $7500 a year were restricted even more tightly. A message to Congress in the first week of September explained the President's order, which, in the absence of congressional objections, took force early in October. Roosevelt then put Jimmy Byrnes in charge.

The success of the new venture, the Treasury believed, depended upon limiting pressure on established or intended ceilings. For that purpose, Randolph Paul and his talented associate, Roy Blough, originated a venturesome scheme that they first showed Morgenthau during the hot, third weekend of August 1942. If the revenue bill, they said, in its final form, could produce $5 billion more than anyone had yet asked for, it would serve better than any set of regulations to hold down the cost of living. The device for raising that additional revenue, they suggested, was a spendings tax, a superior substitute for expenditure rationing. As Blough explained the spendings tax to the Secretary's morning group on August 24, it would be a graduated tax, supplementary to the income tax, on the whole sum which an individual or family spent, less stipulated allowances for necessities. A steeply graduated rate would in itself retard spending except for those necessities. Further, income saved rather than spent would be exempted from the tax. Progressive and efficient, the spendings tax would also yield substantial revenue and obviate the alleged need for a sales tax. The Treasury could administer the tax, though not without some difficulty, and the spur the tax would give to savings would facilitate the sale of government bonds. If the tax reached too far into the pockets of lower income groups, some fraction of the resulting revenue could be defined as a compulsory loan, refundable after the war.

Enthusiastic about the proposal, even its identification with compulsory lending, Morgenthau had Blough explain it to representatives of the Federal Reserve Board, the Office of Price Administration, the War Production Board, the Department of Commerce, and the Bureau of the Budget. "The principle of the plan was sound," they all agreed, as the Secretary then reported to Roosevelt, "and . . . it was a healthy step in the right direction." He believed, Morgenthau continued, that "the tax might well be suggested to Congress even at this late stage in the progress of the tax bill. I am planning, with your approval, to discuss it with Senator George."

Roosevelt permitted the discussion, and George had no objection to the Treasury's presenting its plan to his committee, but political prospects for a spendings tax were poor. Newspapers like the *New York Times* and *Herald Tribune,* as the Secretary put it, wanted "a tax on the poor people so that the rich could escape." Precisely on that basis, Herbert Gaston predicted, Morgenthau would have trouble selling the Department's plan to Congress. There were also other difficulties. Harry White and Randolph Paul tangled over the question of a rate for the spendings tax. A 10 per cent rate, Paul feared, accompanied by withholding at the source, would prove "a swell way to kill it," for it would subtract so much from an individual's total income as to make the plan "look ridiculous and . . . completely jeopardize its acceptance . . . especially in the low brackets." White disagreed. "Harry," Morgenthau interrupted, "you listen to me. . . . It is one thing to propose, and it is another thing to go up there and face the committee. Now it is Paul's responsibility. . . . He has got to present it." White would do better to mind his own business. Stubborn as always, White argued that Tommy Corcoran, Alvin Hansen, and others in Washington were agreeable to a spendings tax only if it produced a substantial compulsory loan. For that purpose Paul's proposed rates were too low. Now Morgenthau lost his temper. "No matter what I do I never can satisfy that group," he told White, "because they will not be satisfied until I am out of the Treasury. . . . So I cannot be influenced by what they think." Paul, the Secretary concluded, would be in charge of the Treasury's field forces on the Hill, and "Paul has got to decide."

Still Morgenthau was ready to go "into either compulsory savings or postwar credit." His personal outline for his testimony to the Senate about the spendings tax expressed his dissatisfaction with the current operations of the volunteer plan, and explained the need to raise "stupendous sums" for financing the war, as well as to make the revenue bill affect "the mass of the purchasing power." After he had "cleared it with the President," Morgenthau on September 3, 1942, admittedly tense and obviously gloomy, read his statement to the Finance Committee:

The legislation which we are proposing has a double purpose. The first purpose is to draw into the Treasury substantial additional funds out of the earnings and savings of the people. The second purpose is even more important. It is to reduce consumer spending directly by withdrawing funds otherwise available for expenditure, and to reduce it also indirectly by creating a strong incentive to saving.

The measures we propose are two: first, a tax on consumer spending which will reach into the lowest income groups above the level of bare subsistence . . . and will provide high penalty rates for luxury spending; second, a further lowering of the exemptions from the income tax applying to family income. . . .

It can be expected that the new spendings tax will reduce . . . the amount which workers can afford to set aside for war bonds under voluntary payroll deduction plans. In the face of present conditions we can no longer afford to rely entirely upon voluntary lending. The new proposals are intended, therefore, to supplement the voluntary bond purchase program. . . .

If the proposals we make seem drastic, I should like to say with all possible emphasis that I believe nothing less drastic will accomplish the results we must have.*

After little deliberation, the Finance Committee rejected the spendings tax flatly. "The plan is dead," Senator Guffey of Pennsylvania commented the day after Morgenthau testified. "Not a man on the committee is for it." In the opinion of Senators Robert Taft and Harry Byrd, the tax was "the most complicated and unwork-

---

* The Treasury asked for deductions at the source of 15 per cent, 10 per cent to be applied against the income tax, 5 per cent against the spendings tax. Exemptions for the spendings tax were set at $1000 for a single person, $2000 for a family, and $500 for each dependent. A normal, 10 per cent rate on spending above those levels was to take the form of a refundable loan, but the rate rose progressively and steeply, and none of the spendings tax paid in above the initial 10 per cent was refundable.

able that has been submitted . . . in nine years." Another senator found it "too complicated for an ordinary man like me to understand." The press agreed. The *Wall Street Journal* considered the spendings tax "an income tax walking about on its hands," and a columnist in the *Washington Post* called it "Morgenthau's morning glory. It opened Tuesday morning and it folded before noon." That was enough for Roosevelt. Though he had permitted Morgenthau to advance the plan, he had himself never mentioned it, and now he refused to give it any support. "I never make any recommendations to Congress while a bill is pending before them," he told Morgenthau. The Secretary was aghast. "It completely took my breath away," he later told Herbert Gaston, "and I couldn't think quickly enough to give him a few examples, because there are plenty of them. . . . But I said something, and then he kind of broke down and laughed, showing that he was trying to put something over on me. Then he immediately made the statement, 'Well, you know, Henry, I always have to have a couple of whipping boys,' to which I replied, 'Yes, I realize that I am one of them and right now I am getting plenty of whippings.' "

Nevertheless, as he told his staff, Morgenthau was "delighted that we had the courage and the foresight to make this recommendation. . . . I don't want anybody around to take the attitude that we have been licked. . . . It is the public who will get the licking."

So did the Treasury, at least in the eyes of the Congress. On September 8, 1942, the Senate Finance Committee officially voted down the spendings tax and adopted instead Senator George's plan for a 5 per cent gross income tax — a tax on all incomes in excess of $624, to be collected at the source, with certain provisions for a partial postwar credit. That measure would produce an additional $3.6 billion before refunds, a net after refunds of $2.5 billion. It would be hard to administer, it would bear unjustly on families with low incomes, it would produce less revenue and less of a check against inflation than the Treasury's scheme. But at the least, George's substitute provided some improvement on the bill that had emerged from the House of Representatives. And the Treasury, while it had lost on the spendings tax, had managed, by its offensive on that matter, to divert congressional attention from, and thus for the time being to defeat, a new development which the Department considered downright dangerous.

5. Tax Forgiveness

While the Treasury was contriving the spendings tax, the Senate Committee on Finance was pursuing a new enthusiasm of its own. Along with some other Americans, most of them men and women from the high tax brackets, the senators were attracted by an idea of Beardsley Ruml, one of the most persuasive American advocates of Keynesian economics, the treasurer of R. H. Macy and Company and the chairman of the board of the New York Federal Reserve Bank.

Ruml had proposed a plan to make taxpayers up-to-date immediately in their obligations to the federal government by getting them out of debt to the government for past taxes due. This plan of forgiveness, as Elinor Morgenthau put it to her husband, was "just 100 per cent against your philosophy of giving no one, especially the very rich, preferential treatment." But Ruml and others, he told the Senate Finance Committee in August 1942, had been concerned about the "awkardness" of taking care of retirement for men who were "perfectly prepared" to leave active business life on a modest income of five to eight thousand dollars, but who could not do so and still pay tax liabilities incurred during a last year of employment at a high salary. It was necessary to provide retiring executives in such cases "first with the income tax, and that became income, and the income tax on that income, and had gotten to a situation that made it impossible for a corporation to get into that sort of thing generally." The same problem, Ruml said, had arisen with young men going into the service from R. H. Macy and Company, for once enlisted they found themselves earning very little but still liable for taxes due on income of the previous year. This embarrassment arose because the taxpayer was always one year behind in his payments. Ruml recommended having taxpayers begin at once to pay taxes on current income for 1942, and forgiving them their taxes for 1941. As he saw it, this would simply move the "tax clock forward, and cost the Treasury nothing until Judgment Day."

The Treasury saw problems in the Ruml plan. To be sure, it took the taxpayer out of debt. It did so, however, by canceling taxes already owed the government. For those who had enjoyed a windfall during 1941, a year in which defense production produced a plethora of windfalls, forgiveness constituted a substantial boon.

Neither Morgenthau nor Paul favored such philanthropy, particularly in wartime. But the need, which the Treasury recognized, for putting all income taxes on a pay-as-you-go basis made the Ruml plan popular with most taxpayers and their congressmen, for if it were adopted, collections at the source for 1942 taxes would proceed without the concurrent payment of liabilities remaining for 1941.

As Paul reported to Morgenthau, "Ruml aroused some interest." The Secretary understood why, but considered the give-away features of the Ruml proposal "rather disgusting." He preferred, if Congress provided the authority, to collect concurrently all 1941 taxes due and also the normal taxes and first bracket of surtaxes for 1942. That scheme would prevent windfalls, bring 87 per cent of all taxpayers up-to-date, and allow the balance of taxpayers to catch up during 1943.

Treasury opposition killed the Ruml Plan in 1942, but meanwhile the spendings tax had also perished, and the bill emerging from the Senate Finance Committee, while perpetuating the hoary inequities of the federal tax system, also failed to provide for enough revenue. With Morgenthau's approval, Randolph Paul in mid-September made a last, futile plea for various improvements. The committee turned down, too, earlier Treasury suggestions for expanding the Social Security System. By extending that system to cover virtually all of the employed and the self-employed population, by promising larger payments for old age and unemployment insurance in the postwar period, but by increasing only the Social Security taxes during the war, the government could pursue desirable social goals while also enlarging wartime revenues and combating inflation. Yet most of the Senate stood with Arthur Vandenberg in favor of freezing Social Security contributions at existing levels. Indeed the Finance Committee went out of its way to display its disdain for the Treasury by voting that its staff should be allowed access to the records of the Bureau of Internal Revenue without permission from the Secretary. "The committee," in the phrase of Senator David Walsh of Massachusetts, "was simply showing its authority."

The 1942 revenue bill passed the Senate on October 10 with no dissenting vote, went to conference committee, and was approved by both chambers on October 21. It would produce, according to Treasury estimates, only $7 billion of new revenue. It raised that sum partly by reducing personal exemptions, partly by applying Senator George's gross personal income tax, most of which was to be collected at the source. The measure also lifted the top surtax on individual incomes from 77 to 82 per cent, the top tax on corporate income from 31 to 40 per cent, and the top excess profits rate from 60 to 90 per cent, but for that last schedule Congress added new provisions for relief instead of blocking existing avenues for avoidance. Other provisions changed without much increasing the estate and gift taxes, regulated the renegotiation of war contracts, and increased various excises on luxuries and on scarce consumer goods. Though the Revenue Act did not include either a sales tax or the Ruml Plan for forgiveness, it also left out the Treasury's important proposals for tax reform — ("The oil folks beat us," Senator George explained) — for Social Security, and for the anti-inflationary spendings tax. Half of the several hundred pages of the act pertained to tax relief, and that at a time when Americans were beginning their offensive against Hitler with landings in North Africa, at a time when they were starting a counteroffensive against Japan at the beachhead at Guadalcanal, at a time when prices and profits and incomes were growing faster than the appropriate circumstances of the wartime economy demanded.

The President saw no alternative to accepting the measure. At a Cabinet meeting of October 22, 1942, he "went into a discussion of the huge tax bill that was put on his desk and the lengthy report from the Treasury on it," Dan Bell informed Morgenthau. "He said the bill might as well have been in a foreign language; he didn't understand it and didn't think the Treasury understood it. . . . He was told he had to sign it that day in order to save some $60 million revenue, so that he was forced to sign it without reading it. He made quite a joke of the whole thing."

Yet the act was no joke. "I am 'plumb disgusted' with the favoritism and privilege," Josephus Daniels, a doughty liberal, wrote Morgenthau. "I do not know," the Secretary admitted, "when we are going to get total war on taxes." Even conservative newspapers acknowledged that the act was insufficient for existing economic needs. Still, perhaps no one could have prevented Congress from rendering so glaring a disservice to the nation. Congressmen did have to face reelection, and the electorate, saving the soldiers and sailors and marines, was enjoying its first prosperity since 1929, a condition scarcely conducive to a spirit of happy sacrifice. Roosevelt, moreover, had long since replaced "Dr. New Deal" with "Dr. Win-the-War." But the very mood of Congress had damped the President's natural zeal for reform, and the passion and hard reasoning of the Treasury had not penetrated the conservative fortresses of the committees on the Hill. Proud of its power of the purse, Congress bore the ultimate responsibility for the timid inadequacy of its act. Morgenthau, depressed, hoped nevertheless that after the election, Congress might respond constructively to the recommendations for 1943 on which the Treasury was already at work.

6. New Revenue "By Various Methods"

In November 1942, while the Treasury was starting a major bond drive and reviewing suggestions about taxation for the President's Budget Message of the following January, the Bureau of the Budget and the Office of Economic Stabilization moved together to take over the direction of revenue policy, particularly to persuade Roosevelt to support compulsory lending. As ever, Morgenthau bridled at a challenge to what he deemed his department's Constitutional prerogatives for making fiscal policy. "I just got to straighten out," he told Randolph Paul, ". . . who's going to . . . prepare the Tax Bill for the President."

The President's order establishing the Office of Economic Stabilization, Morgenthau reminded Jimmy Byrnes, the chief of that office, had said nothing about fiscal or monetary policy. Instead, as the Secretary accurately added, an early draft of the order had explicitly exempted those policy areas, and in announcing the creation of the new office, the President had orally confirmed the exemption. "I had a pretty good talk . . ." Morgenthau reported to his staff. "I went back through the whole business right from the beginning. . . . He tried to sell me that . . . anybody who holds this position and has to present the whole thing on the cost of living has to include taxes. And he said he knew nothing about the verbal statement the President made the night it was announced. He never heard it. . . . He says, 'You don't claim that you are over me, do you?' I said, 'No, and you don't claim you are over me?' He says, 'No.' I say, 'Now, we are both here to lick inflation. We are both here to save the President a headache. Can't we work together?' He says, 'Of course we can.' I said, 'That is what I want to do.'

"Then he went on to say . . . he was relying on the Treasury to prepare the programs. . . . He will have to be watched, that is all."

Before turning to the content of the tax program itself, Morgenthau asked Roosevelt for guidance about procedure. "What I want to know," the Secretary said, ". . . is whether or not you expect us to continue to prepare the tax bill as we have in the past and present it as we have in the past."

"Absolutely," Roosevelt said.

"I didn't know whether Byrnes was thinking of something," Morgenthau said, "and I wanted to find out whether you said anything to him or to the leaders on the Hill." Roosevelt had not.

"This proves to me," Morgenthau later reflected in his Diary, "that Byrnes is groping for power and hasn't gotten any directive from the President. It also proves I am right in thinking that one should not be scared by anyone like Byrnes. The only thing to do is go directly to the President and find out where you stand."

Proposals for new taxes, Morgenthau told his chief aids on December 2, 1942, should not be "too complicated," should minimize difficulties in collection, and should avoid harassment of business. He wondered whether "we can't take a brand new look at the Social Security thing. Now, what they are proposing in England is not only good for today, but it is good for the postwar, and it has many advantages over straight compulsory savings. . . . Every single person in England is going to be insured. They are going to get unemployment insurance; they are going to get sickness insurance, and the whole business.

"Now, the beauty of the study of the social insurance over something else is . . . you have got your mechanics. . . . It wouldn't be an additional burden from the standpoint of machinery. . . . We will just extend it." An extension of Social Security, with higher taxes at once but increased benefits only after the war, "would hit the volunteer war bonds" much less than would compulsory lending, while "last and most important," it would be "a damper on inflationary tendencies."

Yet social reform, Morgenthau had learned, had few sponsors in wartime Washington, even within the Democratic Party, and the Republicans had gained seats in both houses of Congress in the November elections. Accordingly, Robert Doughton opposed opening up the question of Social Security, which would, he predicted, lead only to futile debate. He questioned also any further discussion of tax exempt securities or the percentage depletion allowance. "You tell Doughton," Roosevelt had instructed, "that if the Democrats keep on fighting amongst themselves . . . we are going to elect a Republican President." Doughton needed no convincing on that point. "We had a very nice talk," Morgenthau told his staff on December 3, "and what I said was that I wanted to sit down . . . with him this time and come to as near an agreement beforehand as we could, and that the country knew what I wanted . . . and if we could not agree on it I was not going to go up and bat my head against the wall again.

"I told him that we had a political situation to deal with, and that 1944 was not so far around the corner; that I wanted to try and go just as far as we could to work this thing out, and that I was going to do as much as I could to get an agreement with the . . . committee this time.

"He said, 'Now you are talking my language. . . . If we can't do this, Henry, it would be better that you just say your piece and then withdraw and let the Congress go ahead and write the bill . . . but if we approach it in this manner, I think it would be fine. . . . Let's do it first with the Democrats and agree amongst ourselves, and then pull in the Republicans afterwards. . . . But . . . we have got to be careful this time. The tide is running against us.' "

So was inflation. Treasury studies indicated that in 1943 taxes and savings together would have to absorb $16 billion, the estimated excess of income available to consumers over the value of goods available for them to buy. But Roosevelt was undecided about taxes. "I could tell by the look on his face," Morgenthau said to his staff on December 16, 1942, "that he hadn't seen the budget, and didn't know, and didn't care." The President did, however, approve the Secretary's proposed tactic — "to lay down what the formula is without any specific recommendation." As Morgenthau explained that process to his staff, he wanted them to establish a relationship between productivity and expenditures on the one hand, and disposable income on the other. That would provide a formula for calculating necessary taxation. Roosevelt could then give Congress the formula without specifying what taxes were to be levied. It did no good, Morgenthau said, to sit in the Treasury and decide what was right and just and fair, and then go to the Hill and not get support. In the last Congress even labor, deserting the Treasury, had failed to make the fight for the department's program that William Green had privately promised. Now Morgenthau hoped to produce a plan that the executive establishment could endorse, to commit Roosevelt to that plan, and then to clear it with Democratic and Republican leaders. In this way they could "do the fighting at this end before we go up on the Hill and spend five or six months and have everybody get a heart attack or something."

But almost at once there emerged serious differences between the Treasury and the Bureau of the Budget. The Bureau did not want to use precise figures about the "inflationary gap." Further, Budget Director Smith urged the President to emphasize the need not only for collection at the source, which the Treasury endorsed, but also for compulsory lending and for a sales tax. The Treasury program, as Morgenthau defined it on December 20, 1942, in informal conversation with Roy Blough, included "a very stiff withholding tax, rationing on all scarce articles, increase the personal income and corporate tax and Social Security tax and nothing on the compulsory lending or saving." Morgenthau did not "know how the plan would set with Congress, but I wish I could find out, and I now have a telephone call in for the President to see whether he would let me talk to Walter George and Doughton and try out the plan on them." The President was agreeable. "I'm delighted," Morgenthau told Blough, "and it puts me in a much stronger position when I see him and also a stronger position in relation to the other agencies."

In Atlanta, on December 21, Morgenthau had supper with Walter George — "a very successful party," and he saw Bob Doughton the next day in Washington. "You will remember," the Secretary then wrote the President on December 23, "that when we discussed how to present the tax problem that you and I agreed that it would be best to have you diagnose the case . . . without making any specific recommendations as to how to cure the patient. After we had met with both George and Doughton we all agreed that the Budget Message should be confined to general language, whatever specific recommendations you may wish to have made later. May I remind you that you said, in discussing this matter, that it is better to let them set up the Nine Pins and have you knock them down rather than to let them do the reverse. We here in the Treasury agree with you that this is good strategy and that you will get quicker and more satisfactory tax legislation if this procedure is followed."

That procedure, the Treasury suggested, permitted Roosevelt to recommend an immediate extension of Social Security, a policy desirable in its own right, and immediate congressional action to provide for payroll deductions and other collections of taxes at the source of income. Morgenthau gave the President a memo on those questions on December 29, 1942. "He was in a very good humor," the Secretary later told his staff, "relaxed. I asked him about this memorandum. . . . He read it and said, 'I like it; that is what I want to do.'" When Morgenthau warned him that the Budget Bureau would object, Roosevelt "just grinned all over." The Treasury, he said, should "get busy," revise its memorandum, and send it over to the Bureau for incorporation in the draft of his Budget Message.

The Treasury's recommendations little influenced the first draft of that message, which reached the Department on January 2, 1943, when Morgenthau was ill with a walloping case of flu. The draft called for a "deterrent tax" on consumption — a euphemism, Randolph Paul said, for a sales tax — and for compulsory lending and the cancelation of some 1942 tax liabilities as part of a program to make all taxpayers current in 1943. Defending those departures from the Treasury's policy, Harold Smith told Daniel Bell that Roosevelt had approved the draft and precluded further alterations. The Secretary of the Treasury, Bell replied, was the chief fiscal officer of the government. Since he had to support all of Roosevelt's fiscal policies, he deserved a chance to talk with the President about them before the President announced them in a Budget Message. "I don't know whether you know it or not," Smith objected, "but while I was with the President, Ross McIntire* came in and told the Presi-

---

* Admiral Ross T. McIntire, Roosevelt's physician, whose medical competence Morgenthau never overestimated.

dent that the Secretary was not feeling very well and that he had
been taken to the hospital for a few days' rest." Roosevelt had then
told Smith that neither he nor Bell was to bother Morgenthau.

Suspicious, Bell called Mrs. Morgenthau. He was sure, he said,
that the Secretary would feel badly if he had had no chance to enter
objections before the President went to Congress. On his own Bell
decided against trying to redraft the language of the Bureau of the
Budget. Instead he began a memorandum for the White House criticizing the Bureau's decisions. On Sunday morning January 3, Morgenthau approved of that plan and suggested also that Bell, Paul,
and Gaston draft a letter to the President explaining the conversations that had been going on with Doughton and George. It would
be embarrassing, the Secretary noted, for the Budget Message to
contain specific proposals on taxes when it had already been agreed
with the congressmen that no such proposals would be made.

That night, after reading the Treasury's letter and memorandum,
Roosevelt assured Bell that the Budget Message was not "in final
form by any means." The next day the President met with Bell,
Jimmy Byrnes, and Harold Smith to reconsider the section of the
message on taxation. When Roosevelt reached the words referring
to the "inflationary gap," he stopped, and to the best of Bell's memory, said to Smith:

"Now Harold, we might just as well come to grips with this problem. The Secretary of the Treasury, as you well know, is the chief
financing officer of the Government who has to go up on the Hill
and defend these fiscal programs. He also has to collect the taxes so
that he has to be consulted when we put any tax and borrowing
proposals into the budget. He has . . . with my approval consulted
with Senator George and Congressman Doughton on the matter of
procedure for tax legislation . . . and they have agreed that the
Budget Message should contain no specific proposals on taxes, that
an attempt should be made to work out a tax program between the
Executive Branch . . . and the leaders on the Hill before any program is submitted to the Congress. I have approved this arrangement."

Roosevelt then proceeded to strike out all the recommendations
of the Bureau of the Budget on taxes. He left in a remark to the
effect that the government should strive to collect not less than $16

billion of additional funds, but he deleted the phrase "through taxation and enforced savings," for which he substituted "by various
methods."

The message as Congress received it followed the Treasury's prescriptions. It stated a target for taxes without specifying recommendations for reaching that goal. It also emphasized the urgent need
for more revenue and for anti-inflationary action. Now it remained
for the Treasury to see whether it could persuade the Congress to
move along mutually agreeable lines.

7. Ruml Again

As the Treasury and the Congress agreed, the need to speed collections of revenue surpassed in importance all other aspects of taxation as the year 1943 began. Sentiment in Congress in both parties
ran heavily in favor of the Ruml Plan, now revised to forgive 1942
taxes while making taxpayers current through withholding at the
source during 1943. The Treasury still viewed total forgiveness as
unneccessary, inequitable, and inflationary, though the department
was prepared, for the sake of easing the transition to a pay-as-you-go
system, to forgive a proportion of 1942 taxes, preferably in the lower
brackets.

Though Morgenthau was ill during January and much of February 1943, he supported the proposals that Randolph Paul advanced
in discussions with congressional leaders. Paul suggested separating
revenue legislation for 1943 into two parts, one to consist of forgiveness of 19 per cent of all 1942 tax liabilities, to accompany provisions
for collection at the source as early as April 1; the other to provide
later for a substantial compulsory lending program and new taxes to
raise altogether $20 billion of additional revenue — the $16 billion
Roosevelt had requested, plus $4 billion which would be lost through
diminishing voluntary purchases of bonds. Robert Doughton and
Walter George seemed satisfied with the first part of that program,
but within the executive branch Marriner Eccles and Jimmy Byrnes
disapproved of separating the issues of tax forgiveness and compulsory lending, for they believed that in return for some forgiveness
the Administration should be able to extract a strong compulsory

lending act. Speaking for the Senate Republicans, Arthur Vandenberg, their senior representative on the Finance Committee, was willing to support some compulsory lending but he demanded tax forgiveness of the order of the Ruml Plan, which daily gathered bipartisan support on the Hill and among middle-class Americans.

Privately to Paul, Ruml admitted that his plan benefited wealthy taxpayers far more than those in lower income brackets, but he argued that there was nothing wrong with that. Rather he considered the opposition to his plan "stupid" and Morgenthau "a very unfortunate man" for the country. Back at his desk on February 11, the Secretary made his case in a memorandum to Roosevelt. The Ruml Plan, he wrote, bestowed its greatest bonus on some sixty taxpayers with million dollar incomes in 1942, each of whom would receive a windfall of at least $854,000. In one blow, the plan would add to their wealth more than they could save in six years even if they saved every cent of their income after taxes. The plan presented about $64,000 to individuals with net incomes of $100,000, whereas forgiveness for a man earning $10,000 was only about $2,150, and for a man who had earned $2,000, only $140. Further, accelerating the payment of taxes without any forgiveness would most effectively accomplish the dual purpose of increasing revenue and combating inflation. In contrast, complete forgiveness, which Ruml recommended, would mean that tax collections would increase only insofar as Congress increased tax rates in 1943, and the increases would probably fall largely on lower income groups since earlier increases had impinged primarily on the wealthier. As Morgenthau saw it, the cancellation of a year's taxes would be a psychological deterrent to the war effort, injurious to the morale of soldiers who had every reason to expect some sacrifice at home. It would also lead to the release of funds which had been set aside for meeting taxes already due, funds which would then contribute to inflation.

In an unfortunate public address, Harold Smith inadvertently gave credence to the idea that a shift to the system of collections at the source would assure immediate adjustments in 1942 tax liabilities. Morgenthau was furious. "We've got enough enemies with Germany and Japan," he said, "without having any crossing up wires at home." To Roosevelt, Smith sent an effusive apology, but the damage had been done, and in order to repair it, Doughton and

George, at the Treasury's request, explained on the radio that people
would still have to meet the March 15 installments on their 1942
liabilities.

To Morgenthau's surprise, the day after that speech Doughton
broke ranks. As chairman of the Ways and Means Committee he
had provided indispensable support for the department in its resistance to tax forgiveness. Now, bowing to the growing restlessness of
his Democratic colleagues on the committee and in the House, he
agreed to compromise. "Doughton sold us down the river this morning," Gaston informed Morgenthau on February 16. The chairman
had accepted a proposal for collection at the source to begin on July
1, 1943, with half of 1943 (not 1942) tax liabilities canceled. "This
would give the big boys about two-thirds of what they want," Gaston noted, ". . . If the President or Byrnes want to help this looks
like the time."

But Roosevelt unintentionally multiplied the Treasury's problems. Reverting to his suggestion of 1942, the President wrote
Doughton in behalf of a special total supertax on net income "from
whatever source derived . . . which, after payment of regular income taxes, exceeds $25,000 in the case of a single person, and $50,-
000 in the case of a married couple." That proposal, which the
Treasury had never thought wise, diverted some liberal enthusiasms
from opposition to the Ruml Plan, and further persuaded many
conservatives that that opposition, like the President's suggestion for
a ceiling on incomes, merely reflected a New Deal propensity for
soaking the rich.

During the last week of February, the House Ways and Means
Committee considered various schemes for partial tax forgiveness,
no one of which commanded a majority vote. The ambiguity of the
resulting committee report opened the way for a major Republican
effort to persuade the House of Representatives on the floor to adopt
the unamended Ruml Plan. "We need a white rabbit," Randolph
Paul told Roosevelt on March 11, 1943. The President suggested a
20 per cent withholding tax as an extra, wartime levy for five years,
an "extremely simple" but politically impossible solution. He also
devoted much of his press conference of March 12 to an attack on
the Ruml Plan, primarily because of its favoritism to the rich.
Doughton, while convinced of the need of some tax forgiveness,

agreed, as he said to Morgenthau on March 15, that "we've got to defeat the Ruml Plan," and Morgenthau in turn then promised to support the Democrats on the Ways and Means Committee "with the distinct understanding that we [the Treasury] should be completely free to make our own recommendations before the Senate." Doughton further contracted "to support in conference any reasonable plan recommended by the Treasury and adopted by the Senate . . . provided it is not the Ruml Plan."

The arrangement delighted old Bob Doughton. "It has been very encouraging to me," he wrote to Randolph Paul on March 21, 1943, "to have the support of the Secretary of the Treasury and yourself in our fight against the Ruml . . . Plan, in my judgment the biggest outrage ever attempted to be perpetrated upon the people of the United States. It is also heartening to have the President with us . . . and, win or lose, we will have the satisfaction of knowing that we have stood up in battle for a just cause against a most iniquitous proposal."

The just cause had a close call. In a heated session of March 30, 1943, the House of Representatives first voted 199 to 188 to approve the Ruml Plan, but on a roll call vote then defeated the plan, 215 to 198. The Democrats lacked the strength, however, to put through the bill of the Ways and Means Committee which provided partial tax forgiveness. Instead the House moved to recommit the bill to the committee, thus placing the entire tax question back where it had been in January. In some respects that outcome was a victory for the Administration. "The present law," Doughton at once announced, "is so much better than the Ruml Plan that I am gloriously satisfied." Morgenthau, of much the same opinion, congratulated Doughton on his "magnificent fight." And Roosevelt, as he told the Secretary on April 1, was "very happy about the whole thing." Yet the country had already suffered a considerable loss, for three months of 1943 had elapsed, the question of taxation remained unsettled, collection at the source had yet to begin, and the Republicans in Congress remained determined to put across the Ruml plan.

To postpone further controversy, Sam Rayburn suggested that the Ways and Means Committee report a bill providing only for collection at the source as of July 1, 1943. The question of forgiveness could then be debated later, along with proposals for new taxes.

Doughton preferred restoring 1941 tax rates as a basis for calculating 1942 liabilities, which would give taxpayers some forgiveness under another name while they began to pay 1943 taxes currently. The Republicans, however, were willing to contemplate neither scheme without an Administration promise to freeze rates for 1943 at 1942 levels, a promise that would have subverted the President's Budget Message. It took the Treasury's most ardent advocacy to persuade the Democrats on the committee to oppose that last idea.

With a sense of genuine relief, Morgenthau notified Roosevelt on April 21 that Doughton had at last contrived a tax bill acceptable to the Treasury and to enough Democrats, by Rayburn's count, to pass the House. That bill inaugurated collection at the source on July 1, 1943 and forgave about half of 1942 tax liabilities. On the floor of the House on May 4, 1943, the Ruml Plan again lost out, though only by four votes, while the Doughton bill, also rejected at first, was amended to include slightly more tax forgiveness, and then passed.

The House bill, acceptable to the Treasury as the best available compromise, faced insuperable opposition in the Senate, where there was no one of large influence to fight against the Ruml Plan. Alben Barkley, the Democratic Majority Leader, was ill; Walter George, the chairman of the Finance Committee, was reconciled to a defeat for the Administration; and Robert La Follette, a gritty warrior for democratic causes, swung few votes. The Finance Committee on May 7 rejected the House bill and reported out instead a measure providing full forgiveness of 1942 taxes, for which Senator George proposed a substitute that forgave three-quarters of those taxes, far too much, from Morgenthau's point of view. Even the George version, Doughton argued, deserved a veto. "I think if this swing to the right isn't stopped by the President," Morgenthau commented, "nobody can stop it." But the President stood aside while on May 14 the Senate, defeating George's substitute, passed the committee's bill.

Now Roosevelt intervened. In a letter of May 17, 1943, to Doughton and George, a letter based largely on Randolph Paul's draft, the President again expressed his eagerness to see taxes "put on a pay-as-you-go basis at the earliest possible moment," but his opposition to the Senate bill which "would result in highly inequitable distribution of the cost of the war in an unjust and discriminatory enrichment of thousands of taxpayers in the upper income groups." He asked the conference committee to work out "substantial adjustments to ease" the transition to pay-as-you-go, but, he warned, "I cannot acquiesce in the elimination of a whole year's tax burden on the upper income groups during a war period when I must call for an increase in taxes and savings from the mass of our people."

The President's "very helpful" letter, as Doughton called it, and the "cooperation of the leadership," especially Sam Rayburn, led the House on May 19 to vote against acquiescing in the Senate's bill, but the senators on the conference committee stood fast for the Ruml Plan or its near equivalent. By May 24 Doughton saw no alternative to accepting between 70 and 75 per cent forgiveness of 1942 taxes if any bill were to pass, though the Administration hoped to settle for 62½ per cent. The next morning Morgenthau, back in Washington after five days in New York where his wife had undergone an operation, told Paul that "I am going to sit. . . . I can sit for days. I may get the breaks; I may not." By noon Paul had persuaded the Secretary to urge Roosevelt to intercede again. "This is no time for letters," the President said. "The people aren't interested in letters. What they want is to see a bill get through." As Morgenthau put it to his staff, Roosevelt was tired: "He told me he was tired. He has had ten days of arguing with Churchill,* and the man is exhausted."

So was Doughton. That night, breaking ranks, he voted with the Republicans on the conference committee for a proposal of Arthur Vandenberg for 75 per cent forgiveness of tax liabilities, with 100 per cent cancellation up to $50, and the initiation of collection at the source by 20 per cent withholding from payrolls to begin July 1, 1943. The Current Tax Payment Act of 1943, as Congress then passed it, followed that formula. It made about 70 per cent of all taxpayers current in their liabilities to the federal government. The other 30 per cent were to pay quarterly installments of taxes due according to their annual estimates. Taxpayers were forgiven three-quarters of their liability for either 1942 or 1943, whichever was lower, and were to pay the balance in two installments, in March 1944 and March 1945. The act also provided special relief for members of the Armed Services.

"Well," Morgenthau said when he first heard of Doughton's de-

* About a cross-channel invasion in 1943; Roosevelt lost the argument.

fection, "I'll be damned." Doughton, as he told the Secretary the next day, had felt "in a straight jacket all the time. . . . It's been one of the most bitter experiences I've ever had in my life, but it's got to where I'm not going to make any apology of what I've done. . . . If I made a mistake, why, I always have to take the responsibility of it. There's nothing in the world that's . . . greater pain to me really . . . than to not do the things that I think you up there want done. . . . Now the Treasury has taken the lead . . . about a collection at the source and withholding tax. . . . We just got to where we had to take this or go back and get something worse or take nothing."

"We desperately need more revenue," Morgenthau agreed, ". . . for better or worse, the fat's in the fire now." His own thinking, the Secretary added, "would be considerably cleared if I knew whether or not we could get another revenue bill through the Congress." Doughton was not sure, and though some of the Treasury staff were optimistic, the prospects were poor if Congress continued to write legislation in the pattern of the previous year.

8. Hot Weather

Simply by making Americans current in their tax payments, Congress had added $4 billion to federal revenues for 1943, but $12 billion of the President's stated goal remained to be raised. The problem of reaching that target provoked as much debate within the executive branch as it did between the Treasury and the Hill. Indeed even Roosevelt seemed at first to have lowered his sights. "What we want," he told Morgenthau on May 27, ". . . is to get on the basis where we are paying for one-third of the war through taxes."

"Mr. President," Morgenthau replied, "you are wrong on that. We're on that basis. We are trying to get to a 50 per cent basis."

"You shoot at 50 per cent," Roosevelt said. "Get all you can. . . . You can tell them this for me. If I don't get more revenue before the end of this calendar year, I am going to put the entire blame on Congress."

Yet as Randolph Paul reminded Morgenthau, it would be September or October before any revenue bill passed, and if the new schedules were steep enough to provide additional revenue of $12 billion, they would be too steep for retroactive application to January 1, 1943. The difficulty confronting the Treasury was to persuade Congress to adopt schedules that would add enough new revenue in any calendar year. The cumulative effect of revenue legislation enacted since 1939 magnified public and congressional resistance to taxation, as did the conservative temper increasingly dominant in both parties. Roosevelt, Morgenthau knew, would do little to assist in overcoming those obstacles. "This sort of thing bores the President," the Secretary pointed out to his staff. ". . . It always has been like that. . . . You are going to get very little help out of the President. You never have on this thing."

The negative mood of Congress suggested to proponents of forced lending that only their policy could now serve to check inflation. Perhaps under their influence, Roosevelt in a press conference of June 8, 1943, indicated that both higher taxes and compulsory savings were needed to close the inflationary gap. "I didn't say," he added, "that a compulsory savings plan was an immediate necessity. . . . At the present time the public is supporting bond drives with a great deal of enthusiasm. As long as they continue to do this, I feel . . . the compulsory savings will not be necessary." But newspapers generally predicted, on the basis of the President's remarks, that Justice Byrnes was to take a "leading hand in tax policy."

Morgenthau was aghast. He considered both his bond drive and his authority over revenue policy endangered, and he opposed any compulsory lending or savings program other than a major revision of Social Security taxes and postwar benefits. "If I am to continue to be responsible to you for the development of tax policies," he wrote Roosevelt, "and to represent you before Congress on tax matters, it seems to me that this is the time to clear up the confusion. . . . Until this matter is cleared up, it seems unlikely that congressional leaders will pay serious attention to any suggestions that I or representatives of the Treasury may make." Roosevelt replied that Harold Smith, Jimmy Byrnes, and Byrnes's chief deputy, former congressman Fred Vinson, were cooperating on a draft of a tax message which would deal also with inflation and subsidies. "Each of the departments named," the President wrote, "have responsibilities in connection with the subjects. If I approve a tax program I would, of course, expect you to present it to the Congress as my program. Thereafter there would be no excuse for conflicting views. . . . You and the Director should get together and arrange to cooperate in this matter. Do not let the newspapers disturb you." When Morgenthau pressed him further, Roosevelt said: "This whole question of money is broader than it has been before and I . . . have to consult other people and instead of my coming directly—instead of Morgenthau going directly to Roosevelt and Roosevelt dealing directly with Byrnes, I want you and Byrnes to deal with each other."

But during June and July continuing attacks on his position worried the Secretary, who believed that they were inspired by Byrnes and other advocates of forced lending. Morgenthau also resented Vinson's direct negotiations with the House Ways and Means Committee, though Vinson explained that he was merely trying to establish a unified point of view with his former colleagues in Congress. "What the President has done," Morgenthau told his staff on July 22, "without having the courtesy to tell us, is that he has brought between himself and his Cabinet another group that he looks to to run it.

"He is not going to do it to me, and I am not going to take it. . . . I am willing to take this unjust criticism in the papers, but if the President is stupid enough to let me be undermined. . . . I want him to say so. . . .

"The pattern is perfectly obvious. Those people sit over there in the left wing of the White House and they are going to run the show. If they are going to, let them get the credit publicly, and the blame publicly—I am not going to be a shirt front for Vinson. . . .

"The point of my story is, here are four or five people, very ambitious . . . every one of them . . . a politician. . . . They are maneuverers; they are finaglers. . . . They are much smarter than I am. They are interested in their personal ambition. . . . And that is what we are up against. . . .

"I want it straight from the shoulder. . . . I have been here ten years and your moral fibers begin to weaken after a while. . . . You can take a rubber band and keep pulling it, and after a while the thing just snaps. The things I could take five years ago . . . I can't take now."

He asked his staff to consider overnight the possibility of drafting a strong letter to the White House. Paul and Gaston, agreeing that the situation was intolerable, prepared that letter, which Morgenthau edited and then signed on July 27, 1943. "I am in doubt," he wrote Roosevelt, "whether you want me to go on doing for you what I've done in the past. . . . The whole atmosphere is one of doubt and uncertainty which I think will very greatly prejudice your ability to make recommendations on taxes to which Congress will give serious heed." Morgenthau therefore urged the President to give him "a clear and definite answer to two questions." First, was the Treasury to continue to coordinate the views of others in the Administration, and to present a tax program to the White House for the President's approval? Second, "Do you wish me to be in charge of presenting such a program?" to the Congress.

Roosevelt returned a classic answer, settling nothing, revealing no irritation, teasing but friendly. "AW HEN," he wrote on July 30. "The weather is hot and I am goin' off fishing. I decline to be serious even when you see 'gremlins' which ain't there!"

Back in Washington on August 10, the President had luncheon with Morgenthau. "I sent you a letter just before you left," the Secretary said, "in regard to this tax thing."

"Did you get my very snooty note," Roosevelt asked.

"Yes," Morgenthau replied, "I did and I didn't think it was snooty. I thought it was darling and I enjoyed it. I loved it."

"Now let me do the talking first," Roosevelt said. "In the first place, Jimmy Byrnes feels in his new position that taxes are a part of his over-all responsibility as well as other matters." Morgenthau interrupted. He had not referred to Byrnes but to Vinson. "No, no," Roosevelt said. "Vinson has nothing to do with this. It is Jimmy Byrnes."

"Well," Morgenthau said, "look Mr. President, all I want you to say is that you want me to go ahead."

"You go ahead," Roosevelt replied, "as you always have. Get your tax bill ready — I take it you have a tax bill — and about the 24th I will be ready to see you and Paul and anybody you want to bring over to go over the tax bill with you and give you the okay. After that I would like to see George and Doughton."

"Do you really want a tax bill?" Morgenthau asked.

"You need 12 billion in taxes," Roosevelt answered. "So I think you should put up to Congress various plans which total 18 billion, so that they can pick a number of schemes which will raise 12 billion. . . . Now we used to give Congress a plan which would raise a definite amount and they didn't like it, so we have been giving them suggestions with the result that the newspapers said we had no plan. . . . Now, of course, we have a plan, but we have changed our method of presenting it to Congress. This year let's give them alternative plans to raise 18 billion dollars and then let them select what they want."

"The President," Morgenthau later noted in his Diary "was very firm in that he wanted me to go ahead as I always have done. . . . He also was very definite that he doesn't want to sign any memorandum to Byrnes or Vinson. He said, 'This is all one big family and you don't do things that way in a family.' He was very definite that he wants a strong tax bill."

He was very definite, too, that Byrnes and Vinson had a role to play. "Jimmy Byrnes talked to me," Roosevelt told Morgenthau on August 11, "about what you and I were talking about yesterday morning. . . . Jimmy Byrnes said that Bob Doughton said that he needs Vinson to help him, and that Vinson is the only man that can help him with the bill."

"That would be fine," Morgenthau replied. ". . . If he can give Bob Doughton any help, as far as I am concerned, that would be fine."

Morgenthau's own program also needed help on the Hill. In August 1943, as in January, he was "not willing to lower the exemptions on the working people more than they are now." He preferred to raise taxes on advancing corporate profits. He also endorsed forced corporate (rather than individual) lending according to a scheme that after the war would return funds to the corporations for reconverting their plants to peacetime uses. The heart of his policy, however, he told his staff on August 17, was an immediate, substantial increase in Social Security rates, calculated to yield $5.5 billion in new revenue. That increase, to be followed only after the war with a broad expansion of Social Security benefits, would accomplish the purpose of compulsory lending while at the same time strengthening the fabric of American society. In this manner "at the end of twelve years Mr. Roosevelt will have something to point to for the lower third of this country," Morgenthau said. "To me that is much more important than all the rest of this stuff."

Walter George and Bob Doughton, Harold Smith and Jimmy Byrnes disagreed. On the radio that night Byrnes urged a large compulsory lending program. "I was shocked," Morgenthau wrote him. ". . . This statement is going to cause our State War Finance Committees a great deal of trouble." There was no reason for Morgenthau to be shocked, Byrnes replied, for the Secretary had long known his views, and Senator George was coming to the same position. Morgenthau would be wise to make no effort to censor tax discussions while the revenue bill moved through committees. Unless Roosevelt issued specific orders forbidding him to advocate forced savings, Byrnes would continue to do so — fair warning to the Treasury.

Other warnings followed apace. With the exception of the Federal Reserve Board and the Social Security Board, all the interested executive agencies told the Treasury that the $12 billion goal was too high. Late in August Roosevelt informed Morgenthau that he would accept $10 billion; early in September the Ways and Means Committee suggested eight. After consultation with the President, Morgenthau then grimly redefined the Treasury objective as $10.5 billion, with increases in Social Security to provide about half of that sum. The President would not "put into writing" any definition of Byrnes's responsibilities, but he did promise Morgenthau that he would "see that Byrnes makes no more statements on compulsory savings." As for Morgenthau's "plan to consolidate social insurance with the tax bill," Roosevelt said, "I have been groping for something. . . . This sounds good and I like it."

The only people who really counted would support that kind of bill, Morgenthau replied, the people who were earning $3000 a year or less; "this will be good for those people, and it is good for America, because they are America."

Wholly dissatisfied, Jimmy Byrnes lost his temper at a White House meeting on September 9, 1943. Taxes, he said, as part of the problem of stabilization, had to be under his jurisdiction. Byrnes, according to the account of Randolph Paul, was "pretty bitter and hot. . . . The President tried to stop him a couple of times, but he slugged right on. . . . The Secretary didn't talk very much, but

. . . he called the President's attention to that meeting . . . in which the President had said . . . that this Executive Order* did not contain any authority to issue directives to the Secretary." The Treasury, Roosevelt ruled, was to present and manage the tax bill on the Hill, but the President alone was the "responsible person," and the others "were serving as his agents in presenting the bill." On all questions of basic policy, decision was to lie with the White House. "I am the boss," Roosevelt said. "I realize that taxes fit into the inflation picture. . . . It is all in one picture. We must agree. . . . Then when we agree, I expect you fellows to go in and do the work just like soldiers."

Byrnes said he would not work for the bill unless he had a voice in it. He would take no orders from the Secretary of the Treasury. When he had left the Supreme Court to take over his job, he had done so in spite of a warning from Bernard Baruch that he could never handle it unless he had control over taxes. "I told Barnie," Byrnes said, ". . . 'I will take a chance.' . . . I have never had any trouble getting along with people previously. . . . I get along with Knox; I get along with Stimson; but I can't get along with the Secretary. He is the only man I can't get along with."

Angry as always when his subordinates fought in his presence, Roosevelt pounded the table. "I am the boss," he said again. "I am the one who gets the rap if we get licked in Congress, and I am the one who is in control. You people have to get together on a tax bill and then we can work it the way I want which is for the Treasury to present it . . . and the other people to work behind scenes."

"I think you and I agree on this," Morgenthau said to Byrnes.

"I wouldn't agree with you," Byrnes snapped, "on anything." And in spite of the President's remarks, Byrnes added: "I am going to send for George and Doughton and see if we can't get a bill."

"Livid," as Morgenthau later recalled, Roosevelt again pounded his desk and repeated: "I am the boss, I am giving the orders."

Four days later, on September 13, 1943, the President summoned the principals in the dispute to the White House, where Paul and Morgenthau explained the Treasury's tax program with its emphasis on Social Security. Quietly, Byrnes and Vinson, after recalling their active interest in the Social Security legislation of 1935, ana-

* Creating the Office of Economic Stabilization.

lyzed the political obstacles to expanding Social Security in 1943. The Treasury's intention to include medical insurance in the Social Security plan, they predicted, would stir up "more than a hornet's nest." Roosevelt, after reflecting overnight, told the group the next day that he thought the country would favor an extension of Social Security if the matter were properly presented. For a moment Morgenthau thought he had won his case, but Byrnes interrupted to explain his scheme for enforced savings, and Roosevelt swung over to that idea. In pencil the President wrote out a memorandum of his decision. It called for raising an additional $5 billion through increments in the graduated income tax. After the war taxpayers would have an option of accepting a partial cash refund or a paid-up life insurance policy equivalent to the entire increase in taxes. Those earning less than $3000 a year, who were to be exempt from the new rates, would instead make additional contributions to their unemployment and old age accounts under Social Security. When Morgenthau said that the refundable tax proposal would impede the pending bond drive, Byrnes suggested deferring discussion of the entire tax question until after that drive was completed. There matters were left until the group could meet with the congressional leaders the following day.

At that conference Roosevelt again presided. Working from a Treasury memorandum that reflected the discussions of the two previous days, the President suggested increases in excise taxes to raise an additional $2.5 billion, increases in estate and gift taxes to raise an additional $400 million, and increases in corporate taxes to raise an additional $1.1 billion. He went on to describe the refundable tax scheme he had devised, which would yield, according to Treasury calculations, between $3.5 and $4.5 billion.

That program, Doughton and George immediately said, could not survive in their committees. Their colleagues would vote down any higher payroll taxes. Personally opposed to any scheme involving a postwar rebate, Doughton preferred outright taxation even if it yielded less revenue.

The meeting left Morgenthau dissatisfied. "People like Byrnes and Vinson are going to get Congress in such a frame of mind that I can't work with them," he complained to the President privately. ". . . If they keep this thing up you and nobody but you can stop them." But Roosevelt assured him that "Byrnes was all right." And in his Diary, the Secretary shrugged the matter off: "The President's attitude toward me is always very friendly and I gather he thinks the whole thing is rather funny. So I don't see any sense in my becoming tragic about it, but I will just have to continue to look after my own interests."

To that end, the Secretary enlisted Harry Hopkins, Sam Rosenman, William Green, and Philip Murray behind the Treasury's Social Security plan, but Roosevelt received equally vigorous protests against the plan from Congress. "The only person," the President told Morgenthau on September 27, "who can explain this medical thing is myself. The people are unprepared." And so was the White House. "You don't want, I am sure," Roosevelt said to Walter George at a meeting the next day, "to have anybody come up and present a Social Security program at this time. . . . I know you don't want it. . . . We can't go up against the State Medical Societies; we just can't do it." As Morgenthau interpreted the meeting to his staff: "They're only interested in what they can get through Congress."

Perhaps partly on that account, Roosevelt agreed at the last moment to let Morgenthau present the proposal for a tax refund as a suggestion rather than a recommendation, which seemed to the Secretary to protect the principle of voluntarism in the savings program. "It really worked out wonderfully well," he remarked to Herbert Gaston, and he felt a genuine commitment to the statement he read before the House Ways and Means Committee on October 4, 1943. With Roosevelt's consent, he included two paragraphs about Social Security, but he concentrated, as he had to, on plans for raising another $10.5 billion — $6.5 billion through individual income taxes, $1.1 through corporate taxes, $2.5 through excise taxes, and $400 million through estate and gift taxes. Since the proposed burden was so heavy, Congress might consider lessening its impact on lower income groups by providing for a postwar refund of part of the additional tax. "I should like to suggest," Morgenthau added, ". . . that . . . a substantial increase in the Social Security payroll taxes would be of immediate service in diminishing the threat of inflation. There is no pretence on the part of low income people that they could comfortably pay these additional payroll taxes. It is known by them, and admitted to be a sacrifice; but it is felt by leaders and spokesmen for many such people . . . that because we would be expanding Social Security's advantages and permitting workers to invest in their future, this sacrifice will be made willingly."

The Secretary had made his point. Congress now had officially before it the Administration's recommendations for additional revenue and Morgenthau's personal suggestion for building a better society. Ironically, the revenue program, fashioned with such concern for politics, was to hold no more attraction on the hill than was the bolder call for reform.

9. A Great Defeat

Congress responded adversely to Morgenthau's recommendations. They would, Doughton said, impose "unbearable increased burdens"; the suggestions for excise taxes were "utterly indefensible." Three unidentified members of the Ways and Means Committee told reporters "that relations between Congress and the Administration on fiscal matters would be clarified if Morgenthau did not head the Treasury Department." Though the fury subsided when the Secretary went off for a month in Africa and Italy, the Ways and Means Committee excluded Treasury representatives from its hearings and ignored them in its deliberations.

Back from Africa on November 1, 1943, Morgenthau discovered that the Ways and Means Committee had provided tax favors of various kinds to owners and operators of mines and to the natural gas industry, and had opened new escapes from the excess profits tax. As finally reported out on November 18, the committee bill provided only $2 billion of additional revenue, most of it from increased excises. Morgenthau, as he told Randolph Paul, had had several weeks to think matters over. "After all," he concluded, "we gave them a good recommendation. The fact that they don't take it is their fault, and not ours."

It was also a response to the conservative bias of public opinion. Three-quarters of American daily newspapers had blasted the Treasury's program, "chiefly because . . . it would do much to discourage the spirit of individual enterprise." A fifth of all newspapers considered the country unable to meet the Treasury's demands. A Gallup poll indicated that more than half of the public preferred sales taxes to the Treasury's suggestions.

In the face of that criticism, Morgenthau, as he told his assistants on November 23, had to find some compelling way to restate the Administration's purpose when he appeared before the Senate Finance Committee. While still convinced that the Department had defined the proper techniques for increasing revenues, he was willing to surrender to Congress on the question of means so long as he could get $10.5 billion. He intended to ask again for that amount with "no trimmings, no refunds, or anything else. I want a good stiff tax bill which will help pay for the war while we can afford to pay for it."

A group of "very pleasant and friendly" Democratic senators agreed on the need for $10.5 billion, but Walter George warned Morgenthau that the Treasury would fail to obtain even a significant part of that much money. Since the vote in the House of Representatives had been made public, there was little likelihood of congressmen changing their minds. If the Senate came up with a bill very different from the House version, the two chambers would lock in conflict, and probably pass no tax bill before the following spring. In the interim, the government would lose revenue that the House bill would otherwise provide.

Morgenthau nevertheless read a strong statement to the Senate Finance Committee on November 29, 1943, but the validity of his familiar arguments and the quiet cooperation of Walter George changed no votes. The bill the committee wrote, Morgenthau told the press on December 21, promised only $2.1 billion of additional revenue: "The . . . yield of the bill in its present form is naturally extremely disappointing to the Treasury Department. We had hoped that the unfairness to future taxpayers, including the returning soldiers, of passing on to them war costs that we are able to meet now . . . would have made an appeal to the members of the committees." Further, by freezing Social Security taxes at the existing rate of 1 per cent, the committee had reduced previously scheduled increments in Social Security collections during the coming year by $1.4 billion. As a consequence, the government would have to raise more money in future years for old age insurance.

That statement, Walter George replied, showed "exceeding bad grace." His attitude imbued the whole Senate. Though Roosevelt, in his State of the Union Message of January 1944, characterized the pending bill as "unrealistic" and called for "a truly stiff fiscal program," discussion on the floor of the Senate related only to still further relief for special interest groups. On January 21 the Senate passed a bill no better than the version already adopted by the House.

As the bill went into conference committee for reconciliation of sundry differences, Roy Blough expressed to Morgenthau his grave concern over "a lot of . . . private industry grabs — which are in the guise of highly technical provisions of the tax bill. . . . We have already lost on what . . . will give big steel companies a substantial break [and] . . . some of the big timber outfits substantial breaks. I think we may lose on a lot of the other items." The Secretary saw no remedy. "I don't know any time," he said, "that the Treasury, as far as having influence on the Hill is concerned, was as low as it is right now, and only . . . because you were courageous to go out and talk, because we were right."

As the tax bill emerged from conference committee, it contained so many inequities and produced so little revenue that Randolph Paul, Herbert Gaston, and Dan Bell urged Morgenthau to recommend a veto to the President. Undecided, the Secretary consulted Byrnes on February 1, 1944. "If you ask your mother for a dollar," Byrnes said, "and she gives you . . . a dime, you're not going to turn the dime down. You go back for ninety cents this afternoon." But the arguments of Vinson, Paul, Bell, and Ben Cohen, now his general counsel, moved Byrnes, who sent Morgenthau a message on February 10 that "he had changed his mind about the bill" and now favored a veto. Morgenthau, in contrast, had come to believe the President should let the revenue bill become law without his signature, as he had in 1938. Roosevelt disagreed. With the Secretary on February 13, he said: "I am going to do what everybody is urging me to do. . . . I am going to veto it."

Randolph Paul contributed to the draft of the veto message, which Byrnes, Vinson, and Ben Cohen prepared. As Roosevelt sent it to Congress on February 22, that message condemned the revenue bill as "wholly ineffective" for meeting the budgetary and economic needs of the nation, and as "dangerous" in its provisions for "indefensible privileges for special groups." "In this respect," the President said, "it is not a tax bill but a tax relief bill providing relief not for the needy but for the greedy."

In a quick, hot retort, nineteen of the twenty-five members of the Ways and Means Committee declared that Roosevelt's $10.5 billion goal would have been "oppressive to tax payers and dangerous for the national economy," as well as a threat to "the solvency of all business." Alben Barkley, the Democratic Majority Leader in the Senate, long an effective lieutenant of the White House, went further. Resigning his post on February 23, he called the veto message a "calculated and deliberate assault upon the legislative integrity of every member of Congress. . . . If the Congress . . . has any self-respect yet left, it will override the veto." It did — the House on February 24, 299 to 98; the Senate the next day, 72 to 14. Roosevelt patched things up with "Dear Alben," to whom he wrote a soothing letter and whose reelection as Majority Leader he urged upon the willing Senate Democrats. But the damage was done. Congress had passed a revenue act over a veto for the first time in American history, and Congress had so thoroughly routed the Administration that debate about taxation ceased for the duration of the war.*

The newspapermen covering the Treasury warned Morgenthau that congressmen of both parties, bitterly resentful of the veto message, blamed it largely on Randolph Paul. Paul's prestige on the Hill, the reports added, had vanished, and the Secretary's was fading rapidly. Hoping to temper that hostility, some of Morgenthau's advisers suggested he explain to Doughton that the Treasury had opposed a veto. But Morgenthau preferred to take his beating. As he put it to his staff on March 1, 1944:

> I have followed all of these attacks. . . . I asked everybody's advice, and . . . I decided I would recommend to the President we would sign it. . . . He didn't take our advice. That is his choice. . . . And I am certainly going to stand by my staff. . . . As far as the Treasury is concerned, nobody is going to

---

* Though the Treasury and the Congress worked together in 1944 to prepare a non-controversial act simplifying tax forms and tax collections, and in 1945 on a study of tax adjustments to facilitate postwar reconversion, a study that informed the revenue legislation of that year.

be thrown to the wolves no matter which way they advised me. . . .

The President did it his way; that is his privilege. I will never forget, after all, I am here as an appointed officer. . . .

As far as the press is concerned, my statement, if they ask me, is this: "The President of the United States made up his mind. We gave him certain advice. What we gave him is his business and his business only, and I have no comment to make." . . .

I told my wife — I made the rather trite remark that somebody would have to be the ham in the sandwich, as between the President and the Congress, and I was expecting to be it. He got himself out of it nicely by very fast footwork, and naturally they would like to throw somebody. And I am the natural candidate for that. . . .

Randolph, as the principal man on taxes, carried out a hodgepodge of a tax bill, due largely to the interference on the part of Byrnes and Vinson and the President. . . . Not one of them with the exception of Vinson . . . went up on the Hill and supported us. . . .

Now . . . somebody has to take it. I am perfectly willing to take it, but it does give you a gripe when a man like Byrnes will run to cover just as soon as it gets hot. . . . Anybody who is loyal to the President is going to get it.

Congress, not the Treasury, was the proper object of criticism and attack. Various economists, to be sure, believed the Treasury erred in not sponsoring a program for compulsory lending. Morgenthau years later replied with vigor that in fact the Department had at various times and in various ways presented devices for forced lending, no one of which the Congress accepted. Further, the kind of program that Jimmy Byrnes preferred would have met no better fate on the Hill in 1942 and 1943. Most important, both Morgenthau and Paul remained persuaded that their recommendations, potentially as effective against inflation as were Byrnes's, also advanced the cause of social reform and preserved the voluntary bond program with the income for the federal government which it produced. There were also economists who contended that the Treasury was unwise in resisting a sales tax. Here too, two decades after the event, Morgenthau disagreed, for his staff had calculated again and again that the yield from a sales tax would have been relatively insignificant, while its social impact would have been regressive.

Those issues aside, the Treasury's general policies stood on their merits. The taxes the department recommended were enforceable; they were designed to produce the funds needed to defray on a current basis at least half the cost of the war; they had the capacity to close the inflationary gap; and, unlike the recommendations of any other group in Washington, they reflected the spirit of the New Deal. In rejecting the Treasury's programs, the Congress damaged the economy, weakened the government's finances, rewarded those already overprivileged and penalized the vast majority of Americans. Taxation for war ran counter to the purposes Morgenthau held highest — the mobilization of maximum resources to defeat the Axis; the construction of a good society in the nation and in the world.

III

Financing the Grand Alliance

1941-1944

DURING THE YEAR after Pearl Harbor, the United States and her allies suffered a succession of grave defeats. Japanese forces overran the Philippines, Malaya and the islands of the Central and Southwest Pacific, and were poised for an attack on Australia. In North Africa German troops, advancing past the western border of Egypt, threatened Cairo and British control of the entire Middle East. In Europe the Nazis marched to the outskirts of Leningrad and Stalingrad. While the Grand Alliance was on the defensive, the products of the American arsenal had to be distributed to sustain resistance to Axis gains across the globe, and to prepare for the counterattacks already planned. Launched in late 1942 and 1943, those thrusts turned the Germans back in Russia, cleared them out of North Africa, and drove them north in Italy — all preparatory to the cross-channel invasion of 1944 on which victory depended. So, too, in the Pacific, the Allies began at Guadalcanal the long march north toward Japan.

Morgenthau had no voice in the strategy of the Grand Alliance and very little in the logistics supporting it, but it did fall to him and the Treasury to find ways to finance the alliance in whatever volume the President and his military advisers prescribed. Now and then the Secretary assessed policy from the point of view of his ordinary departmental responsibilities, but when his conclusions diverged from those based upon the political and military considerations of the war, he invariably yielded. His was basically a staff position, and in that role, while candid in his advice to the Presi-

79

dent, he also, like a good soldier, executed unhesitatingly the orders
he received. Those orders, moreover, because of Roosevelt's continuing personal trust in him, involved Morgenthau now and then in
missions extending beyond the ordinary borders of the Treasury to
questions relating to the prosecution of the war and the development of policy for the postwar world.

1. Russia: "This Is Critical"

Three days after Pearl Harbor, Maxim Litvinov, the new ambassador from Russia, called at the Treasury. He and Morgenthau had
known each other since the negotiations that led to American recognition of the Soviet Union in 1933. Now Litvinov, of all eminent
Russians the most popular in the United States, had returned to
Washington. His predecessor, he said, had told him to go to Morgenthau when he needed help. He would be glad, Morgenthau replied, to assist the Russians in any way "that would aid in defeating
Hitler."

An early opportunity arose on January 1, 1942. In order to purchase American materials unavailable through Lend Lease, the Soviet Union arranged through the Treasury to borrow $20 million
against delivery of gold within six months. The transaction resembled several completed during the previous half-year, and as Morgenthau and his assistants remarked, regular Russian gold payments
had confirmed the integrity of the Soviets in meeting their contracts.

The United States was doing less well in fulfilling its Lend Lease
commitments to the Soviet Union. Indeed, in the early months of
1942, deliveries to all allies flagged because of the growing crisis in
shipping. The sea lanes to Russia, exposed both to Nazi submarines
in the Atlantic and to Nazi air attacks from Norway, were especially
vulnerable. Still, Morgenthau suspected that American inefficiency
was contributing to the problem.

At his direction, Gerard Swope, the able president of General
Electric who was on temporary duty with the Treasury, talked with
Admiral Emory S. Land, the chief of the Maritime Commission, who
was taking the brunt of the criticism for American shipping failures.
Land, Swope reported on January 22, 1942, said "that he's been

kicked all around by the President and also by Harry Hopkins . . . and that if anybody can run the thing better than he does, why they're welcome to it; but that they have already . . . sent thirteen ships to Russia, and they will send fourteen more this month." Land needed 639 ships and had only 400; under the circumstances, he was "just doing the best he knows how."

In the following weeks the procurement of supplies for the Soviet Union and the movement of those supplies to port, while erratic, proceeded more rapidly than did shipments. Goods piled up in New York and elsewhere on the East Coast while Russian complaints accumulated at the Treasury. Many of those complaints related to materials the Russians had ordered through the Department's Division of Procurement. Because the War Production Board had not given those orders a high enough priority, deficiencies had developed, largely in various kinds of steel and steel plate.

On Morgenthau's instructions, the Treasury investigated the whole question of Russian requisitions. The First Soviet-American Lend-Lease Protocol called for delivery by April 1, 1942, of 42,000 tons of steel wire, of which only 7500 tons would have been shipped under existing schedules. Commitments for 3000 tools would have netted only 820; of a promised 1200 tons of steel alloy tubes, nothing at all; of 120 tons of stainless steel, only 22; of 48,000 tons of shell steel, only 10,000; of 48,000 tons of cold rolled steel strips, about 19,000; of a promised 42,000 tons of hot rolled steel, barely 18,000. Most of those shortages would persist beyond June 30, 1942, when the protocol expired. To some degree difficulties arose from the Russian failure to submit manageable specifications, but part of the blame fell on American administrators of war production, Lend-Lease, and shipping.

Sure of his facts, Morgenthau took them to Roosevelt on March 11. "I do not want to be in the same position as the English," the President said. "The English promised the Russians two divisions. They failed. They promised them help in the Caucasus. They failed. Every promise the English have made to the Russians, they have fallen down on. . . . The only reason we stand so well with the Russians is that up to date we have kept our promises. I suppose the reason we are behind in our deliveries to Russia is because we got into the war ourselves. . . . I would go out and take the stuff off the shelves of the stores, and pay them any price necessary, and put it in a truck and rush it to the boat. . . . Nothing would be worse than to have the Russians collapse. . . . I would rather lose New Zealand, Australia or anything else than have the Russians collapse."

Morgenthau, the President said, was to see to it personally that "the stuff" moved to Russia. Initialing a chit in his own handwriting, Roosevelt wrote: "This is *critical* because (a) we *must* keep our word (b) because Russian resistance counts *most* today."

As the Secretary explained it to his staff: "The President said he wanted me to get everybody together and say that as far as he was concerned they had made a perfect monkey out of him, that he couldn't stand for it. He would rather lose fifty ships off the Atlantic Coast than have Russia fold up and make peace. It would just have to be done. . . . I am quite excited."

At a conference the next day, March 12, 1942, Morgenthau read the President's order to officials from Lend-Lease, the War Production Board, the Maritime Commission, and other agencies. The President, he added, "just wasn't going to accept any excuses." There were plenty of those. Edward Stettinius, Jr., the head of the Lend-Lease Administration, blamed the Russians for their "failure to bring in their specifications on time." They had submitted "Tiffany requirements. . . . They have asked for steel with a 4 per cent nickel. We are trying to get that down to the same nickel which the United States and the British are using because of the tightness of the nickel content." Speaking for the War Production Board, Donald Nelson said that Roosevelt had promised the Russians only steel rolled according to American specifications. The Russians, Stettinius replied, "have been told constantly for months, that they could have the steel if they would take a standard type." In that case, Morgenthau said, the President ought to have had a memorandum of explanation. "If it was mine to settle," he added later, "and you had a certain kind of steel rolling out and it was 2 per cent nickel and they wanted 4, I would give them the 2 per cent."

For the tie-up of freight cars at Norfolk and Philadelphia, the Russians also bore some responsibility, for they had insisted on using their own methods of designating railroad cars for loading aboard ship. "It seems to me," Morgenthau said, "that before they put in sixteen ships into Philadelphia that somebody might have had the foresight to work out the rail traffic thing so that the thing would flow smoothly to these ships and not have this jam which they have got there now." Representatives of the Railroad Administration admitted that was true, though they also felt that shippers had given them too little advance information to permit proper planning.

Admiral Land foresaw no quick solutions: "You were just singing a song for me here that is going to be sung right along, and that is going to get progressively worse. We haven't got enough ships. . . . I have known it for some time. . . . We have never lived up to our promises; and, as far as I can see, we are probably unlikely to live up to them with exactitude. The repair yards are 300 per cent overloaded. The sinkings are going faster than the buildings, and there are a thousand other excuses that are not worthwhile even to go into. . . . A lot of this trouble . . . is the Russians themselves. It took me months to find out who was the shipping man that I could contact. I was passed around the ring like the ball in a football field. . . . There certainly has been a woeful lack of proper point of contact with Amtorg* mixed up on one side . . . and various and sundry Embassy staff giving orders."

As the discussion ended, Morgenthau asked for assistance in preparing a memorandum for Roosevelt describing the efforts being made to meet the commitments of the protocol. "These confessional meetings," he said, "are good for the soul. . . . From the way the President spoke yesterday, if you are short on something, take it and he will back you to the limit. . . . Filling his promises to Stalin . . . that came first over and above everything else."

The consequences of the meeting were considerable. Within a day, the War Department arranged for a change in authority over inland transportation that promised to accelerate loadings and thereby to relieve the shipping shortage by speeding turnabouts. "That's at least a little something done," Morgenthau reported to the President's secretary. ". . . Tell him I'm keeping after it." Roosevelt kept after it too: "I find that our . . . shipments to Russia are still far behind," he wrote Nelson and Land, after reading

* The Soviet purchasing corporation in the United States.

their memorandum about steel, "and that many of them are placed in preferential lists which fall behind other requirements. I wish that all materiel promised under the Protocol be released for shipment at the earliest possible date regardless of the effect of these shipments on any other part of our war program." To the Cabinet on March 26, the President again stressed the importance of living up to American commitments; his word and the national honor were at stake. "He thought it was very important," Dan Bell, who attended the meeting, reported to Morgenthau, "that everybody understand his position in this connection and make every effort to deliver all of the items required under the protocol by July 1, when it terminates. He said he wanted Mr. Welles* to begin discussing immediately with the Russians the question of renewing that protocol. . . . He also wanted to increase the amount under the new protocol."

During the spring of 1942, as higher priorities for steel for the Soviet Union further strained the limited shipping capacity of the Allies, the British held tightly to the space available for moving cargoes to the North African and Middle Eastern theaters, where their troops and interests were deeply engaged. Litvinov again turned to Morgenthau for help. "Last night," the Secretary noted in his Diary on May 6, 1942, ". . . Litvinov told me that they are only going to get five ships for May, and twelve for the Persian Gulf. He is terribly blue, and says the trouble is the English will not furnish the convoys. He blames this on the Australians, whom he thinks have been working on us. The English have been sending more to Australia, which means less for Russia. He said the President tried to get the English to furnish more convoys, but he has not been successful." On investigation, that complaint struck Clifton E. Mack, the Treasury's Director of Procurement, as unfair. Mack wrote Morgenthau on June 9, 1942, "that there will be an increased number of ships to be made available to the Russians for Lend-Lease shipments this month. It is indicated that fifty-four ships will be provided for July to handle Russian cargo which will almost triple May shipping. . . . Likewise, we are cooperating closely with the British to provide cargo for their proposed increased shipping schedules."

Satisfied by that report, Morgenthau was further encouraged by Roosevelt's attitude. "The whole question of whether we win or

* Undersecretary of State Sumner Welles.

lose the war depends upon the Russians," the President told him on June 16. "If the Russians can hold out this summer and keep three-and-a-half million Germans engaged in war we can definitely win." Losses on convoy runs to Murmansk were staggering, but Roosevelt remained sanguine through the summer. "I don't see any dark spots," he said in early September. ". . . I have said right along that if the Russians can hold on . . . we are all right, and I think they are going to."

"The amusing thing about the President," Morgenthau noted in his Diary, "is that he can state these facts coolly and calmly whether we win or lose the war, and to me it is most encouraging that he really seems to face these issues, and that he is not kidding himself one minute about the war. That, to me, seems to be the correct attitude for a commander-in-chief to take."

Heartening, too, was the improvement in the American delivery of materials to Russia. The first Lend-Lease protocol committed the United States to make available by June 30, 1942, goods estimated at a value of $750 million. By that date, the United States had delivered close to 80 per cent of the quota, and had also provided outside of the protocol other items that brought the value of the total to more than 100 per cent of the original obligation. That record partly reflected improved communications between the Soviet supply mission and American agencies; partly, the pressure on those agencies exerted by the President and Morgenthau.

In diminishing degree, similar pressure had on occasion to correct lags in shipments to Russia during the rest of the war. So it was in September 1942, when Harold Ickes enlisted Morgenthau's assistance in designing and supplying materials for the building of refineries in the Soviet Union to manufacture 100-octane gasoline. Once again, some delays in the project grew out of confusion in the specifications received from the Soviet Union. Further, the Department of the Interior, responsible for supplying the machinery for the refineries, preferred a process for which there would be a $5 million annual royalty charge, whereas the Russians hoped to obtain equipment of equal merit without paying royalties. Both the Treasury and the Interior Departments attempted to find ways in which to save the Russians that cost and to secure from the War Production Board the highest priority for the equipment. By the end of September both Ickes and Morgenthau were satisfied with most of the resulting decisions but unhappy about priority schedules.

With the President on October 4, 1942, Morgenthau said "that there had been delays in purchases for the Russians . . . particularly for gasoline refineries and rubber-making machinery, and I thought it was inexcusable that when he issued an order that it wasn't carried out." The order had been clear enough. Roosevelt had directed all American agencies to "make ships available to fill quota of convoys to North Russia. . . . Make necessary arrangements including production priorities to ensure sufficient priority cargoes in accordance with the protocol. . . . Deliver airplanes in accordance with protocol schedules by the most expeditious means, whether by ship or by flight. . . . Give high priority to projects of the operation and enlargement of transportation facilities on the Persian Corridor." He had also called for monthly reports on progress, "including any recommendations you may have for expediting aid to Russia." Like Morgenthau's complaint, those reports provoked Roosevelt at the end of October 1942, to direct Harry Hopkins to organize a Soviet Protocol Committee, responsible for the coordination of production and deliveries in conformity with the President's policy.

As Roosevelt put it further in a memorandum of early January 1943, "the Army and Navy are definitely of the opinion that Russian continuance as a major factor in the war is of cardinal importance, and therefore it must be a basic factor in our strategy to provide her with the maximum amount of supplies that can be delivered in her ports. . . . In executing the Second Protocol and in planning the over-all program, . . . the necessity of meeting Soviet needs . . . must be regarded as a matter of paramount importance." Armed with that directive, Donald Nelson was able to exceed all obligations to the Russians except for a few items in critical supply, particularly certain kinds of steel and machine tools. By the summer of 1943 American performance, now under the Third Protocol, continuously met the standards the President had set. Morgenthau therefore had no further occasion to intercede. Indeed he had begun instead to think about ways in which to obtain from Russia supplies of manganese, lumber, and fur in return for American services already rendered.

American and British preparations in 1944 for the cross-channel attack contributed to the serenity of the relationship between the United States and the Soviet Union in the first six months of that year. Though Russia's political purposes, according to State Department analysts in Moscow, remained at variance with American expectations, political issues seemed remote with military victory still so distant, and Roosevelt valued Stalin's support for the Anglo-American invasion of Europe that American military planners so warmly advocated.

Still, even those, like Morgenthau, who had most assisted the Russian war effort, were sporadically impatient with the rigidities of the Soviet Government. Russian representatives in Washington, lacking any discretion about questions of supply, demanded, as Morgenthau reported on one occasion, four-pronged barbed wire even though American manufacturers produced only a three-pronged variety. Once Moscow had made an initial order, no one of its representatives in Washington dared alter it, even for a commodity as insignificant as ink.

But the resulting annoyances were transitory as well as trivial, and Morgenthau, like Roosevelt, remained persuaded both of the necessity of the Soviet contribution to the destruction of Nazism and of the probability of postwar cooperation between the United States and Russia. Spontaneously, therefore, the Secretary welcomed the memorandum Roosevelt sent him and other responsible officials on February 14, 1944. "Russia continues to be a major factor in achieving the defeat of Germany," the President wrote. "We must therefore continue to support the USSR by providing the maximum amount of supplies which can be delivered to her ports. This is a matter of paramount importance." That directive governed policy toward the Soviet Union while the United States prepared for the attack on Europe from the west.

2. China: The Price of Friendship

China and Japan, enemies in the field for years, had yet to declare war on each other on December 7, 1941. Partly to show sympathy with the United States, China indicated her readiness to declare

war, though she was delaying, her government said, in the hope —
patently futile — that the Soviet Union might join her. So informed
by T. V. Soong, China's chief financial representative in Washington,
Morgenthau also learned that in the view of the President and the
State Department, China should declare war not on Japan only but
also on Germany and Italy. China did so, but her usefulness as an ally
depended on various uncertainties. Without substantial shipments
of American materials, Generalissimo Chiang Kai-shek remained, as
he had long been, incapable of significant military action. Further
the successful Japanese offensives of December 1941 and January
1942 cut off avenues of supply to China except by air across the
Himalayas from India, a cumbersome and dangerous route. Those
victories also accentuated the vulnerability of the whole South Pacific area, including Australia and New Zealand. The United States
and Great Britain were therefore eager to ensure China's resistance
and to tie up a substantial Japanese force otherwise available for
aggression elsewhere. In Roosevelt's interpretation, China's declaration of war gave her a status equal to that of the English-speaking
belligerents, but that declaration also strengthened the Generalissimo's demands for extensive Anglo-American assistance, which
the corruption within the Nationalist government threatened to
waste.

Long an effective advocate of aid to China, Morgenthau had developed serious doubts about the honesty and efficiency of the circle
around Chiang Kai-shek. Information he received early in December 1941 from a veteran American reporter confirmed his suspicions.
The report counted the Chinese Minister of War among those who
were reluctant to fight. Even more troublesome was the wife of
H. H. Kung, the Minister of Finance, an unscrupulous woman responsible for much of the dissipation of the nation's funds. Her
sister, Madame Chiang Kai-shek, had a better understanding of democratic principles, but lived in splendid luxury while most of China
starved. Chiang himself was financially irresponsible, uneducated,
and brazenly unapologetic for the failure of his regime to advance
the people's rights or welfare.

There was no serious dissent from that analysis by the American
ambassador in Chungking, Clarence E. Gauss, or by most members
of his staff, or most western newspaper correspondents, or Emanuel

Fox, the American representative on the Chinese Stabilization Board, or by the Treasury officials who advised Morgenthau about policy for China. Foremost of those advisers was Harry Dexter White, whose counsel was later subject to particular attack because of postwar accusations, which he denied under oath, that he had been at one time a Communist or Communist agent. Whatever the merit of those charges, the attitudes toward China that White expressed during the war were close to the consensus of informed American observers. Even on questions of monetary policy, his major responsibility, he neither always influenced Morgenthau nor always agreed with him, but he did have a large and continuing voice in Treasury deliberations about many matters, China not the least.

About that there was no secret, then or later. First hired by the Treasury as a specialist in monetary questions, recommended by Jacob Viner, a distinguished economist, White in 1940 became Director of Monetary Research, a promotion he earned by his capacity for hard work, his success in the management of the Stabilization Fund, and his initiative in assisting the Secretary in related matters. "To make life easier for me," Morgenthau announced to his morning group the day after Pearl Harbor, "and . . . better for the Treasury, I want to give Harry White the status of an Assistant Secretary. He will be in charge of all foreign affairs for me. Now, I have talked to each person, in turn, and it's agreeable to everybody but Merle Cochran* and he has asked me to have him transferred back to the State Department. . . . I want it in one brain and I want it in Harry White's brain. He will tell Bell as much as Bell wants to know. . . . When it is some question of foreign matters, Harry will come in and see me and I will give him a decision and when the decision is made he will tell you about it. If it in any way crosses anything that you have got, he will come in first and see you and ask your views."

Cordell Hull, when Morgenthau informed him of White's new role, remarked that "he's a mighty suitable man . . . a very high class fellow." Increasingly of that opinion, Morgenthau in 1943

---

* Merle Cochran had been on loan to the Treasury from the Department of State for seven years, in which he had performed admirably as a special adviser to the Secretary on monetary matters.

asked White "to take supervision over and assume full responsibility for Treasury's participation in all economic and financial matters . . . in connection with the operations of the Army and Navy and the civilian affairs in the foreign areas in which our armed forces are operating." And in 1944 Morgenthau made White an Assistant Secretary of the Treasury. "Harry," he then said to Roosevelt, "has done a swell job."

He had done so, the Secretary knew, against large personal odds. "He could be disagreeable," Morgenthau said years later, "quick-tempered, overly ambitious, and power went to his head." He was rude, abrupt, and impatient with opposition, which he often tried to circumvent by going outside of ordinary bureaucratic channels — a habit that could be identified with furtiveness or even confused with subversion. He appointed some assistants who were almost certainly members of the Communist Party, though Morgenthau did not know they were, and those assistants, in White's view, were as free to pass along information about Treasury policy to the Russians as was Averell Harriman, for example, free to talk to the British. But White did not himself hew to the line of the Communist Party. Further, he was also energetic, unsparing of himself, a bulldog in defense of his chief and the Treasury, and something of a hero to his subordinates who found him considerate, creative, attentive, and helpful. Morgenthau in all his years in office had no reason to question their impression, no reason to doubt White's competence or loyalty or value to the department.

White and his assistants, in the weeks just after Pearl Harbor, agreed with Roosevelt on the overriding need to keep China in the war; with Morgenthau on the desirability of combating corruption in Chungking; and with the Chinese themselves on the gravity of the problem of inflation. Money, early in 1942, provided one obvious means for executing American policy in China. The Chinese treasury and banking system desperately needed dollars to help arrest the accelerating depreciation of the fapi, the Chinese unit of currency. Inflation in China, in the opinion of the American Treasury and Ambassador, arose primarily from the pressure of demand on diminishing supplies of food, textiles, and hard goods, but the financial irresponsibility of the government made things worse.

Politics rather than economics provided the major justification for considering the $500 million loan that Chiang Kai-shek requested on December 30, 1941. It was intended, he admitted, to buttress the morale of the Chinese people after Pearl Harbor. As Ambassador Gauss pointed out, a loan of about $10 million would probably suffice to retard inflation. The primary benefits of a larger loan would be psychological. At the Treasury on January 9, 1942, Assistant Secretary of State Adolf Berle argued that $500 million was necessary to strengthen the position of the Generalissimo who, except for the Communists, represented the only important resistance to the Japanese. That was the President's conclusion, too. "In regard to the Chinese loan," Roosevelt wrote Morgenthau that day, "I realize there is little security which China can give at the present time, yet I am anxious to help Chiang Kai-shek and his currency. I hope you can invent some way of doing this. Possibly we could buy a certain amount of this currency, even if it means a partial loss later on."

Following the President's lead, Cordell Hull defined official State Department policy. "The Generalissimo's proposal," he wrote Morgenthau on January 10, 1942, "has been given very careful consideration. I feel that, as an act of wartime policy and to prevent the impairment of China's military effort which would result from loss of confidence in Chinese currency . . . it is highly advisable that the United States extend financial assistance to the government of China."

Urging quick Treasury approval of a loan, T. V. Soong reminded Morgenthau that the Chinese had expected the coming of war to mean an increase in military and economic assistance, but had found the reverse to be the case. The American War Department was asking them to send troops to Burma at the very time they found their supplies curtailed. Successive and unavoidable Japanese gains had to be offset by some kind of favorable publicity, hopefully the announcement of a large loan. In a separate communication, H. H. Kung, the Chinese Minister of Finance, repeated those points.

Nevertheless Morgenthau hesitated. "The President and the State Department want me to make a loan to China," he told his staff on January 12, ". . . but . . . I would like to do this thing in the way that we could sort of kind of feed it out to them if they keep fighting, but I would hate to put $300 million on the line and say, 'Here, boys, that is yours.' "

With Morgenthau that afternoon, T. V. Soong "went through a long rigmarole, trying . . . to justify this loan." Quoting Chiang Kai-shek, Soong used a military analogy: "I can't tell you where I am going to put my troops, I've got to have my troops, and then I will tell you where I will put them." Responding to that metaphor, Morgenthau said that he would commend the use of American dollars to pay Chinese forces to attack the Japanese. "How about if we could pay these troops with silver dollars," he asked Soong. ". . . How would they like it?" Soong's face lit up. "What I am thinking of," the Secretary continued, ". . . once a month to make you an advance for a month." As the Secretary explained it to his staff: "I was trying to think of some way so that while the boys fight they get their money, and if they don't fight, no money." He was also thinking, he said, of making the American dollar the basic unit of exchange for the whole world after the war. Direct support of the Chinese armies would be a step in that direction. Such support, moreover, was preferable to buying up fapi, for once a loan had been used for that purpose, the Chinese, Morgenthau was sure, would simply print more currency "just as fast as you get it."

After studying the Secretary's suggestion, White and his assistants emphasized its disadvantages. Direct payment to Chinese troops would, to be sure, meet the political necessity of making a spectacular gesture, while it would at the same time relate costs to Chinese military operations. But a tendency to hoard dollars might replace the existing tendency of the Chinese to hoard goods. More important, the Chinese might interpret Morgenthau's scheme as suggesting an abandonment of the fapi, which would destroy the little confidence remaining in the Chinese currency. Further, there would be difficulties in transportation: ten million dollar bills weighed just over ten and a half tons, too much to fly over the "hump" from India at a time when other cargoes deserved priority. Perhaps above all, the Generalissimo would probably regard the Secretary's scheme as a method for making China dependent on the United States, and for depriving her of her own monetary system.

Those formidable objections did not sway Morgenthau. As he told his staff on January 13, 1942: "I was wholly indiscreet last night and enjoyed it. I first tried it out on Halifax*, and it was all right. Then for one hour I got Mr. Churchill thinking about China. . . . I got him quite excited and I got Lord Beaverbrook† quite excited." In the absence of significant assistance, the Secretary had told Churchill, Chiang Kai-shek might move closer to the Japanese and others of the "yellow races." Churchill, as Morgenthau recalled, "conceded they might figure . . . you couldn't count on the white races." "If there is anything the United States Treasury wants to do," the Prime Minister said, "you take the leadership and we will go along with you. We will back you up 100 per cent." At least, Morgenthau concluded, "I got Churchill's mind on it. He was very much interested. They all seemed to like the idea of this business of the soldiers."

The State Department did not. With Morgenthau later in the morning of January 13, Stanley Hornbeck, Hull's chief adviser on Chinese affairs, expressed his hesitation "actually . . . to hire human beings." The problem, he said, was to give "Chiang and his immediate and loyal entourage a sufficient amount of support to enable them to overcome any objections or defections . . . of . . . the defeatist and the appeaser groups. . . . Now, if Chiang can say he has got the financial backing of the United States . . . I think that would take care of that, and it doesn't have to be specified at this moment . . . or in the next two weeks exactly how you are going to do that." Morgenthau disagreed. In the past, he had always told the Chinese exactly how much money they were to receive and on what terms. Now he wanted to discuss with the President the question of how best to use American dollars.

Still later that morning the Secretary called at the White House. Roosevelt, "very enthusiastic" about the payment of Chinese troops, as Morgenthau recalled his words, said: "The State Department doesn't know what they are talking about. Supposing I want to make an arrangement with Chiang Kai-shek, who is Chairman of that Board . . . and I want a million attack troops, and . . . I may want to take Shanghai. I may want to support the Philippines. I

---

* Lord Halifax, British Ambassador to the United States.

† British Minister of Aircraft Production, then with Churchill in Washington for a series of official conferences and dinners, including the one Morgenthau attended.

may want to do anything, but I need a million troops. . . . Now, I expect to pay for them. I will pay for them out of my own funds . . . as Commander in Chief . . . five dollars for maintenance, to the Government . . . per month, and five dollars to the troops themselves. . . . We will call it the D-E-M-O, democracy, the new currency."

That afternoon Morgenthau repeated the substance of Roosevelt's statement to T. V. Soong, and on January 21, 1942, Soong delivered Chiang Kai-shek's adverse reply. The Generalissimo "urgently requests that careful consideration be given to his original proposal. . . . This loan should be regarded in the light of an advance to an ally fighting against the common enemy thus requiring no security or other pre-arranged terms as to its use and as regards means of repayment." The State Department, in a similar vein, recommended a prompt and generous loan in order to secure maximum political effect, as did White, who advised, however, setting definite conditions so as to guarantee the greatest possible anti-inflationary impact of the loan.

Still uncomfortable, the Secretary telephoned Henry Stimson on January 28, 1942. Negotiations with the Chinese were difficult, Morgenthau said: "The attitude that they're taking . . . is — really . . . a hold-up. . . . This is what I'd like to get from you and General Marshall. . . . I'd like to come over and call on you . . . and go to school as to just how much are we or should we be worried that Chiang Kai-shek might stop fighting if certain things happen." At the War Department the next morning, Morgenthau learned for the first time that General Stilwell was going to Chungking to serve as Chief of Staff under Chiang, a development that Marshall considered encouraging. As for China, according to Morgenthau's notation in his Diary, "Marshall regarded the situation seriously" and Stimson had concluded "that at any price we should keep them going." Morgenthau, Stimson also said, had erred in offering to pay Chinese troops. He had done so, Morgenthau replied, only after discussions with Churchill, Rooosevelt, and Soong. "Well," Stimson said, "you can't trust T. V. Soong. . . . In my experience of Orientals, if you say something to them as a proposal, they will always say yes . . . but they will get word to you in some round about way which often makes you think that they have double-crossed you, but they just can't say no to you."

Though his "heart wasn't in it," Morgenthau felt he had to handle the Chinese loan. "The President asked me to do it," he said, "and I would have to go and tell the President I didn't think I could do it, something which I have never done before." In that case, Stimson urged him not to permit any differences between the Treasury and the State Department to interfere. "I am pushing the matter," Morgenthau said. "Please do," Stimson replied, ". . . whatever the cost is."

Though not without personal reservations, push the loan Morgenthau did. "This is nothing but blackmail," Litvinov told him. The Secretary agreed: "Yes, and at a time when we have our back to the wall in the Pacific, I don't like it." But there seemed to be no alternative, and on January 29 he wrote Hull that the Treasury was ready "to go ahead at once. . . . You may wish to consider the desirability of the President and ourselves meeting promptly with the congressional leaders to advise them of the problem and to discuss the . . . methods of financial assistance. With their clearance, it would be possible for the President to make an immediate announcement that he and the congressional leaders are prepared . . . to grant China . . . the financial assistance requested by Chiang Kai-shek. The details could be worked out later."

After the Cabinet meeting the next day, Roosevelt chose to discuss the question of procedures in the Cabinet room, as Morgenthau later told his staff, "with everybody buzzing around and talking at the top of their voices." While they were talking, Hull kept looking around for Jesse Jones, who "was waiting just about three feet away from Hull and he dived right between Hull and the President. It really was funny. I mean, whenever there is anything like that up there, Jesse just sort of crowds himself, sort of leans over on them so he gets in on it. . . . It was going all right, but Hull . . . the last minute he brings him in and Jesse, smelling some new business,* he was only two feet behind . . . So he barges his chair right between Hull and the President, and I tried to explain the thing. . . . The President listened, and of course there was all this talking going on around. It was the most unfavorable circumstances that I ever presented anything in. Jesse . . . tried to get in and the President said 'Well, why can't you, Jesse, buy some goods?' and . . .

---

* For his Reconstruction Finance Corporation or another of the several lending agencies he ran.

Jesse said, 'I could lend them some money against some goods,' and the President said, 'No, no, that won't be any good.' I said, 'Mr. President, you might just as well do it right out in the open. So then . . . there will be congressional action, and that is what Chiang Kai-shek wants. . . . He wants the prestige of a loan backed by Congress to give him face opposite the Japanese.' So then Jesse said, 'Well, wouldn't it be just as good if it was from the President?' Well, of course, there was only one answer I could say. That was 'Yes.' So the President said, 'Well, explore it, Jesse, and if you don't find there is any way that you can do it, then Hull, Jones, and Morgenthau should go up on the Hill together Monday and see the leaders.' . . . I am used to it. It is Washington, and it is the way they do business here. Now, if I didn't want the Chinese to get anything I would just sit tight and do nothing, but I do want the Chinese to get something, so I am going to call up Berle and tell him that."

Jones, to Morgenthau's surprise, proved to be wholly amenable to the Treasury's suggestions for procedure, which Hull also endorsed on January 31. Hull's hands, Morgenthau observed after they had talked, were "the color of pale yellow parchment, and shaking . . . it's terribly depressing." But the Secretary of State agreed to brief the President on the State Department's reasons for recommending the loan, while Morgenthau prepared letters of support to be signed by Roosevelt, Stimson, and Knox. Jones assisted in drafting the text for a Joint Resolution of Congress, which the President immediately approved. It authorized him "to loan or extend credit or give other financial aid to China in an amount not to exceed in the aggregate $500 million at such . . . times and upon such terms and conditions as the Secretary of the Treasury with the approval of the President shall deem in the interest of the United States." It was Jones, not Morgenthau, who altered the original draft of that resolution to include the direct reference to the Secretary of the Treasury. Later, another alteration in phraseology asserted, in the manner of the Lend-Lease Act, that China and her independent future were "vital to the defense of the United States."

"I read to him the joint resolution," Morgenthau noted in his Diary after seeing T. V. Soong that same day, ". . . and told him what we'd done and how we were going up . . . on the Hill, and he should let the Generalissimo know. . . . Soong said this would be very pleasing to the Generalissimo. . . . I told him we appreciated how much the Chinese had done during the last four years, and they of all people should receive help at this time." The next day Morgenthau gave the British a copy of the proposed resolution, and on February 2 they expressed their intention of making available to the Chinese "all munitions and military equipment which it is possible to supply," and a loan "for war purposes . . . up to £50 million."

"This proposal is a war measure," Morgenthau said in testifying for the loan on February 3, 1942. "The effective continuance of the Chinese military effort — so invaluable in our fight against the Axis Powers — depends largely upon the strength of the economic structure of Free China. . . . The Chinese financial and monetary system should be made as strong as possible."

Under questioning in executive session by members of the House Foreign Affairs Committee, Morgenthau admitted that he was recommending the loan at the urging of the Secretary of State and the Secretary of War, as well as General Marshall, and "as a political and military loan." Asked how the loan was to be administered, he replied that the Treasury would open a credit on its books in the amount of $500 million, and then discuss uses with the Chinese, particularly with T. V. Soong. He did not expect the Chinese to draw on the money immediately, but he did believe that it had to be granted in a lump sum and at once in order to buttress Chinese morale. He wanted to make it "taste as good as possible" to the Chinese; he did not want to drive a hard bargain. The loan might be used to curb inflation, but its real purpose was to keep the Chinese interested in the Allied cause.

Again in executive session, now before the Senate Committee on Foreign Relations, Morgenthau on February 5, 1942, confessed that he did not blame Robert M. La Follette, Jr., for lacking confidence in the government of China. He allowed, too, that the Treasury might not be able to control the actual use of the funds. Asked if the loan represented merely an attempt to outbid the Japanese in China, he replied that he did not want to put the matter on that level, but he also said it was not to be regarded as a banking proposition. There was a good chance the United States would never get the money back.

Congress, then, had no illusions about the joint resolution it quickly passed. Yet in his message to Chiang Kai-shek of February 7, 1942, Roosevelt had to maintain the pretense which he and his subordinates had cultivated. "The unusual speed and unanimity with which this measure was acted upon by the Congress," the President wrote, "and the enthusiastic support which it received throughout the United States testified to the wholehearted respect and admiration which the Government and people of this country have for China. They testify also to our earnest desire and determination to be concretely helpful to our partners in the great battle for freedom. . . . It is my hope and belief that use which will be made of the funds . . . will contribute substantially toward facilitating the efforts of the Chinese Government and people to meet the economic and financial burdens which have been thrust upon them by an armed invasion."

Those words, as all American principals to the transactions realized, of necessity put into idealistic cadence the high price of Chinese friendship. Eager for a first payment, T. V. Soong on February 12, 1942, claimed that the attachment of conditions would defeat the purpose of the loan. In the same mood, Sumner Welles the next day wrote Morgenthau "that further political advantage would be gained were this government to take prompt steps . . . whereby there would be immediately available to the Chinese Government some substantial portion of this money." Chiang Kai-shek wanted a quick and free hand in the disposition of American largess.

Morgenthau, though still hopeful that patience and tact would persuade the Chinese to accept some American supervision of the loan, approached negotiations with Soong in "the spirit of the Lend Lease Act." The loan agreement the Treasury drafted attempted to introduce modest controls without seeming to impose conditions. As submitted to Soong on February 21, the preamble enumerated various desirable purposes of the loan but did not obligate the Chinese to those suggestions. American funds could serve to strengthen the Chinese currency, to promote increased production and distribution of necessary goods, to improve means of transportation and communication, to further social and economic reforms, and to meet military needs. Article I of the draft stated that the Secretary of the Treasury of the United States agreed to establish a credit of $500 million and to make transfers of that credit at the request of the

Chinese Government through the agency of the New York Federal Reserve Bank. Article III deferred determination of final terms of the loan until "the progress of events" made clearer the mutual interests of both nations. Article II, the key section of the draft, read: "China desires to keep the Secretary of the Treasury . . . informed as to the use of the funds . . . and to consult with him from time to time as to such uses. The Secretary of the Treasury . . . desires to make available to the . . . Republic of China technical and other appropriate advice as to the ways and means of effectively employing these funds to achieve the purposes herein described. Technical problems that may . . . arise in effectuating the financial aid . . . will be subject to discussion between the Secretary of the Treasury . . . and the Government of the Republic of China."

Immediately upon receipt of the draft, Chiang Kai-shek objected to having the United States pass judgment on the uses of the loan. Since China would keep the American Treasury informed in any case, he argued, Article II was unnecessary. Treasury and State Department officers, meeting on March 7, 1942, bowed to the Generalissimo's wishes. "All agreed," they reported, "that political and military, rather than financial, considerations were of paramount importance," and therefore that the United States should not demand consultation.

Then the State Department had second thoughts. Earlier, in contrast to the Treasury, it had suggested that the Chinese pay interest on the loan. Now Welles, supporting Ambassador Gauss, recommended some American control over disbursements. "The matter," Welles wrote Morgenthau on March 9, ". . . lies primarily with you and the President. In my opinion, retention of Article II of the draft . . . would serve useful purposes both for the Chinese Government and for this Government. . . . Realizing that you have considered both the economic and the political angles of the problem, I am prepared . . . to concur in the conclusions at which you arrive and the course which you propose."

The letter upset Morgenthau and his staff. On the telephone to Welles on March 10, the Secretary criticized him for putting the State Department on record in favor of Article II. "As long as you feel that way," he said, "you take full responsibility . . . for throwing down what Chiang Kai-shek wants."

"No," Welles replied, "I don't take any reponsibility for throwing anything down. As I said in my letter, I think the responsibility in this financial transaction clearly is the President's and particularly yours as Secretary of the Treasury."

"Yeah," Morgenthau objected, "but you're making a record for yourself."

"I'm not in the habit of trying to write smart letters," Welles answered. ". . . I don't think you have any reason to say that. . . . After all, neither you nor I know whether Chiang Kai-shek is going to be murdered tomorrow. . . . If that happens, we will have absolutely no assurance whatever as to the disposition of those funds."

"As Secretary of the Treasury," Morgenthau then said, "I'd like to have all kinds of safeguards; but the spirit under which the thing was taken, I thought we were going to try to please them as much as possible."

Morgenthau was uncomfortable. He knew that in principle Welles was right, but he felt that in practice there was no way to get Chiang Kai-shek to concede. Further, he considered Welles's letter "very tricky." Morgenthau replied formally in writing later that day: "I would welcome any provisions . . . which would protect the financial interests of the United States. . . . If there were not overbalancing political and military considerations, I would insist upon the retention of Article II . . . and even inclusion of stronger provisions. But it has always been agreed at meetings between the State and Treasury Departments that the purposes of the financial aid were predominantly political, diplomatic, and military . . . In view of Generalissimo Chiang Kai-shek's reactions . . . the Treasury was unwilling to risk jeopardizing the value of this financial aid by insisting upon the retention of Article II. . . . I should like to have you advise me as to what our next step should be in replying to the Generalissimo."

By March 12, the State Department had revised Article II: "As a manifestation of the cooperative spirit which underlies the common war effort . . . appropriate officials of the two Governments will confer from time to time regarding technical problems . . . and will exchange information and suggestions regarding ways and means of most effectively applying these funds toward achieving the purposes which are envisaged by the two nations." If Chiang Kai-shek rejected that language, Morgenthau told his staff, "we will stop fussing around . . . and give it to him on an aluminum platter. That is about as rare a metal as there is around here just now."

The Generalissimo again said no. Even the revision, he reported through Soong on March 19, by "limiting the freedom of action in the use of the proceeds . . . would . . . adversely affect the public response to . . . measures . . . based on the loan." He wanted Article II "dropped completely."

Morgenthau was ready to comply, but Welles instructed Stanley Hornbeck "to propose an exchange of letters which would be supplementary to the agreement and which would achieve basically the aims of the proposed Article II. He said that to accept the Chinese position would be establishing a precedent of China's laying down terms to us and that the United States could not let China get away with this." Unable to dissuade Welles and Hornbeck, Morgenthau at the Cabinet meeting of March 21 handed Roosevelt a memorandum that opposed "jeopardizing the important diplomatic and military values anticipated from the agreement by insisting upon the retention of the consultative article." The President agreed.

Welles at once saw Soong, who, he reported to Morgenthau, was "entirely understanding and entirely acquiescent, and what he said that he would do would be of his own initiative . . . to send you a letter . . . saying that the Chinese Government is anxious to keep you informed and would let you know from time to time of the way in which this was done, and to me that's a very happy solution." Soong wrote the letter that day. "I wish to inform you," it read, "that it is the intention of my Government to keep you fully informed from time to time as to the use of the funds provided in the . . . agreement." Still later on March 21 Morgenthau and Soong signed the agreement, less Article II, and issued a joint statement calling it "a concrete manifestation of the . . . determination of the United States, without stint, to aid China in our common battle for freedom."

The official language obscured realities, as it had to in Chinese-American relations. As Hornbeck had said during the negotiations, the Chinese were not fighting for freedom or civilization, but for themselves. Though they had common enemies, China and the

United States had different purposes. Their governments, as Morgenthau knew from experience, had diverse standards of financial
responsibility. He had opposed the loan until the White House, the
State Department, the War Department, and the Army persuaded
him to support it for political and military reasons. He had then,
for the same reasons, overcome the State Department's objections to
making the loan unconditional. He had now to administer the loan
without assurances of Chinese cooperation or safeguards for American funds. For his part, Chiang Kai-shek had obtained half a billion
dollars in return for political and military considerations that the
United States had yet officially to define, and that Chiang had yet to
discharge.

3. China: "A Peculiar and Interesting Situation"

During 1942 and 1943, American military strategy in the Orient
looked to the relief of China through the reconquest of Burma and
the reopening of the Burma Road, and to the build-up of China as
the main base for an attack against Japan. Those purposes, always
remote in these years, informed the increasingly irascible negotiations of General Stilwell with Chiang Kai-shek, guided the allocation of the slim resources that the United States could transport
across the Himalayas, and established the bases for Morgenthau's
responses to problems arising in the disbursement of the Chinese
loan. The Treasury during 1942 and 1943 denied the Chinese nothing that the loan agreement permitted them to request, though the
temptations to refuse were inherent in the persistent inefficacy of
Chinese financial policy, which failed to pursue the most practicable
courses to stem inflation.

In later years, American witch-hunters attributed criticism of
those failures to Communist influence. In fact, however, Communist doctrine remained sympathetic to nationalist China at least into
the summer of 1943. More important, the situation in China spoke
for itself. So it was that Solomon Adler, who succeeded Emanuel
Fox as the American representative on the Chinese Stabilization
Board after Fox died of a heart attack, rendered reports to the
Treasury about monetary affairs that were substantially identical

with the observations of Arthur N. Young. Adler, a friend of Harry White, after the war admitted to membership in the Communist Party; but Young, Chiang Kai-shek's financial adviser, brought to his role both technical competence and an unwavering anti-Communism. The Generalissimo and his Ministry of Finance would have profited from the advices of either man, which they continually rejected.

In spite of his resulting impatience and dismay, Morgenthau bent the Treasury's efforts to the prevailing exigencies, which commanded agreement with China's preferences in the management of the money promised her. He began in April 1942, when H. H. Kung asked for the deposit of $200 million to the Chinese account at the New York Federal Reserve Bank. Kung also requested investment of the money in United States bonds and notes until the Chinese were ready to draw upon it. In time, they intended to use it to back the sale of securities to the Chinese public so as to absorb some of the fapi outstanding. As Harry White pointed out, the Treasury had received no advance information about the project, which was subject to some criticism because of the poor initial response to savings certificates previously issued by the Chinese government. Distressed at the thought of transferring $200 million in a lump sum, Dan Bell also thought it unfortunate that the Treasury would have to pay interest indefinitely on the securities that the Chinese bought with American funds loaned to them. But after several conferences, Morgenthau concluded that "it would be a mistake to show any hesitation in handing over the $200 million." As he later put it, he therefore "held his nose" and transferred the money.

The Chinese Ministry of Finance made a fiasco of its sales of the dollar-backed securities. The conversion terms of the certificates, of which there were three series, vastly overvalued fapi at exchange rates equivalent to five and six American cents, many times their real worth. Still, the securities were hard to sell, for ordinary Chinese had no money to invest and the rich preferred to hoard goods for speculation. In eight months, less than one-tenth of the certificates were sold; after fifteen months, in June 1943, only $47 million had been subscribed. Meanwhile, as inflation boomed and the printing presses turned out fapi, the certificates, at a fixed exchange rate of about twenty to a dollar, became a great bargain. Rumors that the issue would be closed, as it was on August 3, 1943, provoked large sales, in all $56 million, in its last five weeks. Dollar-backed bonds had a similar fate, with sales of only $18 million before a last spurt occasioned by accurate rumors of the closing of the issue in October 1943. In each instance, the rumors helped those in or close to Chiang's coterie. According to Morgenthau's report to Roosevelt in December 1943, the first $200 million of the Chinese loan "made no significant contribution to the control of inflation" and "had little effect except to give additional profits to insiders."

Meanwhile some of China's endemic problems had come into sharper focus. At a Cabinet meeting of February 5, 1943, the President revealed his irritation with continuing Chinese demands. At the Casablanca Conference*, he said, the American and British military staffs had raised the question of China, even though in his opinion it should not have been on the agenda. During the discussion, Roosevelt "got mad," for little could be done to supply the Chinese until the Allies could take Burma from the Japanese, and the controversial and difficult plans for a Burma campaign were still under study. Though he did not say so, the President's attitude probably also reflected his impatience with the continual bickering between General Stilwell and Chiang Kai-shek. Further, though Roosevelt did not like to admit it, the United States had made grander promises of assisting China than it had ever been able to fulfill. Whatever his own shortcomings, the Generalissimo had reason for complaint about the gap between Allied assurances and performances in the China Theater.

The solution, in the view of General George Marshall, General Stilwell, and General Brehon Somervell, the head of the Army Service Forces, lay in pushing the ground campaign against Burma. To that the Combined Chiefs of Staff tentatively agreed over the protest of General "Hap" Arnold, the head of the Army Air Forces, whose preference for a direct aerial attack from China against Japan had the support of Harry Hopkins. Further to explore the matter, Roosevelt in February sent Arnold and Somervell to Chungking, while at the same time Madame Chiang Kai-shek carried her husband's case to Washington.

Preparing at Roosevelt's request to meet with Madame Chiang,

* Between Roosevelt and Churchill and their staffs, January 14–23, 1943.

Morgenthau solicited briefings about the situation in China. In a memorandum of February 23, 1943, Harry White observed that the continuing lack of foreign goods, coupled with the ever-increasing war expenditures of the Chinese government, speeded the course of inflation. Neither increased taxes nor stiffer price controls had relieved the problem. Still, the Chinese were successfully resisting Japanese drives on various fronts, particularly in West Yunnan and along the Burma Road. Further, Chiang Kai-shek had been replacing the pro-Japanese within his government with "very conservative but supposedly anti-Japanese Kuomintang party members." Those developments had nurtured good will between the United States and China, as had the treaty of January 1943 in which the United States abrogated its rights of extraterritoriality and other special privileges in China. Generally optimistic, White emphasized as the central issue for the Treasury the absurdity of the official exchange rate, then holding the fapi at five cents though it was worth little more than a cent. That rate created particular difficulties in the payment of American troops, for had they been paid in fapi at the official rate of exchange, they would have received only a small fraction of the purchasing power of the dollar equivalent. The Army was therefore paying them in dollars, which the soldiers then traded on the black market. Payment of the troops in fapi depended upon a drastic, official revaluation of Chinese currency.

From Eleanor Roosevelt, whose opinions he always honored, Morgenthau received a less happy report. Mrs. Roosevelt sent him a copy of a letter she had had from Pearl Buck, a sturdy but disenchanted friend of the Chinese. "I do not believe," Mrs. Buck wrote, "that Madame Chiang ever had the impulses of real democracy toward her own people. I think she was often ashamed of things she saw about her. . . . This impatient shame and sense of superiority . . . has clouded the life of all the Soongs." The younger members of that family were "wastrels," as were Madame Kung, her husband and family. The Soongs, including the Generalissimo, were "in their present position not by any right or democratic choice but partly by their own ability, partly by their always enormous resources and money, and partly by force of arms. It is a peculiar and interesting situation. It cannot of course, last. I fear an outbreak from the people immediately after the war or at least as soon as the people can recuperate sufficiently to make it." Herself an anti-Communist "of the deepest dye," Mrs. Buck nevertheless could not condone the killing of thousands of young men and women in the name of anti-communism, "a black stain on Chiang Kai-shek and his regime. . . . Some of these young people were communists, . . . some were wholly innocent and even ignorant and died without knowing why. . . . But the people have never forgotten and never will forget, and today the Eighth Route Army, which is the Communist-Agrarian Army, does not forget. Madame Chiang complains that they do not obey orders from Chiang unless they want to do so. The reason is that they are constantly on guard. If they obey they are afraid that they will always be ordered to the front and to the most dangerous places so that they will be killed off."

The question of Chiang and the Communists fell outside of the area of financial responsibility Roosevelt had assigned to Morgenthau, but the problem of corruption affected both the Secretary's custodianship of public funds, and his private sensibilities. In one small but revealing episode, he reacted with special indignation to the selfishness of Madame Chiang Kai-shek. On the morning of February 25, 1943, the chief usher at the White House telephoned Morgenthau's personal secretary. Madame Chiang, he said, then a guest at the White House, was most eager to receive a shipment of a special brand of English cigarettes. That shipment was supposed to be at Pier 90 in New York, and on behalf of Madame Chiang, the chief usher wanted the Collector of Customs to release 1000 cigarettes. During the balance of the day requests for the cigarettes continued, even though the Treasury had ascertained that they were still on board ship. But pressure persisted, and the Treasury "had to get them off the boat and fly them down here." Morgenthau later complained to Mrs. Roosevelt about the high-handedness of Madame Chiang, who then explained that the cigarettes were not for her personal use but for her nurse, whom she fired. From Morgenthau's point of view, the question of who was to smoke the cigarettes seemed unimportant; he objected to the manner in which Madame Chiang had demanded them. "The sooner Madame Chiang Kai-shek gets out of the country, the better, so she won't get some unfavorable publicity," the Secretary said to his staff. "She has done a number of things like that, and has overstayed her time. . . . The President . . . is just crazy to get her out of the country."

Morgenthau's distaste for Madame Chiang grew when in June Randolph Paul reported some curious financial transactions. Since the beginning of 1943, he said, some $867,000 of the Chinese government funds had been turned over to a son of H. H. Kung and to one Dr. S. C. Wu, a representative of the Central Trust Company of China and a member of Madame Chiang's entourage. Some of the transfers had been made directly through Madame Chiang and the others for her account. The Treasury had established that Kung and Wu had withdrawn at least $675,000 in cash. Paul could not further explore the use of that cash without taking the risk that his investigation would become public, so he had had to content himself with the information already in hand, which both he and the Secretary found unsettling. Morgenthau also suspected that the Kungs and the Soongs had profited extensively in trading in dollar-backed Chinese certificates.

In spite of those suspicions, the Secretary followed Roosevelt's wishes for the assistance Madame Chiang requested. At her urging and the President's, he conferred with various Chinese representatives about ways in which the Treasury could help the Chinese government control inflation. Kung particularly wanted to use $200 million of the 1942 loan to purchase gold in the United States for shipment to China and for sale there to absorb much of the currency which had been printed in such vast supply. The Monetary Division was dubious about the scheme. If the gold fell into the hands of the Central Bank, it would provide a further basis for extension of credit, a further invitation to inflation. But the sale of gold in small bars to Chinese merchants and businessmen might help, if the government refrained from printing new currency to replace whatever fapi were retired. In any case, Madame Chiang solicited approval for the plan, which Morgenthau granted in principle.

In July 1943, Kung asked for the $200 million with which to buy the gold. Morgenthau then reminded him of the large costs of shipping and the difficulties in executing the program, which might sacrifice important Chinese assets for postwar reconstruction. But on July 27, 1943, the Secretary agreed to a formal request from the Chinese Ambassador. "In order to avoid unnecessary raising of funds by the United States Treasury," he added, "it is suggested that transfers from the credit of the Chinese Government for the purchase of gold be made at such time and in such amounts as are allowed by existing facilities for transportation. . . . On receipt of requests from . . . China that a specific amount should be transferred . . . and be used for the purchase of gold, the necessary action will be taken." To that suggestion Kung agreed.

Three months later China asked for $50 million in accordance with the Treasury's promise. In a memorandum of a conversation with Morgenthau of September 29, 1943, Harry White wrote: "I said that I thought we ought to be tough with the Chinese on the question of earmarking $200 million of gold for gold sales. . . . The Secretary agreed. He said he thought that we should be tough in this matter and he told me to go ahead and let them have the gold only as rapidly as it could be shipped and sold in China." To effect that purpose, White in November recommended the establishment of a $10 million credit for gold shipments in the Chinese account at the New York Federal Reserve Bank, with the understanding that the Chinese could draw on the credit as they pleased and that the Treasury would then replenish it as necessary. Though Arthur Young approved of that idea of a revolving fund, Kung rejected the plan because of his desire to accumulate reserves greater than $10 million. But the Minister of Finance did not call for much gold. Still, the psychological effects of the announcement of the new arrangements seemed to help retard the rate of inflation during the last two months of 1943.

On that account, Morgenthau on December 18, 1943, suggested to Roosevelt a doubling of gold shipments as a further palliative, though not a cure, for Chinese inflation, for which "the basic reason," he noted, was the continuing "shortage of goods." The Secretary thought that shipments were already at $6 million a month. In fact, as White told him in January, they were far less than that, and farther still from the $12 million a month Morgenthau had suggested or the $25 million a month that Roosevelt then contemplated. Indeed through the first half of 1944 total shipments came to only $2 million of gold, but they were adequate for meeting Morgenthau's justifiable order to let China have gold "as rapidly as it could be shipped and sold." Had sales moved faster, shipments would have, too, especially if Kung had accepted White's proposal for a revolving fund.

Discussions about the gold program during the latter half of 1943 proceeded concurrently with negotiations relating to other aspects of China's inflation. The Stabilization Agreement of 1941 was about to expire, and Kung objected to renewing it except on amended terms. The agreement had called for the appointment by China of both a British and an American representative on the Stabilization Board. Some of Kung's critics interpreted this provision as permitting undue foreign influence, and Kung himself was hostile to the British and their economic counsel. Kung also seemed to resent a provision that permitted the Secretary of the Treasury of the United States to terminate the agreement unilaterally on thirty days' notice, an option unavailable to the Chinese. Too, the 1941 agreement had been the work of T. V. Soong, one of Kung's rivals. A renegotiation on improved terms would diminish Soong's status while enhancing Kung's.

Though Morgenthau was not adverse to renegotiation, Kung permitted the matter to slide so long that in July 1943, no substitute for the lapsing agreement was in sight. Morgenthau therefore directed Adler to submit his resignation as the American member of the Chinese Stabilization Board, effective when the agreement expired at the end of the summer. Kung then reopened discussions, which stumbled over the question of the official dollar-fapi rate. He insisted upon holding the fapi officially at twenty to the dollar, then about five times its actual worth. Morgenthau therefore decided on September 29 that he would not renew the 1941 agreement until China consented to an official rate close to actuality, which would ease the continuing problem of paying American troops. Early in November, Under Secretary of War Patterson endorsed that decision.

The United States was spending on various military and civilian projects close to $20 million a month in China, would soon spend more, and could not conceivably afford to operate at the official rate. With the encouragement of the War Department, Morgenthau therefore instructed Adler, now representing the Treasury in Chungking, to explore the possibility of buying fapi directly from the Chinese government at a reasonable rate. There was little reasonable about Kung, who held that it was impossible to keep secret any special price he gave the United States, and that a departure from the official rate would undermine confidence in the fapi. Instead he particularly suggested having China, under reverse Lend-Lease, provide the United States with one fapi for each that it acquired at the official rate. That procedure would establish a de facto 40 to 1 ratio between the fapi and the dollar, to be achieved through what Kung considered a generous gesture. Yet by November 1943, the real rate had dropped from about 100 to 1 to about 120 to 1, though the United States might settle for as little as 80 to 1 in order to mollify the Chinese. "To obtain even a moderately satisfactory arrangement with the Chinese," Adler later noted, "will require considerable pressure."

The pressure, though Morgenthau and Kung did not yet know it, was moving in the opposite direction. American military strategy was about to change, which would remove the constrictions on Treasury policy of the previous two years. For Morgenthau, who wanted to help China help herself, those had been years of continual exasperation, as they were also for most other Americans involved in China's peculiar situation.

4. China: Reprise

In November 1943, Roosevelt and Churchill conferred with Chiang Kai-shek at Cairo, where "the talks," the Prime Minister later wrote, ". . . were sadly distracted by the Chinese story, which was lengthy, complicated and minor." Complicated it certainly was. The Communists were harassing the Nationalist government, the Japanese were tempting that government to quit the war, the Burma campaign was beginning on a minor scale, and the success of the United States Navy in the Pacific — along with the impressive potentialities of the new B-29 long-range bombers — suggested the possibility of attacking Japan from the air, from China and from oceanic islands alike, without recourse to significant ground warfare on the continent of Asia. But the American Chiefs of Staff, counting on Chinese resistance to Japan to ease the path across the Pacific, temporarily won Churchill to endorse a major operation to recover Burma during 1944, and the Prime Minister also joined Roosevelt and Chiang in the Cairo Declaration that promised that "Manchuria, Formosa, and the Pescadores, shall be restored to the Republic of China."

Churchill and Roosevelt then moved on to meet Stalin at Teheran, where, the Prime Minister later recalled, "I at length prevailed upon the President to retract his promise" for the Burma campaign, though the strictly political agreement of Cairo, unaltered, received Stalin's approval. Stalin's interest was almost exclusively in the Anglo-American cross-channel invasion, which Churchill had resisted. At Teheran it was scheduled definitely for the spring of 1944, and landing craft and other gear needed for the invasion of Europe — the essential step in the defeat of Germany and in victory in the entire war — could not be spared for Asia.

Chiang Kai-shek had to settle for the status as one of the four great powers accorded him, but he was not content. He objected to the postponement of the Burma operation, "so disheartening" for the Chinese people, and he resented, too, Roosevelt's calculated indecision at Cairo about his request for "a billion gold dollar loan." As soon as he heard about the Teheran decision on Burma, Chiang reminded the President of China's economic condition, "more critical than the military," and asked again for the loan.

Back from Teheran on December 17, 1943, Roosevelt told Morgenthau about his resistance to that request. The trouble, the President believed, was that China had too much paper money; he had said as much to Chiang. Roosevelt was thinking about using dollars to buy up fapi in the black market. Then, when the war was over, the United States could redeem the Chinese currency after its value had gone up. The President was vague, as of necessity was Morgenthau when he asked his staff to prepare a memorandum on the plan.

That memorandum, dated December 18, 1943, presented what Morgenthau considered "the unvarnished truth." The Nationalist government had been issuing fapi at the rate of 3.5 billion each month, twice the rate of the previous year. The United States might meet its own expenses in China by purchasing fapi with gold or dollars in the Chinese open market, or it might double shipments of gold for sale by the Chinese government. Together those programs might retard inflation, but never to the degree that would result from increased shipments of food and other goods, which would depend upon future military operations. Certainly there was no need for a further loan, particularly since China had $460 million in unpledged funds in the United States.

The Secretary reported in his Diary that, on December 20, 1943, "the President very carefully in my presence read my memorandum on China for the first time. . . . He said, 'This looks good. . . . What would you think if I send your memo in toto to General Chiang Kai-shek?' I said, 'Nothing the matter with that.' So he said, 'That's what I am going to do.' "

That prospect appalled Cordell Hull. Circumstances in China were already bad, Hull told Morgenthau on January 1, 1944, and it might discourage the Generalissimo and those around him if the President simply dispatched a cable based wholly on Morgenthau's analysis. The Secretary of State wanted to show Chiang Kai-shek "more than what would ordinarily be the case in the way of consideration." He contemplated sending some kind of mission to assure the Chinese that the United States had "every disposition" to get at the merits of the situation. Further, another loan, Hull thought, might provide the cheapest way for steadying China.

Initially sympathetic to that analysis, Morgenthau on reflection concluded that the Nationalist Party could not long tolerate the "grafting family at the head of the Government." In that environment, an American mission could accomplish very little. He therefore urged Hull to follow the President's directive and send Chiang Kai-shek the Treasury's memorandum. But Hull, still reluctant, on January 4 suggested at least softening the text. Further, since Roosevelt had taken kindly to the idea of a mission, Hull felt it might be well to avoid any decision about a further loan until after the mission had reported back. Morgenthau, he suggested, might edit the memorandum with that in mind.

He had no further comment to make, Morgenthau replied. If Hull wanted the message changed, he would have to talk to the President. "To me it is one of the most striking things I have ever heard of," Morgenthau commented in his Diary on January 5, 1944. "Here the President . . . requests the Secretary of State to forward a message to the Generalissimo and . . . Hull tries to block the President and have it changed. I asked Miss Tully* if this had ever happened before and she said, 'No! . . . We didn't ask Hull for

* Grace Tully, one of Roosevelt's secretaries.

any comments. We just asked him to send it. . . . I'd like to know when this message goes forward.'

"If this happens to the President, it is no wonder that sometimes my messages don't go forward for weeks and also that I don't receive answers from them for weeks.

"To me the whole performance is just outrageous."

When the cable went out later that day, Hull had achieved some part of his purpose. Since he knew the Treasury's memorandum would disappoint the Chinese, he persuaded Roosevelt to have Ambassador Gauss deliver the message by hand, and to temper the Treasury's tone by assuring the Generalissimo of the President's confidence and good will. "Sounds all right to me," Morgenthau commented about Hull's new procedure, ". . . and everybody's a good fellow except the Secretary of the Treasury."

In any case, Morgenthau was worrying less about the loan, which he considered a closed issue, than about the growing problems of the United States Army in China. The Army, behind schedule in the construction of major airfields in the Chengtu area, needed fapi to pay Chinese labor and to purchase food and other supplies. General Somervell, in a memorandum to Morgenthau of January 3, 1944, said the "principal concern" was the "exchange situation," for the official rate remained twenty fapi to the dollar, a rate which would make American costs gargantuan. "Progress is being made," the Treasury learned from Chungking on January 13, ". . . on only four of the seven bases which China promised to construct and for which payment is to be made by the United States. . . . The war effort in this theater will seriously be impeded by the delay. . . . The United States Government has not committed itself to pay for these . . . bases at the official exchange rate and China is, therefore, holding up the work on them." All the Treasury wanted, Morgenthau told Somervell, was for the Chinese to build those bases; the question of the exchange rate could wait. Somervell agreed. "Nothing could be more conducive to lowering the prestige of China in the United States," Morgenthau then cabled to Chungking on January 15, ". . . than the knowledge that China was not cooperating fully . . . in the building of these airbases. I firmly believe that I speak in the best interests of China when I recommend that immediate action be taken for the construction of the remaining bases . . .

leaving for future determination the final question of the U.S. currency equivalent."

Chiang Kai-shek replied in what Morgenthau considered "a very drastic cable . . . a very tough cable" to Roosevelt. In it, the Generalissimo argued that China needed the billion dollar loan to finance reciprocal aid to American military forces. If the Treasury opposed the loan, then the United States should bear its own expenses in China at the official exchange rate. The United States, Chiang complained, had been feeding civilians in Britain and Russia, while in China American contributions had been negligible even for military purposes. He had nevertheless consented to delaying the Burma campaign so as to assure essential amphibious equipment for Europe. Now, in the event that the Treasury felt unable to agree either to the billion dollar loan or to unqualified acceptance of the official rate, China "would have to permit her wartime economy and finances to follow the natural course of events. In such a case the Chinese Government would have no means at its disposal to meet the requirements of United States forces in China and consequently the American Army in China would have to depend upon itself to execute any and all of its projects, for to our great regret we would be placed inevitably in a position in which we could not make any further material or financial contribution, including the construction of works for military use."

The cable infuriated Morgenthau. "The billion dollar loan is out," he told White on January 18, 1944. The alternative, White warned, might cost Americans more. "Take it from me, I am not going up on the Hill," Morgenthau replied. ". . . They [the Chinese] are just a bunch of crooks, and I won't go up and ask for one nickle. . . . Supposing we tell them to go jump in the Yangtze River . . . and we go ahead and operate on the black market. And I send a million dollars' worth of gold in jewelers' bars every day to General Somervell. And we take our own soldiers and begin to buy the stuff and build these fields. What are they going to do about it?"

Massive gold sales on the black market, White warned, would involve dealing with big operators whom Chiang, if he chose, would simply shoot. Heads had been cut off in China for less than that. "Well," Morgenthau said, ". . . the first thing to do is to find out from a military standpoint whether we can do this thing in some other way. . . . Chiang Kai-shek . . . is holding a pistol to our head. . . . I am mad as hell. . . . I can't go up on the Hill and ask for a billion dollars' worth of loan. . . . So the question gets down to a military question. Is this something that I have got to stomach . . . or have you got some way to wiggle out and do something else? . . . If the Army tells me that we have just got to, well, that is something else."

The Army had also decided to be tough with Chiang. "China," Henry Stimson noted in his diary on January 19, 1944, "has been riding us pretty hard with the aid of Madame Chiang Kai-shek's influence over the President. . . . I do not fear that the Chinese are going to drop out of the war now that we are so close and I think that their present demands show a good deal of the Chinese bargaining." The Secretary of War had discussed Chiang Kai-shek's message with Generals Marshall and Somervell, as Somervell told Morgenthau that day. All of them were dissatisfied with China's attitude and with the small amount of actual fighting by the Chinese army. The airfield program had faltered, Somervell said, because the Chinese had not delivered the aid they had promised. As things stood, so long as the Army hired and paid its own Chinese workers, they performed well, but when the Army relied on the Chinese government to supply laborers through contractors, few appeared and their work was poor. The Chinese were furnishing supplies at a rate equivalent to $3.25 million a month, whereas the United States had sent over $340 million of Lend-Lease aid to China through the end of the previous November, though much of the materials bought with that money remained stacked up behind the Himalayas in India. Still, the United States was also building a large air transport system for China. In the face of those major contributions, the Army had lost patience with Chinese obduracy. Indeed, the Army was prepared to stop building airports in China and instead to approach Japan from the sea. "Does that mean that the Army has made up its mind," Morgenthau asked, "that it could use other avenues of approach to Japan?" Somervell said it did. Further, the Army might crack down on the Chinese by denying them gasoline or shipping space. Indeed the Army could break the Generalissimo simply by withdrawing American support from him and expending perhaps as much as $100 million to buy out one of his rivals.

With Marshall and Stimson, Somervell had drafted a cable answering Chiang Kai-shek's message to Roosevelt. The United States, it said, was fully prepared to bear all costs of its own war effort in China, but not at a fixed rate of exchange in the spiraling Chinese money market. The Congress would never be able to understand the need for such "unreasonable expenditures." American faith and confidence in China had already been badly shaken. Now Chiang Kai-shek's demands, if they were met, would be disastrous to the war effort and "to both of our futures." But the United States would welcome any arrangement for paying for its military program in China in American dollars at a fair rate of exchange.

Pleased with the draft Somervell had read, Morgenthau telephoned Roosevelt for his approval. Although he was on the whole satisfied, the President censored a few phrases; "large expenditures," he said, would be better than "unreasonable expenditures." He was still opposed to a loan, but he thought a special mission to Chungking might ease the general situation.

The State Department was even more solicitous of Chiang's sensitivities. At meetings of January 19 and 20, 1944, with Treasury and War Department representatives, Alger Hiss, speaking for Cordell Hull, condemned the proposed reply to the Generalissimo as "much too strong." The politics of Chinese-American relations argued for a loan, Hiss said, which would in any case be cheaper than the acceptance of the official exchange rate. For the War Department, General Lucius Clay replied that there were considerations other than costs, especially the question of the Army's relationship with Chiang Kai-shek, who would soon ask for another loan if he received the billion dollars he had requested. There were no military reasons, Clay and Somervell said, for acquiescing in the Generalissimo's terms. With the Treasury, they therefore opposed the temporizing reply to Chiang that the State Department had drafted. But all three departments cooperated in revising and softening the War Department's strong draft of a reply, and Roosevelt approved the amended version for dispatch to Chiang on January 26, 1944. It proposed, as an interim measure, American purchase of one billion fapi at a rate of 100 to the dollar. The official rate would become 40 to 1, but China would add sixty fapi to each forty purchased. At Roosevelt's suggestion, the cable also invited Chiang Kai-shek to send H. H. Kung to Washington for further discussions of monetary problems.

Chiang and Kung responded by demanding a continuation of the official rate of 20 to 1, while they conceded an actual exchange rate for the American purchase of fapi of 40 to 1, a ratio that over-valued fapi by at least a multiple of three. In conversation with Ambassador Gauss on February 3, 1944, Kung held that China could not alter the official rate without breaking her "economic backbone." Even discussions of an alteration weakened confidence in the fapi, which would rally if China received a billion dollar loan for her reserves. He blamed the course of inflation entirely on the growing expenditures of the United States Army, and he claimed that China had actually repaid its previous $500 million loan in the form of various kinds of assistance to the American war effort. Referring to the possibility of Chinese collapse, Kung remarked that the Japanese had been making "some very good offers." Several days later the Ambassador delivered the official American reply: China's proposed exchange rate was unsatisfactory and unreasonable; there was no need for comment on the fatuity of Kung's arguments.

The rejection of the Chinese position forced reconsideration of American plans for China. On February 14, 1944, the Treasury, State and War Departments' representatives agreed that military necessity was the prime consideration in the making of China policy. The State Department nevertheless hoped American policy would prove conciliatory so as to prevent any action that might result in the fall of Chiang Kai-shek. For its part, the Treasury asked that if the United States accepted a rate less than 100 to 1, the record show the military reasons for doing so. Five days later General Clay reported the Army's decision. Recent events in the Pacific, he said, had again altered the strategic picture. American victories in the Marshall Islands made it possible to advance the timetable for a possible attack on the Japanese-occupied Chinese coast. For such an attack, large airfields within Chiang Kai-shek's domain were essential. Clay preferred therefore not to threaten retrenchment in China or to accept the Chinese proposals for a rate of exchange. He suggested instead that the United States, without formal commitment to any rate of exchange, immediately place $25 million to the account of the Chinese government, since the Chinese had already put up one billion fapi against which the Army had drawn. Both the State and Treasury Departments consented at once to that procedure.

During the next few weeks, American policy circumvented questions of principle in order to enhance the military effort. The Army advised General Stilwell on February 20, 1944, to continue to take a firm stand against the official rate, while at the same time expressing American willingness to bear the full costs of the war in China at a reasonable level of exchange. The United States agreed unhesitatingly to a proposal of H. H. Kung of February 25 for $20 million as an advance to the Chinese account, the rate of exchange to be determined later, so that Kung could buy fapi on the black market in an effort to improve their value. For her part, China on March 2 agreed to furnish the American Army up to 5 billion fapi a month, provided the United States printed and transported the necessary currency, and with the understanding that the exchange value of the currency would be left for future negotiations. During March and the next several months, while desultory negotiations about rates continued, the construction of airfields proceded at a relatively satisfactory pace.

Yet the black market rate for American dollars continued to climb, rising above 220 to 1. As Ambassador Gauss cabled the Treasury early in March, the cumulative impact of existing and projected American military activities might destroy China's economy, with disastrous results for American military plans. Deeply concerned, Morgenthau on March 11, 1944, ordered a careful evaluation of the economic situation in China, with particular reference to the Ambassador's assessment. As always, the Secretary wanted to befriend the Chinese. The battle over the rate of exchange grew out of his concern to protect American interests, but while that battle raged, he was determined also to do what he could to sustain the Chinese government and economy, and to forward the Army's plans.

Those motives informed Morgenthau's reaction to a new demarche, a letter from Madame Chiang Kai-shek to Roosevelt, written on February 17 and received on March 20, 1944. "It seems that the amount needed by the American military in China," she wrote, "is of such an astronomical figure . . . that China's economy cannot withstand the strain and is imminently threatened by collapse, for the more paper money is in circulation, the greater the inflation with its attendant evils. Both the Generalissimo and Dr. Kung are studying this question . . . but so far there seems to be no solution. . . .

"Dr. Kung would like very much to go to America in response to your invitation but both he and the Generalissimo feel that unless there is tangible possibility of a loan the disappointment of our people will be such that it would unfavorably affect the fighting morale of the whole nation. The Generalissimo, therefore, would greatly appreciate your sending to China a representative empowered with full authority to consult with our government about methods for the solving of China's critical . . . financial problems."

"Madame Chiang Kai-shek . . . ," Morgenthau told General Somervell on March 20, "wrote another letter to the President and he has asked me to handle it, or prepare an answer for him. . . . She raises this question of a loan again. It's . . . a better tone, and I wondered when you and I could get together. . . . I think this is . . . more of a military matter and I think we should give all the authority to General Stilwell. . . . It seems to me that the Commanding General of the Area has to be in charge, in control and responsible."

That afternoon, Morgenthau, Harry White, Generals Somervell and Clay, and John Carter Vincent — the experienced, astute, and elegant China hand of the Foreign Service who had just returned from Chungking, agreed on a new scheme to relieve the Generalissimo's restlessness while also advancing American strategy. According to the plan, which the Army had worked out with the Chinese, at the beginning of each three-month period, the United States would pay a stipulated sum of dollars to China's account, for which the Chinese would advance fapi to the American Army. For any period of three months the United States would set the rate of exchange for these transactions at a figure between 100 and 200 fapi to the dollar. But while the amount of fapi obtained by the United States would be kept secret, China might publicize the American dollar "contribution" if it seemed desirable to do so in order to enhance the value of fapi. The settlement of accounts would be left for postwar negotiations. The American Embassy in Chungking on March 28 supported the proposal as the most realistic basis for discussions with Chiang Kai-shek, for it would save his face and avoid a showdown. The Embassy also supported a Chinese request, which the Army had approved, for accelerating gold shipments and sales in order to mop up fapi.

On March 30 Morgenthau officially endorsed both undertakings. He also directed Adler to suggest to Kung the sale of both gold and dollars on joint Chinese-American account in a quantity sufficient to meet all American requirements except those of the Army. The Army's costs would fall to the quarterly exchanges of dollars and fapi. It was no longer necessary, Morgenthau had told White the previous day, for Roosevelt to answer Madame Chiang directly. The Secretary had set his face against going to Chungking as a special envoy, which Somervell had recommended. No one representing the President abroad, Morgenthau said, had "had a lasting success. . . . I have always had a rule that if I have any business to do I don't get more than a hundred yards away from the White House. . . . I am not going to China on a mission."

In the ensuing weeks, Roosevelt decided to send to Chungking an official "of the highest standing," as Madame Chiang had requested. At a Cabinet meeting of May 18, 1944, the President announced that Henry Wallace would go. "Things in China are terrible," Roosevelt had told the Vice President. "The currency is 300 yuan to the dollar." Morgenthau commented that the actual rate was about 200. He also contradicted a statement of Henry Stimson that the situation in China was "very critical." "I have been in consultation with General Somervell and General Clay," Morgenthau said. "They are entirely satisfied. The big Army projects for the secret fields are going ahead. We are practically over the hump." Stimson admitted that his own information was not "very recent" — privately Morgenthau later observed it was three months old. Roosevelt then talked on about "a new unit of currency in China," as well as "price control," ideas that suggested to Morgenthau that the President was "badly informed." The Secretary therefore reminded the Cabinet that Chiang Kai-shek had tried to blackmail the President into a billion dollar loan which Roosevelt had refused, that the air bases were nevertheless well along, and that the only thing that would help General Stilwell would be to get him more goods.

Though Harry White, when he heard Morgenthau's story of the Cabinet meeting, maintained that the economic situation in China was in fact deteriorating rapidly, Morgenthau decided that Wallace should hear the Army's point of view. With Stimson's permission, he asked General Clay to see the Vice President before he left the country.* "Somebody filled the President full of a lot of just plain misinformation," Morgenthau told Clay, "and that's why I asked for this brief to be prepared . . . so we can get the President up to date on what is the right story. . . . Just as long as the Army and the Treasury stick together, I'm not going to worry."

Stick together they did, to Morgenthau's gratification. "I should like to take this opportunity to congratulate you," he wrote Roosevelt on June 8, 1944, ". . . upon having faced and passed an important military crises. General Somervell informs me that the United States installations in China are now practically completed. Thus the problem which you faced in January has been overcome and your major objective has been achieved." To be sure, inflation went on at its devastating pace. But with Kung on his way to the United States for conferences about cross-rates, conferences that would also consider a settlement of the quarterly exchanges of currency already made, Morgenthau felt "that despite the financial problems which arose to disturb the cordial relations of this government with the Chinese government, the course of the present financial negotiations is satisfactory and moving in the proper direction."

Though those negotiations were to prove less easy than he hoped†, Morgenthau's pleasure in the apparent achievements of the previous six months had noticeably softened his mood. The quarterly exchanges of dollars for fapi, however much they created unsolved problems for the future, did permit the Army to sustain its program in China. Since the discussion of exchange rates had been deferred, Chiang Kai-shek had kept his prestige without receiving the controversial loan. Most important, the airfields, so far from completion in January 1944, were in June almost ready for use. American victories in the Pacific were soon to render those airfields unnecessary, but for the while they seemed vital for the war in Asia — almost as important as, for the war in Europe, were the bases in Great Britain from which the invasion of Normandy was about to be launched. For two years and more, while China was always a

* The Wallace mission resulted in no change in Chinese-American financial relationships or arrangements.

† See Chapters VI and IX.

problem, the Treasury had also been concerned continually with the financial aspects of relations between the United States and the United Kingdom, the very heart of the Great Alliance.

5. Great Britain: "Nothing Decadent"

Morgenthau's many services to England, as well as his intimacy with the President, earned him a place at the Christmas party at the White House in 1941, when Winston Churchill made his first wartime visit to the United States just three weeks after the attack on Pearl Harbor. "I had the pleasure of sitting opposite Mr. Churchill last night," the Secretary told his associates the next day, "and watching him for two hours. . . . You know, he has a distinct speech impediment. . . . He would say practically nothing because he just wasn't having a good time. . . . You see him on one side of Mrs. Roosevelt and Beaverbrook on the other, and Beaverbrook's face is a map of his life, but on Churchill's face there is absolutely nothing. . . . He looked in good condition. He wasn't flabby, literally in the pink of health. . . . He asked three times to be excused after dinner so, he says 'I can prepare these impromptu remarks for tomorrow.' * . . . After supper I sat next to him all through the movie. . . . When they showed pictures of Libya, he said, 'Oh, that is good. We have got to show the people that we can win.' . . . Beaverbrook, on the other hand, is very cocky. . . . He said that the President and I were the only friends they had right along."

Still a good friend to the British, Morgenthau in his negotiations with them was also a dogged protagonist of American interests. No one had valued more than had he the bravery of the British in their lonesome stand against Hitler in 1940 and 1941. No one had worked harder to get American equipment to them or to establish Lend-Lease, of which they were the first and major beneficiaries. No one estimated more generously their capabilities as an ally in the war, or as a great and amicable power after the war. Yet no one was more certain than Morgenthau that British and American interests were not identical, however much both peoples were dedicated to

* For a speech before the Congress.

destroying Nazism. Like Roosevelt, Morgenthau had long associated the British financial community of the City of London with its American counterpart on Wall Street, and viewed them as basically hostile, often in common concert, to the spirit and aims of the New Deal, and therefore to the good of the country. Morgenthau was admittedly distrustful of what he considered to be the continuing influence of London financiers and of the Bank of England on the British Treasury, and he was unhappy about the appointment of Robert Brand, whom he identified with Lombard Street, as a British negotiator in Washington, first on matters of Lend-Lease, later as a representative of the Chancellor of the Exchequer. More important, Morgenthau considered Lend-Lease essentially a wartime measure, designed to guarantee to Great Britain and other allies of the United States the materials, military and civilian, without which they could not continue to fight. That was the view also, he felt, of the Congress. Consequently he resisted British pressure for associating American Lend-Lease assistance with their needs for dollar and other assets in the postwar period. He did not want to compound British economic problems, or to push England to bankruptcy, which threatened her continually. But he saw no license for using Lend-Lease to build British dollar balances beyond a necessary minimum, which the British thought he underestimated.

His estimations reflected the calculations of Harry White, who sought openly, with the Secretary's approval, to make the dollar the dominant currency in the postwar world. An ardent nationalist in his monetary thinking, White also championed postwar international monetary cooperation, the objective of his tireless efforts to establish the International Monetary Fund.* In that cooperation, White expected the United States and the United Kingdom to provide the lead, but with the United States as the senior partner. Accordingly he, too, resisted, more vigorously than Morgenthau, any deliberate expansion of England's gold and dollar holdings.

In that stance, the Secretary and his assistant were opposed not by the British only but also by Secretary of State Cordell Hull, who considered large British assets indispensable for that free, international trade on which he pinned his hopes for a lasting peace. So, too, did Hull's chief representative on monetary issues, Assistant

* See Chapter V.

Secretary of State Dean Acheson. Further, Acheson, like the British, believed that the Treasury did not understand how poor England had become as a result of her wartime expenditures. He also, unlike Morgenthau, tended to defer to British rather than congressional sensitivities. In contrast, most of the responsible officers of the Lend-Lease Administration and the War Department, whatever their individual preferences or judgments about postwar conditions, realized, as did the Treasury, that Congress was jealous of its authority over appropriations, not the least those for Lend-Lease which had to be renewed every six months. Indeed Congress was spontaneously more generous toward China than toward England, perhaps because no one envisaged China as a postwar rival for power or commerce. In the circumstances, intergovernmental and interdepartmental disagreements affected decisions about the financial aspects of Lend Lease, for which the Treasury carried the American responsibility. Still, those decisions were always eased by the unanimity of all concerned, so often emphasized by Morgenthau, about the overriding necessity for whatever accommodations would best serve the winning of the war.

A first wartime series of discussions about British balances began just after the attack on Pearl Harbor. The war, the British Treasury then warned Morgenthau, was continuing to drain England's gold and dollar holdings. The impending Japanese conquest of Malaya would close off British exports of rubber and tin from that area, with a resulting annual loss of about $300 million. The liabilities that the British were accumulating in India and elsewhere, while quoted temporarily in sterling, would call for postwar payments in gold or dollars. The British therefore asked for the Treasury's assistance in persuading the United States Army to take over for American use $600 to $700 million of contracts which the British had made in the United States before the Lend-Lease Act. Morgenthau thought that Churchill, then in Washington, could make the necessary arrangements with Roosevelt, but Ambassador Halifax said they were wholly involved in the day-to-day problems of the war, and the Secretary agreed to handle the matter: "If Churchill does not want to do it," he said, "let the Chancellor of the Exchequer send it to me personally, and I will do it the best I can for you."

After hearing from the Chancellor on January 25, 1942, Morgenthau consulted Dean Acheson and John J. McCloy, Stimson's responsible assistant. McCloy was willing, Acheson was eager, to assume British contracts if the Army could get the necessary appropriations from Congress. But Roosevelt, as Morgenthau reported to Acheson on February 12, "considered it inappropriate . . . at this time" to settle the question of the contracts. Still the Treasury could not let the related question of Lend-Lease and British balances "drift on forever," the Secretary said, ". . . So I think we will have to move a little bit faster, and the Lend Lease people are going to have to make up their minds, are they going to deal with the British Empire or with the various members; and after that decision is made, then we can get down and talk finances."

Canada, the Treasury calculated, had ample dollar holdings but Australia and New Zealand would need assistance in the Pacific war. South Africa would be able to pay for her own costs of war out of her production of gold. As for the British, Morgenthau promised Lord Halifax on February 19 that the Treasury would make every effort to get them the dollars they needed. In turn, he hoped the Ambassador would work through the relevant federal agencies to minimize England's dollar obligations to American manufacturers and suppliers. Morgenthau felt it especially important to include under Lend Lease as many commodities as possible.

The British-American Lend-Lease Agreement, of February 23, 1942, negotiated by Acheson and approved by Morgenthau, laid down broad principles. Settlement of exact balances and payments, whether for American aid to England or for its reciprocal counterpart, would await the end of hostilities. All settlements, when the time arose, would be made in such a way as to improve rather than burden postwar economic relations. The State Department believed, Acheson told Morgenthau in March 1942, that in all questions of Lend-Lease and reverse Lend-Lease, the United States should take a position which would have as little effect as possible on political relations with the British Empire. Acheson also recommended that the War Department, rather than the British or the Dominions, pay American troops billeted in British territories. Local governments would furnish what supplies they could through reciprocal aid, while within the limits of available shipping, the

United States would send whatever else was needed for American troops. Imports to the United States from the United Kingdom or other British areas would be considered reciprocal aid, for which no payments were needed, but for the time being, the United States would pay for commercial imports, like wool or metals, in order to sustain British balances at a comfortable level.

While Acheson was developing his proposals, Harry White and representatives from the Lend-Lease Administration reached agreement on a proper level for British balances. The British Treasury had suggested $600 million. Accepting that figure, White also endorsed a British estimate that balances would fall below $100 million in 1942 unless the United States took direct action to sustain them. White therefore recommended that the American government purchase the remaining war plants built by the British in the United States, take over for the American army various contracts for airplanes and other materials which the British had let, pay a portion of the wages and other expenses of American military forces in the sterling area in pounds, and buy the current gold production of the sterling area. Those recommendations engendered considerable debate. The British opposed selling South African gold which, they argued, would prove essential for defraying the mounting obligations of the sterling countries to India and other creditors. For its part, the War Department objected to using its appropriations for the purchase of British airplane and general supply contracts without requesting additional funds from Congress. John J. McCloy was willing, however, to assume $100 million of British contracts for ordnance, which the Army badly needed. Morgenthau persuaded McCloy also to do what he could on various airplane contracts.

For some of those contracts, and for facilities the British had acquired to manufacture aircraft, the Army on April 27, 1942, paid Great Britain $70 million and promised another $50 million soon. Meanwhile negotiations moved successfully toward American acquisition of some $100 million of armament plants that the British had bought within the United States, and for American purchase of some $90 million of ordnance contracts. In spite of those developments, and of pending American troop payments in sterling areas, the British Treasury calculated that England's balances would fall below $600 million before the end of 1942. Nevertheless the British still declined to sell South Africa's current gold production, which, according to the estimates of Morgenthau and White, would have closed the gap.

There matters stood in August 1942 when Morgenthau asked Roosevelt's permission to make a tour of American Army camps in the United Kingdom. The President immediately said: "I will announce that I am sending an intelligent civilian observer who can be my eyes and report to me on how he finds the Army. . . . You know I would love to go myself because you and I have got to get close to this thing." General Marshall, however, objected to announcing that Morgenthau was going to inspect troops in England, for Stimson might then also want to go, for which the time was unpropitious. Marshall therefore asked Morgenthau "whether it couldn't be given some financial aspect," and Roosevelt, when consulted, believed it could. The President hesitated to make it look as though Morgenthau were examining only English finances. "I would say," he suggested on August 25, "that you were going over there to study world finance, including German finances, and give it a world outlook." In that case, Morgenthau replied, "I would like to take Harry White with me who is in charge of that in the Treasury." Roosevelt agreed, though the Secretary observed privately that "I really don't think he knows who Harry White is."

Postponed because of the struggle over the tax bill*, plans for the trip materialized in the autumn. "When I came in," the Secretary noted in his Diary for October 11, 1942, "the President said right away that he was very glad I was going, and wanted me to find out certain things which he thought should be observed in England. He said he had heard the English would not let other Nationals trade in certain territories, and he wished that I would find out about it. He said I should ask some questions as to what they proposed to do about the various oil possessions and whether they would let the United States and other countries in there after the war. The President wants all of these Colonies, etcetera, open to all the world. I asked him if he wanted me to give any message to Churchill, and he said, 'Yes. Tell him that my trip around the United States was very successful, that I found production good, and that the whole question is probably one of shipping.' He told me I

* See Chapter II.

should also try to find out how the English are doing their financing."

In London on October 16, Morgenthau began a series of conversations at the British Treasury. Those talks, resulting in no new decisions, confirmed what had long worried Morgenthau about the problems of British finance. But his fortnight in the United Kingdom increased his already large admiration for the courage of the English people. "I think the trip was very, very much worthwhile from every standpoint," the Secretary told this staff upon his return on November 2. "When we first got over there White . . . went right to work with the British Treasury on certain financial arrangements. . . . Harry paid his way on that one conference." * Morgenthau had seen a number of British factories, including the plant where they manufactured engines for the Spitfire airplane. "It is perfectly amazing how smoothly they run," he reported. He had spent one night with an English bomber squadron, one with an American bomber squadron, one day with the celebrated Polish fighter squadron. When the Poles saw a German, he said, "they fly square at him and if he does not give way they just crash him. We saw the very latest Spitfire which is better than anything the Germans have." The British, he went on, had complete aerial control of the English Channel and some fifty or a hundred miles beyond into France. That control enabled them to send convoys through the channel in daytime as well as at night, and thereby to avoid mines.

Morgenthau, much impressed by the British laboring force, was pleased to find nourishing food available at low prices, and cheered by the great amount of activity on the streets, in buses, and in taxicabs — "the place humming with life."

"I think the thing which would interest you the most," he said, "is my own feeling that Hitler has seen his high water mark; that the worst is behind us, and it is not going to be as long a war as I thought it was. I am very, very much encouraged. . . . I think we ought to be able to lick those fellows in 1943 or 1944, because the English are so much further advanced than I dreamt. I mean their production is simply amazing. . . . I have come back definitely feeling that it is going to be very much shorter than I thought. . . .

* About arrangements for military currency during the Anglo-American North African campaign; see Chapter IV.

The English have made their mistakes, recognized the mistakes, and profited by them, and that is the important thing. This thing of calling the English a decadent race is just the bunk. There is nothing decadent about their leaders, the ones they have now."

What the women in England were doing, Morgenthau went on, was "just unbelievable." This was true alike for women in the armed services and in the civilian occupations, true of their housekeeping, their cooking and work in the barracks, their managing of buses and motorcycles. In the services, "as one person put it . . . they treat them like men, and they want to be treated like men. There is no nonsense about it. . . . If it were not for the women England would cave in today." The Secretary compared the contribution of the British women favorably to what the American WACs and WAVEs* were doing, with all of their saluting and pretty uniforms. In contrast, the war for women in England was "a hard, tough job; and do those people hate Hitler. You don't have to have any posters or propaganda — they just hate his guts, and they want to get at him."

The Secretary went on:

> I was with Churchill three times, once on a trip to Dover, once at lunch, and once for dinner. He was in good form every time except the night his wife gave him a supper he did not like and so he did not talk all through supper. She said, "I am sorry, dear, I could not buy any fish. You'll have to eat macaroni." Mrs. Roosevelt was sitting right there. Then they gave us little left-over bits made into meatloaf. . . .†
>
> Here is one little human interest story. When I had lunch with the King and the Queen alone, to make conversation, being an apple grower, when they brought in apples I asked if they had Cox's Pippins, which happens to be their best apple. The Queen was very much upset because she could not produce it, and the next day‡ this note arrived and some apples.

---

* The WACs were Army, the WAVEs Navy personnel.

† Twenty years later Morgenthau recalled the episode differently. As he then remembered either this or another occasion, Churchill "called his wife down for serving fish in aspic, and then sank down in his chair for the rest of the evening and came to life again only with the champagne."

‡ Or that very evening, according to Morgenthau's recollection in 1964.

The package was marked in her own handwriting, too. I think she is an amazing woman — an amazing person.

When we got through the King walked me down about a mile of hall to the front door to see me out. There was one servant present, that is all.

Poor Mrs. Roosevelt, I visited her at the palace. She had four bedrooms and she could not find any light switches. . . . When we went there at night to call on her — there is this big courtyard and you go in, there is complete darkness and nobody in the whole courtyard. I went from door to door trying to get in. . . . Finally I knocked at a door, it opened, and it happened to be the right place, so Mrs. Roosevelt said, "I have not a torchlight. I can't find the switches." . . . So I gave her my torch.

I had another experience. Not having this torch, the night I called for her to take her over to Churchill's I borrowed an Army torch. I came out with Mrs. Roosevelt on my arm and this torch, which had no cover on it — it was just loaned to me by the Army — and this British policeman says, "Don't you know you are supposed to" — I didn't say a word — "what are you doing with a torchlight that — oh, Mrs. Roosevelt!" . . .

The thing that pleased me as much as anything was a little speech Churchill made at Dover, in which he told the crowd I was the man that gave them the 100,000 rifles.* . . . Bracken, to go one better, calls it a million rifles.

As for Brendan Bracken, the British Minister of Information, Morgenthau said he was "perfectly swell. I was really worried about that one and only press conference. They sit you up on a dais. . . . The Army arranged it. . . . There were about ninety or a hundred press people. . . . Brendan Bracken introduced me with a little speech, and like in a radio hall to tell them to applaud he goes like this before I start speaking . . . just like on the radio. . . . In the middle of it I turned to Brendan Bracken and in a very low voice said, 'Am I doing all right?' Bracken could not have been nicer, and he and I hit it off right from the beginning."

* Morgenthau arranged for the sale of those rifles to the British in the critical days just after the evacuation at Dunkirk in 1940.

The hospitality and courage of the British did not alter the Secretary's position about their dollar balances. On January 3, 1942, along with Vice President Wallace, Secretary of State Hull, Secretary of War Stimson, and Edward Stettinius, he reported to the President. The United Kingdom now had accumulated about one billion dollars' worth of gold and dollars, an adequate figure. Any further growth in British holdings depended primarily on factors within the control of the United States, such as the volume of Lend-Lease aid, the volume of American purchases in England, and dollar expenditures for American troops there. Morgenthau and the others recommended that the United States hold British balances between $600 million and one billion, discontinue shipments of civilian goods under Lend-Lease to South Africa, and continue military shipments only on the basis of equivalent reciprocal aid. Conditions in Australia and New Zealand needed further investigation. A final recommendation called for the appointment of a new committee to oversee Lend-Lease policy, and for authorization of the Secretary of the Treasury to obtain full information about exchange resources from all the nations allied with the United States in the war against the Axis.

To Morgenthau's satisfaction, Roosevelt on January 11, 1943, approved those suggestions. He also made the Secretary chairman of the new committee. Pleased with what had been accomplished, with the controlled growth in Britain's asset and the concurrent preservation of the integrity of Lend Lease, the Secretary knew that the build-up of American strength in the United Kingdom during 1943 for the invasion of the continent would raise again, in greater intensity, the very questions that had so consistently marked Anglo-American financial relations. The President's approval, he felt, constituted an endorsement of Treasury policy in the year past and of continuity in that policy for the months ahead.

6. Great Britain: Reprise

It was not until July 1943, when British balances began rising, that Morgenthau became seriously concerned again with the financial implications of Lend Lease. He expected at that time that Congress, with all war expenses soaring, would reduce Lend-Lease aid to the United Kingdom unless reciprocal assistance from Great Britain to the United States, largely in the form of raw materials, held England's net receipts to $200 or $300 million for the fiscal year July 1, 1943–June 30, 1944. Chancellor of the Exchequer Sir John Anderson, however, in a letter to Morgenthau of August 2, 1943, held that the granting of raw materials as reciprocal aid "involves a serious additional burden to the financial position of the sterling area already strained by the four years of war, and in particular to that of the United Kingdom."

Unconvinced by Anderson or British representatives in Washington, Morgenthau returned from his October trip to Italy and North Africa resolved to press his own views. In a memorandum for Roosevelt of November 1, 1943, he called for an examination of Lend Lease policy to British areas, with the goal of reducing British balances to the one billion dollar level that the President had approved in January. American officers in the field, Morgenthau wrote, had informed him that the British, needing only 1,000 tank carriers, had requested 7,000, an inflation of demand that might apply for other arms. Besides cutting down balances, the Secretary wanted to avoid adverse criticism on the Hill and, wherever possible, to stop the practice of employing Lend-Lease for transactions which might better flow through ordinary commercial channels. American goods, he later explained to Lend-Lease officials, were frequently being distributed through British private exporters, who were gaining an unfair advantage over American businessmen.

Those criticisms received a sympathetic hearing from Leo Crowley, who in September 1943 had become the head of the Foreign Economic Administration, a new agency created to direct Lend Lease and other activities.* Crowley, as he told Morgenthau, was meeting continual difficulties in working with the State Department. So was Morgenthau, who knew from Harry Hopkins "that Hull had written a letter to the President . . . objecting strenuously to my heading up this committee on Lend Lease with the Brit-

---

* An Executive Order of September 25, 1943, establishing the Foreign Economic Administration, placed within its jurisdiction the Office of Economic Warfare, the Office of Foreign Relief and Rehabilitation Operations, the Lend Lease Administration, and the Office of Foreign Economic Coordination.

ish." The trouble was not just personal. Whereas Crowley and the War Department agreed with the Treasury's position on British balances and Lend Lease, the State Department held an almost opposite view. That department, according to Dean Acheson, was prepared to support suggestions for eliminating "freakish transactions" from Lend-Lease, but not if the Treasury had the unexpressed but governing purpose of forcing British balances to any particular level.

That purpose, as Morgenthau had often argued, governed the policy of Congress. On November 5, 1943, the Senate Committee to Investigate the National Defense Program, through a statement of its chairman, Harry S Truman, asserted that Lend-Lease was never intended as a device to shift a portion of the United Kingdom's war cost to the United States, but only as a realistic recognition that the British did not have the means to pay for essential weapons and other materials. Further, Congress had been assured that Lend-Lease would be extended only where recipients were already fully utilizing their own resources. The next day Roosevelt discussed the question of British balances with Crowley. "I told Crowley," the President then informed Morgenthau, ". . . to keep them as they were, not to let them get any higher."

On November 14, 1943, Morgenthau explained to Lord Halifax the opinion now common to the Treasury, the Foreign Economic Administration, the Truman Committee, and the White House. British balances were nevertheless rising, the Secretary said, because the British had been lobbying successfully with the State Department. In the long run, that practice might lead Congress wholly to abandon Lend-Lease. As Morgenthau later reported to his staff, he said to Halifax that "just because we were innocent in the international field, it was no reason why they should take advantage of us. I said that there were at least two committees — McKellar and Truman that were hot after us, and something should be done. . . . After all, if you people would only agree with me that your balances should be cut down, I would be glad to tackle your other postwar problem of what you're going to do with your big sterling balances.* I don't know whether I can be helpful, but at least we should look at it as a separate matter, and not try to use Lend Lease

* That is, debts due to other governments within the sterling bloc.

to solve a postwar English problem when Lend Lease was never designed for that. . . . What I was practically telling him was . . . that he should stop fighting me with Stettinius and the State Department and help me solve this thing, and I believe that he will help me. . . . I think this idea of mine of tackling their financial problem as separate from the Lend Lease one is the proper solution and the proper approach."

But it proved impossible to proceed on that basis, Morgenthau admitted to Halifax on November 17, because the Treasury could not commit the United States to any postwar economic policy. For their part, the British could not leave themselves in a vulnerable financial situation simply on the basis of Morgenthau's personal promise that the United States would provide some kind of assistance after the war.

After reviewing recent conversations, White in a memorandum intended for Roosevelt, recommended discontinuing Lend Lease shipments of various kinds of non-military aid in order to bring British balances down to one billion dollars. That proposal met unexpected opposition on November 23, 1943, from Oscar Cox, the major draftsman of the Lend Lease Act, now general counsel of the Foreign Economic Administration. If the Treasury and the Lend-Lease Administration referred to balances, Cox said, the State Department would not agree, and eventually Churchill would raise the issue with the President who would then somehow defer deciding it. It would be much wiser, Cox thought, to attack separately each item that should be cut from Lend-Lease. A first step had already been taken in the elimination of American purchases of fish from Iceland for consumption in England. A next step might terminate American purchases of sugar from the Caribbean for British use. If each such project was broached separately, there would be no point at which the Prime Minister could appropriately complain to the President. Further, the aggregate reductions would reach a total of several hundred million dollars. Crowley and Morgenthau supported Cox's proposal, though Crowley was less than optimistic.

With persisting disagreement, the British blocked every effort to eliminate specific Lend-Lease transfers, as Crowley told Morgenthau on December 15, 1943, and the State Department continued to support the British case. At an interdepartmental conference on December 31, Cordell Hull explained, that, in his view, an American policy for controlling the resources of the British government, even if it were based on reasons of domestic political necessity, would provoke a "very serious international situation." If Congress and the American people found out what British balances actually were, Crowley replied, Congress would criticize the responsible executive agencies, which would have great difficulty in explaining away what they had done. Neither he nor Morgenthau wanted to embarrass the President, but they did feel they had to call the issue to Roosevelt's attention.

They did so in a joint memorandum that described the growth of British assets, reviewed the mood of the Congress, and asked the President to permit the Treasury and the Lend-Lease Administration to discontinue some parts of the non-military assistance rendered to the United Kingdom. There was no need, they said, for decision about the size of British balances. "Listen, you know, it is very interesting," Morgenthau said as he finished reading one draft of the memorandum, ". . . the French are sore at us in Algiers because we stopped Lend Lease. We are trying to cut down Lend Lease to the British; they get sore. I get a snooty, snooty telegram; Chiang Kai-shek sends for our Ambassadors and gives them hell, and this, and that, and the other thing. Just as soon as we quit being Santa Claus we become unpopular."

In a separate memorandum that incorporated Dean Acheson's advice, Hull wrote Roosevelt that he would go along with recommendations about specific Lend-Lease practices, but he also urged forthright conversations with the British about their gold and dollar balances. "I don't know any better way," Morgenthau commented, "to irritate the situation than to bring it to their attention. . . . I should think he . . . wouldn't insist that we continue to keep discussing this whole question with the English and get nowhere . . . as we have during the last twelve months.

"I agree," the President wrote Hull, Morgenthau and Crowley on January 5, 1944, "with the report of the Secretary of the Treasury and Mr. Crowley, and I understand that the Secretary of State approves the report but wished to take the matter up first with the British. Also, I understand that the Secretary of the Treasury and Mr. Crowley feel that they have been doing this for a year and have got nowhere.

"Therefore, I suggest that the matter be taken up once more with the British, but on the distinct understanding that I will be given a final report within thirty days, i.e. February 7, 1944, and will act finally thereon."

Discussions with the British began on January 7. Lord Halifax quickly complained that the United States was taking a more generous position toward the Soviet Union than toward the United Kingdom. Morgenthau replied that the Russians were doing most of the fighting against Germany. The British, "saddened at the trend of events with respect to Lend-Lease," held that at the very time they were increasing their contribution to the war effort, the United States was reducing its assistance. The proposed cuts, they said, while purportedly political, had as their real intention the diminution of British gold and dollar assets, which would "not be very tasty" to the Parliament. Morgenthau then assured them that the question of balances would not enter the forthcoming discussions of Lend Lease.

But after several weeks of continual, futile debate, the Chancellor of the Exchequer on January 27, 1944, urged Morgenthau to put considerations of international finance above those of domestic politics. "We shall have many difficult problems to consider together in the coming months," he wrote. "My financial anxieties arising out of prospective external payments are increasing as the war advances . . . and it may be advisable that we should have an early exchange of views about what the position will be in the early postwar period. I am confident that in the future, as in the past, we can rely on your friendly cooperation."

That confidence was not misplaced, for Morgenthau by the end of January had come almost wholly to accept Acheson's attitude toward the negotiations. With so many issues troubling Anglo-American relations,* the Secretary did not want to strain transatlantic friendship. Still, he believed as he had for some weeks that a debate about British balances would draw blood, while modest and justifiable cuts in Lend-Lease aid would not. Accordingly on February 2, 1944, he approved a program acceptable alike to Crowley and the British. It eliminated from Lend-Lease American purchases for

---

* Especially questions of politics and strategy in Europe, the Mediterranean and the Orient; but also ongoing negotiations of special interest to both Treasuries about military and occupation currencies, postwar international financial institutions, and Argentine relations. On those issues and the problem of Jewish refugees, see Chapter IV and V.

British consumption of Caribbean molasses and sugar, of Icelandic fish, and of Canadian alcohol and petroleum products. Subject to further discussion about details, it also cut out some other non-military items. The Lend-Lease Administration, retreating from an earlier proposal, contracted to continue to provide tobacco, certain paper products, agricultural machinery, and various shipping services. That retreat preserved $245 million of annual Lend-Lease assistance. The mutually agreeable cuts aggregated $288 million — less than Morgenthau had originally hoped for, as much as he thought he could now demand, and about half of what had been in controversy — a reasonable compromise.

Content with the outcome, Morgenthau was disturbed by a reopening of the issue in mid-February. He was ill with influenza when Crowley, at a Cabinet meeting of February 18, 1944, brought up the British dollar position. The President then said "that the three agencies interested in this matter . . . should prepare for his signature a letter to Churchill." Under Secretary of State Stettinius* drafted that letter, but contrary to Roosevelt's instructions, he failed to clear his draft with either Morgenthau or Crowley. "There have been recent discussions," the letter read, as Roosevelt sent it, ". . . concerning the cessation of deliveries under Lend-Lease of certain items which have proven to be embarrassing and no longer required. . . . The subject is far from simple and negotiations appear to have made satisfactory progress.

"Independent of these discussions . . . I have been thinking of the feasibility of your arranging your fiscal matters in such a way as to result in a reduction of the British gold and dollar holdings . . . to a figure in the vicinity of one billion dollars. What are your views as to what should be done and what do you think can be undertaken?"

The last paragraph reopened the very question which Morgenthau had decided temporarily to avoid. Indeed Stettinius himself had hoped to minimize rather than to increase Anglo-American tension. But Churchill, in a testy reply, showed particular irritation about any reduction in British balances. At a Cabinet meeting on March 11, 1944, Morgenthau said that he still believed the United States should hold the British to a ceiling of a billion dollars, but with Churchill protesting that goal, he had become reluctant to pur-

---

* Stettinius had replaced Sumner Welles in that office.

sue it. He was frankly annoyed that the State Department had prepared the cable for the President without clearing it with the Treasury. Further, the cable was unfair to the British, for the Treasury in conversations with Lord Halifax about Lend-Lease had assured him that the question of dollar balances was not involved. Now the President's cable made it seem that the United States was not keeping faith. "You and Hull," Roosevelt said when the Secretary had finished, "better get together on it."

Above all, as Morgenthau put it to his staff, "I don't want to lose sight of the principal thing, and that is this: it is true that the President and Mr. Churchill are having trouble, and that is terrible. I don't want to aggravate it." Neither did Hull, who on March 13 promised to "stand by the position" the Treasury had taken with Lord Halifax. He, Crowley, and Morgenthau also agreed to support no arrangement that would exclude the possibility of reexamining the question of dollar balances if future negotiations did not yield satisfactory results, or if those balances continued to grow. Hull looked "to the Treasury on the matter of dollar balances," and left it to the Treasury to draft a new cable for Roosevelt to send Churchill, and to clear the draft with Crowley and Acheson.

The resulting message, which Roosevelt signed on March 24, 1944, observed that Hull and Morgenthau had reminded the President of the Treasury's understanding with Halifax. "As Secretary Morgenthau stated. . . ," the cable went on, "This understanding did not deal with the dollar position question and did not preclude the possibility of our reopening that question in the future. . . . I raised this dollar position question since it is a troublesome one of continuing concern with us here and doubtless with you. I hope that we may be able together to find some reasonable solution . . . before it becomes more troublesome." In any further discussion of the matter, the Treasury would speak for the United States. That responsibility of course pleased Morgenthau, who had requested it, but as he told White on March 29, he was "scared to death," for he feared any rupture between Roosevelt and Churchill, especially in the weeks remaining before the Anglo-American invasion of Normandy. Until the attack on Hitler could gain momentum, he proposed to defer further debate.*

* Debate resumed in the autumn of 1944, see Chapter VI.

Morgenthau in the spring of 1944 was preoccupied with the course of the war, with issues relating to Allied advances in Europe and in the Pacific. Those and other international problems had been commanding his attention for more than a year. In dealing with them, as in the development of financial policy in China and the United Kingdom, he had found himself often in disagreement with the British or the State Department or both. Indeed the matter of British balances, temporarily put to one side, was the least contentious of the international controversies in which the Treasury was engaged.

IV

Principles and Expedients

1942-1944

OUT OF THE Second World War Morgenthau hoped there would emerge a principled and lasting peace. To that peace he expected the United States to contribute the authority of its power and the inspiration of the spirit of the New Deal — of social justice, humanitarian striving, and popular and responsible government. Yet he realized that the precondition for that kind of peace was the defeat of Germany, Italy, and Japan. The stupendous task of victory again and again demanded expedients that threatened the very purposes of the struggle. In such cases, Morgenthau, like Roosevelt, deferred to military requirements. His style in the financing of the Grand Alliance revealed his general recognition of priorities. Irritated though he often was by the inflexibility of Soviet negotiators, he labored to speed the flow of arms to Russia. Recognizing the corrupt ineffectuality of the Nationalist government, he strove to make the dollar an instrument of the war effort in China. Similarly, he subordinated controversy over Anglo-American finance to the preservation of the most vital partnership the United States had.

Yet British policy in other matters disturbed him, as also did the policies of various of his colleagues in Washington, when they seemed to subvert his definitions of American interests or of appropriate principles for the governing of affairs among men and states. Morgenthau pursued those interests and principles with a calculated toughness and with an intermittent success that depended always on two variables: the degree of support he could elicit from Franklin Roosevelt; and the degree to which principle had to be accommodated to military necessity.

1. Invasion and Occupation Currency: North Africa

In July 1942, the United States began making detailed plans for taking the offensive in the European Theater. At that time the President still hoped for a cross-channel attack in 1943. Although that was to be postponed another year, American forces were within six months of landing in North Africa, and within a year of invading Sicily and Italy. Civilian authorities therefore prepared to meet their obligations in areas occupied by the army, and the Treasury bore special responsibility for the administration of finances.

In mid-July General Dwight D. Eisenhower, in command in the European Theater, asked whether American troops invading North Africa would use British currency, as he supposed, or whether the Treasury had an alternative plan. His own concern was to have available for American soldiers an adequate supply of negotiable currency in invaded and occupied countries. Morgenthau unhesitatingly rejected the thought of paying Americans in pounds sterling. Europeans and Africans, he believed, preferred dollars to pounds. He particularly objected to any system of paying American troops that would in any way appear to make them hired mercenaries; therefore insofar as money and finance were involved, he wanted to distinguish between British and American military operations.

Still, as the Secretary realized, Eisenhower's question raised a number of complicated problems. In a "very preliminary report," Harry White on July 17, 1942, suggested what became temporary guidelines for Treasury policy. As an invasion currency, for use by American and allied soldiers in the period of attack, White recommended the dollar because of its unquestionable superiority in commanding a maximum of goods and services. The conversion rate between the dollar and local currencies would have to lean toward overvaluing the currencies held by friendly people in invaded areas in order to assure their eager reception for the dollar. To facilitate control and to avoid the risk of losses of dollars to the enemy, dollar currency for invasion purposes, White believed, should bear a special overmark which would differentiate it, in experienced eyes, from the currency used at home.

A second problem was more difficult. In some areas, after a successful invasion, the period of occupation might be short; in others it would last for years. In the case of friendly nations with free governments recognized by the United States, White proposed issuing occupation currency similar to the ordinary, indigenous currency as soon as any considerable amount of territory had been won. But in the case of the Axis homelands, he suggested that the dollar should become the only valid currency pending a permanent economic settlement between the Allied Nations and the defeated power.

Those recommendations won the approval of Morgenthau, of Secretary of War Stimson, who considered White's memorandum "excellent," and of Herbert Feis, who represented the State Department in early discussions about invasion currency. Feis further believed, in line with another Treasury suggestion, that local currency should be redeemable in dollars only under license, for in that way the United States could prevent Nazi collaborators and other undesirables from converting profits made during the time of German domination. But Feis and Stimson feared that American troops and local populations would not take kindly to a dollar distinguished by an overmark. Feis also predicted that if sterling and dollar currency circulated side by side in any area, the sterling would soon depreciate, a development he wished to avoid.

Morgenthau and White held out for an inconspicuous overmark consisting of the substitution of a yellow seal for the green seal common to domestic American bills of all denominations. Currency with such an unobtrusive seal, they predicted, would circulate as freely as unmarked dollars. More important, yellow seal currency would have clear advantages. In the event of enemy reoccupation of an area, the United States could prevent its utilization. Where yellow seal currency was circulating, the United States could keep the Axis from using looted American currency of the regular stamp. American soldiers would benefit, too, for the United States could admit occupation currency back into the country with no restrictions, whereas certain restrictions applied to ordinary bills.

On August 5, 1942, Secretary Hull for the State Department and Under Secretary Patterson for the War Department left the question of the marking on the currency entirely to the Treasury, which soon began to print yellow seal dollars. "The military authorities," Morgenthau told Hull and Patterson, "should be completely in charge" of all other aspects of the invasion, but he wondered whether the

Army was planning to use officers or civilians in the administration of occupied areas during the period after the fighting had ceased. Patterson assured him the Army would want assistance, which Morgenthau said the Treasury would be glad to provide. For that purpose, he proposed establishing a committee of War, State, and Treasury Department representatives to make recommendations to the President about the governing of occupied areas. Hull and Patterson agreed.

Treasury representation on the new committee particularly pleased Morgenthau because, as he understood them, questions of occupation policy had large implications both for the prosecution of the war and for the fashioning of the peace. He was especially eager to prevent the British from assuming unilateral authority over European currency and finance. British initiative, he felt, was moving in that direction. Ambassador John G. Winant in London had reported the views of John Maynard Keynes who was working with the finance ministers of the Allied governments-in-exile. Keynes had noted that shortages of goods were more responsible than excesses of currency for the inflation occurring in the parts of Europe under German control. He predicted some unification of European currencies in those areas, arranged in order to check postwar inflation. While concurring in those observations, Morgenthau suspected a British scheme to exclude American influence from the Continent. Eisenhower, the Secretary told his staff, had reported that the British were printing several million pounds with an overmark for use by all occupation armies in Europe, including American forces. Yet the Europeans Morgenthau saw in Washington had convinced him that their countrymen "like American money." More important, "the whole implication of what kind of money you begin to use when you move into a country is reparations, settlement, and so forth."

The Secretary went on:

> My suggestion is that we use for both armies US dollars and that this would be the first foot in the door that the United States, when this war is over, is going to settle . . . what kind of Europe it is going to be. . . . Who is going to pay for it? We are going to pay for it. The English are going to be busted; they are not going to pay for it. . . . We might just as well say it, because we are going to do it anyway. . . . We are now going to say,

"We recognize the fact that the United States is going to have to take the relief over in Europe, and in return for that . . . we will set up once and for all the kind of Europe that we expect."

And the first question that is going to come up is this whole question of reparations. If we are going to go through this whole thing all over again of reparations and grinding the German people down again through malnutrition, through inflation, and through another Versailles Treaty . . . in another twenty-five years we will have another war. . . .

The only way that this thing can be changed so that Europe might live at peace for one hundred years is if the United States will say, "All right, . . . we are going to set up the United Nations peace, tariff walls, and so forth . . . try to set up an ideal state that might be good for a hundred years." If we do, we are going to have to pay for it.

Roosevelt had said only a few days before: "Winston and I will write the Peace Treaty." There was no mention at all of Stalin. "I think," Morgenthau told his staff, "it had better be Franklin Roosevelt without Winston, and also I think it had better be the United States that does the international policing without Winston. I think it had better be the United States that decides that all of these munitions factories will be leveled to the ground and destroyed, and the munitions machinery, airplanes that can't fly more than two or three hundred miles, all the rest of that stuff.*

"Now . . . if we start going into these countries and the English are going to take the attitude right from the beginning, 'We are going to dictate the peace of Europe,' the whole thing is going to be repeated.

"That is a long speech for me . . . maybe . . . very Wilsonian, maybe . . . purely daydreaming, but lacking something like that, . . . my sons' children will be doing the same thing that my sons are doing." †

---

* A prescription for Germany to which Morgenthau returned in 1944, see Chapter VII.

† Henry Morgenthau III served as an Army officer under General George Patton in Europe; Robert Morgenthau, an officer in the Navy, served on ships that were sunk in the Mediterranean and in the Pacific.

Harry White objected that neither Great Britain nor the Soviet Union would agree to the kind of solution Morgenthau was proposing. In three months, the Secretary replied, neither England nor Russia would have a thing to say about it, for both depended on American aid. White then said that no one could yet dare to say the United States was going to shoulder the burden and cost of peacemaking. Morgenthau disagreed: "You have got to begin to say that months in advance before you do it, and . . . at the rate this thing is going, Mr. Roosevelt may have to say something like this in three months. . . . I can say this to the President when I am closeted with him alone. I wouldn't say it before the others, but I wanted you people . . . not to think that I had lost my mind when I am willing to propose that we pay all the expenses of going into Europe. I wanted you to know what is behind it."

White asked if Morgenthau meant the United States to take pounds in exchange for dollars for use in the invading armies. No, Morgenthau replied, he intended instead to Lend-Lease the dollars to the British. They might consider that a blow to their prestige, White said. "I know," Morgenthau said. "I expect all of that. . . . It just gets back — there is nobody, from Hull down, that can handle this thing except the President. This takes tough, hard trading. Our planes are good enough for them, our food is good enough for them, our guns are good enough for them, and our men are good enough for them, and by God, . . . what should be the least of all, is our money."

The United States would certainly have some of the influence Morgenthau described, White suggested, but it was a mistake to assume the United States could dominate the world. If the Soviet Union and Great Britain were out of the picture, the United States would never get into Europe. There would be a negotiated peace. Even Woodrow Wilson, White argued, had not tried to impose an American peace on Europe. Again Morgenthau disagreed. The United States had to play a major part in the settlement of Europe, he believed, on the basis of ideals Roosevelt had yet to define. He had had a taste now of the kind of bickering which would occur after the invasion of the Continent. He had heard representatives of the Netherlands say how they hated the Belgians, and complain about the weakness and corruption of the French. That kind of talk forboded a divided world. The Secretary therefore wanted the President as soon as possible to lift the level of discussion. "I sit around," he said, "and I hear these college students and these young people, soldiers and sailors, and there is nothing inspirational being raised for them." He had come, he admitted, a long way from the question of an overmark on currency; he had, seriously and self-consciously, "been doing a little daydreaming."

The Secretary did not drop his theme. With Under Secretary of War Patterson and Secretary of the Navy Knox on September 4, 1942, he again adverted to the potential significance of currency for the making of the peace. Morgenthau was content to leave the administration of newly conquered areas to military commanders, but he was eager for the United States to work out its own plans for later phases of the occupation, for those plans would be the "first leg in the relay race" to the peace table. If the English, he said, "get a lap ahead of us and should get the civilian population tied up under their thumb, then whatever our peace plans are will be made that much more difficult for us. That is why I think at least we should have a plan. . . . The details could be worked out by experts a great deal better than I could do it. I am just trying to get you two men to think about it."

Morgenthau considered exchange rates at all times within the province of the Treasury. Late in September 1942, as the date approached for the invasion of North Africa, the British Embassy opened conversations with the War Department about cross rates between the occupation pound and the occupation dollar. The English proposed a depreciated rate for the pound, in Morgenthau's opinion an undesirable step that might cause trouble for the dollar in postwar international exchange. The Secretary therefore directed Dan Bell to intercede with Judge Patterson. "I don't care how forceful you are," Morgenthau said, "in telling Patterson that it is perfectly ridiculous to have a British Treasury official dealing with the War Department; he should be dealing with us."

The core of the problem lay in setting rates of exchange between the dollar and the French franc circulating in North Africa, and between the pound and that franc. The British cared primarily about preserving the pound-franc rate that already prevailed in those parts of French Africa in the control of Gaullist rather than

Vichy forces.* Accordingly London proposed for North Africa a rate of 43 francs for a dollar and 172 francs for a pound. The American Treasury, in contrast, wanted to set the rate realistically at 75 francs to the dollar, which was close to the existing black market rate of 100 francs to the dollar. The Treasury believed that a rate of 43 would rapidly slide off. In rebuttal, the British argued that that rate would have a beneficial political effect on the inhabitants of North Africa. After several days of discussion, Stimson and Hull, supporting Morgenthau, decided, in Hull's phrase, to "let it go at 75." So did the British after conversations with White in London.†

For Morgenthau, that decision paled in comparison with larger issues that developed with the invasion of Algeria. To facilitate that operation, the President authorized his personal representative, Robert Murphy, to arrange for the assistance of the French Admiral Jean Darlan, who had remained strictly under the orders of the Vichy government. Murphy succeeded a few days after the fighting had begun; the French troops in Algeria ceased their resistance to American forces; and Darlan enjoyed American support until his assassination on December 24, 1942. As Morgenthau began to understand the degree of American involvement with Darlan, and as he reflected upon the exclusion from the North African operation of General Charles de Gaulle and his Free French forces, the Secretary feared that the United States had surrendered too much to military convenience. The State Department held that the reliance on Darlan had been "decided by the military commanders on the ground of military necessity . . . the chief purpose . . . being to assure . . . that in time of great crisis there would not be any hostilities behind their backs. . . . The President himself was not aware of the details until they had already been arrived at. . . . General Marshall has had the entire thing in his own hands from the beginning."

For the War Department, Judge Patterson offered a rather different explanation. "It was a kind of desperate play," he told Morgen-

* The Vichy French controlled North Africa; de Gaulle controlled parts of French Africa south of the Sahara. The British, who had on occasion fought against the Vichy French, were both cooperating intermittently and trading regularly with the Free French.

† See Chapter III on Morgenthau's trip, with White, to England in 1942.

thau on November 16, 1942, ". . . to get the French fleet. . . .
The White House knows about the thing, and . . . it did not pass
much through the War Department. We only got some very superfi-
cial notice about it, and it was handled through the State Department by this man Murphy." Still upset, Morgenthau replied that
Darlan's record "speaks for itself. It's terrible." Further, the Secretary put full credence in a CBS news report from London that
American sponsorship of Darlan had provoked alarm in Great Britain. Patterson sympathized with those worries. Darlan, he said, was
cold-blooded, loyal to no one but himself. But Murphy was representing the White House, even though he was more or less on General Eisenhower's staff, and Patterson interpreted the situation as
"one of those things where maybe they thought you have to do the
job with the tools you have." Morgenthau shuddered at the "awful
implications" of the policy, which would disgust de Gaulle as well as
"a lot of people in this country."

Hoping to soothe Morgenthau, Henry Stimson asked him to tea
where they were joined by Archibald MacLeish, representing the
Office of War Information, and Associate Justice Felix Frankfurter,
who were also disturbed by the affiliation with Darlan. Stimson and
John J. McCloy, who accompanied him, considered their perturba-
tion "starry-eyed." In Stimson's view, Eisenhower's deal with Darlan had produced enormous benefits, particularly the laying down
of the arms of the French forces in the area. The Secretary of War
therefore gave his guests "a little talk, pointing out first the hazard-
ous nature of our operation in North Africa and the perilous condition in which our troops would have been in case there had been
any delay caused by the obstruction of the French." The Army, he
assured his guests, was not making foreign policy, simply a temporary military arrangement. Responding to Morgenthau's suggestion
that the United States take steps to control the character of French
government after the war, Stimson argued that such an effort, impossible of execution, would violate the principles for which Americans were fighting. The Secretary of War felt that Morgenthau
"after grunts and groans" had gone home "reconciled."

In that conclusion Stimson erred. He had been less persuasive
than he thought, and Morgenthau less reconciled than he perhaps
seemed. In his own Diary on November 17, 1942, Morgenthau recorded his impression of the previous afternoon:

Stimson . . . read a three-page telegram from Eisenhower.
. . . Eisenhower said he felt it was a military necessity to use
Admiral Darlan, and he asked for authority to go ahead, but
that if they didn't want him to do that, they should send a
commission out at once to advise him. Stimson then told us
that both Churchill and Roosevelt had approved what Eisenhower had done.

When Stimson got through giving us all this background,
none of which was very new, showing how necessary it was to
use Darlan, and using him meant the saving of many American
lives, somebody mentioned Edward Murrow's broadcast.* I
had a copy of it in my pocket and I asked Stimson whether he
didn't want to read it. He lost his temper and said he wasn't
interested. . . . I just let it pass. . . .

Then I went on and made a very passionate address on what
I thought about Darlan. I said he was a most ruthless person
who had sold many thousands of people into slavery, and that
to use a man like that in these times, no matter what the price
is, the price is too great. I went on to say that there is something else besides temporary military victories, and I said, "You
can't tell me the whole campaign was set up with the expectation of using Darlan because the President told me that that
wasn't so. . . . There is a considerable group of rich people in
this country who would make peace with Hitler tomorrow, and
the only people who really want to fight are the working men
and women, and if they once get the idea that we are going to
sit back and favor these Fascists, not only in France but in Spain,
which is what we are doing every day . . . , these people are
going to have sit-down strikes; they're going to slow up production, and they're going to say, what's the use of fighting just to
put that kind of people back into power? . . . If something
isn't done about it and that idea once gets into the minds of the
people, you will never be able to get it out. . . . Now for the
English — Darlan is known as one of the most violent British-
haters. How do you suppose the men and women of England
feel about this. General Giraud also hates the English."

When I finished I could tell from MacLeish's face that he

* The CBS newscast from London reporting British criticism of the collaboration with Darlan.

agreed with me. . . . Then Frankfurter said, "Yes, we agree
with what Henry said." Then he began to try to fix a middle
course, and I was never so disgusted in my life. Then he said,
"What would you do if you had the decision to make?" I said,
"That isn't the question. . . . The question is how to explain
to the American people what this means, and we are going to
let the State Department put in this kind of people. . . . If we
do that, nothing will be settled and in another ten years we will
have another war on our hands."

Stimson was quite flabbergasted at my vehemence. McCloy
said nothing, but then one of them spoke up and said, "Well,
you know that last Friday Eisenhower issued orders to Robert
Murphy to take up with Admiral Darlan a matter of rescinding
the Nuremberg Decree* and freeing all political prisoners." I
asked them when that would be made public and they said they
would have to wait until it was carried out. Then I said,
"Well, somebody said that Murphy is living in the pocket of
Darlan, and supposing Darlan refuses to carry out these orders." They had no answer for that.

Shortly before I left, Stimson said, "Give me that copy of
Murrow's address. I want to read it." McCloy said, "Isn't that
typical of the man? He gets mad and then he cools off, and he
does what you ask him."

Frankfurter called me up as soon as I got home, and I was
very disagreeable with him. . . . He wanted me to write the
President a letter telling him that he should say . . . that all
brutality and cruelty in North Africa should be stopped. It was
typical of Frankfurter. He didn't say anything while we were
all together; yet as soon as he got home he wanted to become
"Mr. Fixer."

In his agitated state of mind, Morgenthau called on the President
on November 17. As he entered, he said he wanted to talk about
North Africa, "something that affects my soul." Roosevelt listened
for twenty minutes. The arrangement with Darlan, he then said,
would permit the United States to achieve in two weeks what otherwise might have taken ten. "Darlan," the President continued,

---

* The Nazi Decree calling for various kinds of deprivation for all Jews.

"says he hates Giraud* and the head of Dakar — the governor — hates Darlan, but Darlan drops in our laps because he is the only man who can represent the part of France which is still left. Darlan wants to save lives and in some way keep a semblance of power for Pétain†. . . . It is purely a military matter. . . . There is an old Bulgarian proverb which goes like this: 'You can walk with the Devil as far as the bridge but then you must leave him behind.' "

He was satisfied with that statement, Morgenthau said, but he thought it "terribly important" for Roosevelt to tell the American people that he had rescinded the Nuremberg Decree and urged freedom for all political prisoners in North Africa. He also wanted the President to say he was giving the North Africans the right to vote. "Well," Roosevelt said, "some believe that should be done and some don't." He had, he assured Morgenthau, told Eisenhower to have local people run all public facilities like electric power and water, and also given the General other explicit instructions. Since the President was "running the show," since he had made no promises of any kind to Darlan about the future, Morgenthau "under these circumstances, and knowing that it has saved thousands of lives," concluded that there was nothing more he could say. As he went on in his Diary: "I believe the President when he says he won't tie up with the Darlans and the Flandins‡ and I suppose that Eisenhower is looking at it purely from a military standpoint. McCloy says that both Eisenhower and Clark are soldiers and have no political ideas, that Eisenhower is a farm boy, and that it is merely a matter of military strategy. I hope they are all right, but I do believe the President, and I am confident that Stimson wouldn't be a party to a tie-up with any Fascist because his whole life has been against that kind of thing."

Roosevelt's clarifying public statement about Darlan and his public request for the liberation of all Nazi political prisoners in North

---

* General Henri Giraud, chief of the French Army in North Africa, who succeeded Darlan as High Commissioner in North Africa after Darlan was assassinated. Giraud later signed his authority over to de Gaulle.

† Marshal Henri P. Pétain, head of the Vichy Government.

‡ Pierre-Etienne Flandin, sometime Premier and Foreign Minister in prewar France, at that time a member of the Pétain government in Vichy and a friend of Robert Murphy.

Africa lifted Morgenthau's spirits. When he called the President the next day, November 18, to congratulate him on those statements, Roosevelt said he had decided about voting rights. In Algiers and Morocco the Arabs felt they had been discriminated against, for the Jews there were allowed to vote and the Arabs were not. Roosevelt considered that their domestic problem, and as he put it, removed "all the persecution status of the Jews and I am saying to the Jews and the Arabs, 'Forget about the voting for neither of you is going to vote. There will be no election until we are good and ready.' " All that, Morgenthau replied, was most heartening.

But Morgenthau was soon again disturbed, this time by renewed controversy over exchange rates. The North African French had agreed to the rates of 75 francs to the dollar and 300 to the pound only conditionally. Late in December 1942, General Giraud demanded a higher value for the franc. British authorities had continued to abide by the official rate of 43 francs to the dollar in their trade with Madagascar, where General de Gaulle held authority. Consequently the Gaullists enjoyed a more favorable and more prestigious rate than did Giraud, who resented his situation, and considered the issue political as well as economic.

Seeking remedy, Giraud called on Eisenhower, who in turn appealed to Stimson, who on December 30, 1942, with Hull's consent, asked Morgenthau to handle the whole matter. Morgenthau told Stimson that he believed the problem had arisen because of British ambitions for postwar trade. As Morgenthau saw it, the British hoped to create a pattern of cross rates that would establish a three-dollar value for the pound, a rate at which the pound would presumably compete favorably with the dollar in world commerce. He was therefore eager to sustain the existing North African rate of exchange between the dollar and the franc, especially since it was based on actual economic, rather than theoretical or political, conditions.

With the approval of the War and State Departments, Morgenthau on December 31 sent a long cable to Eisenhower. All responsible American departments, the Secretary noted, considered it unreasonable and impracticable to fix the rate in North and West Africa at 43.90 francs to the dollar, the prewar level. The changed circumstances of the past two and a half years had destroyed the economic basis for that earlier rate. Because of close monetary ties with continental France, French North and West Africa had felt the inflationary forces operating there. Further, German exploitation of French areas had contributed to inflation in Africa, as had various local conditions. An overvaluation of the franc would threaten the stability of exchange, encourage black market activities, and penalize American troops, for if they had to convert their dollars at a rate of 43, they would lose almost half of their real pay. "We find it difficult," the cable concluded, "to understand how anyone fully cognizant of all the factors in this situation could regard a rate of 43.90 francs to the dollar, or any other rate that places a higher rate on the franc, preferable to the rate of 75 francs to the dollar."

Much more exercised than his cable revealed, Morgenthau on January 1, 1943, told others in the Administration: "It is very disturbing to me, because there are so many people who are always looking for something to make trouble between the English Government and ourselves. . . . From what the War Department has told me, handling Giraud is not the easiest thing in the world and General Giraud is bedeviling General Eisenhower, who certainly has got his hands full . . . on the military side. . . .

"Now . . . in our tripartite agreement,* we have always stuck together. . . . We have always had complete frankness and complete cooperation, and I am certainly not going to assume that it will be any different. But here is a situation combining . . . the military, which is the most important . . . and . . . the economic. I hope that the thing can be very rapidly cleared up so that General Eisenhower can put his mind exclusively on fighting and will not have to be bothered by Giraud bedeviling him about what the crossrate is in Madagascar."

The British, however, refused to apply the North African rate in Madagascar and French Somaliland, where it would have reduced their volume of trade. "When we begin to testify on Lend-Lease," Morgenthau warned them, "and the whole question of your balances . . . I want to be in the right frame of mind, and right now I am not. . . . When your Government and ours do business with the French, we have got to have the united front. . . .

* The American-British-French pact of 1936 calling for consultation among treasuries about exchange rates and related matters.

"We can't have one crossrate in Somaliland . . . and another one in Africa if it is upsetting to Giraud. It is only upsetting to me because it upsets him and upsets General Eisenhower. I want to eliminate that . . . and I want a demonstration from the British Treasury towards me — a reaffirmation from the Chancellor that he wants to continue in the future . . . as his predecessors have in the past. . . . In other words, I want a sort of vote of confidence." To the repeated British argument that the Madagascar and Somaliland rate predated the war, Morgenthau replied that "we are starting a new era." He expected the British and American governments to work together toward "having a uniform rate throughout the world . . . with the dollar and the pound . . . with respect to a particular currency."

Buttressed by the warm support of the War and State Departments, Morgenthau fought dogged British resistance to his demand. "Why should the English and the United States governments," he said in concluding the acid talks of January 1, 1943, "let General Giraud throw Madagascar into the face of General Eisenhower? The fact that he has got to sit down and take an hour to read a cable is an hour wasted. It is the Treasury's job to make these things easy for him and see that the civilian situation behind is just as smooth as possible.

"But, if we let a De Gaullist . . . or any other striped Frenchman make trouble for us we will be in constant hot water. It just isn't worth it. Until you get these Frenchmen lined up and get what the President calls French unity . . . they will be making constant trouble for us. It may be Madagascar today; it may be Libya tomorrow; and it may be Central Africa the day after; but if we move on the same front, that is one less cause of friction. I want my mind set at peace so I can face this difficult Lend-Lease thing . . . in the next ten days."

Ill with influenza that New Year's Day, Morgenthau spent nearly a month in bed and convalescing, and Roosevelt in that period settled the currency controversy himself. The British, the President told the Cabinet on January 8, 1943, considered De Gaulle's Fighting French the true representatives of the French people. Roosevelt did not agree. He intended to recognize no one as the head of the French government until France was liberated and the French people could act politically. In the interim, he deemed it essential to make it clear to the people of North Africa that they were under military occupation, with General Eisenhower in complete command. The claims of neither Giraud nor De Gaulle appealed to the President, who, in the matter of crossrates, deferred instead to Churchill and to his own preference for simple mathematics in matters of exchange.

With Churchill at Casablanca, Roosevelt reached agreement on many important matters.* After hearing the President's report, Henry Stimson noted in his diary of February 3 that such questions "as the change of the ratio of exchange between the Morocco franc and the dollar" were resolved. Roosevelt "recollected this all right and told me a good story about it. I retaliated by telling him I knew all about this one because Hull had told me it was an agreement 'signed over a drink' by the President at which he laughed and virtually admitted that the other covenants might have been accomplished the same way."

At a Cabinet meeting on February 5, Roosevelt was full of entertaining anecdotes, which on this, as on many other occasions, obscured, doubtless by design, the seriousness of his purpose, and precluded argument from his subordinates. He said that in North Africa he discovered that the Treasury and State Departments had fixed the rate at 75 francs to the dollar. He did not consider that a very good rate, because in converting francs to dollars, the arithmetic came out unevenly. He also found that the British had fixed a rate with De Gaulle at 43.90 francs to the dollar, again a poor figure for computation. So, as he put it to the Cabinet, Roosevelt decided to make it simple by establishing a franc rate of two cents, 50 to the dollar, which by happy coincidence worked out to 200 francs to the pound. "You have made an excellent story of it," Dan Bell complained, "but that isn't all there is to the picture."

Indeed it was not. The new rate overvalued the franc, precisely as Morgenthau had said it would. Further, the British still objected to applying it in Madagascar and Somaliland, where the Free French held out for the prewar rate. Any change, they argued, would shake confidence in the franc, the unit of currency they associated with the

---

* Among others, adoption of the doctrine of "unconditional surrender" and plans for the invasions of Sicily and Italy.

glory of France. For months to come, the softer rate in North Africa rankled Giraud and others who disliked De Gaulle. Still, Roosevelt's solution sufficiently placated Giraud to relieve the pressure on Eisenhower. However casually, the President had served the interests of military efficiency and the politics of his North African allies, British and French alike.

Then and later, Morgenthau felt that Roosevelt had conceded too much. So also, the Secretary feared that American military government in North Africa moved too slowly toward democratizing the area and ridding it of the influence of those who had collaborated with the Nazis. On that account Morgenthau forced the dismissal of Couve de Murville from the office of Secretary General in the headquarters of the High Commissioner. He considered Murville a Vichyite. Though Robert Murphy and De Gaulle disagreed,* the Secretary believed in taking no chances. As he saw it, the true interests of American finance and politics called for a more forceful, independent, and reformist policy not only in North Africa but also even more in Europe, the target for the next Allied attacks.

2. Currencies for the Liberation of Europe

Planning for the invasions of Sicily and Italy intensified differences of opinion in Washington about policy for the period of occupation. Secretary Stimson, General Marshall, and John McCloy resented the criticisms of "jealous New Dealers . . . cherubs around the throne" who objected to the outlook of the Army training school for military government in Charlottesville, Virginia. The "cherubs," for their part, representing the views especially of Secretary of the Interior Harold Ickes, but also, to a lesser degree, of Morgenthau and his fellows in the Treasury, suspected that Stimson, however innocently, was turning over authority for military government to precisely those Wall Street financiers who had been the most bitter

---

* Murphy's confidence in Murville was equalled by his distrust of Morgenthau, a feeling the Secretary fully reciprocated. The two men, according to Murphy's memoir and Morgenthau's recollection, also clashed when the Treasury canceled the release of $7 million of French funds which Murphy wanted to buy supplies for the African government. The Morgenthau Diary contains no information about that episode.

enemies of the New Deal. With the assistance of Hull, Stimson's critics persuaded Roosevelt early in March 1943, to set up an inter-departmental committee to decide questions of policy concerning personnel to follow the Army into occupied territories and take over jobs that were not strictly military in character.

Continual bickering over the assignment of those positions, as well as interdepartmental and international differences about ex-change rates, exhausted Under Secretary of the Treasury Dan Bell, who asked Morgenthau to relieve him of his duties in those areas. The Secretary assigned those responsibilities to Harry White.* Late in March 1943, White complained that the State Department had assumed leadership over financial, monetary, and economic pol-icy. "Harry," Morgenthau replied, ". . . it is partly my fault." During his illness in January, the Secretary had had no energy for international matters, and through much of February he had been preoccupied with a War Bond drive and the tax bill then before Congress. Now he would again turn to the questions on White's mind. "I am glad you are going to pick up the strings," White said. "You are the only one strong enough to defend our position. I can follow you; and I can follow instructions. But unless you take the initiative . . . we are licked because nobody else in the Treasury can do it."

White had begun discussions with the British and the State and War Departments about invasion and occupation currencies for Italy, an enemy power for which the English and Americans could make policy without reference to the jealousies of native factions. Policy stumbled, however, on the question of an exchange rate at the time of attack and thereafter. According to the Treasury's infor-mation, the Italian lira sold on the black market for about seven-eighths of a cent. White therefore considered the State Depart-ment's suggested exchange rate of 50 lire for a dollar much too high. The President, he said, wanted to be very generous at first, to treat the Italians as much as possible as friendly enemies. But White thought it better to begin at a rate of 100 to 1 and then later, if necessary, increase it, rather than to have to reduce it. A rate of two cents would, moreover, cost the United States twice as much for ex-penditures in Sicily and Italy, and reduce by 50 per cent the value of

* See February 25, 1943 order discussed in Chapter III.

pay received by American troops in those areas, unless of course the troops were to exchange their dollar pay on the black market.

In complete agreement, Morgenthau, as he put it, wanted "less cents but more common sense." Supported by Judge Patterson, he persuaded the State Department to accept the Treasury's rate at the end of April 1943. In return, Morgenthau yielded to the preferences of the War and State Departments about invasion and occupation currency. Receding from his own earlier recommendation for the exclusive use of yellow seal dollars as the "spearhead currency," Morgenthau accepted the British proposal for separate invasion currencies, the yellow seal dollar for American forces and a special, military authority pound for the British. He agreed, too, to abandon his suggestion for printing currency of a new design, adaptable for any part of Europe, to be circulated as lira in Italy during the period of occupation. Instead he again followed British counsel, which the State and War Departments had taken for their own. That called for a common occupation currency, an Allied Military lira with an official exchange rate of 100 to the dollar and 400 to the pound.

Policy in liberated areas, according to a directive of Roosevelt of June 3, 1943, fell under "the leadership of the Secretary of State in the coordination here and abroad of civilian agency activities." The Treasury Department, the President had ruled, was "responsible for fixing exchange rates and should assist on monetary, currency control, and general fiscal matters. This important work must be geared in with the plans and activities of the other agencies." But gearing in was not always easy. Early in August the Treasury objected to the State Department's suggestion of a civilian area director for Italy on the ground that the candidate was too conservative politically. Later that month Harry White opposed a proposal of the War Department, which had originated with the British, calling for the removal from military currency of the statement of the Four Freedoms which had been printed on the lira. And in late September Morgenthau questioned a recommendation of General Eisenhower for a change in the lira rate from 100 to 1 to 80 to 1. "At this distance," Morgenthau wrote, "it is difficult for us to understand why the exchange rate . . . should be changed. Therefore, I wish you would ask General Eisenhower if this matter could rest until . . . I . . . review the whole situation." Even before that review, Roosevelt ruled on October 5, 1943, that the rate of 100 to 1 should prevail.

In North Africa and Italy in late October and November, Morgenthau reacted adversely to conditions that seemed to him to reflect weak and inefficient leadership in military government, and, too often, a reactionary British influence. Back in Washington on November 6, 1943, the Secretary talked at length with Harry Hopkins. As Morgenthau put it into his Diary: "Hopkins was very much interested in what I had to say about King Peter and King George.* He did not realize that they were located in Cairo and was very much upset when he heard it. I told him I felt that neither the King of Italy,† King Peter, nor King George should be picked by us, and he agreed entirely. He agreed there would be a revolution if we forced these people to accept these kings. But Hopkins said, 'You know the President has a warm spot for royalty.' "

With Roosevelt, Morgenthau argued that the Italians and the various peoples of the Balkans should be permitted "the right to select their own form of Government," and should not have "any Kings forced upon them." As he saw it, "there is little evidence that this policy is being followed. There is more evidence to indicate that it isn't." The President just listened, and Morgenthau, without a mandate from him to press the matter, let it drop.

While concerned with the invasion of Italy and the planning that preceded it, Morgenthau was also conducting negotiations about currency questions with the governments-in-exile of the western European nations that had fallen to the Germans. In the face of strong protests from those governments, the Secretary insisted upon using yellow seal dollars as the invasion currency for American troops. He also initially intended to have the United States print supplementary military currencies — Belgian francs, Dutch guilder, Norwegian kroner — for the use of American field commanders in procuring goods and services between the time of attack and the time of reinstatement of legitimate, native regimes. The Army, however, feared that such currency would be suspected as counterfeit. It therefore suggested that, before the United States switched from yel-

---

* King Peter of Yugoslavia and King George of Greece.
† King Victor Emmanuel.

low seal dollars to local currencies, the commanding general should consult both the local authorities and the British, who would have been using their own military government notes.

For their part, the British held that the governments-in-exile would resent the use even of yellow seal dollars. Those governments objected to any outside authority issuing full-value money in their sovereign territories. They therefore supported the British proposal for using notes clearly marked as a military currency for temporary purposes. After the first stages of the invasion, the governments-in-exile would supply currencies of their own to British and American forces. As Morgenthau and White saw it, the governments-in-exile had no vote. The United States had agreed to consult them only about exchange rates. "We feel," the Secretary said, "pretty strongly about this. . . . From what I have seen of some of the representatives recently, I don't worry much about some of these governments."

Postponement of the cross-channel invasion until 1944 permitted discussions about currency to proceed at a leisurely pace. Acting for Morgenthau, White ascertained that the British had accurately reported the views of the governments-in-exile. The Belgians, for one, were determined to prevent occupation dollars or pounds from circulating in their nation. To that end, they were prepared to put at the disposal of the American government a sufficient quantity of Belgian notes to cover all needs of American forces. Further, they interpreted the exchange rate between the Belgian franc and the dollar as falling "within the sovereignty of the Belgian Government guaranteed in principle by the Atlantic Charter." The Dutch and Norwegians took a similar position. In August 1943, Morgenthau promised them all to discuss economic conditions and questions of currency at an appropriate time before he made final recommendations to the War Department. Assuring them of his sympathy, he said he was certain that they could understand his disinclination to make decisions so long before the actual liberation of their territories.

Reversing his earlier position, White in October, 1943 recommended the use of currencies of the governments-in-exile, provided that those currencies were made available in such amounts and at such times as American and British commanders considered necessary. Determination of the resulting costs, including adjustments between the British and American governments and between them and the governments-in-exile, would be deferred until after the liberation of Europe. Morgenthau supported White. Like his subordinate, the Secretary was striving to bring Treasury policy into conformity with the preferences of the War and State Departments. Whatever the advantages of the Treasury's earlier proposal for a common, American-printed currency for all areas liberated in Europe, the greater advantages now lay, as Morgenthau saw it, in easing relationships among the Allies in the months prior to their joint attack on the continent.

But on two matters the Secretary would not budge. First, backed wholeheartedly by the President, he held out for the use of yellow seal dollars for the payment of American troops during the spearhead phase of the invasion. As he put it to the Army on April 10, 1944, "when Ike shoves off, we'll give him . . . gold seal currency and . . . we'll tell these people that we're going to quit fooling around and we'll go ahead and print some up." Once invaded areas were secure and ready for civilian control, then the governments-in-exile could utilize their own currencies. Until then, Morgenthau intended to keep Eisenhower abreast of his needs. "I think our position," the Army spokesman commented, "has been with the Treasury right along."

So also, while ready to accept Belgian and Dutch currency for the period of occupation after the invasion, Morgenthau, in accordance with White's advice and in opposition to the State Department, refused a prior commitment about settling accounts. Advances to the United States of francs and guilders, he insisted, were to remain only bookkeeping transactions until after hostilities were entirely over, when Congress would have some hand in the ultimate settlement. Here, too, Roosevelt supported the Treasury.

The Dutch therefore asked for a loan from the Reconstruction Finance Corporation to facilitate their supply of guilders to the United States. For the State Department, Acheson supported that request on April 28, 1944. The Treasury's refusal to furnish dollars to cover disbursements of guilders for troop pay after the first phase of the invasion, he said, had disturbed the Dutch and other governments-in-exile who interpreted their Lend-Lease agreements with

the United States to include an American obligation to provide
those dollars. The United States was also demanding payments in
dollars for civilian relief to the Dutch. Further, in Great Britain,
Australia, North Africa, and elsewhere the United States was supplying dollars to cover troop payments, and the exiled European
governments felt discriminated against.

Morgenthau asked permission to defer judgment. He might feel a
little more sympathetic to the State Department, he said, if that department were to come over to the Treasury's recommendations for
policy in Argentina.* By May 5, 1944, Morgenthau, as he then put
it, "was like sour cream; I am gradually turning to butter. . . . But
it is a very slow process." Acheson, who was in any case pressing
the Treasury's policy for Argentina, begged Morgenthau not to con-
tend that those two issues had anything to do with each other. In
the end they did not, for though the State Department did not yield,
Morgenthau did mellow. On June 8, 1944, just before the invasion
of Normandy, the Treasury agreed to credit the governments-in-
exile each month or so with dollars equivalent to the amounts of
currencies those governments had advanced for the payment of American troops. "When the Queen of the Netherlands presents you with
a bill for the cost of invasion," Morgenthau told Roosevelt, "you
have a credit."

Meanwhile the Treasury, at the President's request, had deferred
action on a loan to the Dutch. In June Morgenthau believed that a
private loan from the Chase National Bank of $100 million would
obviate the need to turn to the Reconstruction Finance Corporation. Roosevelt, however, had some interest in a reconstruction loan
for the Netherlands as a precedent for other, similar ventures.
"American industry in the postwar period," the President said,
"may probably need all the foreign orders that can be safely accepted in order to benefit employment and dispose of surpluses.
. . . I should like to have us both give further consideration to the
matter." For the while, the Dutch, assured of dollar credits as they
were, did not need the loan. In giving them that assurance, Morgenthau once again had surrendered his own inclination for minimizing American costs and obligations to the State Department's
advices for decreasing tensions within the Grand Alliance.

* See Section 5, this chapter.

That calculated subordination of finance to politics, as the Secretary saw it, in no sense precluded his own continuing interest in the political issues of military government, and in their implications for the postwar world. Just as he had worried about British influence in Italy and the Balkans, so he worried about it elsewhere in Europe. He was anxious particularly about the semi-formal discussions, begun in London in 1943 between British authorities and Ambassador Winant, General Eisenhower, and their staffs, on the subject of occupation policy. Though the Army assured Morgenthau that the Combined Chiefs of Staff in Washington had final authority, the Secretary realized that the planners in London would make telling recommendations. He wanted some one sympathetic to his own opinions to represent the United States in the Army's negotiations about monetary and fiscal matters. Especially was he eager to prevent the assumption of that role by any of the New York financiers so obviously cherished by their old associates, now senior officials in the War Department.

The appointment of a fiscal adviser to the Civil Affairs group in London became a matter of urgency in November 1943. On behalf of Henry Stimson, George Harrison, long the head of the New York Federal Reserve Bank, suggested to Morgenthau the availability of Jay Crane of the Standard Oil Company of New Jersey. Morgenthau had found Crane an able officer of the New York Federal Reserve Bank in the early years of the New Deal, but the Secretary in 1943 opposed recruiting a senior executive of a major oil company. Rather, he urged the selection of a committed New Dealer. Of exactly the contrary view, Henry Stimson complained in his diary that "Morgenthau's appointments in the Treasury have reflected in some of them a narrow political view. . . . I think we can do a little better ourselves."

During the first week in December, when Stimson came up with new names from the banking community, Morgenthau repeated his opposition to any Wall Street man. Stimson for his part sought an outstanding financier whom the British would recognize as expert and accept on even terms. Looking for such a man outside of Wall Street, Stimson offered the position to Herbert Feis, but Feis disqualified himself because he feared that as a Jew he could not function objectively in negotiations concerning Germany.

On December 20, 1943, Morgenthau took the matter to the President. George Harrison, he reminded Roosevelt, while a personal friend of Stimson, had cooperated with the Bank of England in 1932–1933 in creating expectations about American monetary policy that the President had found objectionable.* As Morgenthau put it in his Diary: "I had ample time to tell the President . . . that George Harrison would be sitting there pulling the strings on what was going on in London; I gave him the names of the various people recommended; . . . how Stimson said he did not want . . . anybody . . . connected with any other Department. The President said, 'That's just too bad. . . . Who do you want?' I said either Lauch Currie or Jim Landis. He said, 'I think Lauch Currie would be good. He is doing lots of odds and ends and this will give him a lot to do.' I said, 'If you don't want a repetition of '32 you had better do something.' He said he would."

In Morgenthau's opinion, Lauchlin Currie, a Canadian-born economist then on the White House staff, had the necessary technical training, a dedication to the New Deal, and an understanding of Treasury policy. But when McCloy, at Morgenthau's request, told Stimson about the recommendation of Currie, the Secretary of War became "as mad as a boil." Furious that Morgenthau had spoken to Roosevelt before consulting him, Stimson did not want Currie and would not take him unless the President so ordered. Army men in general had not found Currie impressive. "After all," McCloy concluded, "Stimson is doing the hiring."

Stimson was making a mistake, Morgenthau replied. Because Currie worked for the President, Roosevelt had to be asked about him before any one else was consulted. Stimson need feel no pique. "Let's be perfectly frank about this," Morgenthau went on, ". . . This job in London is very important." Whoever held it would help to shape monetary, financial, and economic developments throughout Europe for the coming decade. Such a man had to represent the President's views, not just the Army's. "Well," McCloy said, "we want someone who will be mutually acceptable."

When no such man appeared, Morgenthau in May 1944, sent Wil-

---

* Especially proposals for preserving the gold standard and for a pound-dollar rate that overvalued the dollar, to the disadvantage of American commerce; those proposals died with the London Economic Conference.

liam H. Taylor to London as the Treasury's — not the Army's — representative on the Combined Civil Affairs Committee. Taylor had earlier worked in the Treasury, served a long term as the alternate American member on the Chinese Stabilization Board, landed with the invasion forces in North Africa, and moved then to the North African Economic Board. He had the kind of experience Morgenthau valued for directing occupation policy in Europe. So, too, did Colonel Bernard Bernstein, a former treasury lawyer who was on Eisenhower's staff. Neither man had much influence on the formulation of policy, but both kept the Treasury informed about proceedings in London of interest to the Secretary. For the time being, he asked no more. In the spring of 1944, the technical and, much more, the political problems of preparing currencies for France and Germany were dominating all other aspects of the Treasury's concern for Europe.

3. The Franc: Mirror of French Prestige

For American policy makers, the problems of France resembled those of no other nation, for, as usual, all France was divided into three parts during the months preceding the Allied attack on Europe. There was occupied France, the area in the north from which the Germans had to be driven. There was the government of France at Vichy, the creature of the Germans, established subject to their change of mind in the south. Roosevelt had dealt with that government of Pétain and Laval in the expectation, only partially fulfilled, that such negotiations would ease the way to victory, as they had in some degree in North Africa. There was also the France of Charles de Gaulle, Free France, Fighting France — the union of brave and patriotic Frenchmen combating the Nazis in the *maquis* of occupied France and of Vichy France, under arms in French colonial areas, in spirit in exile in London, everywhere straining to erase the humiliation of 1940 and to restore France to her station as a great power.

De Gaulle, who personified that France, was head of the French Committee of National Liberation, the shadow-government that a host of loyal Frenchmen served. But the French Committee was not a goverment-in-exile in the view of the United States and Great Britain. De Gaulle's France, while an ally, had a legal status in Washington and London rather less than that of Belgium or Holland. Still, the assistance of De Gaulle's France, of the various resistance groups within geographical France, had special importance for the invasion, in which De Gaulle envisaged a major role for himself and his army. Indeed, for his part, De Gaulle considered the invasion an operation within his sovereignty, within the area under his legal authority. Churchill distrusted and Roosevelt disliked De Gaulle, who in turn resented the treatment he received. De Gaulle thought of himself and of the Committee of National Liberation as the government of France, while Roosevelt and Churchill, though not without disagreement within their own administrations, thought of France as a nation that could have no legal government until after liberation and free elections. Those conflicting assumptions complicated invasion planning, including the planning for a currency for France. And the conflict racked Morgenthau, whose loyalties, as always, were to Roosevelt, but whose sentiments, insofar as those loyalties permitted, lay strongly with the Free French.

A familiar issue confronted the Secretary in the late summer of 1943. Experience in North Africa had demonstrated by that time that the dollar-sterling-franc ratio set by the President at Casablanca overvalued the franc, just as Morgenthau had said it did. British and American financial representatives now advised that the rate of 50 francs to the dollar made it impossible for French Africa to sell its exportable commodities on the world market. The Allied governments therefore had difficulty purchasing strategic materials in French Africa at prices based upon the official rate. A much lower rate was needed, one close to the Treasury's long-standing preference of 75 or 100 francs to the dollar. But the French Committee for National Liberation, interpreting the rate as a symbol of political prestige and a factor in national morale, wanted the 50 franc rate to apply in France after the liberation. After months of doubt, in May 1944, Morgenthau agreed with the understanding that an "equitable adjustment" for American expenditures in France might reflect a lower rate.

The French Committee had meanwhile made concessions to the United States on the question of currency. Initially Morgenthau had endorsed the Committee's proposal, which the State Department supported, for franc currency for use by American troops during their operations in France. The Committee was to issue that currency, though the notes would carry only the legend: "La République Française." Secretary of War Stimson immediately objected. The United States, he argued, did not wish to recognize the Committee as sovereign in France, particularly during the interim between the invasion and a French election. For that period he demanded some kind of military money to be issued on the authority of the Allied commanders. The Free French replied that in Norway, Holland, and Belgium, Great Britain and the United States were planning to use the national currencies, but Stimson pointed out that those nations had governments-in-exile which the United States and Great Britain had recognized; France did not.

Deferring to the War Department, Morgenthau on December 23, 1943, recommended a franc currency for military use inscribed on one side with the words "La République Française," and further "Émis en France." * The currency would not indicate that the issuing authority was the Allied Military Commander. The reverse side of the notes would display a French flag in full color and the words "Liberté, Egalité, Fraternité." Morgenthau also recommended permitting the French Committee of National Liberation to place an order for currency of their own design, which the Treasury would hold for release whenever the heads of government in Great Britain and the United States so ordered.

Those suggestions won the approval of the War, Navy, and State Departments, but not of the President. In a memorandum to Morgenthau of January 6, 1944, Roosevelt objected to the words "République Française." He preferred instead to say only "La France." "In view of the fact that this will be issued by the Allied Military Commander," he wrote, "I would put in the middle, in color, the French flag, supported by the American flag and the British flag on either side. I have no objection to having the French Committee of National Liberation buy finished French currency over here, but it cannot have on it the words 'République Française.' How do you know what the next permanent Government of France is going to be? My guess is that it will be headed by a mandarin."

* Issued in France.

The omission of the phrase "République Française," John J. Mc-Cloy said to Morgenthau on January 8, 1944, would be "fraught with great danger. . . . The more we rap General de Gaulle with republicanism, the better off we are." Morgenthau wholly agreed. Later that day he and McCloy tried to convince Roosevelt, who was adamant. "How do you know what kind of a government you will have when the war is over?" the President asked again. "Maybe it will be an empire."

"That is just what we don't want to imply," Morgenthau pointed out. ". . . It seems to me if you put on the words La République Française, it isn't going to tie your hands at all."

"Henry," Roosevelt said, "you talk just like the British Foreign Office."

"Mr. President," Morgenthau replied, "I have never been so insulted in ten years!"

But as the discussion continued, according to Morgenthau's Diary: "The answer always came back that he didn't want anything on the money which would indicate what kind of a government it was going to be. I argued and McCloy argued and while the President was in a grand humor, he had all his 'Dutch up,' and you couldn't budge him at all. He said, 'I have heard all these arguments. De Gaulle is on the wane.' . . . We got off the 'Liberté, Egalité, Fraternité'; he said we couldn't have that. He also asked for 'La France' . . . off. So it gets back to the flag and nothing else."

Harry White, upon hearing the Secretary's report, asked who Roosevelt thought would supplant De Gaulle. "He wouldn't say," Morgenthau replied. "But besides his own prejudice against De Gaulle, he now says that Stalin has no use for any Frenchman. . . . In the first place, the new government cannot include anybody — this is Stalin speaking — who has ever been a member of the French government before."

"Oh, oh," White interrupted, "Stalin is beginning to issue orders, is he?"

Replying indirectly, Morgenthau said Hull had come around to his position, though the Secretary of State still called "De Gaulle a polecat." Churchill, Morgenthau felt, was the main influence behind Roosevelt, but White noted that most of Churchill's subordinates supported De Gaulle, so that if Morgenthau were correct, the Prime Minister spoke only for himself. Whatever the influence, Roosevelt's views prevailed, and the French Committee, like the American Cabinet, had no choice but to go along.

To ease French feelings, Eisenhower in May 1944, let French authorities organize and provide necessary financial services and facilities, and operate their own economic and fiscal system. He also consented to having the French Committee of National Liberation issue the primary decree declaring the supplemental francs legal tender. But those steps were to be subjected to the "overriding power for emergency action by Allied Commanders in absence of or failure of French authority."

Morgenthau expected the French to perform admirably. With Hull, he signed a memorandum that Roosevelt approved on May 24, 1944, to govern the printing of a new franc currency for the French Committee. Pierre Mendès-France, the Commissioner of Finance for the Committee, had outlined to Morgenthau and others in Washington the measures that the Committee planned for penalizing collaborators, for imposing effective taxation on war profiteers, and for combating inflation. The Committee intended to issue a new and distinctive currency after the liberation, and to call in all outstanding notes issued during the German occupation, as well as those issued during the American military occupation. In order to put the program into effect, the French had to start printing currency at once, for which they needed the assistance of the American Treasury. The Committee understood that the new issue of currency could not bear inscriptions or symbols that raised political issues. It also understood that the new notes would remain under the control of the United States government until that government made the Committee responsible for French civil affairs. As Morgenthau observed, the Committee had now met all of the conditions Roosevelt had prescribed.

For his part, Morgenthau had begun to prepare to assist the Committee's effort to check inflation in France. American troops, receiving far more money than other Allied soldiers or French civilians, would spur inflation unless their pay were diverted from expenditures for consumer goods in short supply in France. General Eisenhower and Secretary of War Stimson, however, objected to any scheme that arbitrarily reduced the pay the soldiers actually received in the field. Morgenthau, also in principle opposed to mandatory withholding, hoped, with the cooperation of the Army, to persuade American troops to increase their purchases of war bonds. Further, he promised Treasury support for War Department proposals to regulate troop expenditures by forbidding all purchases in restaurants and hotels and by retarding the process through which soldiers could exchange dollars for francs. At the Treasury's request, the War Department agreed to adopt a compulsory savings system if the need arose, and to encourage soldiers to partonize postexchanges and other official stores, instead of civilian vendors.

The Army's plans for reducing troop expenditures satisfied Pierre Mendès-France who called at the Treasury to say goodbye just before he returned to London at the end of May 1944. He felt he had made substantial progress while in the United States. He would like to have obtained Roosevelt's agreement to the Committee's authority for issuing francs, but he realized that was a political question Morgenthau could not resolve. He was pleased with the arrangements for printing franc notes, with the Treasury's acceptance of the rate of exchange at 50 francs to a dollar, and with the prospects for Franco-American cooperation in stemming inflation. Most of all, he said, he was grateful for the Treasury's help, and he hoped soon to see Morgenthau in Paris. Morgenthau hoped so, too, and like Mendès-France, felt that negotiations had worked out well. Both men were excessively optimistic.

Mendès-France and Morgenthau had only recently parted, American troops were not yet secure on the Cherbourg peninsula, when De Gaulle provoked a new crisis in Franco-American relations that was embarrassing alike to commanders in the field and to statesmen in Washington. From the Treasury's representative in London, Morgenthau heard early in June that De Gaulle "had been acting up terribly. . . . He was . . . not only arrogant, but . . . actually vicious." He was especially angry that the design for the franc on which his subordinates had agreed did not name the Republic of France or the Committee of Liberation as issuing authority. That omission, he held, undermined his dignity as the leader of the resistance to the Nazis, and challenged the grandeur of the French republic and the French nation.

De Gaulle, so Churchill informed Roosevelt on June 9, 1944, was demanding that General Eisenhower, in a pending proclamation about currency, refer specifically either to the "Provisional Government of France" or the "Provisional Government of the French Republic." If Eisenhower would do so, then De Gaulle would issue a supporting proclamation of his own, putting his endorsement and that of the Committee of Liberation on the new francs. Churchill was worried. If General de Gaulle did not endorse the issue, the notes would not have any backing, and Great Britain and the United States would separately or jointly be responsible to redeem them. Eager to avoid liability for the currency, Churchill was even more intent on preventing De Gaulle from causing difficulties for Eisenhower, perhaps by denouncing the currency as false money. Further, the Prime Minister had examined specimens of the notes and found them very easy to forge. He urged Roosevelt to look at the notes and to decide whether England and the United States should allow De Gaulle to obtain new status as his fee for backing them, or should assume the burden for the time being, improve the issue later on, and make the settlement at the peace table.

Disturbed by Churchill's cable, Morgenthau was embarrassed by a radio broadcast from London that asserted that the French National Committee had never been consulted about the currency. "I am not going to take this," the Secretary told Dan Bell on June 10, "and I want a statement before sunset today that Jean Monnet was in my office and agreed to the whole thing. . . . I don't give a goddamn what the State Department, or the War Department says, I want the public to know that I did this working it out with Monnet . . . and with Mendès-France, the recognized . . . Minister of Finance."

The situation, Bell advised that evening, was too complex to be handled by pointing to that agreement. The Minister of Foreign Affairs for the Committee of Liberation, speaking from Africa, had condemned the Allies for printing any francs. The provisional government, he had said, could not "accord any legal value to the . . . paper." Of course the United States did not recognize the Committee as the provisional government, but there were those in Great Britain who believed that both English-speaking powers should do so at their first opportunity, and the question of the currency as it related to De Gaulle's status had become a matter of large political importance within Parliament and for Churchill. Those hoping to embarrass the Prime Minister, according to reports received in Washington, were using the currency issue as an excuse for demanding recognition of De Gaulle and his group as the government of France. Anything that Monnet or Mendès-France might say about previous arrangements with the United States Treasury would highlight a matter that the United States would do better, for the time being, to obscure.

Nevertheless Morgenthau wanted to proceed. "I would get Jean Monnet in a room," he said. "I'd hold a gun to his head and make him sign a statement that he had approved this thing." But Monnet, Bell remarked, while approving the notes, had never approved of the United States' issuing them. So reminded, Morgenthau concluded that "as Secretary of the Treasury, . . . I should answer the President. . . . Should we assume responsibility for this currency, even if De Gaulle denounces it? . . . And my answer is: We've gone so far that we've got to assume responsibility." As to whether De Gaulle was to sign a proclamation supporting the currency, Morgenthau said that he would not advise the President; that question fell to the Department of State.

De Gaulle's conduct, Morgenthau felt, had been utterly outrageous. "With our men on the beaches of France," he said, "this fellow comes along and holds . . . a gun to our backs." In that mood, the Secretary approved the draft of a reply for Roosevelt to send Churchill which Bell, Harry White, and John McCloy had prepared:

I share your view that this currency issue is being exploited to stampede us into according full recognition to the Comité. Personally I do not think the currency situation . . . is as critical as it might first appear. Nor do I feel that it is essential from the point of view of the acceptability of the supplemental currency that De Gaulle make any statement of support. . . . I propose that De Gaulle should be informed as follows:

1. We intend to continue to use the supplementary franc currency in exactly the same manner as we have planned and as . . . has been fully understood by Messieurs Monnet and Mendès-France of the French Comité.

2. If for any reason the supplemental currency is not acceptable to the French public, General Eisenhower has full authority to use yellow seal dollars and British Military Authority notes. Accordingly, if De Gaulle incites the French people into refusing to accept supplementary francs . . . one of the certain consequences will be the depreciation of the French franc in terms of dollars and sterling in a black market which will accentuate and reveal the weaknesses of the French monetary system. This is one of the important reasons why we accepted the request of the French Comité that we not use yellow seal dollars and BMA notes as a spearhead currency. . . .

I would certainly not importune De Gaulle to make any supporting statement. . . . Provided it is clear that he acts entirely on his own responsibility and without our concurrence he can sign any statement . . . in whatever capacity he likes, even that of the King of Siam.

As far as the appearance of the notes is concerned, . . . I have looked at them again and think them adequate. I am informed by the Bureau of Engraving and Printing counterfeiting experts that they will be extremely difficult to counterfeit by virtue of the intricate color combination. . . . The French representatives here not only approved the note but were satisfied with the design and the color.

After consulting Hull and Stimson, Roosevelt on June 12 sent that message to Churchill.* Hull, Stimson observed in his diary, hated De Gaulle so fiercely that he was almost incoherent on the subject, and Stimson himself distrusted the General greatly. Roosevelt's position, Stimson believed, was correct theoretically and logically, but regrettably unrealistic, for circumstances required an immediate reconciliation between the British and American governments even if that entailed provisional recognition of De Gaulle.

Developments in England forced others to move toward Stimson's view. To Morgenthau on June 16, 1944, McCloy described the heated debate under way in London where Anthony Eden had thrown down a gauntlet to Churchill on the question of recognizing

* The President added only one sentence: "It seems clear that a prima donna does not change his spots."

the provisional government of De Gaulle. Eden was making it a personal issue, on which the future of the Churchill government might depend. Further, the British were making it seem as if the currency were just another American scheme. General Marshall, McCloy also reported, was in a white fury with De Gaulle. If the American people could know, Marshall had said, what De Gaulle had been doing to hamper the invasion — the actual military operations, if that ever leaked out, it would sweep "the whole damn thing aside," but the story was so outrageous Marshall feared that, if he released it, it would provoke too strong a reaction and play into the hands of American isolationists. More important, Marshall, like Stimson, felt that the need for Anglo-American cooperation during the fighting made it necessary to find some way to resolve disagreements about De Gaulle.

Stimson had contrived a formula for that reconciliation. The United States, he suggested to Roosevelt, should authorize Eisenhower to deal with the French Committee as the authority responsible for civil administration outside of the combat zone. That formula involved less than provisional recognition but more than Roosevelt would yield. The President, according to McCloy, told Stimson he did not want to compromise on a "moral principle." That principle, as Roosevelt saw it, guaranteed the French people a free election to determine their government. Accordingly, the President would not now permit that "jackenape" to seize the government. Indeed, he was unmoved even by Stimson's suggestion that he pledge De Gaulle to holding an election.

Yet Roosevelt's reply to Churchill was reducing the temperature of the currency problem. The American threat to use gold seal dollars quieted the Free French and their English supporters. Monnet and Mendès-France, moreover, were taking steps to remind De Gaulle that they had earlier consented to the American design for the supplementary francs. The matter of currency, Churchill believed by June 21, 1944, was no longer critical. Still, the Prime Minister felt that the United States would be morally responsible for redeeming the supplementary francs unless there were some further agreement with the French Committee.

Morgenthau intended to define the terms for any agreement in Washington. With the help of McCloy, on June 23, 1944, he pre-

pared a draft reply for Roosevelt to send Churchill about the redemption of the supplemental francs. There was no need, that draft
held, to assume that the United States and Great Britain were responsible for the currency "merely because no understanding has
been reached with the French Committee." The Supreme Allied
Commander alone had authority to issue currency for France. Ultimately that currency would be redeemed "like any other good currency by the government of the country in which it is issued," just as
in the case of Belgium or Norway.

At first the Treasury's draft displeased the President. "I don't like
issuing money which isn't money," he said at a White House meeting of June 26. After Dan Bell described the proposed scheme in
detail, Roosevelt relented. "These financial matters," he said, "are
very difficult to explain to a layman." With one small alteration, he
then approved the draft. It put to rest Churchill's worries about
redemption.

There remained the fierce French sensitivities about sovereignty.
The French Committee, Mendès-France admitted in a letter to
Morgenthau, had known of the American intention to use the supplemental notes. The Committee, however, had never agreed "on
the matter of the issuing authority." Mendès-France had never
wanted a military currency issued on French territory, and had
never meant to suggest that he believed a major political problem
could be solved on the technical level.

Neither, of course, had Morgenthau, who had, rather, hoped that
the technical solution implied a political understanding. In Wash-
ington on July 5, 1944, during a brief absence from the Bretton
Woods Conference,* the Secretary suggested to John McCloy that
Eisenhower issue a directive recognizing the French Committee and
De Gaulle as a "de facto authority." That phrase, he felt, might suit
Roosevelt better than had Stimson's earlier suggestion of "provi-
sional" recognition of De Gaulle. McCloy, though he feared that
Roosevelt would recognize the new phrase as an old horse, agreed to
join Morgenthau in commending it to the White House. So did
Hull. "We should like to suggest to you a fresh approach to the
French situation," they wrote the President. The United States
should deal with the French Committee either as the "civil author-

* See Chapter V.

ity" or the "administrative authority" or the "de facto authority" in France "to reach agreements on civil affairs administration along the lines of those reached with Belgium, the Netherlands and Norway." The agreements would be temporary, pending selection of a French government by the free choice of the French people, but the French Committee would become the issuing authority for the supplemental francs.

With De Gaulle then in Washington to be entertained and appeased, Roosevelt was unusually malleable. After designating his preference for the use of the phrase "de facto authority," he wrote across the memorandum Morgenthau had submitted: "OK in principle. Let me see the agreement first." On July 7, 1944, he approved the agreement, which followed the lines of the memorandum. "I am very pleased," Morgenthau told his staff, "that I went down and had a little part in it."

The settlement of the currency question relieved Eisenhower of one major irritation but left untouched another matter of concern to the Treasury. Prices in France rose dramatically in spite of the success of the Department and the Army in persuading American troops to save their pay and otherwise discouraging them from stimulating demand. But the obligations of war prevented the United States Army from diverting transportation and supplies to a degree sufficient to relieve inflation. And in the meantime, American troops, during both the fighting and the occupation, like all soldiers in all times and places, looked for relaxation from combat or fatigue and for mementos of their service. In that search they spent some fraction of their pay on luxuries, whether perfume or wine or entertainment, all of which were beyond the reach of the impoverished civilian population. Consequently the presence of the troops occasioned some resentment and contributed some dimension to inflation. The solution to those problems had to await the formulation of civilian policy and the application of necessary controls after normal channels of trade and supply could begin again to function.

Yet the experience in France, like the previous experience in other areas which the Allies reconquered from the Nazis, pointed to the kinds of difficulties which would harass the Allies when in time they gained power over Germany and Japan. There they would again confront the problem of inflation. And before they triumphed, they would have to settle questions of currency that involved the military efficiency and the political cohesion of the Grand Alliance. By June 1944, those questions, as they arose in planning for Germany, were already engaging Morgenthau.

4. Allied Military Marks

Significant planning for occupation currency in Germany commenced early in 1944, some six months before the invasion of Europe and more than a year before Allied troops reached the German border. Germany presented something of a new problem. In Belgium or the Netherlands or Norway, British and American forces were moving into territory held by the enemy but represented by a properly constituted and recognized government-in-exile. In North Africa and France, the French Committee stood ready to assume authority. In Italy a hostile government reigned, but very rapidly that government was supplanted by a cooperative regime. In Germany, however, victory would initiate a long period of Allied military government in which the German people would have no voice. But the United States could not make unilateral decisions about currency or any other aspect of military government, for all plans for Germany began in 1944 with the assumption that the United Kingdom and the Soviet Union would cooperate in the occupation and would pursue unified political and economic policies.*

Experience in North Africa and elsewhere recommended abandonment of yellow seal dollars except, perhaps, during the heavy fighting at the outset. The circulation of the dollars had weakened confidence in local currency, which put a strain on economic life and political stability. In North Africa, too, the maintenance of a uniform rate of exchange had proved difficult. The Treasury and the War Departments now feared that if yellow seal dollars were used in Germany, local vendors would refuse to deliver goods for Reichsmarks and demand dollars instead. That would destroy the value of the Reichsmark, shake the economy, and impede supplies of food and other essentials for military operations. The two Departments therefore preferred printing Allied Military Marks designed

* Later France was also given a part to play; see Chapter VIII.

to circulate alongside of Reichsmarks and serve as currency for payment of troops. In order to guarantee every soldier his full pay, the War Department needed also to establish a military exchange rate. The Army could then convert dollars and marks at that rate on request of any GI. That conversion, however, was to imply no responsibility for redemption of the military marks, which would be the financial obligation of the German government established at the end of the occupation. Further, the Army recognized no responsibility at all for converting Reichsmarks, though their value would partly depend, since they were to be exchangeable with military marks, on the military rate. Finally, the Treasury and War Departments, on the understanding that occupied Germany was to be treated as a political and economic whole, believed the Russians should use a currency identical with that of British and American forces, for a different currency would bring disunity.

With the approval of the British Embassy, Harry White, acting for the American Treasury, first discussed the question of occupation currency for Germany with Russian financial representatives late in 1943. They could only refer the issue to Moscow. Reporting from there on January 26, 1944, American Ambassador Averell Harriman observed that the British Embassy had received instructions different from his own. Great Britain envisaged the use of a currency marked in Russian characters, to be printed in the United States and the United Kingdom and then supplied to the Soviet Union as stocks became available. The Americans, in contrast, expected all occupation currency to employ the Roman-type characters common to the United States and Great Britain. But by January 29, the British Embassy in Moscow had received new instructions from London stipulating that insofar as possible all occupation forces should use identical currency. Since currency plates and printing presses in Germany might be demolished by the Nazis, the British agreed with Washington that it was not safe to depend on an adequate supply of Reichsmarks, and that the United States and the United Kingdom should therefore provide occupation marks for the payment of troops and as a supplementary currency. As Harriman reported it: "Great importance is attached by the British Government to the Russian Government's participation in this arrangement." The British, he said, had envisaged inscribing

Russian characters on the currency precisely for the purpose of pleasing the Russians. The question of the characters was wholly subordinate to the need for uniformity.

The first Soviet opinion reached the Treasury on February 1, 1944. The Russians felt "that the question of the kind of currency that would be used . . . in Germany was too important . . . for them to rush into a decision. . . . They were giving the matter further consideration." That delay, though characteristic, was crippling, for the Treasury and the War Departments considered it essential to begin printing currency not later than February 14, 1944, if production were to take care of Soviet requirements. The Treasury had at least to know whether the Russians expected to use the mark designed for the United States and the United Kingdom, and if not, what alternative they proposed to adopt.

Pressed for a decision, Soviet Foreign Minister Vyacheslav Molotov responded on February 11 in a long letter to Harriman. The Soviet Union, Molotov wrote, shared the wish of the British and American governments to collaborate in the issuance of military currency for Germany during the period of invasion and occupation. The Soviet Union also agreed to American proposals for the design of that currency, and for printing on it the phrase "Allied Military Authorities." The Russians awaited an American suggestion for an exchange rate between the occupation mark and the Reichsmark. More significantly, the Soviet Commissariat for Finance considered it expedient to print serial numbers on all notes, and important to prepare a part of the printing within the Soviet Union "in order that a constant supply of currency may be guaranteed to the Red Army." In order to make the marks printed in Russia identical with those manufactured in the United States, the Commissariat for Finance needed a list of serial numbers, models of paper and colors, and plates for printing the various denominations of the currency.

The Russian request for the plates, received at the Treasury on February 28, elicited an alarmed negative from Alvin W. Hall, Director of the Bureau of Engraving and Printing. "To acquiesce to such an unprecedented request," he wrote Daniel Bell, "would create serious complications." It would make accountability impossible. Worse, by inviolable custom, bank note manufacturers retained possession of all plates they used for the printing of any currency or bonds for any country or bank. Hall urged the perpetuation of that rule. The contractor printing the Allied Military Authorities marks was under strong safeguards and heavy bond to insure against misappropriation, loss, or improper use of the plates, paper, or currency. A scandal might follow removal of those precautions, yet the Treasury could hardly force the Soviet Union to preserve them. Further, the process of manufacture of invasion currency, extremely complex in itself, had to proceed under ideal and controlled conditions which would be hard, if not impossible, to duplicate. Designed to prevent efforts at counterfeit, the AMA marks were manufactured with special inks and dyes intended to produce a quality of color and engraving that Hall believed no one other than the contractor could provide. Opposed to furnishing duplicate plates to anyone for any reason, Hall was "ready and willing to assist the Russian Government in the development of new designs of invasion currency for Germany" and to supply inks and paper for that purpose.

Indirectly, of course, Hall was proposing that the Russians adopt an invasion and occupation currency of their own. That suggestion disturbed Harry White, who at a meeting on March 7, 1944, said that the Russians would construe Hall's answer as an expression of lack of confidence in their handling of the plates. Under Secretary Bell, however, defended Hall. The Treasury, he said, had never made currency plates available to anybody, nor had private companies. The plates in question were the property of the Forbes Company of Boston which, if the Treasury insisted on the delivery of duplicate sets to the Russians, might refuse to print further currency for the United States on the ground that security controls had been removed. Bell was sure that the Treasury through the Bureau of Engraving and Printing could deliver a sufficient amount of currency to the Russians without supplying plates for separate production within the Soviet Union.

Nevertheless White, according to the memorandum reporting the meeting, was "loath to turn the Russian request down without further review. . . . He called attention to the fact that in this instance we were not printing American currency, but Allied currency and that Russia was one of the allies who must be trusted to the same degree and to the same extent as the other allies. He wondered if it wouldn't be possible to talk to the Russian Ambassador here and without settling the question concerning the plates at this time, ask the Russians what their currency needs . . . would be as of a series of specific dates. . . . If the Russians would give us such information it might then be possible to talk to them in terms of delivering the currency in adequate amounts. . . . White said he thought that it would be advisable to review the whole matter with the Secretary before proceeding further. In the event that it was still considered inexpedient to make the plates available to the Russians at this time . . . White further advised that the matter should be cleared with the State and War Departments. Unless State concurrence were obtained . . . it would be possible for the charge to be made . . . that the Treasury, without considering the political implications of its action, had rejected this proposal on a narrow accountancy basis. . . . Bell said that he would review the matter again and would discuss it with . . . White at a subsequent meeting."

The following day, March 8, 1944, Bell drafted a cable to the Soviet Union based on Hall's memorandum denying the Russian request for the plates. In conference with Bell and White, Morgenthau decided to withhold that cable and instead to "discuss the matter orally with the Soviet Ambassador." At the Secretary's home on the evening of March 18, Ambassador Andrei Gromyko said that the Russians, in spite of all the technical problems that Morgenthau had reported, still wanted the plates. In a memorandum about the ensuing discussion, Harry White wrote:

> The Secretary replied that he was sorry that the Soviet government still wanted the plates after his explanation of the difficulties and that he had not expected that they would. He said he would like again to explain the difficulties. . . . He said that since he had last spoken to the Ambassador that the Treasury had again contacted the Forbes Company about the request. The Forbes Company repeated its insistence that it could not go on with the contract if a duplicate set of plates were given out. The Secretary stressed the fact that we were prepared to make available to the Soviet Government the cur-

rency that they needed whereas if we were to give them a duplicate set of plates the matter would be delayed long beyond what
he thought was the time schedule provided to us by the Army.
   He urged the Ambassador to send some of his representatives
to the Forbes Company plant . . . to talk with their people
. . . and to see the magnitude of the task. He thought that if
they would do that they would have a better idea of the difficulties that would beset the Soviet Government printing job. . . .
The Ambassador responded that he would be glad to send
these men up but he doubted very much if it would make any
difference at all in the request of his Government. The Secretary then said he would get the exact information of the time
that would be required to provide the necessary currency if the
Treasury had to take the job over from the Forbes people, and
also the time that it would require for the Soviet Government
to begin production on a large scale if plates were sent to them
now. He . . . would inform the Ambassador within forty-
eight hours of the information he obtained.

On March 21, Alvin Hall sent Morgenthau the relevant data. In
order to meet the existing timetable, the Forbes Company could not
part with the plates. The company also still maintained that the
Russians could not produce exact duplicates of the currency even if
they had the plates. Further, if the plates were sent to Russia, there
would be some delay before the Russians could begin production.
To prepare an extra set of positives would consume a week, air
shipment another week, and delays before production another six
weeks. If the Forbes Company canceled its contract and the Bureau
of Engraving and Printing took over the production of the currency,
the Bureau would need six to eight months to complete the printing. The Forbes Company, on the other hand, working according to
the schedule already begun, could finish by the middle of May the
complete order for 349 million notes of an overall value of 10 billion
marks. Hall noted again, too, that the Forbes Company's schedule
would permit the United States to provide the Soviet Union with
whatever quantities of currency it demanded, at any stipulated
place. Finally, Hall repeated his earlier recommendation that the
Russians produce a currency of their own design with the assistance
of the United States Treasury. Hall believed that a separate cur-

rency would not necessarily present economic or financial difficulties, though he admitted it might prove politically undesirable.

Still eager for a common currency, Morgenthau made another effort to win over the Soviet Union. At the Secretary's instruction, White called on Gromyko on the night of March 21, 1944, and read him the memorandum Hall had prepared. In a report to Morgenthau the next day, White wrote:

> The Ambassador asked a number of questions with respect to the details and I tried to expand on the reasons why it would require six to eight months to produce marks in the Bureau of Engraving and why it might be unwise to have the Army take over the Forbes plant under the War Powers Act and attempt to operate it. He kept coming back with a question which he asked a number of times, namely, why the Forbes Company should object to giving a duplicate set of plates to his Government. He said that after all the Soviet Government was not a private corporation or an irresponsible Government. I explained to him how . . . the Forbes Company . . . felt but I am afraid that he remained unimpressed. . . .
>
> As instructed, I explained to him that Secretary Morgenthau was sending a letter to the Combined Chiefs of Staff containing an explanation of the situation together with a memorandum, asking them for a prompt reply. The Ambassador hoped to be able to get the reply soon, and I told him I thought he would.
>
> He wondered whether our Government was ready to suggest to his Government that it could print its own designed mark currency. I told him that such was not necessarily the view of our Government; but was merely an expression of the possibility of the memorandum and that it would have to be cleared through other departments and doubtless with the British before it could be regarded as an official specific proposal. He seemed interested in the possibility of printing their own currency but he clearly was disappointed and sceptical as to the reasoning contained in the memorandum.

Morgenthau's letter of March 22, 1944, to Admiral Leahy, the senior American representative on the Combined Chiefs of Staff, reviewed the whole problem, the difficulties in acceding to the Russian request for duplicate plates, the insistence of the Soviet Union on those plates, the question of the timetable. The Secretary sent a copy of the letter to Hull. "Under the date of March 7," Morgenthau wrote, "General Eisenhower advised the US War Department that he desired assurances that 40–45 per cent of the initial order for 10 billion A.M. marks would be completed by April 15, 1944. It would not be possible to obtain this objective if the printing of the currency were taken over by the Bureau. . . . It would therefore be appreciated if you would place this matter before the Combined Chiefs of Staff and advise me promptly whether in their opinion the military situation would afford such a delay as would be involved in the event that duplicate plates were made available to the Government of the USSR."

On the following day, March 23, Hull cabled Harriman about the impasse. Gromyko, Hull noted, had received the Treasury's analysis of the technical problems and understood the Treasury's conclusion that meeting the Russian request would delay production. Morgenthau, Hull also said, had referred the question to the Combined Chiefs of Staff. "It is not expected," Hull continued, "that the Combined Chiefs . . . will favor the delivery of plates to the Russians, in view of this very considerable delay."

Yet the Russians held out. Replying to Hull on April 8, 1944, Harriman reported that Molotov would not budge. "The Soviet Government," Molotov maintained, "cannot consider as sound the objections set forth. . . . The Soviet Government finds it necessary to reiterate its previous statement in regard to the necessity that military marks be prepared in the Soviet Union for supply to the Soviet Army. . . . The Soviet Government in this connection has taken into consideration the point of view of Soviet specialists who believe that it would be a disadvantage for the common Allied cause if such military marks were not printed in the Soviet Union." If the United States could not provide the plates, Molotov went on, "the Soviet Government will then be forced to proceed with the independent preparation of military marks for Germany in its own pattern."

As the matter then stood, pending further decision either by Hull or Morgenthau or the Combined Chiefs of Staff, Hall's wholly understandable technical reservations had to be weighed against Molotov's firm, contrary position. While Hall was incontestably correct in his interpretation of ordinary practice in the printing of currency in the United States, Molotov was by no means unreasonable considering the spirit and the exigencies of the time. In April 1944, Soviet-American relations were on the whole excellent. Neither the United States nor the United Kingdom had any palpable evidence to indicate that the Russians would fail to proceed with the developing plan for a co-operative, joint occupation of Germany. Further, just as Eisenhower wanted assurances that he would have in hand the currency he needed for his troops, so did the Russian military commanders want similar assurances, and naturally they and their civilian superiors felt that the supply of currency to Soviet troops would work out most efficiently if facilities for producing the currency were operating within the Soviet Union. In this as in other instances, moreover, Soviet representatives had grave difficulty understanding the posture of the American government toward private enterprise, especially toward a contractor attempting to influence an issue under negotiation with an allied foreign power. Most important, in the United States, as in Great Britain, the dominating concern for unified policy in Germany overbalanced the technical factors that motivated Hall. All those considerations lay behind the cable Hull sent Harriman on April 11, 1944: "We are trying to facilitate a favorable decision in connection with the Soviet request and in a few days we hope to telegraph you the scheme which we think will meet the wishes of the Soviet Government."

In McCloy's office at the War Department on April 12, 1944, General John Hilldring, the Army head of civil affairs, told an interdepartmental conference that the issue of the duplicate plates was almost "too hot" for the Combined Chiefs of Staff. After working over five drafts of a reply to Morgenthau's query to Leahy, the Combined Chiefs had concluded that the question should not be settled on military grounds. They had also suggested that if there was enough mark currency printed by May 1, 1944, for British and American use, then the United States might have the Forbes plant cease production and deliver the original plates to the Russians, rather than providing duplicate plates. As General Hilldring saw it, the final decision on the matter had to be political, but it should not be allowed to hurt American military relations with the Soviet Union.

For the Department of State, Assistant Secretary James Dunn acknowledged the political implications but pointed, too, to the technical problems. The Treasury spokesmen, William H. Taylor* and L. C. Aarons, subordinates in White's office, observed that Morgenthau, after explaining the technical questions in his letter to Leahy, had asked for a judgment comprehending military and political factors. Dunn then told the Treasury men, for the first time, about Molotov's unbudging reply to Harriman. Commenting on Molotov's suggestion for proceeding with an independent currency, both Dunn and Hilldring said they hoped to find a way "whereby the currency that was used in Germany by the American, British and Russian Armies would be identical. Mr. Dunn said that it would have a very nice effect upon the German people if we all used the same type of currency. The General's argument was placed purely upon military terms, as evidence of cooperation between the three nations."

Hilldring also "invited comment as to what was the true reason for the Russian insistence on this matter. Mr. Taylor stated that, in his opinion, the original Russian request was purely for the purposes of assuring themselves that they would have an adequate supply of notes. He added that the Russians, at the present time probably have further reasons for their insistence. In view of our expressed reluctance, the Russians probably feel that it is essential to establish their rights to the plates in order to clarify the future civil affairs arrangements between the three powers involved. It is not unlikely, Mr. Taylor pointed out, that if we fail to furnish the plates the Russians will embark upon a currency of their own. They may also establish a rate of exchange of their own and also establish monetary and financial programs of their own. In such event, the likelihood of developing a uniform and coordinated Allied pattern of action toward Germany would be jeopardized to that extent."

Just that reasoning had informed Hull's cable of April to Harriman, and just that reasoning accounted for the substance of a letter of April 13 from the Combined Chiefs to Morgenthau. The Treasury, that letter suggested, should make the plates available to the Soviet Union unless that step interfered with Eisenhower's re-

---

* Who was soon to leave for London as the Department's representative there, see Section 2, above.

quirements for AMA currency. There would be no interference, Morgenthau ascertained, for Eisenhower's full order was almost ready. Equally important, the State Department supported the decision of the Combined Chiefs, as Morgenthau learned in a telephone conversation with James Dunn on April 14. Morgenthau called Dunn to report that he was planning to tell Gromyko that afternoon that the Treasury would provide the duplicate plates. The Secretary wanted first to be sure the State Department approved. Aside from any military or technical considerations, Dunn replied, it was the opinion of the State Department from a political point of view "that if possible it was highly advisable to have the duplicate plates furnished to the Soviet Government in order that the three Governments and the three Armies entering Germany would be using the same identical currency. The Soviet Government had informed us that if the plates were not furnished to it, that Government would proceed to produce a separate currency for use in Germany. It was our opinion that it would be a pity to lose the great advantage of having one currency . . . which itself would indicate a degree of solidarity which was much to be desired not only for the situation in Germany but for its effect on the relations in many other aspects between the Soviet, British and United States Governments."

Morgenthau was "very glad to have this expression of the Department's views." It would prove helpful if difficulties arose with the Forbes Company — though in the end they did not. And it was essential for interpreting American policy. As the memorandum of the Secretary's conversation with Dunn put it: "It has become perfectly clear to us as a result of the exchanges of correspondence . . . that the Soviet Government is not ready to join in the common use of the same currency unless it receives the duplicate plates. . . . In order to convince the Soviet Government of our sincerity in the desire to have the closest collaboration in these military operations against Germany, it becomes essential that we make every effort within our possibility to furnish the plates to that Government."

The British were of the same mind. It was technically improbable, they noted, that identical notes could be produced in two different places, and they were therefore concerned about the possibility of forgery or of low confidence in the AMA marks. But that was a subsidiary question. "We fully realize," they wrote, ". . . how desirable it is politically . . . to comply with Russia's present request which seems to indicate a welcome readiness to cooperate. Provided US Authorities are satisfied . . . we therefore agree that Russians should be given the plates."

Though Alvin Hall remained passionately unhappy, Morgenthau told his staff that, had he known all the facts earlier, he would have decided even sooner to give the Soviets the plates. "My decision," he reflected twenty years later, "was correct both politically and militarily. The Russians had been holding up the Germans while the United States and England prepared for the invasion. There was every reason to trust them." On that basis, on the afternoon of April 14, 1944, Morgenthau told Gromyko that the United States Government, eager to cooperate with the Soviet Union, would furnish duplicate plates, inks, paper, and, if the Russians wished, supplies of printed currency. As Alvin Hall later recalled, the Secretary instructed him to "do everything you can to give the Russians what they want," and on April 21 the Treasury delivered the plates and other materials to the Soviet Embassy.*

On April 18, 1944, White opened discussion with the Russians about a rate of exchange for AMA marks. The United States, he explained, proposed to give the Reichsmark a value identical with the military mark. The rate established would therefore have to take into account the economic situation in Germany. The United States Army, he went on, needed a rate of exchange for the military mark in order to keep records of expenditures. Those records would have subsequent use in calculating the German liability for military marks placed in circulation. Redemption of the marks would fall entirely to the German government, not to the Allied authorities, but the Germans would ultimately have some offsetting claims for

---

* The foregoing account of intra- and inter-governmental negotiations leading to the delivery of the plates to the Soviets may be compared to the recollection of Elizabeth Bentley, a self-confessed Communist spy who accused Harry White, among others, of complicity in her work. A War Department employee, she wrote, "brought me samples of the marks the United States was preparing for use in the German occupation. The Russians were delighted, as they were planning to counterfeit them. However, due to a complicated ink process this proved impossible — until I was able through Harry Dexter White to arrange that the United States Treasury Department turn the actual printing plates over to the Russians!"

supplies they had furnished, for maintenance of Allied troops, and for other services.

Once again, the Soviet representatives in Washington delayed a reply while awaiting directions from Moscow. As White told a meeting of American experts on April 25, "the USSR had apparently not expected to discuss a mark rate for the period of military operations. . . . The Soviets have shown no interest in a supply of A.M. marks for the initial period and have asked what the United States-United Kingdom authorities expect to do with the proposed records regarding the use of A.M. marks at that time. The Soviets have objected to the word 'liability' in connection with the use of A.M. marks and have asked if this means liability for redemption of A.M. marks currency by the Allies. On the other hand, the Soviets are apparently agreeable to interchangeability within the area of Allied (United States-United Kingdom and USSR) military marks and regular German mark currency without distinction."

Delay in Moscow had its counterpart in indecision in Washington where the Treasury, the War Department, and the British had failed by late May to agree on an exchange rate. The War Department recommended giving the mark a value of 12½ cents; the British suggested 20 cents. At the Treasury on May 25, 1944, White held that "there is no sense in having a higher rate than can be maintained, and the controls are going to break down, prices are going to shoot up. We don't believe you can even hold a 10 cent rate."

"Well," Morgenthau said, "we are going to fight for 10 cents, which we think is much higher than it should be, but much lower than the other fellows say. Germany, of all places, I would like a rate which we could hold. . . . This one I want to take to the President. I want to go in with a rate which will steadily improve from the standpoint of the Germans and not steadily deteriorate. This, I will fight for personally and with the President. . . . I want you to give me a rate at which it will get better and not worse."

The Treasury, White said, might start bargaining for a 5 cent rate, but "there are certain other angles. McCloy has said if we can't settle it, the Army will make its own decision."

"You serve notice on McCloy," Morgenthau directed, "on this one, I am going to really fight. . . . This is the most important thing we have brought up."

That noon, lunching at the White House, Morgenthau and White told Roosevelt that the Treasury favored a 5 cent rate, 20 marks to the dollar. "Why couldn't we go in there without fixing any rate?" the President asked. The Army, White explained, had to pay its soldiers and to purchase goods and services in German markets. "Why can't they do it in dollars?" Roosevelt asked. They could, White said, but since prices in Germany were all stated in marks, they would need some measure for converting dollars to marks.

But on reflection, White was impressed by the President's questions. In a memorandum for Morgenthau, he suggested postponing decision until after the occupation had begun. Invading troops could be paid according to a nominal rate, to be adjusted when the occupation authorities had adequate data about economic and financial conditions within Germany. "We fear," White told the Secretary on June 1, 1944, "that any rate that we set will not be successful in the eyes of Germany, and in the eyes of the Army and the rest of them, for the reason that if we set a rate that is too high, it is bound to depreciate, and depreciation of the rate, once the Army gets in there, is going to contribute very disastrously to further inflation, further breakdown, further disintegration.

"If, on the other hand, we set a very low rate, the inflation which is certain to take place . . . will be blamed against the rate which we have established, and we won't be able to hold the rate unless it is a very low one, and unless we did a lot of things to control prices, which we are in no position to do during the first two or three months. We have to be in there three months, first. . . . It was the President's remarks that led me thinking in that direction."

Morgenthau was dubious. "Haven't you people thought this up," he asked, "because you don't think you can win on a 5 cent rate?" White said that he really believed his new proposal was preferable. Morgenthau then complained that the first time a soldier went into a store with a 40 cent mark, the nominal rate then existing, he was going "to be as sore as hell." The Army did not want soldiers buying in the stores anyhow, White replied, and the soldier would do better buying at a PX. Still, supported by Dan Bell, Morgenthau rejected White's proposal: "No soap. It is a very nice idea — try another one."

From the military standpoint, McCloy told Morgenthau on June

7, 1944, the prime requisite for the initial mark exchange rate was "that it will ensure, to the maximum extent possible, the maintenance of repose and tranquility in the wake of battle and throughout the areas under military administration." That condition concerned the War Department more than did long range financial policy. The determination of the rate, McCloy argued, should therefore give particular weight to price and wage levels existing in Germany, and to curbing inflation. In a further comment two weeks later, he said he especially hoped the Treasury and State Departments could get together on the rate.

No meeting of minds was close, for Morgenthau still wanted a mark of between 5 and 10 cents; the State Department recommended 12 to 18 cents, partly because a lesser value would give the Germans an advantage in competing for postwar trade in Latin America; and the British, preferring 16 to 20 cents, were also attracted by White's suggestion for withholding a decision. In that pass, Morgenthau left the matter to White. "We believe," White told Moscow, after consultation with the British, "that a sound decision with respect to a rate of exchange can only be made after occupation when we have adequate economic data on conditions in Germany. When a rate is finally selected it should be one that the German economy can sustain, so that the Allies can avoid the disastrous political and economic consequences of successive depreciation during the early occupation period. In addition, a rate finally selected in this manner will more accurately reflect the value of the German mark and will avoid injuries to the German internal balances." For the purpose of paying troops, British and American authorities intended not to announce the rate they set, but simply to convert soldiers' money.

Still aloof, the Russians maintained that they needed no rate for paying their troops. They would simply furnish soldiers with whatever amount of marks seemed necessary and, as Ambassador Harriman saw it, deduct those amounts from troop payments according to a convenient schedule. So informed, and eager to agree on a nominal rate for troop payments as McCloy had requested, the Treasury and State Departments settled on a 10 cent mark for temporary use with American forces.*

* Need for decision about a general rate arose only after Morgenthau had left office.

American policy on the mark rate bore a significant relationship to policy on the duplicate plates. Years after the events, when Russian-American relations had deteriorated, critics of the Roosevelt Administration maintained that both policies were unwise, and more important, that the decision about the duplicate plates derived from Communist influence within the Treasury and accounted for the inflation in postwar Germany. The latter assertions were silly. Postwar inflation visited every nation in the world, including the United States, but especially those that had suffered severe war damage, like Germany, France, and Japan. Harry White, who was later alleged to have been either a Communist or a Communist sympathizer, had never doubted, any more than had any other competent economist, that inflation would occur. Indeed White had attempted to set a policy that would minimize the impact of currency on inflation, and reduce any blame that might accrue to the United States, as an occupying power, for inflation in Germany.

The decision about the duplicate plates subordinated technical to military and political judgments. It was not primarily White's decision, but the joint decision of the Treasury, State, and War Departments, the Combined Chiefs of Staff and the British Government, with General John Hilldring, Assistant Secretary of State James Dunn, and Morgenthau as the major contributors to the final policy. No one of those men was in any sense a Communist or Communist sympathizer. All of them in 1944 were dedicated to the advancement of their common hope for successful cooperation among the Russians, the British, and the Americans throughout the postwar world, not least in Germany.

As matters developed after the period of occupation began, in 1945 and 1946 after Morgenthau had left office, controversial negotiations about currency persisted, as one War Department official put it, "ad nauseam" within the Allied Control Council, with Soviet unwillingness to establish central administration as the primary stumbling block. The same official, Assistant Secretary of War Howard C. Petersen, concluded that the total issue of Allied Military Authority marks by all three occupying powers had had little substantial effect on inflation in Germany. Rather, the vastly inflated war and postwar economy of Germany accounted for the tremendous currency overhead in all occupying areas. There had been a tenfold increase during the war in the number of Reichsmarks in circulation, and the Russians, who printed an undisclosed amount of Allied Military marks, had always available to them unlimited supplies of Reichsmarks. The trouble was that by 1946 the premise of 1944 had evaporated, the three wartime allies were no longer disposed to treat Germany as a political and economic whole. To the degree that the Russians printed an oversupply of military marks, moreover, marks for which the responsibility for redemption rested with the German government, the American beneficiaries, if there were any, were the GI's. The cigarettes and candy and soap and wristwatches which they bought in American PX's commanded huge prices in marks from the German people, and from Russian soldiers, too. The Allied Military marks which American soldiers received they could then convert into dollars, often for the purchase, under Army auspicies, of United States War Bonds.

The Army could have stopped the traffic at any time. As Eisenhower informed the War Department in May 1945, Russian-printed marks were distinguishable in various ways, particularly by a dash engraved just before the serial number. Had the Army so chosen, therefore, it could have refused to convert those marks, and it could have ordered American soldiers to decline them. More important, the Army could have limited the privilege of converting AMA marks to dollars to a fraction of the pay of any soldier or officer. Indeed in 1946, when they despaired of Russian cooperation, American authorities did successfully control the barter that had been contributing to inflation in Germany — just as barter had in North Africa, Italy, France, and Japan where the Russians had no currency plates and no share in the occupation.

"Difficult as our financial problems have been," General Hilldring said several years after the decision about the plates, "they would have been immeasurably more difficult" if the invading forces had used different currencies. "It was agreed," he added, "and sensibly I believe . . . that a special Allied Military Mark should be used. . . . The same considerations applied generally to Italy, Austria and Korea. . . . Similar considerations regarding the burden of the internal cost of occupation were present in the case of Japan where . . . the indigenous currency was used almost entirely.

. . . To reverse the thing, I wonder what decision would have been made if, on a matter as important as this, we had been dependent on the Soviets' supplying us with this invasion currenly and Eisenhower's armies would have been the stake involved with us, and it was the stake involved with the Soviets." No government, Hilldring implied, would have permitted its commander in the field to invade enemy territory without confidence in his finances. The Russians had proceeding from a logical assumption in 1944, which the United States and Great Britain had honored for good and sufficient reason, and the decision to deliver the duplicate plates, reached on that basis, uninfected by any communist plot, had had at most a tangential effect on the debilitating course of inflation in postwar Germany.

In the spring of 1944 Morgenthau, as he noted twenty years later, was giving little thought to the problems of postwar Germany, a subject to which he turned only in the following autumn.* He was concerned, rather, with the multifold issues related to the invasion and liberation of Europe. In that concern, he continually put the technical and financial duties of the Treasury at the service of military and political priorities that the President, the State Department, and the War Department established. Yet in that spring and during the preceding months, Morgenthau was also pursuing his own vision of decency and justice in international politics. On that account, he was at odds with the State Department and with the British Foreign Office over policies remote from the European battleground, policies affecting American relations with Argentina and American assistance for persecuted and displaced Jews.

5. Argentina: How Good a Neighbor?

American efforts to eliminate Axis activities in the Western Hemisphere during the Second World War stumbled primarily on the recalcitrance of one nation, Argentina, which remained officially neutral until almost the end of the conflict. Neutral status permitted Argentina to profit as a major supplier of meat and other foodstuffs

* See Chapter VII.

to Great Britain, but also allowed German agents and sympathizers in Buenos Aires to direct Axis activities in Latin America with impunity. The State Department never doubted the persistence of Nazi influence in Argentina; indeed Cordell Hull developed an "almost psychopathic" anti-Argentine bias. But he was also solicitous of the good will of all Latin American nations, and he believed that a hard line toward Argentina would effect small remedy and cost the United States the friendship of good neighbors notoriously suspicious of Yankee imperialism. Jealous of State Department prerogatives for making foreign policy, Latin American policy especially, Hull resented the responsibility of the Treasury for the control of foreign funds in the United States, and even more, the attendant recommendations of the Treasury for economic reprisals against Argentine politics.

Those recommendations first appeared in the spring of 1942 in a report to Morgenthau from his subordinates concerned with foreign funds. Argentina, they informed the Secretary, had yet to take steps to carry out the resolutions of the Pan-American Conference at Rio de Janeiro calling for the severance of diplomatic, commercial, and financial relations with the Axis. Worse, Argentine financial institutions were holding substantial dollar resources in the United States in evasion of controls that applied to the Axis powers. Argentine banks and individuals, operating as fences for looted currency and securities, circumvented American regulations to prevent the Germans from realizing dollars from the sale of those stolen assets. The Treasury analysts therefore suggested extending freezing controls to Argentina. Those controls would make all Argentine financial transactions in the United States subject to license, and the Treasury would permit only those transfers of dollars that were wholly divorced from Axis interests. A freezing order of that kind would serve, too, as a demonstration throughout Latin America that the United States meant business "in this war of survival."

Morgenthau found the report convincing but Dean Acheson, speaking for the State Department, opposed controls of any kind and with whatever exemptions. There was a perceptible trend under way, he said, against the government in power in Argentina. That regime would be strengthened if Argentinians and other Latin Americans felt the United States was persecuting it. The

Treasury, Acheson said, was proposing to use "a club to kill a mosquito"; the recommendation would meet "most violent opposition" within the State Department.

There were also other objections. Officials at the Export-Import Bank predicted that a freezing order would provoke Argentina to a formal alliance with Germany and an attack on Brazil. In the opinion of Secretary of War Stimson, the real trouble in Argentina originated with fifth column agents who provided Germany with information about American ship movements. He could not see how the freezing of assets would relieve that situation. Secretary Hull agreed that Argentina had refused to discipline subversives within her borders, but he hoped to persuade the Argentines to change that policy in return for a share of the armaments the United States was distributing to cooperative South American countries.

The "sudden move" of the Treasury on freezing controls, Hull later wrote, "almost upset" the situation. Morgenthau, Hull went on, with his customary bitterness on the subject, "often interfered in foreign affairs, and sometimes took steps directly at variance with those of the State Department. But since there was frequently a connection between foreign and financial affairs, he had in his hands monetary weapons which he brandished in the foreign field from time to time. . . . Morgenthau was particularly avid on the subject of freezing the credits of foreign countries. . . . Now I suddenly became aware that he was proposing to freeze Argentina's funds." The Secretary of State sent the Treasury's memorandum to the President, with the observation that "you will readily see that this proposes a complete reversal of the Good Neighbor Policy and a substitution of our old discredited policy of coercion . . . by big stick methods."

The President accepted Hull's assessment. "It just won't do," he told Morgenthau on the telephone on May 14, 1942. "It would kill our whole Good Neighbor Policy." Morgenthau replied that Vice President Wallace, at a meeting of the Economic Warfare Board a week earlier, had asked for suggestions for driving the Nazis out of South America, and the Treasury had then volunteered to study the Argentine situation. Hull had attended that meeting and approved the study, from which emerged the recommendation for freezing controls. "Well," Roosevelt said, "as long as it is a study, that's all right, but I don't want to do anything to upset all the good work that has been done in South America."

A day later at the White House, the President with gay exaggeration elaborated upon his views. "I had this question up yesterday," he told Morgenthau, "on how to organize this information group, and they had Rockefeller* in with the others. I told them, 'You know I am a juggler, and I never let my right hand know what my left hand does. . . . I may have one policy for Europe and one diametrically opposite for North and South America. I may be entirely inconsistent, and furthermore I am perfectly willing to mislead and tell untruths if it will help win the war.' "

Did Roosevelt, Morgenthau asked, want him to continue as "your financial detective and give you information we learn of what the Germans are doing in Argentina?"

"You keep out of there," Roosevelt replied. ". . . If the thing gets worse *I* will send for all of the representatives of the South American Republics and tell them what is going on in the Argentine."

Morgenthau withdrew, but Argentine affairs deteriorated. Early in June 1942, the resignation of ailing President Ortiz brought into power the chauvinistic regime of Ramón Castillo. In spite of pressure from Washington, his government retained diplomatic and commercial ties to Germany. In June 1943, an army revolt replaced Castillo with General Pedro Ramírez, who soon revealed blatant pro-Axis leanings. Under his command, Argentina stepped up her efforts to create an anti-Yankee bloc among South American republics, increased the number and intensity of unfriendly acts against American and Allied interests, and abetted the distribution of German propaganda in the Western Hemisphere. At the same time, Argentina continued to cultivate economic relations with England and the United States.

The unabashedly hostile policies provoked American Ambassador Norman Armour in October 1943, to recommend freezing controls and other techniques of economic warfare as part of a campaign to upset the Ramírez administration. That recommendation reached Washington when Hull and Morgenthau were away, the Secretary

---

* Nelson Rockefeller, then an Assistant Secretary of State with special responsibilities for the American information program in Latin America.

of State at a conference in Moscow, the Secretary of the Treasury on
a tour of North Africa and Italy. In their absence, their respective
staffs responded in exactly the pattern of disagreement that had previously prevailed. Once again Roosevelt supported the view of the
Department of State, which Hull had endorsed by cable. "In regard
to blocking Argentine," the President wrote Under Secretary of State
Stettinius on October 25, 1943, "I think we had better keep this matter on our desks, to be reviewed every week or two."

In reporting that decision to the Treasury, Stettinius also said
that Roosevelt thought it might be wise "to let it leak out that
studies along the lines of freezing Argentina are being undertaken,
which would tend to scare the present Government." In interdepartmental conversations on October 26, "it was clear," according to
Randolph Paul's account, "that the State Department was not adverse to the leak but did not want to become too intimately connected with the arrangements." Paul, Herbert Gaston, and John
Pehle — the head of Foreign Funds Control — then agreed that Paul
should plant the leak, which appeared on October 27 in various
newspapers, including the *New York Times,* the New York *Herald
Tribune,* and the Washington *Times Herald.*

The publication, disturbing to Stettinius, also had the predictable
effect of leading to withdrawals of some Argentine assets from the
United States. To prevent those withdrawals, Pehle told the New
York Federal Reserve Bank to refuse to complete the necessary
transactions without further instructions from the Treasury. On
October 28, with the explicit approval of the State Department, he
also designated two major Argentine banks as special "blocked nationals." * Yet the State Department, with the President's support,
remained opposed to a general freezing order, and on November 1,
Stettinius had the Treasury release the Argentine transactions that
Pehle had held up. As Randolph Paul said to Morgenthau that day,
just as the Secretary returned to Washington, the State Department
had been "wobbling all around."

To Paul's surprise, Morgenthau, after studying a long memorandum about the events of the preceding week, criticized his subordi-

---

* An order that froze the funds of those two banks in the United States, even
though other Argentine nationals had been subjected to no controls, just to
rumor.

nates. "I think that Treasury," the Secretary said on November 2, 1943, "is in an absolutely false position. We were outsmarted. . . . We are recommending through freezing of funds that we are in favor of changing the form of government down there in Argentina, which I don't think is any of our damned business. I mean, that is Mr. Hull's responsibility. . . . The other thing which I can't understand is having given this thing out to the press."

Though the Secretary questioned Paul's tactics, he commended his general purpose. He therefore ordered prepared for his signature a strong memorandum for Stettinius that added recent, confirmatory evidence about Argentine activities to advance Axis interests and assist Nazi subversion in the Americas. The Argentine government, Morgenthau concluded in that document, was "rapidly passing from *control* to the *promotion* of such activities. . . . I recognize that freezing Argentine assets involves political as well as economic questions and that decision on the political aspects is clearly your responsibility. However, I sincerely hope that you will again review the Argentine situation and on economic warfare grounds, I again strongly recommend that Argentine assets be frozen."

At Stettinius' request, Morgenthau postponed further discussion until Hull returned from Moscow. On November 24, 1943, the two Secretaries met, and Morgenthau repeated the substance of his memorandum. "I would like to see the present government of Argentina overthrown," Hull said, but his associates did not believe the freezing of Argentine assets would work to that end. Indeed Assistant Secretary of State A. A. Berle argued plausibly that freezing would produce only minor gains in economic warfare while at the same time strengthening the government in office by drawing to it the support of anti-Yankee elements throughout Latin America. Hull then suggested the possibility of consulting the principal Latin American republics to see whether they would approve of an American freezing order, and to determine to what extent they would take similar steps themselves. At Morgenthau's request, he agreed to approach the British with the same question. Meanwhile, entirely on his own, Morgenthau solicited information about conditions within Argentina from General George Strong, the head of Army Intelligence, G-2, whose reports to the Treasury went forward with the approval of Secretary of War Stimson.

By December 7, 1943, the State Department had received replies from Colombia, Peru, and Mexico favorable to a freezing order. Brazil, while not prepared to join in that policy, assured the United States that privately it would approve. At a conference with Treasury representatives on December 20, Hull said that he was working constantly on dropping Argentina from the Inter-American Defense Council and other important Pan-American committees. Such action, he explained, would recognize that Argentina was acting inimicably to the defense of the Western Hemisphere. The government of Argentina, as Hull saw it, now consisted of hard-boiled military men, a group of buccaneers. But the Argentine people — in Hull's view sleek, fat, and lethargic from the profits of wartime trade — would not conceivably exert themselves to overthrow that government.

"You know," Morgenthau told Roosevelt later that day, "on the Argentine thing, Cordell is taking an interest but he's awful slow. . . . [It] looks as though there had been an overthrow in Bolivia as a result of scheming from Argentina. . . . If you want to get the lowdown on it, why don't you send for General Strong and he will give it to you."

"I was sent for," General Strong told Morgenthau on December 21, 1943, "as you warned me this morning. . . . I had quite a talk over there in the presence of Mr. Hull . . . and the Great White Father seemed very much interested. . . . He intimated that he thought the time had come for reexamination of the whole question . . . with the idea of cracking down pretty hard. . . . He directed Mr. Hull to take the matter up with you and have a discussion . . . apparently from the ground up on the whole matter of policy."

Strong had told Hull after their meeting with the President that the British would probably decline to join in a freezing of Argentine assets. Their own devices for exchange control were accomplishing a similar purpose, and they were eager to protect their investments in the Argentine and to sustain the flow of meat to the United Kingdom. Nevertheless Strong thought the United States could make a freezing order at least 80 per cent effective.

Unless the United States, Strong added privately to Morgenthau, countered Argentine activities, Argentina would soon create a Fascist bloc including Uruguay, Paraguay, Chile, Peru, and Bolivia.

The Nazis, Strong said, already partially controlled the Argentine government, especially the clique of Colonel Juan D. Perón, the strongest official in the administration. The Argentines had allowed pro-Axis propaganda to flow into the Western Hemisphere, with results that "kept several countries internally divided and . . . lessened their assistance to the United Nations." Further, Argentina was serving as a base for Nazi purchases of diamonds, platinum, and other materials; one of her government controlled banks was openly aiding the Axis; a former Austrian manufacturer, now establishing a munitions industry within Argentina, had removed $12 million from Germany for that purpose; Argentina's ports served as depots from which Spanish and other neutral ships carried war materials to Germany, and from which couriers engaged in espionage for the Axis. There were indications of Argentine aid to Axis submarines at sea, and indications also that the Nazis planned to use Argentina as a tool to create a disturbance within the Western Hemisphere that would divert American forces from the main war effort.

Understandably, General Strong considered it "insane" for the United States to complete a pending purchase of 75 million bushels of Argentine wheat for distribution for civilian relief in Italy. That prospect, Morgenthau told Strong on January 1, 1944, seemed "more cockeyed than most of the things we do." On January 3, Morgenthau asked John McCloy: "Why the devil should we be spending $75 million on wheat in the Argentine now if it could be bought elsewhere?" The War Shipping Administration, which Morgenthau also approached, reported that transporting wheat from Argentina would be very expensive, particularly since there were no bottoms available to send to Buenos Aires. That agency recommended instead obtaining the wheat from Vancouver, but the War Food Administration considered Canadian supplies already fully allocated, and the War Department, while enthusiastic about disciplining Argentina, could see no way to overrule the War Food Administration. Further, as McCloy told Morgenthau on January 8, 1944, the British had decided that wheat for Italian relief had to come from Argentina rather than from stockpiles in the Middle East. "The English," the Secretary replied, "get together somewhere and they have a policy. We sit around here and cut each other's throat . . . and they just make hay. . . . I think it is all damned nonsense. Here

you have got Italy starving, and we have got to maintain the morale
behind our Armies, and we are stockpiling wheat for the Balkans
. . . because that is a British area. . . . To hell with it!"

Unable to stop the purchase of Argentine wheat, Morgenthau
concentrated again on advocating a freezing order with exemptions
to allow continuing trade in foodstuffs. He wanted an excuse, he
told his staff, to write Hull a letter asking: "What are you going to
do about the Argentine? . . . A little turpentine under the tail.
. . . That's what they use down in the Tennessee mountains." The
wife of the Brazilian ambassador to the United States, just back
from Argentina, had said "she was never so shocked in her life. . . .
She says she has never seen anything like it, that everywhere you
go there are Nazis."

Hull had reached a similar conclusion. The State Department, he
told Morgenthau on January 12, 1944, had satisfied itself that the
Argentine government had inspired the coup d'état in Bolivia.
Concurrently with other American republics, the United States was
preparing to release, probably within the next two or three days, a
statement refusing recognition of the new government of Bolivia,*
and applying a "rawhide" to Argentina. Simultaneously the State
Department would recall Ambassador Armour for consultation, and
agree to the freezing of Argentine assets, which would prove successful, Hull thought, even without British cooperation. But first Armour was to warn Argentina of the contemplated actions on the
chance that that step would in itself provoke desirable changes in
her ways.

Delighted with Hull's plans, Morgenthau directed his staff to prepare the necessary freezing orders, which Roosevelt signed on January 24. Just before their scheduled release, the State Department
reported that Argentina, in response to Armour's warning, was
about to break with the Axis — as she did on January 26, 1944.
Though Randolph Paul believed that such a break would be only
token in character, designed "to forestall action on our part," the
State Department saw no alternative to accepting the Argentine assurances at face value and canceling the freezing orders. The White
House agreed.

---

* Though recognition was soon accorded when Hull was satisfied that the new
Bolivian government was in fact not Fascist or pro-Axis.

The threat and then the abandonment of freezing controls only temporarily accomplished the purpose of the United States. At a Cabinet meeting on February 11, 1944, Stettinius spoke of "very favorable reports from Argentina. He thought they had taken rather drastic steps to eliminate the Axis influence." But within a month the nature of those reports changed. The Argentines freed the German and Japanese naval attachés whom they had put under some restraint. More important, with dissension growing within the ruling clique in Argentina, the various factions rivaled each other in their anti-Americanism. Then on February 15, 1944, a group of colonels, led by Perón, seized control of the foreign office and a few days later replaced Ramírez in the Presidency with Perón's friend, General Edelmiro Farrell. Perón, the real victor in the struggle and intrigue, was manifestly a "pretty ruthless but able manipulator."

The continuing bad news, Morgenthau hoped, would lead the State Department to conclude "that the political situation calls for economic action." He contemplated, he told Dean Acheson on March 3, both freezing controls and sanctions against Argentine exports. Acheson, worried about British food supplies, wanted to hold back until the Argentines resumed relations with the Axis, as he thought they soon would. "Whenever you are ready," Morgenthau said, "I am ready. But I am certainly not ready to move today, any more than you are."

From Stettinius on March 4, 1944, Morgenthau learned that Brazil, like England, depended on Argentina for much of her wheat. "Well," the Secretary said, "if we could get everything else — and by that I mean get the English to join us in complete economic sanctions — on the matter of whether or not Brazil would go along on account of her need of getting wheat from the Argentine, I personally would be willing to wink my eye and let the Brazilians continue to get their wheat. . . . If we start something with the Argentine we have got to be prepared to go through with it, and I think if we take a forceful joint action with the British we can be successful." His subordinates, Morgenthau knew, were impatient, but as he told them, he felt that he made "real progress with Stettinius . . . stiffened him up a lot." The situation, he added, was "so ticklish . . . that I am going to sit here . . . and watch this thing. . . . I think at this time if I don't do everything I can to see that

England and ourselves move as partners then I am falling down on my job. . . . If there is a split . . . over the whole South American thing, it might affect the war effort, because it might give encouragement to our enemies."

Fascism, Morgenthau said to Roosevelt on March 7, 1944, was going "to spread all through South America and what you have accomplished in the last eleven years is all going up in thin smoke. . . . We have really got to get tough with them, and if we get tough they will buckle under." The United States, the President replied, could not prove "anything on the Argentines." At a Cabinet meeting ten days later, as Morgenthau reported in his Diary, Hull, speaking on Argentina, "had come to the decision that inasmuch as the English couldn't go along, it was not feasible. . . . Anything . . . in the way of sanctions . . . would only be an irritant." The President then said: "I agree with that conclusion."

A solution to England's food problems, Morgenthau believed, might persuade the British to cooperate in a program of sanctions against Argentina. Vice President Wallace, whom the Treasury consulted on March 24 in his capacity as head of the Board of Economic Warfare, thought that a ten per cent reduction in meat rations for Americans would not hurt diets in the United States and might conserve enough for British meat and fat requirements. "Unless something is done about Argentina," Wallace also said, "we can write the whole of Latin America off the books." But Marvin Jones, the head of the War Food Administration, maintained on March 29 that Americans would not tolerate a reduction in their rations, and the Combined Food Board, on which American and British representatives sat, considered Argentine meat and wheat indispensable for the duration of the war.

Still restive, Morgenthau, as he told Dean Acheson on April 27, 1944, had reached the point "where I don't feel that I am living up to my responsibility if I don't make a firm recommendation." He no longer cared what England did; he believed the United States, without further delay, should freeze Argentine assets. Conditions in Argentina, Acheson agreed, were "very bad," but Hull was "very tired. He's been through a harassing experience in the last two days* . . . and, he . . . flies off quite quickly. . . . If we could do it

* Negotiating with the British about Anglo-American policy toward Spain.

next week . . . I . . . think that we could discuss the thing more calmly." While leaving Hull alone, Morgenthau continued to press Acheson. The next day they struck a kind of bargain — in return for Morgenthau's concessions on currency arrangements with the Netherlands, Belgium, and Norway,* Acheson drafted a cable, "a humdinger" in Morgenthau's opinion, to Ambassador Armour.

Signed by Hull and dispatched on May 5, 1944, the cable said that the State Department, at the urging of the Treasury, was again considering freezing controls. On May 9 Armour replied that the application of freezing controls would be unwise and dangerous. At that time, moreover, the Combined Chiefs of Staff concluded that "irrespective of the effect upon civilian economies, any cessation of supply from Argentina . . . would have unfavorable military implications."

The Army, Morgenthau told Acheson, always made the wrong political decisions. The Army had been wrong in North Africa and Italy, wrong about the Free French, and now it was wrong about Argentina. Morgenthau therefore once more urged Hull to endorse a freezing order. The recommendation, Morgenthau reported to his staff, was "like lighting a match to a powder keg." Hull was furious. "You always want that," he replied. "That is what you wanted in the case of Japan. You are completely wrong. . . . You wanted to freeze the Japanese. . . . You were all wrong, the Army wasn't ready, and the Navy . . . and that is going to come out, how you people wanted us to do this and that and the other thing."

"It wasn't just freezing," Morgenthau reminded Hull, " . . . we didn't want you to ship aviation gasoline and ship scrap iron. . . . I am fearful that we can win the war in Europe; we can win the war in the Pacific; and lose it right in our own back yard. What we are fighting for will be lost and we will have a fascist state right there — the Argentine." He had a responsibility, Morgenthau concluded, to express his views in writing to the President.

"I have got a lot of responsibility," Hull replied. "I will be glad to swap places with you. . . . If the President wants to do it, that is all right."

The letter to the President went out that day, with a copy to Hull. "Argentina is already emerging as the new champion of fascism,"

* See Section 2, this chapter.

Morgenthau wrote, "and is actively engaged in forcing into its orbit other countries in Latin America. Since October, I have had numerous conferences with Mr. Hull, Mr. Stettinius and Mr. Acheson, all of them amicable, but from the Treasury viewpoint, fruitless. We in the Treasury feel that it is our responsibility to bring this matter again to your attention, and to urge you strongly to take further steps to stop the growth of fascism in the Argentine and neighboring states."

The President settled the issue at the Cabinet meeting of May 18, 1944. "Henry wants to apply sanctions," Roosevelt said, "but you can't do that on account of the English, and the food." Turning to Stettinius, he continued: "Ed, you make a bad face to the Argentineans once a week. You have to treat them like children."

"Mr. President," Morgenthau objected, "I don't think that is quite enough. After all, we can win the war in Europe, win it in Asia, and find out we have a strong, rich fascist country at our back yard." But no one, not even Wallace, supported the Secretary, and Roosevelt ended the discussion by remarking that he had been "trying to build up the Brazilians so they can meet that situation."

Resigned but unconvinced, Morgenthau stopped arguing. He took some solace in June when Hull, angry with the Farrell regime, recalled Ambassador Armour, condemned the Argentine Government, had the Treasury freeze Argentine funds, and had American ships boycott Argentine ports. But the British, though they also recalled their ambassador, would not join the boycott, and the Argentine people, resentful of Washington's policies, remained loyal to Péron and Farrell, who persisted in their pro-Axis ways. As Morgenthau saw it, earlier action supported by the British would have succeeded where the orders of June 1944 failed. Still, he recognized, though he also lamented, the primacy of military considerations in wartime politics. Where military needs did not much intrude, he had a better opportunity than he had had in the case of Argentina to enlist the President's support of the Treasury's ventures. So it was with his efforts to muster American assistance for European Jews.

6. "Those Terrible Eighteen Months"

Years after he had left office, Morgenthau looked back on what he called "those terrible eighteen months. . . . We knew in Washington . . . that the Nazis were planning to exterminate all the Jews of Europe. Yet . . . officials dodged their grim responsibility, procrastinated when concrete rescue schemes were placed before them, and even suppressed information about atrocities."

Long before the war and the worst of the pogroms, Morgenthau had worried about the European Jews whom politics put at Hitler's mercy. He was, for example, a regular and generous contributor to the American Jewish Joint Distribution Committee whose agents were working for the removal of Jews from Germany to the United States and other havens. But, as Secretary of the Treasury, he had little opportunity to deal with the problem. Not a Zionist, always aware of British reluctance to antagonize the Arabs by increasing Jewish migration into Palestine, Morgenthau also knew that American immigration laws, about which Congress took an unyielding position, severely restricted the number of refugees who could enter the United States. With Roosevelt, he therefore seized on other possibilities.

In November 1938, after Hitler had promulgated the Nuremberg decrees to the President's outspoken shock, Morgenthau went to the White House with what he called "the first concrete suggestion to make for the Jewish refugees." He had received a letter, he said, proposing that the United States acquire British and French Guiana in return for canceling the debts of the first World War due from the United Kingdom and France. Roosevelt was unimpressed. "It's no good," the President said. "It would take the Jews five to fifty years to overcome the fever." Roosevelt had instead the idea of a Jewish community in the Cameroons where there lay, he said, "some very wonderful high land, table land, wonderful grass and . . . all of that country has been explored and it's ready." But the geographers whom Morgenthau commissioned to explore the possibility of settlement in the Cameroons considered the probable cost of the project prohibitive and the potentialities for economic development poor.

The Intergovernmental Committee on Refugees, established in

1938, also found no place to which to evacuate European Jews. The whole trouble is in England," Roosevelt admitted to Morgenthau in mid-1939. Since British politics in the Near East prevented the utilization of Palestine as a haven for European Jews, Roosevelt had "talked to the President-elect of Paraguay" and believed that if he could "get two or three people together . . . we could work out a plan." He was even willing to have it called the Roosevelt Plan, and if Morgenthau would give him a list of the thousand richest Jews in the United States, he was prepared to tell each how much money he should contribute. But Morgenthau brought Roosevelt down from his cloud. "Mr. President," he pointed out, "before you talk about money you have to have a plan."

It was no time to bring up the question of Palestine, Roosevelt told Morgenthau in July 1942, for "the English were terrifically worried" about an Arab uprising. By the end of the year, the President had a new dream. "What I think I will do," he said on December 3, 1942, "is this. First, I would call Palestine a religious country. Then I would leave Jerusalem the way it is and have it run by the Orthodox Greek Catholic Church, the Protestants, and the Jews — have a joint committee run it. . . . I actually would put a barbed wire around Palestine, and I would begin to move the Arabs out of Palestine. . . . I would provide land for the Arabs in some other part of the Middle East. . . . Each time we move out an Arab we would bring in another Jewish family. . . . But I don't want to bring in more than they can economically support. . . . It would be an independent nation just like any other nation. . . . Naturally, if there are 90 per cent Jews, the Jews would dominate the government. . . . There are lots of places to which you could move the Arabs. All you have to do is drill a well because there is this large underground water supply, and we can move the Arabs to places where they can really live." But that fantasy was a long way from fulfillment, and by June 1943, Roosevelt had moved only to urge Churchill to bring the Jews and Arabs together for discussion. The President thought the Arabs could be bribed, but the Prime Minister — though himself a long-time Zionist — disagreed. He was straining to avoid the Jewish question and to keep the Middle East quiet at least until the war ended.

Meanwhile "those terrible eighteen months" had witnessed new and frightful stages in Hitler's plan to exterminate the Jews of Europe. Though Morgenthau did not become aware of the full implications of that plan for American policy until 1943, and then, as he later put it, in a "scramble of bits and pieces," a detailed report of the Nazi program reached the State Department in 1942.* It came from a German Jew, Gerhart Riegner who had fled to Geneva, where he represented the World Jewish Congress. Through private channels, Riegner got his ghastly story to Rabbi Stephen S. Wise, the president of the American Jewish Congress. Wise then asked the State Department to confirm the information, and at the Department's request, kept the story to himself while Washington cabled an inquiry to the American Minister at Bern, Leland Harrison. In November 1942, Harrison sent back full documentation for Riegner's report, which the State Department then told Wise he could make public. The United States officially denounced the Nazi policy of extermination on December 17, 1942, and Roosevelt declared that it would be American policy to punish racial and political murder.

A second report from Riegner on January 21, 1943, said that Germans were killing Polish Jews at the rate of 6,000 a day and in Rumania were systematically starving Jews and others to death. Those disclosures provoked requests from Americans of all faiths for governmental efforts to rescue the victims of Nazi brutality. The State Department, however, deferred action. In reply to pleas for assistance, it merely referred to the Intergovernmental Committee on Refugees, which had as yet accomplished nothing significant. The British were still cultivating the Arabs, and within the Department of State itself, those responsible for visas had admitted even fewer Jews than the small quotas for European immigration permitted.

As Morgenthau discovered months later, State Department officials also cut off the communications from Riegner. The Department's reply to Minister Harrison's cable of January 21, 1943, suggested that in the future he should not accept reports submitted to him for transmission to private individuals in the United States except under extraordinary circumstances. Those private messages,

* In order to avoid confusion, the account in this chapter proceeds chronologically, but the Treasury did not obtain the full story until the winter of 1943-1944, and then only in scrambled installments.

the reply said, circumvented the censorship of neutral countries, and in sending them Harrison risked the possibility that neutrals would curtail or forbid communication about important official matters. That directive was signed by Sumner Welles, then still Under Secretary of State, but Welles, who was personally entirely sympathetic with efforts to rescue the Jews, did not understand the implications of the order and may not even have seen it. Indeed in April 1943, obviously unaware of the restrictions he had inadvertently approved, Welles asked Harrison for further reports from Riegner about the Jews. But in the interim, three months of silence had stayed the hands of those who would otherwise have pressed for American action.

In spite of the interruption in communications from Bern, enough information reached the Treasury to alert Morgenthau. On February 13, 1943, the *New York Times* reported from London that the Rumanian government had told United Nations officials that it was prepared to transfer 70,000 Jews to Palestine on Rumanian ships using Vatican insignia. As the *Times* noted, some spies might mingle with so large a number of refugees; further, tension between the Arabs and Jews in Palestine was already high; and there were logistical difficulties in arranging mass transportation for so many people. "The President," Morgenthau told Welles on February 15, "didn't know anything about it, and he said . . . to talk to you about it, and . . . would you discuss it with him." Welles, too, had learned all he knew from the *Times,* but the State Department ascertained through the American Embassy in London on February 18 that in essence the story was correct. "Officials who were in charge in Rumania of Jewish interests" had offered to transfer between 60,000 and 70,000 Jews in return for a per capita ransom of £250. The American Embassy in Ankara, in a cable of February 23, added that the United States and British governments were also to provide assurances of safe conduct and the necessary visas. But the British did not want the refugees in Palestine, and Roosevelt, after months of uncertainty, in a letter to Hull of May 14, 1943, called for strict compliance with American immigration laws and suggested the possibilty of North Africa as a temporary depot for some refugees if local authorities approved.

There matters stood until July when representatives of the American Jewish Congress called at the Treasury to say that certain Nazi officials in Rumania could be bribed at an overall cost of $170,000 to permit the evacuation of 70,000 Jews. The money would have to be paid in local currency. Jewish merchants in Rumania, who had been able to conceal their resources, could make that payment if they were reimbursed either in dollars or Swiss francs, to be held for them in trust until the war ended. The World Jewish Congress would direct the entire operation from Switzerland, and the American Jewish Congress had already discussed the plan in general terms with the Department of State. For the Treasury, the proposal raised the question of whether to release dollars for the purchase of Rumanian currency. On July 19, 1943, Randolph Paul wrote Morgenthau that the matter had "been thoroughly discussed here in the Treasury and we have advised State informally that the Treasury is prepared to approve the necessary transactions on the basis of the facts now before us." Morgenthau then informed Wise that the department was "fully sympathetic to the proposal."

To Roosevelt on July 22, 1943, Wise explained that Morgenthau understood that the alternative to the exchange transaction was the death of the 70,000 Jews. The Treasury, he reported, would retain the dollars it released in escrow in Switzerland so that no funds could reach any representatives of the Axis until after the war. Roosevelt approved the plan orally, but Wise, in a letter to the President written right after their meeting, continued his plea by pointing out that the contemplated arrangements would "create such conditions within the Hitler territories as shall enable many Jews in those countries to survive, to escape deportation and ultimately to come out of those countries. . . . The whole arrangement is to provide especially for the saving of many little children. We feel that these funds may make possible the salvation of thousands of otherwise doomed beings, especially in Rumania, Slovakia and France, without . . . one penny falling into the hands of enemy representatives for the duration."

Morgenthau wrote Wise on July 23, 1943, that the matter was "now awaiting the further exchange of cables between the State Department and our mission in Bern regarding some of the details." In fact it was more complicated than that, for within the State Department, as the Treasury discovered on August 5, there was a division of opinion about the issue, with Herbert Feis in favor of the Treasury's recommendation, while Assistant Secretary Breckinridge

Long, to whom Hull had assigned responsibility, was either opposed or dubious to the point of indifference. Foreign Service officers to whom Long listened, argued that the Germans would never consent to the necessary transportation arrangements, and that neither the British, the Turks, nor local North African authorities would agree to admit the evacuees. So informed, Morgenthau wrote Hull that Foreign Funds Control had been ready since July 16 to "take the necessary action to implement this proposal." Replying on August 7, Hull wrote that "the Treasury itself is entirely free to act on this matter and to grant the necessary licenses if it should so decide. In the latter event the State Department would be pleased to send the appropriate notification . . . to our Legation in Bern. . . . Any view that this would make funds available to the enemy is not correct; the funds would remain blocked in Switzerland until the end of the war."

Hull's quick cooperation reassured Morgenthau. The Secretary of State, unlike some of his subordinates, was clearly eager to assist in rescuing European Jews. Further, he seemed at last to have cleared the way for the dispatch to Bern of a cable communicating instructions to the legation there for the transactions that would permit the execution of the plan for Rumania.

But through no fault of Hull, the appearance remained at variance with reality. Not until September 28, 1943, did that cable go out to Bern. Replying on October 6, Harrison asked for specific orders from the State Department before acting on the authority granted by the Treasury. He then also said that in accordance with standing instructions concerning problems having to do with trading with the enemy, he had discussed the matter with British authorities at Bern who opposed the issuance of the license. It was another ten days before the Treasury learned of the reply, and October 24 before Randolph Paul, acting for Morgenthau while the Secretary was away, succeeded in obtaining a copy of the cable. On October 26 John Pehle, the head of Foreign Funds Control, furious that the State Department had still not directed Harrison to act, told Breckinridge Long that there was no need for British clearance before proceeding. But the British Treasury and the British Ministry of Economic Warfare held that the contemplated license would result in aid to the enemy.

Back in Washington, Morgenthau on November 23, 1943, reviewed the situation with Paul, Pehle, and others on his staff. The Secretary scolded Pehle for neglecting to consult the British himself, since there were, as the State Department had noted, standard instructions for consultation on all activities relating to trading with the enemy. But Morgenthau also realized, as Pehle pointed out, that the root of the difficulty lay in the reluctance of the British and of Hull's subordinates to support the Treasury's policy. The Secretary therefore suggested having "a very careful cable drawn up giving Winant all the facts and asking him whether he would please facilitate this on behalf of the Treasury. . . . That cable has to be signed by Hull, and in that way it does bring it out in the open. A cable going from me to Winant has to be signed by Hull and cleared."

The files, Pehle objected, were filled with cables which Treasury had originated and the State Department had sent. Those cables in turn were full of little remarks "like the Treasury wants this, the Treasury desires you to do this, and the Treasury this, and the Treasury that. And Harrison, unless he is a dumbbell, can see through that, that State is in effect saying this is what the Treasury wants you to do."

Morgenthau disagreed. He believed that Ambassador Winant could bring the British to heel, and he trusted Hull's good will. "So far," he said, "whenever I have gone to him direct he has been very good. . . . No one would like to see this come out in the open more than I. Unfortunately you are up against a . . . generation of people like those in the State Department who don't like to do this kind of thing, and it is only by my happening to be Secretary of the Treasury and being vitally interested in these things, with the help of you people . . . that I can do it. I am all for you. . . . I will do everything I can, and we will get it done. But don't think you are going to be able to nail anybody in the State Department . . . to the cross. . . .

"You men are very forthright . . . very courageous, and I back you up. . . . I will go just as far as you men will let me go. . . . All I can do is to bring this thing and put this thing in Cordell's hands. . . . Then it is up to him to get angry at his own people."

Randolph Paul drafted the letter to Hull, which Morgenthau softened considerably and signed on November 24. The letter reviewed developments in the Rumanian question since the previous June, lamented the delays that frustrated the program, and solicited Hull's assistance. Morgenthau also asked Hull to send Winant a cable requesting him to obtain from the British Ministry of Economic Warfare "the withdrawal of its objections to the issuance of the license."

Morgenthau's letter referred, too, to a related issue which had first arisen toward the end of the summer when two cables from Bern reported the circumstances of Jewish children in France. The Nazis had deported some 4,000 children, ranging in age between two and fourteen, to undisclosed destinations — gas chambers, probably — in windowless box cars without food or water. Under German orders, the French police were attempting to take a census of another 6,000 Jewish children abandoned in France. Many of them had been hidden in private homes, about half in the Italian-occupied area of southern France. Local finances were inadequate for taking care of children who had been evacuated or for providing transportation and subsequent support for the Jewish children hidden near Paris. Relief organizations could not help unless they had permission to convert dollars to francs. Randolph Paul, after examining the problem, concluded that the Treasury should permit responsible philanthropic groups to arrange relief for refugees in enemy territory under stipulated safeguards; the relief organizations were to demonstrate that they had the necessary facilities and contacts, were to ensure that no foreign exchange would reach the enemy, and were to subject their operations to the scrutiny of American officials in neighboring neutral countries. Morgenthau approved that scheme, while also expressing a preference for working through the Quakers or the Y.M.C.A. rather than through Jewish relief organizations. But as in the case of Rumania, the Treasury needed State Department cooperation in order to proceed.

Replying to Morgenthau on December 6, 1943, Hull wrote that he understood the proposals for Rumania and France had never been developed in detail. Consequently Harrison in Bern had been in a difficult position, authorized to issue a license to cover arrangements not yet adequately worked out. Further, Harrison felt the Treasury's conditions for the use of the license could not be met. The

State Department, Hull concluded, had "the deepest sympathy for the desperate plight of the persecuted Jews in Europe. I have always been horrified at the unspeakable treatment which these poor people have received, and it has always been the policy of the Department to deal expeditiously and sympathetically with proposals offering hope of their relief."

Convinced that his arguments were meretricious, Randolph Paul especially resented Hull's tendentious conclusion. In a draft for Morgenthau, Paul argued that Harrison had known how to proceed under the license issued to the World Jewish Congress. There had been no failure to establish safe mechanisms for exchange. Rather, officers of the State Department and representatives of Great Britain had held up the program. By and large, Morgenthau relied on Paul's analysis in the answer which he sent to Hull on December 17, but he also said that existing disagreements were insignificant in comparison with Hull's willingness to review the whole matter and with Hull's assurances that it was State Department policy to deal expeditiously with the proposal. Like Paul, Morgenthau believed that the Treasury's plans had provided proper safeguards for refugee operations in Rumania and France; unlike Paul, the Secretary was willing to subordinate controversy about what had occurred in order to invite cooperation about what had still to be accomplished.

British policy made that task difficult. On December 13, 1943, the Treasury received through Winant a statement of London's position. The Ministry of Economic Warfare, after "very full and careful consideration," agreed to licensing the transfer of funds for the evacuation of Jews from Rumania and France, but only to $25,000, and only under conditions preventing the movement of dollars to Nazi agents or other objectionable persons. The Ministry noted that the Foreign Office saw "grave disadvantages in general," which would be the subject of a longer dispatch. That arrived two days later. The Foreign Office was concerned "with the difficulties of disposing of any considerable number of Jews should they be rescued from enemy occupied territory;" the schemes under consideration were "greatly hampered by difficulties of transportation, particularly shipping, and of finding accommodation in the countries of the Near East for any but a very small number of Jewish refugees." It seemed to the Foreign Office almost impossible to deal with anything like 70,000 refugees, and therefore the British were "reluctant to agree to any approval being expressed even of the preliminary financial arrangements." Those objections perhaps accounted for the decision of the Ministry of Economic Warfare to confine its approval to only $25,000 of transactions, a small percentage of the funds needed to finance the combined Rumanian and French programs.

At last, Randolph Paul said at a Treasury staff meeting on December 18, 1943, they were "down to the real issue." The Ministry of Economic Warfare had accepted the scheme which Harrison had implied was unworkable. The question was not one of safeguards, as Pehle put it, but of foreign policy. The problem lay in removing that question from the State Department to some agency more sympathetic to the Jews. For that purpose, Morgenthau's subordinates urged him to recommend to the President the appointment of a commission on the refugee problem. The Secretary hesitated. He agreed that there was no doubt about the integrity of the proposed licenses, but he was not sure he could go to the President about a special commission without first enlisting Hull. In spite of his staff's continuing pleading, Morgenthau decided that he would return to the Department of State, armed this time with the stiffest possible memorandum.

On December 19, 1943, Morgenthau recruited assistance in the preparation of his case. He called in Oscar Cox of the Foreign Economic Administration, a shrewd lawyer, a loyal counselor on past occasions, and a knowledgeable student of the refugee problem. Throughout Nazi-occupied Europe, Cox said, courageous Jews endeavored to escape to neutral countries, but if they succeeded in evading the Germans, they then ran into immigration laws which demanded that they have money, a job, and inoculations against typhoid, typhus, and other diseases. Unless the United States obtained the cooperation of all the nations bordering occupied Europe, many Jews would be turned back to German control, which would mean certain death. Cox did not consider the financial problem severe, for private agencies in the United States would provide plenty of money. So too, Cox had faith in the European underground assisting the Jews. What was needed were temporary havens from which they could move on to the Western Hemisphere. The

United States, he thought, would have to take "a very strong and firm and persistent position" with all the neutral countries to persuade them to receive Jewish evacuees, and the United States would have to assist those neutrals in preventing epidemics that the refugees might otherwise spread. He also believed that the United States could relax its own immigration laws. "You have," he said, "a good deal of margin in terms of the United States as well as other places in the world to get them out. Then, when you get them at the camps, you need people who are competent and know the job of running the camps, not as concentration camps, but so these people can either be reabsorbed in the community where they are to work, or take the next additional step, to move them to some place semipermanent, whether they want to go back where they came from or not."

For all those purposes, Cox thought the President would have to set up some kind of a committee, "a driving force that brings the viewpoint before the neutral countries, sees to it that the proper personnel is set up, sees to it there is no defect in the financing." There was no point, Cox said, in flagellating the British, for their attitude was no different from that of the Department of State. The trick was to place the refugee question outside the influence of both groups.

Morgenthau agreed. It would not do, he said, to take his case to Hull only in terms of condemning the British Foreign Office. Rather, the time had come to create an effective executive agency, but here as before, the Secretary was reluctant to approach the White House until he had first consulted Hull.

Morgenthau's confidence in Hull's good will was well placed. On December 18, 1943, two days before he received a Treasury memorandum about the obstructionism of the British Foreign Office, Hull had dispatched a severe message of his own. "Your telegram," he cabled the Foreign Office, ". . . has been read with astonishment by the Department and it is unable to agree with the point of view set forth. Very shortly the Department will communicate with you as to the differential between this situation and others which may be related to preventing the enemy from obtaining the foreign exchange. It is desired by the Department to inform you immediately of the fact that the philosophy set forth . . . is incompatible with the policy of the United States Government and of previously expressed British policy as it has been understood by us." That, of course, was precisely the view of Morgenthau, whose memorandum to Hull called for American policy "to facilitate the escape of Jews from Hitler and *then* discuss what can be done in the way of finding them a more permanent refuge."

On December 20, Morgenthau congratulated the Secretary of State on his cable. Back at the Treasury, he told his staff: "This is one of the greatest victories. . . . You fellows don't know old man Hull. He has his teeth in this thing. I have told you fellows consistently not to say a fellow won't come through until the facts are in." Hull had said, Morgenthau went on, that the trouble lay with "the fellows down the line," whose activities the Secretary of State had been unable to review constantly and in detail. Now Hull was himself ripping through the red tape.

The State Department had already taken some important steps. Breckinridge Long, who had accompanied Hull at the meeting with Morgenthau, had personally drafted a license for exchange transactions in Bern and cabled it to Harrison. Long reported confidentially, moreover, that Rumania had attempted to sue for a separate peace. The United States had been unwilling to enter into negotiations at that time but had assured Rumania that if she conducted herself appropriately she would be given favorable terms when a peace could be made. In particular, the United States had urged improved treatment of the Jews, and within two weeks Rumania had replied that Jews in Transnistria were being repatriated in order to protect them from the Germans then retreating though that area. Still, Long was pessimistic about managing by any device, diplomatic or underground, to bring the Germans to assist the rescue.

Later, alone with Morgenthau, Long had complained that there were various people "down the line" who were making trouble in the State Department. "Well," Morgenthau replied, "Breck . . . we might be a little frank. The impression is all around [that] you, particularly, are anti-semitic." Long said he knew that to be the case and hoped Morgenthau would use his "good offices to correct that impression, because I am not."

"After all," Morgenthau said, "Breck, the United States of America was created as a refuge for people who were persecuted the world over, starting with Plymouth . . . and as Secretary of the Treasury for 135 million people — I am carrying this out as Secretary of the Treasury and not as a Jew."

"Well," Long replied, "my concept of America as a place of refuge for persecuted people is just the same."

Morgenthau, as he told his staff, was "very, very happy. . . . We have got Hull on this thing. . . . The most significant thing in my mind in this case, quite aside from the water that has gone over the dam . . . is that by having started on this Rumanian thing . . . it is likely to have a major effect on the whole shooting match." Since Hull was now taking charge, Morgenthau had not even raised the question of establishing a committee.

Hull's intervention produced prompt action. A cable from Bern on December 23, 1943, reported that Harrison had personally delivered to Riegner the license that Long had sent on December 18. Riegner had then selected the Geneva branch of the Union Bank of Switzerland to keep in escrow funds to finance the evacuation of Rumanian refugees, and he now proposed depositing in that bank Swiss francs equivalent to $25,000, the sum which the British had approved. That money was to be in the name of the World Jewish Congress, with authority for drawing on the account confined to Riegner, and to him only with the Treasury's permission in each case that arose. Riegner was ready also to explore the possibility, on the receipt of further funds, of evacuating Jews from France to Spain and Switzerland. On December 24 Treasury and State approved those arrangements.

Building on that good start, John W. Pehle in Foreign Funds Control began that week to help representatives of the Joint Distribution Committee secure the Swiss francs they needed, estimated at about $150,000 a month for 1944, to finance the evacuation of Jewish children from France and to support the 3000 refugees already arriving in Switzerland. By January 3, 1944, the Treasury had prepared the appropriate licenses and authorized the Joint Distribution Committee to make an initial remittance of $200,000 to Switzerland. The Treasury had also asked the legation at Bern to take reasonable steps to facilitate operations under the new licenses and to report promptly on any difficulties encountered. Morgenthau, "surprised and pleased," as he told his associates, at their initiative, considered them "impolitic" for proceeding without explicit approval from the State Department. Further, he issued instructions on January 5 that all organizations in the field should be obliged to help all children threatened by the Nazis, not just Jewish children.

But the Secretary and his staff quickly realized that their energy exceeded their accomplishments. They were disturbed by their discovery at the turn of the year of the way in which State Department subordinates in the previous May had cut off the flow of information from Bern. Worse, State Department officers, perhaps out of sheer bureaucratic inertia, had again interposed a delay by neglecting to transmit the new licenses that the Treasury had prepared for Bern. Most important, Morgenthau learned on January 8, 1944, that the British government felt that the movement of evacuees resulting from the proposed American financial measures would create problems in transportation and accommodation "which might be embarrassing not only to this government but to your own." The United States, Harry White argued on January 10, had permitted the British too long to dominate policy on the whole Jewish problem. Now only the President could break through that obstacle, and he would act only if Morgenthau interceded directly.

The Secretary continued instead to work through Hull. In a long conference on January 11, 1944, Hull was shocked by what Morgenthau reported, but he also seemed "harassed and weary . . . not . . . well informed as to what was going on . . . simply bewildered." Depressed, Morgenthau returned to the Treasury convinced that "Roosevelt wouldn't move on Hull, he never has; and Hull wouldn't move on Long." But the Secretary was ready to try again, to ask Roosevelt to appoint the special committee earlier suggested by John Pehle and Oscar Cox.

The memorandum stating the case was prepared by Randolph Paul. It carried an unequivocal title: "Report to the Secretary on the Acquiescence of this Government in the Murder of the Jews." The first sentence moved that theme forward: "One of the greatest crimes in history, the slaughter of the Jewish people in Europe, is continuing unabated." Officials in the Department of State, Paul maintained, had willfully failed to act to rescue the Jews. Their procrastination, dating back to August 1942, had facilitated mass murder in Nazi Europe, and that in spite of the interest displayed periodically by Congress in a more positive American policy. Paul particularly condemned State Department restrictions on visas. Under the pretext of concern for national security, he said, Breckinridge Long and his associates had held immigration below available quotas. Further, State Department officers had continually frustrated private programs for helping the Jews. The memorandum, Morgenthau suggested, should also describe the role of the British Foreign Office. Otherwise its content and tone provided exactly what he needed for Roosevelt. So did the increasing possibility of congressional action to aid the refugees.

On January 16, 1944, Morgenthau told the President that he was deeply disturbed by conditions in the State Department. The Treasury, he said, had uncovered evidence indicating that subordinates there, defying Hull, were not only inefficient in dealing with the refuge problem, but were actually taking steps to prevent the rescue of the Jews. Pehle then explained the details to Roosevelt who listened attentively. He also glanced at a draft of an executive order creating a War Refugee Board to consist of the Secretary of the Treasury, the Secretary of War, and the Secretary of State. Roosevelt, as Morgenthau later reported to his staff, "seemed disinclined to believe that Long wanted to stop effective action from being taken, but said that Long had been somewhat soured on the problem when Rabbi Wise got Long to approve a long list of people being brought into this country many of whom turned out to be bad people. . . . In any event he felt that Long was inclined to be soured on the situation." But the President was also prepared to take up the matter with Stettinius, whom he expected to find sympathetic, and he agreed with Morgenthau that it was indeed possible to facilitate the escape of Jews from Rumania and France to safety in Turkey, Switzerland, and Spain.

That evening, under Roosevelt's instructions, Morgenthau talked with Stettinius. He told the Under Secretary of State "in plain words," that "he was convinced that people in the State Department, particularly Breckinridge Long, were deliberately obstructing the execution of any plan to save the Jews and that forthright immediate action was necessary if this Government was not going to be placed in the same position as Hitler and share the responsibility for exterminating all the Jews of Europe." Upset by the facts which Morgenthau and Pehle then presented, Stettinius said that he was "not surprised about Breckinridge Long since Long had fallen just as badly and in an equally shocking way in the handling of the exchange of prisoners. Stettinius was very frank in his views on Long's failures and pointed out that in the reorganization of the State Department which he had worked out the only remaining function assigned to Breckinridge Long is Congressional relations." Like Roosevelt, Stettinius doubted that Long had meant to hurt the Jews; rather, he found Long, no longer a young and perhaps never a vigorous executive, inefficient in everything he handled. And like Roosevelt, Stettinius agreed with Morgenthau that the time for action had come. Examining the draft executive order, Stettinius said emphatically: "I think it's wonderful."

His endorsement satisfied the President who on January 22, 1944, established the War Refugee Board to assist the immediate rescue and relief of the Jews of Europe "and other victims of enemy persecution." That board was to cooperate with interested American and international agencies, to utilize the facilities of the Treasury, War, and State Departments in furnishing aid to Axis victims, and to attempt to forestall the plot of the Nazis to exterminate Jews and other minorities. An accompanying order to the Bureau of the Budget set aside one million dollars for initial administrative expenses, and Roosevelt announced that he expected all members of the United Nations and other foreign governments to cooperate with the board in its important task.

The terrible eighteen months had ended, though too late to help most of the Rumanian Jews. "Thousands upon thousands will have the cruel hand of suffering and death lifted from them by what you have done," Oscar Cox wrote Morgenthau. "To feel with and as humans whom you haven't seen in the lands of persecution is one of the marks of your human depth and greatness. Deep in my heart I am warm. Rare individuals like you are what give me, at least, the driving hope to carry on with the war and what comes after."

Pleased and flattered though he was by that letter, Morgenthau then and later grieved over the opportunities lost during the previous year and a half. As he put it, the fight had been "long and heartbreaking. The stake was the Jewish population of Nazi-controlled Europe. The threat was their total obliteration. The hope was to get a few of them out." With the War Refugee Board established, the hope lay, "in the few meagre months remaining," as it had never before, with "crusaders, passionately persuaded of the need for speed and action."

7. The War Refugee Board

Morgenthau, Hull, and Stimson, the members of the War Refugee Board, left the initiation as well as the execution of policy largely to the director of the board, John Pehle. Morgenthau originally suggested Wendell Willkie as director, but Roosevelt felt that Willkie, who had just traveled around the world for the President, had "had all the build-up he has coming to him on that trip." Pehle, in the opinion of the members of the board and their deputies, was the only other attractive candidate for the post. The President named him Acting Director and soon, impressed by his work, made the appointment permanent.*

Pehle and his staff went energetically to work. Before the end of January, they had agreed with the World Jewish Congress on a program for the removal of refugees from France to Spain, Switzerland, and North Africa; and they had granted appropriate licenses for that purpose and also for further operations in Rumania. They had arranged, too, with the Joint Distribution Committee for the evacuation of between five and six thousand children from France, and had issued the necessary licenses permitting expenditure of up to $60,000 during the next six months. They had begun to plan the removal of Jews from Poland and Hungary, and they had assured the Vatican of funds needed for the immediate relief of destitute Jews in Rome. They were cooperating with the International Red Cross in Geneva in its relief efforts; they had provided instructions to American missions in four neutral countries on all aspects of their policy; and they had received $100,000 of private contributions, the first of many larger donations for their work. By mid-March 1944,

* Though Pehle resigned more than a year after his work was well under way, to be replaced by William O'Dwyer, later mayor of New York City.

without complaint from London, the Board had started the rail transportation from Bulgaria of 150 Jewish children every ten days to Palestine via Turkey. The Board had also assisted actual rescues in Poland, Slovakia, and Hungary. In all cases, the licenses issued kept the transfer of funds in escrow or in blocked accounts that precluded Axis acquisition of either dollars or Swiss francs.

Both Stimson and Morgenthau applauded Pehle's efforts. In his Diary on February 1, 1944, Stimson described a luncheon with Morgenthau and Pehle, and the progress of the evacuation of the Jews. "These poor creatures," Stimson wrote, "have lost their homes, are being hunted by the German constabulary and are seeking to get out of the German occupied zone into some place where they can be safe. Apparently enough private money in the shape of private contributions from American Jewish organizations is available to work this out without calling on the Treasury. The principal places where they can get refuge are Palestine, Hungary, a new camp which has been built by the American army in Morocco, and possibly some of the ruined Italian cities. . . . So a meeting which I had rather dreaded turned out to be rather interesting and profitable."

In his Diary of March 7, 1944, Morgenthau reported a session at the White House: "I gave the President the report on what they have been doing in the Refugee . . . Committee. The President was very much interested and he read the stuff very carefully, but I had difficulty getting him to listen to me because he wanted to talk about Palestine and I was trying to get over my refugee story. . . .

"He said . . . 'what I am trying to get the English to do is this. They don't want to change the White Paper*, but I want to get them to say publicly, if I am successful through the Refugee Committee in bringing any Jews out of Europe, that they will let them go to Palestine . . . I want them to say that. . . . I want them to mention Palestine by name. . . .' He said, 'You know the Arabs don't like this thing.' "

Morgenthau, of course, knew that very well, and knew also that British policy would in some degree defer to Arab attitudes. Uninterested in making Palestine a Jewish homeland, the Secretary, like Pehle, was eager to enlarge facilities within the United States to

* On Jews in Palestine and quotas for their entry there.

which Jews could come until the war was over. That possibility troubled Stimson. As the Secretary of War reported in his Diary after a meeting of March 21, "I pointed out the dangers . . . how it was almost impossible to be sure that they would be taken back and that, if they weren't, it would be a violation of our quota policy which I believe in. Of course I feared that this was gall and wormwood to Morgenthau. Hull then said that he supposed that it had better be a policy to go to the President. I told him that it certainly should."

In further discussions of March 31, 1944, Stimson made himself clearer: "I have taken an attitude rather contrary to the one that Morgenthau and Pehle are pushing with the possible support of Hull. McCloy agreed with my position. He has been acting for me when I was unable to be present at the meetings." Together they had prepared a revision of a draft which Pehle wanted to send Roosevelt asking for the President's help in setting up American havens. "I had Pehle come to see me," Stimson wrote, "and I told him of my feeling about the inadequacy of his draft. . . . He took my letter to talk it over with Morgenthau and the others. . . . The main point is that they wish to have the President throw open internment camps in the United States for those refugees and do it without consulting Congress. I think he ought to consult Congress because I fear that Congress will feel that it is the opening wedge to a violation of our immigration laws."

As it developed, both Pehle and Morgenthau immediately accepted Stimson's views, and their recommendation to the President on April 8 suggested four possible modes of action. Roosevelt might create havens in the United States by executive action, or consult with appropriate members of Congress with a view to setting executive policy, or send a message to Congress asking it to act, or send to Congress a draft for necessary legislation. Morgenthau told Pehle that he believed emphatically that Roosevelt should sound out Congress about whether the message would be acceptable. The Secretary also warned Pehle against the dangers of an executive order, which would, he predicted, irritate the Congress. He was going to look after the President's interest, Morgenthau said, as he always had, and he was therefore unwilling to support a recommendation for independent executive action. Hull wholly agreed.

To the President on May 16, 1944, Pehle presented the proposal for American havens in the terms that all three members of the Board had advised. Roosevelt objected primarily to calling the refugee camps "Free Ports." He wanted the name instead to suggest the temporary nature of the establishments, but he liked the plan, and was "very expansive about Army camps in the South, and [the use of] the Navy to bring the people over." He was also eager to have favorable publicity planned from labor and other groups, which had already promised it. Pehle believed that it was too late for the President to delay action pending congressional approval, and Roosevelt was willing to consider independent action, but only for a small group of refugees, perhaps 500 or 1000, that needed immediate help. He would then, he said, send a message to Congress explaining what he had done.

On May 18, 1944, Pehle called the President's attention to the crowded conditions in refugee camps in Italy. There Roosevelt could find an appropriate group of evacuees for a first experiment with an American haven. As other reports indicated, refugees were arriving in Italy at the rate of 1800 a week, far too many for the military authorities to handle. At a Cabinet meeting of May 26, the President instructed the War Department "under no circumstances to turn these people back." While that department examined possibilities for setting up refugee camps in various areas of Italy and North Africa, Roosevelt decided to remove some of the Jews in Italy to what he now called "Emergency Refugee Shelters" in the United States. Pehle supported the President's proposal by an analysis of public opinion. It showed that some 70 percent of Americans approved the creation of havens in the United States, as did the Federal Council of the Churches of Christ, the American Friends Service Committee, the Catholic Committee for Refugees, the Unitarian Fellowship for Social Justice, and many Jewish groups. Approval had been expressed also by the *New York Times,* New York *Post,* the *Herald Tribune,* the *Christian Science Monitor,* the Hearst newspapers, and other leading journals, as well as by outstanding federal officials, including Vice President Wallace and Justice Frankfurter. On June 2, McCloy reported to Morgenthau that one haven was available in a former Army camp, Fort Ontario, at Oswego, New York. In a series of directives, Roosevelt then ordered arrangements made for the transportation of a thousand refugees from Italy.

The War Department was to equip the camp for receiving refugees and to provide security precautions, while the War Relocation Authority was to make arrangements for handling the actual administration of the camp. Until the United Nations Relief and Rehabilitation Administration could assume financial reponsibility, the Bureau of the Budget was to provide funds to the responsible American agencies. In other instructions, Roosevelt noted that he "should . . . like the group to include a reasonable proportion of various categories of persecuted people who have fled to Italy," though of course the largest number would be Jews. And on June 12, the President, in a message to Congress, expressed his abhorrence of Nazi barbarism and described the actions he had just taken. His leadership, Pehle felt, accounted for the British decision at the same time to establish a temporary haven for 1500 refugees at Tripolitania.

By mid-June 1944, the War Refugee Board had begun to fulfill Morgenthau's high expectations. His experience in getting the board established and in helping to oversee its operations constituted his signal wartime success to that date in nurturing humanitarian purpose in American foreign policy. That success compensated, in part at least, for the frustrations the Secretary had met in North Africa, France, and Argentina. But success and failure alike contributed to his growing determination to spend his influence for the construction of a decent postwar world. In June of 1944, moreover, the invasion of France signaled the start of the last great phase of the war. Victory, to be sure, was still far away, but it was at least in sight. And the vision of victory spurred Morgenthau to intensify his efforts, already begun, to create instrumentalities to preserve the peace.

V

A New Deal in International Economics

1942-1944

WITHIN A WEEK after Pearl Harbor, Morgenthau began to think about opportunities for reconstructing postwar international monetary affairs. From the first, he envisaged a kind of New Deal for a new world. He believed, too, that innovations in economic policy, significant for both the domestic and the foreign affairs of the United States, depended upon resolutions of conflicting interests, though those interests were often clothed in the technical vocabulary of economics and finance. The kind of internationalism he sought touched all nations, looked to the wealthy to assist the poor, and envisaged the continuing cooperation especially of three great powers — the United States, the United Kingdom, and the Soviet Union. From that economic cooperation he expected the United States to profit, and he assumed that the United States, the richest of all nations, would contribute the most money to and exercise the largest influence in the institutions through which cooperation was to be managed. Morgenthau's internationalism had a nationalistic bias, just as Roosevelt's did, not the least because both men saw a reciprocal identity between national and international interests.

1. A New Deal for a New World

On Sunday, December 14, 1941, Morgenthau directed Harry White to prepare a memorandum on the establishment of an inter-Allied stabilization fund. That fund, the Secretary said, should provide the

228

basis for postwar international monetary agreements. The planning that then began reflected continually the convictions and experience of Morgenthau and his colleagues in the Treasury.

International monetary instability, Morgenthau knew, had contributed to the coming and the severity of the great depression between the two World Wars. A similar instability would damage the world economy in the future unless some institution prevented it. In his view, private bankers, pursuing selfish ends, had caused most of the trouble in the past. Working alone or through central banks they dominated, they had frequently subordinated national interest to their own purposes. He intended, therefore, that governments should direct monetary policy. He took special pride in his own role in gathering authority over monetary matters within the United States Treasury in the years after 1933, and he valued particularly the achievements of the Stabilization Fund and of the Tripartite Accord of 1936.* Under that agreement, the United States, Great Britain, France, Belgium, Holland, and Switzerland had cooperated to stop competitive devaluations of the kind that had harassed international trade in the preceding decade. Further, the Treasury under Morgenthau had utilized its authority to combat aggressive monetary techniques of the Axis nations. For the future, Morgenthau wanted a multilateral accord, broader than the Tripartite Pact and more powerful, which would provide a central agency for preventing competitive devaluations, for avoiding exchange controls even of a benign type, and to those ends, for assisting nations in solving their international monetary problems. Such an agency, as he saw it, by creating a pool of gold and currencies under unified management, could help weaker members through periods of temporary stringency, promote international monetary amity, and thereby foster international trade. Such an agency would generalize and improve upon the experience of the Tripartite Pact of 1936; it would bring the treasuries of the United Nations into continuing collaboration; and it would assure governmental rather than private direction of international monetary affairs.

By his own admission inexpert about international monetary questions, Morgenthau looked to Harry White to give technical sub-

---

* So-called because its original signers were the United States, Great Britain, and France.

stance and administrative structure to his general scheme. White served both as the architect of the Treasury's international economic planning and as the Department's main advocate, at home and abroad, of the resulting blueprints. In both roles, he exercised a broad initiative and direction, but always with reference to his most immediate client, Morgenthau, who at moments of political crisis brought his own influence to bear on behalf of the evolving program.

On May 8, 1942, White completed his first, elaborate draft proposals for a "United Nations Stabilization Fund" and a "Bank for Reconstruction and Development." The resources of the Fund, he suggested, should consist of gold and of currencies and securities of member governments, with voting rights adjusted to the size of each nation's contribution. Conditions for membership would forbid exchange controls and bilateral currency arrangements, and would demand liberal tariff, trade, and commercial policies. The Fund, as White saw it, was "to provide an instrument with the means and the procedure to stabilize foreign exchange rates and strengthen the monetary systems of the United Nations." The Treasury of each member country would have the privilege of purchasing from the Fund the currency of any other member country, provided that that currency was required to meet adverse balance of payments, but no member could buy a quantity of currency larger than its total contribution to the Fund. Under certain conditions, and by a four-fifths vote of the members — a fraction that gave the United States an effective veto — the Fund could purchase currency in excess of the original contribution of any nation, ordinarily for the purpose of anticipating problems in the balance of payments. As White pointed out, the Fund could also assist the liquidation of blocked accounts that were accumulating during the war. The Fund was to have the power of fixing the rates at which it would exchange the currency of one member for the currency of another, as well as the rates at which it would buy and sell gold. The guiding principle in establishing rates would be stability in exchange relationships, and changes in rates would be made only in order to correct a fundamental disequilibrium, and then only by a four-fifths vote.

Members of the Fund were to contribute a total of five billion dollars, with each nation meeting a quota partly of currency, partly of interest-bearing government securities, and at least one-eighth of gold. Control of the Fund was to fall to a board of directors in which each government would have one hundred votes plus one vote for every million dollars in gold and one vote for the equivalent of every two million dollars of currency it contributed. White's terms assured the United States of the major voice. Those terms also maintained a link of currencies to gold, but they did not reestablish the old gold standard. Indeed the proposal looked to a potential flexibility in exchange rates, whereas the gold standard of the 1920's had been rigid and automatic. Yet it was characteristic of White, as of Morgenthau, not wholly to abandon gold. They considered the American rate for gold, $35 an ounce, an anchor then and for the future for world currencies. The United States, moreover, had acquired most of the world's monetary gold, and as Morgenthau and White saw it, it served the national interest to keep gold a part of an international monetary system.

In addition to the Fund, White proposed the establishment of a "Bank for Reconstruction and Development," which was to be "an agency with resources and powers adequate to provide capital for economic reconstruction . . . to provide relief for stricken people . . . to increase foreign trade, and permanently increase the productivity of the United Nations." For those and related purposes, the Bank would supply capital for financing foreign trade, for strengthening the monetary and credit structures of member countries, for eliminating world-wide economic fluctuations of a financial origin, and reducing the likelihood, intensity, and duration of world-wide depressions, and for stabilizing prices of raw materials. The Bank was to have a capital stock at a maximum of ten billion dollars consisting of ten thousand shares of one million dollars each, with each share to be paid for half in gold and half in currency, and with participating members assigned minimum quotas and allowed voting authority proportionate to their shares — a provision that again assured American dominance. The Bank would have the authority to make short and long term loans to any participating government or, with the approval of that government, to any political subdivision or business or enterprise within its sovereignty. There were to be no conditions about how the proceeds of a loan were to be spent. Most important, the Bank was to have broad powers to issue notes and securities, and to make available resources many times as large as its subscribed capital.* Wherever possible, it was to guarantee loans made by private investors instead of making loans directly, provided the rate of interest was not in excess of a stipulated maximum. Here, of course, White was internationalizing a New Deal practice — the guaranteeing of private loans so as to hold down interest rates and encourage lending. Too, White's concern about the distribution of raw materials and the stabilization of international commodity prices, and about preventing or tempering depressions, reflected his sensitivity to the paramount economic worries of the Roosevelt Administration.

In sending his memoranda on the Fund and the Bank to Morgenthau, White suggested calling a conference of the finance ministers of the United Nations to carry forward plans for both establishments. He urged Morgenthau to take the initiative so that responsibility for future negotiations would fall preeminently to the Treasury.

"I am convinced," the Secretary in turn wrote Roosevelt on May 15, 1942, enclosing White's drafts with his letter, "that the launching of such a plan at this time has tremendous strategic as well as economic bearing. It seems to me that the time is right to dramatize our international economic objectives in terms of action which people everywhere will recognize as practical, powerful and inspiring." If the President agreed, Morgenthau wanted his permission to ask the Board of Economic Warfare, the State Department, and the Federal Reserve Board to work with the Treasury in planning a conference of finance ministers in Washington. "It is my thought," Roosevelt replied the next day, "that the studies now in progress should be continued. . . . You might speak to me about this again after you have . . . got the opinions of the Secretary of State and the Under Secretary of State."

With their assent and the President's, Morgenthau called a first meeting of the interested agencies on May 25, 1942. There was unanimous enthusiasm for the Treasury's general purpose which Marriner Eccles called "most important in the international field from a monetary standpoint." The State Department, Herbert Feis

* A bold provision that was dropped in later drafts in deference to congressional opposition.

said, believed the time had come "to pursue this study," and he and
the others subscribed to a suggestion of Jesse Jones for making
Harry White chairman of a subcommittee to prepare a next report.

In the ensuing weeks, State Department representatives recognized the primacy of the Treasury in monetary planning, but the
two departments soon differed about procedures. While White continued to press for a formal international conference as soon as possible, the State Department feared that a failure of discussion would
have an unfortunate political impact. The State Department also
felt that no formal international conference on either a Fund or a
Bank should occur until the main political elements of a postwar
settlement were determined. And finally, the State Department preferred to confine preliminary conversations to the British who, as
Dean Acheson noted, had the largest stake in the matter, and perhaps to a few other friendly states. The British, Acheson said on
July 2, 1942, "are very nervous that we will produce a large meeting,
have some plan which we will put before that meeting, and that
they will not have an opportunity to go over the whole thing with us
freely, privately, and frankly before the thing starts."

"In other words," Morgenthau said, ". . . anything that they
don't like they just want to be able to kill it."

Not so, Acheson thought; rather, the British were "tremendously
anxious to do almost what we want, but they want a chance to talk
the matter over with us before the thing is crystallized. . . . I think
there is a rather pathetic feeling on the part of the British that we
really are going to write the ticket, and all they want is a chance to
go over it with us, pointing out their views, and to be allowed to
come in on the formulation at the start. . . . In the Department
. . . we felt that there would really be most serious repercussions if
we start out by a large meeting of a great many experts."

Morgenthau suspected that the argument about procedure
clothed an unexpressed State Department opposition to the Fund
and Bank. "What has Mr. Hull got in mind?" he asked Acheson.
"Does he want us to go ahead with this thing? Does he want us to
kind of let the thing peter out, or just what has he got in mind? . . .

"I haven't got energy enough if I disagree with him . . . to get
into an interdepartmental fight. This comes in the realm of foreign
affairs. . . . It is his responsibility and . . . I want to go along

that way. . . . If that is the way he wants to proceed . . . I will take my clue from him. . . .

"I want his complete backing on this thing. . . . So . . . find out what Mr. Hull wants . . . and then proceed from there."

Hull's suggestions received immediate approval on July 21, 1942. First, the United States was to advise friendly governments that American technical experts were examining the economic and financial problems related to creating a Fund and Bank. Second, representatives of the Treasury and of the State Department would initiate exploratory discussions with spokesmen for the United Kingdom, the Soviet Union, China, Canada, Australia, Brazil, and Mexico. If the response of those nations was sufficiently promising, and if Roosevelt was agreeable, the Secretary of the Treasury would then call a preliminary meeting to draft an agenda and other necessary documents for a formal international conference. Prior to that preliminary meeting, the interdepartmental committee and its experts would prepare appropriate studies for the United States.

Those procedures, as Hull and Acheson had expected, quickly resulted in a crucial exchange of views between the United States and the United Kingdom, an exchange which was to continue over many months. The British had been working independently on postwar monetary policy, and their initial proposals, while in important respects sharing American purposes, in other ways diverged significantly from White's formulations.

John Maynard Keynes was the intelligence behind the British plan for an International Clearing Union. After returning from the United States late in 1941, Keynes began developing his scheme, conscious always of the portentous severity of England's growing international debts, dedicated always to the enhancement of British interests within a postwar internationalism, brilliant always in the application to international monetary questions of his own profoundly influential economic ideas. The Clearing Union, which had the support of the British government, incorporated Keynes's purpose: to "obtain the advantages, without the disadvantages, of an international gold currency," to provide stability in both the internal and external value of the pound sterling, and to substitute "an expansionist, in place of a contractionist, pressure on world trade."

As Keynes planned it, the Clearing Union would make available to its members large overdraft facilities related to their prewar share of world trade. The volume of a nation's prewar trade would also determine its proportionate vote within the Union. But unlike White's Fund, the Clearing Union would have no assets, no gold and currencies and securities. Rather, surpluses and deficits in the balance of payments of the member countries would be reflected respectively in credits and debits on the accounts of the Union, expressed in "bancors," Keynes's name for his proposed international units of account. A nation with a credit in bancors would have the privilege of spending them in any participating country, but not of trading them for gold, though any country, through the Union, could convert gold to bancors, which were to be defined in terms of gold by weight.

There would be available to the members of the Union in all some $26 billion for overdrafts — so much that members would be able, Keynes believed, to eliminate all exchange restrictions on current accounts, to maintain stability in exchange rates, and to pursue policies designed to expand domestic economies without fear that resulting price inflation would carry adverse consequences for foreign balances. Naturally Keynes was solicitous of British influence in world affairs, which his scheme for votes preserved. Further, the Union imposed a potentially enormous liability on the United States, economically the strongest country in the world and therefore least likely to need overdraft privileges in the immediate postwar years. Though liability for any nation was limited to the total overdraft rights of all nations, that total was so great as to seem to Americans the equivalent to a blank check against them.

As the British took pains to point out to White and Morgenthau in August 1942, the Keynes plan was put forward only as a basis for discussion. The White and Keynes plans had broad areas in common, while each, in the view of the British, seemed to contribute important elements not fully developed by the other. White had dealt admirably with the problem of liquidating blocked balances and of freeing capital movements. His ideas for the Bank as an agency for stabilizing the prices of primary products ran close to British ideas, as did his treatment of tariffs, exchange controls, and restrictions on trade. But the central element in the Keynes plan

did admittedly differ from what the American Treasury had proposed, for the Clearing Union had powers and responsibilities toward its clients rather like those of an ordinary bank toward its customers. In that situation the British saw advantages. White's plan,
they felt, tended to help only those who had a gold reserve already,
and then only in proportion to the amount of their reserve. A poor
country that needed support might receive little from the Fund since
extraordinary help was available only on the basis of a four-fifths
vote. Too, the Keynes plan went much further in making possible
the adjustment of the total volume of international currency to world
needs. Should a severe world depression threaten at some later date,
success in coping with it, the British believed, would turn largely on
the adoption of generally expansionist policies. The efforts of individual countries might prove futile, as they had in the past, unless
they were given strong support by a common international currency
policy. Last, the British were obviously attracted, though they did
not stress the point, by the internal neatness of the Keynes plan.
Based as it was on the necessary equality of credits and debits, the
Union was a closed system of account which, they felt, could never
meet difficulties in honoring its checks.

Early in October 1942, the American experts prepared for submis-
sion to Keynes a set of questions, some technical, others political. In
general, as Assistant Secretary of State Berle put it, two broad considerations would affect any international monetary plan: first,
would Congress accept it; second, would it fit the financial policies
of the Administration. Though Berle did not say so, the Congress,
like the American business community, still had serious reservations
(not shared by Berle himself) about Keynes's general theory of economics, about Keynes's expansionism, and about the application of
those views to international monetary affairs. Further, the Congress
would almost certainly look askance at any scheme involving American liabilities as large as those that Keynes had suggested, and
would object to a weighting of votes that favored Great Britain.
The British, for their part, had to consider the sentiments of Parliament, where members of the Labor Party would blanch at any move
that seemed to put the nation back on the gold standard, and where
many Conservatives would fight to preserve the policy of imperial
preference. Clearly the politics of the dollar and the pound would

mold Anglo-American discussions more than would technical considerations.

Nevertheless, the technicians, conscious always of the limits of political feasibility, carried the bilateral negotiations forward toward acceptable compromise. With little reference to the Bank, they concentrated on the differences between the Union and the Fund. In the process of proposal and counterproposal, White at one point came up with a rival to the bancor — the "Unitas," a bookkeeping unit to consist, for convenience, of a number of grains of gold equal in value to $10. The large significance of the Unitas lay in its sound, derived from "United Nations" so as to contrast to "bancor" with its tones of Lombard and Wall Streets.

More important, in a draft of December 16, 1942, White satisfied the British demand for some sanction against creditor countries — against nations that accumulated continuing favorable balances of payments, as the United States surely would in the first postwar years. That draft contained a "scarce currency" clause. If debtor nations increased their indebtedness beyond a stipulated point, they would lose their rights to draw from the Fund. If creditor countries increased their credit beyond a corresponding level, their currencies would be declared "scarce" and would be allotted by the Fund, which would also authorize debtor nations to discriminate against the exports of the creditors until a better balance had been established. That provision would prevent an uncorrected favorable balance to continue indefinitely. "This was a very remarkable concession," wrote Roy Harrod, an eminent British economist, and a friend and (later) biographer of Keynes. "If the United States was really to maintain . . . the . . . role of creditor, which all predicted . . . it would mean that she was . . . authorizing other nations to discriminate against the purchase of American goods . . . and to maintain their own full employment. . . . This . . . was the big thing . . . a great event. For it was the first time that they had said . . . they would . . . accept their full share of responsibility when there was a fundamental disequilibrium of trade. . . . I felt an exhilaration such as only comes once or twice in a lifetime."

The "scarce currency" clause brought the treasuries of the two English-speaking countries close to each other, but technical planning and conversations in London and Washington remained confidential until March 1943. The British Treasury then informed the United States that Keynes had discussed a draft proposal for the International Clearing Union at a conference of finance ministers of various governments-in-exile. News of that conference and of the British draft had leaked to the press both in England and the United States, and the news had aroused such interest among the British public and Parliament that the British government considered it necessary to publish the text of Keynes's proposal. That would lead of course to references to the work done in the United States.

In a memorandum for Roosevelt of March 17, 1943, Morgenthau noted that there had already been a number of inquiries about the American plan, including one from Senator Vandenberg asking whether the discussions underway involved any commitments. Though they did not, Morgenthau was eager to provide Vandenberg with a full explanation, for he wanted to win that influential senator to the proposal for the Monetary Fund, and he needed Vandenberg's immediate support for the biennial renewal of the Stabilization Fund then pending in Congress. Consequently Morgenthau asked Roosevelt's permission to issue a press release about the White plan and to give to appropriate congressional groups a summary of the tentative conclusions of American experts. On March 18 at the White House Roosevelt in turn asked only that the Secretary explain that all studies and conversations to date had been "purely exploratory." So informed, Harry White asked whether the President had any interest in a postwar monetary fund. He had read the memorandum carefully, Morgenthau replied, but made no comment. "He very seldom, Harry," the Secretary continued, "shows any enthusiasm these days. It is very rare. So don't be disappointed."

The preparation of an appropriate press release disclosed some of the unresolved differences between the United States and Great Britain. A Treasury draft referred to "fixing values of currencies in terms of gold." The British revision read "fixing values of currency by relating them to gold" — a change designed to avoid offending the large body of British opinion still afraid of linking sterling to gold. So also, Morgenthau intended to say that the Fund might "point the direction for international cooperation." That indicated a degree of commitment greater than the British considered appropriate, and they therefore changed the language to say that a Fund might "form a useful basis for discussions directed toward international cooperation." Yet the British were willing to release details about the Keynes plan, whereas Roosevelt was loath to unveil the White plan. With Morgenthau on April 1, 1943, the President was "very emphatic" that there was to be no "publication of the American plan." "These things are too early," Roosevelt said. "We haven't begun to win the war."

The Treasury, Morgenthau told the Senate Committee on Finance on April 6, had been worried for some time about the threat of international monetary chaos after the war. Only international cooperation could provide the stability in currency essential for world reconstruction and for the resumption of private trade and finance. "No specific plan has as yet been considered by this government," he said, "but preliminary suggestions of our technical experts have been formulated and have been made available for exploratory study of experts of other interested governments. . . . Our tentative proposal is to establish an international stabilization fund in which all the United Nations and those nations which are associated with them in this war could participate. . . . The cooperating governments . . . would . . . undertake not to engage in competitive depreciation. . . . Stability would be in large measure secured by fixing the value of currency in terms of gold, and by providing that changes could not be made without consultation with other members. . . . The voting power . . . would be related to the contribution which each country makes to the required revolving fund." In spite of British objections, then, Morgenthau persisted in his intention to give the United States a commanding voice in the Fund, to link the Fund to gold, and to stress — in contrast to Keynes — the elimination of competitive devaluation rather then the expansion of domestic economies.

Still, the Secretary had not wanted to show his whole hand, particularly after Roosevelt's instructions. He was therefore distressed by the publication in London of the details of the White plan, which were leaked to the press by the finance ministry of one of the governments-in-exile. "As I said to the President . . . ," Morgenthau told his staff, " 'This thing ought to be a lesson for us, that anything that we want to do that is really important, we just can't take all these countries into our confidence.' " The disclosure in London led to an official unveiling of the White plan at a Treasury press conference soon after Morgenthau's testimony to the Senate on April 6, 1943. On that occasion both the Secretary and Harry White reviewed the American position and assessed the Keynes plan.

"Don't underestimate the quality of Keynes's plan," White warned. "You will find that it is very good."

"It is a very British plan, isn't it Mr. White?" one reporter asked. "You don't have to answer him," Morgenthau interrupted. Amid general laughter, White described the method of alloting votes Keynes had proposed.

"I hope that you people won't . . . make it look as though the English . . . are trying to be . . . selfish," Morgenthau added. "We are all in this war together, sink or swim, and we don't want to have it set up as though they were trying to out-trade us or we them. . . . My experience with them since I have been here is that they have put up a good case and we tried to put up a good case, but after we have a . . . chance to rub the edges off they have been fair."

Publication of the two plans produced predictable responses. Both the British and American press expressed preferences for the plans of their own governments, though the London press was not overtly hostile to the American scheme. Financial circles in Washington and London were pleased that both plans maintained a market for gold and looked to the removal of foreign exchange controls. Most important, a Republican resolution introduced in Congress provided for congressional representation at any international conference of Treasury representatives with other nations. On the advice of Cordell Hull, Morgenthau cooperated with Sam Rayburn to persuade Congress to keep its role in postwar conferences on an informal basis. Promised that Congress would be consulted at every important point, Rayburn was able to cut off formal action. The generally friendly reaction to the White plan encouraged the Secretary, as did also the willingness of the British to negotiate reasonably toward a common objective. With the pace of those negotiations about to accelerate, Morgenthau felt that he and his associates had traveled a long way toward a new stage for the New Deal.

THE CABINET, 1941

Left to right around the table: Secretary of Agriculture Wickard, Secretary of Labor Perkins, Vice President Wallace, Secretary of Commerce Jones, Secretary of the Interior Ickes, Postmaster General Walker, Secretary of War Stimson, Secretary of State Hull, President Roosevelt, Secretary of the Treasury Morgenthau, Attorney General Biddle, Secretary of the Navy Knox

"War called forth their last reserves of energy."

Morgenthau, Congress, and the Sales Tax

Cartoon by C. K. Berryman in the Washington *Star*, May 10, 1942

Secretary Morgenthau Sells Bonds
on his Trip to the Mediterranean Theater, 1943

"Americans at home had too much to spend."

Secretary Morgenthau's Solution to the Cost of War
Cartoon by C. K. Berryman

Secretary Morgenthau Consults with the Fiscal Chiefs
of Supreme Headquarters in England, 1944

"England was broke."

IT CAN'T BE OURS! IT'S GOT GOLDEN HAIR!

Cartoon by Low—The Bretton Woods Conference, 1944

Left, above: Secretary Morgenthau Greets Troops in the
European Theater, 1944

"The boys are wonderful."

Left, below: Secretary Morgenthau with General Omar Bradley
in France, August 9, 1944

Bradley: "Very quiet, complete self-control, complete balance."

President Roosevelt and Secretary Morgenthau
End the 1944 Campaign Touring Dutchess County

"That mortal friendship was immortality enough."

2. Staging for a Conference

The circulation of White's revised draft for the Fund was the first of many stages between the confidential Anglo-American discussions and the calling of an international conference on monetary affairs. The draft reached finance ministers of the nations united against the Axis late in April 1943. Australia, Paraguay, the Philippines, then China and soon Russia expressed approval of the American objective and arranged to send experts to Washington for technical conversations. In Parliament in May, the Chancellor of the Exchequer announced that those conversations would continue for several months, during which Anglo-American negotiations would also go on. The treasuries of the two nations, he said, would consider the views that had been expressed by bankers and economists within their own countries. Toward the end of the period, the American Treasury hoped that a general but informal meeting in Washington could synthesize the suggestions that would by then have emerged. If at that point the area of agreement was large, plans could go forward for a conference of finance ministers.

The omens of the summer pointed to an emerging consensus. *Fortune* in a major article emphasized the need for international monetary cooperation and drew heavily on the proposals of the United States Treasury in making its principal points. More important, the interdepartmental working committee in Washington rapidly agreed on revisions of the White draft designed to attract British support. Pleased by that progress, Morgenthau in July asked Hull to approve Treasury leadership during the coming stages of negotiation. That approval was already implicit in Hull's earlier understanding with the Treasury, but Assistant Secretary of State Berle had raised questions about procedure, and Morgenthau took them directly to Hull so as to avoid further tensions between the departments.*

The Secretary of State was bitter, irritated by his relationships with the President, but not uncooperative. As Morgenthau put it in his Diary on July 9, 1943:

> He kept saying, "What is it we can do to improve the situation? . . . The President runs foreign affairs. I don't know

* Then at odds about American policy in Argentina and North Africa.

what's going on. . . . I asked to see the political part of the cables between the President and Churchill, because I have to find out from Halifax what's going on between the President and Churchill. . . . The President said . . . he would give it to me and, three hours later, I got a message that the President had decided he would not do it. . . .

"There is somebody over there who passes on everything the State Department sends to the President. . . . I know the President is running foreign affairs and I know the President will not let me help him any more. . . . Since Pearl Harbor he does not let me help in connection with foreign affairs. . . . I just don't know what's going on. . . ."

I told Hull I think the trouble with the President is that some of the old line agencies don't run to his satisfaction. Then he creates an independent agency and then another independent agency and before he's through he has thirty or forty independent agencies. Then he needs a coordinator and then a commission to run the independent agencies and the commission fails and my answer is he has ten Cabinet members and if they don't function properly, fire them, but leave this responsibility with them. . . . I said, "The President tries to do it all and he can't do it." Well, Hull agreed with me. . . .

Then he also went into a long criticism of Senator Connolly.* He's terrible! This thing has gone to his head and, he said, he just can't work with him. . . .

Then, after we got all through this, I said, "Now, look, Cordell. It's just this kind of thing that you are complaining about that I don't want to happen between your department and mine. That's why I came over. . . . I take it from my conversations with you that where we are dealing with foreign exchange, World Bank, and such matters . . . you would like me to continue to handle it." He said, "Absolutely! . . . I can't keep track of all these back-scene intrigues."

And shortly thereafter Hull withdrew the objections to Treasury procedures which Berle had earlier entered.

* The Texas Democrat who had recently become Chairman of the Senate Committee on Foreign Relations.

His mandate confirmed, Morgenthau prepared to meet J. M. Keynes who was about to return to Washington. Recognizing that the United States, as White had said, would have to guard its commitments if Congress were to act favorably, Keynes had noted that for similar reasons the British would have minimal requirements of their own, but those, he was confident, would prove compatible. He was impressed, moreover, by the revisions of the White proposal that had reached him. In Washington on September 13, 1943, Keynes told Morgenthau that he believed Anglo-American talks would lead quickly to the appointment of a drafting committee to be selected from among all the United Nations. The British Treasury, however, had promised to permit Parliament to debate the question before the proposal for the Fund took final form, so he hoped the United States would agree to some statement of general principles for Parliament to use as a basis for debate.

Morgenthau asked Keynes whether the British experts were prepared to talk about the Bank. They had no instructions, Keynes said, though they hoped to be able to explore the question with their American counterparts. As it worked out, both subjects received some attention, though conversations focused on the Fund.

Keynes opened his negotiations with White with the foreknowledge that Great Britain would have to yield, in the end, to the greater wealth and strength of the United States. But the Englishman, resolved to fight his case on every point, brought to his advocacy his extraordinarily subtle and quick intelligence, his talent for stinging repartee, his mastery of prose, and his incomparable professional prestige. He had, moreover, a respect, ultimately a liking, too, for his antagonist. White for his part knew he held the trumps and rarely hesitated to play them, but White also knew that the Fund, with which he identified himself inseparably, could not be created and could not survive without the hearty participation of the British. Truculent as ever, as dogged as Keynes about every issue, White also respected his adversary as a man and as an economist, and though the two sometimes offended each other, they continually recovered their bearing and together carried their difficult task to a successful conclusion.

Both had to make concessions, as both already had. Though Keynes could hardly bear the jargon of American economics (he called it "Cherokee" and contrasted it to his own "Christian English"), he took White's draft of a "Joint Statement on . . . an International Monetary Fund" as the basis for discussion. Accordingly he abandoned the system of credits and debits he had made the basis for his own Clearing Union and accepted once and for all the American scheme for providing assests for the Fund, and the American principle for establishing quotas and voting rights, though the size of those quotas remained unsettled. The earlier American proposal on "scarce currencies," though now somewhat modified to England's disadvantage, made that concession possible. So also did White's resolution of another major British concern. The early plans for the Fund assigned it an active role in the internal economies of its members, for it could buy and sell their public securities as well as their currencies, and thus directly influence their internal interest rates and the conditions of their public debts. Indeed White had conceived of the Fund, in that respect, as an international equivalent of the American Treasury during the New Deal, an activist, shaping instrument of public finance. Keynes, however, insisted on making the Fund "passive," that is, on eliminating the possibility that the Fund might challenge national sovereignty and the authority of central banks. The American consented to the principle of passivity, though procedures were still to be defined. Further, the British demanded a provision for the right of any nation to withdraw from the Fund instantaneously and without penalty. White balked, but according to the account of Roy Harrod, Edward M. Bernstein, second only to White among the American experts, whispered that the impossibility of withdrawing "may mean a lot of trouble for us in Congress." With that, White let the British win the point.

A sensitivity to congressional conservatism had already led White also to modify his ideas about the Bank, which, according to current drafts for its charter, was to have much less authority for lending and for dealing in currencies than had at first been contemplated. That change had significance for the Fund. In White's original scheme, the potentialities of the Bank, as the British saw it, compensated in part for the relatively small assets White planned for the Fund, only one-fifth of what Keynes had in mind for his Clearing Union. But the British by September 1943 had agreed in principle to the smaller dimension for the Fund in spite of the reduction in scope of the Bank. Even in its diminished form, the prospectus for the Bank bothered the British. They did not expect to seek financial assistance, while their financial situation did not permit them to make substantial contributions to the Bank for loans to other nations. They therefore wanted to restrain the Bank from large-scale direct lending and to be sure that it would call up only a small fraction of its total, pledged capital. Those points, which were to be conceded only after another six months, in the fall of 1943 impeded planning for the Bank without interfering with conversations about the Fund.

The "Joint Statement" to which Keynes and White agreed impressed Morgenthau who obtained Roosevelt's permission to explain the revised plans on the Hill, as he did on October 5, 1943. The treasury would proceed no further, he promised, without consulting Congress. To facilitate communications, Morgenthau the next day encouraged the appointment of an informal liaison committee representing both houses to which the Treasury could continually refer questions. The Secretary, at his first meeting with that group in mid-November, presented the most recent drafts for the Bank. White then reported on negotiations with the British concerning the Fund. His remarks resembled the statement from the floor of Parliament earlier that month by the Chancellor of the Exchequer who, under interrogation, had said that there had been an appreciable advance toward agreement on principles, though important points remained outstanding. Parliament, the Chancellor added, would have ample opportunity to debate the question before it was closed.

By November 1943, Morgenthau had begun to worry more about the Russians than the English. Though Ambassador Gromyko had assured the Secretary that the Soviet Union was keenly interested in the proposals for the Fund and the Bank, Moscow had yet to send an observer to the technical conferences in Washington. Morgenthau asked Hull to "encourage them to send their experts," and when that tactic failed, Morgenthau himself prodded Gromyko. The first week in January 1944, to the Secretary's relief, Gromyko reported that two of the five Soviet technicians had arrived.

"There remains only one important difference between ourselves and the British," White wrote the Secretary two months later, ". . . and they have promised to give us their answer within the next two weeks. Discussions with the Russians are proceeding favorably and though it is too early to know definitely it looks hopeful that we may be able to come to an agreement so far as the technical people are concerned within the next couple of weeks. Sometime soon I would like to discuss with you what we ought to do next."

He was concerned, White told Morgenthau on March 21, 1944, about the timing of the general conference. He hoped that conference could complete its work before the Republican convention met in late June, but unless the Treasury received approval from the British by the end of March, no conference could meet in the spring, and in that case White feared the matter would have to wait until after the election. Pressing the issue again in April, White urged Morgenthau to ask the President to consent to a conference in 1944. "Don't worry," the Secretary told him. "I haven't let you down yet, have I? . . . I have it very much in mind and I promise you that I will see the President." On April 5, Roosevelt endorsed a joint request from Morgenthau and Hull for the conference, provided that the British agreed.

Domestic politics underscored the desirability of speed. At a Treasury meeting of April 8, 1944, White reported that Republican Congressman Charles S. Dewey of Chicago had admitted that his opposition to the Fund and Bank was "wholly political." Dewey believed the Republicans would win a majority in the House of Representatives in the autumn election and would then be able to defeat any proposal resembling either White's or Keynes's. He was therefore collaborating with friends in the New York and Chicago banking communities on a scheme that would accomplish a few of the purposes envisaged for the Bank but none of those proposed for the Fund. White and his advisers judged that Dewey would be unable to defeat a single plan suitable not only to the British and Americans but also to the experts of thirty-five other interested nations. Nobody, Morgenthau said, could move any faster than he had been moving. He could only await a reply from Great Britain before taking the next step.

"We now feel that it is vital," White told Morgenthau on April 10, 1944, "that you appear before the hearings of the Dewey bill which . . . will be on the 25th." But vital or not, as Ambassador Winant cabled from London, the British government could not endorse any tentative agreement or call for a conference without the consent of Parliament. "Unless we hear immediately," Morgenthau cabled Winant on April 10, "that the Joint Statement can be published next week (in time to clear with the technicians of other countries before my meeting with the congressional committees) then it is my personal opinion that we shall not be able to hold a conference this year." A cable to Moscow on the same date made the same plea.

Chancellor of the Exchequer Sir John Anderson and J. M. Keynes, Winant replied on April 12, were doing everything in their power to help Morgenthau meet his timetable, but they faced strong opposition within Great Britain. A majority of the directors of the Bank of England opposed the program, as did their spokesman in the Cabinet, Lord Beaverbrook. They argued that the plan for the Fund would damage London as a financial center and lead to the replacement of sterling exchange by dollar exchange. Right-wing Conservatives were especially disturbed by the challenge of the Fund and the Bank to the special trade and economic relationships within the British Empire. Churchill, who never felt that he had a grasp of financial questions, postponed decisions about them because of the strength of the opposition. Yet Winant was confident that a satisfactory solution would emerge. Morgenthau answered that the circumstances Winant had described did not constitute a reason for delaying any longer the publication of the Joint Statement.

Under continuing pressure from Morgenthau and Winant, the British Treasury agreed on April 15 to release that statement, provided that the technicians could settle a few outstanding issues. In particular, the British opposed any reference to White's Unitas, because they were defined in terms of grains of gold. They also asked that the announcement indicate the tentative nature of the plans and emphasize that the Fund and Bank were conceived as parts of broader schemes for international cooperation, which looked to the progressive development of international trade, active employment, and reasonable stability of prices.

Those were acceptable conditions, but the Treasury had heard nothing from Moscow, and some State Department subordinates were working unabashedly to combat the proposal for the Bank. "We're moving heaven and earth to get the English and Russians lined up," Morgenthau told Dean Acheson on April 17, 1944. ". . . I've told the English I'm going on the Hill . . . whether they agree or not, but they practically agreed. . . . I saw the Russian Ambassador . . . and I told him I was going up . . . and I hoped that they'd agree. Now the reason we're rushing it this week is because we've got to testify on the Dewey bill . . . and the Dewey bill is simply a Republican trick to get something . . . which will have the Republican label. . . . I hope very much that you can go with me because I want this an Administration matter, and the State and Treasury, we've got to be together on this." Acheson was of exactly that opinion.

At a strategy meeting on April 18, 1944, Morgenthau said that he intended to talk to Congress before Dewey could introduce his bill; the Treasury would not let itself be put on the defensive. "We felt," the Secretary continued, "that it was good for the world, good for the nation, and good for the Democratic Party, for us to move. If anybody doesn't like that, he can leave the room. Anyway, that is the mood I am in. I made Acheson laugh! Have to get a little political around here, Dean. Looking around the room, I think I am fairly safe."

In the ensuing discussion Acheson said that the conference planned on the Fund and Bank would be the first truly world conference since the war had begun. He recommended the inclusion of some members of Congress within the American delegation, a suggestion which Morgenthau accepted. "It was decided," the Secretary later told his staff, "that we would send a joint telegram tonight to the President . . . recommending that the President authorize us to say . . . that if such a conference took place, he would appoint members from Congress as delegates. . . . I . . . felt that the State Department's attitude was very cooperative and sympathetic." The telegram went out that day, and Roosevelt replied: "I heartily approve."

Still awaiting Russian endorsement of the Joint Statement, Morgenthau on April 20 "took an awful chance" and cabled Harriman to tell the Soviet Union that the British had already agreed to the American draft, which in fact they had not yet officially done. That day he also telephoned Harriman in Moscow and the Russian Embassy in Washington to urge a quick and affirmative answer from the Soviet Union "so that it would seem that all the United Nations were together." The Soviet Union, Harriman replied later in the day, could not yet agree to the text. Soviet experts still demanded a provision for unilateral Russian definition of the gold value of the ruble, and they still objected to White's requirements for payments of gold to the International Fund. But Moscow agreed "to instruct its experts to associate themselves with Mr. Morgenthau's project" if it were necessary for the United States government to have the concurrence of the Soviet Union in order to secure "due effect in the rest of the world."

England on April 20 devised a similar solution. The British Treasury was willing to go along with American plans for an early conference, though the British questioned the possibility of travel and communication in the spring of 1944 since severe security regulations associated with the pending invasion of France limited departures from the United Kingdom. More important, the British Treasury disagreed in various ways with the American statement about the Bank, and most important, the British believed that many of the United Nations would receive their first understanding of the Fund and Bank from the Joint Statement about to be published, and would need considerable time for further study. In those circumstances, it seemed to the British premature for Morgenthau to tell Congress that the Joint Statement had the approval of the experts of a number of countries. He might better describe the Joint Statement as representing the views of the United States.

In his testimony of April 21, 1944, Morgenthau announced that technical experts of the United Nations had agreed on the basic principles for the Fund. The Joint Statement, however, did not bind any government to participate, though it did mean the Fund would be recommended to each government as a practical means of meeting postwar monetary problems. Plans for the Bank, Morgenthau went on, were not yet completed, but he said that there was considerable support for the idea among the thirty United Nations. In keeping with the British request, the Secretary made no mention of the Unitas, but he did say that the par value of currencies of member countries of the Fund would be expressed in gold. He also reported Roosevelt's intention, once a conference was called, to "invite direct congressional participation in the work of the United States delegation."

Relieved that he had met his own timetable, Morgenthau wrote

Roosevelt about the developments of the last few days: "Only by telling the English that I would go up and testify whether I heard from them or not were we finally able to get an agreement out of them to go along with the principles involved. The Russians also have been stalling us, and yesterday I called up both Harriman in Moscow and Ambassador Gromyko here to put all the pressure I could on them to get the Russians to come along. I never got an answer from the Russians until I was in the middle of my testimony before the . . . committees this morning. . . . I thought you would be most pleased that the Soviet government decided to go along with us 'to secure due effect on the rest of the world.' In other words, they want to be associated with us in the eyes of the world. State and Treasury both think this is highly significant, as I am sure you will also.

"Before leaving the hearing in the Senate, Senator Vandenberg whispered to me that he would support this program. The fact that I was able to tell the Senate that you would appoint members of Congress to the American delegation made a great hit."

The Secretary had yet to obtain agreement from Great Britain and the Soviet Union on a date for the conference. "I feel that in this year," he said to White, "England and Russia have to make up their minds on two vital things for them. . . . 1. Is Russia going to play ball with the rest of the world on external matters, which she has never done before and, 2. Is England going to play with the United Nations or is she going to play with the Dominions? Now, both of these countries have to make up their minds, and . . . I am not going to take anything less than a yes or no from them. I am not, because this . . . is a terrifically important thing, not the monetary conference as such, but what is their position going to be? And once they come in, then they have crossed that bridge. . . . I am not running for office. I haven't the whole postwar problem on my shoulders but he [Roosevelt] has. . . . Unless we get a clean cut answer from Russia and England, I will not ask the President to call this conference. . . .

"In all of these years that I have worked with Mr. Roosevelt, I have always been prepared to let him have what is good, and I have always been prepared to take what is bad. I can afford to take it. After all, if it gets too bad, I can always go back and raise apples.

But this is very important for him, and I am thinking of him. . . .
He may have to sit at the peace conference. He should have a
record of success for his first conference. If it is a failure, it is a black
mark against him. . . .

"I am not worried about getting a bad press myself. I am used to
it. . . . I am not worried about Hull running out on me if it gets
hot. I am expecting all of that at a discount, but I . . . have to do
everything to look after the President's interest, because the President's interests are the country's interests."

In that mood, Morgenthau on April 26, 1944, told Roosevelt that,
subject to British and Russian consent, he would like to send out
invitations for the conference on May 1, to commence informal
drafting on May 10, and to open a first plenary session on May 26.
"Well done," Roosevelt replied on April 28. "You are hereby authorized to go ahead." But the schedule was too fast. It was May 3
before the Russians officially agreed to the conference, and the British asked for a postponement in order to permit them to consult the
Dominions. Morgenthau acceded to that request subject to Roosevelt's willingness to hold a conference at a date so close to the Republican convention.

The President on May 25, 1944, endorsed plans for arrangements
which Morgenthau, Harry White, and Dean Acheson had made.
The conference itself, they decided, would take place at Bretton
Woods, New Hampshire, where there were excellent hotel facilities
in a cool, handsome and accessible environment. "In an excellent
humor," the President "approved wholly of the program presented
him," including a draft of a letter of invitation, a suggested list of
American delegates, and a title for the meeting: "The United Nations Monetary and Financial Conference." "That's good," Roosevelt remarked. "Here's where you get a medal, Henry."

The American delegation, as it worked out, included Morgenthau
as chairman; Fred Vinson, the deputy chief of the Office of Economic Stabilization, as vice chairman; Dean Acheson from the State
Department; Edward E. Brown, president of the First National
Bank of Chicago, a large, industrious, outspoken man who represented the tractable element of the banking community; Leo T.
Crowley, the head of the Foreign Economic Administration; Marriner Eccles, the president of the Board of Governors of the Federal

Reserve Board; Mabel Newcomer, a Vassar professor of economics and the one woman in the group; Harry White, and four members of Congress. Three of those four were chosen for their positions and parties: Democrat Brent Spence, the chairman of the House Banking and Currency Committee; his senior Republican colleague, Jesse P. Wolcott; and Democrat Robert F. Wagner, chairman of the Senate Committee on Banking and Currency. Morgenthau and Alben Barkley, the Senate Majority Leader, decided to bypass Republican Robert Taft, a possible candidate to balance Wagner, because Taft had said membership in the Fund would be "like pouring money down a sewer." They turned instead to Republican Charles W. Tobey, of New Hampshire, a member of Wagner's committee, whom Morgenthau described as "all milk and honey for the program." Besides the delegation, the Treasury planned to send to the conference a group of experts from its own ranks and from the State Department and Federal Reserve Board.*

With the delegation selected, the stage was almost set. There remained only a preliminary meeting among the experts to bring the agenda for the conference into a condition for debate. Morgenthau had employed the prestige of his office and his influence with the President to advance the planning from which he expected so much. Now White, with the Secretary's continuing support and encouragement, faced the penultimate, technical round in the negotiations he had been carrying so ably.

3. Conflicts of Interest

The American technicians joined their counterparts from other countries for two weeks of important, preliminary negotiations in mid-June 1944, at Atlantic City, New Jersey. They were trying,

---

* Apart from the American delegation, the most distinguished delegation at the Bretton Woods Conference was the British. Keynes was chairman of that group, which also included Professor D. H. Robertson, the talented economic adviser to the British Treasury; Redvers Opie of the British Embassy in Washington; and R. H. Brand, the British representative at the American Treasury. As a technical adviser, the British added G. L. F. Bolton of the Bank of England, who had been a frequent correspondent of Morgenthau in the months prior to the negotiation of the Tripartite Accord of 1936.

White told Morgenthau, to isolate the issues on which there would be disagreement when the delegates convened at Bretton Woods, and to prepare a draft of the Fund for final approval. But the Secretary, for the first time during the many months of preparation, objected to White's assumptions. Technical subjects, Morgenthau knew, continually involved conflicts of political interest. The technicians could not and should not resolve them. As Morgenthau said to White, the proposed procedure was "leaving me completely high and dry, and all the rest of the American delegates." He felt that White expected them all to sign on the dotted line, and that "it won't work." The Secretary therefore instructed Edward Bernstein to keep him fully informed about developments at Atlantic City. What he learned revealed the range of controversy both among American interest groups and between the American government and the other participating nations.

Randolph Burgess of the New York Federal Reserve Bank, designated by the American Bankers Association to act as their spokesman, wrote Morgenthau on June 22, 1944, to introduce severe objections to the plan for the Fund. Few New York bankers, Burgess said, understood the proposal, and most of them were suspicious of it. "They are distrustful of any program," he wrote, "for giving away American gold; they are distrustful of all spending programs, especially when sponsored by Lord Keynes. . . . I am sure the opposition to the experts' plan is very widespread and vigorous." The United States, Burgess believed, should not commit itself "to put up money until other countries are prepared to make some commitment as to how they will use it and how they will pay it back." Further, Burgess felt that "making a big pot of money available . . . would accentuate . . . inflationary tendencies," that the South American nations already had ample gold and dollar reserves, and that the monetary plan would therefore relate largely to what he considered an exclusively British problem. He objected especially to the proposed contribution of the United States to the Fund, some 60 or 65 per cent according to the preliminary draft, and he interpreted Keynes's views as expressing "the philosophy of deficit spending over again — the use of credit as a cure-all." As Burgess' comments indicated, the New York banking community, as ever, wanted to minimize government control in monetary affairs, and wanted as rapidly as possible to see the United States and the rest of the world return to the automatic gold standard of the pre-depression years.

Less jaundiced observers realized that the revised drafts for the Fund and Bank that emerged from the Atlantic City meeting represented a marrying of the White and Keynes plans in a fashion that favored the more conservative American proposal, that maintained the link to gold that Morgenthau and White had always championed, and that built the proposed postwar institutions on the basis of the long prewar experience from which Morgenthau and White had continually drawn. Only naïve critics of the Fund, White wrote in a long memorandum for the American delegation, could conclude that a bilateral monetary arrangement between England and the United States would be adequate for postwar purposes. After the war, when smaller nations met economic trouble, they might begin to depreciate, and depreciation anywhere would infect the countries most likely to be in competition with the devalued currency. The little countries would follow each other into rounds of devaluation that would ultimately affect the great nations unless some international institution assisted all nations to maintain stability. Contrary to Burgess' argument, the Fund was not intended to be a source of long term credit, but rather to provide short term loans for currency stabilization and equilibrium.

The United States was not about to waste money. If the United States had dollars in the Fund and another country, needing dollars, borrowed part of them, that country would have to turn over to the Fund an equivalent amount of its own currency, thus keeping the overall value of the Fund constant. The United States would on occasion need that currency for imports, would use dollars to buy that currency from the Fund, and in time would restore the ratio that had existed before the other nation had borrowed dollars from the Fund. In the long run all transactions would tend to return the holdings of the Fund to their initial ratios. Of its original holdings, worth some $8 billion,* the Fund would have some $2 billion in gold. It would not have to expend that gold until some particular currency was wholly depleted from its stocks. At that point, the Fund would employ gold to buy that currency. In time, as its hold-

---

* Revised upward from the original draft that called for $5.5 billion.

ings of the currency in question increased, it could repurchase the gold. Even if the Fund were one day to exhaust its gold in procuring a currency in high demand, for example dollars, the Fund could continue to trade in all other currencies, and it might also negotiate a dollar loan from the Federal Reserve Board.

Americans, White continued, should not think of the Fund as an arena in which the United States would compete against the rest of the world. Rather, the Fund was to establish "the rate of the various exchanges of the countries of the world on a multilateral basis and . . . provide a mechanism for keeping orderly exchanges. Now, that is in itself very important.

"Another thing that it does, it points up very directly the position of the creditor nations. It puts the pressure on the creditor nations to recognize realistically that foreign trade is not just a means of selling goods; that a country that expects to sell goods and services has got to be prepared to buy goods and services or take gold or give long term credits which are bad because you never know when you are going to get paid. It does point up for the first time that relationship."

The case of the Bank was somewhat different. The plans completed at Atlantic City called for an initial capital for the Bank of $10 billion. Its chief business would be to promote private investments for special projects of reconstruction and development. According to the plan, the initial subscription would equal about 20 per cent of the total expected from each participating nation. The determination of each nation's subscription would take into account the national income of that nation, its gold, and its foreign exchange resources. The net result would lead to a subscription by the United States of a little less than a third of the total amount, with the United Kingdom subscribing approximately half as much. The Bank, White explained, was to have two separate operations. Through the more important one, it would guarantee loans made by private investors through regular channels. Loans were to be guaranteed also by national goverments. So, for example, if a municipality wanted to borrow, then the government of the country in which that municipality existed would have to guarantee the loan. The investor would have the additional guarantee of the Bank — in effect the guarantee of the thirty or forty governments subscribing to the bank. "As far as the investment is concerned," White said, "he couldn't get a safer one." The charges the Bank collected for guaranteeing a loan would go into a reserve against possible defaults. World conditions, White noted, warranted the creation of a Bank: "The situation is that there probably has never been a time in history when countries are more in need of capital to reconstruct their economy, get back on a working basis, and also develop some of the necessary industries without which they couldn't have any hope for full employment or anything like it."

The Bank would also have a second function — to make direct loans of its own. Those would have to come from the original 20 per cent of the total subscription. Further, borrowing countries would have to agree to spend the currencies they borrowed in the countries from which those currencies came. For example, if Yugoslavia negotiated a loan of sterling and dollars, she would have to spend the pounds in the United Kingdom and the dollars in the United States. But such direct loans, as White saw it, would prove far less significant than the guaranteeing of private loans.

The Atlantic City drafts for the Fund and Bank left unsettled a number of questions that only the Bretton Woods Conference could resolve. Some of those questions involved considerations of prestige. So, for example, both China and France pressed for the fourth largest quota in the Fund, to be exceeded only by the quotas, and thus the votes, of the United States, the United Kingdom, and the Soviet Union. Other problems remained where this nation or that sought some special advantage, as the British and Russians both did by advancing formulas for gold contributions that would minimize their own subscriptions. Characteristically, the Russians also believed that the determination of voting power should relate to political rather than financial considerations. In character too, the Mexicans and other Latin Americans advocated a partial substitution of silver for gold in the resources of the Fund. Countries devastated by the Germans wanted the Bank to emphasize loans for reconstruction; countries in the southern hemisphere had a contradictory preference for development loans. But in spite of those and other disagreements, the technicians at Atlantic City worked together in good temper and in the end endorsed in principle the major purposes of both Fund and Bank.

Naturally pleased, even cautiously optimistic, Morgenthau nevertheless expected no cessation of debate when the international conference met. "I've just received three . . . delegations," he told Dean Acheson on the eve of their departure from Washington. "I'm exhausted. . . . We had no fights. . . . If I can only keep my sense of humor, I'll be all right."

4. Bretton Woods: The International Monetary Fund

The conference at Bretton Woods, Roosevelt wrote in his greeting to the delegates on June 29, 1944, was only one phase of many needed for an orderly and harmonious postwar world. "But it is a vital phase," he said, "affecting ordinary men and women everywhere. For it concerns the basis upon which they will be able to exchange with one another the natural riches of the earth and the products of their own industry and ingenuity. Commerce is the life blood of a free society. We must see to it that the arteries which carry that blood stream are not clogged again." Further, the President expected the meeting at Bretton Woods to furnish evidence "that men of different nationalities have learned how to adjust possible differences and how to work together as friends."

So did Morgenthau, whose opening speech as chairman, on July 1, noted that "prosperity has no fixed limits. It is not a finite substance to be diminished by division. On the contrary, the more of it that other nations enjoy, the more each nation will have for itself. . . . Prosperity, like peace, is indivisible. . . . Poverty, wherever it exists, is menacing to us all. . . . It can no more be localized than war."

The physical environment at Bretton Woods contrasted vividly with the conditions of poverty and war. The hills and woods of New Hampshire's vacation-land invited delegates to leisure their duties precluded. Even in the White Mountains the days were hot, but the nights were ordinarily pleasant, fortunately, for the pressure of work — of committee meetings, caucuses, plenary sessions — continued almost round the clock. No one got enough sleep; everyone was soon tired. The resort hotel where the senior delegates stayed was comfortable and commodious, though it lacked special equipment designed for a large conference. Yet Morgenthau, whose room was just below Keynes's, later remembered most sharply the penetrating rhythm of the exercises of Lady Keynes, a *prima ballerina* who was unaware that her routine practicing could be heard through the ceiling beneath her. Doubtless the Secretary would have slept more soundly had he been less tense, less worried about the outcome of the conference and the esprit of his associates.

To his colleagues on the American delegation, Morgenthau stressed the need for bipartisanship. "As far as I am concerned," he said, ". . . this has no party politics. . . . It is bigger than either the Republican or the Democratic Party. . . . I think we are fortunate in having both Senator Tobey and Congressman Wolcott here." For their part, Tobey and Wolcott, along with Ned Brown, the Chicago banker, agreed that it was essential to build a backfire to criticisms of the conference emanating from the financial community and from the Republican Party. The conference, Tobey said, had to be linked to a definite American commitment to world cooperation. For that purpose, Morgenthau put the ablest of the Treasury's specialists in press relations at the service of the American delegation. So, too, the Secrétary warned Roosevelt of the efforts of Thomas Lamont and Winthrop Aldrich of New York to "unsell" various foreign delegations on the work of the conference, and of their contention that the agreements reached at Bretton Woods "would never get the approval of Congress."

But the American delegation also realized that its "two major difficulties," as Brown put it, "are going to be with the British and with the Russians. The British have a very strong bloc at home which believe they are better off keeping the sterling bloc. . . . Any plan that is put up is going to have very rough sledding in the House of Commons. They may give something, but they will break off if we insist on too much. As far as the Russians are concerned . . . one of them will raise his hand in a sub-committee and ask for a recess and come back after ten minutes with a typewritten statement which says, 'This is the Russian position.' Somebody asks them the reason for it, then they read the memorandum over again and say, 'This is the Russians' position.' "

"Russia doesn't need the Fund," Brown went on. "It has a complete system of state trading — state industry. . . . I have the idea

that in the case of the British . . . and in the case of the Russians
. . . we are going to have a good deal of difficulty trading with
them."

That was a fair statement, White said, which exactly described
the Russian technique in negotiation, but the Fund needed Russia.
Senator Tobey concurred: "World cooperation must have Russia."

It needed Great Britain, too, and White warned his associates that
the British delegates could not make "too many compromises," for if
they did, "Parliament will throw it out." The British delegates,
Morgenthau added, were deeply worried by the persisting problem
of British balances. The enormous debt in sterling accumulated
during the war, though it was never mentioned, governed their approach to economic issues. But the Fund and the Bank, the Secretary believed, would help the British overcome the troubles the war
had engendered.

The Soviets provoked the first crisis of the conference. They had
thought, Morgenthau reported to the American delegation on July
3, that they were to have a quota equivalent to 10 per cent of the
holdings of the International Monetary Fund, a quota of about a
billion dollars, which was more than the $800 million that the Amer-
ican plan assigned. In Morgenthau's view, the Russians were not
bargaining but were "very much disturbed." White said that he had
earlier assured the Russians they would have a quota of about 10
per cent of the total Fund, but when they objected that that was not
enough, he had told them that they were free to raise the question
at committee meetings at Bretton Woods. They were confused. They
had thought that the one-third increase in their quota promised
before the meeting would bring them to one-tenth of the total fund,
whereas in fact it brought them to the $800 million assigned them,
which was less than that tenth. The United States, White admitted,
set the figure of $800 million rather arbitrarily because of the un-
availability of data about the Russian economy. The whole problem
had arisen only because the Russians wanted ten per cent of the
votes.

They were reasonable to ask for a vote as large or almost as large
as the British, Morgenthau said, as he turned to Dean Acheson for
another opinion. From an economic point of view, Acheson said,
that did not make much sense, but it made great sense from the

point of view of military power. "I think that the best thing to do with the Russians," Acheson continued, "is to tell them that you think there is a complete misunderstanding about this, that we have been thinking of 800 million . . . and in view of the misunderstanding, we are willing to go along and increase it to 900 and we think that solves the problem for them, and we hope they think so." That higher figure would still leave them short of the British quota of about $1250 million, but even so, Acheson was not alarmed by the Russian position, though he agreed with Morgenthau's prediction that the Soviet delegation would have to cable Moscow before reaching any conclusion.

"If we start in by giving them the whole of the request on quotas," Edward Bernstein objected, "we will have given away the best thing we have in talking to the Russians while we still have untouched all their other questions." Bernstein wanted leverage especially for negotiation on the question of the initial gold contribution to the International Fund, but with Marriner Eccles, Morgenthau supported Acheson. "I started it in 1933 at the President's request," the Secretary said, ". . . I started the negotiations with them . . . and I have dealt with them ever since . . . and . . . I believe they are sincere." Now White protested that a readjustment of the Russian quota would lead to renegotiations of all quotas, a prospect he was reluctant to face. Morgenthau nevertheless asked Acheson to write out his formulation, because, as he put it, "I do not want to trust myself to present it to them verbally."

"As we have explained to you orally," Acheson's memorandum read, "there has unfortunately been a misunderstanding between us regarding the amount of the Soviet quota. It was always our understanding that the Soviet quota would be in the neighborhood of 800 million dollars, i.e. approximately 10 per cent of the total quota of the whole fund.

"Notwithstanding this regrettable misunderstanding, I want to assure that the US delegation will associate itself with the Soviet delegation in efforts to obtain an increase in the quota for the USSR at this conference."

At that juncture, Morgenthau had briefly to return to Washington, and in his absence Harry White and Fred Vinson together negotiated with the Soviet delegation. Its chairman, Finance Commissar Stepanov, emphasized that considerations for the fixing of quotas should take into account other "than the purely economic." The authorities in Moscow, he said, "felt that the proposed formula was based upon past economic data such as foreign trade and that since it was hoped that the foreign trade of all countries would be increased, particularly that of the Soviet Union and the United States, the calculations for the quotas should be based on future prospects rather than past statistics." As Vinson and White recognized, those words were a circumlocution for "prestige." White replied that the Americans had always known their formula was arbitrary, and Morgenthau had therefore been able to provide the written assurances the Soviets had received. "Under such circumstances," Stepanov said, the Soviet quota should equal the British. White then suggested reducing the British quota to $900 million and giving the Soviets a quota of $850 million, but Stepanov replied that his government would not accept that figure and the British would doubtless also balk.

"The time has come," Ned Brown said to his fellow American delegates while they were reviewing the Russian question on July 5, "when unless it is resolved . . . the conference will fail just because it can't complete its task within . . . two weeks . . . it is necessary for us at this time to show our teeth, something I dislike to do."

"Not unless they are good teeth," White said.

Brown suggested raising the Soviet quota to a billion dollars and at the same time telling the Russians that they would have to give up their demand for a reduction in their initial gold subscription. Congressman Wolcott, supporting Brown, also believed that "we had better understand and give them to understand that this Fund is going to operate more to their benefit that it is to ours, and we can get along better without this Fund than perhaps they can." Marriner Eccles thought that if the conference broke up because of the Russian quota, it would alienate American opinion, then so warm toward the Soviet Union. Eccles therefore was ready to increase that quota and also to concede to the Russians on the issue of gold subscriptions for the few years after the war, though not "eternally." Harry White, though he did not want to be out-traded by the Russians, agreed, as did Dean Acheson.

The Soviet quota had become a "pretty hot subject," Fred Vinson told Morgenthau by telephone on July 6. The Russians wanted 1 billion 200 million; how did Morgenthau feel about that? "They're doing such a magnificent job in the war," the Secretary replied, ". . . that I've got a weak spot for them."

"We feel the same way," Vinson said.

Later that day the American delegation, with Vinson presiding, recalculated quotas and also increased the aggregate sum enough to allow the Russians $1 billion 200 million. White wanted the Soviet Union in return to withdraw claims on all other matters. Morgenthau, he said, had left a message with him that stressed two points: the Americans should maintain a substantially larger vote for themselves and for the British than for the Russians; yet it was very important for the Russians to come along. To those points there was no dissent, but Acheson feared that the Russians, after accepting a $1 billion 200 million quota, would then bargain sharply on every other question, too. After further discussion, the delegation passed a motion of Marriner Eccles that endorsed Acheson's position. It resolved to submit in writing to the Russians a single proposal for a quota of $1 billion 200 million on condition that the Americans would make no other concessions. So informed on July 7, Morgenthau said: "I'm pleased."

Back at Bretton Woods on July 10, Morgenthau learned that the Russians had yet to answer the American offer. Further, they were still insisting that countries occupied or devastated by the Germans receive a reduction in their gold contribution to the International Fund. He was "very much surprised," Morgenthau told the Soviet delegates on July 11. He had understood that they had been "determined to work side by side in the solution of an international monetary and financial problem." But now, he said:

"After having the most friendly relations with your people, I am quite shocked that two great nations should begin what we call 'to horse trade,' and that you people should say to us, 'We want one billion, 200 million *and* the 25 per cent.' * That isn't the spirit which my Government has approached this problem with; it isn't the spirit expressed by Mr. Molotov to me. . . . I have never had anything like this happen to me in dealing with the Russian Government so there must be some misundersanding.

* Reduction in gold subscription.

"I don't know the vernacular, but we are dealing with all our cards face up. . . . So I must ask the Russian Delegation please to reconsider. . . . I feel that very deeply, because I have only one desire, and that is the continued friendly relations side by side of our two Governments."

"We have regarded this provision," Stepanov replied on the question of the gold subscription, "not as purely an economic one, but as a political provision." He felt he had made a concession by asking for a reduction of only 25 per cent in the initial gold contribution rather than the 50 per cent to which the Russians had earlier leaned. The figures on Russian national income, he said, would persuade the American delegation of the justice of his views. He had sent a cable home and could not "decide anything right now without the consent of Moscow." Stepanov concluded on a reassuring note: "As we say in Russian, there is no black cat running between us!"

He was neither a diplomat nor a lawyer, Morgenthau replied; just a farmer. Stepanov interrupted that he was neither a lawyer nor a financier, just a businessman. Resuming, Morgenthau said there was room for a difference of opinion about the quota, on which the Americans had made a concession without asking for any further data. Now he hoped the Soviet Union would accept the American position on gold, particularly since the gossip at Bretton Woods held that the Russians had $4 billion in gold, as well as an annual production of between $300 and $400 million dollars of that metal.*

"Well," Stepanov said, "you can't stop the gossiping."

"We have made you an ultimate proposal," Morgenthau said. ". . . We have honestly gone as far as we can. . . . This is only one of many agreements which we hope to have with Russia. . . . I don't think from your standpoint it is a matter of life or death. . . . If your Government has any confidence in me . . . you will have to accept my word . . . that we have gone as far as we can go. . . . And once this is finished, I am ready any time . . . to take up the next question, which seems to me the question of how Russia is going to get manufactured goods in this country."

The Secretary was throwing into the scales the possibility of a

---

* Soviet reticence about gold production, a reticence Morgenthau had often encountered, was attributable in part to Soviet reluctance to let the world know how many prisoners, especially political prisoners, were engaged in gold mining.

postwar credit, already under discussion between the Soviet Union and the American Treasury, as well as his own personal standing, which he was urging Stepanov to test with Moscow. Stepanov replied laconically that in his view $1 billion 200 million was a fair quota, and he hoped Moscow would go along with the Americans on gold.

Within twenty-four hours, the newspapers reported the Russian-American disagreement about gold subscriptions. Morgenthau immediately telephoned Stepanov. As the Secretary later put it in his Diary, he told Stepanov "that I was very sorry that the press had gotten word . . . of the negatiations going on. . . . I said I had followed the practice of trying to keep the American delegation and the experts informed, and I was afraid that there was somebody who didn't want to see Russia and the United States get too friendly and . . . was making trouble. I also said that he should remember that Mr. Roosevelt was running for President, and the Republicans didn't lose a single opportunity to do something to hurt Mr. Roosevelt's prestige. He said he understood that, and he realized the success of this Monetary Conference would be useful to Mr. Roosevelt when he ran for President.

"Mr. Stepanov was most friendly. . . . He said that there were really no grounds for misunderstanding between us, and that he was simply waiting word from Moscow before taking the matter up with us again."

From Ambassador Harriman in Moscow, to whom he had telephoned for information, Morgenthau learned by cable on July 13, 1944, that the Russian delegation had authority to talk with him, but Harriman had been unable to find out what the Soviet answer would be. Vishinsky had told Harriman personally that he could not see why the size of the quota and the question of a gold deduction for devastated countries should be coupled, but when Harriman started to argue the point, Vishinsky said that he preferred to study it further.

Expecting trouble, Morgenthau on July 14 informed Keynes that he was about to tell the Russians "that we can't wait any longer for their decision." If the Russians were to "kick very hard," the Americans would let them keep their newly mined gold outside of the Fund for several years. "It is all right," Keynes replied after further conversation. ". . . We will support you on this matter."

To Stepanov later that day, Morgenthau said the Russians were holding up the conference, the American delegation had taken its final position, and the Americans were not going to trade. The United States, the Secretary added, was willing to permit the Russians for a few years to handle their newly mined gold entirely apart from any provisions relating to the International Monetary Fund. That concession was far more important than the issue of the original gold contribution.

The Russians conceded nothing then or on the following day. Rather they brought up again their demand for authority to change the value of the ruble on their own initiative and without concurrence of the members of the Fund. As Morgenthau put it at the end of the meeting of July 15, the Soviet Union had presented an agenda that would have kept the group busy for ten hours. The Americans would "stick to their guns" and leave the outstanding disagreements for decision by the whole conference. In the end, those decisions adopted the American formulas.

As the negotiations with the Russians indicated, Morgenthau and his associates were prepared to make concessions to another nation's interpretation of its own grandeur when those concessions did not damage the integrity, as the Americans defined it, of the International Monetary Fund. So it was also in negotiations with several Latin American nations. Since Argentina was not one of the United or Allied nations, she was not represented at the conference, nor was she considered for a quota within the Fund. The two largest Latin American quotas fell to Mexico and Brazil. Difficulties arose because the Cubans wanted the third largest Latin quota, which available statistics showed they deserved, but Chile wanted status at least equal to Cuba's, though in economic terms she did not merit it, and Colombia, while satisfied with a small quota, insisted on equality with Chile. As Marriner Eccles noted, the whole tempest related to prestige and politics. After several long discussions, the American delegation, following a suggestion of Dean Acheson, left Cuba with the third largest quota, gave Chile the next place, and assigned Colombia just a little less.

Mexico had a protest of her own. Her delegation, of which the chairman was Minister of Finance Suarez with whom Morgenthau had often worked before, called for a statement by the conference requiring the Fund to determine the feasibility of using silver collaterally with gold for the settlement of international balances. Alternatively, the Mexicans were willing to accept a promise that the Fund would take such action as it deemed adequate to protect the stability of silver in international markets. Under pressure, the Mexicans agreed to settle for the still more innocuous commitment that the Fund would determine the proper role and function of silver within the international monetary structure. But Morgenthau had long since swallowed more silver than he could digest, and Keynes disliked the idea of introducing silver into international monetary plans in any manner whatever. In order to placate Mexico, as well as Bolivia and Peru, Keynes was willing to mention silver in a context divorced from the Fund, but the very word "silver," as Ned Brown and Dean Acheson saw it, would cause trouble in Congress. Ultimately the Americans, with British assistance, worked out phraseology authorizing the Fund to study questions involving monetary policies — of which silver, though it was not named, might be one. Reluctantly the Mexicans accepted that solution.

Domestic and international politics combined to affect the question of the Polish quota. The British, champions of the smaller nations, recommended a larger quota for Poland, though with less apparent enthusiasm than did Senator Robert Wagner, whose central concern was with the Polish-American vote in New York City and Buffalo. "If we decide to do anything on improving the quota of Poland," Morgenthau wrote Fred Vinson on July 13, "Senator Wagner wants to be the delegate to inform them, for obvious reasons." But as it worked out, there was nothing of substance to be communicated.

France, too, had complaints. During the period of the conference, sharp political disagreements between Roosevelt and De Gaulle heightened the tension in Franco-American relations.* On that account unusually sensitive, Pierre Mendès-France, the Gaullist chairman of the French delegation to Bretton Woods, protested bitterly against a reduction in the French quota from an original sum of $500 million to $450 million. He reminded the Americans that he had disliked granting the Chinese the fourth largest quota. He had not then expected his own quota to be diminished, and now his nation's prestige was at stake. Sympathetic to that claim, Dean

* See Chapter IV.

Acheson said the French had suffered as much as had the Russians from the refusal to permit deductions in gold contributions on account of Nazi devastation. But Morgenthau would concede nothing. France, he said, had already received two prestigious favors — a seat on the executive committee of the International Monetary Fund, and an increase from four to five in the number of national depositories for the Fund's assets, so as to include France as one.

As ever, the Chinese worried about face. In order to bring the Russian quota up to $1 billion 200 million, the Americans had taken $50 million from the original Chinese quota of $600 million. On July 17, 1944, H. H. Kung asked Morgenthau to restore the Chinese figure so as to permit the Chinese themselves to announce that out of friendship for the Soviet Union, they would surrender $50 million. Morgenthau, who was about to begin negotiations with the Chinese about the still troublesome dollar-fapi exchange rate, had reason to placate Kung, but the Russians objected to the Chinese suggestion, and the Secretary, without explanation, thanked Kung "for his very nice gesture" but also declined it. Kung then demanded restoration of the original quota, but Morgenthau refused. "I didn't realize until the other day," he told Acheson after Kung had departed, "that Russia and China refused to sit together. . . . I don't know what the trouble is between the two countries, but there evidently is . . . something which is burning in there. . . . I wonder if it wouldn't be worth our while to . . . go out of our way just to mention China?" That reference, as well as a flattering reference to France, might be included in a pending speech by Fred Vinson to the final general session on quotas. Acheson was agreeable so long as Vinson confined his remarks to quotas and said nothing that put the State Department in the position of having to do something for China. That reference was all Kung got.

Great Britain was more successful. Early in the conference Keynes objected to a provision in the American draft permitting the Fund to inform a nation that it was pursuing inflationary policies. "How would you like it," Keynes asked Harry White, "if the Fund informed your government that the OPA wasn't doing a good job and as a result of that you had rising prices?" In reply White suggested empowering the Fund to make informal reports at any time, but allowing the publication of formal reports only with the permission of the government whose affairs were under consideration. Under that scheme, Keynes could assure Parliament that the Fund could not butt into British domestic policy. Somewhat wryly, Keynes said: "I should think that is exactly what your country would want." The revised draft incorporated White's suggestion.

The Norwegians, ordinarily uncomplaining, raised another issue that temporarily split the British and American delegations. Before the conference, Morgenthau and Keynes had concurred on the desirability of using the Fund to replace entirely the Bank of International Settlements, the international institution at Geneva on which were represented the central banks of the major Western powers. Fully persuaded, as was Morgenthau also, that Nazi collaborationists dominated the BIS during the war years, the Norwegians pressed for its abolition. Morgenthau counted on Keynes to support that policy. "I don't know what the experience of the rest of you has been with Keynes," Morgenthau told some of the American technicians on July 19, "but mine is, I feel that he has been absolutely sincere and wants this meeting to be a success, and tonight* the man unhesitatingly impressed me with the fact that he wants to do away with the BIS. . . . B. M. Baruch has fed me full of this stuff that you can't believe Keynes, and Keynes double crossed him at Versailles, and so forth and so on, and I have been looking for it, but I have seen no evidence of it."

With the endorsement of Cordell Hull, Morgenthau had the American delegation take the initiative against the BIS, but Keynes and the British proposed a resolution on the matter that failed to suit the Secretary. "The United Nations Monetary and Financial Conference," the British draft read, "recommends that at the date of the constitution of the Board of the Fund the necessary steps will be taken to liquidate the Bank for International Settlements." Morgenthau wanted a stronger statement saying that the conference "recommends that the Bank of International Settlement be liquidated at the earliest possible moment." That, said Keynes, was "not very early!" But Keynes also commented: "I don't think we want to keep the damn thing alive, do we?" The British then agreed to vote for the American phraseology.

Keynes was most concerned about the location of the headquarters of the Fund. The American delegation wanted that office in the

---

* That night, Keynes, who ran upstairs to his own suite after dining with Morgenthau, suffered a minor heart attack.

United States. The British, though they knew they would have to concede sooner or later, did not want yet to endorse a symbol of the loss of prestige in international finance they had suffered in the previous five years. As a delaying tactic, they moved to defer the question to the first meeting of the Board of Governors of the Fund. He was under orders from the Chancellor of the Exchequer, Keynes told Morgenthau, not to recede from that position without express authority from London. Though he had asked for further instructions, the Chancellor, rejecting the American proposal, had said that "the decision is a political matter and therefore to be decided by Governments," and not, by implication, by the conference. Further, like the Chancellor, Keynes maintained that the location of Fund headquarters could not be settled without reference to the location of other international offices, particularly that of the United Nations, not yet created.

The American delegation dismissed Keynes's objections categorically. New York, Harry White maintained, had become the financial center of the world and was entitled to appropriate recognition. Furthermore, the United States had the votes at the conference to enforce its will. Fred Vinson agreed, and the congressmen in the delegation said that the House and the Senate would insist on having the headquarters within the United States, and that the Latin American nations and the Russians expected as much.

Morgenthau, who felt less strongly about the issue than did his colleagues, accepted their advice. At a private meeting with Keynes he found his companion at first "very combative." When the Secretary said that the American delegation held unanimously that the conference should vote to put the headquarters of the Fund and the Bank within the United States, Keynes "got sort of angry and said that it left him no choice, either to withdraw from the Conference or to make a protest. And of course if they made a protest and were defeated by countries like Nicaragua and Costa Rica, it would look very bad, and he would have to report to the Chancellor of the Exchequer, and he was afraid he would be instructed to withdraw. He said two or three times that he would have to withdraw."

He could not help himself, Morgenthau replied, for "that is the way our delegation — particularly the congressional delegation, feels."

"Well," Keynes said, "the trouble with you people is, all the time you are thinking about the Presidential election — everything is Congress. You keep throwing it at us all the time."

"We have had considerable discussion," Morgenthau said, "over a long period about how we should handle Congress this time so we shouldn't make the same mistake Woodrow Wilson made. . . . You know that Senator Lodge's papers show that if Wilson had ever sent for him and talked to him, he, Lodge, would have gotten the thing* through the Senate." Keynes said he knew, and Morgenthau then explained that the congressmen in the delegation were there "solely for the purpose of getting this legislation through, because they are sensitive to their constituency." The question of Roosevelt's reelection did not enter the matter at all.

Keynes admitted that the American congressmen had been "perfectly magnificent." He also said that Ambassador Halifax was hyperconscious of the election, about which he reported to London at every opportunity.

"I know Lord Halifax is," Morgenthau said, "because I know he keeps sounding out Republicans all the time as to who is going to win, and take it from me, President Roosevelt is going to win, hands down." Some Americans, the Secretary continued, had the feeling that there were those within the British government who wanted Roosevelt defeated. "The very heads, of course," Keynes replied, "are for Mr. Roosevelt, but we can't account for the people like Lord Beaverbrook and some of the others who may not want Mr. Roosevelt reelected."

But Keynes agreed that the spirit of the conference had been wholly free of politics. Apparently appeased by Morgenthau's manner, he also promised to dispose gently of the issue of the headquarters. He would send a cable to the Chancellor of the Exchequer, he said, indicating that he would himself make a mild protest on the floor "and let it go at that." Delighted, Morgenthau felt that he had "left Keynes in an excellent humor."

Later Keynes agreed to have the British delegation support a revised American motion. Without naming any country, that motion, which the conference adopted, called for locating the headquarters of both the Fund and the Bank within the nation with the largest quota. The motion happily satisfied the congressmen in the American delegation and spared the British unnecessary insult.

* The League of Nations in 1919.

The conference's agreement on the Fund, which the forty-four signatory countries had still to ratify, had an unmistakably American stamp. The White plan, modified and improved in successive compromises and accommodations, prevailed in its essentials, as did also the earliest and strongest of White's purposes and Morgenthau's — the prevention of a repetition of the international monetary rivalries and battles of the interwar years. The Fund provided machinery for international consultation, for establishing a postwar structure of exchange rates, for orderly adjustment of those rates when necessary to correct basic disequilibriums in balances of payments, for aid to member nations in achieving balanced trade without recourse to deflation at home or monetary aggression abroad, and for the gradual removal of foreign-exchange restrictions that burdened international commerce. The experience of two ensuing decades would point to possibilities, indeed to necessities, in international monetary management for which changes would be needed in the holdings, structure, and procedures of the Fund, and some of those desirable changes were to be reminiscent of parts of the Keynes plan. But the agreement of 1944, in its day or in retrospect, was nonetheless a stunning achievement, the first and one of the most important in creating a basis for practical internationalism.

5. Bretton Woods: The International Bank for Reconstruction and Development

Midway through the Bretton Woods Conference, which had been giving most of its attention to the Fund, it became clear that the committees working on the Bank would need extra time and help to unsnarl their disagreements. Dean Acheson, the leader of the American subcommittee concerned with the Bank, reviewed the negotiations up to that time for the rest of the American delegates on July 11, 1944. The most important unsettled issue, he said, was the ratio of loans to assets. The committee on the Bank, of which Keynes was chairman, had agreed on a capital of $10 billion, one-tenth to be paid in at once, one-tenth on call. With that fifth the Bank could make direct loans; with its entire capital, including the 80 per cent promised but not subscribed, it could guarantee private loans. The Bank's guarantee would of course greatly increase the security of those loans and thus facilitate their sale in world money markets. If there were few or no defaults, there would be no need ever to call for the other 80 per cent of the subscription. But if the loans were defaulted, then the subscriptions would have to be called in, at least in part. Further, any loan the Bank guaranteed was guaranteed also, willy-nilly, by its member nations. If a member defaulted on a loan, then the 80 per cent of its subscription not yet demanded might not be forthcoming. Against that background, the conservative Dutch held out for a ratio of loans to assets of only 75 per cent. Underdeveloped nations, and nations that had suffered extensive war damage, favored a ratio as high as 200 per cent. Within the American delegation, opinion ranged between those figures, with Wolcott close to the Dutch and White at the other extreme.

"There is nothing," White argued on July 12, "that will serve to drive these countries into some kind of ism — Communism or something else — faster than having inadequate capital to reconstruct their railways, their port facilities, their power development — things which have been destroyed during the war, or things which have deteriorated." In the absence of a reasonable source of foreign investment, war-torn nations would suffer from severe unemployment and unrest. On the other hand, as White saw it, the United States in the years after the war would for some time have difficulty finding markets to absorb all that it produced unless the potential consumer nations had a source of money with which to buy American goods. In the absence of those markets, the United States would also experience depression. But in meeting world capital needs, the United States could not go it alone, for that would put too big a risk and burden on the American taxpayer. Therefore White believed in the Bank which would reduce risk by making it multilateral, while at the same time it encouraged the necessary lending and opened the desirable markets. For those reasons, White considered it preposterous to hold the ratio of loans to assets to as little as 200 or 300 per cent. He thought they had to run as high as 400 or 500 per cent.

Impatient with the conservative leanings of some of his colleagues, White complained to Acheson on July 13 that Ned Brown, while meaning well, was mishandling negotiations on the Bank. Acheson disagreed. Brown, he said, "had worked terrifically hard . . . for a long time, and he is a big fat man, and that takes a lot. . . . He is really simply exhausted." He was also, as White was not, in tune with prevailing conservative sentiment. "Expansion," like "Keynes," remained a nasty word in the vocabulary of American congressmen, whose opinions accounted in large degree for the decision of the American delegation to settle for a ratio of loans to assets of 100 per cent, a figure that also suited the Dutch and the British.

As Acheson had said, Brown was tired, and so were most of the delegates who had lived and worked closely together for several hot weeks in a situation of unrelenting pressure. "It is as though," Keynes wrote, ". . . one had to accomplish the preliminary work of many interdepartmental and Cabinet committees, the job of the . . . draftsmen, and the passage . . . of two intricate legislative measures of major dimensions, all this carried on in committees and commissions numbering anything up to 200 persons in rooms with bad acoustics, shouting through microphones, many of those present . . . with an imperfect knowledge of English, each wanting to get something on the record which would look well in the press down at home, and . . . the Russians only understanding what was afoot with the utmost difficulty. . . . We have all of us worked every minute of our waking hours. . . . Harry White told me that even he was all in. . . . But all of us . . . are all in." Keynes, who was chairman of the discussions of the Bank, expressed his weariness partly by his impatience with delay and with the interminable bickering about quotas. The session of the afternoon of July 13 particularly disturbed Morgenthau who found one delegate "so mad he shook," and another, an Indian, "just as furious as he could be." Vinson agreed that many delegates were raising "the very devil" about the way Keynes was driving matters to conclusion before some of them could even find the pages of the documents to which he was referring.

Acheson considered Keynes's performance tactless but understandable. There simply was not enough time. The work for the Fund had gone much further before the conference began than had the work for the Bank, and now Keynes, charged with completing an acceptable draft for the Bank, was being rushed "in a perfectly impossible and outrageous way." So, too, Acheson had inadequate technical assistance for developing the American case. Morgenthau volunteered to tell Keynes "in a nice way" to slow down. The Secretary also took steps, at Acheson's request, to permit him to play the role of the barrister, to present on the floor the brief on which the other American delegates and technicians had agreed. "I regard myself," Acheson explained, "as . . . the trial lawyer. . . . What does my client want?"

The chief of those clients, Morgenthau, on July 14 told Keynes that he had "seemed to rush things," a criticism Keynes took "in very good spirit." The two, with support from the French and the Russians, agreed to extend the conference for a few days so that all of the delegates could "ease up." And with the assistance of the entire American delegation, Morgenthau defined the important outstanding issues that Acheson had to argue.

Quotas for the Bank differed perceptibly from quotas for the Fund. In the Fund, the larger the quota of a nation, the larger the vote of that nation, and also the greater the capacity of the nation to borrow for the purpose of stabilizing its own currency. In the Bank, the vote of a country also depended upon the size of its quota, but the opportunity to borrow related not to quotas but to need. The poorer nations, those with the smallest quotas, would borrow the most, while the wealthier nations, with the largest quotas, would undertake the greatest risk. The very countries that had scrambled for larger quotas in the Fund tended to demand smaller ones in the Bank.

There were differences, too, about lending policy. As White reported to the American delegation on July 18, the Russians were attempting to amend the declaration establishing the Bank so as to give special weight to expediting loans for reconstruction. Like other countries overrun by the Germans, Russia would benefit from a lending policy that favored reconstruction. That policy, however, would be detrimental to underdeveloped countries outside of Europe. Ned Brown thought the phraseology unimportant. The real consideration, he judged, would be the rate of interest, and the rate of interest would depend on the riskiness of the loan. Whatever the language, he believed it would be easier for Brazil to get a loan at low interest rates than it would be for the Soviet Union. But Dean Acheson opposed the Russian proposal because of the trouble it would certainly cause with the Latin Americans. Acheson favored Keynes's phraseology, which gave equitable consideration to both types of loans and stressed the question of need. White disagreed, but Morgenthau settled the matter by directing the American delegation to sound out the major South American countries whose views, as it developed, paralleled Acheson's.

The Secretary had more trouble with the Soviet demand that their quota for the Bank be no greater than $900 million. "Talking as a grandfather," Morgenthau on July 19 urged Stepanov to take a position in the eyes of the world like that he had assumed with respect to the Fund. Stepanov replied that the Russians would have especially heavy reconstruction expenses, but at Morgenthau's request, he agreed to cable Moscow. Still without an answer on July 21, Morgenthau decided to put Russia down for a subscription of $1 billion 200 million. Acheson objected. The United States, he said, should avoid any kind of a row, and could not commit the Russians who, in his opinion, could not go beyond one billion dollars. Brown thought the Russian subscription would make little difference to the Bank, since the private money market put no faith in Russia's guarantee. Tobey and Spence agreed.

At a committee meeting on quotas on July 21, Fred Vinson reported for the United States that total subscriptions came to $7 billion 318 million, wholly apart from the Russian subscription which he expected to be another billion. The American share was $2 billion 750 million; the total goal, $8 billion 800 million. Whatever the Russians decided, the conference had almost reached that goal, and Vinson hoped the other delegates would now accept the list as it stood. Keynes at once supported that proposal. Several nations, including Cuba, China, and Poland, volunteered to increase their quotas. Keynes then appealed to the Soviet delegates to follow that example, but Stepanov instead, in a long speech, maintained that India could afford more than Russia since India had suffered so little from the war.

Surprisingly, the following evening at seven o'clock, one hour before the final plenary session, Stepanov called on Morgenthau. He had heard from Molotov, he said, "and the answer is that he is happy to agree to your proposition . . . to increase our quota . . . to one billion two hundred million dollars."

"Well," Morgenthau said, "you tell Mr. Molotov that I want to thank him from the bottom of my heart. . . . This confirms the long-time respect and confidence that I have in the Union of Soviet Socialist Republics." Minutes later, in his closing speech at the terminal banquet, Morgenthau announced that the Soviet Union had increased her subscription. That remark, according to the *New York Times,* "came like the proverbial bombshell."

The Bretton Woods agreement for the International Bank for Reconstruction and Development, like the agreement on the Fund, followed primarily American lines. Though the original White plan was much reduced, the agreement incorporated on an international basis the New Deal experience in direct government lending and in government guarantees of private lending for desirable local projects and regional economic development. The Bank was to have a capital of $9.1 billion, subscribed by forty-four nations (if they ratified the pact)*, with 10 per cent paid in immediately and that sum, plus another 10 per cent on call, available for direct loans. But essentially the Bank was to be an underwriting and guaranteeing institution which would supplement rather than supplant private international investment.

As Morgenthau said in his closing address to the conference, the Fund and Bank were "two . . . foundation stones for the structure of lasting peace and security." The delegates to the conference, he also said, had shown "that the people of the United Nations can work together to plan the peace as well as fight the war." The agreements, he went on, employing the vocabulary of Franklin Roosevelt's first inaugural message, drove the "usurious money lenders from the temple of international finance," freed world capital from "monopoly control," and made that capital available to war-torn and underdeveloped countries.

"I am perfectly certain," Morgenthau continued, "that no delegation to this Conference has lost sight for a moment of the particular national interest it was sent here to represent. The American delegation . . . has been, at all times, conscious of its primary obligation — the protection of American interests. . . . Yet none of us has found any incompatibility between devotion to our own country and joint action. Indeed, we have found on the contrary that the

---

* Of all the signatories, the most important not to ratify or join either Fund or Bank was the Soviet Union, but that development seemed unlikely in 1944, especially after Russian cooperation at the conference.

only genuine safeguard for our national interests lies in international cooperation."

Earlier the Secretary had talked informally with his fellow American delegates and their technical assistants. "I really wanted to thank you each and every one," he said, ". . . for the splendid work. I have never in my eleven and three-quarters years in Washington . . . participated with a group, and this is not blarney, that worked so well together. . . . I think it has demonstrated to me that on this sort of thing it is the way we should work with Congress. There has been lots of discussion about the Executive infringing on the authority of Congress and vice versa, but I think I certainly am going to recommend as strongly as I know how, to the President, that he follow this method at any other similar international conference." The Republican delegates responded in the same spirit. "Much of the harmony," Congressman Wolcott said, "is due to the splendid leadership you have exhibited and the fairness with us all. I shall leave here thinking that this is one of the greatest experiences of my life and one of the most pleasant."

Morgenthau was gratified, too, by the eleventh-hour gesture of the Soviet Union. Molotov's agreement to lift the Russian quota to $1200 million, the Secretary wrote Roosevelt on July 22, demonstrated the Russian "desire to collaborate fully with the United States. Dean Acheson has just said that this was almost unbelievable, and that he regards it as a great diplomatic victory . . . and as a matter of great political significance." Keynes agreed. In a private letter to a friend, he wrote: "Our personal relations with the Russians have been very cordial. . . . Given time, we should . . . gain their confidence. . . . They *want* to thaw and collaborate."

"There are two kinds of people," Morgenthau told Roosevelt a month later, "one like Eden* who believe we must cooperate with the Russians and that we must trust Russia for the peace of the world, and there is the school which is illustrated by the remark of Mr. Churchill who said, 'What are we going to have between the white snows of Russia and the white cliffs of Dover?' "

"That's very well put," Roosevelt replied. "I belong to the same school as Eden."

He had been able, Morgenthau added, "to work with Russia at Bretton Woods, and Dean Acheson said I seemed to have a sixth

* Anthony Eden, British Foreign Secretary, now Lord Avon.

sense of those things. At first he told me he thought I had handled
the Russian situation entirely wrong, and then he was man enough
to come around at the end and say I was completely right and
Keynes said the same thing."

Still, Morgenthau knew there was a long way to go. The Bretton
Woods agreements had yet to run the gamut of congressional hearings and votes. The banking community and the conservative press
in both the United States and Great Britain were already building a
case against the Fund and Bank. Concerned about the ordeal of
ratification, Morgenthau was worried even more by the many remaining problems of constructing a peace. At Bretton Woods, as he
had said, he had found the Russians in the end cooperative, but he
had also found them stubborn antagonists, polite but impossible to
move except by direct appeal to Moscow. Still, he expected that the
United States could count on them because he expected Moscow to
yield to the urgent requests that Roosevelt might make. Equally
important, Morgenthau had discovered the British to be as reliable
in their friendship as they were sturdy in the pursuit of their own
national interests. He had, of course, worked longer and more intimately with the British than with any other ally, but he had also in
recent months had his difficulties over the question of dollar balances and the matter of occupation currencies, over policy in Argentina and policy toward the Jewish refugees. Those problems had
bothered him when he arrived at Bretton Woods, but he left with
his confidence in the English-speaking alliance renewed, and on that
account with increased sympathy for the positions the British were
adopting on their dollar balances and particularly on Lend-Lease.*

The success, as Morgenthau saw it, of Bretton Woods, the first
United Nations conference, fortified his hopes for genuine cooperation among the United States, the United Kingdom, and the Soviet
Union in building the postwar world. The satisfactory resolution of
their national interests seemed to him the only firm basis for future
peace. The establishment of the Fund and Bank appeared to him as
much a political as an economic venture. Now, in both respects, in
midsummer 1944, he prepared to further other plans he had begun
to design.

* See Chapter VI.

VI

In the National Interest

1944-1945

THE BRETTON WOODS negotiations revealed the generous but purposeful nationalism that underlay Morgenthau's genuine but careful internationalism. He sponsored American participation in international economic and financial affairs, and American assistance to other nations, because he believed that no other course would permit the United States in the future to avoid a repetition of the depression and war of the previous decade and a half. Only a guarded altruism, as he saw it, would strengthen the national interest and assure the safety and prosperity of the country in a peaceful postwar world. It was his duty, he felt, to minimize the costs of internationalism, both during and after the war, to the American people. It was his intention to cultivate well-being at home and, where possible, to induce other nations to adopt the democracy and liberal economy for which he worked in the United States. Those objectives, as they pertained to domestic matters, demanded the extension of the New Deal; as they pertained to Europe, the rebuilding of a prosperous Great Britain, the cultivation of Soviet relations "not tainted with mutual suspicion," and the incapacitating of Germany for future aggression; as they pertained to Asia, the support of decent government and economic growth in China. Those goals, as Morgenthau interpreted them, in large decree depended on each other, and all, he was convinced, advanced the national interest.

1. Reconversion to a Liberal Society

The problems of reconverting the American economy from a wartime to a peacetime basis began to concern Morgenthau even before the Allied invasion of Europe. With his chief adviser on reconversion, Robert E. McConnell, who had earlier reorganized the General Aniline Company,* the Secretary believed, as he long had, that the protection of small business and the prevention of monopoly were necessary for a healthy, free economy. He therefore encouraged Vice President Henry Wallace who was urging the Administration to "do something for the little businessman," and he directed the Treasury's General Counsel to assist Supreme Court Justice Robert H. Jackson in his efforts, ultimately successful, to establish the Small Business Administration.

Morgenthau was uncertain, however, about the desirability of renominating Wallace as Roosevelt's running mate in 1944. "The President," he told Steve Early, Roosevelt's press secretary, that June, "ought to have him run again mainly so that people couldn't say that he, the President, was disloyal to Wallace. Well, we went on talking and by the time we got through I said I wouldn't want to see Wallace President of the United States. . . . Then Early asked me what I thought of Senator Lucas† and I said as far as I knew I thought he was fine. He said he was a wonderful speaker, and he said that the governor of Georgia told newspapermen yesterday that the President told him that after the armistice and after the Peace Conference, he, the President, wanted to go home and look after his private affairs. Steve said that if that got around it would be terrible. . . .

"Pa Watson took a couple of seconds to tell me how terrible he thought Wallace was. Steve said that yesterday at the state convention in Kentucky the delegates got up and tore Wallace's picture down from the wall, and everybody cheered."

The southern and conservative Democratic mood, inimical to Wallace, worried Roosevelt.

Morgenthau noted in his Diary for July 6, 1944:

> When I saw the President this morning, he brought up the question of Vice President Wallace. He said that Mrs. Roosevelt is trying to force him to insist on Wallace . . . and he wanted to know what I thought of Wallace. I said I was devoted to him personally, but I said, "In the final analysis, you and I are both

---

* See Chapter I.
† Scott Lucas, the Illinois Democrat, more conservative than Wallace.

only human, and if something should happen to you I certainly wouldn't want Henry Wallace to be President. . . . I know how loyal you feel towards him." I could see that he was trying to find a way of not having Wallace. He asked me, "What about Winant?" and I said, "I think you might have trouble with him. You know he has a tax case pending." So he said, "What about McNutt?" * And I said, "Mr. President, I will crawl from here to the Capitol on my stomach and back again if it will keep you from taking McNutt. . . . The man's record is very bad." Then he said, "What about ex-Senator Minton?" and I said, "Well, I don't know him very well."

Then I told the President I thought he ought to get somebody from west of Chicago, and he said, "I don't want Sam Rayburn." I said, "I think Bill Douglas† would be fine. He comes from the right part of the country. He is young and he could tell this fellow Dewey‡ off. He isn't a stickler for rules and regulations." "Well," the President said, "Kaiser§ has been suggested." I said, "I think he is too old." I didn't say it but I was thinking that he is the same age as the President, and I think they ought to have a younger man.

Then I said to the President, "After all, the last time they raised a Third Term question. This time they aren't raising the Fourth Term question, but they do feel — if you don't mind my saying so — that you forced Wallace down their throats, and this time they would like to have the matter undecided and have the Convention open." He said, "That's what I hear. You are right. . . . I think it is terribly important to let the Convention pick their own man. I think it would put them in a good humor."

With Roosevelt's quiet approval, the Convention selected Harry S Truman, whom Morgenthau knew scarcely at all, and the President provided a small palliative for Wallace's feelings by nominating him

---

* Paul McNutt of Indiana, a handsome Democrat who had held various federal posts and whom Morgenthau distrusted.

† Supreme Court Justice William Douglas.

‡ Governor Thomas E. Dewey of New York, the Republican Presidential candidate.

§ Henry Kaiser, the industrialist.

to be Secretary of Commerce in place of Jesse Jones, with whom Roosevelt at long last had lost patience. But the nomination of Wallace for Secretary of Commerce blew up a storm in Congress. Jones, a conservative Texan, had many friends on the Hill, who had smiled upon his accumulation of lending responsibilities within the Commerce Department, particularly his chairmanship of the Reconstruction Finance Corporation. Republicans and Democratic conservatives, especially those from the South, set out to block confirmation of Wallace unless the Commerce Department were divested of the lending agencies.

Walking down to work with Morgenthau on January 24, 1945, Wallace said he had made up his mind that he would lose confirmation unless he surrendered the RFC. He therefore favored making the corporation a totally independent agency. "The thing to do," Wallace said, "is to clean it up and have an audit made . . . to give it a good send-off." Morgenthau asked Dan Bell to help Wallace prepare a memorandum for that purpose. The Secretary also that day described Wallace to a hostile critic as a "supremely loyal public servant, able and devoted, . . . well qualified to direct the work of the Department of Commerce, and of the lending agencies attached to it." Further, he gave Wallace, for whatever use he cared to make of it, a Treasury study on prospects for postwar full employment. Wallace leaned on that material in his testimony to the Senate committee on his appointment.

"I believe," Morgenthau told the press on January 26, "he has done the country a genuine service in offering a concrete program for achieving the President's goal of sixty million jobs after the war. Without attempting at this time to weigh the merits of each of his proposals, we can all thank Mr. Wallace for the courage he has displayed in coming forward with specific suggestions. . . . Intelligent planning for problems we know will arise after the war spells the difference between an orderly transition period and a logjam of poorly considered measures. . . .

"I think too that Mr. Wallace is correct in stating that the real issue involved is not his lack of experience in the financial field. As Secretary of the Treasury during most of the period Mr. Wallace was in charge of the Commodity Credit Corporation, the Farm Security Administration and the Rural Electrification Administration, I can say that I know that Mr. Wallace's record in making loans in excess of $6 billion is beyond reproach. He is in the truest American tradition — a Yankee businessman with the horse sense to recognize that we are living in a world of change. I know that Henry Wallace made a genuine contribution to good government and free enterprise as Secretary of Agriculture. I believe he can make an even greater contribution as Secretary of Commerce."

The struggle over Wallace's confirmation, Morgenthau warned Roosevelt in February, "can be fairly interpreted as a fight not only against Wallace personally, but also against the liberal and forward-looking character of your domestic program." That was an accurate judgment, as was Wallace's after his victory that Morgenthau had had "a lot to do with it."

In the fight for a liberal program, domestic and foreign, Morgenthau, as ever, depended on the steady assistance of his senior subordinates in the Treasury. In late 1944 and 1945 only a few of those he had most valued were still in the department. Those veterans were Under Secretary Daniel Bell, Assistant Secretary Herbert Gaston, and Harry White, now also holding the rank of Assistant Secretary. Randolph Paul had retired from public life, exhausted by his struggles for equitable taxation, and John Pehle, often in the past a member of the Secretary's morning group, was on his way to becoming head of the Surplus Property Office in the Department of Commerce. The recruits to Morgenthau's personal cabinet began with Joseph J. O'Connell, Jr., a Treasury official since 1938, who replaced Paul as General Counsel in May 1944. There was also Ansel F. Luxford, who had served the department with one brief interruption since 1935, ordinarily within the office of the General Counsel, with duties pertaining to foreign funds, economic warfare, and international monetary questions. The chief legal adviser to the American delegation at Bretton Woods, Luxford became Assistant to the Secretary in December 1944. His close companion within the Treasury, also an Assistant to the Secretary, Josiah E. DuBois, Jr., was, like Luxford, a devotee of liberal causes, and had earlier been in Foreign Funds Control. The other new regular at the morning group was Frank Coe, an economist, a Treasury official from 1934 to 1939, later an adviser to the National Defense Council and a special assistant to the American ambassador in London, also for more than a year assistant to the Director of the Board of Economic Warfare and an assistant within the Foreign Economic Administration. Coe, whose labors as a technician on the American delegation to Bretton Woods especially impressed Morgenthau, succeeded White in 1945 as the Director of Monetary Research for the Treasury. Like White, he was later accused of communist sympathies and affiliations.

Morgenthau enjoyed the youth and admired the energy of the men on his staff. Eager, ambitious, and impatient, they demonstrated their worth to the Secretary not only in connection with the International Monetary Fund and the World Bank, but also in the battle for the War Refugee Board, in the first stages of planning for Germany*, and in the preparation of papers about economic warfare in Argentina and economic cooperation with Great Britain. In their zeal for disciplining big business and assisting small enterprise they exceeded the Secretary himself, and most of them, in their commitment to Keynesian economics, differed sharply from Morgenthau. As he saw it, those differences were an insignificant price to pay for the loyalty and the esprit de corps his young staff brought to the Treasury. Nevertheless, the Secretary missed the greater maturity and wisdom of men like Oliphant and Paul. He had trusted them more than he ever trusted their successors. And though he delighted in the persistence of the liberal spirit within the department, Morgenthau in 1945 found his office more lonesome than it had been before.

Confident always of the counsel of Bell and Gaston, usually responsive to the advices of White, Morgenthau often tempered the recommendations and the pace of the younger men. He did so, except when he was tired, with an avuncular good will. So it was in March 1945, when the group urged him to promote the candidacy for Secretary of Labor of Murray Latimer, then the Chairman of the Railroad Retirement Board. "I have your memorandum," the Secretary wrote them, "in regard to Murray Latimer, suggesting that I throw my weight around. It seems to me, inasmuch as I have taken on five pounds recently, that your suggestion about my weight is untimely. Furthermore, don't you think that Latimer is a little bit too left of center and might not be acceptable to some of the big

* See Chapter VII.

businessmen who are in favor of Bretton Woods. After all, we must have big business as usual.

"In your memo you constantly refer to the C.I.O. Just at this time I think it is unfortunate that you bring up the C.I.O. because after all big business does not like them. . . . In strictest confidence, and by that I exclude your various pipelines, you will be interested in knowing that I have recommended Senator Kilgore* to the President for the position."

Joking aside, Morgenthau looked to his staff to give force and substance to his own broad ideas for liberal wartime and postwar policies at home and abroad. His convictions, he liked to say, were those of "an apple-farmer and a democrat." He claimed for them neither originality nor profundity. Yet on that account he held them no less dear, and he considered them as pertinent for any other country as for the United States. A liberal economy, he believed, constituted one requirement for a liberal democracy and therefore for a peace-loving and decent nation, a good neighbor in international affairs. And the American interest, in his view, demanded a world constructed of such nations. Those convictions, along with his custodian's prudence toward the expenditure of American funds, guided his continuing negotiations with the major partners in the alliance against Germany and Japan.

2. Balance Sheet for Chengtu

The meeting at Bretton Woods presented a new opportunity for settling the corrosive financial problems relating to American participation in the war in China. In June 1944 there remained at issue the question of an exchange rate between the dollar and the fapi and the calculation of the Chinese contribution to the war effort in the Asian theater.† For some months, the War Department had been attempting to reach the necessary agreements with the Chinese,

---

* Harley M. Kilgore, West Virginia Democrat, a United States Senator since 1940, and in 1945 the chairman of the senate committee investigating big business and wartime business. As it worked out, Frances Perkins remained Secretary of Labor for the balance of Roosevelt's tenure.

† See Chapter III.

but on June 23, 1944, George Harrison, who had been handling the matter for Secretary Stimson, proposed to turn the problem back to the Treasury. Stimson approved, as he put it in his diary, because he did not want to have any catastrophe occur while he was dealing with the Chinese.

The Chinese rate of exchange, Stimson observed, was still declining, and yet no one had been able to show the Chinese how to stabilize it. Further, the United States had been incurring debts for the construction of airfields in China which, in terms of the official, inflated value of Chinese currency, amounted to billions of dollars. To press the Chinese case, and also to attend the Bretton Woods Conference, Finance Minister H. H. Kung was on his way to the United States, along with his wife, a sister of Madame Chiang Kaishek. As Stimson reported it, when Roosevelt learned she was arriving, "the President at Cabinet . . . threw up his hands in horror and said he thought he'd take to the woods!" So, in effect, did Stimson, by returning to the Treasury responsibility for the financial negotiations.

Aware of the difficulties ahead of him, Morgenthau welcomed the promised assistance of the Army, but at the same time took pains to prevent the Chinese from playing one American agency off against another, as they so often had. "I just talked to Admiral Leahy," the Secretary noted in his Diary on June 27, 1944, "and I told him I understood the President was going to see H. H. Kung and that State and War and Treasury hoped that the President would not discuss exchange rates with Kung and that if he brought it up would the President tell Kung to take it up with the Treasury." At the White House the next morning, Roosevelt "immediately started off by saying that he had seen Kung, and from the way he talked I gather he got my message . . . because he said that he had told Kung to take this matter up with me. The President said . . . 'Why not give the Chinese a new currency similar to what we have done for France? * . . . I am not recommending it. I just want you to think about it.' Then he said that he had also talked to Kung about getting more goods over the Hump† . . . because he said the only way to handle the inflation problem was by getting more goods. . . .

* See Chapter IV.
† The mountainous air route into China from India.

"The President said . . . 'What I am trying to find out, where is the Chinese Army and why aren't they fighting because the Japanese seem to be able to push them in any direction they want to.' "

The Americans had never been able to influence the Chinese when questions of money were at stake. As the Secretary knew, the Chinese, guarding their sovereignty with as much vigor as the French, would resist any American proposal for a new currency or for any other device that threatened to cost them either face or cash. For his part, Morgenthau wanted to give the Chinese everything they deserved, and everything beyond that which seemed to the Army necessary to strengthen Chinese participation in the war, but he was determined to resist the demands which the Chinese would certainly make for an exchange rate that would milk American taxpayers of hundreds of millions of dollars. Those were the views also of the able group whom Morgenthau recruited to work with him in the forthcoming negotiations. Senior among them was General Lucius Clay, at that time second in command in the Army Service of Supply, a tough-minded soldier with a broad knowledge of finance and supply, and a ranging and acute intelligence in personal relations. Besides Clay, Morgenthau's associates included John Carter Vincent, a veteran Foreign Service Officer with long experience in Chungking and an extensive knowledge of Chinese affairs, and Solomon Adler, for several years the Treasury's special representative in Chungking.

The Chinese had recently offered to settle past and future obligations on the basis of an exchange rate of 60 to 1, whereas the actual rate was many times that figure. They also proposed that for each 60 fapi for which the United States paid them in dollars, they would credit 40 to reverse Lend-Lease. The Americans intended only to fulfill the precise commitment of Roosevelt's January 28, 1944 message to Chiang Kai-shek. "Since you say," Roosevelt had then cabled, "that your government is not in a position to continue any direct maintenance of American troops in China, this government, in order to cover all of its military expenditures, including such maintenance as well as construction, is prepared to place to your account the United States dollar equivalent of any Chinese funds made available under general arrangements that will be suggested by General Stilwell and the Ambassador." In keeping that promise, the Americans did not want to overvalue fapi or to place the Chinese in a position to claim that they had made a large, uncompensated contribution to the American war effort. A reasonable figure, reflecting an actual exchange rate of about 120 fapi to the dollar, Dan Bell advised Morgenthau, came to about $115 million as the equivalent for the outstanding American debt of 13.6 billion fapi. Since the United States had already paid the Chinese $25 million, there remained due them $90 million. Bell further suggested the United States reach future settlements every three or six months. "The theory of this approach," he wrote, "is to negotiate with the Chinese on the basis of their contribution to our war effort in China without any reference to an exchange rate." Adler supported Bell's proposal, and on July 16, 1944, at a meeting of the American negotiators, the Secretary, to the complete satisfaction of the others, summed up by saying: "We are going to be tough with them, very political, very courteous, but tough."

Later that morning, General Clay explained the American position to the Chinese. To date, he said, the Army had paid $25 million toward financing airports and other installations. Now the Army proposed a final settlement, exclusive of food and lodging, as of June 30, 1944, of another $75 million.* Though Clay did not say so, that figure presumed an exchange rate of 120 to 1. In the future, the Army would settle accounts every few months.

In a passionate reply Kung stressed his concern for Chinese-American friendship, his pride in Chinese sacrifices, and the difficulties of Chinese inflation, but he avoided a direct answer to Clay. Morgenthau reminded Kung of the many displays of American friendship and of the exorbitant prices the Army had had to pay for most of the articles it needed in China. As he had planned to, Clay then offered to raise the lump sum payment to the Chinese from $75 to $90 million, with the increment earmarked to cover the food and the lodging that the Chinese had earlier said they wanted to give the United States.

Now Kung, dropping his mandarin manner, came to the question of cash. The Chinese, he claimed, had understood that the Army expected its expenditures to total $25 million a month exclusive of

---

* Dan Bell's estimate of $90 million included the month of July, the first month of fiscal 1945. Clay's $75 million for the period through June represented a substantially identical estimate.

the costs of the airfields. The Army had meant no such thing, Clay objected, but Kung, persisting, said that he had a document, which he did not produce, supporting his interpretation. After acrid debate, Clay volunteered, in the interests of a "quick and prompt settlement," to raise the American offer to $100 million. Still dissatisfied, Kung focused his case on one item, the air base at Chengtu, which had been constructed for the use of B-29 bombers in attacking Japan. At the Cairo Conference, he said, Roosevelt had promised to pay for the Chengtu base. The Americans, Morgenthau replied, had no record of that promise.

During an adjournment for luncheon, Clay told the other Americans that the Army had itself paid by contract for much of the work done at Chengtu. He considered his last offer of $100 million more than generous. The others agreed, but when negotiations resumed, Kung was willing to accept $100 million only if it excluded costs at Chengtu, which he reckoned at another 4 billion yuan ($200 million at the official rate of 20 to 1).

After another American caucus, Clay made another concession. The United States, he told Kung, would proceed "with the understanding that the 4 billion for the Chengtu airfield . . . would be presented by you as a claim under reverse Lend-Lease. . . . We would pay you the lump sum of 100 million dollars immediately, and in any reverse Lend-Lease agreement . . . you could, in addition to the food and lodging which you would put forward as a claim, include also this 4 billion." But still Kung balked. The private conversation between Roosevelt and the Generalissimo at Cairo, he said, made it impossible for him to accept Clay's formula; he could not yield without explicit instructions from Chiang Kai-shek. "Then we'll just have to wait," Morgenthau said. ". . . That is the best we can do."

Overnight the Americans drafted a telegram to Roosevelt reviewing the discussions. As Morgenthau saw it, the record proved that they had caught Kung "red-handed." Rather more generous, Adler suggested that Kung was utterly irresponsible in his use of details, perhaps because he had never taken the time to master them. But whether Kung was sly or sloppy, the American negotiators stood behind Clay's final offer of a total settlement of $125 million, of which $25 million had already been paid, for the five-month period February through June 1944. Without reference to the official exchange rate, and without trying to suggest a realistic rate of exchange, the $125 million, according to Clay, bore a close relationship to what it would have cost the American Army in the United States to obtain services similar to those received from China.

The disagreement, the telegram to Roosevelt explained, arose over whether the figure of $25 million a month was intended to include the construction costs of airfields, particularly those in the Chengtu area. "We maintained that it did," the telegram read. "Kung maintained that it did not. . . . We feel that the terms offered are more than fair . . . and we recommend a firm stand. We do not feel that there will be political repercussions in China which would warrant material deviation from the stand we have taken."

There matters stood for the rest of the summer of 1944. In that time, conditions in China deteriorated. The hostility between General Stilwell and Chiang Kai-shek, still growing, impeded military operations, while increasing dissatisfaction within China at the corruption and inefficiency of the Kuomintang threatened Chiang's government as, in equal degree, did the persisting opposition of the Chinese Communist forces. Brooks Atkinson, writing for the *New York Times* from Chungking, in mid-September described Chiang Kai-shek's administration as a "moribund regime," an assessment which American military and political representatives were also making in secret cables from the Chinese capital. Deeply concerned, Roosevelt dispatched still another special mission, this time under General Patrick Hurley, Herbert Hoover's Secretary of War, and the President moved also toward the recall of General Stilwell. Morgenthau, generally familiar with those developments, shared Roosevelt's hopes for buttressing Chiang Kai-shek, for galvanizing the military campaign in the China theater, and if necessary for those purposes, for finding a rapprochement between Chiang Kai-shek and his domestic opponents. But Morgenthau had no responsibility for the large issues of Chinese politics; rather, as in July, so in September, his duties were confined to financial questions, and as before in executing his charge, he leaned on the Army's advice.

In a letter to Morgenthau of September 9, 1944, Kung wrote that, since their conversations in July, he had received information from

China substantiating his claim that the costs for the Chengtu airfields had always been regarded as a separate account which the United States government was to pay. An American communication of January 8, 1944, which Kung quoted, cited General Marshall as stating that "the United States will bear the cost of labor and material for Chengtu airdrome construction at a rate of exchange to be arrived at under negotiation now in progress." A message from Stilwell to Chiang Kai-shek of January 12, 1944, quoted a cable from Roosevelt saying, with reference to the Chengtu airfields, that "I'll undertake to make available the necessary funds through Lend-Lease appropriations if that will hasten the completion of the work on the desired schedule." Once more, Kung proposed that the United States reimburse China at the official rate of exchange but receive a reverse Lend-Lease contribution from China, which would have the effect of reducing that rate.

With the explicit endorsement of General Clay, Morgenthau replied to Kung on September 20, 1944:

"There was never any doubt as to whether the United States government would pay for the costs of the construction of the Chengtu airfield. The President's telegram, which was transmitted to Generalissimo Chiang Kai-shek on January 28 by Ambassador Gauss, states explicitly that the United States 'in order to cover *all* of its military expenditures in China, including such maintenance as well as construction, is prepared to place to your account the US dollar equivalent of any Chinese funds made available under general arrangements that will be suggested by General Stilwell and the Ambassador.' The United States thus recognized its obligations for its military expenditures in China, including the cost of the Chengtu airfields as one item in those expenditures, and is anxious to make a settlement which will cover them all.

"I share with you a desire to reach a settlement at the earliest possible moment. It is for this reason that I would suggest that we avoid the question of the rate of conversion, an approach which was tried in the past without any success, and which raises many difficult, technical, and highly involved issues precluding a speedy settlement. To my mind, therefore, an approach on the basis of a lump sum payment for all our outstanding yuan obligations offers the best possibility for a speedy settlement equitable to both sides."

Yet the exchange rate remained for Kung the crux of the matter. Even if conversations were confined to a lump sum payment, Kung constantly calculated the ratio between the dollars he was to receive and the yuan he claimed. In that pass, there lay open a new approach for the Americans. A recalculation of estimates that resulted in a reduction of the amount of yuan expended would yield, if payment remained at the figure offered in July, an exchange rate better than the 120 to 1 ratio of yuan to dollars which had then been tacitly proposed. Whether for that purpose or because of complications in its bookkeeping, the Army in the first week of October did submit revised figures, and those figures did establish an actual but unstated exchange rate of about 100 to 1.

On October 6, 1944, Morgenthau apologized to Kung for the changes in American calculations but also pointed out that the revision produced in effect a more favorable rate of exchange. Still, he would not and could not, he added, play a numbers game. Urging quick agreement, now partly to facilitate Kung's plans for necessary hospitalization, he repeated Clay's July offer. As the Secretary put it privately to his staff: "I have the rate in mind . . . but I still pay . . . in US dollars. I am not going to pay . . . in yuan."

On the telephone to Clay that afternoon Morgenthau tried to work out a figure that would appease Kung. "I'm going to make one final offer," the Secretary said. "I am going to offer him a gross of $150 million, of which we've paid 25 . . . and the rate will be effective up to June 30th. . . . In other words, I'm going to take advantage of that extra $25 million that you . . . said I could use if I wanted to." Wholly agreeable, Clay proposed going up, if necessary, to $185 million by adding $35 million to make the settlement cover the period through September 30. If that later period were to be included, the United States, Morgenthau suggested, should offer Kung about $200 million and let him interpret it at any "goddamn rate he wanted to."

Later that afternoon Morgenthau made Kung the last offer he had described to Clay. As the Secretary put it, he was taking $125 million for the period through June 30, adding another $60 million ($20 million a month for July, August, and September), and then adding still another $25 million, for a grand total of $210 million which the Chinese could view as indicating any rate they liked. But

Kung, increasingly prickly, suggested the United States pay the Chinese in fapi rather than dollars; the Americans could go into the Chinese open market and buy the currency they needed. Morgenthau declined to take that possibility seriously, but he had to admit, when pressed, that the Army had kept altering its calculations.

Kung, Morgenthau told his staff, had been "very nasty," and a month later Stimson described the Chinese Finance Minister as "the same oleaginous . . . gentleman as of yore," but Kung's case gained from the President's growing anxieties about the deterioration of the Chinese government and economy. Back from the White House on November 20, 1944, Morgenthau wrote Harry White: "Kung convinced the President that there's something in writing that said we would pay separately for these airfields. I told the President I'd never seen any such thing in writing. The President said he would send over to me the memorandum that Kung had left with him. . . . Please be prepared . . . to come in with a very condensed memorandum telling the President what we've done, pointing out the fact that Mr. Stimson has asked us to do it."

What was in writing, it developed, was the cable from Roosevelt to Chiang Kai-shek of January 28, 1944, that the Treasury had long since seen. "Our interpretation of this cable," Morgenthau wrote Roosevelt, employing White's draft, "gives Dr. Kung no ground for any additional demand except for payment for board and lodging of American troops. . . . We have stated our willingness to pay for this item in US dollars but the Chinese indicated their preference for treating it as reverse Lend-Lease. . . . No agreement was reached . . . because of the insistence by Kung that Chengtu airfield expenditures were not included and our insistence that they were included. . . . My offer of October to Dr. Kung works out at a rate of around 100 yuan to one US dollar on the basis of our Army's gross figures, around 90 on the basis of the Army's net figures, and around 110 on the basis of Dr. Kung's figures. This is most reasonable to the Chinese, in view of the exceedingly low purchasing power of the yuan and of the fact that it compares favorably with the black market rate which has risen . . . to 400 recently. . . . In order to facilitate settlement we have informed Dr. Kung that we have no objection to his putting in a claim for the cost of the Chengtu airfields on reverse Lend-Lease, making it clear, however, that we regarded the lump sum payment that we were offering as a final settlement of our outstanding obligations."

That analysis must have persuaded Roosevelt, for with his support, Morgenthau remained firm. "I am operating here as the agent for Mr. Stimson," the Secretary told Kung on November 25, 1944. "I can't do any more than I have done." Kung also held fast. "I think maybe it would be much better," Morgenthau then said, "if I would simply write Mr. Stimson . . . that I have tried my best to get together with you with the information which he has given me. I have been unsuccessful." Now Kung complained. He had not been dealing with Stimson, he said, but with Morgenthau and the President, and Roosevelt, he asserted again, had promised to pay for Chengtu. "I feel very badly about this," Morgenthau replied. "I have tried my best to stretch every possible point. I feel that we have done everything within the spirit of the message from the President."

With the President, the War Department, and the State Department backing the Treasury, Kung could turn for aid to no important official or agency. On November 28, 1944, he yielded at last to the American terms. That day Morgenthau summarized the long negotiations in a memorandum for Roosevelt:

I finally got Dr. Kung to agree to the offer I made him on October 6 of $185 million, in addition to the $25 million already paid, in liquidation of our yuan obligations for US Army expenditures in China. This offer of October 6 was substantially that we made to Dr. Kung at Bretton Woods on July 16 . . . except that we added $25 million to induce the Chinese to settle, as the American representatives . . . had agreed among themselves we should do, should it turn out to be necessary. . . . This settlement is without prejudice to the Chinese contention that the cost of the Chengtu airfields is not included in the amounts referred to . . . but should be treated as an item of reciprocal aid. . . . Our offer was in fact based on the figures supplied us by the Army, which it insists, include the cost of these airfields. But Dr. Kung stood out for a higher figure by constantly refusing to accept our position with respect to Chengtu. . . . We regarded the lump sum settlement we were offering as a final settlement. . . . There are, in fact, some discrepancies between our Army figures and the Chinese figures. These are not substantial enough to have justified any revision in our offer. We asked the Army to check on the Chinese figures. They reported back that they'd stick to their own figures, including their figures on the cost of the Chengtu airfields, adding that there is no satisfactory way of checking on the Chinese figures as the Chinese have failed to fulfill their agreement to submit itemized lists of their expenditures for the Army's account.

There remained almost a month of dickering over details before the settlement was completed, but as Morgenthau's memorandum indicated, the major issues had been resolved to the satisfaction of both principals, though there lay ahead a reopening of the Chengtu issue, which the Chinese were bound to raise in reckoning a final accounting for Lend-Lease. But against that time, as Morgenthau wrote on November 30, 1944, to Harry White: "We have settled with China. In paying them in dollars instead of yuan . . . I have saved the taxpayer millions of dollars." He had done so, moreover, with a calculated generosity toward the Chinese, who gained at least $25 million more than either Morgenthau or Clay believed them entitled to. And he had done so with the ultimate support of the President, and the continuing support of the State Department, of Secretary of War Stimson, and of Generals Somervell and Clay. In the view of all those participants, he had treated China with friendship and decency, while at the same time protecting the legitimate interests of the United States.

3. Chinese Politics and American Gold

In October 1944, when Kung reopened discussions about Chengtu, he also asked the Treasury to expedite shipment of $20 million of gold which China had earlier requested. Sales of that gold, which was to be supplied as a part of the $500 million American loan of 1942, were to absorb some of the huge quantity of fapi outstanding in China, and thereby in small degree to combat inflation, unless the government of Chiang Kai-shek issued more fapi, as it probably would. In the opinion of Morgenthau and his staff, gold sales did provide some palliative for Chinese inflation whose cure could result only from military victories that would permit American delivery of vast amounts of commodities to China, that would remove the Japanese occupation, and that would also, perhaps, prepare Chiang Kai-shek to adopt and enforce positive economic policies. At the least, gold shipments constituted a token of support and prestige for the Generalissimo.

During the summer of 1944 Harry White, as he told Morgenthau on October 5, had "stalled" because of the discrepancy in China between the official price of gold and the price at which banks actually sold the metal. Someone, White suspected, was making a profit from the gold sales, probably T. L. Soong — a brother of T. V. Soong — whose bank handled much of the gold the United States supplied. In spite of his suspicions, White now recommended that Morgenthau tell Kung that evening that he was going to get his $20 million. "Is that," the Secretary asked, "what I am going to pay for my dinner tonight?" Later in the month the Army transported the bullion, though it had to move it by ship because of the shortage of air space.

Morgenthau had little interest in the transaction. He had delegated responsibility for assessing the Chinese request to White because the matter seemed relatively trivial. Yet the Secretary had a large interest in the condition of Chiang Kai-shek's government, to which the gold shipment of October gave a public American blessing. In assessing the state of affairs in China, Morgenthau turned neither to his subordinates, who were aggressively bearish about Chiang Kai-shek's future, nor to his own judgment. Rather, he looked to General Patrick Hurley, Roosevelt's chosen agent.

Roosevelt had assigned Hurley a threefold mission: to maintain the existing government and work through the Generalissimo, to keep China in the war, and to unify the Chinese Army for a more effective military effort. But Hurley, as he informed the Treasury on November 15, 1944, considered the situation in Chungking distressing, the government "traditionalist" — confident that no matter what the Japanese did, they would be absorbed, as had all previous conquerors, into Chinese society. In Hurley's view, most of the officials at Chungking were interested only in preserving their own position. They regarded the American taxpayer as "a sucker," whom they could exploit indefinitely. Though they claimed to be democratic, they were really fascists, in favor of dictatorship, and opposed to the concessions necessary for the achievement of national unity. The Communists, in Hurley's opinion, genuinely wanted multiparty government. Indeed he was impressed by a statement he had had from Molotov while in Moscow on his way to China which held that the Chinese Communists were not really Communists at all, but a kind of farmer-laborer group. Further, Hurley had found that the Chinese Communists had done a better job of organizing for war than had the subordinates of Chiang Kai-shek, that the Communists favored the unification of China and of the Chinese army, and that on the whole they "offered a fine, liberal program." He was certain they were not receiving Soviet support. The Kuomintang, Hurley said, was resisting Communist overtures largely because of T. V. Soong, whom Hurley considered a "crook." The achievement of unity in China would be a difficult task, but Hurley rejoiced in believing that he had brought the Communists to the American side. He also took heart from Roosevelt's recall of General Stilwell and Ambassador Gauss. Both men, he thought, out of sheer disgust had favored "pulling the plug and allowing the show to go down the drain." Now Hurley planned a more constructive approach. To abet that purpose, Roosevelt in December made him Ambassador to China, and Morgenthau on December 13 sent his "heartiest congratulations" for a "difficult and important assignment" in which the Secretary promised "every assistance" from the Treasury's representative, Solomon Adler, then about to return to Chungking.

On the following day White reported that the Chinese were requesting an acceleration of gold shipments. "We think it is unwise," White said, "in this very uncertain state of political development for them to get out as much gold as they want to get. . . . What we would like to do is raise a lot of objections. . . . We can continue to stall indefinitely. Is that all right with you?" Morgenthau said it was "as long as we let Ambassador Hurley know what we are doing." Because Hurley was attempting to bring the Chinese Communists into closer cooperation with Chiang Kai-shek, Morgenthau also approved a letter White drafted introducing Adler to Chou En-lai. At White's suggestion, the Treasury instructed Adler to ask Hurley "whether or not he feels it would help him to have this letter sent to . . . Chou En-lai." The Secretary, too, told Adler to offer his services to General Albert C. Wedemeyer, who had been appointed to succeed Stilwell as Commanding General in the China Theater. And in a letter of December 16 which expanded on his earlier telegram, Morgenthau wrote Hurley: "I need not say what a feather it would be in your cap if you were instrumental in bringing about political unity in China which would be the basis for the more effective participation of China in our common war effort. I do hope that you succeed."

In mid-December 1944, then, Morgenthau had taken Roosevelt's instructions to Hurley as the guideline for Treasury policy, had put the Treasury's Chungking staff at the disposal of Hurley and Wedemeyer, and had made the Treasury's policy on gold shipments conditional on Hurley's judgment. "I need not say," the Secretary wrote Chinese Ambassador Hu Shih on December 30, "that I have always favored that as much aid as possible should be given to the Chinese people in their fight for freedom and independence. I also need not say that this is the established policy of the U.S. government.

"I have shared with you fears and misgivings about the current military situation in China. Therefore, I am sure that you will agree with me when I express the hope that the situation may improve in such way as to make possible increased military aid to China and that steps will be taken within China to make possible the maximum utilization of the aid which is given."

In that spirit, Morgenthau on January 8, 1945, sent Adler a cable about gold. White had recommended denying Kung's request for speeding shipments on the ground that deliveries were justifiable only when they helped to fight inflation, whereas under the current conditions they were benefiting only hoarders and speculators. Rejecting that advice, Morgenthau explained to Adler that the Chinese had asked for $80 million of gold bars and $100 million of gold tokens, with another $100 million or more in the very near future. Thus far, the Secretary cabled, he had not given his assent because of the uncertainty in China and because of her postwar needs for foreign exchange. Now he instructed Adler to discuss the matter thoroughly with General Hurley and "inform me as quickly as possible of his view."

Before Adler could reply, Morgenthau on January 16, 1945, received a Chinese request for $5.5 million to train financial technicians. The Secretary had learned confidentially that day from the State Department that fighting had broken out between the Kuomintang and Communist troops. That intelligence brought his quick endorsement of the request, in which White concurred. As both men knew, the Chinese Ministry of Finance badly needed technicians to define and enforce an anti-inflationary program. And both were encouraged by a report of the same day from Donald Nelson, just back from China, that the Generalissimo "was giving definite evidence of his desire to cooperate fully with the United States."

But pending word from Hurley, Morgenthau was not ready to let $100 million or $200 million of gold move to Chungking. On January 26, 1944, H. H. Kung again pleaded for those large shipments. Typically, he cited a statement Roosevelt was alleged to have made in private. The President, he said, had told Madame Chiang Kaishek when she was last in the United States that China could have $200 million in gold. Morgenthau was skeptical.* Further, data received from Adler cast doubt on the usefulness of large gold sales. During January 1945, alone, prices in Chungking rose at least 20 per cent, with the black market price for gold moving from 25,000 to 34,000 fapi per ounce, though the official government price remained at 20,000 an ounce. Given that gap, profits from gold sales would accrue to speculators, particularly those favored by the government. Gold sales even in the dimension of $200 million would provide limited remedy for the inflationary wave. Those statistics provoked Morgenthau to continue to delay, especially since he had no advice from Hurley.

In February, at the urging of Adler and of representatives of the State Department and the Foreign Economic Administration in Chungking, Morgenthau agreed to a small shipment of gold designed to finance Chinese tin production. Later that month, Kung asked for $47.5 million of gold bullion as well as for an early decision about the minting and shipping of another $100 million of gold tokens, as a supplement to earlier requests. Yet little had changed

---

* On the question of an American promise of gold shipments, see Chinese-American discussions of May 1945, Chapter IX.

for the better in China. Hurley had failed to arrange the political rapprochement which he had thought close to hand the previous November. Adler, like others in Chungking, foresaw only disaster as a product of the Generalissimo's relentless opposition to American advice. And at the end of February, while still hoping for improvements in China, Hurley recommended holding down gold shipments to about the same magnitude as in the past years. On that account, after reviewing Kung's various requests, Frank Coe advised Morgenthau on March 2, 1945, to export to China during the coming three months only about $7 million of gold earmarked at the New York Federal Reserve Bank, with one half of that sum designated as payment for exports of tin to the United States.

Without mentioning specific figures, Morgenthau in a letter to Kung of March 3, 1945, remarked the "many difficulties involved in making arrangements for the export of gold to China." Military necessity, he wrote, took precedence in this as in all activities. Yet the Secretary had "instructed my men to raise again with the military authorities the possibilities of shipping gold to China during the next few months. They will inform your representatives of their findings on this matter."

A cable from Adler of March 11, 1945, argued for a negative finding. The Chinese government, he said, was now relying on sales of gold as its main source of revenue. Receipts from those sales in January and February had reached 14 billion yuan, with another 20 per cent of that sum arising from the purchase of Chinese Treasury certificates required of those who bought gold. That total substantially exceeded returns from taxation in the same period. Over seventy-five per cent of the gold sales were for delivery after six months, for in the absence of American shipments, the government had almost no gold to sell, and the short position of the Central Bank had reached about one million ounces. Though the public deficit was nevertheless soaring, and the black-market price had gone up to 39,500 fapi per ounce, the government maintained it could not raise the official price without having more gold at hand,* but the recent

---

* A position also taken by the American adviser to the Chinese Treasury, Arthur N. Young, in a memoir two decades later. Spot prices for gold, Young there held, had risen on the black market precisely because the government could deal only in future sales, pending favorable action by Washington.

heavy purchases of gold for future delivery had followed a rumor that the government was going to increase that price on the first of March. The government's further contention that raising the price of gold would push up general prices failed to take into account the skyrocketing of prices under existing policy. Adler therefore recommended sending as little gold as possible to China, precisely the conclusion at which Hurley and Morgenthau had earlier arrived.

In keeping with it, the Secretary agreed only to the shipments Coe had suggested. "You'll be pleased to learn," Morgenthau wrote Kung on April 12, 1945, "that of the $7 million of gold to be exported to China during the next few months, the first shipment of more than $1 million has already left this country." Seven million, of course, was far less than Kung had expected. In the same letter, the Secretary rejected Kung's complaint, recently repeated, about American dealings in the Chinese black market. "As for the question of United States civilian and military personnel in China exchanging U.S. dollar currency in the open market," he wrote, "both of our governments have acquiesced in this practice because of the general recognition that the official rate of exchange has not reflected real conditions. . . . I would be glad to consider any proposal which would give fair Chinese national dollar equivalent for the expenditure of United States civilian and military personnel in China as a substitute for the present practice."

In politics as in finance, in the spring of 1945 as in the spring of 1944, the problems of China defied American efforts to find solutions. In Washington on March 8, 1945, Patrick Hurley called on Henry Stimson, who reported their conversation in his diary: "Hurley told me of his experiences with Chiang Kai-shek. . . . He was sent there . . . with a direct order to do everything he could to hold up the Chiang Kai-shek regime and therefore he had a hard time with a lot of the American and Chinese there who are trying to pull down Chiang. He told me of his trip to the Communists and his efforts to reconcile them to Chiang. He said they were not really Communists and that he was certain that they had no relations with Russia . . . that the Russians were frank and sincere in saying they didn't want to have them. . . . He has no great opinion of T. V. Soong and he told me that the leader of the Communists was very ambitious for power too. He told me that Madame Chiang Kai-shek is separated from the Generalissimo now but, as it is about their fortieth 'permanent separation,' nobody takes it seriously."

Had it not been for the enormous stakes at issue — the winning of the great war in the Orient, the future of China in the world — it would have been hard not to laugh at the opéra bouffe in Chungking. Even those like Hurley and Wedemeyer, who later conveniently forgot it, blanched at the unabashed nepotism and corruption in the Kuomintang. Even they, moreover, misconceived the purpose of Chou En-lai. And both of them, like the more veteran observers of the Army, the State Department, and the Treasury, believed that Chiang Kai-shek had contributed far less than lay within his grasp to the war against Japan; that the Generalissimo and his associates had failed, even within their limited capacities, to combat inflation; that conditions of life and of morale in China were at a distressing remove from the minimum requirements of decency and democracy.

Relying on Hurley's judgment, Morgenthau had established a policy toward gold shipments that delayed substantial aid while offering token support. In the situation, there was no other logical choice. The policy he followed protected American gold which the Chinese would otherwise have squandered. Even had gold been sent in the quantities Kung requested, it could not have saved China from the economic and political disasters bred of prolonged enemy occupation, inept government, and internal revolution.

Yet Morgenthau's policy of friendship tempered by caution was in later years attributed to the influence of pernicious advisers. Critics of the Secretary's decisions maintained that White, Adler, and Coe, Communists or Communist-sympathizers, had fashioned their counsel to the demands of a world-wide Communist conspiracy. That claim drew some plausible support from the recourse by Coe and Adler, during interrogations at congressional hearings, to the Fifth Amendment and from their associations, soon thereafter, with Chinese Communists. But the question of the political affiliations of the three men, whatever those affiliations may have been, bore only an oblique relationship to Morgenthau's policy. The Secretary had consulted them, to be sure, but he had leaned much more on Secretary of War Stimson, Generals Somervell, Clay, and Wedemeyer, and Ambassador Hurley, no one of whom had ever had any attachment to Communism or its masters. When in time Hurley and

Wedemeyer condemned the Treasury, they chose to overlook the unanimity of American assessments — including their own — of Chinese conditions and of appropriate American policy in the early months of 1945. Without exception, all responsible counselors had then concurred in the decisions Morgenthau made. And they had then all recognized, as Henry Stimson once said at a dinner party, and as Ambassador Hu Shih agreed: "There are in this room two real friends of China — Mr. Morgenthau and myself." But so, too, and above all else, was Morgenthau the guardian of what he deemed American interests.

4. Compensation for American Assistance

From the first, American Lend-Lease had as its purpose the defeat of the Axis. Without Lend-Lease, the nations allied with the United States could not have fought the war, and without its allies, the United States could not have carried the battle. The ultimate compensation for American assistance was victory. But with the progress of the war, questions arose about the terms of American assistance during the coming period of reconstruction, for which Lend-Lease had never been designed.

The French, for one, wanted the United States to include under Lend-Lease substantial non-military aid for the postwar period. "If I wasn't Secretary of the Treasury," Morgenthau commented, "but just a citizen, I would be arguing 'give them all of it,' but I am supposed to look after the taxpayer's interest." Further, as he noted, Congress never intended Lend-Lease to cover relief or reconstruction. With that interpretation Stimson and Hull agreed. Indeed Hull particularly feared establishing a precedent with France that would open the way for British and other requests for postwar aid. Of the same mind, Roosevelt told the Cabinet that he opposed non-military Lend-Lease for France either during or after the war. And Morgenthau, as he had in the case of the British, approached Lend-Lease negotiations with the French with a determination to prevent the program from increasing French gold and dollar balances beyond the minimum necessary for preserving confidence in the franc. As a result, the terms for French compensation for non-military aid were more severe than the State Department had recommended, though Jean Monnet considered them "entirely fair."

The Soviet Union, Morgenthau believed, should also provide compensation for non-military assistance, but in the Russian case, he preferred compensation in the form of strategic materials, first under reverse Lend-Lease, later, after the war, in exchange for American capital goods. Instructing White to prepare a memorandum on the subject, Morgenthau early in 1944 asked "What is the maximum we can absorb, and what is the maximum that they can export . . . over thirty years" of such commodities as mercury, manganese, and chromium? White's memo suggested a $5 billion postwar credit for the Soviet purchase of American agricultural and industrial products, to be repaid over thirty years by the export of strategic materials. The credit, he wrote, would assure the United States of an important market for industrial goods. The terms, he and Morgenthau concluded, should include a carrying charge on outstanding Soviet indebtedness calculated at one-eighth of one per cent above the average rate of interest that the Treasury had to pay for borrowing in the American market, a figure that worked out to about 2.1 per cent at 1944 rates.

The Russians, in preliminary discussions of the proposal, were agreeable to paying in full for any equipment they received after the end of the war, but they first deferred consideration of interest and then, in August 1944, refused to pay any, unless they were assured that they could purchase industrial products below market costs so as to offset all interest charges. The Treasury in September suggested eliminating interests, but the State Department and Foreign Economic Administration rejected that possibility.

There matters lay until January 1, 1945, when Morgenthau turned to Roosevelt. The Secretary described the Treasury's plan "for comprehensive aid to Russia during her reconstruction period. We are not thinking of more Lend-Lease or any form of relief but rather an arrangement that will have definite and long-range benefits for the United States as well as for Russia. Ambassador Harriman has expressed great interest and would like to see the plans. . . . I understand from him that the Russians are reluctant to take the initiative, but would welcome our presenting a constructive program. . . . It would contribute a great deal toward ironing out many of the difficulties we have been having with respect to their problems and policies." As the plan then stood, it envisaged a credit of $10 billion for 35 years at 2 per cent interest. Insofar as the Soviet Union failed to meet payments through the export of strategic materials, her gold resources would provide more than enough dollars to guarantee the credit. In a memorandum for Roosevelt Morgenthau emphasized the importance of the proposal for "conserving our depleted natural resources" and as a "major step in your program to provide sixty million jobs in the postwar period." He hoped that the President would open discussions of the plan during the forthcoming conference at Yalta.

From Moscow Harriman had cabled that Molotov placed great importance on a large credit. "An implication that development of our friendly relations . . . depended upon a general credit," the Ambassador said, "was sensed by me." But the State Department and the President did not consider the issue appropriate for the Yalta conference. Back from the White House where he talked with Roosevelt and Stettinius on January 10, 1945, Morgenthau told his staff: "On the Russian proposal, I tried to show it [Harriman's cable] to him. He wanted to read it. Stettinius wouldn't let him read it. . . . The President said, 'Well, after all, we are not having any finance people with us and I will just tell them we can't do anything until we get back to Washington. . . . I think it's very important that we hold this back and don't give them any promises of finance until we get what we want.'" Morgenthau, who disagreed openly, later told Admiral Leahy at luncheon "that both the President and Stettinius were wrong and that if they wanted to get the Russians to do something they should . . . do it nice. . . . Don't drive such a hard bargain that when you come through it does not taste good."

Still hoping to persuade Stettinius and through him Roosevelt, Morgenthau that afternoon reopened the argument over the telephone. "I feel very, very strongly," he said, ". . . with all due respect to the President and you, I think you are 100 per cent wrong on the approach to Russia. And I think that the carrot should be put before their nose when you first get there and let them know that there's going to be financial aid for them while they're at war and financial aid for them when the war is over."

"Henry," Stettinius replied, "I don't think you'd feel that way if you knew all . . . if you had all the chips before you."

"Well," Morgenthau said, ". . . I've been through very difficult negotiations with the Russians myself . . . at Bretton Woods. . . . I'm just going to be so bold as to set myself up against the President and you. . . . Only within the family."

"All right, Henry," Stettinius said. ". . . Let me give that some study and we'll talk about it next week."

During that week, Morgenthau learned for the first time what was disturbing Stettinius. The Russians were imposing a police state in the Eastern European countries they entered. They had done so in Bulgaria and to a degree in Hungary. Without consultation with the United States or Britain, they had taken some 170,000 Germans from Rumania to Russia for forced labor. While lamenting those developments, Morgenthau still thought that an American offer of a generous postwar credit would soften the Soviet mood on all outstanding political questions.

The State Department decided irrevocably against that offer on January 25, 1945. The United States, the Department held, should wait at least until it knew what its other allies were going to ask for, and then consider all requests for credit together. The State Department had decided also against making any of the concessions the Russians had requested in the renewal of the Lend-Lease protocol. Morgenthau felt that those decisions were "a great mistake." His proposal, he believed then and twenty years later, would have produced important political and economic compensations.

5. British Finances Again

The course of the war introduced questions of wartime relief and postwar reconstruction into Anglo-American financial negotiations. At the time of the attack on Europe, the British, in an aide mémoire to the State Department, proposed that the procurement of relief supplies for liberated areas should fall half to England, half to the United States. But "any . . . final settlement," they suggested, ". . . must be on an equitable basis and must be based upon a recognition of the relative financial strengths of the countries concerned. In this connection, His Majesty's Government desires to place on record their view that in the light of the difference in financial strengths between the United States and the United Kingdom, they would not be able to regard an equal sharing of the burden of relief in the military period between the two countries as an equitable settlement."

Though Dean Acheson approved of that proposal, the Treasury objected. Since England's contribution of relief supplies came largely from Lend-Lease goods shipped to the United Kingdom by the United States, Morgenthau would not interpret the division of responsibility as actually fifty-fifty. He was even more unhappy about predicating a final settlement on relative financial strengths. Acheson, he complained, "always takes the British view."

It was Morgenthau's opinion that it would cost less politically and financially to furnish 90 per cent of the relief supplies than to defer to the British. In Italy, he said, the United States had provided 80 per cent of relief but Churchill had used his 20 per cent as a lever for obtaining recognition of King Victor Emmanuel III and Marshal Badoglio, whom Morgenthau considered reactionary. Now the Secretary wanted the United States to assert itself, and if necessary to pay all relief costs. He also insisted on negotiating the final settlement on the basis of all relevant factors, of which relative financial strength was only one. Acheson satisfied Morgenthau by replying to the British that "the final settlement should be on a fair and equitable basis, in the determination of which no relevant factor should be excluded," but Morgenthau nevertheless wrote Roosevelt on June 16, 1944: "I cannot agree with the position of the United Kingdom . . . that any final settlement as regards supplies to the liberated areas . . . must be equitable but be based upon a recognition of 'relative financial strengths' of the two countries. I believe that the adoption of such a principle would be contrary to the best interests of the United States and would be so regarded by Congress and the people."

The issue was still unresolved when the Secretary flew to England in August 1944, to talk directly with Churchill and the Chancellor of the Exchequer about Lend-Lease and British balances during the coming period of the war.* Both governments, expecting the defeat of Germany by the end of the year, had begun to examine their

---

* Morgenthau's interests during that trip also related to postwar planning for Germany, see Chapter VII.

financial problems for the continuing operation against Japan. During Stage II — the British phrase for the period between the surrender of Germany and the surrender of Japan, which the Americans called Phase II — by joint agreement the United States would make the larger military contribution, with Great Britain and the Dominions bearing a fair share of the fighting. The Churchill government also hoped that with victory in Europe they could at last ease their severe controls on civilian life. Morgenthau sympathized with that hope but felt himself responsible for confining Lend-Lease aid to England during Phase II to reasonable proportions.

The Secretary found the British much worse off than he had supposed. Back in Washington on August 19, 1944, he reported his observations to Roosevelt and their conversation in his Diary:

> I told the President I had seen Churchill, who started the conversation by saying that England was broke. The President said, "What does he mean by that?" I said, "Yes, England really is broke." That seemed to surprise the President, and he kept coming back to it. I said that Churchill's attitude was that he was broke but not depressed about England's future. The President said that that was well put. . . . I said, "Well, he is going to tell Parliament about their financial condition at the right time after the armistice, and that when he does that he is through." So the President said, "Oh, he is taking those tactics now. More recently his attitude was that he wanted to see England through peace."
>
> I then told the President I had been very frank with Churchill, particularly after he told me that he had heard that I was unfriendly toward them. I said that I wasn't unfriendly but I didn't like their playing one person against the other, and that they had the temporary advantage over us. I said that I had merely been trying to carry out the President's decision given to me in January 1943, to keep the British balances down to a billion dollars. I then told him I thought the British should put all their cards on the table and approach this thing in a completely frank manner. I said that I thought Mr. Churchill should appoint a committee which would consider all these financial questions . . . and then he . . . should approach the President. I said the President should appoint a similar com-

mittee and he might ask me to do it. I said that we did make a
study of suggestions for the President before I went to England
. . . that there should be a committee here having to do with
all financial matters. . . . I also told Churchill . . . that I
made a similar suggestion to Halifax and nothing had happened.

During the course of the conversation, the President kept
coming back to England's being broke. He said, "This is very
interesting. I had no idea that England was broke. I will go
over there and make a couple of talks and take over the British
Empire." I told him how popular he was with the soldiers and
how unpopular Churchill was. I told him about the difficulty
of finding someone to take me through the shelters because
Churchill . . . had been jeered . . . recently, and that finally
they decided on Mrs. Churchill and Lady Mountbatten."

Morgenthau also called on Harry Hopkins on August 19. The
British, the Secretary said, wanted to reduce their production of munitions so as to increase their production of civilian goods. They
realized that the United States had similar expectations, but the two
nations were far from agreement about how much each might cut
back. Any arrangements, Hopkins said, would have to await a complete review of conditions in both countries.

That review began in Morgenthau's office on August 24, 1944,
with a report from Robert Brand, representing Chancellor of the
Exchequer Sir John Anderson. During Stage II, Brand said, the
British people would not tolerate 100 per cent mobilization. They
needed fewer hours of work, more holidays, more consumer goods,
and the economy needed to begin to reconvert for export trade.
Though he had no exact figures, Brand was sure that the United
Kingdom would continue to require food, oil, and shipping under
Lend-Lease. The figures would become available only when
Churchill had decided about the extent of Great Britain's par-
ticipation in the Japanese war. At that point, settlement of the outstanding problems would be urgent, as would the beginning of
discussions of Lend-Lease during Stage III, the period following the
Japanese surrender.

He was eager to help, Morgenthau replied, but if he was to have
anything to do with the matter, "it would have to be centralized in

the Treasury; . . . he could not have the British Government representative going around back doors to various agencies. . . . The British would have to cooperate fully and make available . . . all of the information . . . wanted, and the British Treasury would have to deal only with and through the Treasury on the matter."

The suggestion, as Brand understood it, called for Churchill to appoint Anderson to work directly with Morgenthau on Lend-Lease questions. That was rather "too definite," Morgenthau replied. There would have to be a committee representing several agencies on both sides of the ocean. The President had yet to appoint one in Washington, and Morgenthau could not be sure that it would fall to him to head the American group. "I don't want to get over the idea that it's an accomplished fact," he said, ". . . because it isn't." But he and Brand agreed on the desirability of asking Churchill to stand by to appoint a responsible group to carry the British case. The next morning, August 25, 1944, as the Secretary wrote in his Diary:

"I asked the President what was happening in regard to the suggestion for an over-all committee on finance in this country and in England, and I said that Grace [Tully] had told me that he had sent a memorandum to Hull. He said, 'That's right,' and he seemed very much pleased with himself . . . but he said he had not yet heard from Hull.

"I then told the President that Sir John Anderson had asked me to let him know whether the President would consider the suggestion in a favorable light, and I had sent for Bob Brand and told him the President had received the suggestion favorably, and that he could send word back to that effect."

Far more than he told Roosevelt, Morgenthau as a result of his trip had persuaded himself of the need to sustain the British economy. As he said in private on August 25, "this has to be approached from the standpoint that Great Britain made this fight for democracy. Now we have got to help her. She is a good credit risk, a good moral risk, and we have to put her back on her feet. . . . Somebody smart enough has to think up a new name, other than Lend-Lease, because that will have been worn out. But we have got to do the thing to put her back . . . for a permanent world peace, and I look at this peace thing — a lasting peace, to me is becoming a religion."

In his official communications, Roosevelt was more restrained. "There has been a good deal of discussion within the several Government Departments relative to our Lend-Lease policy after the collapse of Germany," the President wrote several interested offices on September 9, 1944, "It is my wish that no Department . . . take unilateral action in regard to any matters that concern Lend-Lease, because the implications of any such action are bound to affect other Departments . . . and, indeed, our whole national policy. I am particularly anxious that any instructions which may have issued, or are about to be issued regarding Lend-Lease . . . to our allies after the collapse of Germany, be immediately canceled and withdrawn."

That directive cleared the slate for Roosevelt's scheduled meeting with Churchill in mid-September in Quebec, where the two would arrange military and financial cooperation for the prosecution of the war against Japan. Summoned, to his surprise, to that conference,* Morgenthau received when he arrived a memorandum for Roosevelt from the British Treasury. The objective of Lend-Lease, it read, had been to satisfy England's justifiable military and civilian requirements beyond the reach of the fully-mobilized British economy. Of the munitions which British forces had used during the war against Germany, still under way, Great Britain herself had furnished a little less than 60 per cent, the United States about 27 per cent, Canada 10 per cent, and the rest of the British Empire, the balance. If the British Empire had to provide total British munitions requirements during Stage II, there could be insignificant reduction from conditions of full mobilization. Yet after five years of war, a considerable reduction was necessary for civilian morale, for rebuilding damaged cities, and for taking the first steps towards restoring the British economy. The British therefore suggested, as a yardstick for Stage II, that the proportion of their total munitions supplies received from Lend-Lease should be the same as in 1944. Besides munitions, they asked for Lend-Lease foodstuffs and raw materials sufficient to meet the reasonable needs of the United Kingdom, though not primarily for purposes of reconversion. The aggregate requirements would be about $3 billion during the first year of Stage II, as compared to about $3.9 billion for 1944.

---

* On the Quebec Conference, and on the relationship between British and German questions there and later, see Chapter VII. The account in this chapter relates only to the issue of British finances.

It fell to Morgenthau to discuss the British memorandum with Lord Cherwell, Churchill's controversial and intimate adviser. A personal friend of the Prime Minister for many years, Cherwell — "the Prof." — had been a professor of physics at Oxford, a courageous experimenter in British aviation, and a steady and strong Conservative. Morgenthau found him "very keen . . . wonderful to work with — very frank, very direct . . . a breath of fresh air from the sea." Together they brought negotiations to the point where Roosevelt and Churchill were quickly able to reach agreement. They did so on September 14, 1944, in a conversation which Cherwell reported from memory the next day in a memorandum that Churchill and Roosevelt initialed:

The Prime Minister said that when Germany was overcome there would be a measure of redistribution of effort in both countries. He hoped that the President would agree that during the war with Japan we should continue to get food, shipping, etc. from the United States to cover our reasonable needs. The President indicated assent.

He hoped also that the President would agree that it would be proper for Lend-Lease munitions to continue on a proportional basis even though this would enable the United Kingdom to set free labor for rebuilding, exports, etc. E.g., if British munitions productions were cut three-fifths, U.S. assistance should also fall to three-fifths. The President indicated assent. Mr. Morgenthau, however, suggested that it would be better to have definite figures. He understood that munitions assistance required had been calculated by the British at about 3.5 billion dollars in the first year on a basis of the strategy envisaged before the . . . Conference. The exact needs would have to be recalculated in the light of decisions on military matters reached at the Conference. The non-munitions requirements had been put at three billion dollars gross against which a considerable amount would be set off for reverse Lend-Lease. The President agreed that it would be better to work on figures like these than on a proportional basis.

The Prime Minister emphasized that all these supplies should be on Lend-Lease. The President said this would naturally be so.

The Prime Minister pointed out that if the United Kingdom was once more to pay its way it was essential that the export trade, which had shrunk to a very small fraction, should be re-established. Naturally no articles obtained on Lend-Lease or identical thereto would be exported or sold for profit; but it was essential that the United States should not attach any conditions to supplies delivered to Britain on Lend-Lease which would jeopardize the recovery of her export trade. The President thought this would be proper.

To implement these decisions the Prime Minister suggested there should be a joint committee. It was held that it would be better to appoint an ad hoc committee for this purpose on an informal basis in the first instance which could be formalized in due course. Pending its report the United States departments should be instructed not to take action which would prejudge the committee's conclusions, e.g. production should not be closed down without reference to Lend-Lease supplies which it might be held should be supplied to Britain. The President thought that the committee should be set up but suggested that Mr. Morgenthau should head it representing him, and that Mr. Stettinius, who had taken such a large part in Lend-Lease, should also be a member.

Another memorandum of September 14, 1944, also initialed by Roosevelt and Churchill, confirmed and elaborated Cherwell's report. The two documents were the subject of further discussion on September 15, 1944. "I met at twelve today," Morgenthau noted in his Diary, "with Roosevelt, Churchill, Eden, and the Under Secretary for Foreign Affairs. We took up the question of Lend-Lease agreement for Phase II. The President read the thing through very carefully, and the only suggestion he made was where it read, 'Naturally no articles obtained on Lend-Lease or identical thereto should be exported.' He included the words 'or sold . . . for profit.'*

"Churchill was quite emotional about this agreement, and at one time he had tears in his eyes. When the thing was finally signed, he

* That phrase, according to a clarifying memo of Cherwell of September 16, meant that the British should not sell Lend-Lease goods for more than the price at which they were entered in American books, plus a reasonable allowance for transportation. The American Foreign Economic Administration agreed with that interpretation.

told the President how grateful he was, thanked him most effusively, and said that this was something they were doing for both countries."

At the State Department on September 20, 1944, Morgenthau told Hull, Stimson, and Forrestal that Roosevelt had been casual about Lend-Lease while at Quebec. Hull complained about the President's failure to consult the State Department and to demand British concessions for postwar commercial policy in return for American aid. Roosevelt, he said, had given away the bait. Harry White, who had accompanied Morgenthau to Quebec, defended the Lend-Lease memorandum, but Stimson, siding with Hull, said: "There may be some flexibility, but not much." Cherwell and Halifax, Morgenthau said later that day, were ready to open negotiations about the exact figures for Stage II. "The way I would like to proceed," Morgenthau went on, "would be to sort of put them on the witness stand and ask them how much they wanted and why they wanted it, and then start in with whatever was agreed on at Quebec as to what . . . they would contribute in the Pacific. Then we would expect the Military to testify. . . . Churchill knows that the President is willing to give them the works. . . . This committee is appointed . . . with the attitude that . . . this agreement will be carried out cheerfully. . . . Cherwell knows that the British have to justify these figures." Were they to be justified, McCloy asked, "in terms of the Japanese war?" Morgenthau said yes.

When Cherwell arrived soon thereafter, he proposed beginning discussions on non-munitions, and he admitted at once that the British requirement stated at Quebec was by no means exact. The amount would probably run between two and three billion dollars, with the larger figure including the entire empire, not just the United Kingdom. Munitions and non-munitions bore little relationship to each other, he said: "We can't grow more food than we are growing, and we must have a certain amount of food to live. We are down already to 80 per cent of prewar, and we can't go much lower. In fact, we want to go higher, because the people have had four or five years of it, and they will expect some relaxation. So with the non-munitions, I don't think there is any difficult question, except questions of quantity. The munitions is, perhaps, rather more difficult, because broadly speaking, . . . the President first agreed that . . . we should get a sort of proportion to what we have been getting heretofore. But you said that that was not much good to the Treasury. . . . We then said we . . . thought we would be able to manage with 3.4 billion dollars in the first year of Stage II. That figure was tentatively regarded as reasonable. . . . It will have to be varied in the light of the decisions at Quebec . . . very possibly diminished — if that figure could be regarded as an upper limit, and the service and supply people could begin discussing exactly what proportion of munitions were wanted . . . then I think we could go ahead with the munitions just the same as with the non-munitions."

The British, Morgenthau replied, were eager to reestablish their position in world trade. That goal related to their Lend-Lease requests. To assess those requests, he therefore needed all the information he could get that bore on the British economy. "I want it all," Morgenthau said. "Not just information on food and munitions, but also on the whole British economic program."

Cherwell answered obliquely. Food, he said, was not the only worrisome shortage: "We must build. We can't let the soldiers come home if they haven't got any houses. If they have no place to live there will be a riot." Clothing stocks were less than 60 per cent of normal, as were household goods. There was need, too, for more gasoline, especially for doctors and professional men. "Our civilians," he continued, "have been very hard pressed . . . for a long time. . . . When we get the people back from the war we won't have the same power of directing labor that we had before." Cherwell also repeated what Morgenthau had heard before, that British exports had dropped 30 per cent in terms of production and 50 per cent in terms of price, that the British had growing external debts, that they would have quickly to double their prewar exports.

Morgenthau asked if the British could provide data to support those statements, and provide, too, a detailed breakdown of their requests for both munitions and non-munitions. Cherwell promised to do his best.

Later, alone with Morgenthau, Cherwell said that Sir John Anderson wanted to send J. M. Keynes to Washington as head of the British committee on Lend-Lease for Stage II, but not if Morgenthau thought there would be unfortunate political repercussions.

The Secretary replied that he would be "delighted to have Lord Keynes." He also told Cherwell that in reporting statistics and other matters of detail, he should "look to Mr. White." White, for his part, was disturbed by the appointment of Keynes, always a tough negotiator. "Shouldn't monkey with the buzz saw," he said to Morgenthau. But the Secretary, confident of the American position, replied: "Not as long as the saw can keep turning. Sometimes its teeth get kind of dull."

The British, Morgenthau knew, would have to bargain from weakness. But that weakness, that accumulated strain on the British economy, he now understood better than he had four months earlier. Without intending in the least to surrender his obligations to American interests, he wanted to help a brave and steadfast ally, whose postwar recovery he considered essential for a stable world. He expected Keynes to make large demands, but he also expected to reach with him an equitable agreement on Stage II beneficial to both the United States and the United Kingdom.

6. Lend-Lease for Phase II

Morgenthau and White approached negotiations for Phase II of Lend-Lease from opposite points of view. The spirit of the Quebec Conference, the Secretary said on October 6, 1944, was to prevail during the discussions with Keynes. British dollar balances had not entered the agreement between Roosevelt and Churchill. "Here is a client or customer or friend who is broke," the Secretary continued, "but who is a good moral risk, and we should ask this friend to state his entire program so that we can analyze it. Then . . . we should . . . do a job for England to make it possible for her to stage a comeback and gradually meet her obligations. . . . I don't consider that the dollar balances are yardsticks anymore. I think we might just as well have this thing straight from the beginning." White objected to incurring any responsibility for putting England back on her feet. The United Kingdom, he argued, could absorb endless billions of dollars, and any vague commitment to England's future prosperity would threaten both the financial and political position of the United States in the postwar world.

The British, Morgenthau replied, had made a magnificent fight. England had been the bulwark against German aggression, the jumping-off place for the American Air Force. The United States could not now permit her to "go under financially." He did not believe the British would ask for ten billion in order to get five; Cherwell and Keynes would be honest with the Americans. In return they deserved the most "careful attention" to the "domestic problems" that Great Britain faced.

Morgenthau also hoped that American generosity would induce the British to support his own political views. "The old man," he told White on October 18, 1944, "was doing a little bargaining last night* . . . and I am going to keep doing this . . . while this is before me." But the Secretary did not bargain hard. The British, as it developed, rapidly receded from their temporary endorsement of his proposals for the treatment of Germany.† They also held to their policy toward Argentina.‡ Still, Morgenthau did not let his disappointment affect his judgment about Lend-Lease needs. He did not even take offense at Keynes's irritation in response to his suggestions for reducing both British and American forces in India and other British colonial areas. Such a reduction Morgenthau believed, would pave the way toward the independence of the colonial people, who would feel freer in the absence of British troops. Expenditures for imperial troops abroad, Keynes replied, were a matter exclusively for British decision; the British would be master in their own house. The Secretary did not press the point.

The military spokesmen on the informal American committee on Phase II were more hesitant about aiding England than was Morgenthau. At a caucus of that committee on October 19, 1944, Judge Patterson, the Under Secretary of War, held that the Army should restrict munitions for Great Britain during Stage II to military weapons for actual use in operations against the Japanese or in the occupied areas of Europe. British requests for military equipment, he believed, were excessive, and the British were remiss in not volunteering to redeploy most of their air force to the Pacific. General Somervell recommended reserving shipping for the movement of

* About planning for Germany, see Chapter VIII.
† See Chapter VIII.
‡ See Chapter IV.

military supplies to the Pacific even at the cost of delaying the redevelopment of British export trade. Somervell also suggested that American production of any military item during Stage II should be held below the level of production for 1944. That policy would assure the increase of available consumer goods in the United States, though it would also reduce the size of a similar increase in Great Britain. Morgenthau considered those arguments too much concerned with "ifs, ands, and buts." In the "spirit of the Quebec Agreement," he wanted the American committees working on particular categories of British requests to avoid rigid rules, and instead to examine "the reasonableness of the British requirements from this broad point of view."

By mid-November, however, as both the British and the Americans agreed, the prospect that the war in Europe would continue into 1945 altered the presumptions of the Quebec Conference. Allocations of munitions for 1945 had to take into account operations against Germany as well as Japan, and also the usual problems of procurement. Nevertheless discussions had begun in good temper about removing Lend-Lease restrictions that inhibited the rebuilding of British export trade, and about protecting British dollar balances. Morgenthau had also assured Cherwell that the Treasury would begin to consider British problems that would arise after the surrender of Japan as soon as Churchill could get Roosevelt's consent.

But the Secretary had had, too, to deny some British requests for non-munitions during Phase II. Keynes had asked for a resumption of American tobacco shipments to the United Kingdom, but the Secretary and his associates saw no way to reverse the earlier decision to take tobacco off Lend-Lease, especially in view of the cigarette shortage in the United States. So also, in line with the policy established toward France and other nations, the Americans would not consent to using Lend-Lease for the purposes of rehabilitation, and they therefore turned down a British request for assistance in replacing and repairing bombed-out homes.

For their part Morgenthau and his colleagues asked the British for reciprocal help in the form of supplies for the campaign in the Pacific, especially meat from Australia and New Zealand. Keynes wanted to reduce the request. American troops, he said, were demanding more meat than the British and Dominion troops regularly consumed, more than the Dominions could furnish without cutting meat shipments to the United Kingdom. But Morgenthau insisted on extending the geographical range of existing reciprocal aid agreements to the most forward point of American action.

While postponing a reply until Morgenthau could compile precise figures on meat, Keynes sent the Secretary an eloquent summary of the United Kingdom's finances. The increase in British indebtedness outside of the United States, he wrote, arose largely from military expenditures in the Middle East and India. For five years Great Britain alone had been responsible for practically the whole cash outlay for the war in the vast territories from North Africa to Burma. That program had been essential for driving the Germans back in Africa at a critical point in the war. Further, early in the war the British Treasury virtually abandoned control over overseas expenditures. The principles of good housekeeping had had to give way to the necessities of fighting a battle for life in three continents far from home. The British, moreover, had received no Lend-Lease from the nations in the British Commonwealth except Canada. Indeed Great Britain had had less favorable arrangements with the Dominions than the United States had had, and the British had considered it improper to ask for contributions from the Crown Colonies, which were trusteeships. The British had also abandoned their export business in order to devote the whole of their manpower to the manufacture of war materials. And they had paid nearly all of their gold reserves to the United States in the period before Lend-Lease. "No doubt," Keynes concluded, "the above makes collectively a story of financial imprudence which has no parallel in history. Nevertheless, that financial imprudence may have been a facet of that single-minded devotion without which the war would have been lost. So we beg leave to think that it was worthwhile — for us, and also for you."

Morgenthau, as Keynes had ascertained in the previous fortnight, believed exactly that, but by mid-November 1944, Roosevelt had become uncomfortable about "the spirit of Quebec." "These speeches that Churchill has been making . . . have ruffled him tremendously," Morgenthau told Ed Stettinius. The President had been nettled, particularly during the recent election campaign, by the Prime Minister's devotion to the royal families of southern Europe and by the delays in Anglo-American planning for Germany. Consequently, Morgenthau went on, when it came to Lend-Lease, Roosevelt acted "as though he never heard" of the Quebec agreement. Morgenthau was therefore sending "a delegation," including Dean Acheson, Lauchlin Currie, Harry White, and various military officers, to explain to Admiral Leahy what the American Lend-Lease committee was attempting to arrange with its British counterpart. Stettinius thought that it would be useful also to inform the chairman of the Committee on Appropriations of the House of Representatives, as well as some ranking Republicans, of the nature of Anglo-American discussions, so that the ultimate agreement on Phase II would in effect have prior approval from the Congress.

Morgenthau's "delegation" to the White House achieved nothing, as the Secretary learned on November 18, 1944. Admiral Leahy, he told White, had reported that "the President said he never promised them anything at Quebec and that we should handle this just the same as any other Lend-Lease operation. Admiral Leahy says he thinks we could work it out so that the thing is not binding. . . . Leahy seemed to be thoroughly sold on the program . . . but . . . the President . . . seems to be confused."

As Morgenthau explained the situation further on November 21, 1944, Roosevelt and a few members of the American Lend-Lease committee were afraid that the British might "sound off in public" in such a way as to make the American people feel that England was "getting a jump . . . in export trade." Somebody, Morgenthau did not know who, had apparently persuaded the President that agreement on Phase II would create a political problem on the Hill. On that account, the Secretary thought, Roosevelt was reluctant to give Churchill what he wanted, and what Morgenthau thought Churchill wanted was "the feeling that he could sew the silver lining to the black cloud which has been hanging over England for four years." Further, continuing changes in military plans for the campaign against Japan upset tentative agreements about munitions, and the persistence of the war against Germany dispelled the optimism of September.

The hardening of Roosevelt's opinion meant that the Americans on November 22, 1944, gave the British considerably less than Morgenthau had hoped for two weeks earlier. Still, the commitments for Lend-Lease in Phase II to the army, air, and fleet programs promised substantially all the British had asked. The pinch came on non-munitions. The American subcommittee on those items, reflecting the President's attitude, reported against any changes in policy on exports of raw materials prior to the end of the war in Europe, whereas the British had hoped for changes as of January 1, 1945. There would be no easing of British food shortages until after the surrender of Germany, though here again the British had hoped for earlier relief.

Keynes complained especially about the delay in the removal of restrictions on British export policy. That delay, he said, would surprise London and offend British public opinion. He had also some other, minor criticisms, and one major reservation: the United Kingdom could not "underwrite," as the United States expected it to, reciprocal aid from Australia and New Zealand. The paragraph in the American draft calling for that British responsibility had to come out. Morgenthau, who had of course expected those objections, thanked Keynes and the other English committeemen for their consistently fair approach to the negotiations. He also called the completed agreement consistent with Roosevelt's instructions at Quebec.

The Secretary's letter to the President of November 25, 1944, began with the same judgment. It then reviewed the points of agreement between the two English-speaking countries. The British, Morgenthau wrote, had asked initially for themselves and for the Empire for $3.2 billion of munitions, $3 billion of non-munitions, and $800 million of other special items — in all $7 billion of goods and services. After screening all the requests, the American committee had recommended $2.7 billion of munitions and $2.8 of non-munitions, a total of $5.5 billion — a substantial reduction from the first British estimates and some 50 per cent less than the level of Lend-Lease for 1944. "All schedules," Morgenthau continued, "both munitions and non-munitions, are subject to the changing demands of strategy as well as to supply considerations and the usual considerations of procurement and allocation."

The program, the Secretary explained, consisted of articles and services which the United Kingdom could not produce in time to meet the demands of war, or which the United States could produce much more effectively. Coupled with decreases in overall munition and manpower requirements for Phase II, the Lend-Lease agreement would make it possible for both the United States and the United Kingdom to release some resources for reconversion, for raising living standards, and for reviving exports. The American committee had recommended "no change in the present export policy be made until V-E day," Morgenthau reported, "and thereafter . . . to prohibit the reexport of goods delivered under Lend-Lease." The British for their part had assured the United States that the flow of supplies and services to the United States from the United Kingdom and the Dominions under reciprocal Lend-Lease would continue "as in the past."

Privately Morgenthau felt that he had obtained for the British everything possible, less than Cherwell had expected at the time of the Quebec Conference, more than Roosevelt would have yielded on his own. Winston Churchill would have been surprised had he known how much more generous Morgenthau had been than were such presumed friends as Bernard Baruch, a critic of the Phase II agreement. "American production and standards have held the world up for many years," Baruch had written Morgenthau. ". . . I am sure that those standards can win the peace. . . . But we ought not to do all of it. . . . Nothing can hold up many of these countries unless they modernize their business structure. For instance, does anyone know what England or France or any other country will permit an American to do in those countries?" Baruch, though he spoke only for himself, would have insisted, like Cordell Hull, on commercial privileges for American businessmen and investors. Indeed Baruch believed that the British had overstated their case. He wrote Cherwell:

Your statement that the English were bankrupt . . . provoked the following thoughts: Germany in preparation for the Second World War through sweated labor and subsidized exports, cluttered the export market of the world everywhere, reducing prices and profits and causing reduction in scales of wages and standards of living. During that time they were enabled to keep up a certain standard of living uncomplainingly, to obtain through their enforced exports stockpiles of necessary materials and make unhappy the population of the rest of the world. The removal of the sweated labor and subsidized exports for these two countries will enable the rest of the world to increase employment, profits and standards of living.

After the Phase II agreement was made public, Baruch on December 1, 1944, again wrote Morgenthau:

> Today I saw that certain agreements had been entered into between us and England, in which they get 5 billion and one-half dollars of Lend-Lease a year. . . . No one need think that by giving too much and weakening ourselves that we can help the rest of the world. We can weaken ourselves so much by giving away so many things before peace is here that no one will pay any more attention to us when we talk of world peace than they did at the Paris Conference. We must also measure the cost, not only in dollars, but in the derangement of our enconomy which inflation is bringing. . . . Winston Churchill said that he did not accept a portfolio to liquidate the British Empire. I should like to see either a full explanation of why all this is done . . . or simple Americans like myself will wonder if this action is of such a nature as to tend to liquidate the American standards of living.

After his usual fashion, Baruch also enlisted Arthur Krock of the *New York Times* in his cause. In a column of December 12, 1944, Krock used Baruch's exact words in a lament that the United States was weakening itself "while trying to help the rest of the world." Continuing from that point, in another letter to Morgenthau of December 13, 1944, Baruch wrote that "the English people have not commenced to touch their ability to produce either in quantity or at a price. They have been crying poor mouth so long it reminds me of a number of my southern friends who do the same thing but do not try to help themselves. Why should we help England or anybody else until they have learned to help themselves?"

For Baruch, and for thousands of like-minded Americans, Morgenthau had a ready answer. "The recent agreement on Phase Two of the Lend-Lease program," the Secretary wrote Baruch on December 23, 1944, "has no other purpose but to bring all of Britain's resources to bear on the earliest possible defeat of the enemy. By mobilizing the full strength of our allies in this struggle . . . we can shorten the war and in this way diminish the ultimate burden on our own economy. Defeating the enemy has been the sole purpose of the Lend-Lease program from the beginning and that is all that Phase Two of the . . . program is intended to do while the war with Japan continues." Great Britain, Morgenthau noted, had yet to ask for financial aid in the postwar period. Her problem would be to expand her exports enough to enable her to purchase food and other necessary raw materials. With the deterioration in her economic position that had already taken place, she would have to increase her prewar exports, as she had often pointed out, by at least 50 per cent in order to pay for her prewar level of imports. She could do so only in a world in which international trade and investment maintained a high level, and in which nations cooperated in stable and orderly exchange arrangements, such as those designed at Bretton Woods.

"What worries me most about your comments," Morgenthau continued, ". . . is not that you feel as you do, but that these arguments play right into the hands of the isolationists who are only too eager to capitalize on issues of this character to further their own objectives. Recent events in Greece and Italy* are already being exploited and it is not difficult to anticipate a recurrence of a wave of cynicism that will destroy the hopes for international cooperation until we are in the throes of another war. It is going to tax our capacity for self-restraint if we are going to give international cooperation a trial — let alone make a success of it."

Since his trip to Great Britain in August 1944, Morgenthau had moved to the van of those Americans who believed, as he put it in another context, that the future peace of the world depended first of all on "an economically strong and prosperous Britain." Yet as he had written Baruch, the Secretary, under Roosevelt's orders, had confined the agreement on Phase II to the period ending with victory over Japan. He had as yet only hopes, not instruments, for

---

* Demonstrations of democratic discontent, in some degree exploited by local communists, under the conservative regimes restored after liberation.

rendering to England the assistance she would incontestably need thereafter. And as he implied in his letter to Baruch, for all of his differences with the British about political questions, he had made England's economic stability the criterion second only to military necessity for establishing the terms of aid during Phase II.

Lord Cherwell, Winston Churchill, and Chancellor of the Exchequer Sir John Anderson all understood the magnitude of Morgenthau's efforts in their behalf. "I share the feelings of my colleagues," Cherwell wrote the Secretary on December 20, 1944, "in my gratitude to you for your appreciation of our difficulties and your readiness to help in solving them. I am sure that there should be no obstacle in our two countries working together for the benefit of all, given good sense and good will. Unfortunately, as you must have observed on your side as well as we do on ours, these attributes are not quite as universal as one might hope. It is easy for a few grains of sand to bring a big machine to a standstill." Two days later Sir John Anderson sent Morgenthau his "warm thanks . . . and in particular the Prime Minister has asked me to associate his name . . . for the very great, and indeed indispensable task of adjusting the Lend-Lease programme to the new circumstance. . . . We . . . especially appreciate the part you played . . . in securing so satisfactory a final outcome. Our financial problems do not get easier or their future settlement less perplexing as time goes on. . . . Only on the basis of complete frankness on both sides about the difficulties with public opinion and with Parliament and Congress which each of us has to face, can we hope to reach understandings and arrangements which are fair and advantageous to all parties. We have done our best, and will continue to do so, to let you know the factual position in full detail; and the frankness with which you have let us know how your mind is moving in these matters and in all that concerns the future of Europe, as reported to me by Lord Keynes . . . makes our task easier. . . . In the course of the coming year we shall have to pass on to the question of Stage . . . III. I hope that you and I will have the opportunity of discussing that personally."

That opportunity was not to arise, but Morgenthau had already demonstrated the direction in which he would move American policy if the responsibility fell to him. As he remarked early in January of the next year, Churchill had not exaggerated in his statement of the previous summer that without Phase II and III of Lend-Lease, England would be unable to make the transition to a tolerable peacetime basis. For a similar objective, as Morgenthau saw it, the Soviet Union would benefit from the credit he had proposed. And for its part, the United States, he believed, would have to follow a program for reconversion geared to the needs of its wartime allies and the control of their wartime enemies. The latter goal had brought him deeply into the debate over postwar policy for Germany.

The Morgenthau Plan

A u g u s t - S e p t e m b e r , 1 9 4 4

THE MOST controversial and agonizing episode in Morgenthau's public career grew out of his involvement in American postwar planning for Germany. When in 1944 he first approached that issue, the Secretary proceeded on the assumptions that guided his general thinking about the making of peace. His views on Germany both conditioned and were conditioned by his other major objectives: a prosperous Great Britain, a cooperative and friendly Russia, a liberal community of democratic nations in a world free from war. His views on Germany reflected, too, his personal interpretations of the particular conditions of the time and his personal assessments of the possibilities for changing them.

1. Background to Involvement

By the summer of 1944, the peoples and the leaders of the nations of the Grand Alliance had ample reason for their almost universal animosity toward Hitler's Third Reich. The Nazis had brutalized Germany, annihilated millions of human beings, stormed across Europe, and mistreated those whose lands they conquered. The British people, the sturdiest of Hitler's intended victims, believed almost to a man that, with victory, the Allies should punish the German war criminals, eradicate nazism, disarm Germany, and impose upon her a period of military occupation. About the details of a victorious settlement there was less British unanimity, but public opinion polls estimated that two-thirds of all Englishmen favored the permanent separation of the Ruhr, the area containing some 40 per cent of Germany's industry, from the rest of the Reich, and an even larger percentage believed the Germans should help rebuild the nations they had damaged or destroyed. At least a majority wanted Germany broken up into several smaller states, while an articulate minority, of which Lord Vansittart* was the foremost spokesman, deemed the German people "incurably bellicose," and on that account proposed occupying Germany for at least a generation, controlling German industry, and eliminating its capacity to produce arms. The Russians, who had felt the full bestiality of the Wehrmacht, at the very least expected victory to bring with it a time of judgment for Germany, long the most active threat to Soviet security.

Though geography had put them beyond the reach of Hitler's forces, the American people were close to unanimity — 81 per cent according to the polls — in support of the policy of "unconditional surrender" that Roosevelt and Churchill had announced at Casablanca. Most Americans believed Germany would begin planning a new war as soon as she met defeat, and most therefore favored a reduction of Germany to a "third rate" nation.

Roosevelt, Churchill, and Stalin both reflected and shared the sentiments of their countrymen. The insistence of the President and Prime Minister upon unconditional surrender marked their refusal under any conditions to negotiate with Hitler. Beyond that, the foreign ministers of the three powers in Moscow in October 1943, had agreed on the occupation of Germany by forces of all three countries, on the creation of an inter-allied control commission, on the complete disarmament of Germany, and on the dissolution of the Nazi party. For the Russians, those were minimum terms. Foreign Minister Molotov also called for the partition of Germany. He demanded extensive reparations, but Cordell Hull proposed limiting them to a dimension consistent with a healthful "postwar world economic and political order." Yet Hull, unlike Anthony Eden, had no concern for legal formalities in the ultimate treatment of Nazi leaders and war criminals. The foreign ministers, with the later approval of Roosevelt, Churchill, and Stalin, agreed that after the war

---

* As Sir Robert Vansittart for many years Permanent Under Secretary in the British Foreign Office.

the Germans responsible for atrocities would be "sent back to the countries in which their abominable deeds were done in order that they may be judged and punished according to the laws of the liberated countries," and major criminals, those "whose offenses have no particular geographical localization," would be punished "by joint decision of the Governments of the Allies." Finally, in order to draft terms for surrender and to suggest machinery to oversee the fulfillment of those terms, the foreign ministers created the European Advisory Commission, a three-power organization which was to begin its work in London.

A month later, in November 1943, the Big Three met for the first time at Teheran. There, as in Moscow, there were differences about significant questions but also agreements about important principles. So, to begin with, Germany was to be divided into three zones for occupation purposes, with a fourth, combined inter-Allied zone to be located in Berlin from which common policies would be administered during the period of occupation. But Stalin had ambitions for German territory which Churchill would not yet concede, and Roosevelt put off for later consideration Stalin's demand for great quantities of German machinery to replace the Russian industry that the Nazis had destroyed. Without prejudice to later decisions about boundaries, the three also considered the partition of Germany, at the least a separation of Prussia from the rest of the nation and some form of special isolation and control for the industrial areas of the Saar and the Ruhr.

In the months immediately following the Teheran Conference, planning for the treatment of Germany fell to three major groups — two in London, one in Washington. In London, Ambassador John G. Winant joined Feodor T. Gusev for the Soviet Union and Sir William Strang for the United Kingdom as the senior members of the European Advisory Commission. There Winant, working without specific instruction from Washington, had three influential assistants: George F. Kennan (until mid-1944), Philip E. Mosely and E. F. Penrose, all of whom tempered their views toward Germany with an abiding suspicion of the Soviet Union. Wrangling over the definition of zones of occupation, the European Advisory Commission settled on a scheme that Roosevelt vetoed. The President's views and the preferences of the American Joint Chiefs of Staff contributed to the demarcations which the EAC approved in April

1944. Those lines established an eastern Russian zone as the EAC had originally envisaged it, consisting of about 40 per cent of the German territory of 1937 and about 36 per cent of the population, and including all of Berlin, though the city was to be jointly occupied by the three powers. An east-west line of latitude divided the rest of Germany into northern and southern zones. It remained unclear which of those zones would fall to the British, which to the Americans, but Roosevelt in mid-1944 much preferred the northern area. Fearing that France would succumb to a postwar revolution, the President wanted to stay out of the southern part of Germany, for which access was available only through France.

By July 1944, the European Advisory Commission had also adopted a draft of a surrender document. Here, too, there was need to reconcile disagreements among the three powers. The Soviet Union preferred to confine the document to military questions; the United States, to assert also the right of the Allies to control German political, economic, and social life; the British, dissatisfied with a brief assertion, called for describing in detail both political and economic policy. The draft document as approved, while postponing questions of detail, provided for the disarming of Germany but left unsettled the question of the disposition of prisoners of war. It proclaimed the Allies as supreme political authorities in Germany and announced that they would impose "political, administrative, economic, financial, military and other requirements." But Winant and his staff hoped that the surrender and occupation would leave behind for the long-range future a disarmed but unified Germany with a strong economy under democratic government.

Meanwhile other plans had emanated from Supreme Headquarters, Allied Expeditionary Forces, where General Eisenhower presided. In April and May 1944, SHAEF received drafts of pre-surrender directives from the Combined Chiefs of Staff in Washington. Those orders called for the arrest of high Nazi leaders and government officials, for the dissolution of the Nazi Party, for purging the German courts of Nazis, and for forbidding all political activity except by special permission of the Supreme Commander. They also directed Eisenhower to provide for the revival of German agriculture, to import food and other supplies so as to "prevent disease and unrest," to restore public utilities, and to operate coal mines and transportation facilities. On the basis of those provisions, Eisen-

hower's military government officers in June 1944, completed the
draft of a "Handbook for Military Government in Germany." For
the occupying armies in Germany, that volume set the task of assuring "that the machine works and works efficiently." The armies
were to preserve the centralized German administrative system, and
to retain and rehabilitate enough light and heavy industry to make
Germany self-supporting and also to keep the whole European economy on "a reasonably even keel." The Germans, moreover, were to
have a relatively high standard of living, including an average food
supply of 2000 calories per person per day, which was more than
their neighbors could expect. Above all, SHAEF stressed the primacy of military considerations during the period of occupation.
Since the War Department and the Army expected the German
economy to be in a state of collapse, Eisenhower's planners also asserted the authority of the occupying forces over economic affairs.

Finally, American planners were at work in Washington in various committees of the State Department. In January 1944, Edward
R. Stettinius, Jr., had succeeded Sumner Welles — who had resigned — as senior officer for postwar planning. Welles had favored
a harsh peace, but Stettinius adopted the more generous views of his
chief advisers. Foremost among them were Mosely and Leo Pasvolsky, a professional economist and valued counselor to Cordell Hull.
In the spring of 1944, the Department's postwar committee, with
Hull's approval, recommended against the partitioning of Germany
and against a harsh peace, though it accepted the idea of zones of
occupation. Further, it endorsed a statement on economic policy
toward Germany by the interdepartmental Executive Committee on
Economic Foreign Policy. That statement owed most of its content
to Pasvolsky and most of its form to Dean Acheson. Harry White,
who represented the Treasury on the interdepartmental committee,
had been preoccupied with the Bretton Woods negotiations during
most of the discussions of the memorandum, which was ready for
circulation on August 4, 1944. The memorandum advocated a
limited control of the German economy and the elimination of
Germany's economic domination of Europe, but the eventual re-
absorption of Germany into the world economy. It also called for
short-term collections of reparations in kind, to be taken from current production rather than German capital equipment, and for
maintenance of German production at a level sufficient to maintain a

tolerable standard of living. The memorandum constituted one part of the State Department's emerging policy of a "stern peace with reconciliation."

At the end of July 1944, Morgenthau knew nothing about the State Department memoranda or about the planning for Germany that had gone on at Teheran and in London. Except in his discussions of occupation currency,* he had given little thought to German questions. Still, he had distrusted the Germans since the time of the First World War, which he attributed to their aggression, and he never forgot the cruelty that he had personally observed on the Turkish front. He disliked German manners and abominated Prussian autocracy as much as he admired French civilization and applauded British democracy. The advent of Hitler and nazism had confirmed those feelings, and Nazi policies repelled Morgenthau as they did all civilized men. Even before the Munich Conference of 1938, and certainly thereafter, he considered the elimination of nazism the first requisite for a peaceful and democratic world. That belief hardened in 1943 with his intimate involvement, for the first time, in the fate of the European Jews. As a Jew himself, Morgenthau had naturally resented Nazi racial doctrines, but their sting, he often later recalled, dated from his horror when he began to investigate the whole, hideous record of Nazi atrocities. It was then, in December 1943, as he indicated in a remark to his staff, that he applauded what seemed to him a "trend . . . for a much more aggressive approach towards our enemies."

Even earlier, Morgenthau had advocated breaking up German industry so as to eliminate the power of German cartels in international trade and the war-making capacity of the German nation. Those purposes had marked his policies on matters falling within the jurisdiction of the Alien Property Custodian.† Those purposes also provoked his sympathy for the recommendations of July 1943, of Robert E. McConnell, whom he had put in charge of General Aniline and Dye. To render Germany impotent for the prosecution of war, regardless of what the German people might one day intend, McConnell proposed removing Germany's facilities for the production of synthetic gas and nitrogen and prohibiting German stockpiling of raw materials, like oil, on which military capacity depended.

* See Chapter IV.
† See Chapter I.

The Germans, Morgenthau believed, would cultivate dreams of world domination even in defeat. "Last night," he noted in his Diary on June 17, 1944, "I phoned Miss Tully and asked her to find out from the President whether it would be all right for me to say in my speech in Chicago* that if the Germans thought they were losing, there was danger of the German general staff's wanting to sue for peace while the fighting was still on French, Italian and Finnish soil, and to warn the American people against this. I would also say that in this way the Germans could save their Army and be ready for another war in the next generation." The next day both Roosevelt and Hull approved the proposed text. "The German war machine has plans for survival," Morgenthau said. "We can be sure of that. Such plans have worked before. . . . It is an easy guess that Germany may offer Hitler and the Nazi gang to bribe conditions out of us. We won't be bribed. Our terms are unconditional surrender."

It was not enough, in Morgenthau's view, to settle for the capture or the execution of Hitler and his aides, not enough even to liberate the nations the Germans had overrun and to occupy Germany itself. A lasting peace also required the education of the German people in the meaning and the ways of democracy — at best a long and laborious process, and the elimination from Germany of the industrial capacity for making war. Only under those conditions would Europe and the world be safe. Only those conditions would permit the early and complete withdrawal of American troops from Europe, a withdrawal that the American people were demanding and the President was expecting. Only those conditions, finally, would permit the United States, after victory, to turn its full energies, moral and economic, to the advancement of prosperity and of the New Deal's liberal goals. But if Morgenthau had strong convictions about Germany, he had no specific recommendations until he learned that planners in Washington and London were charting courses that seemed to him to risk German resurgence.

2. Portentous Misgivings

The catalyst of Morgenthau's involvement in German planning was the Acheson-Pasvolsky memorandum on economic policy. "I was

* To sell war bonds.

not in agreement with the recommendations . . . ," Harry White
wrote, "and I felt that it was not in line with the Secretary's views.
Knowing that the Secretary was interested in the subject and not
wanting to take any action until he had had an opportunity of
going over the report, I instructed the Treasury delegates to reserve
the Treasury's position." The Treasury never approved the report,
for Morgenthau reacted to it precisely as White thought he would.

The story really began, Morgenthau later wrote, on August 6,
1944, on "an airplane to Europe. I was making the trip primarily to
see how the Treasury's financial arrangements for the liberated
areas of France were working out. . . . But as we were swinging
out over the Atlantic, one of my assistants* pulled out of his brief-
case a copy of a State Department memorandum on reparations in
Germany. I settled back to read it, first with interest, then with
misgivings, finally with sharp disagreement." In England, Morgenthau learned more from Colonel Bernard Bernstein, a former Treasury official who was then with the Civil Affairs section of SHAEF.
As White later put it: "Bernstein described . . . the directives
which were being prepared for the occupation of Germany. The
Secretary regarded them as reflecting the wrong policy decision. His
later discussions of the post-surrender terms followed from the necessity of taking a position." That was also Morgenthau's recollection.
"When I planned the European trip," he reflected, "I did not expect to become involved in the question of the future of Germany.
But as a result of the trip, I found myself projected unexpectedly
into the very center of the German discussions." At that center
Morgenthau found not only the State Department's memorandum
on economic policy but also the "Handbook for Military Government in Germany," and the policy papers of the European Advisory
Commission, to all of which he took strong objection. And close to
the center, in London where German V-1 bombs were working their
nightly havoc and on the front in Normandy where the battle for
Europe raged, Morgenthau saw at first hand the ravages of the war
the Nazis had begun. From Churchill and Sir John Anderson he
heard again, with more force than ever before, the accounting of the
material cost of the war to Great Britain,† with its implications for

* White. Also on the trip were Fred B. Smith and Josiah E. DuBois.
† See Chapter VI.

American Lend-Lease during Stage II, while the conversations conducted by his subordinates about asylums for refugees reminded
him continually of the face that nazism had shown the world.

Firsthand impressions of the war, mingling with discussions of
high policy, fed Morgenthau's interest in planning for Germany
during his entire trip. As he told his staff after his return: "We
started right in with General Eisenhower to find out where he stood
on this business of how he is going to treat Germany when he first
gets in. He was very positive that he was going to treat them rough.
He was perfectly willing to let them stew in their own juice." According to the Secretary's later recollection, White noted that the
Civil Affairs Division of SHAEF "would have a different job in Germany from its job in the liberated countries. The goal in the liberated countries was to build up the economy as quickly as possible; to
repair transportation, to restore the necessary services of life, to improve the standard of living as fast as we could. Surely, my assistant
said, this would not be our goal in Germany." Eisenhower replied:
"I want to say that I am not interested in the German economy, and
personally would not like to bolster it if that will make it easier for
the Germans." Demands for a soft peace, Eisenhower continued,
came from those who wanted to make Germany "a bulwark against
Russia." Soviet strength was "fantastic," but the General thought
the Russians would be busy for generations digesting what they had
already swallowed. "I never saw Eisenhower in such good shape,"
Morgenthau reported. "He made the best impression he has ever
made on me."*

From London the Secretary went to Cherbourg, which, he said,
was

> to hell and gone. . . . But . . . the speed and tempo is just
> unbelievable. . . . I have never seen any place where the elec-

---

* Eisenhower, in his own memoir, recalled expressing himself "roughly as
follows: . . . The German people must not be allowed to escape a sense of
guilt. . . . Prominent Nazis . . . must be . . . punished. . . . The German nation should be responsible for reparations. . . . The warmaking power of the
country should be eliminated. . . ." His memoir notes no reference to Russia
but asserts that he opposed Morgenthau's suggestion for flooding the mines in
the Ruhr, though Morgenthau did not remember having made that suggestion
at that time. Later, beyond any question, both White and Eisenhower opposed it.

tricity is so in the air. . . . The loss of lives was something
terrific. . . . In American troops, something like 16,000 dead
and when I left there there were 78,000 wounded. And the
dead is twice that of the English. . . . The wisecrack they say
over there is "If you are not careful, we [the Americans] are
going to encircle Montgomery!" . . .

We were at Bradley's Headquarters. He makes an excellent
impression. . . . Very quiet, complete self-control, complete
balance. . . . He planned our trip. . . .

They let me go down within 5,000 yards of the Germans . . .
but they wouldn't let you go any further, because the thing is
so fluid. . . . We were west of Avranches and east of . . .
Villedieu and due south of St. Lo . . . where the fighting was
most severe and they had five German Divisions right opposite
there. Three were SS Divisions. . . .

Of course, General Patton has been perfectly magnificent.
. . . The air people . . . completely misfigured. . . . The
German air strength, the production, is just four times what
Arnold told me. But it doesn't make so much difference, because they have licked them anyway. . . . Our flights are definitely limited by the amount of aviation gasoline . . . and
they are short of heavy ammunition, too. . . . I went to the
evacuation hospitals in France, and in some cases it is unbelievable. Men are there four hours after they have been wounded.
I saw them put in, went into the planes and these air nurses are
the finest body of women I have ever seen. . . . And the boys
are wonderful.

So were the English whom Morgenthau observed during German
bombings of London. He said,

Going into these shelters in England, I just can't tell you. . . .
There was one family there that had no home and they had been
there for six weeks, living there. . . . I saw one mother with five
children. I saw another mother with an eight-month-old baby.
. . . But the spirit of those people! . . . And Mrs. Churchill
is just marvelous. She is like Mrs. Roosevelt. . . . And in the
whole of England there was only one person had a little kick.

God! I don't know how the American people would be, but, of course, the thing that this has done is toughen them [the British] up, so that . . . any idea of any negotiated peace, or anything like that, is finished.

I asked the fellow in the hotel who looked after me, "How do you feel about the Germans?"

He said, "Well, we want to stamp them out, but the high finance doesn't!"

These little buzz-bombs* go over — they make a note very much like a single engine fishing vessel. . . . Nobody pays any attention to them — I mean, when they go over! . . . But everywhere you go you see damage in London, the damage is unbelievable; it is terrific.

In London Morgenthau spent two hours with Winston Churchill. "I got a great kick," the Secretary told his staff, "he took me through his own map room . . . which was quite a thrill. He is a great fellow." The Prime Minister, to Morgenthau's delight, showed great affection for Franklin Roosevelt. "Just to hear the President shout 'Hello'," Churchill said, "is like drinking a bottle of champagne." Churchill then, as Morgenthau recalled, "started off, bang, on how England was busted.†. . . He and I got along very well. We put it right on the line. . . .

"The interesting thing with Churchill was — he said, well, he was practically seventy and it was time he made peace with his Maker, and as soon as the war was over he would resign and be the most unpopular man in England. . . . I got the impression he wanted the Germans treated in a stern manner."

British opinion on Germany, according to Morgenthau's later account, "fell into two main camps. Sir John Anderson, the able Conservative Chancellor of the Exchequer, represented one side. He favored letting the Germans continue to manufacture non-military items. . . . Many British Tories were thinking in terms of a strong postwar Germany partly as a potential market, partly as a counterweight to Russia.

---

* The V–1's.

† See Chapter VI on the discussions of Stage II Lend-Lease as they developed before the Quebec Conference.

"Anthony Eden, then Foreign Secretary, represented the other side. He stressed the fact over a pleasant luncheon . . . that a soft policy would only rouse Russian suspicions and make postwar cooperation among the three powers more difficult."*

On August 12, 1944, Morgenthau invited Ambassador Winant and several of his advisers on German questions to luncheon at the country house in Wiltshire where the Secretary was staying. After luncheon, according to the account of E. F. Penrose, one of Winant's group, discussion of plans for Germany "took place in bright August sunshine, on the wide lawn which surrounded the house. As we lounged on the grass Mr. Morgenthau in brief, simple terms expounded his views." Then Harry White, amplifying Morgenthau's statement, came as close as possible, in Penrose's opinion, to "clothing a bad thesis with an appearance of intellectual respectability." Germany, Morgenthau and White argued, should never again be in a position to wage war. To attain that objective, which would keep the peace, it might be necessary to reduce Germany to the status of a fifth-rate power. Philip Mosely, frankly hostile to that analysis, said that any attempt to "smash" the German economy would drive the Germans to dependence on Russia, which would in turn expose all of Europe to Soviet control. For his part Winant, who agreed with Mosely, nevertheless confined his remarks to a description of the status of the European Advisory Commission. "It was not doing very much," Morgenthau later recalled, ". . . because it lacked clear authority and instructions." To get that authority and to block Morgenthau's purpose, Winant after this meeting, without the Secretary's knowledge, cabled Roosevelt for instructions compatible with EAC attitudes, but he did not receive them.

Before leaving England, Morgenthau again saw Anthony Eden. "Very much surprised," as Morgenthau put it, that Winant considered the EAC so powerless, Eden ". . . exclaimed that this had all been settled at Teheran. To prove his point he sent out for the minutes of the Teheran Conference.

"I was astonished to hear that the Big Three had already specifi-

---

* Eden was silent when Morgenthau suggested dividing Germany into numerous, small, agricultural provinces, and stopping industrial production. Morgenthau took that silence to mean agreement — an erroneous interpretation, as he later discovered.

cally instructed the EAC to study the problem of partitioning Germany. Stalin, determined that Germany should never again disturb the peace of Europe, strongly favored its dismemberment. Roosevelt backed him wholeheartedly, and Churchill reluctantly agreed that the European Advisory Commission consider the proposal.

"Eden and I were both amazed to learn that the EAC was cheerfully drawing its plans on the basis not of German dismemberment, but of German unity. Winant had been at Teheran. But having received no instructions from the State Department to proceed along the Teheran lines, he felt that they might not know of the Big Three decision and that it was not his business to inform his superiors on such matters."

Shaken by much he had learned, Morgenthau had been even more disturbed, he later wrote, by the sight of London — "that bombed city with its courageous people." On the eve of his departure he made his deepest convictions the theme of a broadcast to the English people:

"There can be no peace on earth — no security for any man, woman or child — if aggressor nations like Germany and Japan retain any power to strike at their neighbors.

"It is not enough for us to say, 'we will disarm Germany and Japan and *hope* that they will learn to behave themselves as decent people.' Hoping is not enough."

Back in Washington on August 17, Morgenthau called early the next morning on Cordell Hull. Immediately after their conference he dictated his memory of it for his Diary:

I told him I had called on General Eisenhower and asked him how he felt about the way Germany should be treated the first few months after we entered Germany, and he said that his impression was that they should be treated sternly and that they should be allowed to stew in their own juice.

Then I told Hull that I had a talk with Churchill . . . and I got the impression he wanted the Germans treated in a stern manner. I then told him that I had done a lot of probing, and through talking with Winant and with the people who assist Winant, and also based on a memorandum . . . of Mr. Pasvolsky I found that from all appearances it seemed that the Germans were going to be treated in a manner so that they could be built up over a number of years to pay reparations, and that at the end of ten years, they would be prepared to wage a third war.

I also told Hull that . . . with Eden . . . I learned, by having Mr. Eden read from the minutes of the Teheran Conference, that during discussions about Poland the President switched the conversation to a discussion of Germany, and it was then and there decided* that Germany should be dismembered in either three or fifteen parts, and that a commission would be appointed to study this question. . . .

When I made this statement, Mr. Hull literally gasped and he said to me, "Henry, this is the first time I have ever heard this. . . . I have never been permitted to see the minutes of the Teheran Conference. . . . I have asked and I have not been allowed to see them, and what you have told me is the first time I have ever heard this." . . .

And I said, "Well, now Pasvolsky has made a study along quite contrary lines, and Winant has also made a study . . . along different lines." I said that when I was in Winant's office I didn't think he was telling the truth because he first said he was making a report on reparations for Germany, but that about two weeks ago he began to make a new study which would take into consideration the dismemberment of Germany. I really don't think that anybody has made a study along the lines the President and Churchill decided on at Teheran.

When I first mentioned the European Advisory Committee, Hull said, "That has been a complete failure. The trouble is that Winant is trying to do two big jobs and he can't do them both." So I had to treat the next thing very carefully. I said, "I am not quite sure whether at Teheran Winant knew about the clause for the dismemberment of Germany or whether he didn't." I said he was a little vague about it, but Winant kept saying right along that he had no instructions. However, at one stage in the game Winant did say that the reason he was hesitat-

* In fact Roosevelt and Stalin supported partition, Churchill did not, and the matter was discussed rather than decided at Teheran. It was also referred for study to the EAC.

ing telling me all the facts about this Conference was that Mr. Hull had not seen the minutes. . . . He said that he was there, but it put him in a very embarrassing position because he didn't know how much to tell back home. . . .

The sum and substance of this is that here a meeting takes place sometime last November in Teheran where . . . Roosevelt, Churchill and Stalin, agree to the dismemberment of Germany, and all these people go ahead and make studies without taking that into consideration and without explicit instructions. It is like telling an architect to build a new house and not telling him where it should be built, how it should be built, or how many people it is to house.

Hull was quite upset, so I said to him, "You know, Cordell . . . I appreciate the fact that this isn't my responsibility, but I am doing this as an American citizen, and I am going to continue to do so, and I am going to stick my nose into it until I know it is all right. . . . If I find out anything I will come over and tell you about it." He said that was all right.

I said to Hull, "Where do you stand on this?" And he said, "You know the reason I got along so well with the Russians was because when I was in Moscow I told the Russians that I would hold a secret trial before which I would bring Hitler and his gang and Tojo and his gang, and I would shoot them all, and then I would let the world know about it a couple of days later." . . . I asked him what he was going to do about the state of Germany, and he said, "I don't have any chance to do anything. I am not told what is going on. . . . I am told that that is a military affair. . . . I am not even consulted." . . .

Then I went on and told him about the plans which the Army is making where we would go into the south of Germany and England in the north of Germany. That is contrary to the way the President wanted it, but the only way they could have carried out the President's wishes would have been to have the two armies cross each other, so the army decided to do it the other way. . . .

I also told Hull that Russia had kept completely aloof from the European Advisory Committee, and I told him the reason they were keeping out of it, in my opinion, was because they realized how the American and English delegates were proceeding on this matter, and they wanted no part of it.

From my talk with Hull, I am sure if Hull got a directive on the dismemberment of Germany he would go to town. My trip to Europe was many, many times worthwhile just for what I learned and what I told Hull, and we will see what happens when I see the President.

With Roosevelt on August 19, 1944, Morgenthau, according to his recollection right after their conversation, said: "Mr. President, here in the State Department . . . Pasvolsky has been making a study, but he didn't know about the Teheran Conference agreement." The Secretary then told Roosevelt about his conversation with Hull. "The President didn't like it," Morgenthau wrote, "but he didn't say anything. He looked very embarrassed, and I repeated it so that he would be sure to get it." Morgenthau also told Roosevelt about Winant and the work of his committee. Nobody, the Secretary said, "has been studying how to treat Germany roughly along the lines you wanted."

"Give me thirty minutes with Churchill and I can correct this," the President said. ". . . We have got to be tough with Germany and I mean the German people not just the Nazis. We either have to castrate the German people or you have got to treat them in such manner so they can't just go on reproducing people who want to continue the way they have in the past."

"Well, Mr. President," Morgenthau replied, "Nobody is considering the question along those lines. . . . In England they want to build up Germany so she can pay reparations."

"What do you want reparations for?" Roosevelt asked. Morgenthau, though he did not reply, opposed them.

As the Secretary put it, Roosevelt "left no doubt whatsoever in my mind that he personally wants to be tough with the Germans. He said, 'They have been tough with us.' "

Confident that the President shared his own opinions, aghast at the policies of EAC and the Army, Morgenthau soon after leaving the White House appointed a special committee of Harry White, John Pehle, and Ansel Luxford "to draft the Treasury's analysis of the German problem." That committee began at once, with strict attention to the Secretary's specific instructions, to define what became of the Morgenthau Plan.

3. The Morgenthau Plan

Morgenthau dominated the work of the Treasury's committee on Germany. The members of that committee followed the Secretary's instructions to the letter even though they sometimes disagreed with him. Further, in the tradition of high departmental morale that had long existed, the committee presented a united front to others in Washington. To assist the Secretary, his staff assiduously collected materials supporting his position. It used various remarks of Warren A. Seavey, a Harvard law professor who believed the Germans incorrigible and advocated depriving them of "the raw materials, the machines and the 'know-how' " with which otherwise they would "menace . . . the future peace of the world." The writings of James B. Conant, the president of Harvard and a chief scientific adviser to Roosevelt, and several letters of Bernard M. Baruch also helped in the building of the Treasury's case, as did a report of the British Parliament that called for subordinating "any attempt to put Germany economically on her feet . . . to the necessity of preventing Germans directly or indirectly preparing for another war . . . and to the prior claims of the nations victimized by Germany, and the restoration of their economic prosperity." General Hilldring told Harry White that the prime concern in treating Germany, as he saw it, was to be sure that the United States did nothing to put the Germans in a position from which they could again wage war. And according to White's report to Morgenthau, J. M. Keynes in a conversation of August 20, 1944, agreed "with our view of the desirability of dismembering Germany and as to the relative unimportance of reparations. He explained . . . that in a report he submitted . . . last year he was specifically given terms of reference which did not include the assumption of partition of Germany. He said that he had wanted to add a sentence at the end of his report . . . to the effect that he disagreed with the whole recommendation and preferred another solution, namely, the partition of Germany. In short, Keynes seems to be wholly in our corner."

But others, more important to Morgenthau than Keynes, were not. In his Diary, the Secretary reported his conversation of August 23, 1944, with Henry Stimson and John McCloy:

> Stimson was . . . anxious to see me. I told him the whole story even including the part that Hull had never seen the minutes. . . . McCloy's interest is the immediate one — what is the Army going to do as soon as they go in there? Stimson's interest is the long-range one. . . . He is thinking along the lines that you have to have a long Armistice or a period of at least twenty years to police Germany while the present generation is in control and until a new generation grows up. He was also very much interested evidently in a proposal made by Jean Monnet to internationalize the Saar Basin and have joint control by some international body and permit the Germans to work there but not run it. They thought if we could control the Saar we could keep the Germans from going to war again. So I said, "Well, if you let the young children of today be brought up by SS Troopers who are indoctrinated with Hitlerism, aren't you simply going to raise another generation of Germans who will want to wage war? . . . Don't you think the thing to do is to take a leaf from Hitler's book and completely remove these children from their parents and make them wards of the state, and have ex-US Army officers, English Army officers and Russian Army officers run these schools and have these children learn the true spirit of democracy?" . . .
>
> I also gave him my idea of the possibility of removing all industry from Germany and simply reducing them to an agricultural population of small land-owners. He said that the trouble with that was that Germany was that kind of a nation back in 1860, but then she only had 40 million people. He said that you might have to take a lot of people out of Germany. So I said, "Well, that is not nearly as bad as sending them to gas chambers."
>
> I got the impression that Stimson felt this was a very important subject . . . but he hasn't given too much thought to it. . . .
>
> I then said that I thought a committee of Hull, himself and

myself ought to draw up a memorandum for the President so that he will have it before he meets Churchill again. . . . I said, "I don't think Churchill is going to worry about it and the President hasn't time to think about it." . . . I asked him whether when he saw the President again he wouldn't suggest that to him, and he thought he would rather do it in a memorandum.

More than Morgenthau yet realized, Stimson opposed his ideas about the German economy, as did two important Treasury officers, Robert E. McConnell and Ansel Luxford. McConnell, to be sure, advocated dismantling much of German industry, including heavy forging works, gas plants, and nitrogen plants, but he also proposed installing American management to run most of German industry in order to manufacture materials for Allied use during the war against Japan, to offset some of the costs of the occupation in Germany, and to defray parts of the expense of the war to the Allied nations, presumably through the delivery of reparations in kind. Luxford also believed that German industry should be used to produce reparations.

Morgenthau, however, considered reparations insignificant; his objective remained the elimination of all industry in Germany that might relate to the manufacture of military goods, and he considered undesirable the imposition of Allied control over the German economy. Those responsible for that control were bound, he felt, to strive for efficiency and order, whereas he hoped "to strike a keynote of toughness . . . to let the German economy sort of seek its own level."

On that account, when the question of the exchange rate for Allied Military Marks arose again on August 24 and 25, 1944, Morgenthau supported a recommendation for a military rate of 20 marks to the dollar. The British proposed 5 marks to the dollar; the State Department, 8, for both felt "that a low rate of exchange for the German mark and high purchasing power for our soldiers' dollar will disrupt the price and wage structure in Germany, unbalance the Germany economy thus retarding its rapid rehabilitation and recovery." That suited Morgenthau. "Somebody's got to take the lead about let's be tough to the Germans," the Secretary told McCloy. ". . . And I'm going to propose that we have a military rate

. . . of 20 German marks for the dollar. . . . Just for the soldiers. . . . This is a military rate. We can keep our books on that basis. We start out this way . . . then after we're there a month we reexamine it."

As Morgenthau saw it, the military rate was simply a "straw in the wind as to how we're going to treat Germany." Much more important was the "Handbook of Military Government" which SHAEF had prepared in London. To Roosevelt on August 25, 1944, Morgenthau took memoranda on both questions. That on the "Handbook," which was designed to guide American and British military government officers, quoted a number of excerpts which the Secretary found objectionable. "Your main and immediate task," one excerpt read, ". . . is to get things running, to pick up the pieces, to restore as quickly as possible the official functioning of the German civil government. . . . The first concern of military government will be to see that the machine works and works efficiently." Other excerpts called on the officers of military government to reorganize the German police so as to maintain law and order, to control German finances, to establish and maintain adequate standards of public health, to promote agriculture, to restore public utilities, to provide for the gradual rehabilitation of peacetime industry, to employ labor and prevent industrial unrest. The Allied officers were also to assist in the conversion of industrial plants to the production of consumer goods, and to reconstruct German foreign trade with priority for the needs of the United Nations. "The highly centralized German administrative system," the "Handbook" ordered, "is to be retained unless otherwise directed by higher authorities. . . . All existing German regulations and ordinances relating to . . . production, supply or distribution will remain in force unless specifically amended or abrogated. Except as otherwise indicated by circumstances or directed by higher authority, present German production and primary processing of fuels, ores and other raw materials will be maintained at present levels. . . . The food supply will be administered so as to provide, if possible . . . a diet on the basis of an overall average of 2000 calories per day. Members of the German forces will be rated as normal consumers. . . . Should the indigenous products of Germany be insufficient to provide such a basic ration, the balance will be made up by imports. . . . All possible steps will be taken to insure the utilization of German economic, material and industrial facilities to an extent necessary to provide such raw materials, goods, supplies and services as are required for military and essential civilian needs. . . . The main objective of Allied Military Government in the financial field is to take such temporary measures as will . . . minimize the potential financial disorder . . . that is likely to occur. . . . International boundaries will be deemed to be as they were on 31 December, 1937."

At first, the quotations from the "Handbook" bothered Roosevelt less than did the memorandum about the military exchange rate. As Morgenthau told White and Bell when he returned from the White House, "I gave the President the memorandum on twenty marks to the dollar, and he doesn't like it. . . . He . . . says, 'I don't want any rate. I want to give the American soldiers dollars and let them make their own rate as they go along.' . . . You can't budge him on it."

Roosevelt's suggestion, White objected, might cost as much as $50 million. "There are . . . other things pending . . . which are important," Morgenthau replied, "and he has certain ideas when he gets these things, and . . . I don't want to fight him on this, because I have bigger fish to fry with it. . . . This is just going to raise hell with the German economy, and I said good; this is what the President wants." Privately in his Diary on August 25, Morgenthau described those "bigger fish":

"I called on the President this morning, and I really was shocked for the first time because he is a very sick man, and seems to have wasted away. . . . I . . . gave him my memorandum [about the "Handbook"] which he read very carefully, and he said to me, 'Well, you could read this thing two ways,' meaning that you could interpret it both hard or soft. So I said, 'Look, Mr. President, this is based on a handbook which we picked up in England and which I understand has not yet been approved, but lacking a directive from the top this is what is going to be used. . . . I told McCloy to tell Stimson that I was going to speak to you about it, but I understand you are seeing him* and I don't want to annoy him so I think maybe you'd better give me back the memorandum and the handbook,' but the President said, 'No, if you don't mind, I would like to keep it and read it tonight and then I will return it to you.' . . . I'm going to continue to feed the President suggestions, but it is quite

---

* Later that morning.

obvious that he wants to keep me very much in the background, and wants to do it his own way as usual."

The President's "own way" appalled the War Department. Informed by Morgenthau of Roosevelt's views about the marks, McCloy warned that "the British won't permit it without a fight, nor will the Russians and all the work of six months . . . goes out the window." Morgenthau disagreed: "I think the Russians will love it." He went on to explain that he had advocated a rate of 20 marks to the dollar, but Roosevelt absolutely rejected it. "This leaves me a little staggered," McCloy said. "I've got to think what we've got to do." Gradually in the ensuing days McCloy, with Morgenthau's approval, brought the British reluctantly to accept a rate of 10 marks to the dollar, which Roosevelt, who had lost interest in the matter, endorsed.

But like Stimson, McCloy was less troubled by the rate of exchange than by the Treasury's criticisms of the "Handbook" and its implications for German policy. After talking with Morgenthau on August 23, Stimson prepared a memorandum that he delivered to the President at luncheon two days later. In conversation with Roosevelt, as in his memorandum, the Secretary of War opposed Morgenthau's position. To be sure, like Morgenthau, Stimson considered "Robert Murphy not sufficient" as a political adviser to Eisenhower. Stimson also favored the reeducation of German children, the disarmament of Germany, and the punishment, after trial, of leading Nazis. But he objected to breaking Germany up into several small states and he proposed international control of the industries of the Ruhr and Saar. Dismemberment and deindustrialization, he told Roosevelt, would result in the starvation of thirty million people, a barbaric prospect.

Of the two Cabinet members, Morgenthau left the deeper impression on Roosevelt on August 25. After reading the Treasury memorandum on the "Handbook" that night, the President the next day sent Stimson a sharp letter. It quoted the excerpts Morgenthau had quoted, incorporated some of his phraseology, and carried the sting of Roosevelt's own prose:

This so-called "Handbook" is pretty bad. I should like to know how it came to be written and who approved it down the line. If it has not been sent out as approved, all copies should be withdrawn and held until you get a chance to go over it.

It gives me the impression that Germany is to be restored just as much as the Netherlands or Belgium, and the people of Germany brought back as quickly as possible to their pre-war estate.

It is of the utmost importance that every person in Germany should realize that this time Germany is a defeated nation. I do not want them to starve to death, but, as an example, if they need food to keep body and soul together beyond what they have, they should be fed three times a day with soup from Army soup kitchens. That will keep them perfectly healthy and they will remember that experience all their lives. The fact that they are a defeated nation, collectively and individually, must be so impressed upon them that they will hesitate to start any new war. . . .

There exists a school of thought both in London and here which would, in effect, do for Germany what this Government did for its own citizens in 1933 when they were flat on their backs. I see no reason for starting a WPA, PWA or a CCC for Germany when we go in with our Army of Occupation.

Too many people here and in England hold to the view that the German people as a whole are not responsible for what has taken place — that only a few Nazi leaders are responsible. That unfortunately is not based on fact. The German people as a whole must have it driven home to them that the whole nation has been engaged in a lawless conspiracy against the decencies of modern civilization.

Please let me see the revision of this and also let me have this original copy back.

That revision would have to reflect the deliberations of the committee Roosevelt appointed, at the suggestion of Stimson who in turn was following a recommendation of Morgenthau. The two Secretaries and Hull, the President had directed at the Cabinet meeting on August 25, were to confer about the treatment of Germany. Roosevelt then sent the Treasury and State Departments copies of his note to Stimson about the "Handbook," surely with the purpose of guiding the interdepartmental discussions. Characteristically, Hull resented having to share command for policy with Morgenthau, whose opinions about the German economy he rejected, and with Stimson, whose interpretation of military and political necessities conflicted at various points with those of the Department of State. Here, too, according to Morgenthau's account of the Cabinet meeting: "The President was more firm about this opposite Hull than I've ever seen him, and so was Stimson." The Treasury's intercession, Morgenthau felt, had accomplished his first purpose. "McCloy can't — Stimson can't — wash their hands of the fact," the Secretary told his staff, "that if we hadn't gone to Europe and dug this stuff up, that 'Handbook' would have gone into effect."

Stimson was distressed less about the President's response to the "Handbook" than about Morgenthau's point of view. In Saranac, New York, over a long Labor Day weekend from August 26 through September 3, 1944, Stimson confided to his diary his grave reservations about Morgenthau's "very bitter atmosphere of personal resentment against the entire German people without regard to individual guilt and I am very much afraid that it will result in our taking mass vengeance . . . in the shape of clumsy economic action. This in my opinion will be ineffective and will inevitably produce a very dangerous reaction in Germany and probably a new war."

Morgenthau, whose convictions were equal and opposite, also left Washington for the Labor Day weekend. As he departed, he instructed White and Pehle to devote their whole time to their studies of Germany. "The President is hungry for this stuff," he told them by telephone two days later. "This thing is so much a . . . psychological matter, it's a question of how to handle the Germans who have been inculcated with this fanaticism. . . . It's a question of attacking the German mind. . . . I wouldn't be afraid to make the suggestion just as ruthless as is necessary to accomplish the acts."

By telephone daily through the weekend Morgenthau reviewed the memorandum White and Pehle were drafting. Their first efforts struck the Secretary as not tough enough. "I wish," he said on August 31, 1944, "that your men would attack the problem from this angle, that they take the Ruhr and completely put it out of business. . . . And also the Saar. Now, the reason I said particularly the Ruhr, you can find out very easily what their production of coal and steel and that sort of thing is, and consider what it would do in the way of helping England and Belgium if they stage a come-back because, after all, the Ruhr — it was partly responsible for the great unemployment in England, and one of our problems is to put England back on its feet. And both of these studies and all other studies that I've ever seen are contemplating keeping the Ruhr in existence. And I'd like to approach the thing from — just putting the whole Ruhr out of production. And also, as a separate thing, what would happen if we put the Saar out of production? . . .

"And . . . as I say, what competition the Ruhr gave to both the Belgium coal and steel and England coal and steel, and an estimate to guess how long it would take before Russia could be in production and that she could take care of customers — I mean, England, Belgium and Russia could take care of the customers that Germany used to have — with coal and steel."

"This Ruhr," White objected, "is the most difficult problem. You see . . . crushing it as you say presents us with about fifteen million out of eighteen million people who . . . will have absolutely nothing to do, and . . . some of the boys feel . . . that we'd never get away with it politically. . . . That's the problem with the Ruhr. If you internationalize it, it has other problems. You can't give it to France; it's too big. You can't give it to Belgium and Holland; it will swallow Belgium and Holland. It's . . . the most difficult problem and, we'll . . . work along the lines that you're suggesting. I think that the question of how it will help Britain and France . . . will be a good selling argument, but it certainly oughtn't to be the decisive consideration. . . . But we'll investigate it."

"I can tell you this," Morgenthau replied, "that if the Ruhr was put out of business, the coal mines and steel mines of England would flourish for many years." When White continued to express doubts, the Secretary said categorically that "the Ruhr ought to be put out of business." Further, in answer to White's question of what to do with the Germans in the area who would lack employment, Morgenthau proposed "an international T.V.A." manned by "a couple of million Germans" at work on reclamation and hydroelectric projects all over the world.

While redrafting proceeded at the Treasury, Morgenthau on September 2, 1944, gave the President the preliminary version of the Treasury's memorandum on Germany. They met, as they often had before, in the handsome, spacious family house that Morgenthau had rebuilt on his farm in Fishkill, New York. It was a peaceful setting, with the great trees in their late summer glory and the nearby orchards laden with the apple crop. Both men relaxed in that stately but pastoral environment. The Secretary's Diary entry for the day recounted their conversation:

> The President and Mrs. Roosevelt came to tea this afternoon, and stayed about an hour and a quarter. Fully an hour of the time we used to discuss the German situation. I gave him the memorandum of the outline of suggestions plus a map. The President said, "I wonder if you have the three things in it that I am interested in." . . . I explained to the President this was preliminary and had not yet been circulated fully in the Treasury, and that my own criticism of it was that it didn't go nearly far enough.
>
> The President read this memorandum very carefully, and as soon as he got to the map he said, "This isn't what we agreed to at Teheran or since then," and he started to talk about Poland. I said, "Mr. President, we have been working wholly within the Treasury, and we just don't know what anybody else has been doing for you. . . . This is approximately correct except that, as I remember it, from the Kiel Canal north toward Denmark they made that an international zone, and they made the Saar district an international zone." He was keenly interested in the memorandum and read it very slowly and very carefully. When he got through, he told me about the three things he wanted, and I think that his thinking is along these lines — Germany should be allowed no aircraft of any kind, not even a glider, and that Germany should be served from the air by other countries. The second was that nobody should be allowed to wear a uniform, and there was no marching, that would do more to teach the Germans than anything else that they had been defeated. So I said, "That's very interesting . . . but I don't think it goes nearly far enough. . . . Where this memorandum falls down, as far as I am concerned, is that the heart of the German war machine is the Ruhr, and I would like to see the Ruhr dismantled, and the machinery given to those countries

that might need it. . . . I realize that this would put eighteen or twenty million people out of work, but if we make an international zone of it it is just time before Germany will attempt an Anschluss. . . . This will have a tremendous effect on England and Belgium, and ought to guarantee their prosperity for the next twenty years because their principal competition for their coal and steel came from the Ruhr, and this ought to go a long way towards solving the economic future of England."

Well, the President liked all of this, and I said, "Then the other problem which this memorandum doesn't touch on is the mentality of the German between the ages of 20 and 40 . . . who have been inculcated with Nazism. . . . I am convinced that you could change them, and you may even have to transplant them out of Germany to some place in Central Africa where you can do some big TVA project. . . . The other big problem is what to do with the children of these people so that they will get the right kind of education."

The President listened very closely and seemed to be in complete sympathy with what I was saying. I don't think he had done any thinking along these lines. He did interrupt me to say, "You know you will have to create entirely new textbooks for the Germans," and I said that I realized that. . . .

Towards the end of the conversation, I said to the President, "How did you ever appoint Robert Murphy as political advisor to Eisenhower?" . . . Then the President went into a long discussion about . . . how he had directed the business with Darlan and how he had saved 10,000 lives of American soldiers. . . . He got quite excited about it as Mrs. Roosevelt pushed him on this. So I said, "Mr. President, why not let bygones be bygones? . . . I don't want to discuss what has gone in the past, but why pick Robert Murphy for this job? In the minds of the people it connoted Darlan and everything that goes with it." . . .

During my discussion with the President on Robert Murphy, Mrs. Roosevelt said that with the attitude of the Pope, she thought it was a mistake to send a Catholic to Germany, and the President came to the Pope's defense particularly in regard to this last speech the Pope made on private property. He said the Pope had always been for private property, and was against Communism. His arguments weren't very reassuring or convincing. . . .

I felt it had been distinctly worthwhile to see Mrs. Roosevelt because I never knew just how she might feel towards treating the Germans so harshly. She had been slightly pacifist before the war and I thought she might think we should go a little easy on the Germans, but she doesn't.

Again at the Treasury on September 4, Morgenthau instructed White to include in the memorandum on Germany the President's wishes forbidding the Germans aircraft, uniforms and marching. The Secretary also said that Roosevelt was in accord with his idea for the Ruhr. "I think that somebody is going to be confronted," White protested, "with what to do with fifteen million people." The President, Morgenthau replied, would feed them from the Army's soup kitchens. Pehle asked how long that would last, and Morgenthau said Roosevelt would not worry about that, but Pehle predicted that "he is not going to be able to sell that kind of program." White then, as he had before, proposed an alternative "of making the Ruhr an industrial area under international control which will produce reparations for twenty years."

"Harry," Morgenthau said, "you can't sell it to me at all. . . . You just can't sell it to me, because you have it there only so many years and you have an Anschluss and the Germans go in and take it. The only thing you can sell me, or I will have any part of, is the complete shut-down of the Ruhr. . . . Just strip it. I don't care what happens to the population. . . . I would take every mine, every mill and factory and wreck it. . . . Steel, coal, everything. Just close it down. . . . I am for destroying it first and we will worry about the population second."

White, Gaston, and McConnell continued to enter objections, but Morgenthau persisted. "That is the place where war can spring from," the Secretary said, "and that is the place that closed down the steel mills in Birmingham, the coal mines in England, that caused the misery and the low standards of living in England. . . . It is the competition. . . . I would close down those things tight. There is nothing left. . . . I want to see as good a job done as I can on the war criminals, but over and above that, my interest is the future. . . . Looking to the future peace of this world . . . and the only way I know is to shut that thing down.

"I don't know how much the Saar has or how much their production is; if necessary, shut that down or give it to France. But certainly if that area [the Ruhr] is . . . stripped of its machinery, the mines flooded — dynamited — wrecked — it would make them impotent to wage future wars. . . .

"Now, as soon as you start arguing with me, and I begin to give way, let this in or that in, or let that area or that population continue their skills, they will do just what they do in the hills of Pennsylvania — they will mine bootleg coal. . . . A fellow will have a coal mine in his basement, and those fellows are so clever and such devils that before you know it they have got a marching army. . . .

"I am not going to budge an inch. . . . Sure it is a terrific problem. Let the Germans solve it. Why the hell should I worry about what happens to their people? . . .

"It seems a terrific task; it seems inhuman; it seems cruel. We didn't ask for this war; we didn't put millions of people through gas chambers, we didn't do any of these things. They have asked for it.

"Now, what I say is, for the future of my children and grandchildren I don't want these beasts to wage war. I don't know any other way than to go to the heart of the thing, which is the Ruhr, and I am not going to be budged. I can be overruled by the President, but nobody else is going to overrule me."

The destruction of the Ruhr, Morgenthau admitted, would impose some sacrifices on Great Britain and the United States, at the least reduce export markets, but that seemed to him a small price. He had already told the President, he went on, that the preliminary memorandum had not gone far enough. He wanted army engineers to go "into every steel mill, in every coal mine, every chemical plant, every synthetic gas business, . . . and put dynamite in and open the water valves and flood and dynamite." And as Morgenthau interpreted the President, "he is willing to go as far as I am, or he is willing to go farther than I am. . . . The man is hungry, crazy to get some stuff to work with. When he saw what we were talking about he said, . . . 'It will be tough sledding with Churchill.'

"But he is very, very anxious to get something down in black and white on this thing. . . . You put your Ruhr under lock and key and make it a ghost area, the Germans cannot wage war with what they have left."

Adamant though the Secretary clearly was, his subordinates continued to try to persuade him to soften his views. White suggested permitting the Ruhr to produce coal so as to alleviate the "terrific coal shortage" that Western Europe and Great Britain would face after the end of hostilities. "To answer," Morgenthau said, "as to letting them produce coal, that doesn't answer what I have in mind. . . . I am not going to give in while I have got breath. . . . I want to make Germany so impotent that she cannot forge the tools of war."

That statement ended the argument within the Treasury. The destruction of the Ruhr formed the core of Morgenthau's plan for Germany. The plan itself, Morgenthau believed on September 4, 1944, would win Roosevelt's full support. It would also, he was sure, contribute to the awakening of prosperity in England; to the relief of Russian fears of German resurgence, and therefore to Russian-American friendship; to the elimination of Germany as a threat to the world, and therefore to a lasting peace. And by nightfall of September 4 his staff, their objections vetoed, had completed the draft which was to remain for Morgenthau the essential statement of his ideas. Its form that day was identical with the form he later published in facsimile in his book of 1945, *Germany Is Our Problem*.

Entitled "Program to Prevent Germany from Starting a World War III," the Morgenthau Plan began by calling for "the complete demilitarization of Germany in the shortest possible period of time after surrender. This means completely disarming the German Army and people (including the removal or destruction of all war material), the total destruction of the whole German armament industry, and the removal or destruction of other key industries which are basic to military strength." With regard to geography, the plan proposed giving Poland that part of East Prussia which did not go to the Soviet Union, and also the southern portion of Silesia. France was to get the Saar and adjacent territories bounded by the Rhine and Moselle rivers. And an International Zone was to contain the Ruhr and its surrounding territory. The remaining part of Ger-

many "should be divided into two autonomous, independent states
. . . the South German state comprising Bavaria, Wurttemberg,
Baden and some smaller areas and . . . a North German state comprising a large part of the old state of Prussia, Saxony, Thuringia
and smaller states." There was to be a customs union between the
South German country and Austria, which was to be restored to her
pre-1938 borders.

The plan next discussed the Ruhr, including the Rhineland, the
Kiel Canal, and all German territory north of that canal: "Here lies
the heart of German industrial power. This area should not only be
stripped of all . . . existing industries but so weakened and controlled that it cannot in the foreseeable future become an industrial
area." To that end, if possible within six months after the end of
the fighting, "all industrial plants and equipment not destroyed by
military action shall be completely dismantled and transported to
Allied Nations as restitution. All equipment shall be removed from
the mines and the mines closed."

The Morgenthau Plan went on to hold that "reparations, in the
form of future payments and deliveries, should not be demanded,"
though it did make provisions for restitution and some reparations
through the transfer of existing German resources and territories,
including forced German labor outside of Germany and the confis-
cation of German assets outside of Germany.

Within Germany, "all schools and universities will be closed until
an Allied Commission of Education has formulated an effective reorganization program. It is contemplated that it may require a considerable period of time before any institutions of higher education
are reopened. Meanwhile the education of German students in foreign universities will not be prohibited. Elementary schools will be
reopened as quickly as appropriate teachers and textbooks are available.

"All German radio stations and newspapers, magazines, weeklies,
etc. shall be discontinued until adequate controls are established
and an appropriate program formulated."

Taking a strong stand for the dismemberment of Germany, the
Morgenthau Plan contemplated the military occupation as a step
toward an eventual partitioning of the country. On that account,
military authorities were to dismiss all policy-making officials of the

German government and deal instead with local governments. Those governments were in time to organize federal governments both in North Germany and South Germany.

"The sole purpose of the military in control of the German economy," the Morgenthau Plan continued in direct contrast to the "Handbook," "shall be to facilitate military operations and military occupation. The Allied Military Government shall not assume responsibility for such economic problems as price controls, rationing, unemployment, production, reconstruction, distribution, consumption, housing, or transportation, or take any measures designed to maintain or strengthen the German economy, except those which are essential to military operations. The responsibility for sustaining the German economy and people rests with the German people with such facilities as may be available under the circumstances."

For a period of at least twenty years after the surrender of Germany, the United Nations were to maintain controls over foreign trade and capital imports. Those controls were to prevent the establishment or expansion of key industries "basic to the German military potential." They were also to break up all large estates and divide them "among the peasants, and the system of primogeniture and entail should be abolished."

The Morgenthau Plan, after noting the need for a program for the punishment of war crimes, proceeded to incorporate Roosevelt's particular suggestions: "No German shall be permitted to wear . . . any military uniform or any uniform of any quasi-military organization . . . no military parades shall be permitted . . . and all military bands shall be disbanded . . . all aircraft . . . will be confiscated for later disposition." No German was to be allowed to "operate or to help operate any aircraft, including those owned by foreign interests."

"Although the United States would have full military and civilian representation on whatever international commission or commissions may be established for the execution of the whole German program," the Morgenthau Plan concluded, "the primary responsibility for the policing of Germany and for civil administration in Germany should be assumed by the military forces of Germany's continental neighbors. Specifically, these should include Russian, French, Polish, Czech, Greek, Yugoslav, Norwegian, Dutch and Belgian soldiers." And in its last sentence, the Morgenthau Plan stated

categorically what the President expected the American people to
demand: "Under this program United States troops could be withdrawn within a relatively short time."

The Secretary had now to attempt to make his program the policy
of the United States.

4. Discord in Washington

At a dinner at his home on September 4, 1944, with Henry Stimson,
John McCloy, and Harry White, Morgenthau unveiled his newly
completed plan for Germany. "With temperateness and good will,"
which Morgenthau returned in kind, Stimson immediately attacked
the economic features of the plan. As Harry White later recalled the
remarks of the Secretary of War, "he stressed the fact that to destroy
much of the German industry would be to force thirty million people into starvation. In answer to an inquiry as to how he arrived at
thirty million, he said that that was the difference in the population
of Germany before it was industrialized . . . and its present population. Mr. Stimson said that he favored slicing off Silesia and a part
of East Prussia and that he also desired a rigorous prosecution of war
criminals. However, he did not believe that the proper way to treat
the Germans and to prevent future wars was to destroy German industry."

Stimson expanded that argument at a meeting the next day of the
Cabinet committee on Germany, of which Roosevelt had made
Harry Hopkins chairman. Immediately after the meeting Morgen-
thau described it to his staff:

> Stimson is opposed to making Germany a barren farm coun-
> try. I gathered he wanted an international Ruhr and Saar and
> let them continue to produce. . . . More and more Stimson
> came out very emphatically, very very positively, that he didn't
> want any production stopped. He said it was an unnatural
> thing to do, it ran in the face of the economy. . . . And more
> and more it developed that Hull did want to take very drastic
> steps.* . . . Stimson kept making these speeches about why we
> must keep up production in Germany. . . . Nothing we told

* Stimson in his diary called Hull "as bitter as Morgenthau."

them last night made any impression. . . . In the beginning Hopkins stated both sides of the issue . . . but as Hull more and more made himself felt — Hopkins finally said to Stimson that he disagreed with him in his conclusions. So Stimson said, "This is just fighting brutality with brutality."

So Hopkins said to him, "Well, look, do you mean to say that if we stopped all production of steel in Germany that that would be a brutal thing to do?" . . .

I came away with a very clear picture that Hull . . . is approaching this thing with the same viewpoint that I have. . . . He said . . . : "This Nazism is down in the German People a thousand miles deep and you have just got to uproot it, and you can't do it by just shooting a few people." . . .

Stimson didn't even seem to like that and he went into a long legal discussion of how you would have to have legal proceedings before you shot the people. . . . Well, Hull doesn't want to wait; he just wants to shoot them all at dawn.

The three Cabinet members could agree only to submit separate memoranda to Roosevelt and to see him together the next afternoon at four. "That was most encouraging," Morgenthau told Hopkins over the telephone. ". . . I wanted to get up and kiss Cordell."

"You probably knew," Hopkins replied, ". . . what you were going to get from the other fellow [Stimson]. My God! He was terrible. . . . Henry, . . . it hurts him so to think of the nonuse of property. . . . He's grown up in that school so long that property . . . becomes so sacred. . . . Do you think he disagrees with us so sharply? . . . I think it's fruitless to talk with him any more. . . . And . . . I feel confident . . . about where the President is going to land."

So did Morgenthau, who believed that Roosevelt would blow up if Stimson were to say to him, as he had to the others, that "kindness and Christianity" would have to play a part in the reconstruction of Germany. What Stimson really wanted, Morgenthau suggested to Hopkins, was for Germany to serve as a buffer to the Soviet Union. Here Morgenthau misread the Secretary of War, for Stimson was less worried about the implications of the Morgenthau Plan for Russia than about its implications for the future economy of Europe and ultimate rehabilitation of Germany. Yet if Morgenthau had understood Stimson exactly, he would have opposed him nonetheless.

Politely but vehemently, Stimson attacked the Morgenthau Plan in his memorandum for Roosevelt:

> I cannot conceive of such a proposition being either possible or effective, and I can see enormous general evils coming from an attempt to so treat it. During the past eighty years of European history this portion* of Germany was one of the most important sources of the raw materials upon which the industrial and economic livelihood of Europe was based. Upon the production which came from the raw materials of this region during those years, the commerce of Europe was very largely predicated. Upon that production Germany became the largest sources of supply to no less than ten European countries. . . . The production of these materials from this region could not be sealed up and obliterated . . . without manifestly causing a great dislocation to the trade upon which Europe has lived. . . .
>
> I cannot treat as realistic the suggestion that such an area in the present economic condition of the world can be turned into a . . . "ghost territory." . . .
>
> I can conceive of endeavoring to meet the misuse which Germany has recently made of this production by wise systems of control or trusteeship or even transfers of ownership to other nations. But I cannot conceive of turning such a gift of nature into a dust heap.
>
> War is destruction. This war more than any previous war has caused gigantic destruction. The need for the recuperative benefits of productivity is more evident now than ever before. . . . Moreover speed of reconstruction is of great importance if we hope to avoid dangerous convulsions in Europe.
>
> We contemplate the transfer from Germany of ownership of East Prussia, Upper Silesia, Alsace and Lorraine (each of them except the first containing raw materials of importance) together with the imposition of general economic controls. We are also considering the wisdom of a possible partition of Ger-

* The Ruhr and Saar.

many into north and south sections, as well as the creation of an internationalized state in the Ruhr. With such precautions, or indeed with only some of them, it certainly should not be necessary for us to obliterate all industrial productivity in the Ruhr area. . . .

Nor can I agree that it should be one of our purposes to hold the German population "to a subsistence level" if this means the edge of poverty. This would mean condemning the German people to a condition of servitude in which, no matter how hard or how effectively a man worked, he could not materially increase his economic condition in the world. Such a program would . . . create tensions and resentments far outweighing any immediate advantage of security and would tend to obscure the guilt of the Nazis and the viciousness of their doctrines and their acts.

By such economic mistakes I cannot but feel that you would also be poisoning the springs out of which we hope that the future peace of the world can be maintained.*

At the White House late in the afternoon of September 6, 1944, the two Secretaries repeated their opposing arguments about the Saar and Ruhr, with Hopkins supporting Morgenthau's position and Hull, in contrast to his behavior on the previous day, moving closer to Stimson's side. It was a "very unsatisfactory meeting," Morgenthau told his staff:

Stimson started off right away . . . and when Stimson got through the President took the same position I have been taking, on the Ruhr; namely, that the English would have the advantage of the steel business if the Ruhr were closed. . . .

But the President kept saying, "Well, you can do this economic thing in six months — a year; there is no particular hurry." I tried to explain to him what that was. . . . Then the President went into something quite new. He said he was thinking of Dutchess County and how it was back in 1810, and how the people lived in home-spun wool. He went back to

* Though Morgenthau did not know it, General George Marshall fully agreed with Stimson.

when he was a boy. . . . That there is no reason why Germany couldn't go back to 1810, where they would be perfectly comfortable but wouldn't have any luxury. . . . He expounded on that at great length. . . .

What seemed to be in the President's mind was that while he wouldn't touch the steel mills right away — he would leave them there and sort of decide gradually what would happen to them — he had the idea that this thing was good for England, but he didn't have the whole picture.

Hopkins, on the other hand, made a very forceful argument against there being any steel mills at all, or any other war factories. . . .

The unfortunate thing is that the President gave us barely a half hour. . . . He certainly gave aid and comfort to Stimson.

On the other hand, when they got on this question of Germany, on trade and her position, he turned to Hull and said, "Now, of course, Mr. Hull, you and I together, for the last fifteen years, have stood for increased trade, and increased prosperity and peace and . . . I am sure you agree with me that we have got to do that in Germany," and Hull didn't answer him. . . .

But the sad part about this thing is . . . although I pointed out to the President that he had to do this thing right away . . . he just won't give you time enough to talk the thing out. I mean, this thing is a matter of hours. . . . I said, "This is the directive which is enforced by the Combined Chiefs of Staff, on which this Handbook is based, and this directive is still in existence." . . .

I went immediately to Hopkins' office on the way back and left word there I wanted to talk to him.

Hopkins did not call back, but before evening, Major John Boettiger arrived at the Treasury. The President's son-in-law, Boettiger had been involved in the work of the Civil Affairs section of the Joint Chiefs of Staff. With his wife Anna, the President's daughter, Boettiger was also living in the White House and was with the President daily during the fall of 1944. His mission on September 6 was to obtain Morgenthau's approval for changes in the directive covering the "Handbook," which the War Department had drafted in response to Roosevelt's criticisms. Boettiger believed the changes both desirable and sufficient. They appeared on the flyleaf to the "Handbook" and listed three principles to govern the occupation of Germany: "No steps looking toward economic rehabilitation of Germany are to be undertaken except as may be immediately necessary in support of military operations in occupation. . . . No relief supplies are to be imported or distributed beyond the minimum necessary to prevent disease and such disorder as might endanger or impede military operations in occupation. . . . Nazi officials will be removed from office and Nazi organizations will be abolished without regard to consideration of administrative or other expediencies."

Harry White considered those orders a definite improvement, but Morgenthau wanted to read the revised "Handbook" before endorsing a cable to SHAEF. Boettiger objected. It would be a mistake, he said, to bring the "Handbook" to the Treasury, since there was only one copy of it, which no senior American officer other than Eisenhower and no British officer had yet seen. Nevertheless, Morgenthau insisted. The "Handbook," he knew, would control American policy in the first few months of the occupation, and in spite of the President's apparent inclination to defer deindustrialization during that period, Morgenthau still hoped to persuade him to impose the Treasury's program on the War Department and SHAEF.

The debate between the Treasury and War Departments, continuing on September 7, 1944, focused that day largely on the question of denazification. Morgenthau and his assistants considered the terms in the "Handbook," which McCloy permitted them to examine, still too gentle. For the sake of efficiency, McCloy explained, the Army would have to keep some members of the Nazi Party at work — stenographers, for example — just as they had had to use some Fascists in Italy.

"What you didn't do in Italy," Morgenthau replied, "is what I had hoped to do in Germany."

"Oh, well," McCloy said, "there may be arguments as to how far down you should go, but we can't undertake to eliminate immediately every member of the Nazi Party." When Morgenthau asked why not, McCloy said there were too many, some thirteen million, many of them day laborers and clerks. The Army would not be able to provide enough personnel of its own to replace all those Germans. But Morgenthau disagreed, as did White, who argued that the American Army should employ only non-Nazis.

General Hilldring then said that Eisenhower would be moving into hostile territory where he would confront difficult problems. If he deliberately undertook in each village to destory all governmental authority, he would contribute to chaos behind his own lines and delay the defeat of the German army. With that explanation, Morgenthau agreed to the idea of using Nazis in the period before the surrender of Germany, but the Secretary continued to oppose the employment of any Nazi Party members after surrender, and continued also to demand more stringent restrictions on the importation and distribution of food than those which the Army had drafted.

Later that day Morgenthau took heart from Roosevelt's attitude. "I saw the President," the Secretary noted in his Diary, "and before I could say anything, he said, 'Don't be discouraged about yesterday's meeting. . . . The whole question seems to be about closing down the plants, and we have got to do the thing gradually.'

"But the amazing thing was that he should have greeted me the way he did because he must have realized the way I felt and this was most encouraging."

So was a conversation with Cordell Hull on September 8, 1944, which Morgenthau reported in his Diary:

> I found him looking very tired and very badly. . . . Hull said that the President had asked him to go to Quebec,* but he told him he couldn't go because he had been working so hard on this South American thing . . . that he was exhausted.
>
> I told him that I was discouraged after the meeting with the President because he seemed to be influenced by Stimson, and Hull just brushed Stimson aside and said that the President wasn't going to listen to Stimson and that I should forget about it. . . .
>
> Through the whole conversation I felt Hull was holding back on me, and I got the feeling that he wasn't telling me every-

---

* For Roosevelt's pending conference with Churchill.

thing. He went on another one of his tirades that the President didn't consult him. . . .

I feel from what Hull said that he didn't want the President to discuss the economic future of Germany at Quebec. He said that Churchill would listen to some squeaky-voiced man from the Foreign Office. He said that he had asked the President to take a representative of the State Department with him to Teheran so that if they accused the President of making any statements at Teheran, the State Department man would be a witness that this had not taken place. I asked him whether a State Department man went with the President and he said, "No."

He said that there were inter-departmental committees on this German business set up in Europe, and they should make a report. . . . I said, "The trouble is, Cordell, the President has never given a directive on how he feels Germany should be treated. . . . The first thing we know we will be in Germany and we will have no policy." He said, "Well, you heard the President say he wants to put the Germans on a soup kitchen diet and Stimson wants to give them luxuries." I said, "I know but I still say the President has got to give out a directive on how to treat Germany." . . . I said that during the next three months the thing in Germany will have to be settled. . . .

Hull said he hoped that the President wouldn't take up the question of the partition of Germany and the economic future of Germany at all at Quebec and just confine the conference to military matters. He said that Russia wouldn't be at the conference and it might get them upset if the matter was discussed. . . . I said . . . that I thought we ought to try to get the President . . . to decide on some kind of statement which would clarify his position in regard to Germany, and Hull thought that we might do that.

Whatever Hull's preferences, the President, Morgenthau believed, would discuss German questions with Churchill at Quebec. So, too, the issues of Lend-Lease during Stage II were bound to arise at their meeting. The Secretary therefore had his staff prepare a set of memoranda — a "Black Book," he called it — on German and British problems. One of them simply restated the Morgenthau Plan. Another contended that "the British could supply all the coal for coking purposes if we lose the coal mines in the Ruhr." Still another held that "the statement that a healthy European economy is dependent upon German industry was never true, nor will it be true in the future. Therefore the treatment to be accorded to Germany should be decided upon without reference to the economic consequences upon the rest of Europe. At the worst, these economic consequences will involve relatively minor disadvantages. . . . At best . . . they will speed up the industrial development of Europe outside of Germany. But any disadvantages will be more than offset by real gains to the political objectives and economic interests of the United Nations as a whole." His staff, Morgenthau said, had done "a perfectly amazingly good job. . . . I should think it would be very useful to the President at Quebec. . . . It is very, very necessary. And out of this thing, what I am hoping is, there will come a directive from the President as to his policy."

At the White House on September 9, 1944, Morgenthau, Stimson, and Hull delivered the papers presenting their several cases for the treatment of Germany. According to Morgenthau's report:

> Hopkins brought up the question of partition, and . . . the President . . . said that he is in favor of dividing Germany into three parts. . . . During the discussion Stimson said that we must get along with Russia.
>
> The President kept looking through the book* and wanted to know whether I had the part put in about uniforms and marching, and I said that it was there. The President read out loud . . . "It is a fallacy that Europe needs a strong industrial Germany." The President said, "This is the first time I have seen this stated." He says that everybody seems to disagree on that point, but he said, "I agree with this idea. . . . Furthermore, I believe in an agricultural Germany." (I evidently made a real impression on the President the time he came to my house, and the more I talk to him the more I find that he seems to be coming around to our viewpoint.) . . .
>
> The President put up this question, "Supposing the Russians

* The Treasury's set of memoranda.

want to insist on reparations, and the English and the United States don't want any, what happens then?" So I spoke up and said, "Well, my experience with the Russians at Bretton Woods was that they were very intelligent and reasonable, and I think that if the matter is put to them about reparations, that there is a good chance of their going on with us, providing we offer something in lieu thereof."

As a result of this conference, I am very much encouraged and if I could only have a chance to talk to the President alone I think I could get somewhere.

I kept saying, "Don't you want this committee to draft for you a suggestion for the American policy toward Germany?" I said it a couple of times and got nowhere and then Hull said that he had sent some paper on the economic future of Germany to Stimson, and he had not heard from Stimson. Stimson said he didn't know what he was talking about.

Hull just won't get in on the discussion, and just what his game is I don't know. As I came in, the President was asking Hull whether he didn't want to come to Quebec, and Hull said he was too tired. At the beginning of the discussion the President said, "Well, I think there will be two things brought up in Quebec. One is the military and the other is the monetary because Churchill keeps saying he is broke. . . . If they bring up the financial situation, I will want Henry to come up to Quebec." This is the second time he has said that.

But Morgenthau was nevertheless surprised by the telegram that reached him on September 12, 1944: "Please be in Quebec by Thursday, 14 September, noon. Roosevelt." The Secretary had never before attended one of the top-level Anglo-American conferences. Now, with Hull absent by his own choice, and with Hopkins temporarily in some disfavor with the President, Morgenthau had his first chance to observe, even to participate in, negotiations between the President and the Prime Minister. In part those negotiations would pertain to the problems of financing Lend-Lease that fell regularly within the Treasury's domain. In part, however, the Quebec conference — its code name was OCTAGON — would deal with Germany, about which the departments had conflicting opinions. As he left for Quebec, Morgenthau of course hoped that his goals would prevail, while Hull, in spite of his self-willed absence, resented the presence of any alternative Cabinet member, and Stimson, who believed erroneously that Morgenthau had contrived to be invited, hoped that the President would reject the Treasury's "very dangerous" counsel.

5. Octagon*

His first evening in Quebec Morgenthau attended a state dinner where the President asked him to explain the Treasury's proposals for Germany. As the Secretary wrote in a reminiscing article several years later, "I had barely got under way before low mutters and baleful looks indicated that the Prime Minister was not the most enthusiastic member of my audience. . . . I have never seen him more irascible and vitriolic than he was that night. . . . After I finished my piece he turned loose on me the full flood of his rhetoric, sarcasm and violence. He looked on the Treasury Plan, he said, as he would on chaining himself to a dead German.

"He was slumped in his chair, his language biting, his flow incessant, his manner merciless. I have never had such a verbal lashing in my life.

"The President sat by, saying very little. This was part of his way of managing Churchill. He let the Prime Minister wear himself out attacking me; he used me, so to speak, to draw the venom. Then, when the time came, he could move in with his superb and infectious humor and compose the situation. But I went unhappily to bed just the same and spent a sleepless night."

The next morning Lord Cherwell cheered Morgenthau. Churchill's attitude the previous night, Cherwell said, had surprised him; the Prime Minister had not altogether understood what Morgenthau was driving at. Cherwell himself, in contrast, seemed to agree with the Morgenthau Plan, which he and the Secretary discussed prior to their meeting at noon that day with Roosevelt, Churchill, and Eden. Morgenthau described that noon conference in his Diary only a few hours after it ended:

* For details of the negotiations at the OCTAGON Conference about Lend-Lease, see Chapter VI.

Churchill, turning to Lord Cherwell and myself, said, "Where are the minutes on this matter of the Ruhr?" Then according to our agreement we said that we didn't have them. The reason we didn't have them was because I felt, when I read the minutes which Lord Cherwell had written, that it presented much too weak a case, and I thought that we could get Churchill to go much further. He seemed quite put out that we didn't have the minutes of the previous meeting, and the President said the reason we didn't have them was because Henry interspersed the previous discussion with too many dirty jokes, and that sort of broke the ice. So Churchill broke in and said, "Well, I'll restate it," which he did, and he did it very forcefully and very clearly. Then he suggested that Lord Cherwell and I withdraw and try to do a job on dictating it, which we did. It only took us a few minutes, and we came back up to the room where they were meeting and just calmly walked in. When Churchill read our very short memorandum, he said, "No, this isn't what I want." Then he started to talk and dictate to us, and I said, "I don't know what the rules of the game are, but is there any reason why we can't have a stenographer present? Then you could dictate directly to her." He said, "By all means" and Cherwell went out and got Churchill's secretary and she came in and he began to dictate to her. He dictated the memorandum, which finally stood just the way he dictated it. He dictates extremely well because he is accustomed to doing it when he is writing his books.

While Churchill was dictating, he used the memorandum which I had dictated as a sort of a text.

Roosevelt's important contribution, while Churchill was dictating, was that when he got talking about the metallurgical, chemical and electrical industries, Roosevelt had him insert the very important words "in Germany." What Roosevelt meant — because it came up later — that he didn't have in mind just the Ruhr and the Saar, but he had in mind entire Germany and that the matter we were talking about, namely, the ease with which metallurgical, chemical and electrical industries in Germany can be converted from peace to war, does not only apply to the Ruhr and the Saar, but the whole of Germany, which of course is terribly important.

When Churchill got through, Eden seemed quite shocked at what he heard, and he turned to Churchill and said, "You can't do this. After all, you and I publicly have said quite the opposite. Furthermore, we have a lot of things in the works in London which are quite different." Then Churchill and Eden seemed to have quite a bit of argument about it. Roosevelt took no part in it, and I took a small part and kept throwing things in. Churchill's main argument was what this meant in the way of trade; they would get the export trade of Germany. So Eden said, "How do you know what it is or where it is?" and Churchill answered him quite testily, "Well, we will get it wherever it is." I was quite amazed and shocked at Eden's attitude; in fact, it was so different from the way he talked when we were in London. Finally Churchill said, "Now I hope, Anthony, you're not going to do anything about this with the War Cabinet if you see a chance to present it. . . . After all, the future of my people is at stake, and I when I have to choose between my people and the German people, I am going to choose my people." Churchill got quite nasty with Eden and I understand from the President that all the rest of the day Eden was not at all helpful. The President was quite disappointed.

Of course the fact that Churchill has dictated this himself strengthens the whole matter tremendously. Naturally, I am terrifically happy over it as we got just what we started out to get.

So Morgenthau had, for Churchill's dictated memorandum, dated September 15, 1944, and initialed by the President and the Prime Minister, expressed a stern view toward Germany:

"At the conference between the President and the Prime Minister upon the best measures to prevent renewed rearmament by Germany, it was felt that an essential feature was the future disposition of the Ruhr and the Saar.

"The ease with which the metallurgical, chemical and electrical industries in Germany can be converted from peace to war has already been impressed upon us by bitter experience. It must also be remembered that the Germans have devastated a large portion of the industries of Russia and of other neighboring Allies, and it is only in accordance with justice that these injured countries should be entitled to remove the machinery they require in order to repair the losses they have suffered. The industries referred to in the Ruhr and in the Saar would therefore be necessarily put out of action and closed down. It was felt that the two districts should be put under somebody under the world organization which would supervise the dismantling of these industries and make sure that they were not started up again by some subterfuge.

"The program for eliminating the war-making industries in the Ruhr and in the Saar is looking forward to converting Germany into a country primarily agricultural and pastoral in its character."

At Roosevelt's invitation, Morgenthau returned for an evening conference that day. According to the Secretary's account in his Diary immediately thereafter:

"I got in about 6:00 and stayed until after 7:30. I tried several times to get up to go because I thought the President wanted to rest, but he evidently just wanted to sit and talk. We haven't had a talk like this since almost going back to the time when he was governor. He was completely relaxed, and the conversation was entirely on the week's work.

"While I was waiting for the President . . . I was sitting there talking with Grace Tully and Admiral Leahy. . . . He said that they had only settled that afternoon what part of Germany the English would go into, and what part the USA would go into. In the morning when I arrived at 12:00 the President was sitting alone in his room with three different colored pencils and a map of Europe, and he then and there sketched out where he wanted to go and where he wanted the English to go. . . . He had before him a map of the Combined Chiefs of Staff, which he said was terrible. According to Admiral Leahy, this afternoon the President showed Churchill his map and got what he wanted. . . . Leahy . . . was very happy because he said that the English were going to occupy the Ruhr and the Saar and they would have to carry this thing out.*

"Late in the afternoon in my discussion with the President, to my surprise he told me that Leahy had been favorable to my plan. The President said that he had withheld bringing up this question of where our armies should go because he wanted to get Churchill in a good humor and wanted everything else settled.

* The United States would occupy the southern zone, contrary to Roosevelt's earlier preferences at Teheran.

"The President was very relaxed and not at all tired. I asked him what he meant about the suggestion of having the United Nations meet at the end of October*, and he said he felt it had taken much too long to bring up the League of Nations after World War I, and he wanted to do this in October. So I said, 'Well, it makes good window dressing for the campaign,' and he said, 'Yes.' "

Back in Washington, Morgenthau told his staff that "the thing up at Quebec . . . was unbelievably good. . . . As far as I went personally, it was the high spot of my whole career in the Government. . . . And the thing that attracted Churchill the most was a suggestion that they would get the German export business that is the bait that he bit and swallowed and got hooked so deep that he couldn't . . . cough it up. Of course, the parallel all through this was the so-called Phase II — Lend-Lease — . . . which was agreed to. . . .† I can't over-emphasize how helpful Lord Cherwell was because he would advise me how to handle Churchill. . . . Roosevelt was very firm through the whole thing, and I imagine the reason he sent for me was he had tried this [the Morgenthau Plan] out on Churchill and got nowhere. He then cabled me to come on up."

Herbert Gaston observed that the Quebec memorandum "goes beyond what you proposed making it primarily agricultural and pastoral." Morgenthau said that had been his intention from the time that he had visited England, but the word "pastoral" — "that was Churchill."

Harry White, who had accompanied Morgenthau to Quebec, suggested a month later that Churchill had accepted the Morgenthau Plan as a quid pro quo for American assurances about Stage II of Lend-Lease. Churchill, White recalled, had had difficulty persuading Roosevelt to sign the Lend-Lease document. "What do you want me to do," Churchill asked at one point, "stand up and beg like Fala?" But Roosevelt had agreed to the document after Churchill's oral consent to Morgenthau's proposals for Germany.

Morgenthau thought White's memory was wrong. At dinner, the Secretary recalled, Churchill had indeed opposed the German plan, but "the next morning he came around, but Mr. Roosevelt wouldn't discuss the Lend-Lease thing until the second morning." The Prime Minister, Morgenthau had reported within a few days of the Quebec

---

* Later postponed six months.
† See Chapter VI, above.

meeting, "agreed to the policy on Germany prior to the final drafting" of the memo on Lend-Lease. Still, White believed that in the minds of the British, the German and the Lend-Lease matters were tied together.

Morgenthau recognized then and later that the two questions had had some bearing upon each other at Quebec, but he never thought that he and Churchill had struck a bargain in any direct sense. Further, during the autumn of 1944 he continued to advocate American assistance to Great Britain during Stage II even though Churchill in that time backed away from the agreement on Germany. The Prime Minister then responded both to his own second thoughts and to the pressures on him from Eden, from others in his Cabinet, and from the Parliament. During the same period, Morgenthau was fighting to prevent similar pressures from influencing Roosevelt.

VIII

The Problem of Germany

1944-1945

THE QUEBEC MEMORANDUM on Germany settled less than Morgenthau at first believed. As he discovered, the language of the agreement needed interpretation. The provision for closing down the industry of the Saar and Rhur did not necessarily demand the degree of destruction of mines and other installations that Morgenthau had contemplated in earlier comments to his staff. A country "primarily agricultural and pastoral" might remain secondarily industrial. There was no indication of the amount of deindustrialization that Roosevelt and Churchill had in mind. Further, their memorandum did not indicate precisely what territory Germany was to include, whether or in what manner Germany was to be partitioned permanently, if at all, and how those and other objectives were to be reached. Most immediately, the President had yet to approve any directive for the American occupation of Germany, and primary responsibility for the drafting of such a directive still lay with the War Department, just as the State Department retained a primary voice in the formulation of American policy for the period after the occupation. Roosevelt had given Morgenthau and the Treasury a place on the committee concerned with those questions, but in spite of his success at Quebec, the Secretary had by no means committed either Hull or Stimson to his program.

1. Retreat from OCTAGON

Morgenthau reported to the Secretaries of State and of War on September 20, 1944. "He did it marvelously," Stimson noted in his

Diary, "and without rubbing it in, but it was the narration of a pretty heavy defeat for everything that we had fought for." Where Stimson was saddened, Hull was disgruntled because in his absence Roosevelt had made foreign policy at Quebec. Both, moreover, were resolved to fight to overturn the Quebec memorandum.

That fight entailed a direct confrontation between Morgenthau and Stimson. In his earlier memoranda to the President, the Secretary of War had attacked the Morgenthau Plan for being vengeful toward the Germans and dangerous for the economy of Europe. Morgenthau replied to those criticisms in a memorandum for Roosevelt of September 20, 1944. Stimson's suggestion for leaving the German economy virtually intact, Morgenthau argued, "would permit Germany within a period of fifteen to twenty-five years to become so strong economically, and as a consequence politically and militarily, that she could again be instrumental in bringing to these nations of good will even greater death, horror and destruction than she has caused in this war. It was this same attitude of appeasement that was so fruitful in helping Germany plunge the world into the present war."

Stimson, as Morgenthau interpreted him, labored under misconceptions about the Treasury's program. The Treasury's objective was not punitive; rather, "its purpose is highly humanitarian. . . . The motivating factor is the welfare of human beings throughout the world." Regardless of the nature of the program for Germany, the German people would have a hard time during the several years after their defeat. The very fact of defeat would result in intense suffering. But after a transition of five or ten years, the Treasury program, Morgenthau maintained, would permit the Germans to adjust to a fuller life. More important, outside of Germany the welfare of some two billion people was at stake. During the war Germany had caused the death of more human beings than there were within her own borders, and in another war she would destroy still more if she were permitted to rebuild her army. "The more effective it is in preventing World War III," Morgenthau said of his plan, "the more humanitarian it will be." The Morgenthau Plan, he went on, would not arrest Germany's economic development. Rather, it would channel that development along lines fruitful for peacetime pursuits. The energies that Germans had previously devoted to war would be devoted to social services. Accordingly, there was no need to presume that the Morgenthau Plan would give rise to suffering or bitterness, beyond that inherent in defeat itself.

Morgenthau did not write about one foundation for his convictions. His profession, he frequently said, was that of an apple farmer. He had always loved life on the land. More than that, he believed that those engaged in agriculture achieved a contentment that managers and workers in industry could only rarely and incompletely enjoy. He was a Jeffersonian, a devotee of agricultural society as the nearest equivalent to an Eden on earth, as the garden in which men cultivated not only the land but also their souls, from which they reaped their understanding of each other, of community, of human dignity and democratic behavior. In a pastoral country, then, the German people would not only lack the means to embark again on a mission of conquest; they would also find the means to reconstruct themselves. By contrast, Stimson's vision of postwar Germany struck Morgenthau both as menacing to the world and as preventing the reformation of the German spirit.

For his part, Stimson could see the Morgenthau Plan only as a function of Jewish vengeance. Yet there were eminent, Christian men, like James B. Conant, who in 1944 supported the plan, and eminent, influential Jews, like Felix Frankfurter, who opposed it. Neither Stimson nor Morgenthau understood the motives of the other, perhaps largely because both were so confident of their own integrity and so zealous in their quest for the allegiance of the President.

Roosevelt, close to Morgenthau at Quebec, soon returned to the ambiguous position he had struck before the Secretary's trip to England. Churchill's change of heart surely influenced the President, as possibly also did the continuing Russian demand for reparations out of current production, which the Morgenthau Plan forbade. Doubtless, too, Stimson's arguments made some mark. But the precipitating factor in the President's new caution about German policy was the public reaction to a series of leaks that divulged the contents of the Morgenthau Plan and of the Quebec Agreement, still officially secret.

In the Washington *Post* on September 21, 1944, Drew Pearson reported on the rift within the Cabinet about the "Handbook" for

Germany. His column, based on an unauthorized but informed account, referred to the blistering letter that Roosevelt had written
Stimson about that "Handbook." Arthur Krock published a similar
story in the *New York Times* on September 22. The next day the
Wall Street Journal described the main details of the Morgenthau
Plan, noting that it was not yet official policy and that there was
considerable opposition to it within the Cabinet. On September 24,
John Hightower wrote further on the same subject for the Washington *Evening Star* in the first of three articles that provided a remark-
ably accurate narrative of much of the debate within the Cabinet
since Morgenthau's return from England. And Krock on September
29 wrote about the "value of publicity" in a column that announced
that the President had returned the responsibility for planning for
Germany to the Department of State. Adverse reactions to the Morgenthau Plan, Krock judged, had influenced the President, as had
the propaganda of high-ranking Nazis who were spurring the Germans to renewed resistance to the Allied troops by warning them of
the Quebec program for the Reich.

Krock's conclusions were only partly true. Goebbels had attacked
the Morgenthau Plan on the German radio and in the German
press, but the Office of Strategic Services doubted that propaganda
any longer made a difference within Germany. Rather, the state of
the battle for Europe, and in particular the attenuation of Allied
lines of supply just at the time when the Germans were mounting a
counteroffensive, explained the growing difficulties on the Western
Front. But some American newspapers had criticized the Morgenthau Plan severely, and while others had endorsed it, the criticism
troubled Roosevelt during the early weeks of his campaign for a
fourth term. Further, his opponent, Governor Thomas Dewey of
New York, not only attacked the Morgenthau Plan but also blamed
it for the intensity of the fighting near the German border.

On several counts Morgenthau lamented those developments. He
had never condoned the disclosure of classified information by anyone in any department. More important, he considered the question of planning for Germany not yet a proper matter for public
debate. Rather, it seemed to him essential for Roosevelt first to reconcile divergent views within the Administration. Morgenthau also
realized that the leaks militated to the Treasury's disadvantage. So

it was that he resented an editorial in the Washington *Post* that called the Morgenthau Plan "the product of a fevered mind." More significantly, he worried about the effects of the leaks on Roosevelt. With the President characteristically shy of any unnecessary controversy during a campaign, with the Republicans condemning the Morgenthau Plan, the Secretary knew, as he put it to his staff, that he would have to lie low until the election was over. "This isn't the first time that I have been the whipping boy for the President," he said, "and I have taken it on taxes again and again. . . . So don't worry; I can take it. . . . I have not yet had any indication from the President that he has changed. I don't agree . . . that he is going to change."

But for the time being, Roosevelt was also not going to associate himself with the Morgenthau Plan. The President dissolved the Cabinet committee on German policy. Further, as Morgenthau noted in his Diary on September 29, 1944: "I went . . . over and saw Anna Boettiger, and I gave her all of my clippings on the German Plan, and asked her to particularly show the President the one of Krock's. . . . So she said, 'Oh, the President knows all about this.' So I said, 'Please take it in and show it to him. . . . I think he ought to get Hull, Stimson and me together in the room and read the law to all of us, and tell us to stop talking. . . . The first thing you know they're going to spread it that the President has signed an agreement with Churchill on this thing. It is bad politically and it is bad by the inference on the Jewish angle. . . . I will stay here outside the President's door in case he should want to see me.'

"She came out in a couple of minutes, and put her hand on my arm and sort of gently but forcibly started to move me away, and she said that the President didn't want to see me, and she kept moving me toward the elevator. She said, 'All I know is that the President said he definitely doesn't want to see you.' . . .

"Then I dropped in to see Hopkins and told him I had taken his advice, but the President said we were both wrong. Hopkins for the first time read Krock's article, and he thought it was very vicious. Nobody hates Roosevelt as much as Krock does, and I pointed out to him that the next story would be that Roosevelt bribed Churchill with $6 billion Lend-Lease to be favorable to what he wanted to do in the Ruhr and Saar, and Hopkins said, 'He practically says that in this article.' . . . Hopkins said that he was convinced that if this matter had been left to Hull and me, we would have had no trouble but that Stimson . . . had made trouble. He didn't imply that Stimson had talked to the newspapermen at all."

Indeed Stimson had not, and neither had Morgenthau, but Roosevelt did. At his press conference on September 29 he denied flatly that there had been a breach within the Cabinet about Germany. In the course of the denial, moreover, Roosevelt made public a letter he had written Leo Crowley, the head of the Foreign Economic Administration, instructing him to work out an economic policy for Germany, a policy relating to the control of exports, to strategic and critical raw materials, to the control of Germany's war-making power, and to Lend-Lease during the remaining war against Japan, as well as to the reconstruction of Europe and future foreign trade.

On the same day Roosevelt privately instructed the State Department alone to "study and report upon the problem" of Germany, and he told Hull that "no one wants 'complete eradication of German industrial productive capacity in the Ruhr and Saar.'" Further, the President sent a memorandum to the Secretaries of State, War, and Treasury, that suggested a division of functions in planning for Germany which restricted the Treasury to questions of finance. "It is desirable," the President's memorandum read, "that civilian experts be recruited for the American section of the Allied Control Commission for Germany. For such recruiting, I suggest that the Army call upon the State Department for civilians for political work; upon the Foreign Economic Administration for civilians for economic work; and upon the Treasury for experts in finance and exchange."

The President had already told Stimson, according to Stimson's report in his diary, that he did not really intend to make Germany a purely agricultural country. His motive, Roosevelt said, was to help pull England out of its postwar depression. Later he said as much to Hull, too. On October 3, 1944, again according to Stimson's diary entry, Roosevelt "grinned and looked naughty and said 'Henry Morgenthau pulled a boner' or an equivalent expression, and said that we really were not apart on that; that he has no intention of turning Germany into an agrarian state and that all he wanted was to save a portion of the proceeds of the Ruhr for use by Great Britain which was 'broke.' . . . He got so affirmative to this effect that I warned him that the paper which Churchill had drawn and which he had initaled did contain the proposition of converting Germany 'into a country primarily agricultural and pastoral in its character,' and I read him three sentences. . . . He was frankly staggered by this and said he had no idea how he could have initialed this. . . .

"I told him that in my opinion the most serious danger of the situation was the getting abroad the idea of vengeance instead of preventive punishment and it was the language in the Treasury paper which had alarmed me on this subject. . . . I said throughout the war his leadership had been on a high moral plane. . . . Now during the post-war adjustment 'you must not poison this position.' "

Morgenthau, of course, knew nothing of Roosevelt's conversation with Stimson, nor was he aware of the instructions the President had given Hull. The directive for Crowley, Morgenthau judged, had been a kind of red herring intended by Roosevelt to lay to rest newspaper reports about a split within the Cabinet. But red herring or no, it demonstrated that the President would tolerate no statement from a Cabinet member suggesting that such a split had occurred. Morgenthau therefore, as he told his staff on October 5, planned to draw back from further consideration of Germany until after the election. "I think we have seen the worst of this," the Secretary said. "My mail seems to indicate that . . . we have turned the corner, and I think the thing is going to get better for us. If it doesn't, I want to do something. I don't want to go into a long explanation, but take it from me . . . I have tried everything I could possibly do . . . and I was unsuccessful. . . . I'd like to mark time and see what happens. . . . I don't want to do much more between now and the seventh of November. . . . Then . . . I'd like to sit around and have a real discussion of where do we go from here." Meanwhile White, Luxford, and DuBois were to begin to draft a book explaining and defending the Morgenthau Plan.

In the month before election day Morgenthau tried to find the source of the leaks to the press. Privately Stimson attributed the blame to the Treasury, for he felt that Drew Pearson had been attempting to advance its point of view. Morgenthau thought the trouble lay with the State Department, largely because Krock had for so long been so close to Hull. But an investigation that Morgenthau conducted with Stettinius yielded only negative evidence. Though Stimson's suspicions were obviously misdirected, the culprit remained unidentified, while whoever he was, he had offended the Secretary of the Treasury as much as he had irritated the Secretary of War.

There was for Morgenthau a further painful episode. In the last speech of his campaign, Governor Dewey charged that the Morgenthau Plan had cost American lives needlessly. "The publishing of this plan," Dewey maintained, had done as much good as "ten fresh German divisions." Replying to an inquiry from Morgenthau, Stimson wrote on November 17, 1944, that there was no "basis whatever for such criticism of you as that made by Governor Dewey. At the time when the rumors as to the Treasury Plan became public the rapid advance of the Allied armies through France had already reached their finish. The German retreat had already reached the Siegfried Line, and the Germans had begun to make their still defense behind those fortifications. . . . I do not think that the use of the rumor by the Nazi propagandists made any substantial change in the situation whatever."

But the leaks and the responses to them had made a substantial change in the balance of influence within the Cabinet. On the basis to Roosevelt's instructions of September 29, Hull had presented a revised State Department plan for Germany that called for postponing a decision about the partition of the country and for destroying only those factories "incapable of conversion to peaceful purposes." While the President replied only indirectly to those proposals, noting that he disliked making "detailed plans for a country which we do not yet occupy," he made no mention whatsoever of the Morgenthau Plan or of its terms in his carefully moderate comments about Germany in a speech of October 21 before the Foreign Policy Association in New York. At that time it no longer seemed, as it had in September, that Germany was about to surrender, and Roosevelt apparently intended to postpone final decisions about German policy for weeks or even months. The President's mood, on the whole encouraging to Hull, weakened without eliminating the influence of the Treasury on the ongoing drafting of a military directive for the occupation of Germany, JCS 1067. All in all, by election day Morgenthau had lost most of the ground he had gained just before and during OCTAGON. On November 7, with Roosevelt's reelection accomplished, he hoped soon to recoup.

2. JCS 1067

During the fall of 1944, the War Department supervised the drafting of the directive on post-surrender policy in Germany which was eventually issued by the Joint Chiefs of Staff under the title JCS 1067. In Washington both the Treasury and the State Department participated in the work on JCS 1067, over which John J. McCloy exercised a general command. Though the Washington drafts governed the supplementary work of the United States Group Control Council, that group, like its British counterpart, continually advocated a moderate policy toward Germany. The Civil Affairs Division of SHAEF in London, however, insisted that the United States Army should administer its zone of occupation in Germany with scant reference to overall control from Berlin. The Army's professional concern in some degree sustained the Treasury's position on German policy. So, too, did the particular influence of Colonel Bernard Bernstein, long associated with Morgenthau, who served both as chief of the Finance Division of the Civil Affairs Division of SHAEF and as the Director of the Finance Division of the Group Control Council in London. Bernstein sponsored Morgenthau's objectives and kept the Secretary informed about his opponents. Within Washington, Treasury officials received similar assistance from Colonel David Marcus, a member and later the chief of the Planning Branch of the Civil Affairs Division in the War Department. More important, the Quebec agreement on Germany, even after Roosevelt retreated from it, exerted a subtle, lingering influence on War Department officials.

Morgenthau therefore operated from a position of strength when in November 1944, he turned his attention to JCS 1067. He had worried about occupation policy in Germany since he had first seen the "Handbook." Now he adverted to that question with renewed interest on two accounts. First, he learned from McCloy on November 1, 1944, about the President's reply to the October memorandum of the State Department on Germany. As McCloy explained it, Roosevelt had "made it very strong" that he did not want to consider questions of partition, reparations, and deindustrialization of the Ruhr. Rather, he preferred to postpone discussion of those and related matters until after Germany surrendered. That order in itself gave a priority to the shaping of occupation policy, which in any event had to be ready for Eisenhower's guidance once the fighting in Europe stopped. So informed, Morgenthau was moved to examine JCS 1067 by his dismay over a British draft for occupation policy in Germany which he had also received from McCloy.

In a memorandum severely critical of the British policy, the Treasury especially objected to its failure to eliminate or destroy heavy Germany industry, its failure to partition Germany or to internationalize or otherwise control the Ruhr, and its ambiguity about restitution and reparations. In the Treasury's view, the British paper would not prevent the reemergence of a powerful industrial Germany, would not break up the Prussian Junker estates, and would not adequately punish war criminals. Further, the British seemed to have produced a long-range document inadequate for the purposes of the occupation, and overly concerned about maintaining the German body politic.

It fell to McCloy to respond for the War Department to the Treasury's objections. Stimson had removed himself from the controversy over Germany. The Secretary of War was tired, deeply engaged in other affairs, including the planning of the war in the Pacific, and above all dismayed by the Morgenthau Plan and by the President's meandering sympathies for it. Determined to let others settle policy for the ultimate treatment of Germany, Stimson delegated to McCloy responsibility for overseeing the interim policy, for negotiating with the State and Treasury Departments about it, and for fashioning it in a manner that would ease Eisenhower's initial management of the occupation. McCloy, a wise and adaptable man, devoted to Stimson and dedicated to public service, was also a tactful and effective bargainer. Though he objected to the industrial provisions in the Morgenthau Plan, though he had also some sharp reservations about its political content, he was as resolved as was Morgenthau himself to crush nazism, and as resolved as was Eisenhower to make the functioning of military government in Germany as easy and as efficient as possible. On occasion therefore in agreement with Morgenthau, McCloy was always friendly, cooperative, and patient. When he disagreed with the Secretary, he ordinarily avoided controversy by saying nothing, while at the same time yielding as little as he could to Morgenthau's preferences. He did so, moreover, with an unvarying charm and restraint that won Morgenthau's trust and affection. Indeed in the Secretary's opinion no one in Washington had contributed more than had McCloy to the management of the war against the Axis, and no one responsible for planning for Germany, outside of the Treasury, was as compatible a colleague.

When on November 1, 1944, they reviewed the British directive for Germany, Morgenthau warmed to McCloy's criticisms, many of which were identical with the Treasury's. Like Morgenthau, McCloy found the British document unsuitable for interim use, too much addressed to the preservation of the German state, too little focused on the arrest and detention of Nazis. So also, he agreed that the only practical policy for education in Germany was to close all schools until they could be purged of Nazi influence and doctrine. "The English definitely take the line," McCloy said, "they think they are going into a country where there will be a government, and they are going to have control of that government. We have taken, perhaps, too purely the other line, that there will be no government. . . . But the military government is the only government that exists in Germany, and although we can use functionaries throughout Germany, they are instruments only, and they are responsible to the military. Yet we, at the same time, say to the General [Eisenhower] 'you are not responsible for the fundamental economy of the country,' and we sort of recognize that the Germans themselves will have to cover a certain field there, subject to our stepping in." The British approach, he continued, treated Germany as if there were to be an armistice rather than an unconditional surrender, retained German administrative structures to an undesirable extent and assumed a uniformity of conditions throughout Germany which would, as McCloy saw it, deprive American commanders of the full freedom of action they needed. Finally, McCloy encouraged Morgenthau to explain the Treasury's attitude, and the War Department's too, to Lord Cherwell, who was scheduled for luncheon with the Secretary.

The United States, Morgenthau told Cherwell, was not yet ready to formulate a long-range program for Germany. The British document, in the American view, was too lengthy and too detailed for an interim program, and, more important, it deviated from the general principles that guided JCS 1067. Cherwell, after examining the Treasury's memorandum on the British draft, endorsed Morgenthau's criticisms. He promised to pass them along in Great Britain and to urge the English military to bring their directive into line. But in London, as it developed, the British military remained unhappy with JCS 1067, particularly with those parts most directly derived from the Morgenthau Plan, while in Washington, the War Department continued to try to soften the American draft.

Replying to an inquiry from Morgenthau, Stimson on November 27, 1944, noted that the British would probably refuse to throw the Germans on their own responsibility. Rather, the British would tend to place responsibility for the German economy as well as for German government on their own occupation forces. As for the Russians, Stimson continued, they had yet to comment on the American directive. The only indication of their attitude toward the occupation came from studies of the Office of Strategic Service. Those studies, which the Secretary of War enclosed, predicted that Russia's long-run aims in Germany, as well as her desire for reparations, would dictate a policy designed to prevent the economic collapse of the zone she occupied. OSS expected the Russians to emphasize the collection of reparations out of current output rather than out of standing machinery and equipment. That would turn the Russians away from deindustrialization. For political and ideological reasons, the Russians would try to cleanse from the German economy the Nazis and their collaborators among industrialists and landowners, they might well take over the railroads and utilities, and they would probably confiscate large-scale enterprises and estates, but their emphasis on reparations would lead them away from the core of the Morgenthau Plan.

Insofar as American intelligence could ascertain, then, the Russians, like the British, would govern their zone of occupation according to standards unlike those of JCS 1067. Only in that document, in the draft version he received on December 7, 1944, could Morgenthau find any expression of his own objective. According to that draft, the essence of American policy was "that no effort will be made to rehabilitate or succor the German people. Rather, the sole aim of Military Goverment is to further military objectives." Germany was not to be "liberated" but to be treated as an occupied and defeated nation. The German people were to be made to realize that all necessary steps would be taken to prevent them from again attempting to conquer the world. Army personnel would be disabused of the doctrine that it was the American job to make Germany a "happy land" again. Soldiers were not to fraternize. And "no steps will be taken looking toward the economic rehabilitation of Germany nor designed to maintain or strengthen the German economy except those needed to prevent epidemics or serious diseases and serious civil disorder which would endanger the forces and to prevent the dissipation or sabotage of German equipment required for Allied countries."

That last statement, so important to Morgenthau, remained the subject of debate in Washington. Neither Stimson nor McCloy would have tolerated it had not the Treasury interceded in September to sponsor it. By December, most army officers in the field, at SHAEF, and in the Civil Affairs Division in Washington, opposed it, largely because of the difficulties in applying it. On December 19, 1944, John Boettiger, speaking for McCloy as well as for himself, explained to Morgenthau the problems the Army had met in Aachen. As the Secretary reported their conversation to his staff, Boettiger had told him there were visible no Germans who were "sympathetic to the Allies." The Germans, moreover, had been systematically uncooperative. And Aachen was in shambles — "there isn't a building . . . which has a roof on it." Boettiger therefore believed that the occupation authorities would have to assume control in Aachen, not only to prevent disorder there but also to use local production facilities to supply other parts of Europe.

"He thinks," Morgenthau said, "that we ought to tell the Germans what they should pay for wages, prices, and supervise distribution to keep them from going into chaos, and that the economists . . . people in the War Department say that Europe needs the coal from Germany. . . . He said that Bernstein is an extremist. . . . He said there was a lot of food in Germany. Should we build up the mines, or shouldn't we? If we build up the mines, we have to feed the people who do the mines. We have to transport the coal out. He thinks that we should have a very tough administration of the Germans.

"Boettiger . . . . says we have to supervise lower down wages, prices, and distribution, or throw Germany into . . . complete chaos . . . have revolutions, and all of Europe will have a revolution."

Boettiger had asked Morgenthau whether he agreed. "Now that I understand what you mean," the Secretary had replied, ". . . my answer is no. . . . We don't want that responsibility. . . . That is what the President had been saying right along, 'Let the Germans decide. . . . We don't want to be responsible for the price of the mark.' . . .

"You can tell McCloy I will be delighted to see him, but as of today my position hasn't changed one iota. . . . I don't want to destroy Germany, I want them to take care of themselves as we leave it."

Once again Boettiger had said that "if you don't do something, there is going to be complete chaos," and once more Morgenthau had replied that, as he understood it, the President since Quebec had wanted "to wait and see." Boettiger and others in the War Department, Morgenthau told his staff, "dislike us heartily."

Boettiger, the Secretary also remarked ruefully, was eating two meals a day with the President; it was "getting lonesomer and lonesomer." But when Dan Bell suggested that the Treasury position was too extreme, Morgenthau criticized the Army and the State Department for being too soft. He intended to stay tough, and he was "tickled to death" that "these people have a wholesome respect for the Treasury opinion."

Stiffened rather than moved by Boettiger's report, Morgenthau responded identically to criticisms from the State Department. That department sent him a cable from Winant which contained a message from Robert Murphy, Eisenhower's political adviser. Long convinced that Murphy was an appeaser, Morgenthau rejected his plea for revising JCS 1067 so as to instruct the occupation authorities to take steps to prevent inflation. More important, Murphy argued that a large-scale removal of German governmental, industrial, and financial officials would create a vacuum in government that would in turn encourage chaotic social and economic conditions. The first of those points, Morgenthau believed, ran counter to the President's purpose as well as his own; and the second contemplated the retention and thus the rewarding of high-ranking Nazis.

Seeking exactly the opposite objectives, Morgenthau successfully demanded that McCloy restore to JCS 1067 a sentence stating that "it may generally be assumed in the absence of evidence to the contrary" that any German holding even minor positions in government was a Nazi or Nazi sympathizer. That sentence, as Morgenthau read it, put the burden of proof on the Germans rather than on American military officers. He also had McCloy incorporate in JCS 1067 a phrase asserting that in arranging for the collection of taxes in Germany, American officers assumed no responsibility for German fiscal affairs. That responsibility, by implication, remained instead with the Germans themselves, as did responsibility for the control of inflation.

Most markedly, the section of JCS 1067 on financial matters reflected the Treasury's policy, molded largely by Colonel Bernstein, who advanced Morgenthau's views. Bernstein saw to it that the Treasury's draft of the Financial Directive made explicit the responsibility of the Germans for taxation and public finance. He and others in the Treasury also wrote into the directive orders to the zonal commander, subject only to a veto by the Allied Control Council, that forbade him to establish any general rate of exchange between the Reichsmark and the dollar and other currencies, except for use in the payment of troops and for military accounting. Further, without his specific authorization, no government or private bank or agency could issue bank notes or currency. He could require German authorities to make available Reichsmarks or bank credits free of cost and in amounts sufficient to meet all expenses of the forces of occupation, including the costs of Allied Military Government. He was to prohibit or regulate dealings in private or public securities and real estate and other property. He was to close stock exchanges and insurance companies and similar institutions until he had completed the de-nazification of their personnel. He was to prohibit the payment of military pensions or other emoluments to former members of the Nazi Party or its affiliates. He was to prohibit or regulate all dealings in gold, silver, foreign exchange, and all foreign financial and trade transactions of any kind. He was forbidden to authorize any outlay of German foreign exchange assets for imports, and forbidden to make credits available to the Reichsbank or any other public or private bank or institution except on an emergency basis.

With the completion of the draft of the Financial Directive, Morgenthau felt that he had, for the time being, done all he could to mold occupation policy. After January 1945, he left further negotiations about that subject largely to his subordinates. His own interests, even before that date, had come to focus again on long-range policy for Germany, especially on the State Department's emerging proposals.

3. To Yalta and Beyond

During the late fall of 1944, the State Department strengthened its voice in the making of German policy. A new State-War-Navy Coordinating Committee facilitated the cooperation of Cabinet officers of moderate opinions — Stimson, Stettinius, and Secretary of the Navy James Forrestal, who was to announce his disapproval of the "enslavement" of Germans and of the industrial devastation of their country. Charles E. Bohlen, for whom Harry Hopkins arranged an appointment as liaison officer between the State Department and the President, brought intellectual vigor, broad experience with Soviet affairs, and a suspicion of Soviet motives to the preparation of memoranda on Germany. Perhaps most important, the President's apparent indecision encouraged State Department officers to press their objections to the Morgenthau Plan.

They did so emphatically in a draft statement on economic policy submitted to Roosevelt on November 10, 1944. The paper asserted that both Great Britain and the Soviet Union intended to retain much of the existing organization, structure, and productivity of the German economy. That purpose, the argument continued, would not threaten Britain's export markets. A conflicting American purpose, however, would endanger tripartite cooperation, while any "sweeping deindustrialization" would undermine international security programs in Europe. It would be essential, the State Department concluded, for the occupying powers to guide the German economy away from autarky but also to prevent "development of a chaotically unmanageable economic situation."

Morgenthau's contrasting opinions won timely support on November 13, 1944, from the Senate Subcommittee on War Mobilization, of which Harley M. Kilgore of West Virginia was chairman. "A real disarmament program," the Kilgore Committee then reported, "requires not only the dismantling of all direct munitions industries but also the dismantling and removal to the devastated areas of Europe of the primarily indirect munitions industries including the metallurgical and chemical industries. . . . Those who have urged that all industry, other then direct armament manufacture, be left intact have overlooked the fact that for more than thirty years all of German industry has been closely integrated as a munitions economy." In order "to crush German imperialism permanently," the committee recommended altering "the structure and control of German industry . . . so . . . that it cannot again serve the purposes of war."

"I thought you got out a swell report," Morgenthau told Kilgore. His committee had been working on German materials for a year, the Senator replied, and he had personally concluded that "you were badly misinterpreted. . . . I think your plan and mine fairly well coincide. . . . And I think it's the real solution."

The report also impressed Roosevelt. "Yesterday the President said that since the Kilgore Report came out," Morgenthau told his staff on November 16, "as far as he is concerned, what the public thinks now he doesn't care. He thinks the Kilgore Report was so wonderful." Roosevelt also told Morgenthau to examine the draft paper on the German economy which the State Department had sent to the White House. "I didn't know anything about it," Morgenthau told Stettinius on November 16, "but he brought it up and said that this was in the works and he wanted my advice and wanted me to go over it. . . . Since the Kilgore Committee and the publicity they got, his attitude on this whole business is just like lifting a cloud." The State Department memorandum, Stettinius replied, "might not go far enough to satisfy you and if it doesn't . . . we ought to thrash it out." Morgenthau agreed that the two departments should exchange views before either made final recommendations to the President.

Roosevelt's invitation to Morgenthau to review economic policy probably surprised Stettinius, who had gathered from the President earlier in the day that the draft paper met his general approval. Now, with the Treasury again a factor, the State Department modified its position. Its "Summary . . . Views on Economic Treatment of Germany," dated November 22, 1944, also reflected the President's statement, reported by Stettinius, that "he was still in a tough mood and . . . is determined to be tough with Germany." The "Summary . . . Views" called for a "rock-bottom standard of living for the Germans," for transfer of industrial equipment as reparations "limited only by necessity for maintaining a minimum German economy," for the conversion of that economy to peacetime production, for the elimination of those identified with nazism from high industrial positions, but also for the operation of the economy "as nearly as possible as a unit." There was no mention of deindustrialization, and there was a strong reminder of the importance of Germany in the long run in the economic interdependence of the European nations. The two departments were still far apart.*

Nevertheless Morgenthau liked Stettinius, who had been acting as Secretary of State for several months. Hull, ill and bitter, had deferred resigning only to avoid embarrassing the President before the election. When at last Hull left, Morgenthau supported Stettinius for the vacant office, most candidly on November 27, 1944, in a conversation with Eleanor Roosevelt:

"I said that I didn't think Stettinius would be ideal, but I thought he was the best man I could think of from the President's standpoint as the President likes to be his own Secretary of State, and what he wanted was merely a good clerk. I said, 'If he puts Byrnes in on the theory that he has a lot of influence on the Hill, I don't think the President could get legislation through that way. . . . The only way for him to do it is to go directly to the people.' Eleanor agreed. I said, 'Furthermore, I don't think the President would be comfortable with Byrnes, and from past experience I wouldn't be, and it would be only a matter of a couple of months before I would want to get out because I couldn't and wouldn't take that sort of thing any more.' She said, 'What about Wallace for

* The November 22 draft became part of the material included within the pouch the State Department prepared for Roosevelt to take to Yalta, see below, this section.

Secretary of State?' and I said, 'No.' . . . Mrs. Roosevelt said, 'What about Winant?' and I said no, that he wasn't a good enough administrator."

The matter was settled that day. In a note to Morgenthau mailed some hours later, Stettinius wrote: "I appreciate with all my heart your having taken the trouble to call me as I went into the President's office for lunch. . . . Your support and your confidence means more to me than you know." Like McCloy, Stettinius had already established a good working relationship with Morgenthau, though again like McCloy, the new Secretary of State disagreed with his colleague about German policy. Yet unlike Hull, Stettinius knew how to disagree without rancor, and unlike Stimson, he understood Morgenthau's motives without on that account approving of them. During the coming weeks he and Morgenthau invariably dealt with each other with tact, candor, and mutual trust, though their subordinates continued to bicker.

Candor characterized Stettinius' long memorandum of December 18, 1944, reviewing the State Department's communications to Roosevelt about Germany since the previous October. "The State Department," Stettinius wrote Morgenthau, "has . . . submitted several . . . memoranda . . . particularly with reference to our economic objectives. The President has . . . informed the State Department that he is in favor of restitution of looted property of all kinds and that Germany should be allowed to 'come back industrially to meet her own needs but not to do any exporting for some time until we know better how things are going to work out.' The President also expressed himself as being opposed to reparations."

Eager to examine the memoranda which Stettinius had mentioned, Morgenthau sent DuBois and Luxford to the State Department where Stettinius' subordinates denied the existence of the papers the Treasury requested. Luxford, outraged, urged Morgenthau to demand a meeting of representatives of both departments, and at Morgenthau's request, Stettinius agreed without hesitation. The two Secretaries agreed further to see the President together on January 10, 1945.

In preparation for that occasion, Morgenthau instructed his staff to write for his signature a stiff reassertion of his position on Germany, one that would rebut the objections advanced by both the

War and State Departments. Continuing study during the last few months, that reassertion read, had confirmed Morgenthau's convictions that the German people had the will to try again to conquer the world; that democracy and reeducation and kindness could not destroy that will within any brief time; and that heavy industry gave Germany her war-making potential:

> The more I think of this problem, and the more I read and hear discussions of it, the clearer it seems to me that the real motive of most of those who oppose a weak Germany is not any actual disagreement on these three points. On the contrary, it is simply an expression of fear of Russia and communism. It is the twenty-year-old idea of a "bulwark against Bolshevism" — which was one of the factors which brought this present war down on us. Because the people who hold this view are unwilling (for reasons which, no doubt, they regard as statesmanlike) to come out in the open and lay the real issue on the table, all sorts of smoke screens are thrown up to support the proposition that Germany must be rebuilt. Examples are:
>
> A. The fallacy that Europe needs a strong industrial Germany.
>
> B. The contention that recurring reparations (which would require immediate reconstruction of the German economy) are necessary so that Germany may be made to pay for the destruction she has caused.
>
> C. The naive belief that the removal or destruction of all German war materials and the German armament industry would in itself prevent Germany from waging another war.
>
> D. The illogical assumption that a soft peace would facilitate the growth of democracy in Germany.
>
> E. The fallacy that making Germany a predominately agricultural country, with light industries but no heavy industries, would mean starving Germans. . . .
>
> This thing needs to be dragged out into the open. I feel so deeply about it that I speak strongly. If we don't face it I am just as sure as I can be that we are going to let a lot of hollow and hypocritical propaganda lead us into recreating a strong Germany and making a foe of Russia. I shudder for the sake of our children to think of what will follow.

There is nothing that I can think of that can do more at this moment to engender trust or distrust between the United States and Russia than the position this Government takes on the German problem.

On reflection, the Secretary decided not to submit that statement on January 10. As he put it to his staff on returning from the White House that day: "I decided before I went over not to give him the German thing. The President was very tired . . . and I am awfully glad I did not. We will put this in the . . . pouch. It will be much better. He will be at Hyde Park." So also, Morgenthau decided against trying to persuade key Democratic senators of the virtues of his plan for Germany, though Claude Pepper of Florida advised him to.

If the Secretary's tactics were subdued, his purpose was not. Prior to the scheduled meeting with the representatives of the State Department, White, Luxford, and DuBois tried to get him to soften his views. "We all feel," White said on January 17, "that it would be easier and helpful if you would in your discussions leave yourself a little vague in the treatment of the coal mines. . . . We think that one of the strongest objections of the other side will be centered on the closing of the coal mines and the elimination of the industry, and they'd pick on that one point and assume that that is indicative or illustrative of your entire program." As he had before, so again Morgenthau said: "I am not going to change on that. There is no use pounding me on it." Luxford hoped the Secretary would at least leave the question open, for coal was not crucial. "I don't agree with you," Morgenthau replied. From coal the Germans made dyes and other synthetics. If the Germans were permitted to make bicycles or baby carriages, they could just as well make airplanes. "We are just in an impossible position," White objected, "if we say they can't have any factories, because then we are taking an indefensible position when we don't have to." But Morgenthau held fast.

With Stettinius and a number of his subordinates, among them James Dunn, Dean Acheson, and Leo Pasvolsky, Morgenthau later that day reaffirmed his dedication to his plan for Germany, his belief that that plan would abet the economic recovery of Great Britain, and his hope for a genuine friendship with Russia, to be cemented at the outset by a $10 billion American credit. The meeting proceeded in good temper, but the two departments had reached an impasse on German policy.

Stettinius and his colleagues put forward their proposals in memoranda on Germany included within the "Briefing Book" that was prepared for Roosevelt to take to his coming conference with Churchill and Stalin at Yalta. Afraid that the Russians would attempt to establish permanent control in Germany through a puppet government, the State Department recommended an overall inter-Allied administration, rather than a partitioning, of the country. "The establishment of comprehensive military government," one memorandum said, "would prevent . . . the undesirable development of the importation into Germany of a substantially ready-made provisional government perhaps recognized by and functioning under special foreign auspices." The memorandum went on to applaud the demilitarization of Germany; the destruction of German war materials and of plants and machines "incapable of conversion to peaceful uses"; the prohibition of aircraft production; and the dissolving of the Nazi party, its laws, and its fronts. It also recommended the arrest of war criminals and "the principal political malefactors," as well as the removal from office of some two million "active Nazis," but it made allowance for the retention for service during the occupation of some four million civil servants who were only "nominal" members of the Nazi party. It sought educational reforms "as unobtrusively as possible." It defined the long-range American objective in Germany as "the assimiliation of the German people into the world society of peace-loving nations." To that end, the memorandum warned against indefinite coercion of "so many millions of technically resourceful people." The disruption of the German economy, the State Department argued, would carry with it a general lowering of European standards of living. The Department therefore stood by its "Summary . . . Views" of November 22, 1944, on economic policy.

In rebuttal, White and other Treasury officers presented to James Dunn and his colleagues the Treasury memorandum originally drafted for the President on January 10 with its sharp attack, A through E, on the premises which it attributed to State Department planners. That memorandum also became a part of the collection of briefs which were handed to the President before he left for Yalta.

Dunn, at a meeting with White on January 19, denied the charge that the State Department was trying to build up Germany as a bulwark against Russia. Will Clayton then spoke for international control of the Ruhr so that its industries could contribute to the rebuilding of the economy of Europe. He rejected White's elaborate argument that deindustrialization would provide new markets for the Belgians, Dutch, and British. There was clearly no important issue about which the two departments could agree.

The Treasury was at odds, though less bitterly, with the conclusions of the Foreign Economic Administration, to which Roosevelt had referred the question of the German economy. The FEA report to the President of January 10, 1945, urged the control rather than the destruction of German industry. It recommended only that "economic and industrial disarmament" which would do "a minimum of damage to the economic fabric of Europe," but it approved the elimination of some German industries, particularly "any substantial war potential in the aircraft industry." On the matter of the Ruhr, it suggested only further study.

The Treasury objected also to some of the recommendations of Judge Samuel Rosenman whom Roosevelt had directed to report on the treatment of war criminals, another subject scheduled for the attention of the Big Three at Yalta. With Stimson and Attorney General Francis Biddle, Rosenman proposed instituting international legal action against the leading Nazis. Morgenthau would have preferred simply to shoot the arch-criminals, but he confined his protest to a suggestion of Joe DuBois. Accepting the necessity of a trial, DuBois wanted to facilitate proceedings by establishing a simple and binding definition of conspiracy according to which all members of an organization like the SS would be found guilty of a crime against humanity simply by virtue of their membership, and would be subject to a standard, minimum punishment without further trial. DuBois drafted the memorandum on war criminals which Morgenthau signed and sent to Rosenman on January 19, 1945. It demanded "the greatest possible effort . . . to avoid legalistic red tape" and technical delays and defenses, including defenses based on pleas of sovereign immunity or of obedience to superior orders or of insanity. Apart from questions of procedures, the Treasury held that the trials should cover the punishment of crimes committed by Germans against other Germans as well as by Germans against other nationalities. "If the conspiracy charge is used," the memo said, "it should cover . . . the murder of Jews and other minority groups of Axis nationality." Though Rosenman incorporated some of the Treasury suggestions in papers he sent Roosevelt on January 22, DuBois was not satisfied, and Morgenthau encouraged him to continue, while Roosevelt was at Yalta, to press the Treasury's case.

At the end of January 1945, Morgenthau had yielded in his views toward Germany neither to his fellow New Dealers, nor to his colleagues in the Cabinet, nor to the arguments of his subordinates. So also, he had conceded nothing to the objections of Churchill, Eden, and Sir John Anderson. Nor was he moved by Russian plans. In conversation with Herbert Gaston, Vladimir Pravdin, a Washington correspondent for TASS, held that the real solution to the German problem was socialism. "They would have large scale industry," Gaston reported to Morgenthau, "operated by the government and would give the Allies a dominating position in directing the industries for years to come." That solution did not satisfy the Secretary, for it left the heavy industry intact, and he feared a renaissance as much in the Russian zone of occupation under socialism as in the British or the American zones under capitalism. In January as in September, for the future containment of Germany, he trusted only the Morgenthau Plan.

But in January Roosevelt was even more reluctant to settle the long-range future of Germany than he had been in October. After his reelection, the President had continued to postpone decision while his subordinates wrangled. Morgenthau's criticisms accompanied the State Department papers that the President took to Yalta, but on his way to that rendezvous, Roosevelt, obviously more tired than he had ever been before, gave no attention whatsoever to the documents in his pouch. And at Yalta, the President approached the German problem in the context of a multiplicity of issues about which the United States, Great Britain, and the Soviet Union disagreed.

In his characteristic way, Roosevelt at Yalta tried to plaster over differences by directing deliberations toward general policies on which the Allies could agree. The President also made some concessions to the Soviet Union, concessions in any event implicit in the military positions and potentialities of the various armies, in return for Russian cooperation on issues important to the United States, including the prosecution of the war against Japan and the establishment of the United Nations. In the circumstances, the Yalta agreements on Germany bore the marks of British, Russian, and American preferences.

Most of the discussion about Germany at Yalta fell to the three foreign ministers, Stettinius, Eden, and Molotov. Their decisions, which their chiefs approved, assigned to the United States, the United Kingdom, and the Soviet Union "supreme authority with respect to Germany." In the exercise of that authority, the three nations were to "take such steps, including the complete disarmament, demilitarization and the dismemberment of Germany as they deem requisite for future peace and security." The ambiguous last phrase, which Eden demanded, left undetermined, subject to future interpretations of the requirements of peace, the very issues the article raised. Similarly, a long debate among the Big Three about reparations ended inconclusively. They agreed to refer the matter to a three-power commission to meet in Moscow, but the instructions to that group stated that "the Soviet Union and the United States believed that the Reparations Commission should take as a basis of discussion the figure of reparations as 20 billion dollars and fifty per cent of these should go to the Soviet Union." That phraseology revealed the British dissent from the Soviet-American view, and left open the question of what proportion of reparations should come from current production. The Soviet figure, however, was so large that current production would have to supply some part of it, contrary to the provisions on reparations in the Morgenthau Plan.

Other agreements on Germany were of less interest to Morgenthau. The Big Three turned over the question of major war criminals to the foreign ministers "for report in due course." Reluctantly Stalin agreed to permitting France a zone of occupation in Germany which was to be carved out of the area previously assigned to Great Britain and the United States. The French were also to join the other three powers in the Central Control Council in Berlin. There was no agreement about the western boundary of Poland or about the ultimate disposition of the Ruhr and Saar.

On February 12, 1945, Roosevelt, Churchill, and Stalin published an official communiqué about Germany. "It is our inflexible purpose to destroy German militarism and Nazism," they said, "and to insure that Germany will never again be able to disturb the peace of the world. We are determined to disarm and disband all German armed forces; break up for all time the German General Staff . . . remove or destroy all German military equipment; eliminate or control all German industry that could be used for military production; bring all war criminals to just and swift punishment and exact reparation in kind for the destruction wrought by the Germans; wipe out the Nazi party, Nazi laws, organizations and institutions, remove all Nazi and militarist influences from public office and from the cultural and economic life of the German people; and take in harmony such other measures in Germany as may be necessary to the future peace and safety of the world. It is not our purpose to destroy the people of Germany, but only when Nazism and militarism have been extirpated will there be hope for a decent life for Germans, and a place for them in the community of nations."

In Washington again on February 28, 1945, Roosevelt commissioned Stettinius to carry out the political understandings of the Yalta Conference. The assignment of that task to Stettinius, as well as the implications of the public communiqué from Yalta (the detailed agreements were still secret), seemed to Morgenthau to guarantee dominance to the State Department in further planning for Germany. Yet he was not ready to leave the field of controversy, and Roosevelt was not ready to reach any final decisions. The debate about Germany had only entered a new phase.

4. Two Black Weeks

"I am anxious to see," Roosevelt wrote Morgenthau and Stimson on March 12, 1945, "that the decisions we reached at the Crimea Conference should . . . be carried forward as expeditiously as possible in conjunction with our Allies. I have, therefore, charged the Secretary of State with the responsibility for implementing the Crimea decisions exclusive . . . of those dealing with purely military matters. . . . Mr. Stettinius will . . . wish to tell you personally of those decisions . . . which are of interest to you in connection with your duties."

"Delighted to cooperate with Mr. Stettinius," as he replied to Roosevelt on March 14, Morgenthau was shaken by the report he received the next day from John J. McCloy. As the Secretary recorded in his Diary:

"McCloy called me up this morning in great excitement and came over to see me. He had gotten a copy of the document on reparations which was agreed to at Yalta, which he feels is terrible, and then another document which he had gotten somehow on the sly which had been prepared in the State Department, and agreed to . . . by the President yesterday. This is a substitute for 1067, and, according to McCloy sets up complete authority for central control of Germany. . . . One of the reasons McCloy was so excited was that . . . Stettinius told the President that the War Department had seen this and agreed to this, which was untrue. . . . Nobody in the War Department had seen it and McCloy feels it's up to Stettinius to tell this to the President. . . .

"It is quite evident that he wanted me to go to this meeting . . . with Stettinius and raise hell. Well, I am not going to do it . . . ; it's up to Stimson to take the lead on this thing."

The State Department paper to which McCloy had referred was a "Draft Directive for the Treatment of Germany," dated March 10, 1945, which the President had initialed without consulting either the Treasury or War Department. That paper, following the State Department's interpretations of the Yalta decisions, departed from the thrust of JCS 1067 and from what Morgenthau later construed to be the meaning of the Yalta agreements on Germany. The "Draft Directive" did not call for the dismemberment of Germany. According to its terms, the inter-Allied control machinery for Germany was to take the place and assume the functions of the central government of Germany, and the authority of the Control Council was to be paramount throughout the Reich. The zones of occupation would be areas for the enforcement of the Council's decisions rather than regions in which the zone commanders possessed much autonomous power. While the "Draft Directive" generally satisfied Morgenthau in its remarks about denazification, its sections on the German economy did not provide for the destruction of a significant proportion of Germany's heavy industry. Rather, they instructed Allied Military Government to provide "a minimum standard of living for the German people," including food, shelter, and medical supplies. The Allies were to meet the requirements of the occupation forces and of the German people before directing any excess goods and services to restitution and reparations payments. The proposed schedule for the delivery of reparations permitted Germany to discharge its obligations within ten years, and the volume and character of German reparations were to be defined so as to reduce Germany's relative predominance in the capital goods industries and so as to strengthen and develop those industries in other European countries. Though the memorandum forbade the production or the maintenance of facilities for the manufacture of aircraft, synthetic oil, synthetic rubber, and light metals, it recommended restraining rather than removing the metals, machinery, and chemical industries, and it ordered the facilitation of German production of coal and light consumer goods.

Besides initialing the directive, Roosevelt, at the State Department's suggestion, on March 15 appointed an Informal Policy Committee on Germany, which Washington quickly called IPCOG. Assistant Secretary of State William L. Clayton held the chairmanship of that committee, on which the other members were John J. McCloy, Harry White, Ralph A. Bard, the Under Secretary of the Navy, and W. H. Fowler of the Foreign Economic Administration. As Morgenthau's representative, White of course examined the "Draft Directive" of March 10, and his description of its contents prompted Morgenthau to "take the lead" he had wanted to relinquish to Stimson in attacking it.

The Secretary turned first to the particular question of reparations. Bernard Baruch had completed a statement on that subject which he had tried without success to show to the President. "The gist of this thing," Morgenthau told his staff, "is we must not build up Germany industrially in order to pay reparations. . . . He doesn't know whether he shouldn't let the English have some of the Ruhr coal. . . . [But] Baruch . . . is all right on this German business." Since Baruch hoped to represent the United States at the Moscow conference on reparations, Morgenthau set out to win him completely to the Treasury's plan for Germany. "Joe," the Secretary told DuBois, "if he took a liking to you, I would let you go with him. . . . This is very important and if you could sell yourself . . . I would encourage you to go." On March 16 DuBois talked about reparations with Samuel Lubell, who was working on the matter for Baruch, and then on March 19, along with Frank Coe, DuBois saw Isador Lubin, the labor economist whom Roosevelt had by that date designated instead of Baruch to head the American delegation to Moscow. In appointing Lubin, the President, according to one report, had said "it is a very nice thing to have the man in charge of reparations over in Germany to be a Russian Jew." Lubin's religion interested Morgenthau less than did his sympathy for the Treasury's program. In conversations with DuBois, Lubin said that his reparation policy would leave Germany with only light industries except for coal. Indeed Lubin's was the "toughest" memorandum on reparations that Will Clayton had seen, and Lubin assured DuBois that he was going to fight the issue out with the State Department. Unless he got 95 per cent of what he wanted, he added, he would not take the assignment that Roosevelt had given him.

While DuBois was talking with Baruch and Lubin, Morgenthau was hounding the State Department about its "Draft Directive." "I had a very frank talk with Stettinius," Morgenthau told McCloy on March 17, 1945. ". . . I shook him terrifically. . . . He as much as said this thing [the German question] was given to him the day after he returned, and he was tired and he really didn't know what was in it . . . and I believe him. . . . When . . . somebody asked him had the President read it [the "Draft Directive"] he didn't answer. . . . So I am preparing a very careful report . . . showing where this interpretation of the protocol is quite different from 1067. . . . He's away and I am going to give it to Grew* at his request. . . . I am calling you up to find out what you were going to do."

Stimson had seen the President, McCloy replied, and told him that he did not want to reinvolve himself in the German issue. The War Department, its Secretary held, had worked out a document, JCS 1067, which had now been changed without consultation. Stimson would therefore henceforth interest himself only in seeing that

---

* Joseph Grew, Under Secretary of State at that time, career diplomat, formerly Ambassador to Japan in the years before Pearl Harbor.

the administration of Germany was militarily possible. Roosevelt, according to McCloy, had then told Stimson not to pay much attention to the State Department's "Draft Directive." Consequently McCloy was arranging for the War Department to restudy JCS 1067 in the light of the Yalta decisions. The question of how far the occupation authorities went on economic controls was not of interest to the military, McCloy said, but the military did care about being able to carry out effectively whatever program was defined. McCloy promised to examine whatever the Treasury prepared. "This business is all pretty delicate," he said, "because of the relations with the State Department, but I think that now, that in the light of the fact that they went off on a frolic of their own . . . that . . . we've got a right to sulk on it."

"We've got a right to talk," Morgenthau said. ". . . It's damnable, an outrage."

In order to exercise that right, Morgenthau instructed his staff to prepare for his signature a memorandum criticizing the "Draft Directive," especially for its incompatibility with the Yalta agreements and for its economic policy. He was encouraged by his luncheon conversation on March 19 with the Soviet ambassador. As the Secretary put it in his Diary:

"He told me that at Yalta the Russians and the US Government agreed in connection with reparations that the Germans should pay $20 billion over a term of years in kind. I questioned him very closely whether they intended to build up German industries so that they could pay reparations and he said definitely not. . . . I said, 'If Germany needed electric power to produce reparations, would you want us to send electrical machinery into Germany in order to build her power plant?' And he said, 'No.'

"On dismemberment . . . he said that it was agreed that they would dismember Germany, and again England said she hadn't had time to study it. I said that there were some people . . . who believed that in running Germany during the occupational period all occupational zones should be treated alike, and that we should establish a strong central authority. He said, 'What's the use of doing that? If we start to dismember Germany, we might as well start right.' "

Interpreting those remarks to indicate full support of the Morgenthau Plan, the Secretary that afternoon told Harry White to sharpen the tone of the Treasury memo criticizing the "Draft Directive" and to indicate that the Treasury assumed Germany was to be dismembered. White objected that unless Morgenthau knew it was to be dismembered, he was taking a dangerous tack, but Morgenthau replied only that he felt sure he was on safe ground.

With only insignificant changes from the Secretary's instructions, and with some help with phraseology from McCloy, White on March 20, 1945, produced a memorandum for the State Department and one for the President, both of which Morgenthau signed. "On the basis of decisions made at Yalta of which I have been informed," the memorandum for Stettinius read, "it seems clear that the directive has adopted certain definite views on the most fundamental issues involved in the treatment of Germany, which views are not required by or even implied in the Yalta decisions. I understand that these views were advanced prior to Yalta within the State Department; they are completely opposed to the Treasury's views on these issues; are contrary in major respects to decisions made by this government prior to Yalta; and are opposed in their most important implications to the views which I understood the President holds on Germany." The memo went on then to urge the administrative decentralization rather than integration of Germany, and the elimination of German heavy industry. The industrial provisions in the State Department directive, the Treasury memo held, were "contrary to the Quebec Agreement." Further, the Treasury maintained that "the Yalta decisions clearly did not contemplate that the collection of reparations requires the Allies to take steps designed to rehabilitate and strengthen the German economy." If any decision had been reached to dismember Germany, the memo went on, "or if there is a likelihood that such a decision will be reached, then the directive will . . . undermine this basic policy." The memorandum concluded with two suggestions:

"That for the time being we allow JCS 1067 to remain unchanged as the statement of policy for the US forces during the first period of occupation, and that we attempt to get immediate agreement through the European Advisory Commission on JCS 1067.

"I am informed by the Army . . . that after the collapse of Germany initial operations by the Army can take place satisfactorily under JCS 1067.

"On reparations and other longer-run policies for Germany, the

Treasury is of course prepared to meet with you and your representatives for further discussion."

Morgenthau's March 20 memorandum for Roosevelt on the
"Draft Directive" restated the Treasury's familiar position on Germany:

> From many conversations that I have had with you, as to how
> to deal with a defeated Germany, I am confident that this Di-
> rective goes absolutely contrary to your views. I would like to
> call your attention to some of the fundamental points con-
> tained in the March 10 directive which seem to me to be con-
> trary to the views you hold and the views that were contained
> in JCS 1067 which I understand you collaborated on.
>
> (1) *Decentralization of Germany* — it required the Control
> Council to "utilize centralized instrumentalities for the execu-
> tion and implementation of its policies to the maximum extent
> possible" and requires that for this purpose "central German
> agencies . . . shall be revived or replaced as rapidly as pos-
> sible."
>
> (2) *Elimination of German Heavy Industry* — it allows Ger-
> many to maintain "metal, machinery and chemical industries"
> with controls on exports; and forbids "aircraft, synthetic oil,
> synthetic rubber and light metals" industries.
>
> (3) *Control of German Internal Economy* — it states that "a
> substantial degree of centralized financial and economic control
> is essential" and requires the Allies to "direct, control and ad-
> minister" the German economy in order to collect reparations
> and for other purposes. It requires the Control Council to for-
> mulate policies governing "public finance," "prices and wages,"
> "rationing," "international commerce," etc.
>
> Carrying out the above directions would build up a strong
> central German Government and maintain and even strengthen
> the German economy. You, of course, would know whether or
> not it was decided at Yalta to move in that direction.
>
> I strongly urge that the directive of March 10 be redrafted in
> accordance with the three principles indicated below which, in
> my opinion, reflect your views.
>
> 1. We should avoid assuming responsibility for the function-

ing of the internal German economy and its economic controls. The maintenance and rehabilitation of the German economy is a German problem and should not be undertaken by us in order to collect reparations or for any other reason except the security of the occupying forces.

2. We should aim at the greatest possible contraction of German heavy industry as well as the elimination of her war potential. The occupying forces should accept no responsibility for providing the German people with food and supplies beyond preventing starvation, disease, and such unrest as might interfere with the purposes of the occupation.

3. During the period of military occupation policies in the separate zones should be coordinated through the Control Council, but the actual administration of affairs in Germany should be directed toward the decentralization of the political structure.

With General Hilldring, McCloy examined both Treasury memoranda on March 20. McCloy agreed with Morgenthau that the State Department had jettisoned JCS 1067 and that Ambassador Winant had worked continually to that end. McCloy agreed, too, that the three policies Morgenthau recommended to Roosevelt would clear up the basic confusion. But he reminded Morgenthau of Stimson's opposition to the Quebec Agreement, and he warned Morgenthau, who was about to have luncheon with the President, against getting Roosevelt's signature before the War and State Departments had had a full hearing.

"The President's thought was this," Morgenthau told Joseph Grew immediately after luncheon, "that he'd like something along the lines which I prepared as a draft, if we could come to an agreement. He wants to withdraw this memorandum that he and Eɑ signed as of March 10 . . . and he wants us to come to an agreement as to what we do from here on. . . . The thought is that this committee of Clayton, White and McCloy should prepare something to take the place of this March 10th memorandum; he had absolutely no recollection of having seen it or signed it."

"Amazing," Grew replied.

Though he did not say so to Grew, Morgenthau was "very low."

He was disturbed alike by the President's obviously bad health and by the constant presence in Roosevelt's company of Anna and John Boettiger. To McCloy that afternoon Morgenthau said:

"This is sort of embarrassing, but, everything is embarrassing. . . . I gave the President the documents we prepared. . . . He read them very carefully. . . . He was in thorough agreement. . . . Boettiger . . . was there . . . to keep me from making my case. Now the thing that Boettiger is talking about so earnestly is that we must regulate prices, we must tell the Germans how much they eat . . . we must tell them how much coal they mine, and all the rest of it. . . . I told Boettiger in front of the President that I had spent four hours with you and Hilldring, . . . and that Hilldring said that . . . as a professional soldier that he was satisfied with 1067 . . . and that General Eisenhower was satisfied. . . . Well, Boettiger kept saying that people down the line didn't understand it, and it wasn't workable, and Winant wouldn't accept it. . . . So we got all kind of mixed up. . . . But the thing ended this way: . . . Boettiger wanted the President to call the three Cabinet members together. And I said, 'No, we have a committee' . . . and this committee should go to work and make recommendations to the three Cabinet members, and then from that to the President. . . . And I told him I didn't want to pull on him what the State Department pulled on us. He [Roosevelt] was perfectly ready to sign that document. . . . I didn't ask him. . . . I stuck by my guns . . . and I did accomplish this — that March 10th is to be cancelled and something new in its place."

Morgenthau had also talked with Roosevelt specifically about German coal production. The President, according to the Secretary's report to McCloy, admitted he had not given that question much thought. He was also, as was Morgenthau, aware that Europe would need some coal from Germany, but again like Morgenthau, he did not want the occupation authorities supervising mining. As the Secretary recalled Roosevelt's statement for McCloy, the President had said: "All right, I'll appoint a committee of three German businessmen to run the coal mines, and we'll supervise them in Washington. If they don't get out the coal . . . we'll shoot them."

The Informal Policy Committee on Germany met on March 21, 1945, to begin to formulate a substitute paper for the abandoned

"Draft Directive" of March 10. At that meeting Frank Coe represented the Treasury. Will Clayton, according to Coe's report to Morgenthau, attempted to have IPCOG produce only an interpretation of the directive of March 10, but McCloy demanded a replacement. Most of the discussion centered on the Army's insistence on flexibility in military government. On practically every point the State Department gave way. But when Coe tried to obtain agreement on a positive statement in favor of decentralization, McCloy said that Stimson had only an administrative interest in the matter, and Coe's suggestion failed. Only in the last ten minutes of the meeting did the group consider economic matters, too late for useful discussion. As Coe saw it, the new paper would leave more latitude to the Control Council than had the memo of March 10. "That would be satisfactory to me," Morgenthau said. Obviously surprised, Coe replied that he thought the Secretary had not wanted any central control. "That would satisfy me," Morgenthau repeated, "because I would put myself in the hands of the generals, and there would be a Russian general there, an American general, and a French general." Together, the Secretary implied, those three would be able to ride herd on any British effort to restore the German economy.

Whatever optimism Morgenthau gained from Coe's report he had to surrender the next afternoon. McCloy then stopped at the Treasury on his way to the White House. There had been a meeting, he told Morgenthau, between him and Clayton from which the State Department had definitely excluded the Treasury. There McCloy had seen a State Department paper replying to the Treasury memoranda of March 20. The paper, McCloy thought, was wholly unfair to the Treasury. The document emerging from IPCOG, furthermore, reflecting the influence of Will Clayton and others in the State Department, would come down strongly in favor of centralization in Germany.

Distressed by the news, Morgenthau was nevertheless grateful to McCloy, "a straight shooter." "The cards are stacked against us," the Secretary said to White, "because here is McCloy taking the position that he mustn't talk on the economic front. Boettiger is making this a cause." The Treasury's best hope lay in the "long stretch between their making this directive and the result, and they will change the orders and the Administration policy, not once but twenty times."

Morgenthau had come to expect from the State Department the furtive treatment he was receiving. Still later in the afternoon of March 22, 1945, Joseph Grew telephoned to say he was sending over the State Department's answer to the Treasury "which I think is going to be good to be used to bring our ideas together." But while that paper was on its way, Grew went to the White House to urge Roosevelt to approve the IPCOG paper advocating centralization in Germany. Morgenthau would probably never have known what Grew said to the President had not McCloy, who was there at Roosevelt's request, related the story. On his return from the White House, McCloy on the telephone to Morgenthau said that Roosevelt started out with the statement that he "thought he had been sold a bill of goods. . . . That is what he said — that there were many elements in this thing that he didn't like. . . . That rather backed the people [from the State Department] off a bit. . . . Then he [Roosevelt] said that he thought there was a little too much emphasis on centralization . . . that it was pitched that way, and that he agreed, however, that there had to be some controls from above on what he called . . . the public services. By that he meant telephones, transportation, and the services necessary to carry those out. . . .

"And the President talked about his experiences in Germany as a boy. Then he went from that into how he would run the thing if he were running it."

"Did he talk about a committee of three," Morgenthau asked.

"Yes," McCloy replied. ". . . A committee of three, and if they didn't behave, he'd take them out and shoot them in the morning.

"Then he said, 'In short, I would say that you have to have these controls, to some extent, but that you should exert them to the minimum extent possible in order to carry out the objectives of your occupation.' . . . He wanted a political decentralization, and . . . he wanted as much economic decentralization as possible, but with the recognition that there would be some necessity for some central administration, but what he kept coming back to were public services. . . . Clayton spoke about the chaotic conditions — the necessity for some controls if we were going to . . . make anything out of this affair at all. . . . Clayton said that he wanted to point out that there would be a very large measure of central administration. . . . The President said maybe so; he said he didn't know. He thought you would have to go in and take a look and see. . . . Then there was a lot of conversation. . . . Then Grew said, 'Well, then I think . . . we're very close. We think . . . you agree generally with the paper that Mr. Stettinius submitted to you.' "

"My God," Morgenthau interrupted.

"And the President said," McCloy continued, " 'Why, yes, I guess so.' Then he caught himself. And he said, 'Oh, you mean the March 10 paper? . . . No, that will have to be rewritten.' "

"Oh," Morgenthau interpolated, "wonderful."

"Yeah," McCloy said. "Then Mr. Clayton said, 'Well, I wonder whether it's desirable to rewrite that. Hadn't we better try a new shot at it? . . . This . . . paper which was prepared at the State Department this morning, Mr. President, . . . I think you will agree with that.' He [Roosevelt] said, 'Well, let me think about it a little bit,' and that was about all he said. . . . Then we adjourned . . . and it was at that point that Grew decided that he thought he had better cancel his appointment with you, because he didn't know just where he did stand . . . and see if we couldn't get together and redraft something that would be suitable in the light of that conversation. But the general tone that the President took was definitely one in which he didn't agree with the strong emphasis upon centralization that runs throughout March 10th."

After the White House meeting, McCloy went on, Will Clayton had come up to him. "I want you to understand," Clayton had said to McCloy, "that I came into this thing cold with only the education that I got from my own people, and I am beginning to see now things that I didn't see before, and I am quite ready to say that I am convinced now that March 10th, as it was drawn up, is a mistake."

"I'm a new man," Morgenthau said.

"I would gather," McCloy pointed out, as their conversation continued, "that the President is trying to take the view that there was more control than you would do . . . but a long way off from the tone that the State Department was taking."

"Well," Morgenthau replied, "I don't think that we are apart at all because the control that you people explained to me would take place when General Eisenhower went there. . . . But that's a long way from saying how many grams of food and what price and all the rest of the stuff. I mean that it is one thing to have communications and a railroad, and it is something else to have an OPA."

McCloy wanted Morgenthau to labor under no misunderstanding. The Secretary's statement had reminded him of still other remarks of the President. As McCloy reported it, Roosevelt at one point had said: "I don't want you to eliminate German industry — not at all. . . . I want you to change the character of it, but I don't want you to eliminate it. I'm not for throwing salt into the mines and doing all those things. . . . I want to have German industry maintained to the fullest extent necessary to maintain the Germans so that we don't have the burden of taking care of them. I think that means a very substantial degree of preservation of the German industry, but I am very leery of their exports."

In spite of that added information, Morgenthau, as he said, was "very happy," and particularly grateful to McCloy. "It may sound silly," the Secretary told McCloy as their conversation ended, "to say thank you because when I'm treated squarely it is so unusual that I have to say thank you. . . . It has happened so rarely in Washington . . . it is something unusual and I do say thank you. . . . It's a pleasant surprise."

Will Clayton, also tired of intrigue, took the IPCOG directive on Germany to the Treasury on March 23, 1945, where he, Morgenthau, McCloy, and a group of their subordinates quickly agreed to endorse, with small revisions, a new War Department paper, "Summary of U.S. Initial Post-Defeat Policy Relating to Germany." McCloy had designed that paper to bring the departments together and to incorporate the President's opinions. Later in the day Roosevelt approved it: "O.K. F.D.R., superseding the memo of March 10, 1945." Morgenthau, McCloy, and Clayton also signed it.

"The authority of the Control Council to formulate policy," the March 23 memo read, "with respect to matters affecting Germany as a whole shall be paramount, and its agreed policy shall be carried out in each zone by the zone commander. In the absence of such agreed policies, and in matters exclusively affecting his own zone, the zone commander will exercise his authority in accordance with directives received from his own government."

Going on, the memo reflected what Roosevelt had told Grew and

McCloy on March 22. "The administration of affairs in Germany," it stated, "should be directed toward the decentralization of the political structure and the development of local responsibility. The German economy shall also be decentralized, except that to the minimum extent required for carrying out the purposes set forth herein, the Control Council may permit or establish central control of . . . essential national public services such as railroads, communications and power; . . . finance and foreign affairs, and . . . production and distribution of essential commodities."

There followed a paragraph drafted by Herbert Feis, inserted at the behest of John Boettiger: "Germany's ruthless warfare and fanatical Nazi resistance have destroyed the German economy and made chaos and suffering inevitable. The Germans cannot escape the responsibility for what they have brought upon themselves."

The memo then continued, rather in the vein of the Morgenthau Plan:

> Controls may be imposed upon the German economy only as may be necessary . . . to carry out programs of industrial disarmament and demilitarization, reparations, and of relief for liberated areas as prescribed by appropriate higher authority and . . . to assure the production and maintenance of goods and services required to meet the needs of the occupying forces and displaced persons in Germany, and essential to prevent starvation or such disease or civil unrest as would endanger the occupying forces. No action shall be taken, in execution of the reparations program or otherwise, which would tend to support basic living standards of Germany on a higher level than that existing in any one of the neighboring United Nations. All economic and financial international transactions, including exports and imports, shall be controlled with the aim of preventing Germany from developing a war potential. . . . Recurrent reparations should not . . . require the rehabilitation or development of German heavy industry and should not foster the dependence of other countries upon the German economy.
>
> In the imposition and maintenance of economic controls, German authorities will to the fullest extent practicable be or-

dered to proclaim and assume administration of such controls. Thus it should be brought home to the German people that responsibility for the administration of such controls and for any breakdown in those controls, will rest with themselves and their own authorities.

Morgenthau was pleased, too, by provisions relating to the dissolution of the Nazi Party and its affiliated organizations, to the elimination of Nazi and militarist doctrines from German education, and to the repeal of laws of the Hitler regime relating to race, creed, and public opinion. He could see his influence also in the demand that "all members of the Nazi Party who have been more than nominal participants in its activities . . . will be removed from public office and from positions of responsibility in private enterprise." The memo provided further for the arrest and trial of Nazi leaders, for a suitable program of restitution, and for the demobilization of the German army and general staff.

Though the March 23 memorandum preserved much of the Morgenthau Plan, Henry Stimson judged it a "fairly good paper." He and McCloy applauded the initiative left with the zone commanders and the references to considerable centralized economic control. Morgenthau, for his part, accepted that degree of centralization. The March 23 memo, he told his staff, was "the first step toward a kind of peace which I think will last. . . . The fact that they have got this thing out and we got them to . . . change it completely was a very satisfactory thing. . . . We have got a good tough document with decentralization responsibility on the Germans. . . .

"I have never been under such pressure in my life to give way on principles, and I didn't. . . . We stand for something worthwhile. . . . It was one of the most important conferences that I have ever participated in, and it is very encouraging that we had the President to back us up. . . . They tried to get him to change, and they couldn't — the State Department crowd. Sooner or later the President just has to clean his house."

"It's a very good job," McCloy told Morgenthau. "Good progress, great thing, and the Treasury should be given credit for it."

"I'm happier," Morgenthau replied, "than I've been since March 10th."

5. The Last Evening

The President had been clear in mind but exhausted in body during his conferences of March 22 and 23. Indeed, he had seemed old and ill since his return from Yalta. As he prepared to leave Washington for a long rest in Warm Springs, Georgia, Morgenthau asked his consent for the project on which some of the Secretary's staff had been working, the publication of a book on Germany written to persuade its readers to support the Morgenthau Plan.

"Since you are going away for a time," Morgenthau wrote Roosevelt on March 23, "and events are moving fast, I should like your permission before you go to get some facts on the German economy ready for publication in book form* when Germany falls.

"The people of this country are going to need information of this nature if they are to understand our policy.

"With your approval, I want to get to work on this at once. It will take several months to get the material ready."

Through Mrs. Roosevelt, the President inquired "why a book now?" When she explained that the Secretary would withhold publication until the war in Europe was over, Roosevelt said: "That's all right. Let him go ahead and make the study." But on reflection, Roosevelt on March 28 asked Morgenthau to delay: "The plan you outlined . . . is laudable in purpose, but I find it difficult to know just what to say. The people of the country are going to need information on the German economy.

"The spirit of the Nation must be given articulate expression. But it's not so easy to say when the Nation will or can speak. Timing will be of the very essence. We must all remember Job's lament that his enemy had not written a book.

"Anyway, we'll have to keep thinking about it."

During the next fortnight, Morgenthau had little chance to think about the book or anything else relating to Germany or other public affairs. His subordinates, to be sure, worked along with their counterparts from the State and War Departments on evolving drafts of

---

* *Germany Is Our Problem* was published in the fall of 1945 by Harpers, after Morgenthau had left office, and at a time when American public opinion was moving away from his point of view. Most reviews of the book took positions close to Stimson's.

JCS 1067, and worked also with Lubin on plans for the Moscow conference on reparations. But the Secretary had to leave Washington for Florida where his wife Elinor was in the hospital suffering from what he described as "heart trouble." Distraught, he hoped to refurbish his spirits and to explain the purpose of his book during the evening he spent at Warm Springs on April 11, 1945, at Roosevelt's invitation. For his Diary, before he went to bed that night, Morgenthau dictated a long account of his visit:

Around 7:30 P.M. Eastern War Time, I called on the President. He had been out for a two-hour drive. When I came in, he was sitting in a chair with his feet up on a very large footstool with a card table drawn up over his legs. He was mixing cocktails.

I was terribly shocked when I saw him, and I found that he had aged terrifically and looked very haggard. His hands shook so that he started to knock the glasses over, and I had to hold each glass as he poured out the cocktail. He had a jar of Russian caviar, and I asked him whether he wanted some. They had eggs and onions to go with it, and I said, "If I remember correctly, Mr. President, you like it plain," and he said, "That's right," so I fixed him some. I noticed that he took two cocktails and then seemed to feel a little bit better. I found his memory bad, and he was constantly confusing names. He hasn't weighed himself so he didn't know whether he had gained weight or not. I have never seen him have so much difficulty transferring himself from his wheelchair to a regular chair, and I was in agony watching him.

I brought him a box of candy, and I said, "That's for the ladies of your house." He said, "Why the ladies? I would like it," and he seemed very much pleased, and after supper he took some.

At supper, the President sat at one end of the table and I sat at the other. There were two ladies on each side. . . . We had veal and noodles for dinner, and then a marvelous chocolate waffle with whipped cream and chocolate sauce, which the President seemed to enjoy very much. . . .

Just before supper, I went into the President's own bedroom

and bathroom, and they seemed exactly the same as they had
been years ago when I spent several nights at the cottage.

During supper we joked about the early Valkill furniture*
with which the cottage is decorated. I carried on a conversation
at my end of the table, and the President's hearing seemed so
bad that it didn't disturb him. . . .

The President said he would be in Washington on the 19th
and up until noon on the 20th.† At first I said that I wouldn't
be there, and then I said I would stay until he left and that
seemed to please him. He said, "I have been offered a beautiful
apartment by a lady in the top floor of some hotel [in San Fran-
cisco], but I am not taking it. I am going there on my train,
and at three o'clock in the afternoon I will appear on the stage
in my wheelchair, and I will make the speech." Then he made
a grimace and clapped his hands and said, "And then they will
applaud me, and I will leave and go back on my train, go down
to Los Angeles and dump my daughter-in-law, and I will be
back in Hyde Park on May first."

Early in the evening he had been very solicitous about Mrs.
Morgenthau and he let it slip that he was in touch with some
heart doctor — I think he said at the Presbyterian Hospital in
New York. . . .

When the President and I started to talk, I said, "Mr. President, I am doing a lot of things in regard to Germany and I
want you to know about it. We are having a lot of troubles,
and I don't want to be doing these things if it isn't agreeable to
you." He didn't say anything, so I went on and said, "You
know what happened on that March 10th memorandum on
Germany." The President said, "Oh, wasn't that terrible? I
had to rewrite the whole thing." So I said, "Yes, it was pretty
bad. . . . A lot of the things I am doing really should be done
by Leo Crowley and the Foreign Economic Warfare, but the
War Department seems to want to work with me."

I told the President that Clay‡ had called on me and I had

---

* Which Mrs. Roosevelt was having manufactured at Hyde Park.
† Before departing for the United Nations Conference in San Francisco.
‡ General Lucius Clay, who was to be in charge of the American military
occupation in Germany.

asked him what he was going to do about Robert Murphy, and
he said that he realized that was one of his headaches. The
President said, "Well, what's the matter with Murphy?" And I
said . . . 'Murphy was too anxious to collaborate. . . .' *

The President said, "Well, what have you got on your
mind?" I said, "In order to break the State Department crowd
. . . just the way you broke the crowd of Admirals when you
were Assistant Secretary of the Navy, my suggestion is that you
make Claude Bowers† political adviser to Eisenhower . . ."
The President thought that it was a wonderful idea, and so that
he wouldn't forget it, I made him write it down. . . .

I then got on to the question of my writing a book, and I
showed the President the photostat of the letter he had written
to me. . . . The President said, "Where did you get that from?
I have never seen it before." So I said, "Well, the reason I am
bringing it to your attention is because I want to know what it
means." He said, "I don't know what it means. . . . Somebody told me you wanted to get a book out right away, and I
thought it was a mistake." I said, "No, what I want is to get out
a textbook after V-E Day. For example, I would like to write a
chapter on how 60 million Germans can feed themselves." He
said, "I said they could." . . . I told him that when the book
was written I wanted to show it to him, and that I hoped he
would write the preface. I told the President that if he didn't
write the preface I would like to have Stettinius do it. He said,
"I think that's fine. You go ahead and do it. I think it is a
grand idea. . . . I have a lot of ideas of my own. I would like
to put something in there about my conversations with Dr.
Schacht." Then he went on and told me the story about how
Dr. Schacht came over here and wept on his desk about his poor
country. He said that Schacht came over three or four times
saying that the Germans were going broke and they never did.
This is a story that I have heard the President tell about three
different times, but he seems to enjoy telling it.

Then I told the President that I wanted him to know about

* With Darlan and the Vichy regime.

† Bowers, a perfervid liberal and Democrat, then Ambassador to Chile, in
1932 keynoter of the Democratic National Convention; also a sprightly historian
whose biases always showed.

Lubin. I said, "You have appointed him, and he doesn't know what to do. . . . We are helping him, and we have written the things for him." The President said, "Oh, hasn't he gone yet?" And I said, "No."

I said to the President, "General Hilldring couldn't get in on this reparations matter, and he called me up and asked me to arrange it for him, and I did arrange it. . . . McCloy is away you know." Then the President said, "McCloy is all right now, but he was all wrong about De Gaulle, but I explained things to him and now he has been loyal to me." I said, "I am glad you feel that way." . . . I was glad to hear the President say that because I think some people around town have been trying to poison him against McCloy. . . .

I asked the President if he wanted me to interest myself in the future treatment of Germany. He didn't answer me directly. I said, "Look, Mr. President, I am going to fight hard, and this is what I am fighting for. . . . A weak economy for Germany means that she will be weak politically, and she won't be able to make another war. . . . I have been strong for winning the war, and I want to help win the peace." The President said, "Henry, I am with you 100 per cent." I said, "You may hear things because I am going to fight for this," and he made no comment, but I certainly put him on notice as to what I was going to do. I repeated it two or three times. . . .

I had just about concluded my conversation when the four ladies came in. I asked whether I could use the telephone. . . . Then I came back and said good-bye to the President and his company, and when I left them they were sitting around laughing and chatting, and I must say the President seemed to be happy and enjoying himself.

The next morning he died.

Americans mourned Roosevelt. The faces that lined the streets along the route of his cortege revealed a sorrow greater than any the nation had known since Lincoln's death. The world mourned him, too, and rightly so. Particularly for those who had known him well, nothing ever replaced Roosevelt's spirit, Roosevelt's leadership, Roosevelt's very presence.

For Henry Morgenthau, Jr., the President's death was a catastrophe. He had lost his sponsor, his chief, his closest friend. For years he felt the shock of personal deprivation. From the first, as he suspected immediately, he faced also the lesser loss of the support without which he could no longer effectively pursue his public purposes, his plan for Germany not the least. The evening of April 11 was, in a special sense, the last evening of Morgenthau's public career, as well as the last evening of Franklin Roosevelt's life. After April 11, there remained for Morgenthau as a public figure only a tense and trying epilogue.

IX

Epilogue:
Harry S Truman

April - July, 1945

MORGENTHAU, like the others in Roosevelt's Cabinet, scarcely knew Harry S Truman. Like them, too, he could not foresee what his relationship with the new President would be. The Secretary's entire public career had hinged on his friendship with Franklin Roosevelt. Now, bereft by Roosevelt's death, weary after twelve years in Washington, upset by the continuing illness of his wife, Morgenthau hoped to remain in office only until the war in Europe ended and only in order to advance the programs he had nurtured for international monetary cooperation, for economic aid to Great Britain, and for the occupation of Germany. For the months ahead, as in the years behind, he could succeed only if he had the support of the President.

1. President Truman

In his Diary Morgenthau recorded his first conversations with and impressions of President Truman. Immediately after Roosevelt's death on April 12, Truman summoned the Cabinet. "I want every one of you to stay and carry on, and I want to do everything just the way President Roosevelt wanted it," he said. "Nobody said anything," Morgenthau recollected later that day, "so I nodded to Stettinius to say something, and he did. He simply said that we would all be back of him. Then I spoke up and said, 'Mr. Truman, I will do all I can to help, but I want you to be free to call on anyone else

in my place.' Then Wickard said that I had expressed his sentiments also."

Two days later Morgenthau called on the President at nine in the
morning. As the Secretary recalled that meeting: "He didn't keep
me waiting a minute. I went in, and he started to tell me how
badly he felt and he said, 'I think I admired Mr. Roosevelt as much
as you did.' I said, 'I don't think that's possible. . . . Mr. President, I am ready to help, but I want you to feel that your hands are
untied as far as I am concerned.' He said, 'That's what everybody
has been telling me. . . . I need the help.' I said, 'I feel this war
very strongly. I have one son with General Patton and another in
the Pacific, and his ship has just been torpedoed for the second time.
. . . My idea is to win the war and then I want to win the peace,'
and he said, 'That's what I want to do.'

"I said, 'I have been doing a lot of things which Mr. Roosevelt has
encouraged me to do that aren't strictly Treasury business. . . . In
my job, I am very vulnerable because we have moved the financial
capital from London and Wall Street right to my desk at the Treasury.' He said, 'That's where I want to keep it,' so I said, 'Well, the
big boys will be after me, and I can't do what I have been doing
unless I have the complete backing of the President.' He said, 'You
will have that from me.'

"Then I said, 'I would like to talk to you sometime about Germany. I have some very definite ideas, and I would like to explain
them to you and explain the Morgenthau Plan.' He said, 'I would
like to know about it.' I said, 'There are no differences between
Stettinius and me, but the differences are down the line. They
haven't carried out the President's orders. . . . A lot of people in
the State Department were there in Hoover's time, and they aren't in
sympathy with the New Deal and Mr. Roosevelt.' So he said, 'Well, I
will get rid of them if they give us any trouble. . . . I have already
talked with Stettinius about Germany, and he said there is no difference of opinion. . . . I don't want any fussing between you and Stettinius.' I said, 'There is no fussing between us. We get along very
well together, but what I am worried about is the people under him.
. . . I get along with all members of the Cabinet,' and he said, 'I
know you do.' . . . Truman has a mind of his own. As he took me
to the door, he said, 'Now I want you to stay with me,' and I said, 'I

will stay just as long as I think I can serve you.' He said, 'When the time comes that you can't, you will hear from me first direct.'

"The man has a lot of nervous energy, and seems to be inclined to make very quick decisions. He was most courteous with me, and made a good impression, but, after all, he is a politician, and what is going on in his head time only will tell."

Morgenthau returned to his Diary on April 16, 1945, to record his memory of Roosevelt's funeral at Hyde Park and of the train ride back to Washington that followed it:

"It was a brilliant, clear day, and the flowers stood out just like so many jewels, and I have never seen such an impressive ceremony. The thing that finally got me was the blowing of the taps. I was worried about Joan* because she cried so, and I took her down to the train and gave her tea and a sandwich, and then she felt better.

"After a while I went and looked up Grace Tully and asked her to come back to me. She came back and spent about an hour with me. We just nicely got started talking when Frances Perkins barged in. She made me so intensely nervous that I couldn't take it, and didn't see why I had to, so I told her Miss Tully and I had to talk about some financial matters in which the President† and I were partners, and she took the hint and got out.

"I can't remember whether I got this from Tully . . . but immediately after the President's first attack his blood pressure went up to 300 and subsequently dropped to 200. They said that they did something about removing the saliva and pulling the tongue out in order to assist him in breathing. When the President finally passed away, there were just a couple of heavy breathing sounds, and that was all. This Commander in the Navy who attended him is a heart man from the Presbyterian Hospital, but I gathered that Admiral McIntyre was telling everybody in the train that this was wholly unexpected, and that they hadn't looked for it, which, of course, is just sheer damn nonsense because I have heard from two or three sources that the President had an enlarged heart. I don't think they had sufficient medical care or attention down there, considering the man's condition.

---

* Morgenthau's daughter, Joan, then a student at Vassar, who had accompanied him to Hyde Park for the funeral.
† President Roosevelt.

"I told Tully that if she wanted it she could have a job here in the Treasury. She was very much touched, but she said she didn't know what she would do, and that the first thing she was going to do was to go away and take a rest. I told her that I wasn't making an offer to anybody else over there.

"I asked her if the President had been satisfied with me and whether I had annoyed him in any way, and she said, 'Absolutely not — quite the contrary.' She said that . . . the Department that bothered him and worried him the most was the State Department. She said that I was never a source of worry.

"After lunch I asked to see Mrs. Roosevelt, and you had to go through President Truman's car to get to Mrs. Roosevelt's car. I saw Hannegan,* and I told him I would like to see him afterwards.

"I had a very nice talk with Mrs. Roosevelt. . . . Mrs. Roosevelt was very sweet and calm, but she looked rather drawn. . . .

"I . . . told Mrs. Roosevelt that she ought to get her business affairs rounded up as soon as possible so that she could speak to the world as Eleanor Roosevelt, and that I thought it was most important that her voice be heard. . . . She sort of questioned whether now that she was the widow of the President anybody would want to hear her. . . . I assured her that they would want to hear her. . . .

"Then I went back and I asked to see Hannegan. He and I went into one of the compartments of Truman's car, and we must have talked about a half to three-quarters of an hour. . . . I said . . . 'Maybe I will be cutting my own throat with what I am going to say now. . . . I don't like Byrnes, and I don't get along with him. . . . I think Truman would make a great mistake if he made Byrnes Secretary of State. . . . It is my belief that Byrnes, in the last three months, has lost a lot of popularity and prestige in the country . . . and on the Hill they think he has a swelled head. I don't think he would do Truman any good because he just can't play on anybody's team. . . . I think it would be bad if Truman takes it. I don't know how you feel.' Hannegan said, 'I agree with you completely.'

"I also said, 'Another thing you can pass on to Truman is that this idea of having twenty people at Cabinet is ridiculous. You just

* Robert E. Hannegan, chairman of the Democratic National Committee, close friend of Truman, soon to become Postmaster General.

can't do any business with that many people around.' Hannegan agreed with me and said, 'Why the night I came in there when the President died it looked like a carnival.' I said, 'We ought to have a War Cabinet; we should have an agenda, and we should have a Secretary, and if I want to bring up Bretton Woods I should notify the Secretary of the Cabinet and find out if it is agreeable to the President for me to talk about Bretton Woods.' He said, 'Henry, you aren't saying anything that I am not wholly in accord with.' . . .

"Then I told Hannegan about my talk with the President when I told him that I was accustomed to running my own Department, and he said, 'That's what Truman wants. He will give you complete independence. That's the way he operates.'

"Hannegan told me that at lunch with Truman and Byrnes, he took great pains to bring out the question of Bretton Woods because he wanted to see where Byrnes stood and Byrnes said that this is an absolute must, and so did President Truman. . . .

"Hannegan at no time gave me any indication as to whether he wanted me to stay, but everything I suggested he pass along to Truman he agreed with. . . .

"Later on, Sam Rosenman came in and he was very much down in the dumps. . . . Rosenman . . . said he thought recently anybody could get the President [Roosevelt] to sign anything, and that was very dangerous. He said that often the President didn't know the contents of the document he signed. . . .

"It seems that Vandenberg* had been with Truman, and Truman had asked Vandenberg's advice on whom he should keep and whom he shouldn't and that they had agreed to get rid of Biddle and Perkins, but that they also agreed they should keep me for the time being. Truman said he didn't think I would want to stay indefinitely because I had been there so long, but they wanted me to stay, and Vandenberg advised him to keep me. I gather that Dewey† agreed with that. It seems that Truman doesn't like Biddle at all, but that I am acceptable."

Morgenthau next saw Truman on the morning of April 20, 1945. "Before you were President you called me Henry," the Secretary said. "I wish you would continue to do that." Truman said he

---

* Republican Senator Arthur Vandenberg of Michigan.
† Thomas E. Dewey.

would like to. He then went on, according to Morgenthau's Diary, to say "that the evening of the President's death was the most difficult period he has ever gone through in his life, and I said, 'Mr. President, if you don't misunderstand me, as a citizen I would like to say that I think you have done extremely well in the first week.' He said, 'I have had all the breaks.' "

He had still another when on May 7 the Allied forces completed the conquest of Germany. Truman made the next day, his birthday, V-E Day, the symbol of a victory that had seemed much more remote, if possible at all, four years earlier.

"I am not going to make any speech," Morgenthau told his staff when first they heard the news of the end of the war in Europe, ". . . but I would like to say this much. I think that those of you who have been associated with me since Pearl Harbor and before . . . can all feel we have had a little share in this victory. . . . We gave them some orders to start with — the French engines. I think the Air Corps got at least one full year's headstart due to the fact that airplane factories, engine factories, had been working on Allied orders, and all of that was done from this office. I think that Mr. Purvis and I were with President Roosevelt, and he got the idea of lending the ships to the English rather than selling them, . . . the idea of the Lend-Lease was sort of born there that day . . . , and there was no question that the Treasury wrote the Lend-Lease Bill and got it through the House and Senate. . . . Certainly we have raised the money that the war has cost from the people. It has been the people's financing, and the people themselves have gotten in on this war the way they have as far as financing is concerned. . . . I think each one in his own heart can feel he had contributed something here at home toward quickening the end of this phase of the war. Now, we have got another very tough one ahead of us. . . . And when the last phase is through and the Japanese quit, then I think for the first time in my life — I have never really been drunk — I think I will get drunk then."

But first, while the war against Japan continued, the Secretary was involved in four important issues about which he had written the President: the legislation before Congress concerning the Bretton Woods agreements, which Truman supported vigorously; the ongoing negotiations about American aid to China, so long a difficult and controversial matter; the problem of American assistance to the United Kingdom during Phases II and III; and the planning of occupation policy for Germany. With the President on May 9, 1945, Morgenthau said "that I just wanted him to keep it in the back of his head . . . that he might want to use me on the Russian situation. He said, 'I will use all the tools I can lay my hands on,' but in this case . . . I got the feeling he was just being polite and he didn't welcome the suggestion.' " It remained to be seen how many of Morgenthau's other suggestions Truman would accept.

2. Confirmation for Bretton Woods

Truman's enthusiasm for the Bretton Woods Agreements eased the Treasury's task in obtaining congressional approval for American participation in both the International Monetary Fund and the International Bank. That objective had been Morgenthau's responsibility since the time of the New Hampshire conference. The Secretary in turn had made Luxford and White his chief agents, for public and for congressional relations respectively. But Morgenthau remained deeply involved in the planning and execution of legislative strategy, and determined to avoid the mishaps that had frustrated Wilson at the end of the First World War.

The chief opposition to the Bretton Woods Agreements sprang from the New York financial community, including officers of the New York Federal Reserve Bank, and from isolationist senators and newspapers. The latter simply rejected anything tainted with internationalism. The newspapers hostile to Bretton Woods were mostly continuing an old antagonism to the New Deal. In New York City alone, the *Wall Street Journal,* the *Sun, World Telegram, Mirror,* and *Journal American* opposed American participation in the International Bank, except on radically altered terms. In New York and elsewhere, newspaper support for the Treasury was uncommon and often equivocal. Even the influential *New York Times* took an editorial position indistinguishable from that of the financial critics of the Fund and Bank, and Morgenthau's personal efforts to move the *Times*'s publisher and editors produced hours of polite conversation but no positive effect.

Morgenthau and his aides also attempted, again without success, to elicit the cooperation of the American Bankers Association and its president, Randolph Burgess. Closely associated for many years with the Treasury's quarterly financings, Burgess regretted his unaccustomed role as an opponent of the Department, but his personal convictions, as well as his office in the American Bankers Association, gave him no alternative. Still, he welcomed a chance to discuss the question of the Fund and the Bank with Treasury experts early in 1945 and periodically thereafter. In spite of their arguments, Burgess remained disapproving of the Fund because "it would give credit automatically to countries which were not credit worthy." Many bankers, moreover, interpreted the Fund as still another attack on the traditional, pre-1933 gold standard, which they would like to have restored. They drew support for that interpretation from the debate in Great Britain where the government had to dissociate the Fund from the gold standard, the bête noir of the British left.

Burgess and his fellows in the ABA therefore recommended setting up an advisory committee to include, among others, the chairman of the Board of Governors of the Federal Reserve Board, and the presidents of various of the Federal Reserve banks. That committee would then guide the policies of the American representative on the Bank. The United States, Burgess argued, was putting up most of the money, and should therefore depart from the Bretton Woods pacts in order to advance American interests. By American interests, as Morgenthau saw it, Burgess really meant the habits and preferences of downtown Manhattan.

In rebuttal to Burgess, Morgenthau and his staff explained that the function of stabilization and the function of investment, quite distinct from each other, should not be combined. A long-term stabilization loan had a different purpose and effect from the kind of broad cooperation in maintaining exchange standards which the Fund would cultivate. Indeed the International Fund was not to be essentially a lending institution. Rather it was a means of securing international cooperation for establishing standards of monetary exchange. Further, its method for giving help to countries in trouble through the sale of exchange under a gold-value guarantee had proved successful in the past in the experience of the United States

Stabilization Fund and in recent bilateral agreements between the British and the Belgians and the British and the Dutch. The Fund, moreover, would not begin exchange transactions with countries unless they were able to keep their exchange rates stable without excessive recourse to currency loans. According to the rules of the institution, no country could purchase exchange except to help to make payments for current imports and similar, current transactions. The Fund could prevent any nation at any time from buying exchange for purposes contrary to those defined at Bretton Woods. And all of the currency holdings of the Fund were guaranteed against depreciation in terms of gold. In reply to the assertion of the ABA that few nations lacked dollar and gold holdings, the Treasury noted that many countries would need exchange loans during the period of reconstruction and would need increases in their monetary reserves in order to sustain a stable exchange. The bankers, with characteristic gloom, had asked: "Who knows the kind of world we are facing for the next five years — the political, social and economic conditions?" The Treasury answered that if nothing constructive were done during those five years, the world would know a time of economic, social, and political disturbance.

Those and other arguments failed to impress either the ABA or the Senate isolationists who, unlike Burgess, opposed the Bank as well as the International Monetary Fund. Those isolationists, moreover, would be able in time actually to vote against the Bretton Woods pacts. Their leader, Robert A. Taft, rested his case on characteristic reassertions of nationalistic politics and traditional economics. By his own account always "suspicious" of the Treasury's program, Taft had denounced the Bank "as part of the general New Deal program to create new methods of deficit spending." All the money the Bank loaned, he said, would come from the United States, and all of its loans should therefore depend on specific congressional authorization. The Bank, in this view, violated both the strictures of sound finance and the provisions of the Constitution. As for the Fund, Taft predicted that "it would be like pouring money down a sewer. . . . All the real assets of the Fund will come from the United States. . . . It will not be long before all of our assets are gone and the Fund is entirely made up of weaker, worthless currencies." As he saw it, the Fund also placed power in a representative of the President "without approval of the Congress, to change the gold value of the dollar." Thus it too challenged the Constitution. In advancing those and other views, Dean Acheson held, Taft made continual errors of fact and, along with likeminded associates, indulged in an "utterly unscrupulous misrepresentation" of the Bretton Woods Agreements.

In order to correct misunderstanding, the Treasury undertook to reach the uninformed and the indifferent, to explain the Bretton Woods Agreements in the press, and to enlist support for them. Morgenthau and his assistants persuaded the *New York Times Magazine, Foreign Affairs,* Walter Lippmann, and Raymond Gram Swing to publish articles advocating American participation in the Fund and Bank. In an appeal to a less intellectual audience, the Treasury assisted in the writing of pieces for *Liberty Magazine* and the *Reader's Digest.*

Those articles doubtless made less impact on Congress than did the efforts of pressure groups with which the Treasury worked. Among those groups were the League of Women Voters, the CIO and the AFL, the National Foreign Trade Council, the National Council of American Importers, and the Advertisers Club of New York. Morgenthau especially welcomed an endorsement of the Fund and the Bank by the Independent Bankers Association whose report he sent to the House Committee on Banking and Currency. That association had a membership of over two thousand country banks in some forty states. "While we can hardly claim to speak for Wall Street" its reports said, "we do believe we can speak for Main Street." The Secretary also delighted in a poll of the American Economic Association that indicated that 90 per cent of its members advocated adherence to the Bretton Woods Agreements. He was gratified, too, by the approval of some two hundred leading scholars of the Economists Committee on the Bretton Woods Program. "I think that was a wonderful job getting all those economists together," Morgenthau wrote Harry White, "and if you would write a letter to Professor [Seymour] Harris . . . congratulating on this, I'd be glad to sign it."

Morgenthau also encouraged White to muster influential individuals behind the Treasury's program, among them Alvin Hansen, the celebrated Harvard economist, Dean James M. Landis of the Harvard Law School, and Harold Stassen, the then liberal, then Minnesota Republican who declared himself "tremendously interested" in the Bretton Woods Agreements but remained officially noncommittal. Morgenthau himself wrote Senator Carter Glass, then old and ill, who was unable to reply, and Walter George, a conservative with credentials as good as those of Glass. As the Secretary put it to his staff: "I had a very good forty-five minutes with Walter George and he ended up by saying, 'I will say a good word for Bretton Woods.' "

Most important was the continuing cooperation of the members of the American delegation to Bretton Woods. Dean Acheson was a steady and effective advocate of the agreements while the Congress considered them, as were Ned Brown, the Chicago banker, and Republican Congressman Wolcott, who helped to persuade Governor Thomas E. Dewey to reject Taft's advice.

Morgenthau presided over the conferences about tactics which profited from the continual presence of Fred Vinson and Senator Robert Wagner, the chief sponsor of the Bretton Woods pacts in the Senate. Against the advice of his subordinates, Morgenthau joined Acheson in advising the President to link the Bretton Woods proposals to other recommendations for international economic policies, including new lending authorizations for the Export-Import Bank, an extension of the Trade Agreements Act, and participation in the United Nations Food and Agricultural Organization. With Acheson, Luxford attended meetings on the Hill to set a schedule for the hearings on the Bretton Woods Act, for which Roosevelt had provided specific endorsement in a message to Congress in February 1945. "International political relations," the President then had said, basing his remarks on a draft the Treasury had prepared, "will be friendly and constructive . . . only if solutions are found to the difficult economic problems we face today. The corner stone for international economic cooperation is the Bretton Woods proposal for an International Monetary Fund and an International Bank for Reconstruction and Development. These proposals are . . . concrete evidence that the economic objectives of the United States agree with those of the United Nations. . . . What we need and what they need correspond — expanded production, employment, exchange and consumption."

Confident of victory in the House, Morgenthau was uncertain

about the Senate. He attempted to circumvent Taft by going to
Arthur Vandenberg, but Vandenberg declined to involve himself in
the contest. "I tried to follow this thing for a couple of months,"
Vandenberg said, ". . . and it is just too damned complicated. It is
a terrible thing to say, but I am busy and we have divided this thing
up under Republican organization and this is Taft's bomb. . . . I
will be very frank with you. Bob Wagner never was any good, and
he isn't worth a damn. The thing you have got to do is get some
Democrat who knows this thing . . . and who will make the fight.
Otherwise, you are sunk." But Morgenthau felt he had to work
through Wagner on the Democratic side, while Vandenberg's position left the Treasury without a Republican advocate.

In an effort to appease the Republicans, Dan Bell opened discussions in April with Randolph Burgess about a compromise between
the Treasury and the American Bankers Association. Burgess was
willing to drop his demand for the elimination of the International
Monetary Fund if the Treasury would agree to the appointment of
one American to serve both as executive director of the Fund and as
governor of the Bank. The Treasury, according to that plan, would
also urge the Canadians, British, Dutch, and Belgians to follow the
same practice. In that manner the two institutions, as Burgess put
it, would have "a single Board of Directors." Burgess also continued
to insist on the appointment of an advisory board on the operations
of the Fund and the Bank. Further, he wanted Congress to lay
down explicit rules for guiding American representatives on those
institutions. The rules he proposed, as the Treasury saw it, needlessly elaborated upon the meaning of the Bretton Woods Agreements.

As it developed, the leading officers of the New York Federal Reserve Bank declared themselves opposed to the Fund even under the
terms Burgess had suggested. "My own feeling," Morgenthau told
Dan Bell, "is this. I think we should move very slowly on what we
agree to. . . . I think that it would strengthen our hand enor-
mously before the Senate if we got it through the House without any
amendment. Then if we've got to do any horse trading, let's do it in
the Senate." Persisting in that view in spite of Roosevelt's death,
Morgenthau on April 13, 1945, stood fast against compromise. "The
very group that had been pushing us hardest," he told his staff, "was

the group that put him [Roosevelt] in an untenable position in the London Economic Conference. . . . It is that crowd, plus their descendants." Loyalty to Roosevelt and to the New Deal, the integrity of the Bretton Woods Agreements, and the tactical situation in Congress, all called for a hard line. Dean Acheson agreed. "It would seem to me to be most desirable," he said, "if it is possible to get this through the House with a large vote. . . . I think that will do more to strengthen this in the Senate than anything else." And on April 14 and later, President Truman took the same position and promised his assistance. Bretton Woods, he said, was "an absolute must."

The enabling legislation for the Bretton Woods Agreements started on its way through the House at just the time that the San Francisco Conference completed the charter for the United Nations. The spirit of internationalism then ebullient in the United States applied to economic as well as political prescriptions for the postwar world. Most of the forty-four original members of the United Nations, as Morgenthau noted in April 1945, would need economic assistance. "The conservative thing to do," he said, "is to help these people so they won't go either Fascist or Bolshevik. . . . The radical thing is to do nothing and sit by and let them go to hell. . . . If we let Europe go to hell we will have either Fascism or Bolshevism. It's going to spread. That's what we fought to keep from spreading." He would therefore agree to no "picayune" compromises with the American Bankers Association. If there were going to be any conditions for American participation in the Fund and Bank, Congress would have to set them on its own.

The Treasury did consent to an amendment to the enabling legislation that created an Advisory Council to report to Congress and to oversee American policy in the Fund and Bank. Morgenthau worried about that amendment largely because the State Department persuaded the House Committee on Banking and Currency to leave open the question of which Cabinet officer should serve as chairman of the council, but initially he accepted Truman's advice not to "hold up Bretton Woods on account of this." Later, however, when Acheson and Will Clayton suggested that the chairmanship should fall to the Secretary of State, Morgenthau bristled. "We might just as well settle," he said, "who's going to represent the President of the United States . . . on financial matters." He therefore urged Truman to support a draft of the amendment that gave the Secretary of the Treasury specific responsibility "for conducting . . . financial and monetary negotiations — working, of course, in close cooperation with the State Department." At the White House on May 18, 1945, Truman read Morgenthau's memorandum carefully, "waved it in the air and said, "This is all right and I'll tell Stettinius this is what I want.' "*

By that date, the Banking and Currency Committee had rejected Republican amendments to the enabling legislation. Before the end of May, it approved three amendments which Morgenthau backed, one on the advisory council as Truman had endorsed it, a second noting that the Bank could make stabilization loans — a possibility inherent in its charter but dear to Burgess, and a third authorizing American representatives on both the Fund and the Bank to get interpretations from Congress with regard to the powers of those institutions. On May 24 the committee reported the bill out favorably. "I think you handled it beautifully," Morgenthau told Wolcott and Spence. On June 8 the House passed the committee's bill. As Congressman Spence put it, "we didn't have anybody against us except the confirmed isolations." Indeed the eighteen Republicans who opposed the Bretton Woods legislation had also to a man opposed extending the draft in 1941, and had opposed the Lend-Lease Act and appropriations to implement it. Now, Wolcott told Morgenthau: "Everything turned out splendidly. . . . I thoroughly enjoyed working with you. . . . After all the bad things I had heard about you before that . . . I had to change my mind."

The vote in the House by no means dispelled opposition to the Bretton Woods agreements in the Senate. Morgenthau, working with the Democratic leadership, especially Senators Barkley and Wagner, tried to extend the sponsorship of the bill. The Secretary also bolstered Wagner when the need arose. It was important, he said, to have the press and the radio praise Wagner. "He doesn't think he is getting enough publicity," Morgenthau explained.

---

* The amendment provided for a council consisting of the Secretary of the Treasury as chairman and, as members, the Secretaries of State and Commerce, the chairman of the Board of Governors of the Federal Reserve System, and the chairman of the Board of Directors of the Export-Import Bank. No president of any federal reserve bank was to sit on the council.

". . . It is a chronic illness with him. . . . And I wondered if . . . they couldn't tie him in with what a wonderful job he is doing for Bretton Woods." The Treasury found unexpected help among Senators in the silver bloc, for whatever the ABA condemned, they tended to applaud. As one of them put it: "I am against all god-damned New York bankers!" Yet the silverites insisted that nothing in the bill should militate against the use of silver as one basis for American currency. Agreeable to that condition, Morgenthau was surprised when the silver men, going further, pushed an amendment through the Senate that eliminated from the enabling legislation a definition of the dollar in terms of gold. That deletion had only symbolic significance, for the Treasury, along with other treasuries, would continue to define the value of the dollar as it had before.

As the Treasury and Democratic leadership realized, some concessions to Taft and his associates were necessary. During the hearings in the House and the Senate, the Department consented to provisions requiring the American director on the Fund to have the approval of the Advisory Council before voting on any issue for which his support was required by the Fund agreement. The Council had also to approve any waiver of the conditions set for the Fund's lending operations, and any definition that the dollar was a "scarce currency" — a definition that would have led to the imposition of restrictions on American exports. The Director, too, was to oppose the use of currency stabilization loans for "relief, reconstruction . . . or to meet a large and sustained outflow of capital." As Morgenthau saw it, those restrictions were already inherent in the Fund Articles. The language in the Bretton Woods Agreements Act was merely confirmatory. His critics believed that that language, by stressing the conservative bent of the Senate, embarrassed the British, who hoped the Fund, once it began to operate, would pursue liberal policies. The Secretary, however, felt that such policies remained probable, for he believed that Truman would select a Director with liberal leanings on questions of international finance, and that the Advisory Council would encourage those leanings.

Yet Treasury spokesmen before the Senate committee continually reassured their conservative interrogators. Again and again they said that the Fund's resources would not be made available except to nations satisfying the conditions of the Fund Articles. They also emphasized the potential benefits that the operations of the Fund would confer on international trade. Some of their statements implied that, with the establishment of the Fund, exchange controls and currency devaluations would soon vanish. That implication, an excessively sanguine forecast, rested on assumptions that the Treasury could not seriously defend, especially Morgenthau's assumption that large American support for the British economy would be forthcoming during Stages II and III of Lend-Lease. Had American policy toward Great Britain in particular developed as the Secretary hoped it would,* the Treasury's high expectations for the Fund would have had a far better chance for fulfillment in the immediate postwar period. So, too, with the Treasury's sunny predictions about postwar Anglo-American balances of payments. And so, finally, with the Department's optimism about the international financial problems of the transition from war to peace. The assurances that Morgenthau's associates offered doubting Senators distorted the immediate future, but the distortions resulted largely from the caution and penury of conservative congressmen who chose later in 1945 to interpret narrowly American interests that Morgenthau would have interpreted more broadly. Further, during the hearings, those assurances did sufficiently pacify the opposition to the Bretton Woods pacts.

As the bill moved toward the floor of the Senate, Morgenthau was skittish about the unpredictable silver bloc and even more concerned that the debate about the UN charter might generate an isolationist resurgence injurious also to the Fund and Bank. He tried without success to get Truman to have the vote on Bretton Woods precede that on the charter; he kept pressure on Senator Wagner; he had several of his staff "devote themselves exclusively" to answering any "wild statement" that the opposition might contrive. There was no cause for alarm. The enabling legislation, tabled during the debate on the United Nations, made its way through the Senate at the end of July. It was, Morgenthau believed, the single most important act that the Treasury had sponsored during his tenure.

* See Section IV, below.

3. Assistance for China: Last Round

In mid-April 1945, Harry White warned Morgenthau that T. V. Soong had left the United Nations conference in San Francisco early in order to come to Washington "to put on a drive" for extensive gold shipments from the United States to China. The Treasury, on White's advice, had been holding down such shipments for several years, primarily because they had so little impact on the inflation in China which they were intended to palliate. Now Soong was trying to persuade Truman to reverse this policy. "The story that they have," White said, "appears to be a very defensible one, that they are going to . . . order reforms in China, but that is not the real reason in either Soong's mind or the Generalissimo's mind. . . . The political ramifications are the most important things. . . . I don't think you will be in a position to discuss it intelligently with the President. . . . I think you will have to go into it in . . . detail."

Morgenthau, as White implied, had been out of touch with the situation in China because of his overriding concern for German questions. The Secretary therefore needed time before he could brief the President. As White also said, the demand for gold arose, perhaps in major part, from the need of the Kuomintang to buttress its political prestige. But inflation, following its familiar paths for familiar reasons, was still eroding the Chinese economy, and White feared that Soong would draw support for his request from Leon Henderson who had recently returned from China. Soong had set a high target. Of the $500 million credit of 1942, the Chinese had yet to use $240 million; Soong now wanted $180 million of that balance to purchase gold for sale by the Chinese government to mop up billions of outstanding fapi. The gold was needed, too, to cover substantial forward sales of gold that the Chinese had already made.*

The Treasury's Monetary Division, according to a memorandum of Frank Coe, judged that the $27 million of gold already shipped had been wholly wasted, sold at inexcusably low prices to favored speculators and hoarders. Further, the Chinese government, Coe held, had sold both forward gold and certificates calling for payment

---

* That is, the Chinese government had sold gold futures, for which it received fapi in return for promises to deliver gold at a later date.

in dollars at rates far below their black market price to privileged buyers who could now redeem them at more than fifteen times their original cost. In Coe's view, individuals and organizations intimately connected with T. V. Soong and H. H. Kung had been the primary beneficiaries, and would make outlandish profits if the United States acceded to Soong's proposal for the shipments. The Chinese, Coe wrote, were still overcharging the United States Army for services and supplies, and were asking not only for gold but also for $75 million worth of trucks from Lend-Lease, and for huge quantities of textiles which they proposed to sell for anti-inflationary purposes. Those requests ignored the difficulties of transportation into China and the tightness in textile supplies within the United States.

Soong, Morgenthau discovered in conversation with the President, had visited Truman and "it wasn't clear . . . what Soong wanted. So I said it was a gold question, and on questions like that where it was a monetary question I felt it should be one Treasury opposite another treasury, and he said, 'Absolutely.' I said, 'If you would like me to see Soong and in consultation with State and War work out whatever he has, I would be glad to do it.' And he said he would like me to do it. He brought it up again in Cabinet and he confirmed it there again."

During the next two weeks Morgenthau learned that the Army was eager to have the Treasury cooperate with China on an anti-inflationary program, even though Under Secretary of War Patterson recognized that the Chinese "do an awful lot of lying." For the State Department, Will Clayton endorsed the Treasury's reluctance to increase gold shipments which, Clayton agreed, had been consistently ineffective in fighting inflation. Yet Clayton, like Morgenthau, wanted to strengthen Chiang Kai-shek. So did Leon Henderson, who had discovered at first hand how corrupt and unreliable was the Nationalist government, but nevertheless concluded that it could still be saved. "I think unless we do something," Henderson told Dan Bell, "we will lose a lot, provided we think our eggs are all in the Nationalist Government basket. It is a high political question which I am not qualified to pass on. I think the thing could be held together if given help. . . . I am a friend of theirs." Leo Crowley for the Foreign Economic Administration also sympathized with China's plight. Nevertheless he and his staff were dubious about meeting the Chinese request for 4000 trucks and 176 million yards of cotton textiles. In allocating such critical materials, he told Morgenthau, the FEA had to consider the needs of the liberated areas in Europe and of the various recipients of Lend-Lease, as well as of American civilians.

In a preliminary analysis of May 1 and a memorandum of May 8, 1945, for interdepartmental discussion, Frank Coe set forth the recommendations of the Monetary Division. The American agencies dealing with the Chinese, Coe argued, agreed that any program designed to stabilize China's currency and check inflation should include a broad series of measures, among them the rehabilitation of the monetary and banking system, the stabilization of foreign exchange, and fiscal and administrative reforms, as well as increases in the delivery and distribution of supplies from the United States. Coe therefore favored using the balance of the 1942 loan to establish a new Chinese stabilization fund. He went on to demand a cessation of forward sales of gold in China and to offer the Chinese only very limited quantities of gold within the next few months, unless the State Department ruled otherwise for political reasons. He concluded by urging an investigation of previous gold sales and a cancellation of those made to speculators.

Morgenthau objected on two counts. He was not at all sure, he said, that he should use a "preachy tone" with Soong. More important, he felt that Coe was too assertive. At the most, Morgenthau said, the memorandum should suggest that an unfortunate impression had arisen within the United States that there had been speculative sales of gold in China. Any stronger statement, the Secretary felt, would cost Soong "face."

Incorporating that suggestion, but otherwise leaving his memorandum unchanged, Coe read it aloud to representatives of the State Department, the War Department, and the Foreign Economic Administration who met at the Treasury on May 8. The State Department approved the general policy outlined. At the suggestion of Leo Crowley, the Army agreed to let Morgenthau tell Soong he would get his trucks, but the question of textiles would have to be deferred for further study. When Soong arrived to join the conference, the Americans faced him with a "unified front."

Soong concentrated his protest against the Treasury's position on gold. The Treasury memorandum, he said, while clearly intended to be constructive, gave no indication of just how a stabilization fund would help to combat inflation. Morgenthau replied that the only remedy for inflation lay in relieving shortages of goods in China. He looked forward to the day when China would again have an open seaport, but meanwhile a stabilization fund would provide a more orthodox weapon against inflation than would the Chinese suggestions for sales of gold. Soong objected that China could not wait. He admitted that the Treasury had not been consulted about the forward sales of gold, but he promised to tax those who had made speculative profits, and more important, he quoted a letter Morgenthau had sent to the Chinese ambassador on July 27, 1943. "The Treasury," that letter read, "agrees to the request of . . . China . . . that $200 million be made available . . . for the purchase of gold. In order to avoid unnecessary raising of funds by the United States Treasury, it is suggested that transfers from the credit of the Chinese government for the purchase of gold be made at such time and in such amounts as are allowed by existing facilities for the transportation to China of the . . . gold." That letter, Soong noted, gave him "a definite commitment," and on the basis of that commitment China had made its forward sales.

The letter and Soong's related argument disturbed Morgenthau more than he at first revealed. When Soong left the conference, the Secretary commented that he was going "to stick to the memo," but the next day he scolded Coe and others on his staff. "Look," Morgenthau said, "you people, I think, should be severely criticized for letting me go into court and try my case before T. V. Soong, and the letter . . . where I gave the Chinese Government a firm commitment . . . I think it's inexcusable. After all, you were so worried about saving face, what about my face? I have given, in writing, the Chinese Government a firm commitment that they can have $200 million worth of gold and . . . I don't remember it, I can't remember it. I do ten things a day. . . . And you put me in an absolutely dishonorable position, and I think it's inexcusable." Coe wriggled; his recommendations, he said, had not categorically refused gold to the Chinese. Now clearly angry, Morgenthau replied: "That has nothing to do with it."

"I was worried last night wholly independent of this," the Secretary continued, ". . . and I figured these people were being kicked around from pillar to post and I was worried. Will Clayton called me twenty minutes to nine and asked if he could see me. I told him yes and he dashed over to the Navy Department to sit there waiting to see me and he brought this stuff.* . . . This morning with Forrestal and King I wanted figures so I could talk about the . . . War Loan. . . . So I got them on China, and Admiral King tells me that the Chinese are doing much better. . . . They are really getting somewhere, and they are really fighting and moving. . . . They are going to have eleven or twelve Chinese Divisions . . . and they are good Divisions. The Chinese are really doing it, and here I am acting like a huckster over something which has been settled on . . . 1943. I don't like it."

Coe and his associates, Morgenthau ordered, were to reconstitute the Treasury recommendation to show that the gold belonged to China and that China would get it, though for the sake of future relationships, the Treasury was to suggest also the establishment of a new Chinese stabilization fund. Conversation with Soong later in the day made Morgenthau still more favorable to the Chinese request. Soong, he told his staff, "shouldn't be held responsible for things which were done while he was not in charge . . . this matter of gold is of vital importance to him, and . . . after all . . . I had promised it. . . . He said . . . that he didn't think they wanted a stabilization fund because it would have been bilateral and they should wait for Bretton Woods. So I suggested, 'Well, why not have it called a reconstruction fund.' . . . He stressed that they were going to tax these people [who had speculative projects]. They were even willing to recall some of the certificates, but he thought they could do it better through taxes." Further, Soong wanted the gold as an indication of the confidence of the United States, for that, he said, would strengthen him in his pending negotiations with the Russians.

Later on May 9 Soong incorporated Morgenthau's suggestion for a reconstruction fund in a memorandum he delivered to the Treasury. The reconstruction of China, Soong wrote, was an integral part of both Chinese and American policy for making China a strong

* On China's contribution to the war effort.

power and enabling her to fulfill her role in the politics of Asia and the Pacific. But no stabilization fund alone would serve China's needs. Any such fund had to be part of a broad plan based primarily on projects for industrialization. That plan would depend on China's getting from the United States capital goods, machine tools, transportation facilities, and investments. Only a true collaboration of the two nations could assure a successful program, which Soong was prepared to discuss at once. Meanwhile, Soong asked once more for the delivery within the next three months of at least 1,131,000 ounces of gold.

The memorandum impressed the Secretary who nevertheless remained reluctant wholly to abandon the project for a stabilization fund. Supported by Will Clayton, Morgenthau told Soong that the creation of a stabilization fund "would enable me to be in a position that I wouldn't have to explain. . . . While I want to do everything possible, I can't do it as enthusiastically as I would like to. Now, what is it worth to you to have the United States Treasury enthusiastically back of this new regime which you're heading . . . so that you have the full support which you deserve? . . . Mistakes . . . were made during your absence, and I'm not going into details but you and I know what I'm talking about. No matter how strict taxation reforms you put in, the very fact that you haven't put in very strict taxation shows that the money is there, otherwise you wouldn't be recommending these high taxes. . . . The impression I received and the impression I gave Congress . . . was that we would be consulted as to the spending of the money. . . . Certainly if we had been consulted as to this method of the use of the $500 million we never would have given our consent. . . . I would like you to think about it some more. . . . There's no question of making the gold available, but it's a question of the speed with which it can be done. I think that I've . . . tried to be helpful, and . . . if you help me to help you . . . I think I could say . . . that we are talking this way for the Administration. . . . Frankly, I hope I will not be called before Congress to have to explain. . . .

"We stand ready to fulfill any commitment which was made, but that's one question. The other question is that you have to decide . . . how I think I could be helpful to you. Now you decide what my friendship is worth. . . . There are no hard feelings."

But there were hard feelings on the part of White and Coe. On May 15, 1945, Coe suggested that Morgenthau send a letter to Truman emphasizing the public scandal attending Chinese gold sales and urging the United States to ask China to withdraw her request for gold shipments. White that day insisted that discussions between the Treasury and the Chinese in 1943 had made gold shipments conditional on their wise and effective use. Those evasions irritated Morgenthau. "These people own this gold," he reminded his assistants." . . . I think that the Treasury up to this time, has been correct. And I certainly am part and parcel of this policy of slowing down the shipment of gold just as much as we could, because it wasn't good for them, and looking forward to the day they really need the money. And it's there. . . . We have two targets. One is we have to first defeat Japan, and the other target is to liberate China. . . . The Chinese are beginning to fight now. That seems to be fairly well substantiated, and there's a determination to fight, and if we can get these people to fight . . . that means saving lives, many lives, and it's a very expensive investment. . . . I suddenly made up my mind that this was all wrong, . . . particularly when I see that my written word and the promise of Franklin Roosevelt is at stake. . . . Never mind what I told the Congress. Never mind what I say they told me. . . . There is my written word you can have $200 million worth of gold. . . . That influences me greatly. . . . I don't think we have a leg to stand on. Even if the Chinese weren't fighting . . . they could have this."

Still unhappy, White suggested Morgenthau write to Will Clayton asking him to recommend the gold shipments for political reasons. Then Morgenthau could take a note to Truman approving the Chinese request on political rather than economic grounds. The Secretary did ask Clayton for such a letter, but he also warned White that "I'm going to live up to my word."

A day later, on May 16, 1945, Morgenthau expressed increased dissatisfaction with his advisers. He had discovered that, contrary to Coe's report, Soong and Kung had not profited from the Chinese sales of forward gold and dollar certificates. "There's no reason for me to believe that that is Soong's," the Secretary said. ". . . They are simply corporations. . . . You boys have been telling me right along that Soong owns most of this stuff, and that's misleading."

Fully persuaded of Soong's honesty, Morgenthau was not upset when Clayton reported that there was no "political reason at the moment to urge you to do anything . . . whatever the commitment is" in China. The State Department wanted of course "to maintain this particular government," but it saw no direct relationship between the gold question and that objective. Morgenthau would like to have had the State Department "ease my conscience," as he put it, but "I'm going to tell the President of the United States that my recommendation is that we fulfill our contract." Clayton applauded that decision.

Later that day, May 16, Soong called at the Treasury. "I had a chance to talk this morning with President Truman," Morgenthau said, ". . . and he told me that you had told him that mistakes had been made in the past with regard to the handling of this gold and that you assured him in the future that these mistakes would be corrected.

"I am just back . . . and I would like to write you a letter pointing out the mistakes we think have been made. . . . So there will be no future misunderstanding . . . also pointing out in this letter the steps that we hope will be taken to correct them, we are writing this letter and the rest is up to you. We recognize that the United States Government had made this commitment and we are prepared to carry it out. . . .

"I am pointing out that how you use this gold will have great influence on any future assistance which this government may or may not be prepared to make. . . . We'll be influenced by what you do about the suggestions which I have made about a fund."

Morgenthau's letter of May 16 did just what he had said it would. He also persuaded Joseph Grew, the acting Secretary of State, to send him a letter expressing State Department support for Treasury policy. That letter, while finding "that the sale of gold by China has not proved and is not likely to prove a very effective anti-inflationary device," commended the proposal for the establishment of a Chinese stabilization fund. "Since there appears to be no doubt," Grew continued, "that the Chinese Government attaches a greater importance to the immediate delivery of the gold than to the longer run benefits which might result from the establishment of the fund . . . and since the continued stability of China and her increasing military efforts in the war . . . are of great concern to the United

States, the Department recommends that the Treasury . . . deliver the gold to China in accordance with the time schedules put forward by Dr. Soong."

Unfortunately, the State Department neglected to consult or even inform Ambassador Hurley in Chungking about the conversations with Soong. Hurley was therefore abrupt in a cable of June 11, 1945, replying to a report from Morgenthau about the gold shipments and the stabilization fund. Like the Treasury, Hurley had found gold sales almost useless; like the Treasury, he was disturbed by the "vicious speculation" in China and the "unfavorable publicity and the so-called gold scandals." But like Soong, he doubted that a stabilization fund would provide any immediate remedy for inflation. Most important, he was upset that the United States had "reserved no power to control the situation in its gold commitment to China." He would, he cabled, have withheld the gold until China had actually established the fund, and he regretted that he had not been consulted before Morgenthau acted.

For his part Morgenthau, who had expected the State Department to handle communications with Hurley, had developed greater confidence in the Generalissimo and in Soong than had the Ambassador. Indeed in June 1945, Hurley stood much closer to White and Coe than he did to Morgenthau. As for the Secretary, he was, as always, setting his course in China on the basis of his reading of American interests. As much as his own promise of 1943, the assurances of Admiral King and of the Army that the Chinese were fighting and would continue to be valuable allies had accounted for Morgenthau's decision about the gold. He did not stop there. "As a straight military matter," he urged the Army and the Foreign Economic Administration to provide "45 million yards of cotton goods for China over a three month period," with further and larger shipments to follow. In behalf of that project Morgenthau went to Truman on May 23, 1945. "I talked to him about cotton for China," the Secretary noted in his Diary, "and I told him how slow everybody was. . . . He pounded the desk and said, 'What the hell is the matter with these people? Don't they know we have a war on our hands? . . . I want to give China some cotton.' I told him that up to now all we had given them was promises, . . . I said that I would have something for him by next Wednesday."

And so Morgenthau did, by arranging to have the cotton move

not under Lend-Lease but through the Army which, independently of the Chinese government, would trade the textiles for the goods and services it needed. Those transactions, both Morgenthau and Judge Patterson believed, would assist Army procurement in China and, by moving textiles into the Chinese economy, help to reduce inflation. "It is a source of great satisfaction to me," Morgenthau wrote Patterson on May 31, 1945, "that because of the active support of the War Department, China will receive substantial quantities of textiles during the second half of this year. I am pleased that safeguards will be taken to bring about the most effective use and disposition of these textiles for the prosecution of the war against Japan."

On June 1 at the White House, Morgenthau delivered a final report of the committee on Chinese requests which he had signed along with Patterson, Clayton, and Crowley. As it noted, the Foreign Economic Administration would furnish China 4000 trucks over and above the previous allocation. For the third quarter of 1945, moreover, China would receive 45 million yards of textiles, with the probable allocation of another 65 million yards in the fourth quarter. The Treasury was shipping gold of a value of $189,-224,000. "I read the report . . . for China," Morgenthau noted in his Diary, "and the President said that T. V. Soong ought to be very pleased with that."

So, of course, was Morgenthau. At his direction, in spite of the continuing objections of White and Coe, the gold was on its way. The Secretary had been able also to procure trucks and textiles for the Chinese because Truman had given him direct support. He had already discovered how difficult it was to accomplish anything when the President was hostile.

4. No "Brain Wave" for England

The end of the war in Europe gave a new urgency to Great Britain's economic problems. With the Allied victory in Germany, Lend-Lease entered Stage II, for which Morgenthau had made plans with his American and British colleagues in the months immediately after the Quebec Conference. But Stage II was commencing in May 1945, instead of in January, as Roosevelt and Churchill had hoped it might when they met at Quebec. By May, the American Joint Chiefs of Staff considered the military requirements for Stage II significantly changed from their estimates of five months earlier. The army now held that strategic plans necessitated a reduction in Lend-Lease shipments to Great Britain previously contemplated. Morgenthau agreed that military considerations would govern the allocations of weapons and civilian supplies, but he also felt that the United States had incurred a moral commitment to assist the United Kingdom during Stage II, particularly to help England ease restrictions on civilian consumption and begin to reconvert to a peacetime economy. Further, the Secretary knew that the British were disturbed about their prospects during Stage III, the period to follow the defeat of Japan. As J. M. Keynes had put it, there was need for some new "brain wave" to inspire a plan for American assistance to Great Britain. Pending that "brain wave," the British were deliberately holding back in making or disclosing their plans for postwar economic policy in Europe, for those plans would depend heavily upon the willingness of the United States to strengthen British finances.

While convinced that American contributions toward British prosperity constituted one essential of a stable peace, Morgenthau recognized, as he told President Truman, that the entire Lend-Lease program had to be surveyed and overhauled as soon as possible. For reasons of his own, Truman agreed. As he later recalled, he doubted that Congress would continue Lend-Lease once the fighting was over. Without consulting the Treasury, the President on V-E Day, May 8, 1945, accepted the advice of Leo Crowley of the Foreign Economic Administration and Acting Secretary of State Joseph C. Grew, and signed an order which Roosevelt had approved. It authorized FEA and the State Department "to take joint action to cut back the volume of Lend-Lease supplies." Interpreting the order literally, Crowley immediately "placed an embargo on all shipments to Russia and to other European nations." Soviet protests quickly persuaded Truman to rescind the order, but the British had suffered even more than the Russians. For the benefit of both Allies, the President on May 23 "explained that the order . . . was intended to be not so much a cancellation of shipments as a gradual readjustment to conditions following the collapse of Germany. . . . All al-

locations provided for by treaty or protocol would be delivered and
. . . every commitment would be filled."

Yet Truman chose not to have Morgenthau interpret the commitment to Great Britain, though in the weeks after Quebec the Secretary had been responsible for defining it. "I don't want to give them
everything they ask for," Truman told Morgenthau on May 23. "I
never have," Morgenthau replied; "in fact, they have complained
about it." Morgenthau suggested that a committee representing the
Treasury, State Department, and Foreign Economic Administration
review Lend-Lease policy for Stage II. Truman agreed to study that
suggestion, but he soon rejected it.

While the President was ruminating, Chancellor of the Exchequer
Sir John Anderson, in a cable to Morgenthau, expressed his fear that
the forthcoming Lend-Lease appropriation would not cover British
needs during Stage II. The War Department, Anderson noted, had
already indicated to British representatives that the United States
was not bound by the principles of the agreement of the previous
fall. Morgenthau, who disagreed with that interpretation, could do
nothing about it. As he told his staff on May 28, the President had
yet to decide who was to handle Lend-Lease negotiations with the
British: "It's a nice mix-up."

The confusion distressed Winston Churchill. "When I met President Roosevelt in Quebec," Churchill cabled Truman on May 28,
". . . we both initialed an agreement about Lend-Lease after the
defeat of Germany. In accordance with that agreement a detailed
plan was worked out. . . . I now hear that your War Department
has told our people in Washington that they are expecting so large a
cut in their . . . appropriation for the US Air Corps that supplies
to us must be drastically curtailed below the schedule of our requirements as agreed last autumn. These requirements were, of
course, subject to subsequent modification in the light of changes in
the strategical situation. I am hopeful that our requirements . . .
can now be reduced, but the details of the reduction depend upon
discussions between our respective Chiefs of Staff, which will not
have been completed before 31 May. Meanwhile I hope that your
people can be told that the principles your predecessor and I agreed
on at Quebec will stand."

Informed by Robert Brand, the head of the British Lend-Lease mission in Washington, of the general content of Churchill's cable, Morgenthau replied that the fault was not his, though he was often blamed. Now he would not intrude without a direct invitation from Truman. "I am waiting for the President," he said on May 29, 1945, "to tell me whether he wants me in on it. . . . I want it in writing and I want it made public. . . . The French are starving and freezing, and I'm the one who is holding this up,* and this is wrong and that is wrong, and Churchill gets on the floor in Parliament and thanks Lord Keynes for the wonderful job he did, and I never get a line. I'm not going to take it. I was willing to take it from Roosevelt because I was his friend, but I want a little more now."

Truman turned not to Morgenthau but to Judge Fred Vinson, his close friend and now the head of the Office of War Mobilization and Reconversion. During the first week of June, Vinson consulted representatives of the State and War Departments, the Foreign Economic Administration, and the Treasury. Frank Coe, as Morgenthau's surrogate, reported that they were proceeding on the basis of principles entirely different from those established at Quebec. Yet Coe initialed a draft of a reply which Vinson's associates prepared for Truman to send to Churchill. That draft held that the general policy laid down at Quebec did not "necessarily mean that either the military or the non-military program for the coming year will be equal to the Lend-Lease requirements as in the meetings of last October and November. Those estimates were subject to changing strategic demands as well as to supply considerations . . . and to the provision of the necessary funds by Congress. I have requested Congress to appropriate funds that will make possible Lend-Lease deliveries to the British Commonwealth in accord with the spirit of these earlier understandings. . . . In connection with the foregoing, it has come to my attention that the British gold and foreign exchange holdings are now considerably higher than was anticipated. . . . I do not wish to propose reopening the . . . discussions on this account. However, I would like to request that your government relax its position with respect to permitting dollar payments on certain items."

---

* That is, he was accused of holding up Lend-Lease and other supplies, though he had not.

The draft angered Morgenthau. He criticized its reference to British balances which, he pointed out, while higher than the British estimate of November 1944, were no higher than the American estimate of that time. The reference to a reopening of negotiations was "very bad judgment." More important, the Secretary said, Truman should tell Churchill that the United States expected to carry out the Quebec agreement on Lend-Lease "just the way I expect you to carry out other agreements which were made at Quebec."* In his very first sentence, Morgenthau believed, the President should say, in effect, that "what you and Mr. Roosevelt agreed on, bingo, I carry out." Rebuking White and Coe who had urged him to initial the draft, Morgenthau concluded: "I certainly am not going to go along with that. . . . You shouldn't put Truman in that position. . . . He gives no reason why he's welching."

Under Morgenthau's orders, Coe then prepared an alternative draft for the President. "We shall of course," that version read, "carry out in full the understanding reached between you and President Roosevelt at the Quebec Conference. The War Department officials concerned with the Lend-Lease program understand this and I am confident that there will be adequate appropriation to carry out the decisions reached by the Combined Chiefs of Staff." That phrasing suited Morgenthau entirely, but Fred Vinson, by the end of June, had yet to decide which of the two drafts to send to the President.

While Vinson hesitated, Morgenthau, again rejecting the advice of Harry White, on June 28, 1945, endorsed an estimate of Will Clayton that the British would need $3 billion during Stage III.† The State Department wanted to provide that money not as a grant but as a loan carrying perhaps 2½ per cent interest and due in about thirty years. As conditions for the loan, the State Department suggested requiring the British to make substantial modifications in the system of imperial preference, to make sterling freely convertible to dollars on all current and future accounts, and in other ways to cooperate with the United States in the establishment of a worldwide liberal trade program. Morgenthau doubted that Great Brit-

---

* Including, presumably, the agreement on Germany.

† The Congress had meanwhile voted against the use of any Lend-Lease funds for reconstruction or rehabilitation.

ain would accept a loan on those or any other terms, but he stressed the importance of finding some way to provide the needed billions of dollars.

Still, the Secretary admitted he was "fed up." When he had reminded Truman that Churchill had yet to receive an answer to his inquiry about Stage II, the President had said emphatically: "I am going to take care of that personally." The State Department, obviously with White House approval, had assumed control of planning for Stage III. Morgenthau felt left out. Even more, he resented what appeared to him to be the drift of Anglo-American politics in Europe, especially in Germany, where the pace of de-nazification in the British zone of occupation seemed slow. Consequently, as he told his staff on July 3, 1945, he did not want "to be part in helping to finance England." Someone else could undertake that task. He would stand back "until they help us rid Germany of the top Nazi businessmen and Italy of the top Fascists. . . . I have about reached the end of my rope."

By early June 1945, Morgenthau had centered his interests almost exclusively on policy for Germany. All other considerations, he felt, were secondary. And by that time he had found that Truman, cool to the Treasury's recommendations for Great Britain, was antagonistic to the Department's German program.

5. Demise of the Morgenthau Plan

His policies for Germany, Morgenthau liked to believe, had had the support of Franklin Roosevelt. That support, if ambiguous at times, had been exhibited, as the Secretary saw it, during his conversation with Roosevelt the night before he died, and in the late President's apparent sympathy for the Treasury's suggestions for revising JCS 1067.* Truman's position was less clear. While in his early weeks in office the new President listened cordially to Morgenthau's comments about Germany, he tended to rely on the State Department and the War Department for counsel about matters diplomatic or military, and German questions fell primarily into those categories. According to his later recollections, Truman from the

* See Chapter VIII.

first shared Stimson's views about Germany, but at the time he did not so inform Morgenthau. Further, the President feigned indecision about the appointment of a new Secretary of State, though he had decided to replace Stettinius with Jimmy Byrnes, to whom Morgenthau was openly antagonistic.

Truman's reserve encouraged Morgenthau to continue to press his own objectives. During the spring of 1945, the resulting contest within the executive establishment centered on the related questions of reparations and of the occupation directive, JCS 1067, which had not yet achieved final form. The Treasury wanted to speed the removal of reparations in kind from Germany to deserving Allied nations. For the War Department, Robert Lovett objected to that policy as just another effort to make Germany a "pastoral" country. He and his associates, concerned about the administration of occupied Germany, held that the Reparations Commission "should not plan for the removal of facilities, equipment or goods unless the Control Council determines that they are not needed for the support and protection of the occupying forces or to prevent disease and unrest endangering the occupying forces." That recommendation left decisions about reparations to the unanimous agreement of all four zone commanders. For the State Department, Will Clayton took a similar stand. It was in the American interest, Clayton argued, to leave machinery, plant, and equipment within Germany in order to maintain the German economy and to produce enough goods for export to pay for what Germany had to import. In particular, he noted, the Germans would need to import cotton for clothing. Clayton, Morgenthau felt, was twisting policy to serve his own interests, and those of his fellow Texans, in the cotton business.

"Things weren't going very well on reparations," Morgenthau told Stettinius, then still Secretary of State, on April 20, 1945. The State Department seemed to be carrying a "grudge" against the Treasury. In contrast, Bernard Baruch "was unbelievably good." Just back from England, Baruch, according to Morgenthau's assessment, "was much stronger for the decentralization of Germany than when he left. . . . He wants to do everything to be helpful. He said the English still haven't made up their mind on account of the fear of Russia, which is more important, to build Germany up or get the business which they might get by de-industrialization."

Aware of Baruch's influence with Truman, Morgenthau on April 20 also spoke to the President: "I said I was worried about the way things were going with regard to German reparations. He said, 'Well, this is confidential that I have stopped Lubin from going. I don't think he is a big enough man. . . . I am sending somebody else. He is a wonderful person. You will be pleased.' " That "somebody else" was Edwin W. Pauley, an old friend of Truman's, a California oil executive, and major contributor to the Democratic Party. To Morgenthau's relief, Pauley referred the question of reparations to the Informal Policy Committee On Germany (IPCOG), on which the Treasury was represented. That committee was already the arena for continuing interdepartmental debate about JCS 1067.

As that debate evolved during a series of meetings on April 24, 25, and 26, 1945, Morgenthau reacted much more favorably than did his subordinates to the restrained and persuasive arguments of John J. McCloy, the representative of the War Department. That reaction brought the Secretary closer also to the point of view of Clayton and the Department of State. Their discussions dealt first with the arrest of members of the Nazi party. The Treasury wanted the paragraphs in JCS 1067 concerned with arrest to prevent special favor for eminent industrialists like the Krupps or veteran diplomats like von Papen, who had been willing servants of Hitler. So also, the Treasury urged the imprisonment of all officers of such Nazi organizations as the SS. The War Department explained that Eisenhower would not have facilities enough to lock up all those offenders — some two or three million people. "We don't say we are not going to arrest them," McCloy said, "but give the fellow with responsibility some freedom to act. . . . In administering a country you just can't do it." Had the Treasury's policy prevailed in Frankfurt, the Army would have had to keep in jail the only man in the city who understood the water system. "You have got to give Eisenhower," McCloy went on, ". . . the discretion before he determines that he can arrest three million people when he has got twelve million people."

Though Morgenthau agreed to phraseology permitting Eisenhower to recommend to the Joint Chiefs of Staff a deferment in the arrest of individuals whose services were essential to the occupation, the Secretary was still eager to assure harsh treatment for Nazis of high industrial or diplomatic rank. The Army, McCloy replied, preferred to put some such men, like von Papen, in a villa rather than in a prison so as to elicit from them valuable military and political information. "That is something for Eisenhower to determine," McCloy said. ". . . I have suffered at the hands of von Papen . . . and I know all about his wickedness, and I don't want to be in the false position of arguing in favor of a high class Nazi, but I am thinking about your trying to tell Eisenhower how he shall run the prison. . . . It may very well be that Eisenhower would want to put that fellow in a protective custody status rather than an inner dungeon." Convinced, Morgenthau consented to allowing Eisenhower discretion to except from harsh treatment leading Nazis important "for intelligence or other purposes."

The Treasury especially opposed language in JCS 1067 that authorized the Control Council to direct and to empower German authorities to maintain and establish controls over prices and wages, and to take fiscal and financial steps necessary to that end. The Control Council, the Treasury argued, should only permit German authorities to use the means at their disposal to prevent inflation, with the understanding that if inflation assumed dangerous proportions, the commanding general in each zone could make recommendations to his home government and request instructions for policy. The restraint of inflation, the Treasury held, should not constitute grounds for importing supplies, for rehabilitating the German economy, or for limiting the removal or destruction of productive facilities. "Let's make it perfectly clear," Morgenthau said, "that the Treasury doesn't want to see inflation in Germany. . . . But it doesn't want to be held responsible for it in case there is. . . . And in discussing this a number of times with President Roosevelt, he was very clear on it, and the point was that the responsibility should be the Germans' and not ours. . . . The American Army should not be held responsible for inflation if it should happen."

There was bound to be inflation, Will Clayton replied, as "a natural consequence of the unsound measures on which the war was run" by the Nazis. Still, if that inflation got out of hand, it would break down the supply of food and the Army would have to act. Without disagreeing directly, Morgenthau repeated his case against "assuming this responsibility. We don't think that you are going to be able to accomplish it, but if that's what you want, we will accede, and since it has been decided we will put everything at our disposal to assist you." That statement satisfied McCloy. "I want to get the point clear," McCloy said, "that we don't think we are going to stop inflation in Germany. We don't have any such idea as that but we think it's rather fantastic to suppose that we will not be blamed for the inflation that takes place. We'll be blamed for everything that takes place, so that is a rather academic consideration as against the doubtful advantage of trying to throw off or disclaim responsibility for something that may occur if you give the zone commander the authority to do what he feels he may have to do. Give him that flexibility."

While concurring, Morgenthau repeated that the Army would be taking on "an impossible task." More important, the Secretary reminded McCloy that Roosevelt had often said, "Let the German economy seek its own level." Morgenthau was willing to let the Army "attempt to peg that level," but he regretted that there was nothing within JCS 1067 "to say . . . that the Germans brought this thing on themselves." Clayton then agreed to incorporate the language of the March 23 directive in JCS 1067, which was altered to read: "It should be brought home to the Germans that Germany's ruthless warfare and the fanatical Nazi resistance have destroyed the German economy and made chaos and suffering inevitable and that the Germans cannot escape responsibility for what they have brought upon themselves."

"The Treasury of the United States," Morgenthau said, turning to reparations, "wants the minimum of inflation in Germany. . . . But I can't visualize two agencies in Germany, one administering the civilian population and the other administering reparations. . . . It all has to come under this control."

That control, the Secretary went on, should take no steps to rebuild the German economy. Accepting his argument, Clayton and McCloy agreed to add to JCS 1067 another sentence the Treasury had drafted: "Prevention and restraint of inflation shall not constitute an additional ground for the importation of supplies, nor shall it constitute an additional ground for limiting removal, destruction or curtailment of productive facilities in fulfillment of the program for reparation, demilitarization and industrial disarmament."

Conversation moved on to the disposition of the landed estates in Prussia. McCloy urged "fundamental agrarian reform. . . . It is my philosophy that it's the kernel of the whole damn Prussian business." But Clayton objected to saying categorically that the United States approved of taking land from anybody without compensation. He also thought that the commanding general would not immediately be able forcibly to expropriate the Prussian estates, for their produce would be needed until the Army had solved the problem of feeding the Germans. Though reluctantly, Morgenthau endorsed Clayton's purpose and phraseology which called on the Commanding General to "direct the German authorities to utilize large landed estates in a manner which will facilitate the accommodation and settlement of Germans and others or increase agricultural output."

Clayton was satisfied with the section of JCS 1067 directing the Control Council to "prohibit immediately and prevent the production of merchant ships, synthetic oil and rubber, aluminum and magnesium and any other products and equipment on which you will subsequently receive instructions." McCloy, however, worried about any further destruction of facilities for the production of synthetic rubber and oil. The Army had been utilizing certain synthetic plants "to very great advantage," he said, and he saw no harm in carrying on production "for the purpose of our occupation." Morgenthau feared that unless those facilities were destroyed at once, the Germans would continue to have access to them after the period of occupation. But the Army emphasized the shortage of fuel in Europe, especially in France, which would need German coal and oil during the coming winter. "The thing we are talking about is a broad line policy," Morgenthau said. "If there are tons and tons of oil at stake, it would be one thing, but . . . whether we are going to go ahead and destroy these things with which they could make war or whether we are going to begin to find excuses not to destroy them . . . I think the principle is more important than the little synthetic oil which is left."

Yet without further argument, Morgenthau left the subject, satisfied that JCS 1067 was sufficiently sound on the question of German productivity. Enough facilities were to be left in Germany to permit the German people to supply the occupying forces and to achieve for themselves a standard of living no higher than that of any of their neighbors. Germany would have to adjust to the conditions prevailing not only in France, which was substantially poorer, but also in the still more impoverished areas of Poland and Czechoslovakia. All in all, Morgenthau commended the redrafted version of JCS 1067. "I feel all these documents," he said, "are so far better than I had any hope for that I am perfectly willing to sit tight. . . . They are . . . completely satisfactory to me."

On April 27, 1945, just before the other members of IPCOG delivered the revised occupation directive to the White House, Morgenthau called on Truman. In the privacy of their conversation, the President agreed to look at the book on Germany which Morgenthau's staff had begun to prepare. He also applauded Morgenthau's suggestion for the appointment of a liberal political adviser to Eisenhower. The others then arrived, and according to Morgenthau's report in his Diary: "Clayton presented the thing very formally, and he said, 'This document is based on President Roosevelt's memorandum of March 23rd,' and McCloy said, 'Yes, I gave it to the President [Truman].' The President said that he had read it last night. He said, 'I have read a million words since I became President, and I am ready to read another million words. . . . I am very much interested in this Directive on Germany, and I am going to read every word of it.' "

While Truman was studying the directive, IPCOG on May 1, 1945, resumed discussions of reparations policy. No reparations plan, the committee agreed, should be "of such a nature as to promote or require the building up of German economic capacity." Morgenthau, eager for more precise guidelines, persuaded the State Department to try to define a program for conscript labor. Further, he predicted that public concern about Germany would soon flag. The occupation troops, he feared, would then have to sustain themselves by utilizing any German industry still standing. On that account he again urged a tough policy at the outset of the occupation. "If these important plants," he said, "which would be used again to make war are eliminated the first six months, I don't believe there would ever be another war, and I think that the Army . . . has been advocating that these important plants be maintained. I think that they have got a very, very grave responsibility as far as future wars are concerned. . . . I wish the Army would give it another look."

That was a futile wish, directly contrary to Stimson's view and without immediate relevance to the document on reparations, which in its final form, Morgenthau nevertheless described as "wonderful." That document, an instruction for the American commission, called for a general program designed to exact from Germany payments in kind for losses caused the Allies during the war. The Allied plan for reparations should assist in the elimination of industrial capacity deemed dangerous to the security of the United Nations. It should aid in strengthening and developing the industries and trade of the devastated nations of Europe, and in raising their standards of living. The burden of reparations should fall equitably on each of the four zones. No reparation plan should lead an occupying country to finance "directly or indirectly" any reconstruction of Germany, nor should it require the building up of the German economy. Insofar as possible, reparations should be taken from the natural wealth of Germany existing at the time of her collapse, with first emphasis on the removal of machinery and plant, particularly in the metallurgical, electrical, chemical, machine tool, and shipbuilding industries. Reparations in kind should not include arms or ammunition or implements of war. In order to prevent other nations from becoming dependent upon German reparations and thus on German recovery, recurrent reparations, to be exacted over any length of time, should be held to a minimum and should take the form primarily of raw materials and natural resources. While limiting the Germans to a standard of living no higher than that of surrounding nations, the reparations plan should not place on the United States responsibility for sustained relief of the German people. Reparations in the form of the "use of German labor" outside of Germany should be used only for the reconstruction and repair of war damage and not for current production, except the production of food and fuel. Compulsory labor should be required only from war criminals and individuals determined by appropriate legal processes to be members of the Gestapo or the SS, or to have been leading collaborators of the Hitler regime. The Reparations

Commission should, furthermore, survey the use of compulsory labor to ensure that it enjoyed a humane standard of living.

Those American stipulations had yet to be discussed in Moscow with British and Soviet representatives to the Reparations Commission. In later months that commission failed to reach agreement, so the American plan served in the end, as it had begun, only as an instruction for Edwin Pauley, who appeared to Morgenthau wholly to approve it. Perhaps on that account, Will Clayton, as Morgenthau noted in his Diary, protested "vigorously" against Pauley's appointment. In strict confidence, Pauley informed Morgenthau that "he had told the State Department to go to hell." For his part, Morgenthau on May 2, 1945, said to Truman that "Pauley would do all right." Truman agreed, and added, according to Morgenthau's Diary, "two or three times, 'I have complete confidence in you . . . and if I ever haven't, I will tell you.' I said, 'Well, I hope that day will never come.' He said, 'I am sure it never will.'"

Two days later Truman was more guarded. "The President asked me to stay after Cabinet," Morgenthau recorded in his Diary on May 4, "and he handed me this chapter [of the book on Germany] . . . and he said that he had read it twice, and for two hours last night he couldn't sleep because he was worrying about it. He said . . . 'I read over the Yalta Agreement again, and Churchill, Stalin and I have to agree on a plan. . . . It's up to me. . . . You have to give me time. . . . I wish you wouldn't do anything about it,' so I said, 'All right. I really have only two aims in life — the first one is to win the war and then to help to win the peace, and . . . I will abide by your request.'"

On May 9 Morgenthau resumed the conversation. As he put it in his Diary, "I got on the Plan for Germany, and I said, 'Mr. President, I realize you don't want me to publish this thing . . . but I have accepted your decision.' He said, '. . . I have got to see Stalin and Churchill, and when I do I want all the bargaining power — all the cards in my hand, and the plan on Germany is one of them. I don't want to play my hand before I see them. . . . I am studying this myself.' . . .

"I said, 'I got the impression you liked my plan,' and he said, 'Yes, by and large, I am for it.' So I said, 'Well, here is the part on agriculture.' I went over the charts with him, and he was amazed when

I showed him that Germany was fourth in production on the various important food items. . . . He was very anxious to have this chapter, and he said he would read it and study it. . . .

"I went away with the distinct feeling that the man likes me and has confidence in me. . . . He gives me the impression of being completely frank. . . . In discussing IPCOG . . . I urged him to give it [JCS 1067] out quickly as the next move. He didn't say that he would or wouldn't."

On May 10 Truman did sign the revised version of JCS 1067 and also the document on reparations, developments that Morgenthau felt made "a big day for Treasury." The Secretary hoped "somebody doesn't recognize it as the Morgenthau Plan." He felt, apparently, that Truman would come his way just so long as that way seemed to be the President's own, not a path borrowed from somebody else. He had yet to understand Truman's grave objections to the sections on industry and agriculture which Morgenthau considered the heart of his plan for Germany.

Painfully, little by little, Morgenthau came to see his distance from the President. In the last week in May 1945, the Secretary criticized the plans formulated by Supreme Court Justice Robert Jackson for the trial of German war criminals. Morgenthau felt that Jackson, absorbed in the niceties of legal procedure, would unduly prolong the work of the Allied tribunal and delay indefinitely any convictions. As Morgenthau put it to French Foreign Minister Bidault on May 22: "The thing that worried me was this Crime Commission. . . . The way the matter was drawn up, I doubted if they could get around to trying these various organizations like the Gestapo and the SS, and getting a conviction before Christmas. . . . By that time all of these organizations would have gone underground and they would have a hard time finding them. . . . I finally said . . . 'My motives are not revenge but one hundred years of peace in Europe.'" To Truman on May 23, 1945, Morgenthau made the same point. The President disagreed. Jackson, he said, would do a good job; as for himself, Truman said: "I don't want to do it the way the English want it without a trial. . . . Even the Russians want to give them a trial."

Bothered by that reply, Morgenthau was even more anxious about the gossip predicting the appointment of Jimmy Byrnes as

Secretary of State. On June 1 he asked Truman whether the rumors were true. "I can't get along with him," Morgenthau said, adding that Byrnes was not a good team man and was not expert on foreign affairs. Truman answered by describing his difficulties in completing arrangements for the conference at Potsdam where he was to meet with Stalin and Churchill. "You don't know how difficult the thing has been for me," the President said. "Everybody around here that should know anything about foreign affairs is out." Further, the Democratic leaders considered it dangerous to have Stettinius next in line for succession to the Presidency. They wanted a better party man as Secretary of State, and although they did not insist on Byrnes, Truman was "studying the situation." The gossip about Byrnes, Morgenthau could conclude privately, was not without foundation.

There was nothing evasive about Truman's next refusal of a request by Morgenthau. In mid-June, at the instigation of Jean Monnet and René Pleven, the French Government invited Morgenthau to open an exhibit of War bonds in Paris early in July. "I only want to go," Morgenthau told Acting Secretary of State Joseph Grew, "if it is completely agreeable to the President and to the State Department. . . . I'm going to ask the President if I go . . . to let me go up into the Ruhr and the Saar and see what is going on." On June 13, 1945, Morgenthau discussed the proposed trip with Truman. "I saw the President," the Secretary noted in his Diary,

> . . . and asked him if he had received the invitation for me to go to France. He said he had. . . . The President seemed very much distracted and fidgety, and sort of jumped around the room and paced up and down. He said, "I just haven't had time to think this thing through." I said, "Well, the French feel that it would help to teach democracy to their people, and that is important to them." He kept saying, "Just let me read the thing. I want to take it home and read it. I want to think it through." I said, "I have talked to Mr. Grew about it, and they approve." He said, "I know but I have certain things in mind." I asked him if he were going to Paris, and he said, "No."
>
> All I can say is that there is a definite block in his brain on this thing. . . . I said to the President, "I certainly don't want

to go without your blessing," and he said, "I don't want you to go without it, and if you do go you will go with my entire blessing." I said, "I think my going could supplement your going," which didn't make any hit at all.

I told him that when I went over there for President Roosevelt last August I found that the Army was building up a strong Germany, and that I would like to see what they are doing now. I said that General Clay surrounds himself with a lot of Wall Street people, and I wanted to find out about it. I said, "I don't think anybody but Senator Kilgore or myself would tell you the truth." Then he jumped at this like a life preserver, and he said, "I am waiting to talk to Kilgore. . . ." I said, "You know Kilgore has asked me to come up on the Hill and talk about my plan for Germany." The President said, "Yes, I know about that. . . . I want to talk the whole thing over with Kilgore."

It could be any one of a half dozen things. From a remark he dropped once before when I asked him, he knew about the trouble I had gotten into over the Morgenthau Plan, and he may just not want me to start something again. He may think that it will get him into more trouble on the Hill and that is why he is going to check with Kilgore, or he may think that my going two weeks in advance of his going might steal some of his thunder or that I may mess things up. It could be any one of a dozen things, but I have talked to him at least three times, and each time I have gone up against a stone wall.

Finally, the President said, "When I make up my mind, I will put all my cards on the table," and I said, "I certainly expect you to do that."

By June 18, 1945, the President had made up his mind. As Morgenthau reported that day in his Diary:

I had been prepared to make a little speech to him to the effect that my going to France wasn't a matter of life and death. . . . As soon as I came in, the President opened up right on me very direct, and said, "I have been thinking about your going to France . . . and I don't want you to go. I want you to stay here. I don't want you and myself over there at the same time. When I come back you can go any place, any where you want to in September. . . . I won't go to France, I will leave that to you. . . . I have got to work out with Stalin and Churchill a plan for Germany," and I don't know just how he put it, but the idea he conveyed to me was he didn't want me messing around over there at the same time because it might make it difficult for him. I said, "Mr. President, that's all right with me." The President said, "I don't want to go over there now because I think it is the wrong time, but Stalin has invited me and I have got to work out a plan with Stalin and Churchill for Germany." The implication he left me with was that he and I saw pretty much eye to eye on Germany. Again, he didn't say just those words. He said that they were not going to invite the French in at the beginning so that they could get something worked out amongst the three of them.

The President said, "I don't want you to be out of the country while I am," so I said, ". . . When Mr. Roosevelt went to the Crimea, he told the Cabinet that . . . if anything happened or if any emergency arose I should call the Cabinet together." He said, "That's so. I want you to be here. You are the ranking man by law." * I said, "I would much rather have it come from you than by law, and I would like you to say something to the Cabinet before you leave." And he said that he would.

During this discussion, he said that he felt like a brother toward me, and he wished I would feel that way towards him, and I said that I would like to. I said, "Mr. President, about my own affairs you have been wonderful, and you have made my position much easier." He said, "I want to do that. I like to do that." He said that if the time ever comes that we can't get along we will separate company, and I said, "That suits me." He treated me more on a man-to-man equal basis today than he ever had before. He made one remark that didn't make sense. He said, "I have no ambitions, there is nothing I want." I would like to remind him about that two years from now

* Since there was no Vice President and the new Secretary of State, Byrnes would be at Potsdam with the President.

when he begins to run for reelection. I said, "Well, I certainly haven't anything I want except to serve you." . . .

Then I told the President that Kilgore . . . wanted to start hearings on the Hill on Germany, and that he wanted me to come up and talk about the Morgenthau Plan. The President said, "Well, I feel about that just the way I do about your going to Europe. I don't want Kilgore to hold hearings until I have my feet on the ground on this conference." . . .

Then I said . . . "What would you think of Kilgore as Secretary of State?" He said, "I can't spare him on the Hill. . . ."

Then I said, ". . . What would you think of Patton to take Clay's place? Kilgore says that Clay is nothing but a Fascist." The President laughed very heartily, and then said, "That's what we used to call him when we were in the Senate."

But Truman trusted Clay more than Morgenthau. At the end of June the Secretary learned that the President, worried about coal supplies in Europe, had overruled the Treasury's recommendations about German mining. Jean Monnet, Morgenthau recorded in his Diary, had reported that Truman was sending a cable "which is going to set up the production of coal in the Saar and the Ruhr. . . . What they need is another million tons of coal per month which would give a half a ton of coal to every family in France. . . . I certainly want to be informed about what is going on."

That was not to be the case. Early in July Truman joked with Henry Stimson about Roosevelt's reliance on Morgenthau at Quebec. Morgenthau and Baruch, the President said, were alike; "they couldn't keep from meddling in" German questions. It was not they, but Stimson, that Truman wanted at his side at the Potsdam Conference. Within two days, Morgenthau was to learn at last the full implications of that decision.

6. After Twelve Eventful Years

On July 5, 1945, Morgenthau sat in his office with Dan Bell and Herbert Gaston, those old reliables who had been with him longer than had any others on the Treasury staff; Henrietta Klotz, his private secretary and friend for more than twenty years; and Edward Greenbaum, his family lawyer and close personal friend for some three decades. They were the first to learn about the Secretary's meeting with Truman, just ended:

I called on the President and said, "Look, Mr. President, the last time I was here you said you felt like a brother to me, and I would like to reciprocate that feeling. . . . I would like to reciprocate that feeling and have an official family talk. . . . You are leaving, and there is all this gossip which has been increasing more and more about my being through, and I would like to raise the question with you before you leave because I am assuming a great responsibility while you are away." He interrupted me and said, "Oh, I am going to say that you are the man in charge while I am gone." I went right on though and said, "Well, I would like to know whether you want me to stay until V-J Day." He said, "Well, I don't know. I may want a new Secretary of the Treasury." I said, "Well, Mr. President, if you have any doubts in your mind after my record of twelve years here, and after several months with you and when I have given you my loyal support, you ought to know your mind now, and if you don't know it, I want to get out now."

"Well," he said, "let me think this thing over." I said, "Mr. President, from several remarks you have dropped you must have something in your mind. Either you want me or you don't, and you know it now." He said, "I can't make up my mind." I said, "Well, Mr. President, I am going to write you a letter of resignation. . . . Would you like me to stay while you are abroad or would you like to have it take effect immediately?" He said, "I would like you to stay while I am abroad." I said, "Well, I will write you a letter. Do you want me to put in a draft of an answer for you?" And he said, "Yes."

I said, "Do you want me to break in Vinson as my successor while you are gone?" And he said, "Oh, Vinson is going with me on account of Lend-Lease."

He said that he would say publicly that I was staying and I told him that I believed him but unfortunately the public didn't. I told him I was willing to stay until after he came back and he said, "You are rushing it." He repeated that several times. Then I said, "Well, if you don't give it out tonight I will be forced to give it out tomorrow, and I wouldn't like to do that while you are on the high seas," so he said that he would do it tonight.

He said several times . . . that he wanted to think this over, and I said, "Either you want me to stay until V-J Day or you don't. . . . After all, Mr. President, I don't think it is conceited to say that I am at least as good or better as some of the five new people you appointed in the Cabinet, and on some of them I think you definitely made a mistake." He said, "Well, this makes me feel very badly," and I said, "Well, don't feel badly." . . .

I found him very weak and indecisive, but I sensed definitely that he had it in mind that I was on the way out, but he wanted to choose the time, and I am very glad that my intuition was correct and that I picked the time rather than having him pick the time.

I said to him, "It is unfortunate that you haven't taken anybody from the Treasury with you because we have information nobody else has," and he made no comment. Then I asked him whether he would like to have the Morgenthau Plan with him and he said "Oh, I have read it, and I know everything that is in it, and I think it is very good." Then I said, "Well, once I am a private citizen, you won't have any objection to my giving it out?" And he said, "Oh, no, I am in complete accord with that."

Later on July 5 Morgenthau gave a similar report about his meeting with Truman to others on his staff, including Harry White, Frank Coe, John Pehle, and Ansel Luxford. "I feel sorry," the Secretary then said, "only on account of the great disturbance it will cause you people, rather than it will cause me, because the disturbance caused me happened when Mr. Roosevelt died; that is when I was disturbed. This doesn't disturb me now. In fact, I am beginning to feel kind of good. . . .

"Nobody, especially after being Secretary of the Treasury for twelve years . . . can take that, and I don't see why I should have to. . . . I couldn't hold my head up and have this man say to me he was uncertain about me. After all, I didn't ask him to appoint me for the next three and one-half years as Secretary of the Treasury. I would have liked to have stayed but I didn't say that to him. I would like to have stayed until the war was won, but I didn't say that to him. . . . It has been a good twelve years, and we've worked hard."

Morgenthau's letter of resignation, dated that same day, July 5, 1945, revealed none of his tension.

The Secretary wrote Truman:

> When Franklin D. Roosevelt came to Washington, he asked me to come with him, stating that when he was through we would go back to Dutchess County together. For twelve of the most eventful years in American history I was associated with him, actively participating in meeting the important problems confronting the country both before and during the war.
>
> Immediately after President Roosevelt's death I told you how I felt, and stated that I wanted you to know that your hands were untied as far as I was concerned. You were good enough to say that you needed my help and urged me to remain.
>
> Since then, with your support, I have completed many of the most urgent tasks that were then pending. As I told you this morning, I feel the time has now come when I can appropriately be released from my responsibilities. Accordingly, I now tender my resignation as Secretary of the Treasury. My preference was to have this resignation effective immediately, but since you stated this morning that you wish me to remain until you return from Europe I will, of course, comply with your wishes.
>
> Permit me to express my appreciation of the fine support you have given me since you became President.
>
> I most fervently hope for the great success of your Administration in solving the difficult problems which lie ahead.

Truman's reply, which the President had agreed would accompany the resignation, was drafted in the Treasury and carried the same date. It said that the President was sorry to learn of Morgenthau's decision but grateful that the Secretary would remain in office until the end of the Potsdam Conference. The letter remarked on Morgenthau's long and efficient service in peace and war, and mentioned particularly his work in the formulation and administration of the Federal tax programs which had raised unprecedented revenues, the Treasury's war bond campaign and other financial activities, the Treasury's close cooperation with Allied governments during the war, and Morgenthau's advocacy of the agreements reached at Bretton Woods.

On July 6, the very day of the President's departure from Washington, Truman announced his intention to appoint Fred Vinson to succeed Morgenthau, and when the Secretary called to congratulate him, he learned that Vinson, contrary to Truman's earlier statement, was remaining in Washington while the President went to Europe. Morgenthau therefore saw no reason why he should continue as Secretary of the Treasury. Neither, as it developed, did Truman, who sent Judge Rosenman, one of his special assistants, to urge Morgenthau to depart at once.

"Judge Rosenman has just been here for one hour," Morgenthau told some of his staff on July 11, 1945. ". . . It seemed that . . . people had been calling up President Truman, insisting that he accept my resignation and send up Vinson's name.

> He said that Truman had told . . . the whole story of what happened . . . practically the same as I did. He said that I wanted to resign immediately, but that he had insisted that I stay while he was gone. . . . He didn't want to change his position, but . . . he was under great pressure to have me resign on account of the people worrying about the succession. So the President* asked Sam Rosenman whether he wouldn't come over to see me and put the matter up to me. He said, "The President didn't do anything about it, leaving it entirely to me," but he said that if I did send in my resignation it would make the President very happy.
>
> I told Sam that I would have to think the matter over because . . . now it was a matter of public relations. I asked him what he thought, and he said he didn't know and that he felt very

* Who had sailed for Potsdam.

uncomfortable. I told him that there was no reason to feel uncomfortable. . . . I said the one thing which might influence me was if I thought Congress was going to adjourn and not convene until October because if that were going to happen then I would want the President to send Vinson's name up at once because I wouldn't want to stay that long.

Rosenman asked me what I had in mind for myself, and I said, "Nothing." He said, "Do you want to stay in public life because if you do I think it would put Truman definitely under obligation to yourself if you would resign. . . . Then if you had any idea of doing something with Bretton Woods he would be under obligation to you." I said, "Well, I have no such ideas but people around me are talking about my being Governor of both the Bank and the Fund or possibly President of the Bank. . . . But I haven't really thought about it." Rosenman said, "Well, I can't promise you anything, but if you did resign he would be under obligation to you."

That's Sam, the politician, talking. I told him that I would have to think it over very carefully. Then I said, "I'm going to ask you on your word of honor not to send any message to Truman unless he sends you a message whether you saw me and whether you did anything about it." Rosenman said that he wouldn't.

I think that perhaps with the worry and bustle of leaving, the President might have been concerned about it, and when he gets on board he might not be worrying about it. Rosenman said he wouldn't do anything about it. . . .

I asked him if he knew what Truman had in mind when he didn't want to give me any assurance about staying, and he said, "I just think that he wants to have his own people around him." I asked about Byrnes and when he thought the President decided that,* and Sam said he thought that was decided the day after Roosevelt's funeral at Hyde Park. I said, "Well, Truman knows I don't like Byrnes and that I can't get along with him because I told him so," and Sam said, "I told him that, too."

* The appointment of Byrnes as Secretary of State had been announced on June 30.

Then he said that it was only that afternoon that they had pulled Vinson off the boat.* . . . He said that it didn't make sense but that they did it and that there must have been something in their mind.

What Truman had in mind was to have Vinson in Washington as the senior Cabinet officer during the Potsdam Conference. Aware of this, Morgenthau, who wanted to get out of an uncomfortable situation, prepared another letter to the President which he reviewed with Rosenman on July 13, 1945, along with two replies for Truman to use if he wished. "I showed him my letter," the Secretary later told a few of his subordinates, ". . . and he thought it was excellent. He first thought that as to the timing of my resignation, he would make it after Bretton Woods had passed,† but then on second thought, he seemed to think that he wouldn't do that, and I didn't try to urge him. I didn't want to do any selling, so when he said he didn't think that would be so good I let it go at that.

"Then I showed him the letter from the President to me, and he thought that was all right. Then I showed him the other letter from the President to me — the one having to do with his putting me in as Governor,‡ and he liked that. I made it perfectly clear that this letter had nothing to do with the exchange of the other two letters, and that there were no strings tied to the other letters.

"He said that he would cable these letters immediately to the President and would read to me his introductory remarks before they went.

"When we came to this last letter to me he asked me whether that was to be made public and I said, 'No, Sam, I wouldn't make it public.' I told Sam I thought he ought to tell the President that it was his idea because Rosenman told me that it was his idea and that the President hadn't suggested it. Sam said he would do that.

"Sam asked me whether I would want the signed letters before it was made public, and I said, 'No, I will be satisfied if you send the cable and get an answer back from the President. Then when the President comes back he can sign his letter to me, and I will sign my letter to him.'

* For Potsdam.
† Which was to occur on July 31, 1945.
‡ Of the Fund and Bank.

"He hesitated about sending the third letter to the President because he said that Byrnes would be there and he might discourage the President from acting on it. So I said, "Well, it is just as good a time now as ever to find out where Byrnes stands. . . . That doesn't matter anyway because no matter where Byrnes and the President are, the President might consult him, and from the President's own standpoint, I think he will have to make up his own mind whether he wants somebody like myself or whether he wants to have some important New York Wall Street banker.'

"Then I said that Vinson was coming over for lunch, and I would like to show him these lettters and Sam said, 'Fine.' Then I got what I thought was a brilliant idea, and I said, 'I will call Vinson on the telephone and tell him that you and I have been talking things over, and before the letters go I would like to be sure that they meet with his approval, and that I would like him to see Judge Rosenman at once.' Sam said that would be wonderful because he would like to put in the cable that all three of these letters had been shown to Vinson and that they met with his approval, and he said he thought that would have a lot of weight with Byrnes — which I thought was rather revealing."

Vinson, though he bore no animosity towards Morgenthau, declined to associate himself with the messages for Truman. Morgenthau explained the situation in his Diary after Vinson had left the Treasury on July 13:

"Judge Vinson said that he had no idea about what Rosenman had talked to me about, and that the idea of my resignation becoming effective earlier than was originally planned came as a complete surprise to him. . . .

"He gave me an opening to ask him the question about why he didn't want to let Rosenman send a cable saying that he, Vinson, concurred in Rosenman's suggestion that the President name me as Governor of the Bank and Fund. Well, he did some hemming and hawing, but I kept his feet to the fire, and . . . he said that the President might get a false impression from it. I said, 'How?' He said, 'Well, the President might feel that he, Vinson, was in collusion with me and Rosenman to rush the President into an early appointment of Vinson as Secretary of the Treasury. . . .' I told him that Rosenman . . . had suggested that I ask him what his reason was. Finally after lots of talk, always beating around the bush and saying that he had kept completely away from the Treasury and hadn't talked to anybody about the Treasury plans, he said, 'Well, it would be very nice if you were the Governor.' That's all he said.

"He asked me what my plans were, and I said that I would stay here in Washington at the apartment until Mrs. Morgenthau was well enough to be moved. He said that he would want to consult with me, and I told him that I was ready at any time and would be at his disposal. I said that I had made that same offer to President Truman, but the President had said that Vinson was going on the boat with him. Vinson said . . . that even his baggage had been sent ahead, and it was only decided last Friday that he shouldn't go, which checks with what Rosenman told me. . . .

"Vinson said that Rosenman had suggested sending the letter on Bretton Woods one day later, but he said he didn't think that was a good idea because if the President got them together he might agree. I said, 'I don't even know if I want it, but the boys around the Treasury would like me to take it, and if the President decides to offer it to me, I will have to take time to carefully consider it.' "

Later that day, after checking his covering note with Morgenthau, Rosenman sent Truman the three letters. In the first Morgenthau wrote:

"Since you have now made your decision as to my successor, it seems to me that the delay we contemplated is no longer necessary but, on the contrary, may prove a handicap to Judge Vinson for whom I have the highest admiration. It is my earnest desire to be of every assistance to him in taking over the great responsibilities of this office.

"Such matters as the continuation of war financing, the tax enforcement drive, revenue legislation and many other Treasury problems call for prompt decision. My successor should be given the opportunity to make these decisions, since it will become his duty to carry them out.

"These considerations are given added weight by the recess of the Senate, which would delay Judge Vinson's confirmation.

"Accordingly, I urge that you appoint my successor at your earliest convenience, and make my resignation effective upon his appointment and qualification."

Assenting to that letter, Truman also agreed to a reply which

Morgenthau had drafted for his signature: "I have given careful consideration to your letter of July 13. . . . I am inclined to agree with you that for the reasons you mentioned it would be preferable to take this action now instead of waiting for my return from Europe. I appreciate very much the fine spirit and keen sense of public responsibility in which you have thus approached this matter." But that was as far as the President would go. As he cabled Rosenman July 14: "I have received your dispatch . . . in reference to Secretary Morgenthau. I concur only in the exchange of the first two cables. . . . Do not . . . release third cable." That was the President's way of declining the appointment of Morgenthau as the American Governor of the Fund and Bank.

It was also the last official word that Morgenthau received from the White House. He did not really want a position with the Fund or the Bank, but he would like to have been asked. He later remembered resenting the way Truman had handled the resignation, just as Truman recalled his impatience with Morgenthau. But on Morgenthau's part resentment quickly disappeared. Indeed, in retrospect the four months he spent in Truman's Cabinet seemed to the Secretary trivial, anticlimatic. To be sure, Morgenthau took pride in the success of the legislation for Bretton Woods, but the major work on the Fund and the Bank had occurred before and during the Bretton Woods Conference. The final negotiations that he conducted with the Chinese struck him as just another chapter in the morass of Chinese-American relations. He had been allowed, he knew, no real part in the negotiations with England, and for all of his hopes in the early spring, his plan for Germany, while it had some persisting influence on the phraseology of JCS 1067, made a negative impact on Truman. For his part, Truman had made little impact on Morgenthau, though later the Secretary was to admire many of his policies and support his election. In office and out, Morgenthau thought of the President of the United States as Franklin Roosevelt. The twelve eventful years, the twelve good years, had ended when Roosevelt died. Roosevelt had made possible Morgenthau's participation in those years, Morgenthau's contributions to the New Deal and to the war. Roosevelt had imbued those years.

The Secretary's last annual report emphasized the policies naturally related to the Treasury — policies pertaining to taxation, finance, and the domestic and international management of money. Those were important, of course, but in looking back over the whole record, Morgenthau twenty years later cared much more about what he had accomplished for the least privileged Americans, the beneficiaries of New Deal housing, relief, and farm loan policies. So it was that in memory the sharp differences he had had with Henry Wallace and Harry Hopkins seemed less important than their common concern and common effort, under Roosevelt, to lift the distress of the bankrupt farmer and unemployed laborer. So it was that Morgenthau always rather enjoyed recalling the ways in which Hopkins, after spending too fast, had made him the cooperative victim in the "squeeze plays" that produced new funds to provide more help for men and women needing it. "I took a lot from Hopkins," Morgenthau said in one moment of reflection, "with cherries, too, and Franklin didn't help any; Franklin would never call a proper conference on unemployment, though I begged him to a dozen times. Harry had a tough job, and Harry down at the bottom was all right; he was a New Dealer and so was I and there weren't many of us and we didn't get much thanks."

So, too, Morgenthau liked to remember his struggles to discipline the great corporations, especially those engaged in banking and finance. "They were selfish," he said. "They put themselves above the interests of the people and the interests of the country. I had to police the Prohibition racketeers, and I had to police the Wall Street profiteers. The only flag they followed was their own gain. Franklin and I moved the money capital from London and Wall Street to Washington, and they hated us for it, and I'm proud of it. Business should make profits, and government should be glad when business does, and that's why I was for a balanced budget no matter what the economists had to say, but the budget wasn't the important issue. The important issue was who governs, and the New Deal made the government govern American banking and monetary affairs, and I'm proud of my part in bringing that about."

Even more, Morgenthau drew retrospective satisfaction from his role in assisting the victims of Nazi aggression, in preparing the United States for war, and in assisting the prosecution of the war. "If Hitler had won," he said, "there wouldn't be any democracy anywhere, here or in England or in Europe. We were all too weak;

we were all too slow to wake up. And then we had to move fast, and the United States had to supply all the armies that fought the Axis. It was unbelievable. I don't know how we did it. I don't think we'll ever have time enough to do it again. But we did do it. And Franklin gave me a chance to do a lot of it, to stick my neck out and be the whipping boy if I failed. And we got the airplanes produced, and the goods to Churchill, and Lend-Lease; and none of them, not the English or the Russians or the Chinese could have fought without us, and we didn't get much thanks after it was over. But it was worth it, more than worth it. We've got problems now [1965] but none of them is as bad as the Nazi threat. I had an opportunity, thanks to Franklin, to help beat back that threat, and it was the greatest thing in my life. Sure, we made mistakes, but the greatest mistake would have been to lose, and we won, and I don't need any decorations, any orders of the garter or the red star, because we did win, and if we hadn't, there wouldn't be anything worthwhile left. I was lucky. Franklin gave me the chance to help in the most important job this country's had to do in this century — beating the Nazis, demolishing Nazism."

His record in office, the Secretary often said, could speak for itself. He had kept the evidence, his Diary. He was prepared to "let the chips fall where they may." He knew what his critics thought — that he had been too orthodox in fiscal policy, that some of his subordinates had been communists, that he had been too harsh toward Germany. He disagreed. He also thought his critics missed the major points — the central significance of the New Deal's large domestic policies, and of victory in the second World War.

When he left office, Morgenthau stood fast to the root ideals of his early manhood. The source of the good life, he believed, was the land. The purpose of the good life was helping those who needed help. The land and the people were the important things, the things he cared about. He did not think he knew the secrets of the universe, but he did think he knew good from evil, and he believed the land and people good.

He was a farmer, a reformer, a democrat, one of the children of American plenty whose spirits transcended the material advantages of their personal inheritances. With another man of wealth and independence and high purpose he tried, to the exhausting limits of his energy and determination, to make the world a better place in which all men could live a better life. In that, he felt, he had succeeded. More important, he knew he had tried without stint or let or compromise.

He knew Roosevelt had trusted him and that he had never breached that trust. The long, close, rewarding relationship with Franklin and Eleanor Roosevelt gave Elinor and Henry Morgenthau, both at the time and in the Secretary's recollection, a measure of satisfaction and comfort that no one could adequately describe, no one could overestimate. For Morgenthau, public life had been a long adventure in collaboration and friendship with the Roosevelts. He rejoiced in having had the chance for service, but still more, in having had the confidence and companionship of the President. For Morgenthau, when the scales were balanced, that mortal friendship, no matter what the other weights, was immortality enough.

Notes and Index

Notes

THE NOTES that follow are intended to indicate only the immediate sources of the quotations and other materials on which this book is based. Though I have drawn most heavily on the Morgenthau Diaries, I have also consulted the Franklin D. Roosevelt Papers at the Franklin D. Roosevelt Library in Hyde Park, New York, and the Henry L. Stimson Papers at the Yale University Library in New Haven, Connecticut. I have also examined relevant government documents — of which several contain extensive selections from the Morgenthau Diaries — newspapers, biographies, autobiographies, and special studies, ordinarily not listed here but readily available to any student of the period.

The Roosevelt and Stimson Papers contain many documents also collected within the Morgenthau Diaries. I have invariably, however, referred to the location of such documents only in the Morgenthau Diaries, and always, in those and other references to the Diaries, volume numbers precede the colon and page numbers or dates follow the colon. Stimson and Morgenthau often recorded their separate recollections of joint conversations. Without exception, their accounts agree about the substance of those conversations, though the two men naturally differed in their interpretations of the significance of their exchanges.

The Morgenthau Diaries, more than eight hundred bound volumes, are in the Franklin D. Roosevelt Library. They are not "diaries" at all, though they occasionally include reflective observations. Rather, the Morgenthau Diaries consist primarily of papers that

479

crossed the Secretary's desk, letters and memoranda, incoming and outgoing; of verbatim minutes of meetings held in his office; of stenographic transcripts or summaries of other meetings that he or his subordinates attended; and of verbatim transcripts of conversations he had on the telephone. At their fullest, the Diaries provide a minute-by-minute account of his days in office. They are supplemented by other papers of the Secretary at the Franklin D. Roosevelt Library, cited as "Morgenthau MSS," and by volumes of transcripts of press conferences, cited as "Press Conferences." They are supplemented further by a collection of papers still in Mr. Morgenthau's estate. Those papers, often revealing of his most private opinions, consist largely of his accounts of conversations with Roosevelt, accounts dictated within hours of the event. Though the papers are bound, they are not paginated. I have referred to them by date under the title "Presidential Diary." Material derived from conversations between Mr. Morgenthau and me is cited as conversations.

The officers of the National Archives and of the Franklin D. Roosevelt Library have done their best to open for research and citation the many documents for the period 1941–45 which were originally classified for reasons of national security. Still, some of those documents remain classified and will so remain for some years to come. Yet only in relatively few instances have considerations of security prevented me from access or reference to significant material. In other important cases, I was able to obtain valuable material from the records or memories of men who must for the time being remain anonymous. I have not been able to cite those sources, but I shall deposit all of my notes in the Franklin D. Roosevelt Library, and those notes will be open to interested researchers when the director of that library concludes that the material embodied in them is no longer sensitive.

This book depends continually on the works of a number of scholars to which I have turned again and again with particular reward. For the sake of brevity, I have not continually listed those volumes below. Had I done so, their titles would have appeared with impressive frequency. In my discussions of taxation, debt management, and inflation, I drew heavily on the authoritative Randolph E. Paul, *Taxation in the United States* (Boston, 1954). In my treatment of Chinese-American relations, I found indispensable Herbert Feis, *The China Tangle* (Princeton, 1953), while Arthur N. Young, *China and the Helping Hand* (Cambridge, 1963) was also exceptionally useful. Vital for discussions of German problems were John L. Snell, *Wartime Origins of the East-West Dilemma over Germany* (New Orleans, 1959) and Paul Y. Hammond, "Directives for the Occupation of Germany" in Harold Stein, ed., *American Civil-Military Decisions* (Birmingham, 1963). On questions relating to Lend-Lease for England, to Anglo-American relations in general, and to the negotiations of the Bretton Woods pacts, I relied continually upon H. Duncan Hall, *North American Supply* (London, 1955), Roy F. Harrod, *The Life of John Maynard Keynes* (New York, 1951), Richard N. Gardner, *Sterling-Dollar Diplomacy* (Oxford, 1956), and E. F. Penrose, *Economic Planning for the Peace* (Princeton, 1953). Of special importance, for the various topics they covered, were Herbert Feis, *Churchill, Roosevelt, Stalin* (Princeton, 1957), Julius W. Pratt, *Cordell Hull* 2 vols. (New York, 1964), and Elting E. Morison, *Turmoil and Tradition* (Boston, 1960) — an incisive biography of Henry L. Stimson. Essential, too, were the available volumes covering the years 1941–1945 in the invaluable State Department series, *Foreign Relations of the United States.*

CHAPTER I. STRAINS OF WAR

1. Emergency Unlimited, pp. 1–4

The December 7 quotation is from Diary 470:47, 58. On security measures at the White House, see Diary 470:16, 19, 92, 102. The discussions of the control of Japanese funds and businesses are in Diary 470:1–7; Diary 471:140–43, 148, 155–69, 242; Diary 472:106–109; Diary 473:60; Diary 504:175–78.

2. Alien Property, pp. 4–10

On the activities of Foreign Funds Control, see Diary 474:106–19. Morgenthau's views on the jurisdictional question and his conversation with Roosevelt are from Presidential Diary, December 19, 1941; his talk with Byrnes, from Diary 480:194–95; and the proposed jurisdictional compromise appears in Diary 480:212–13. There is a preview of Treasury policy toward General Aniline in Diary 484:232; for Morgenthau's conversation with the President on that issue, see Diary 484:238. The conversation with Bullitt is from Diary 491:1; for Mack's views, see Diary 492:64–70; on the vesting and the ensuing Treasury orders, see Diary 492:127; Diary 497:134, 166–69; Morgenthau's remarks to Hopkins are from Diary 501:222–33; his report of the Cabinet meeting of February 27, from Diary 502:7–10. Roosevelt's directions of March 5 are in Diary 504:70-72; Morgenthau's letter to McConnell, in Diary 506:128–30. For the Executive Order of March 11, 1942, see Diary 507:51. For Morgenthau's conversation with Rosenman on July 7, 1942, see Presidential Diary of that date.

3. Producing for War, pp. 11–14

For the episode of the trucks, see Diary 479:1–3, which includes Morgenthau's conversation with Patterson about general procurement problems. For further discussions of those problems among the principals from government and labor, see Diary 480:42–43, 63. The Executive Order establishing the WPB is in Diary 485:310. On silver policy, see A. S. Everest, *Morgenthau, the New Deal and Silver* (New York, 1950), Chapter VIII, and Diary 511:165–66, 341; Diary 512:81–88; Diary 514:68–70, 246; Diary 521:273–82; Diary 522:14–17; Diary 562:321 — the last reference relates to Oak Ridge. Morgenthau's crisp talk with Stimson about secrecy, and the ensuing developments, are from Diary 782:211–16; Diary 785:1–6; Diary 788:24–27.

4. A Tremendous Program, pp. 14–16

This section and the following sections of this chapter owe much to H. C. Murphy, *National Debt in War and Transition* (New York, 1950). For Morgenthau's remarks to Bell on December 23, 1941, see Diary 477:57. Eccles's reply to *Time* is in Diary 580:3–6.

5. Voluntarism — Treasury Style, pp. 16–22

Roosevelt's remarks about the bond program and the G. M. plan are from Presidential Diary, April 15, 1942, as is Morgenthau's statement about war-mindedness. Smith's comments, along with other miscellany, are in a file on "War Savings" in the Morgenthau MSS at the Franklin D. Roosevelt Library. On the question of advertising, see Morgenthau to Francis Case, February 21, 1942, Morgenthau MSS. The Secretary complained about mink in Diary 503:386. His speech of April 20, 1942, is in Diary 518:117, and his off-the-record comments are in Press Conferences, 20, for the same date. For the exchange with F. S. Allis, Jr., see Allis to Morgenthau, April 21, 1942, Morgenthau's reply of the same date, and Allis's response of the following day, all in Morgenthau MSS, where are also the Secretary's other wires and letters of exhortation and thanks. On intimidation, see Diary 530:317. The statement of June 4, 1942, is from Diary 536:217; the report of the July 10 Cabinet meeting, from Presidential Diary, that date, and also July 16, 1942. The Secretary praised his staff in Diary 587:46–60, and talked about the December 1942 drive in Diary 601:87.

6. Two Hundred Billion Dollars, pp. 23–32

On the Victory Loan groups, see Press Conferences, 23: March 3, 1943; on Morgenthau's worries, Press Conferences, 23: April, 1943; Diary 666:136. The analysis of the Third War Loan is from the "War Savings" file in the Morgenthau MSS; the discussion and quotations pertaining to the Secretary's North African and Italian trip are from Diary 671:84–94; Diary 672:21; Diary 677:152, 155. For Morgenthau's views of March 1944, see Diary 712:134–47. He called for only three drives in 1944 in Diary 683:99. There is an excellent discussion of "free riding" in M. S. Eccles, *Beckoning Frontiers* (New York, 1951), pp. 360–366; see also Diary 762:80–83; Diary 774:70–83. On Treasury plans for the Sixth War Loan, see Diary 779:260; Diary 783:271; on the results of that loan drive, Diary 809:317–18; Diary 810:49–55, 126–29. For the development of policy toward and the assessments of the Seventh War Loan, see Diary 821:83–84; Diary 824:4–6, 177, 193, 199–200; Diary 863:108; and Eccles, *op. cit.* For the summary of Treasury borrowing policy, see "Raising Funds for Victory," a Special Report of the Secretary of the Treasury, July 17, 1945, Morgenthau MSS. On postwar recommendation, see Diary 795:59–72; on the exchange with *Fortune,* Diary 841:248. Morgenthau's retrospective views are from conversations.

CHAPTER II. TAXATION FOR WAR

1. The Social Point of View, pp. 34–36

On the general question of wartime taxation, see R. E. Paul, *Taxation in the United States* (Boston, 1954), Chapter VI, which was of large importance for this chapter. For the discussion about taxes of Jan. 7, 1942, see Diary 483:3–12; for the Treasury's initial program, and its opposition to a sales tax, see Diary 488:19–43; Diary 499:10–53. The remark about Roosevelt is from Diary 501: 107; about the bathtub, from Diary 501:242; and the testimony appears in Diary 503:183 ff.

2. Weeks of Particular Hell, pp. 36–39

On the committee on inflation, see M. E. Eccles, *Beckoning Frontiers,* 370–74. The Paul program is in Diary 512:251–52; the April 3, 1942, memo in Diary 513:81–92. Morgenthau's comment about the Keynesians comes from Diary 513:333–42; about the knife in the back, from Diary 514:183. For the meeting with Roosevelt, see Diary 514:310–13; for the Cabinet meeting, Diary 515:87–103; for the April 15 comments to Roosevelt, Presidential Diary for that date. On the President's address of April 27, 1942, see Diary 521:18, 204, 342.

3. A Most Hostile Committee, pp. 39–42

The question of corporate taxes is summarized in Paul, *Taxation in the United States,* and in the second volume of this work. For the May 6, 1942, conference see Diary 524:199–201. For the comments on collection at the source, see Diary 529:262. The May 25 remarks are from Diary 531:207–39, 265–74. On the draft by the Ways and Means Committee, see Diary 539:184–203, which includes the exchange between Morgenthau and Rayburn.

4. A Couple of Whipping Boys, pp. 42–48

The testimony before the Senate Finance Committee is in Diary 553:16–45. Morgenthau was shocked during conversations in Diary 552:171–207. For Rosenman's July 27, 1942, report, see Diary 554: 28–32. On expenditure rationing, see Diary 554:197–216; Diary 555:2–4, 89–123, 132–52. The bit in the teeth advice and other remarks to Roosevelt are from Presidential Diary, Sept. 2 and 4, 1942. On the spendings tax and related discussions, see Diary 561:17–38, 47–97; Diary 562:1–13; Diary 565:1–60, 74–120, 175, 178–79; Diary 566:3, 151–60 (the testimony), 312–14 (the response), and Presidential Diary, Sept. 7, 1942 (the whipping boys remark), as well as Diary 567:61–65 (no regrets).

5. Tax Forgiveness, pp. 49–52

On the genesis of the Ruml Plan, see Paul, *Taxation in the United States;* Elinor Morgenthau's comment is in Diary 488:162. Paul's remark about Congressional interest is from Diary 554:68; the Secretary's sense of disgust, from Press Conferences, 21, Aug. 24, 1942. On the social security proposals, see Diary 562:215; Diary 574:212–15; and on the Senate committee's mood, Diary 574:216–217. For the comments about the Revenue Act of 1942, see Diary 578:155; Diary 579:117.

6. New Revenue "By Various Methods," pp. 52–58

Morgenthau wanted to straighten things out in Diary 586:4; he talked with Byrnes in Diary 586:32, and with Roosevelt in Presidential Diary, December 3, 1942; and he gave directions to his aides in Diary 592:92–115. On his talk with Doughton, see Diary 592:228–33. On Roosevelt's December 16, 1942, indecision, see Diary 597:26–44; on Treasury disagreement with the Budget Bureau, Diary 597:234; Diary 598:48 (including the talk with Blough); on Morgenthau's Atlanta journey and report to Roosevelt, Diary 598:187, 266–67. For the Dec. 29 meeting with Roosevelt, see Diary 599:160–61. For the episode of the rewriting of the Budget Message, see Diary 601:168–80 (which includes all quoted material).

7. Ruml Again, pp. 58–64

For developments during January 1943, see Diary 603:5–11; Diary 606:46–47; Diary 608:131–55. Morgenthau's Feb. 11 memo is in Diary 608:161–62; his remark about enemies, in Diary 607:145. Gaston described Doughton in Diary 609:235 and Roosevelt wrote him in Diary 609:342–43. On the need for a white rabbit, see Diary 615:295–97 (including Roosevelt's new plan). Morgenthau's March 15, 1943, talk with Doughton is in Diary 616:141, 154–60; the

Doughton letter to Paul, in Diary 619:120; Doughton's and Roosevelt's comments on the House bill, in Diary 621:275; Diary 622:8. The April 21, 1943, notification to Roosevelt is in Diary 628:49. On the "swing to the right" and on the President's intervention and the responses thereto, see Diary 634:103–05, 112–17; Diary 635:1, 29. For the developments of May 24–26, 1943, see Diary 636:10–15, 158–61, 171–79, 189–91; Diary 637:5–11.

8. Hot Weather, pp. 64–73

For the May 27, 1943, conversation, see Diary 637:126–39; on the June 8 statement by Roosevelt, Diary 640:44. Morgenthau complained to Roosevelt in Diary 640:215–16 and Roosevelt replied in Diary 641:173. Morgenthau's lament of July 22, 1943 is in Diary 650:126–27, 170–85; his July 27 letter in Diary 651:118–20 and Roosevelt's July 30 reply in Diary 652:227. Their Aug. 10 and 11, 1943, conversations, from Presidential Diary, those dates. Morgenthau's statements about not lowering exemptions and about August tax plans generally are from Diary 656:146–66; his letter to Byrnes, from Diary 656:197–99; Byrnes's reply, from Diary 657:50–52. Morgenthau's redefined objections met Roosevelt's approval in Presidential Diary, August 29, 1943. The argument of Sept. 9 is from Diary 663:26–46; the discussion of September 13, from Diary 663:244–48; that of Sept. 14, 1943, from Diary 664:22–25. Doughton and George objected to the new proposals in Diary 664:150–54. For Morgenthau's complaint to Roosevelt, see Presidential Diary, September 16, 1943. On the September 27 talks, see Diary 667:32–40. Morgenthau's testimony is in Diary 669:374–414; his preceding comment to Gaston, in Presidential Diary, Oct. 3, 1944.

9. A Great Defeat, pp. 73–78

There is a summary memo of importance for this section in Diary 705:27–36. On the congressional and public responses to Morgenthau's testimony, see Diary 670:62; Diary 675:181. Morgenthau commended the Treasury's proposals to Paul in Diary 672:9–11, and talked to his staff on Nov. 23, 1943, in Diary 679:52–81. On the friendly Senators, including George, see Diary 679:238–40. Morgenthau's Dec. 21, 1943, statement to the press is from Diary 685: 182–83; George's rejoinder, in Diary 686:108. For Blough's *cor* cerns, see Diary 697:126–32. Morgenthau's Feb. 1, 1944, talk with Byrnes is from Diary 699:1. On developments leading to the veto, see Diary 700:17–18, 57, 114; Diary 701:1, 25, 194, 268–70; Diary 703:30; Diary 704:163–64. See also Paul, *Taxation in the United States*. Morgenthau reflected upon the veto, with his staff, in Diary 705:3–12.

CHAPTER III. FINANCING THE GRAND ALLIANCE

1. Russia: "This Is Critical," pp. 80–87

The Morgenthau-Litvinov conversation in early Dec. is from Diary 471:80–81; the gold arrangement of Jan. 1, 1942, from Diary 481:134. For Swope's remark on Land, see Diary 487:228. On deliveries under the First Protocol and Morgenthau's March 11, 1942, talk with Roosevelt, see Presidential Diary, that date. The "this is critical" chit is in Diary 507:26; the Secretary's report to his staff and conference of March 12 are from Diary 507:27–35, 85–118; the follow-up through March 26 is from Diary 507:261; Diary 508:355–56; Diary 510:334. For the May 6, 1942, report on shipping, see Diary 524:153; Mack's June 9 report is in Diary 538:53; Roosevelt's June 16, 1942, and Sept. 9 remarks, from Presidential Diary, those dates, which include Morgenthau's reflections. On the refineries, see Diary 569:247, 249, 263–80; Diary 572:193–94. Morgenthau's related comment to Roosevelt is in Diary 575:58a–58d; for the President's order, see Diary 575:67–68. The Jan. 1943 memo is in Diary 602:36; the Feb. 1944 memo in Diary 703:36.

2. China: The Price of Friendship, pp. 87–102

Morgenthau's talks with T. V. Soong about a Chinese declaration of war are from Diary 470:226; Diary 471:55–56. The sensitive question of Harry D. White, along with other issues relating to China which this and later chapters cover, is treated, too, in the excellent volume of Herbert Feis, *The China Tangle* (Princeton, 1953); in the reliable personal memoir of Arthur N. Young, *China and the Helping Hand, 1937–1945* (Cambridge, 1963) — with which this study sometimes disagrees about matters of judgment, but not matters of fact; the introduction, in my view untenable in its claims, to *Morgenthau Diary* (*China*), Subcommittee . . . of the Committee on the Judiciary, United States Senate, 89 Cong. 1 Sess., 2 v. (Washington, 1965), in which are reprinted most of the Documents on which I, too, have relied — a circumstance true also of *Foreign Relations of the United States, Diplomatic Papers, 1942, China* (Washington, 1956). For Gauss's view of the Chinese loan proposal, see Diary 482:209; for Berle's opinion of Jan. 9, 1942, see Diary 483: 216, and for Roosevelt's, Roosevelt to Morgenthau, that date, Roosevelt MSS. Hull's Jan. 10 letter is in Diary 484:289–90. The meetings of Jan. 12, 1942, are reported in Diary 485:74–81, 93–97, with the Monetary Division's reservations to the currency scheme in Diary 485:98–99; the Jan. 13 staff meeting in Diary 485:207–17, including Hornbeck's views, with Roosevelt's in Diary 485:252–54, 264. China's adverse reply appears in Diary 487:275–77. Morgenthau talked to Stimson on Jan. 28 and 29 in Diary 489:366; Diary 490:1–3. Litvinov spoke of blackmail in Diary 490:5–6. For Morgenthau's January 29, 1942, letter to Hull, see Diary 490:46–47; for his report on the Jan. 30 Cabinet meeting, Diary 490:153–67, followed by the draft of the resolution in Diary 490:272–75, which Morgenthau read to Soong in Diary 490:305, and to the British in Diary 491:2–3, who promised assistance in Diary 490:94. On Morgenthau's testimony to the congressional committees, see Diary 490: 302–21; Diary 492:293–99. Roosevelt's message to Chiang is in Diary 493:278. The material quoted about the Treasury-State-Chinese exchanges concerning terms of the loan is from Diary 497:89; Diary 499:421–23; Diary 505:242–43; Diary 506:162–75, 212–13; Diary 509:111; Diary 510:1–6. The peak of the Welles-Morgenthau controversy came in the material cited from Diary 506.

3. China: "A Peculiar and Interesting Situation," pp. 102–110

On general questions in this section, see works cited in paragraph above. Kung's April 1942 request is discussed in Diary 515: 269–70, 279, 287. For a summary of the Chinese securities sales during 1942–43, see Diary 685:140–42. On the Cabinet meeting of Feb. 5, 1943, see Diary 606: Bell report of that date. White's memo of Feb. 23 is in Diary 611:216–18, Mrs. Bucks's analysis is quoted with her permission. On the episode of the cigarettes, see Diary 619:29–30. Paul's June report is in Diary 641:65; the July negotiations with

Kung, in Diary 647:242–44; Diary 648:195; Diary 649:91, 93; Diary 651:214–15. The Sept. 29, 1943, memo appears in Diary 668:68. Morgenthau's views in Dec. are in Diary 658:140–42.

4. China: Reprise, pp. 110–122

On general and background issues, see Feis, *The China Tangle*. The December 18, 1943, memo is cited above, Diary 685:140–42. Roosevelt's response is in Presidential Diary, Dec. 20, 1943. Hull and Morgenthau talked on Jan. 1, 1944, in Diary 689:24; but Morgenthau quickly expressed distrust of the Soongs in Diary 689:32. Hull's Jan. 4 views are in Diary 690:256–57, and Morgenthau's adverse response of the next day in Diary 691:50–51. The cables sounded all right to Morgenthau in Diary 691:111–14. Morgenthau's recommendation of Jan. 15 is from Diary 694:147. On the "drastic" reply from Chiang, see Diary 695:51–56, which also reveals Morgenthau's anger and White's rejoinder; see also Stimson Diary, Jan. 19, 1944. Morgenthau and Somervell talked that day in Diary 695:176–79, which includes Roosevelt's editing. On State-Treasury conferences of Jan. 19 and 20, see Diary 695:181–82, 272–75. There is a good summary of developments during Feb. 1944 in Diary 705:160–61. The Feb. 14 conference is in Diary 701:276–78. Morgenthau's March 11, 1944, response to Gauss is in Diary 709:97. On Madame Chiang's letter and the American response, see Diary 712:1, 53–55; Diary 716:76, 80–85; Diary 719:24–28. The report of the May 18, 1944, Cabinet meeting is in Diary 733:32–36, which includes White's comment. Morgenthau talked to Clay in Diary 733:120. He wrote Roosevelt on June 8, 1944, in Diary 741:91–93.

5. Great Britain: "Nothing Decadent," pp. 122–131

On Churchill, see Diary 478:5. On the dollar drain in England, see Diary 476:126–27; Diary 487:231, 233; Diary 488:132 — where Morgenthau talked with Halifax. The views of Acheson and McCloy are in Diary 492:211–13; Diary 493:53–57. For Roosevelt's Feb. 12, 1942, opinion, see Diary 496:36–62. The Feb. 19 promise to Halifax is in Diary 498:111–13. The March discussions of Lend-Lease are in Diary 508:225–48. On the level of British balances, see Diary 508: 260. Efforts to sustain those balances are reported in Diary 518:146–48, 260; Diary 521:50; Diary 523:161–62. On plans for Morgenthau's

trip to England, see Presidential Diary, Aug. 22 and 25, 1942; Diary
562:200a–200b, 212; Diary 567:237a; Diary 578:69a. The trip is reported in Diary 581:2–25. For the report to Roosevelt of Jan. 3,
1943, on balances, see Diary 601:34–38; Roosevelt approved in Diary
603:143.

6. Great Britain: Reprise, pp. 131–139

On the question of balances in August, 1943, see Diary 653:214–
240, 257–58, 262–64; Diary 654:1, 23, 26, 166. The November 1,
1943, memo is in Diary 672:216; it was discussed with Crowley and
Acheson in Diary 672:173–209, 223–26; Diary 673:295–97; see also
Presidential Diary, Oct. 11, 1943. Roosevelt "told Crowley" about
balances in Diary 674:70; and Morgenthau talked with Halifax on
Nov. 14, 1943, in Diary 676:34–36, and on November 17 in Diary
678:43–45. On White's memo and Cox's opposition, see Diary 678:
152; Diary 679:91–92. For the December 31, 1943, conference, see
Diary 687:128–70. Hull's memo is in Diary 690:130, with attendant
discussion in Diary 687:182–88; Diary 689:38–40, 200. Hull's own
Jan. 4 memo is from Diary 690:128, and Roosevelt's reply in Diary
691:132. Halifax, Morgenthau, and others talked, and the British
were "saddened" in Diary 692:2–5. The Chancellor's Jan. 27, 1944,
letter is from Diary 697:114. Morgenthau's Feb. 2 cooperation, from
Diary 699:294–95. For the Feb. 18, 1944, Cabinet meeting, see Diary
702:102–03; for Roosevelt's message to Churchill, see Diary 703:142;
and for the March 11, 1944, Cabinet meeting, see Diary 709:1–13.
The message of March 24 is in Diary 713:277–78, Morgenthau's remark to White, in Diary 716:75.

CHAPTER IV. PRINCIPLES AND EXPEDIENTS

1. Invasion and Occupation Currency: North Africa, pp. 141–156

For a good general discussion of the question of invasion and
occupation currency in all theaters of operation and throughout the
war, see W. Rundell, Jr., *Black Market Money* (Louisiana State
University, 1964). On those issues in North Africa, see also R. Murphy, *Diplomat Among Warriors* (Garden City, 1964). White's preliminary report on Eisenhower's request is in Diary 550:271–82.

For the views of Feis and Stimson, see Diary 553:159; Diary 554:266; Stimson Diary, July 17, 1942. The issue of the marking on the currency was resolved in Diary 556:99–100, 145; Diary 557:33–35. For Keynes's opinion on inflation, see Diary 557:241–43. Morgenthau spoke about the "implication of what kind of money you begin to use" on Aug. 5, 1942, in Diary 557:16–27, which includes his exchange with White. The Sept. 4 quotation is from Diary 566:212–236. The Secretary gave directions to Bell in Diary 572:22a–22g; on cross rates, see also Stimson Diary, Sept. 25, 28, 1942. For the successive conversations about Darlan, see Diary 584:170a–170g; Stimson Diary, Nov. 16, 1942; Diary 585:190a–190e; Presidential Diary, Nov. 17, 18, 1942. The inquiry and response about changing cross rates at the end of Dec. are in Diary 600:48, 174–78; Diary 601:24. For Morgenthau's Jan. 1, 1943, statement see Diary 601:1–23, which includes his talk with the British. The report of the Jan. 8 Cabinet meeting is from Diary 602:104; on Casablanca, see Stimson Diary, Feb. 3, 1943; on the Cabinet meeting two days later, see Diary 606: 102–06. The matter of Couve de Murville is in Murphy, *op. cit.*, and from conversations.

2. Currencies for the Liberation of Europe, pp. 156–165

On the "cherubs," see Stimson Diary, Aug. 27, Nov. 4, 1942. Morgenthau's Feb. 25, 1943, order is from Diary 612:68. White's late March lament and Morgenthau's reply appear in Diary 619: 247. On the lira rate, see Diary, 622:10–12: Diary 625:180–87; Diary 628:33–39. Morgenthau accepted part of the British plan in Diary 629:145–52; Diary 656:229–33. On Roosevelt's directive of June 3, 1943, see Diary 639:213–21. Treasury objections to State and War Department plans appear in Diary 654:179–81; Diary 659:192; Diary 668:48 (Morgenthau's letter on the lira rate); and Presidential Diary, Oct. 5, 1943 (Roosevelt's ruling). The Nov. 6, 1943, talks with Hopkins and Roosevelt are from Presidential Diary, that date. On invasion currency for Europe, see Diary 597:145; Diary 675:100–02. Morgenthau's August 1943 letter is in Diary 653:151; White's memo reversing his position, in Diary 669:83–84. The Secretary's statement of April 10, 1944, appears in Diary 719:162–66; his view on bookkeeping, in Diary 706:255. On the Dutch loan, see Diary 725: 23–31. The May 5, 1944, conversation is from Diary 728:49–52.

The June 8 remark to Roosevelt appears in Diary 741:81. For Roosevelt's statement about industry and foreign orders, see Diary 727:66; the Chase Bank discussed a private credit in Diary 739:158–164. Material about the fight over the appointment of a Civil Affairs officer is in Diary 661:76; 680:156; 681:1; 682:179–90; 686:31–33; 687:70; 727:205–06; Stimson Diary, Nov. 29, Dec. 3, 1943; Presidential Diary, Dec. 20, 1943.

3. The Franc: Mirror of French Prestige, pp. 165–177

On conditions in late summer 1943, see Diary 661:93–98. The Treasury-State agreement on design for the franc appears in Diary 679:268; Stimson's objection in Stimson Diary, Nov. 25, 1943. The Dec. 23, 1943, recommendation is in Diary 686:253; Roosevelt's Jan. 6, 1944, objection, in Diary 691:220; the Jan. 8, 1944, conferences in Presidential Diary, that date; see also Diary 692:116–47. Eisenhower's policy of May 1944 is reported in Diary 733:58–59; the Treasury-State memo, in Diary 734:181–82. On the anti-inflation program, see Diary 736:61; Diary 737:35; Diary 734:139–42. Morgenthau spoke to Bell on June 10 in Diary 742:4–10, 30–44, 51–56. On the gun in the back, see Diary 742:149. Stimson's views are in Stimson Diary, June 14, 1944. For McCloy's June 16 report, see Diary 744:59–68; for the June 23 draft reply, Diary 746:226, 230–31; for the June 26 meeting, Diary 747:68–69. Morgenthau talked to McCloy on July 5, 1944, in Diary 750:137–41 and they wrote Roosevelt, with Hull, in Diary 750:328 (including Roosevelt's endorsements). On inflation in France, see Diary 762:157–59; Diary 814:242–46; Diary 824:72; Diary 836:251.

4. Allied Military Marks, pp. 177–194

On the background to this issue, see Rundell, *Black Market Money*. The Morgenthau Diaries are singularly thin on the subject matter of this section, which is drawn instead from two well-indexed publications: *Occupation Currency Transactions,* Hearings Before the Committees on Appropriations, Armed Services, and Banking and Currency, U. S. Senate, 80 Cong., 1 Sess. (Washington, 1947) and *Transfer of Occupation Currency Plates,* Hearings Before the Subcommittee on Government Operations Abroad of the Permanent Subcommittee on Investigations of the Committee on Government

Operations, U. S. Senate, 83 Cong., 1 Sess. (Washington, 1953). On the question of the mark rate of exchange in May 1944, see also Diary 735:149–51; Diary 738:80–96. Morgenthau's retrospective views are from conversations.

5. Argentina: How Good a Neighbor? pp. 194–206

Material of the first importance for this section appears in Cordell Hull, *Memoirs* (2 vols., New York, 1948), Chapters 99–103; J. W. Pratt, *Cordell Hull* (2 vols., New York, 1964), Chapter 21; S. Welles, *Time for Decision* (New York, 1944), Chapter 5, and S. Welles, *Where Are We Heading?* (New York, 1946), Chapter 4. The recommendations of May 1942 are in Diary 524:235–38, with the response of Acheson and others in Diary 528:217–20. Roosevelt's May 14 and 15 statements are in Presidential Diary, those dates; see also Stimson Diary, May 21, 1942. On the developments of Oct. 1943, see Diary 672:7, 22, 33, 38–39, 45, 54. For Morgenthau's view on Nov. 2, 1943, see Diary 672:142–59, 164, 166–72 (the memo for Stettinius). Hull and Morgenthau met on Nov. 24, 1943, in Diary 679:199–202, and on Dec. 20, 1943, in Diary 688 II:161; see also Presidential Diary, Dec. 20, 1943. Stone's comment of the next day is from Diary 686:45–48. Stone and Morgenthau conferred on Jan. 1, 1944, in Diary 689:14, and Morgenthau saw McCloy on Jan. 3 in Diary 689:137–38. For the opinions of the War Food Administration and the War Shipping Administration, see Diary 690:61–62, 89–91. McCloy's Jan. 8, 1944, report is discussed in Diary 692:153–57. Morgenthau sought an excuse for action in Diary 692:115; Diary 693:70–75. Hull explained his Jan. 12 plans in Diary 693:98–101. The Treasury lamented delay in execution in Diary 696:99–101. For the Feb. 11, 1944, Cabinet meeting, see Diary 701, Bell's report of that date. Morgenthau's opinions of March 3 and 4, 1944, are from Diary 706:38–53, 168. The Secretary explained himself to his staff in Diary 706:214–41, and to Roosevelt on March 7, 1944, in Presidential Diary, that date. For Wallace's views and Jones's, see Diary 713:308–09. Morgenthau talked with Acheson on April 27, 1944, in Diary 724:256–67, 279–82. On the "bargain" of the next day, see Diary 728:49–52 (which quotes the cable). The Hull-Armour exchange is reported in Diary 730:27. On Morgenthau's hot exchange with Hull, see Diary 730:134, 148–49 (the letter to Roosevelt); Diary 733:29–31 (the May 18 Cabinet meeting).

6. "Those Terrible Eighteen Months," pp. 207–223

Diaries 688 I and 68 II, both well-indexed, contain most of the important material pertinent to this section, and except as otherwise noted, are the sources for the account and quotations in the text. Morgenthau's charge in the first paragraph of this section is from his article, "The Refugee Run-Around," *Collier's*, Nov. 1, 1947, which is based on the same material. On Nov. 1938, see Diary 151:32–35; see also Presidential Diary, June 19, 1939; July 7, 1942; December 3, 1942. On June 1943, see Diary 642:75–79. Morgenthau's Feb. 15, 1943, statement to Welles is from Diary 609:39–41; the report from the embassies, from Diary 610:208; Diary 611:276. Diary 688 I picks up the narrative in May 1943, but on Rabbi Wise in July 1943, see also Diary 652:230–31; on developments of Jan. 10–16, 1944, see Diary 692:289–92; Diary 693:51–52, 88–90, 186–229; Diary 694:190–92, 204–11. For Cox's letter, see Diary 694:212.

7. The War Refugee Board, pp. 223–227

On the matter of the director, see Diary 696:124, 127–48, 168–77. The early successes of the Board are reported in Stimson Diary, Feb. 1, 1944; Presidential Diary, March 7, 1944. On the question of havens, see Stimson Diary, March 21, 31, 1944; Diary 719:3–7; Diary 732:62–64 (May 16 meeting); Stimson Diary, May 26, 1944; Diary 738:42 (memo on supporting newspapers, etc.); Diary 738:177–82 (June 2 report); Diary 742:296–97 (message to Congress).

CHAPTER V. A NEW DEAL IN INTERNATIONAL ECONOMICS

1. A New Deal for a New World, pp. 228–240

This section and this entire chapter owe much to three important studies of the subjects here discussed: Richard N. Gardner, *Sterling-Dollar Diplomacy* (Oxford, 1956); R. F. Harrod, *The Life of John Maynard Keynes* (New York, 1951); and E. F. Penrose, *Economic Planning for the Peace* (Princeton, 1953). The 1941 memo to White is in Diary 473:16; the May 9, 1942, memo of White, in Diary 526:111–312. Morgenthau wrote Roosevelt on May 15, 1942, in Diary 528:321–22; the reply is in Diary 529:7; the May 25 meeting, in Diary 531:256–64. For the conversations of July 2, 1942, see

Diary 545:90–114; for the July 21 agreement, Diary 552:142–43. On Keynes, see Harrod, *op. cit.* The American questions of October 1942 appear in Diary 575:91–93. On the December American draft, see Diary 596:181–98. Morgenthau's memo to Roosevelt of March 17, 1943, is in Diary 617:123–25; for Roosevelt's response, see Diary 617:153. On the press release, see Diary 619:160–61; Diary 620:32. The April 1, 1943, conference and April 6 testimony are in Diary 622:9, 178–93. Morgenthau worried about the leak in Diary 622:246; see also Press Conferences, 23, April 6, 1943. On the congressional reaction, see Diary 625:66–70, 73, 81–83.

2. Staging for a Conference, pp. 241–252

International responses to the White draft are recorded in Diary 630:358–59; Diary 638:160; Diary 649:108–09; Diary 632:24–27 (the British). On the *Fortune* article, see Diary 654:44. Morgenthau and Hull talked on July 9, 1943, in Diary 647:169–83, and with Keynes on Sept. 13, 1943, in Diary 664:29–30. On Keynes and White and their negotiations, see works cited in section 1 above. I drew also on the oral accounts of two of Keynes's British associates who asked to remain anonymous. The testimony of Oct. 5, 1943, is in Diary 670:2–15; the preceding permission in Diary 667:59; Diary 668:73–74; the following liaison with Rayburn, Diary 670:53; the mid-November conference, Diary 678:289. Morgenthau spurred the Russians in Diary 670:20; Diary 686:173, 211; Diary 689:119. White's memo about differences remaining with the British is from Diary 709:14; his March 21, 1944, worries are expressed in Diary 712:224. Morgenthau urged him not to worry, and proceeded further with Roosevelt and Hull in Diary 717:63–64, 68, 185. The April 8, 1944, meeting is from Diary 719:36; see Diary 719:203–06 on April 10. For the reply from London, see Diary 720:139; Morgenthau's objections are in Diary 720:232–33; the British consent, in Diary 721:284–85. Morgenthau talked to Acheson on April 17, 1944, in Diary 722:57–59 and discussed strategy in Diary 722:179–94. On the exchange with Harriman, see Diary 723:1–2, 18–22, 35–38; on the British position, Diary 723:178–82; on Morgenthau's testimony of April 21, 1944, Diary 723:206–23. His letter to Roosevelt of that day is in Diary 723:232–33; his long statement to White, in Diary 724:150–76. The exchange with Roosevelt of April 26 and 28 is from Diary 725:43–45, and Roosevelt's May 25, 1944, statement, from Diary 735:152–54. On Tobey's mood, see Diary 744:84.

3. Conflicts of Interest, pp. 252–257

Morgenthau complained to White in Diary 746:133–39 and heard from Burgess in Diary 746:139nn, 139tt–139uu. White's memos to the delegation are in Diary 747:141a–141l, 232–41.) Morgenthau spoke to Acheson in Diary 747:210–13.

4. Bretton Woods: The International Monetary Fund, pp. 257–271

For Roosevelt's greeting and Morgenthau's speech, see Diary 748:172–74; Diary 749:63–77. The Secretary talked privately with his associates in Diary 749:1–53. The Americans discussed the crisis over Russia's quota in the IMF in Diary 749:254–88, 294, and continued discussions on July 5, 1944, in Diary 750:77–132 and on July 6 in Diary 750:229–31, 248–98. Morgenthau was "pleased" in Diary 751:44–46, and expressed his surprise to the Russians on July 11 in Diary 752:202–16, which includes his talk with them. On the ensuing leak, see Diary 753:40–41, 47; for the July 13, 1944, cable, see Diary 753:117. On the developments of July 14, see Diary 754:14–20, and Morgenthau MSS, Memo of the Secretary about a conversation with Keynes, that date. The problem of the quota received further attention on July 15 in Diary 754:115–53. On the Latin Americans, see Diary 751:253, 293–301; Diary 752:1–40; on Poland and Wagner, see Diary 753:165; on France, see Diary 754:164–79; on China, see Diary 755:242a; Diary 756:184–91. Keynes and White discussed the question of the IMF and inflation in Diary 751:252. On the problem of the Bank of International Settlements, see Diary 756:53–62, 132–136, 137, 151–57. On the matter of the location of IMF headquarters, see Diary 753:122–32, 161–63; Diary 754:3–6; Morgenthau MSS, Memo of conversation with Keynes, July 14, 1944; Diary 755:161–170, 197–98, 201.

5. Bretton Woods: The International Bank for Reconstruction and Development, pp. 271–278

Negotiations about the Bank are reported in Diary 752:217–76 (July 11, 1944); Diary 753:1–15, 21–39 (July 12); Diary 753:77–83, 133–42 (July 13); Morgenthau MSS, Memo of conversation with

Keynes, July 14, 1944; Diary 755:69–94 (July 17); Diary 755:203–10 (July 18); Diary 756:1, 16–40, 53–70 (July 19); Diary 756:236–56 (July 21); Diary 757:13a (July 22 — with Morgenthau's thanks to Molotov). For Morgenthau's closing comments, messages, and retrospective conversations, see Diary 756:282; Diary 757:1–12, 15–16, 100–14, 115; see also Presidential Diary, Aug. 25, 1944.

CHAPTER VI. IN THE NATIONAL INTEREST

1. Reconversion to a Liberal Society, pp. 279–285

On reconversion and small business, see Diary 657:105, 113; Diary 667:118. On the nomination for Vice President, see Presidential Diary, June 28, July 6, 1944. On the Wallace confirmation, see Diary 812:7–9, 320; Diary 815:86, 138–54; Diary 816:1, 29–30; Diary 820:44, 55. On Latimer, see Diary 826:35.

2. Balance Sheet for Chengtu, pp. 285–295

Stimson's observations are from his diary, June 23, 1944. Morgenthau talked to Leahy in Diary 747:133, and with Roosevelt in Presidential Diary, June 28, 1944. Bell summarized the questions at issue with the Chinese in Diary 753:171–73, as did Adler in Diary 754:31–43. Morgenthau and his associates prepared to meet Kung and the Chinese in Diary 755:1–9 and met them in Diary 755:13–64. The telegram to Roosevelt of July 17, 1944, is in Diary 755:105–107. Kung's letter of Sept. 9, 1944, is in Diary 771:87–88; Morgenthau's Sept. 20 reply, in Diary 773:93–94; the two met on Oct. 6 in Diary 780:59–80, 85 (Clay's views), 90–109. Stimson described Kung in Stimson diary, Nov. 17, 1944. Morgenthau's memo to White of November 20 is in Diary 797:100. On the Treasury's interpretation of Roosevelt's controversial cable, see Diary 798:215–16. Morgenthau and Kung conferred on Nov. 25, 1944, in Diary 798:222–46; Morgenthau wrote Roosevelt on Nov. 28 in Diary 798:249–51, and wrote White on Nov. 30 in Diary 800:251.

3. Chinese Politics and American Gold, pp. 295–303

The works by H. Feis and A. N. Young cited above in references to China for Chapter III, are of large importance here, too.

The October 5, 1944, conversation about gold is in Diary 779:277–280. On Hurley's three-fold assignment, see Diary 801:263–64, which includes his views of Nov. 15, 1944. Morgenthau's Dec. 13 message is from Diary 802:263; his Dec. 15 talk with White, from Diary 802:272–76. On the instructions for Adler and Morgenthau's letter of Dec. 16, 1944, see Diary 803:155, 158–60. The Dec. 30 letter to Hu Shih is in Diary 805:252; the Jan. 8, 1945, cable to Adler, in Diary 807:327–29; Kung's Jan. 26 plea, in Diary 812:269–89. For Adler's analysis, see Diary 814:315–18. On the tin, see Diary 816:349; Diary 819:233; Diary 821:137. Coe's analysis of March 2, 1945, is in Diary 824:230; Morgenthau's March 3 letter, in Diary 825:171; Adler's March 11 cable, in Diary 827:53–55; Morgenthau's April 12, 1945, letter to Kung, in Diary 836:240–43. See, too, Stimson Diary, March 8, 1945.

4. Compensation for American Assistance, pp. 303–306

On France, see Diary 773:4–8; Diary 813:9–10, 159–73; Diary 819:36; Diary 823:263. Morgenthau put White to work on the Russian question in Diary 691:104–21. White's memo is in Diary 707:59–62, and it was discussed in Diary 711:218. Conversations about interest rates, held in Aug. 1944, are from Diary 764:158–59; Diary 766:39–40; for Sept., see Diary 773:4–8; Diary 774:178. Morgenthau's Jan. 1, 1945, letter is in Diary 806:168. The Treasury proposal and the Jan. 10, 1945, conversations are in Diary 808:196–203, 294–96, 310–11, 315–16. On eastern Europe, see Diary 810:17. The Jan. 25, 1945, decision is in Diary 812:209–10.

5. British Finances Again, pp. 306–316

The problem of Lend-Lease for Phases II and III, as discussed in this and the following section, receives invaluable treatment in the works of H. Duncan Hall, R. N. Gardner, and R. F. Harrod, all cited in connection with Anglo-American issues in references to Chapters III and V, above. On the British aide-mémoire and Treasury-State disagreement about it, see Diary 739:26–36, 72–73, 201, 210–33; Diary 741:125. Morgenthau's June 16, 1944, memo for Roosevelt is in Diary 744:80. Morgenthau reported on his trip to England in Presidential Diary, Aug. 19, 1944, and to Hopkins in Diary 764:34–39. The Aug. 24, 1944, talk with Brand is from Diary

765:107, 118–23, and see also Presidential Diary, Aug. 25, 1944, and, for private comments too, Diary 766:25–30. Roosevelt's September 9 letter is in Diary 770:232. For the memos about Sept. 14, 1944, discussions, see Diary 771:223–25. On developments of Sept. 15, 1944, see Presidential Diary, that date. See also Diary 772:61. The meetings of Sept. 20, 1944, are reported in Diary 773:4–8; 35–75. On the "buzz saw," see Diary 772:215–16.

6. Lend-Lease for Phase II, pp. 316–326

For the discussions of Oct. 6, 1944, see Diary 780:1–13; for Oct. 18, Diary 783:35–39. On Argentina and on British colonial areas, see Diary 789:1–3. The caucus about munitions is reported in Diary 783:126–41; see also Diary 784:22. Key negotiations of Nov. 1944 are in Diary 791:46–69, 78–92; Diary 793:220–23; Diary 794:79–84. Keynes wrote about imprudence in Diary 795:275–76. Morgenthau reported Roosevelt was ruffled in Diary 795:150–54. On the White House meeting of Nov. 18, 1944, see Diary 796:146; on the Nov. 21 conversations, see Diary 797:166–207, and on Nov. 22, 1944, proposals, see Diary 798:63–67. The letter of Nov. 25 is in Diary 798:268–70. Baruch's opinions appear in Diary 787:164–65, 305; Diary 805:262, 267, 271–73, with Morgenthau's reply in Diary 805:263–64. The letters of Cherwell and Anderson to Morgenthau are in Diary 806:248–52.

CHAPTER VII. THE MORGENTHAU PLAN

1. Background to Involvement, pp. 327–333

The Morgenthau Plan, its development, modification, and impact, has received extensive treatment in memoirs and history alike. For this chapter and the next, I am indebted to a large number of published works, of which only the most fruitful are listed here. I drew often upon Henry Morgenthau, Jr., *Germany Is Our Problem* (New York, 1945) and "Our Policy Toward Germany," *New York Post*, Nov. 24–29, 1947. Arthur M. Schlesinger, Jr., was the anonymous collaborator in the second of those publications, which is meticulous in its detailed narrative. Indispensable for any study of the Morgenthau Plan is Paul Y. Hammond, "Directives for the Occupation of Germany: The Washington Controversy," in H. Stein, ed., *American Civil-Military Decisions* (Birmingham, 1963). It contains, among other thing, an excellent bibliography on the subject. I found particularly useful also the following works, many of which have been cited in other connections above: Cordell Hull, *Memoirs* 2 vols. (New York, 1948); H. L. Stimson and M. Bundy, *On Active Service in Peace and War* (New York, 1947); W. S. Churchill, *Closing the Ring* and *Triumph and Tragedy* (Boston, 1951 and 1953); Lord Moran, *Churchill* (Boston, 1966); E. F. Penrose, *Economic Planning for the Peace* (Princeton, 1953); D. D. Eisenhower, *Crusade in Europe* (Garden City, 1948) — all memoirs, and E. E. Morison, *Turmoil and Tradition* (Boston, 1960); J. W. Pratt, *Cordell Hull* 2 vols. (New York, 1964); and J. L. Snell, *Wartime Origins of the East-West Dilemma Over Germany* (New Orleans, 1959). The account in this chapter begins to rest primarily upon the materials in the Morgenthau Diaries and related sources with Morgenthau's remark of December 1943 which is in Diary 688 II:254. For the telephone call of June 17, 1944, see Diary 744:238, 298.

2. Portentous Misgivings, pp. 333–343

White's memo of disagreement with the State Department is in Diary 767:176. Morgenthau recalled the beginning of his involvement in the *New York Post* articles, *loc. cit.;* see also a file folder on the 1944 trip to Europe in Morgenthau MSS. The Secretary talked to his staff on his return in Diary 763:93–105, 111–12. For his meeting with Winant, see Penrose, *op. cit.,* and for his radio speech, Morgenthau, *Germany Is Our Problem.* His talk with Hull is reported in Diary 763:202–05; his conversation with Roosevelt of Aug. 19, 1944, in Presidential Diary, that date. The committee within the Treasury was appointed in Diary 764:120.

3. The Morgenthau Plan, pp. 343–359

For Seavey's views, see Diary 764:61; for the report of the Parliament, Diary 764:91; on Hilldring and Keynes, Diary 764:90, 154, 176–77. On Morgenthau's meeting with Stimson of Aug. 23, 1944, see Stimson Diary, that date, and Diary 765:14–16, 39–43. McConnell's views appear in Diary 764:232, Luxford's in Diary

765:39–43. Discussions of Aug. 24 and 25 about the exchange rate are in Diary 765:100–05, 109–14; Diary 766:1–12 (which also includes discussion of the "Handbook"). Memos for Roosevelt on the rate and the "Handbook" are in Diary 766:13–16; see also Presidential Diary, Aug. 25, 1944. Morgenthau reported to Bell and White that day in Diary 766:35–38, and was shocked when seeing the President in Presidential Diary, August 25, 1944. McCloy and Morgenthau discussed the rate in Diary 766:47–51. On Stimson, see Stimson Diary, Aug. 25, 1944. Roosevelt's letter about the "Handbook" is in Diary 766:167–70; Stimson's reflections, in Stimson Diary, Aug. 26–Sept. 2, 1944. For Morgenthau's messages to and conversation with his staff in that same period, see Diary 766:58; Diary 767: 1–29, 159–68; Diary 768:1–22, 66. On the tea with the Roosevelts of Sept. 2, 1944, see Presidential Diary, that date. The Treasury discussions of Sept. 4 are reported in Diary 768:104–27, 134–45. For the Morgenthau Plan, see Diary 768:158–65.

4. Discord in Washington, pp. 359–369

On the dinner of Sept. 4, 1944, see Diary 768:156; Stimson Diary, Sept. 4, 1944. On the Cabinet committee meeting of Sept. 5, see Stimson Diary, that date; Diary 769:1–19 (including the conversation with Hopkins). Stimson's memo attacking the Morgenthau Plan is in Diary 769:22. For the report about the White House meeting of September 6, 1944, see Diary 769:118–45 (which includes the discussion with Boettiger). See also Stimson Diary, Sept. 6, 1944. On the Sept. 7, 1944, Treasury-War Department meeting, see Diary 770:17–33, and see, too, Presidential Diary, that date, for Morgenthau's talk with Roosevelt. Morgenthau saw Hull on Sept. 8 in Diary 770:120–22. The "Black Book" memos and Treasury discussion of them are in Diary 771:6–29. The White House meeting of Sept. 9, 1944, is reported in Stimson Diary, that date, and Diary 771:41–49, as well as in Presidential Diary, that date. The telegram of Sept. 12, 1944, is in Diary 771:140.

5. OCTAGON, pp. 369–374

The introductory quotation is from the *New York Post, loc. cit.* For Morgenthau's contemporaneous account of the Quebec Conference, and for the documents there drafted and initialed, see

Presidential Diary, Sept. 15, 1944; Diary 772:1–3, 153–63, 208–12. White and Morgenthau disagreed about the relationship of German and British problems in Diary 783:35–39.

CHAPTER VIII. THE PROBLEM OF GERMANY

1. Retreat from OCTAGON, pp. 375–383

Important for this entire chapter are the works cited in the reference for Chapter VII, above. On the Morgenthau-Stimson-Hull conference of Sept. 20, 1944, see Stimson Diary, that date; Diary 773:4–8. Morgenthau's rejoinder to Stimson's anaylsis of the Morgenthau Plan is in Diary 773:85–87. On the leak to the press, see Diary 774:122–32, Diary 775:1, 3–22, 25, 29, 32–37; Stimson Diary, Sept. 25, 27, 1944. For the material on Sept. 29 see Diary 777:1–18, 21–22, 29–30, 90; and see Stimson Diary, Oct. 3, 1944. Morgenthau talked to his staff on Oct. 5 in Diary 779:291–301. On Dewey's charge, see Diary 781:210; Diary 783:159–60, 163, 178; Diary 784: 174; Diary 790:263–66; Diary 792:66–71; Stimson Diary, Nov. 4, 1944; Presidential Diary, Nov. 4, 1944; Diary 798:289 (Stimson's letter).

2. JCS 1067, pp. 383–390

The November 1, 1944, conversation with McCloy is reported in Diary 790:11–20. See Diary 790:36–37 for the Treasury view of British preferences. Stimson's letter of Nov. 27, 1944, is in Diary 800:139; see Diary 800:144–47 for the OSS report. The December 7 draft is from Diary 801:208–09; the Dec. 19 meeting with Boettiger, from Diary 804:13–28. Murphy's views are in Diary 810:159–61, and Morgenthau's demand to McCloy is in Diary 808:124–27. On the Financial Directive, see Diary 809: 89–90; Diary 817:146–49.

3. To Yalta and Beyond, pp. 390–400

On the Kilgore Committee, see Diary 794:9, 14, 277; Diary 796: 21. Morgenthau's report of the President's opinion of that committee is from Diary 795:203–05, and his conversation with Stettinius, from Diary 795:154–57. The State Department papers of Nov. 10 and 22 are detailed in Hammond, *op. cit.*, as is the FEA report of the following January. Morgenthau's Nov. 27, 1944, conversation with Mrs. Roosevelt is in Presidential Diary, that date, and Stettinius' letter, in Diary 799:81. For the Dec. 18 memo, see Diary 803:314–17; for Luxford's outrage, Diary 804:96–104. Morgenthau's memo of reassertion is in Diary 808:297–99; he talked with his staff on Jan. 10, 1945, in Diary 808:312; and argued with them about the terms of the German plan in Diary 810:141–45. The Treasury-State meeting of Jan. 17, 1945, is from Diary 810:149–58. Dunn and White and others met on Jan. 19 in Diary 811:95–98. On the question of war criminals, see Diary 811:1–8, 49–52; Diary 813: 293–95; on Russian plans, see Diary 812:214. The discussion of Yalta is from relevant works cited in references to Chapter VII, and also H. Feis, *Churchill, Roosevelt, Stalin* (Princeton, 1957); see, too, Diary 827:64–66.

4. Two Black Weeks, pp. 400–414

Roosevelt's March 12, 1945, letter appears in Diary 828:109; and Morgenthau's reply in Diary 828:107. The State Department's "Draft Directive" is in Diary 827:1; McCloy and Morgenthau discussed it on March 15, 1945, in Diary 828:259. On IPCOG, see Diary 829:230. On Baruch and reparations, see Diary 827:159–66; Diary 828:327, 331–34; Diary 829:222–29, 232–33; Diary 833:17–18. Morgenthau's March 17, 1945, conversation with McCloy about the "Draft Directive" is from Diary 829:1–15. The first Treasury memo criticizing the "Draft Directive" is in Diary 829:68–72. For Morgenthau's March 19, 1945, luncheon with the Russian ambassador, see memo of that date, Morgenthau MSS. Morgenthau and White discussed revising the Treasury memo in Diary 829:239–55; McCloy participated in Diary 830:1–12, and the March 20 draft is in Diary 830:13–18, with the memo of the same date to Roosevelt in Diary 830:19–20. Morgenthau talked later that day to Grew in Diary 830: 26–32 and to McCloy in Diary 830:37–45. On the March 21 IPCOG meeting, see Diary 831:16–23 (including Morgenthau's response to Coe's report). The Secretary met McCloy on March 22 and discussed his report and phoned Grew in Diary 831:44–51. Later, on March 22, 1945, McCloy reported on the White House meeting in Diary 831:55–68. On the March 23 conference, see Diary 835:87–94; and also Diary 831:183–90, 197–200, 205, 223–24 — references that include the memo of that date and report Roosevelt's response to it and Morgenthau's satisfaction; see also Stimson Diary, March 29, 1945.

5. The Last Evening, pp. 415–420

Morgenthau's March 23, 1945, letter to Roosevelt is in Diary 831:231; Roosevelt's question in reply, in Presidential Diary, that date; Roosevelt's letter, in Diary 833:45. On the last evening, see Presidential Diary, April 11, 1945.

CHAPTER IX. EPILOGUE: HARRY S TRUMAN

1. President Truman, pp. 421–427

On all this section through April, 1945, see Presidential Diary, April, 12, 14, 16, 20, 1945. On May 7, 1945, see Diary 845:12–14; see also Presidential Diary, May 9, 1945.

2. Confirmation for Bretton Woods, pp. 427–436

On newspaper opposition, see Diary 763:116, 138; Diary 833: 13. On the general issues involved and their resolution, see works cited above in connection with Chapter V, section 1. On Burgess and the ABA, see also Diary 802:266; Diary 807:151–56; Diary 816: 120–45. On Taft, see Diary 820:38–43; Diary 825:120; Diary 854: 43. The Treasury worked on the press in Diary 759:75–76, and on pressure groups in Diary 821:119; Diary 825:204; Diary 836:161; and on influential individuals in Diary 824:25; Diary 828:309; Diary 829:52, 197. For Roosevelt's message, see Diary 818:210; on Vandenberg, see Diary 820:38–43. On Bell and Burgess and the question of compromise, see Diary 834:227–33; Diary 835: A–E; Diary 836:163; Diary 837:10–39; Diary 839:102–04; Diary 843: 251 — references that include Morgenthau's views on the issue. See also Presidential Diary, April 14, 1945. Morgenthau's opinion of "the conservative thing to do" is from Diary 841:228–30; see also Diary 843:252. On the chairmanship of the council, see Presidential Diary, May 16, June 6, 1945; Diary 847:116–18, 268–83, 289–90; Diary 848:378. Morgenthau's response to victory in the House, and the opinions of his allies in the fight, appear in Diary 848:420; Diary 853:2–6, 37; Diary 854:53. For Morgenthau's view of Wagner, see Diary 856:7. On the silver bloc, see Diary 860:4–8, 12; Diary 861:305, 327. Morgenthau worried about wild statements in Diary 864:22.

3. Assistance for China: Last Round, pp. 437–446

Important for this section are the works of H. Feis and A. N. Young, cited above in references to China for Chapter III. White's warning is in Diary 837:259–60. On Soong's requests, see Diary 839:40–43, 139–40 — references that include the Monetary Division's analysis. Morgenthau talked to Truman in Presidential Diary, April 20, 1945. For the views of Patterson, Clayton, Henderson, and Crowley, see Diary 839:189–91; Diary 840:98–100; Diary 843:102–23, 250–51; Diary 844:113–20. Coe's memos of May 1 and 8, 1945, are in Diary 843:230–31; Diary 845:170–80 (which includes Morgenthau's objections). The memos were discussed with State, War, and FEA representatives, and with Soong, in Diary 845:211–225, 232–48. Morgenthau scolded Coe and others in Diary 845:314–322, and reported on his talk with Soong in Diary 845:329–32. Soong's memo is in Diary 845:346. Morgenthau discussed it with Soong and others in Diary 845:333–45. The Secretary argued with Coe and White on May 15, 1945, in Diary 847:33–55 and again on May 16 in Diary 847: 75–97 (which includes Clayton's opinion). The May 16 talk with Soong is in Diary 847:101–07 and the letter to him in Diary 847:130–31. Grew's letter is in Diary 847:144–45, Hurley's cable in Diary 854:30–32. On the cotton goods, see Diary 848:147–169; Diary 849:27–30, 177–81, 216; Diary 850:27–44, 52–54, 219, 226; and Presidential Diary, May 23, 1945. The June 1, 1945, report is in Diary 851:45–46.

4. No "Brain Wave" for England, pp. 446–451

The excellent studies of British financial problems cited in Chapters III and V are relevant for this section, too. On England's problem and the need for a "brain wave," see Diary 835:121. On Truman's order, see Presidential Diary, April 20, May 23, 1945. In Diary 849:175–84, Morgenthau talked to his staff on May 28. On Churchill's cable (quoted with permission of Randolph S. Churchill) and the May 29 conversations, see Diary 850:45–46, 230. Coe reported on his meeting with Vinson in Diary 852:16–19. The draft reply for Churchill is in Diary 856:214–15 (which includes Morgenthau's criticism of it). The Treasury draft is in Diary 858:157–58; the developments of June 28, 1945, in Diary 859:135. Truman said he would operate personally in Presidential Diary, July 5, 1945; Morgenthau's reflections of July 3 are in Diary 861:271.

5. Demise of the Morgenthau Plan, pp. 451–464

Essential for this and the next section is Harry S Truman, *Year of Decisions* (Garden City, 1955); for this section, see also the works cited in reference to Chapter VII, section 1. On the opinions of Lovett and Clayton, see Diary 837:175–76. Morgenthau talked to Stettinius on April 20, 1945, in Diary 839:3; and about Baruch in Diary 839:105–07, 149; and to Truman in Presidential Diary, April 20, 1945. The meetings of April 24, 25, and 26 are reported in Diary 839:247–300; Diary 840:3–90; Diary 841:1–58. The memo of April 26, 1945, for Truman is in Diary 841:148–81. Morgenthau saw Truman on April 27, 1945, in Presidential Diary, that date. On the May 1, 1945, meeting of IPCOG, see Diary 843:12–76; the statement on reparations is in Diary 844:187–96. Pauley confided in Morgenthau in Diary 844:211; see, too, Presidential Diary, May 2, 4, 9, 1945, for Morgenthau's conversations with Truman. Morgenthau's remarks of May 10 are from Diary 846:18; his statement to Bidault, in Diary 848:207–08; his May 23 and June 1 talks with Truman, in Presidential Diary, those dates. Morgenthau consulted Grew about the French invitation in Diary 854:143; and Truman on June 13, 1945, in Presidential Diary, that date. Truman had made up his mind in Presidential Diary, June 18, 1945; the President criticized Morgenthau and Baruch in Stimson Diary, July 13, 1945; and Morgenthau had talked with Monnet in Diary 858:105.

6. After Twelve Eventful Years, pp. 464–476

The developments of July 5, 1945, are reported in Presidential Diary, that date, and Diary 862:8–17, 26, 35, 47, 57, 80 (the letter of resignation), 83 (Truman's reply), all of which contrasts with Truman's memoir, *Year of Decisions*. Morgenthau talked with Vinson on July 6 in Diary 862:119. The conversations of July 11, 1945, are reported in Presidential Diary, that date, which is the source, too, for the developments of July 13, 1945, under that date. For the resulting letters and cables, see Diary 863:230; Diary 864:75, 94, 101, 152–54. Morgenthau reflected on his twelve years in office and their significance in conversations.

Index

Aachen, army problems in, 387

Aarons, L. C., 186

Acheson, Dean, views on British monetary problems, 124, 125–126; and British dollar balances, 133, 135, 136, 138; supports Dutch request for RFC loan, 161; presses Treasury policy for Argentina, 162; opposes controls on Argentina, 195–196, 203, 204–205, 206; on the British attitude toward the Fund and Bank, 233, 234; and planning for the economic conference, 248; and the Bretton Woods conference, 251, 259–260, 261, 262, 265, 266–267, 271, 272–273, 274, 275, 277; and Anglo-American financing of relief and reconstruction, 307; and Phase II of Lend-Lease, 320; statement on economic policy toward Germany, 331; on Taft and the Bretton Woods Agreements, 430; and the Bretton Woods Agreements, 431, 433; mentioned, 257, 395

Adler, Solomon, reports to Treasury on Chinese monetary affairs, 102–103; Communist sympathies, 103, 302; and negotiations with the Chinese regarding exchange rate, 109, 110, 120, 287, 288; returns to Chungking, 297–298; and the question of gold for China, 298–299, 300–301

Advertisers Club of New York, 430

Advertising War Council, 17

Afga-Ansco Division, General Aniline Corporation, 6

Airplanes: B-29, 110; Spitfire, 128

Aldrich, Winthrop, 258

Algeria, invasion of, 147; problems developing from, 147–152. *See also* North Africa

Alien property, regulation of, 4–10

Allis, Frederick S., Jr., 20

American Bankers Association, 253; opposed to Bretton Woods Agreements, 428, 429, 432, 433; silverite Senators of contrary mind to, 435

American Economic Association, 430

American Federation of Labor (AFL), 430

American Friends Service Committee, 226

American Jewish Congress, 209, 210, 211

American Jewish Joint Distribution Committee, 207, 219, 223

Amtorg, 83

Anderson, H. W., 20

Anderson, Sir John, and Lend-Lease negotiations, 132, 309, 310; faces opposition on Fund and Bank, 247; wants to send Keynes to Washington, 315–316; thanks Morgenthau for efforts on behalf of Britain, 325; and postwar planning for Germany, 337; fears Lend-Lease to Britain will not suffice for Stage II, 448; mentioned, 334, 398

Argentina, 162; neutrality as problem to Allies, 194–195; Treasury proposals of economic reprisals against, 195–202, 203–206; anti-Yankee bloc in, 197; breaks with Axis, 202; freezing controls abandoned, 202–203; not represented at Bretton Woods, 265

Stettinius, Edward, Jr. *(cont'd)*
tary of State, 392; proposals in "Briefing Book" for Yalta, 396; at Yalta, 399; assigned to carry out political understandings of Yalta, 400–401; Morgenthau suggests to write preface to his book, 418; in Truman's Cabinet, 421, 422; replaced by Byrnes, 452, 461; mentioned, 319, 405, 434

Stilwell, General Joseph, to serve as Chief of Staff under Chiang, 94; bickering between Chiang Kai-shek and, 102, 104, 290; and the exchange rate problem in China, 118, 119, 120, 287, 291; recalled by F.D.R., 297

Stimson, Henry L., and Pearl Harbor, 1; and funds for the atomic bomb, 13–14; distrust of Orientals, 94; advises Morgenthau regarding Chinese loan, 94–95; on Army problems in China, 115, 120, 121; and British dollar balances, 131; approves White's memorandum on invasion currency, 142; and exchange rates for North Africa, 147, 152, 155; and problems of Darlan and North Africa, 148–150, 151; and plans for the occupation of Europe, 156, 157; and the appointment of a fiscal adviser to the Civil Affairs group, 163; and problems of French currency, 167, 169, 173; formula for reconciliation with De Gaulle, 174; opposes reprisals against Argentina, 196; and the War Refugee Board, 223, 224; opposed to Jewish havens in U.S., 225; discusses problem of Chinese rate of exchange with H. H. Kung, 286, 293, 294, 295; on his conversation with Hurley, 301–302; and Chinese policy, 302–303; and postwar Lend-Lease policies, 303, 314; and postwar planning for Germany, 344–345, 347, 348, 349–350; opposed to Morgenthau Plan, 359–362, 363, 365, 366, 367, 375–377, 379, 380; suspicions regarding press leak on Morgenthau Plan, 381–382; on Dewey's criticism of the Morgenthau Plan, 382; removes himself from controversy over Germany, 384, 403–404; on probable British and Russian aims in Germany, 386; on Coordinating Committee, 390; opposed to Quebec Agreement, 407; approves new War Department paper, 414; Truman

Stimson, Henry L. *(cont'd)*
wants at Potsdam, 464; mentioned, 70, 96, 127, 199, 397, 401, 409, 458

Strang, Sir William, 329

Strong, General George, 199, 200–201

Suarez, Eduardo, Minister of Finance, 265

Sulzberger, Arthur Hays, 21

Supply Priorities and Allocations Board, 12

Supreme Headquarters Allied Expeditionary Forces (SHAEF), 330; "Handbook for Military Government in Germany," 331, 334, 346–347, 348, 349–350, 358, 363, 364, 377–378, 383; Civil Affairs section, 334, 335, 383; and JCS 1067, 387

Swing, Raymond Gram, 430

Swope, Gerard, 80–81

Taft, Robert A., on the spendings tax, 47; opposed to International Monetary Fund and Bank, 252, 429–430, 431, 432; concessions to, 435

TASS, 398

Taxes, 33–78; sales, 35, 37, 42, 78; corporation, 36; income, payroll withholding of, 40–41, 43, 58, 63; spendings, 45–48

Taylor, William H., 164–165, 186

Teheran Conference, 111, 329, 338–339, 340, 342, 366

Time magazine, 16

Tobacco, excluded from Lend-Lease, 318

Tobey, Charles W., 252, 258, 259, 275

Trade Agreements Act, 431

Treasury Department: and alien property regulation, 4–10; wartime interest policy, 14–16; relations with Federal Reserve System, 15; War Bond program, 16–32; Morgenthau's suggestions for enlarging authority of, 31; offensive against inflation, 43; differences between Budget Bureau and, 55–58; $12 billion objective considered too high, 69; staff (1944–45), 283–284; and preparation of the Morgenthau Plan, 343, 345, 347, 350–351, 354, 356

Tripartite Agreement of 1936, 153, 229

Tripolitania, refugee haven at, 227

Truman, Harry S, on the purpose of Lend-Lease, 133; selected as Vice Presidential candidate, 281; Morgenthau's first impressions of, 421–423, 425–426; supports the Bretton Woods

Date Due